THE GERMAN SUBMARINE WAR

Printed and bound by Antony Rowe Ltd, Eastbourne

THE following is the opinion expressed by Admiral Earl St. Vincent in 1804, upon hearing of the proposal, made by the American inventor Robert Fulton, that the British should build a submarine for use against the French fleet :—

'*Don't look at it, and don't touch it. If we take it up, other nations will; and it will be the greatest blow at our supremacy on the sea that can be imagined.*'

FOREWORD

THE Authors of this very interesting book mention in its opening pages the fact that German naval officers in pre-war days had not realised the influence that submarines would exert upon naval warfare, as the capabilities of the new arm to undertake oversea operations at long distances from their bases, and unescorted by surface vessels, had not been fully appreciated.

Similarly, the Royal Navy had looked upon the submarine as a vessel dangerous to surface craft, but possessed of but a limited range of action.

When German submarines began to be reported outside the North Sea, it was considered probable that they were obtaining fuel supplies from some source, either afloat or ashore, other than their home bases.

The possibilities of the submarine as an offensive weapon came, therefore, as somewhat of a surprise to both sides after the commencement of the war in 1914.

The existence of these vessels influenced naval strategy and tactics to a considerable degree. Unless an adequate anti-submarine escort of destroyers was available to accompany the Fleet when at sea, serious risks from submarine attack were incurred. It was not until late in 1915 that the number of destroyers attached to the Grand Fleet was sufficient to screen the Battle Fleet adequately, and an anti-submarine screen for the Cruisers was not available until the end of 1916.

But it was, of course, the depredations of the German

submarines on Merchant Ships which caused the Allies by far the greatest concern and the heaviest losses, particularly their work in what was known as the Unrestricted Submarine Warfare, *i.e.* the sinking of merchant-ships by torpedoes at sight and without warning.

In the pages which follow, the fullest information is given in regard to the German submarines, particulars of their design, numbers, and distribution, the rate at which they were commissioned and were lost, and in most cases the fate which overtook them. There is little indeed about the German submarines that this book does not mention, and I feel sure that it will be read with the greatest possible interest both by naval officers and by the general public.

A statement is given of the losses sustained by the Royal Navy and by the Merchant Navy both from submarine attack and by mines laid by submarines.

The methods by which the submarine menace was eventually overcome are dealt with very fully and completely, and will certainly form not the least interesting portion of the book.

Mention is made on pages 147 and 148 of the invaluable work of the Anti-Submarine Division at the Admiralty in this connection, and the immense development of the depth-charge offensive is dealt with on pages 149, 178, and 339. Without this development, the institution of the convoy system could not have met with the success which it achieved.

The difficulties attending the introduction of convoy are well brought out on pages 173-175 and 213. On these latter pages the fact is mentioned that even as late as September 1917 we still needed 41 cruisers and 55 destroyers or sloops to complete the convoy system

FOREWORD

in the Atlantic, and 74 escort vessels (destroyers, sloops, and trawlers) to establish the convoy system in the Mediterranean. This statement is very clear proof of the difficulties with which we were contending during the year 1917.

It was only the splendid work of the Royal Navy, with the invaluable assistance of the small craft attached to it, manned by fishermen and R.N.R. and R.N.V.R. officers and men, and in combination with the devoted courage of the officers and men of our Mercantile Navy, whom no dangers could daunt, that enabled us to tide over the period during which our anti-submarine measures came into fruition. The memory of those days should serve to remind us of the fate which will assuredly overtake the Empire if our dependence upon the safety of sea communications is allowed to be forgotten.

JELLICOE, A.F.

AUTHORS' ACKNOWLEDGMENT

THE Authors desire to make full acknowledgment of the use they have made of the following sources of information :—

I. OPERATIONS

'Naval Operations,' vols. i.-iv. (Corbett and Newbolt).
'The Grand Fleet' and 'The Crisis of the Naval War' (Earl Jellicoe).
'Germany's High Sea Fleet in the World War' (Scheer—English translation).
'The Dover Patrol,' vols. i. and ii. (Bacon).
'Battleships in Action,' vol. ii. (Wilson).
'The Auxiliary Patrol' and 'Q-Ships' (Chatterton).
'The Merchant Navy,' vols. i.-iii. (Hurd).
'My Mystery Ships' (Campbell).
'The Victory at Sea' (Sims).
'The Story of our Submarines' ('Klaxon').
'Submarine and Anti-Submarine' (Newbolt).
'Raiders of the Deep' (Lowell Thomas).
'The World Crisis,' vols. i.-iv. (Churchill).
'Six Ans de Croisières en Sous-Marins' (Spiess—French translation).

Considerable use has been made of Captain A. Gayer's work 'Die deutschen U-boote in ihrer Kriegführung 1914-18,' and of the English translation of his lecture, 'Summary of German Submarine Operations in the Various Theatres of War from 1914 to 1918.'

Another lecture, containing useful historical information, is that delivered by Captain C. V. Usborne, C.M.G., R.N. (on March 19, 1924, at the Royal United Service Institution). entitled 'The Anti-Submarine Campaign in the Mediterranean, subsequent to 1916.' Of this, use has also been made.

II. Technical Data

For the design and constructional features of German submarines the following authorities have been consulted:—

'Der Bau von Unterseebooten auf der Germaniawerft' (Techel).
'Die Technik im Weltkrieg' (Schwarthe).
'U-bootskrieg 1914-1918' (Michelsen).
'Taschenbuch der Kriegsflotten,' 1922 (Weyer).

Also the following three articles, by German naval architects, which appeared in 1919 issues of 'Schiffbau':—

'Die deutschen Unterseeboote' (Schürer);
'Das Hochsee Minenunterseeboot' (Werner);
'Deutsche Unterseeboote für Küstengewässer' (Schürer);

and the lecture, read by the present Director of Naval Construction, Admiralty, at the 1920 (Spring) Meetings of the Institution of Naval Architects, entitled 'German Submarines.'

Details for the Austro-Hungarian submarines are derived from a full report, specially prepared for the information of the authors by the 'Kriegsarchiv' (Official War Archives Office) of Vienna, during August 1930. So far as can be traced, no naval annual, work of reference, or war history has ever published a complete and authentic list displaying the technical features of the Austro-Hungarian submarines, 1914-1918. The 'Kriegsarchiv' particulars embodied in this book reveal, at last, the real strength of the Austro-Hungarian Navy in vessels of the under-water type during the period of the conflict.

III. War Losses

The most authoritative statements upon the casualties suffered by the British war and merchant fleets are those embodied in the two Official Returns, 'Navy Losses,' and 'Merchant Shipping (Losses),' dated from the Admiralty, August 1919. Considerable use has been made of these two White Papers. The Authors have taken special care in collecting and comparing all accounts relative to the destruction or disablement of German and Austro-Hungarian submarines. The majority of the authorities that they have consulted are those cited above under the headings of 'Operations' and 'Technical Data,' but they have also made reference to many other minor documents which are cited by means of footnotes. Some allusions to losses suffered by the combatant and non-combatant fleets of the Allied and Associated Powers, and by neutral shipping, are founded upon statements published in the British and Foreign Press, official returns, etc.

IV. Text

To Admiral of the Fleet Earl Jellicoe the Authors desire to tender their simple thanks for the Foreword contributed to this book. They do not venture to offer him any praise as a mark of their gratitude, since no praise of theirs could add to that renown which he has already won, both as a great seaman and as a great administrator. But in all sincerity they would say that, had this work been prefaced by but a single line from him who took so prominent and distinguished a part in the Naval War, they would have considered it a reward more than ample for their years of labour.

That the present work should ever have been carried on, until it reached its present and final form, is, in a large measure, due to the kindly encouragement given to the Authors by their valued friend, Mr. Francis E. M'Murtrie, A.I.N.A. Not only has Mr. M'Murtrie read and revised the manuscript and proofs, but he has also eliminated certain errors, elucidated doubtful points, and made many helpful suggestions. The Authors consider themselves to be most fortunate in that their narrative has undergone the scrutiny of so kindly and competent a critic before its presentation in printed form.

To the Intelligence Division of the Naval Staff, Admiralty, the Authors wish to express their appreciation of the assistance so kindly rendered to them through the communication of information which has only recently become available.

V. ILLUSTRATIONS

The Authors desire to express their gratitude to the Imperial War Museum for permission to reproduce several remarkably interesting photographs relating to the Submarine War ; to the Cunard Steamship Company for their courtesy in supplying the block of the photograph depicting the *Franconia* sinking ; and to Dr. Oscar Parkes for the two photographs of the *Dover Castle* attack.

Further, appreciation must be here expressed of the valuable services rendered by Dr. Oscar Parkes. He not only undertook the work of collecting the photographs, but also greatly assisted the Authors by his skilled advice upon the illustrative treatment of their book.

CONTENTS

	PAGE
FOREWORD (by Admiral of the Fleet Earl Jellicoe, G.C.B., O.M., G.C.V.O., LL.D., D.C.L.) . .	vii

CHAP.
I. AN ARM NEW TO NAVAL WARFARE . . . 1

II. TRIAL AND ERROR: THE FIRST WAR ON SHIPPING (February–September 1915) 23

III. THE MEDITERRANEAN: SOWING THE SEED (1915) . 67

IV. THE WAR OF LIMITATIONS AND THE RESPITE (January–May 1916) 81

V. THE SUBMARINE AS A MILITARY WEAPON (May–September 1916) 96

VI. CRUISER WAR RESUMED (October 1916–February 1917) 113

VII. THE MEDITERRANEAN: REAPING THE WHIRLWIND (1916) 124

VIII. THE CRISIS (February–April 1917) 137

IX. THE STRUGGLE FOR MASTERY (May–September 1917) 173

X. THE PENUMBRA OF ECLIPSE (September–December 1917) 204

XI. THE MEDITERRANEAN HARVEST (1917) . . . 236

XII. THE MEDITERRANEAN FREED (January–November 1918) 263

XIII. DOWNFALL AND NOT WORLD POWER (January–November 1918) 282

XIV. SURRENDER 330

APPENDICES

I.	The Triumph of Convoy	338
II.	A Short History of German Submarine Design, 1904-1914	340
III. *A–L.*	German Submarine Construction and Losses	351
M.	German Submarine 'Aces'	378
N–O.	The Toll of Merchant Shipping	380
IV. *P.*	Austro-Hungarian Submarine Construction, Losses, etc.	383
Q.	Turkish Submarines	390
R.	Summary	390
INDEX		391

LIST OF ILLUSTRATIONS

FACING PAGE

I. THE LAST MOMENTS OF THE U 8. (*Imperial War Museum*) . . . . } 32
THE EXTERMINATION OF UC 39. (*Abrahams*) .

II. THE DEATH THROES OF THE *ANGLIA*. (*Imperial War Museum*) 60

III. PRIZE OF WAR. (*Imperial War Museum*) . . . 94

IV. LOTHAR VON ARNAULD DE LA PERIÈRE AND OFFICERS OF U 35. (*Imperial War Museum*) . . 124

V. A MEETING IN THE MEDITERRANEAN. (*Imperial War Museum*) . . . . } 130
FRIEND OR ENEMY? (*Imperial War Museum*) . .

VI. THE SINKING OF THE *RUSSELL*. (*Abrahams*) . . } 132
THE MINES' LARGEST VICTIM. (*Imperial War Museum*)

VII. THE ORDEAL OF THE NEUTRAL TRADERS. (*Imperial War Museum*) 146

VIII. THE HOSPITAL-SHIP *GLOUCESTER CASTLE* BEACHED. (*Imperial War Museum*) 164

IX. THE DESTROYER *TETRARCH* KEEPING WATCH OVER A PATCH OF OIL. (*Imperial War Museum*) . 170

X. SNATCHED FROM THE MAW OF THE SEA. (*Imperial War Museum*) 192

XI. AMERICAN WARSHIPS SINK A SUBMARINE. (*Imperial War Museum*) 226

XII. THE BEGINNING OF A WAR CRUISE. (*Imperial War Museum*) . . . . } 236
THE LAIR OF THE SEA GUERILLAS. (*Imperial War Museum*) . . . .

		FACING PAGE
XIII.	WHAT IS YOUR SHIP ? WHERE ARE YOU BOUND ? (*Imperial War Museum*) . . . . . . THE ANTI-SHIPPING WAR IN OPERATION. (*Imperial War Museum*)	242
XIV.	A TROOPSHIP PLUNGING TO THE DEPTHS. (*Imperial War Museum*)	244
XV.	THE ATTACK ON THE HOSPITAL SHIP *DOVER CASTLE*. (1) (*Dr. Parkes*)	250
XVI.	THE ATTACK ON THE HOSPITAL SHIP *DOVER CASTLE*. (2) (*Dr. Parkes*)	250
XVII.	U 38 AFTER COLLISION. (*Imperial War Museum*) .	256
XVIII.	THE END OF THE *FRANCONIA*. (*Cunard*) . . THE TORPEDOING OF A TROOPER. (*Imperial War Museum*)	262
XIX.	A VIKING'S PYRE. (*Imperial War Museum*) . .	270
XX.	THE END OF H.M.S. *BRITANNIA*, OFF CAPE TRAFALGAR. (*Abrahams*)	276
XXI.	AN OCEAN TRAGEDY. (*Imperial War Museum*) . .	306
XXII.	THE LARGEST TYPE OF U-BOAT. (*Imperial War Museum*) . . . . U 153 : ONE OF THE *DEUTSCHLAND* TYPE MERCANTILE SUBMARINES. (*Gieves*)	310
XXIII.	THE CONVOY'S GUARD COMES TO GRIEF. (*Nautical Photo Agency*) . . . . THE LARGEST VESSEL TO SUCCUMB TO TORPEDO ATTACK BY SUBMARINES. (*Nautical Photo Agency*)	312
XXIV.	THE IMMOLATION OF THE FLANDERS U-BOATS. (*Nautical Photo Agency*) . . . . . . SURRENDER. (*Reproduced from an official photograph by permission of the Controller, H.M. Stationery Office*) .	330

LIST OF CHARTS AND GRAPHS

		PAGE
1.	THE MEDITERRANEAN CAMPAIGN	79
2.	THE NORTH SEA, AUGUST 19, 1916	108
3.	THE SUBMARINE BLOCKADE ZONES	138
4.	MONTHLY RATE OF U-BOATS COMMISSIONED	142
5.	MONTHLY TOLL OF SHIPPING DESTRUCTION	161
6.	MONTHLY STRENGTH OF U-BOATS	205
7.	THE DOVER BARRAGE	223
8.	THE OTRANTO STRAITS	265
9.	MONTHLY LOSSES OF U-BOATS	305
10.	THE GRAVES OF THE U-BOATS	327

The coloured charts in this reprint are placed before chapter one.

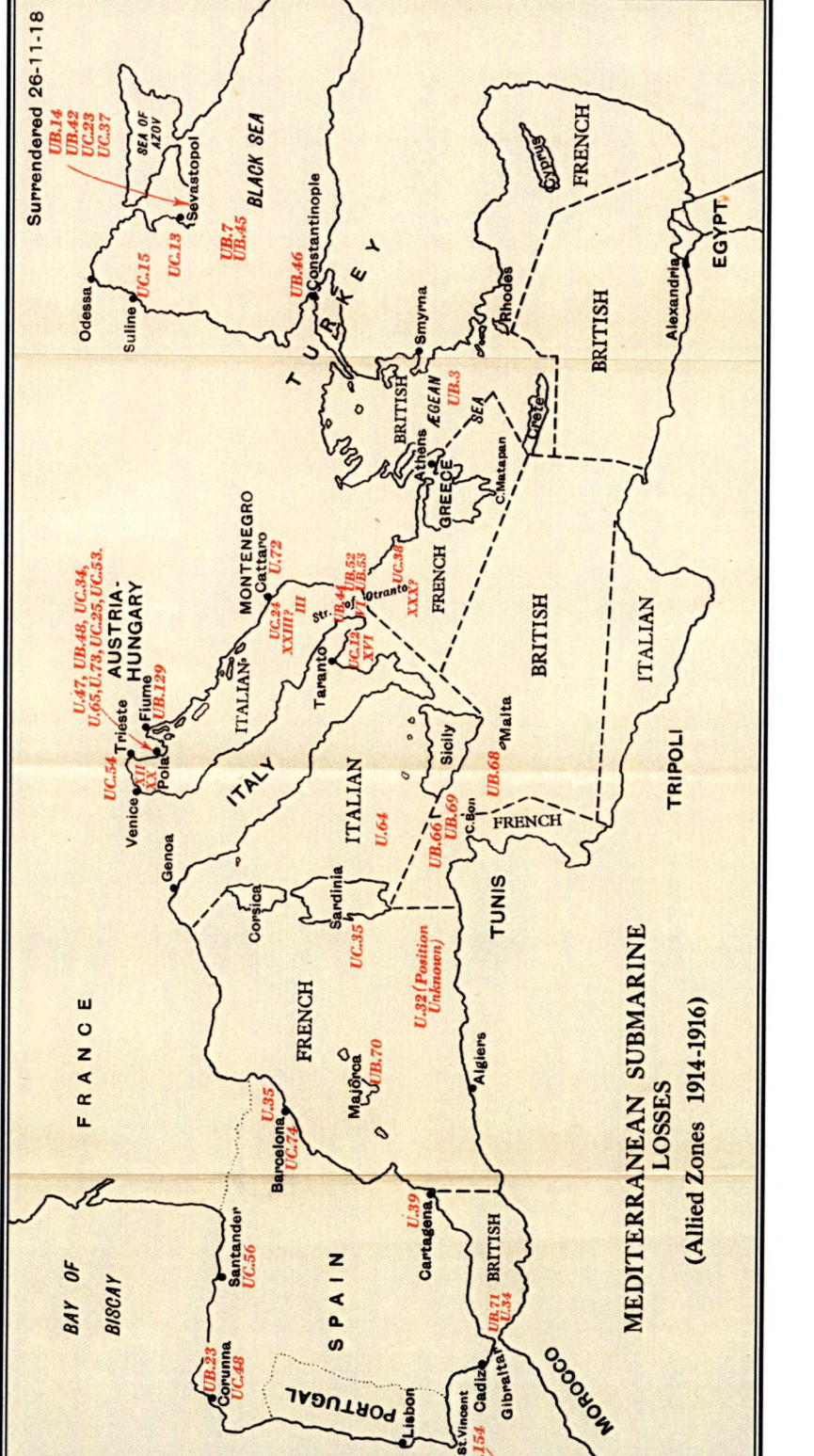

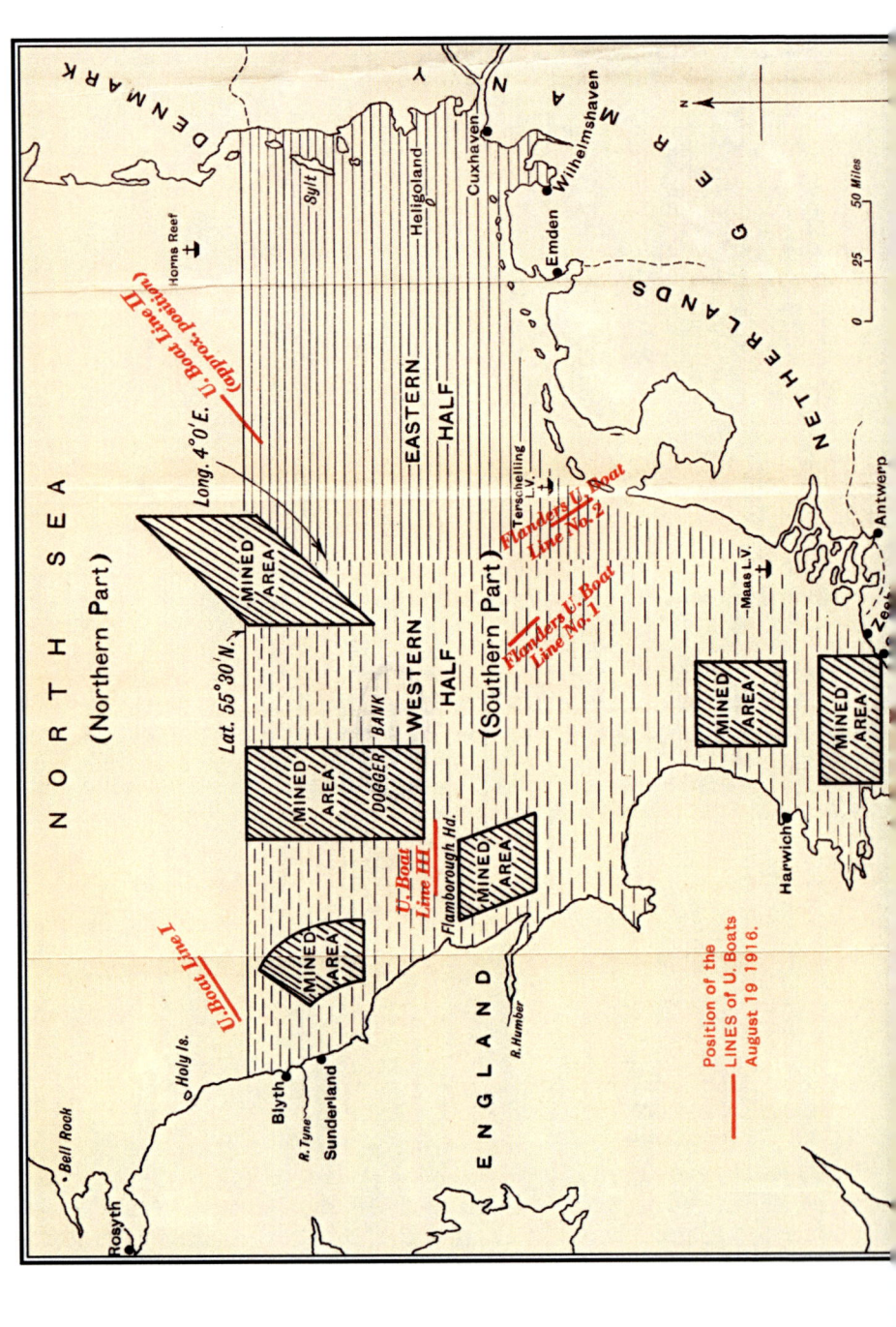

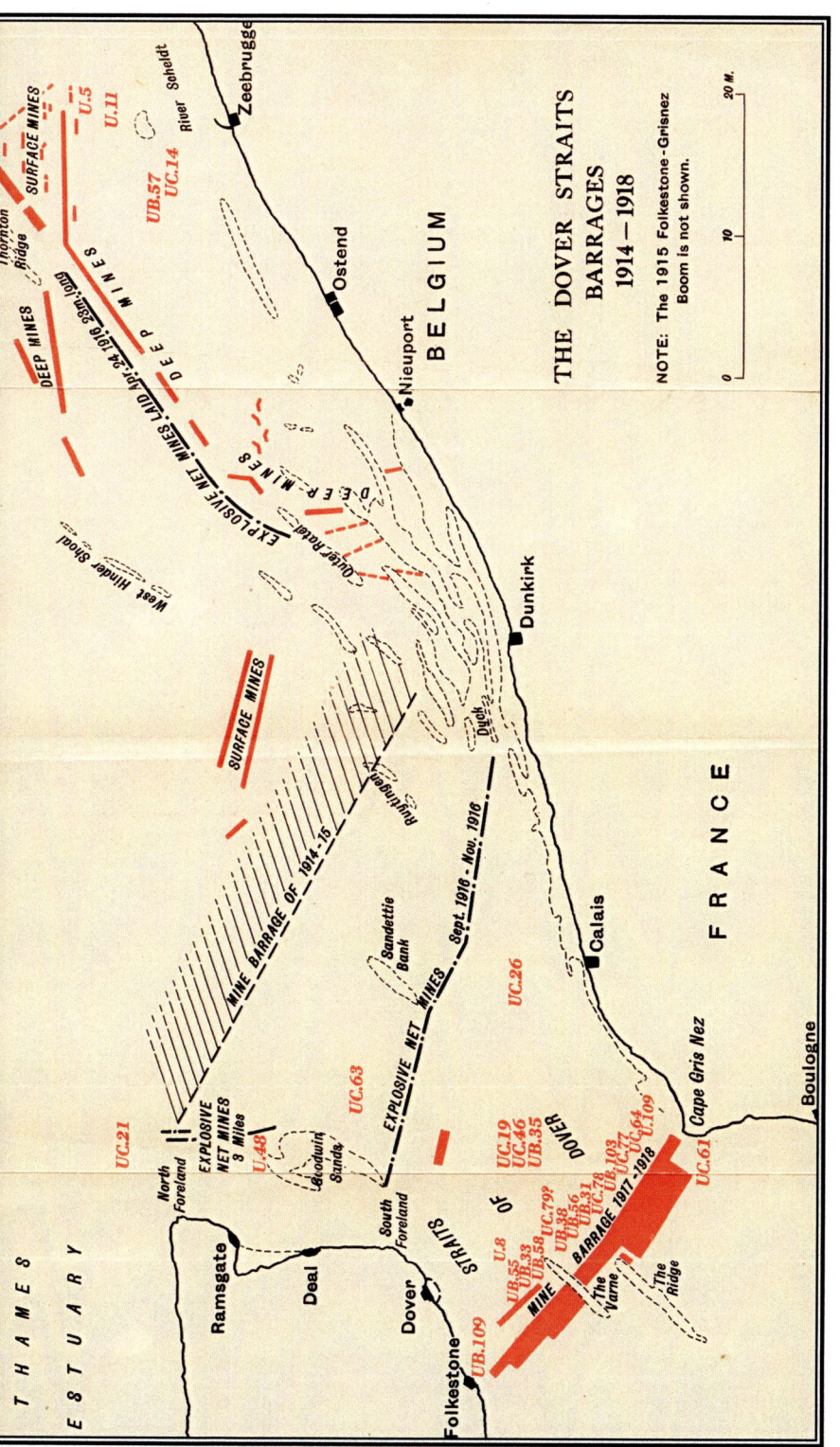

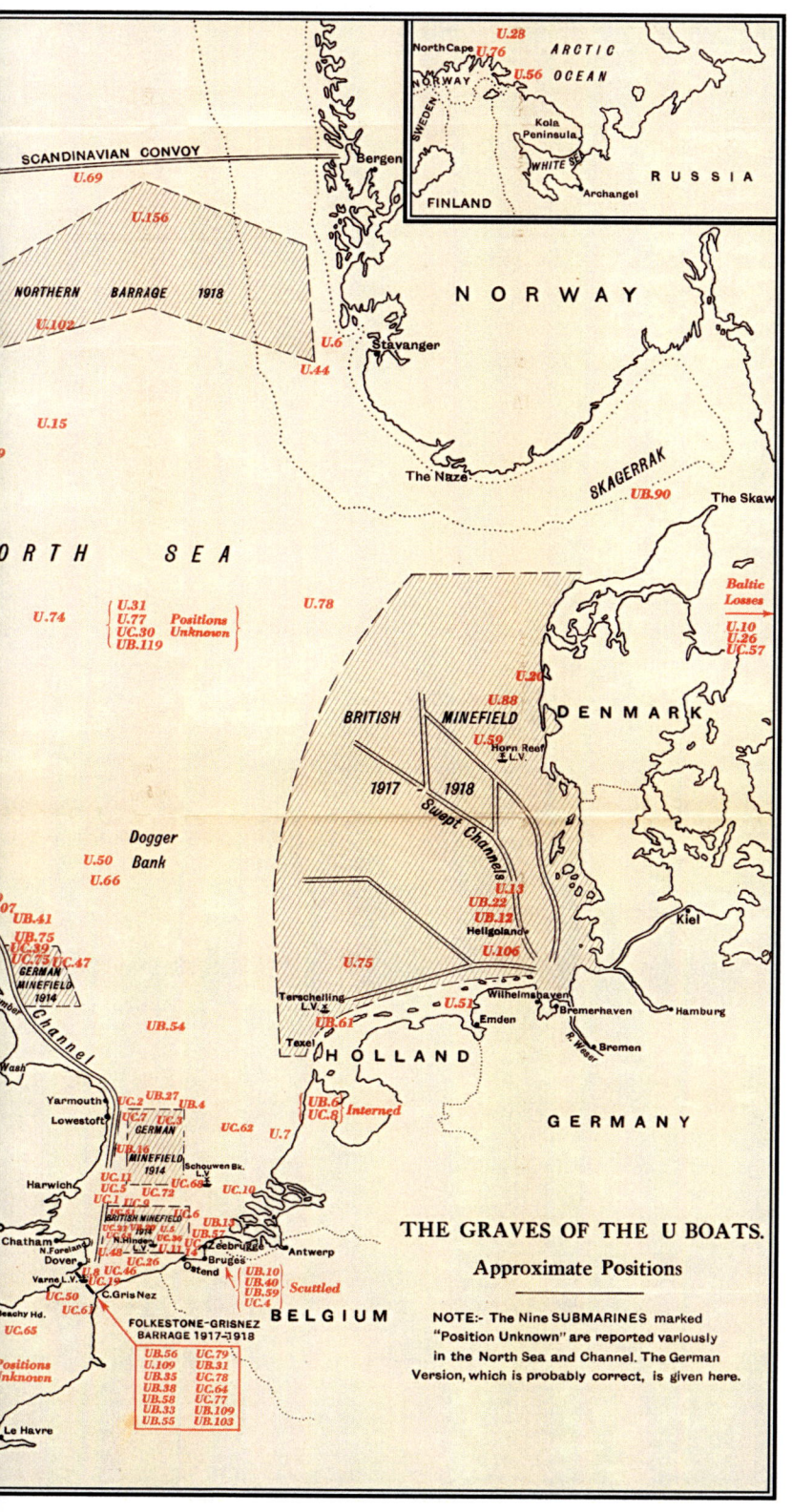

CHAPTER I

AN ARM NEW TO NAVAL WARFARE

(August 1914–February 1915)

EARLY on the morning of August 2, 1914, the German submarines quitted the port of Heligoland, in company with their escort vessels. They were charged with no enterprise of hazard. The diving boats had been ordered to move out to sea and take up assigned observation stations around the island fortress. Once arrived at those positions, they were to moor and keep watch during the daylight hours; in the evening they were to return to harbour. The escort vessels, having seen their charges safely berthed in the allotted stations, steamed back in the freshness of the summer morning to Heligoland.

So little faith had Germany then in the capabilities of her submarines! She could not trust them beyond sight of land without a mothering convoy of surface ships; she could find no better employment for them than that of buoyant sentry-boxes! Crude and none too reliable were the majority of her *Unterseeboote*; cautious to the point of timidity had been the peace-time training of their officers and crews. Outside of the submarine branch, the Imperial Navy had little or no faith in the New Arm of the Underseas and its war value.

Upon their return to Heligoland, during the evening of August 2, the submarines received their first definite orders 'to take war measures against Great Britain forthwith.' Still, their routine of forming immobile barrages around the island continued for the next few days. The submarines moved out at 3 A.M., and all day rode to their moorings amongst the sandbanks of the Bight. As an advanced line of outposts, it was their duty to give their Fleet first and timely warning of the impending great drive down the North

Sea by the British Navy. For implicitly was it believed by the German naval command in those days that, even before any declaration of war, Britain would launch a massed attack with her entire sea forces upon the German coast.

Nothing happened. Great Britain declared war at midnight on August 4. Still nothing happened; the dreaded onslaught did not arrive. Then a foray of unprecedented intrepidity, range, and duration was planned for the submarines. In extended scouting formation and unescorted by any surface vessels outside home waters, the U-boats were to advance up the North Sea, as far as the line Norway-Orkneys, in an endeavour to divine the British naval dispositions. No cruise so adventurous, so far-reaching, had ever been attempted before : the Bight, the Baltic, and Kiel Fjord had hitherto been the restricted, peace-time cruising-grounds of the submarine flotillas.

At 4.30 A.M. on August 6, ten boats set out on the first war cruise. The numbers of these pioneers are worthy of record. They were U 5, 7, and 8, units of the first class of serviceable submarines ever built ; U 9, commanded by an officer already distinguished for his enterprise and skill ; the unhappy U 13 and 15, and U 14, 16, 17, and 18. At 1.40 P.M. the escort vessels turned sixteen points and made off at full speed southward, to regain the protection of Heligoland's big guns and howitzers. The submarines were left alone in the open sea—face to face with war.

They carried on northwards. Nearing the Horns Reef, the crews went to diving stations, expecting to sight, at any moment, the most advanced of the British blockading lines. No such contact was made ; farther and farther north they pushed, hoping to fall in with British squadrons between the Shetlands and Bergen. During their advance they lost the services of one unit. On the morning of August 8 (when 225 miles out from Heligoland), one of U 9's engines broke down, and she was compelled to turn about and make for home. The other nine continued their quest for the British battle-fleet. Off Fair Island, on this same day (August 8), U 15 (Pohle) sighted the battleships *Ajax*, *Monarch*, and *Orion* carrying out battle practice ; she made an approach

AN ARM NEW TO NAVAL WARFARE

and fired a torpedo at *Monarch*, but without success. This attack put the British ships on their guard. Towards evening, the presence of hostile submarines, already suspected, was confirmed, a periscope having been sighted both by the flagship *Iron Duke* and the *Dreadnought*. The leviathans sheered out of the line to ram, but did not crush their opponent underfoot by their mighty bulk. The first attack and counter-attack therefore failed.

About dawn next morning, the 1st Light Cruiser Squadron, forming a screen ahead of the battle-squadrons, came into contact with the elusive foe. The look-out of the questing *Birmingham* suddenly sighted, amidst the wraiths of mist, the hull of U 15, lying immobile and hove-to. It would seem that no watch was being kept in the submarine, and, from the sounds of hammering which pierced the haze, the crew was apparently trying to remedy an engine breakdown. Altering course, and making sure that U 15 was within her turning circle, the *Birmingham* bore down, opening a rapid fire at close range. The submarine slowly began to move through the water, but it was too late. The bows of the light cruiser caught her fair and square, cutting her completely in two. The two severed parts of U 15 appeared to float for a short time, possibly because the sheared plating was folded over at the point where her hull had been rammed, so partially sealing and making water-tight the severed ends. Only temporary repairs could be effected to the light cruiser, owing to the urgent demand for her services; and for several months the *Birmingham* bore evidence of her success in the shape of two long scars, almost exactly symmetrical in length and pattern, which defaced her bows.

Three days later, August 12, seven submarines returned to Heligoland. Not only had U 15 been surprised and destroyed by the British forces: there was another boat missing—U 13. Her commander, Graf A. von Schweinitz, had reported his position during the day, and it is surmised that his boat soon afterwards struck a mine and blew up.

The first attack on the Grand Fleet had therefore failed. Losses—the first of a long tale—had been suffered. Not even the hardiest optimist could pretend that the submarine had vindicated its war value by this expedition. Yet, had the Germans known, the effect of the cruise had caused uneasiness to their opponents. That these under-water foes should have been encountered so far north proved the falsity of previous estimates as to the German boats' radius of action. The security of the Grand Fleet in the unprotected anchorage of Scapa Flow was already open to question.

In several respects this initial cruise was noteworthy. Against the *Monarch* had been launched the first war-headed torpedo ever delivered by a submarine with intent to kill. Never before in naval warfare had an under-water vessel essayed the destruction of a fully-manned, moving, hostile ship-target. Within twenty-four hours U 15 had made the first submarine attack under war conditions; had missed her target, and later had herself been attacked and exterminated. Dramatic had been the opening gambit of the great game, and it had ended by Germany losing her pawn. The ease with which U 15 had been destroyed, in the first attack by fleet scouts upon an enemy submarine, encouraged the idea that submarines, after all, were no serious menace to surface warships. Arguing a universal rule from a particular example, it was confidently predicted by some—but not by naval officers—that all other U-boats would soon follow U 15 to the bottom. Hence the later events of 1914 descended with dire force, not on minds prepared for disaster, but on minds lulled into a complacent over-confidence.

On August 8—that is, two days after this northward s⸺ began—four other U-boats were sent to scout in the 'Hootaen,' the German name for that area lying south-west of the line Terschelling-Flamborough Head. Neither did this expedition meet with success. The boats selected were the Diesel-engined U 19, 21, 22, and 24; and all but U 21 (Hersing) were forced to put back. This solitary boat pushed on with the intention of interfering with the passage of the British Expeditionary Force to Belgium. As is well known, the Force did not actually land on French soil until August 15-17, although the advance party did cross on the 9th. So complete was the failure of the German Intelligence Service, that the German Staff was unaware of these large troop move-

AN ARM NEW TO NAVAL WARFARE

ments up to the 22nd. Even more remarkable was the desire, expressed by the German military party, that the passage from England should not be interfered with, because they wished to crush the British Army on French territory !

Hersing, nevertheless, returned with most valuable information concerning the patrol system off the East Coast ; and, in company with U 19, he set out again on the 14th, to sweep across from Egersund to Peterhead. At the same time, U 22 (Hoppe) was sent to scout off the Humber before the minelayers *Albatross* and *Pelikan* laid their mine-field in that area on the 24th. The three U-boats returned safely from their cruises, although the two northern ones reported numerous patrols which had kept them under for many hours at a stretch. Hersing in U 21 was particularly successful : he covered 1600 miles without the slightest inconvenience, a feat which even his superior officers had thought to be impossible of achievement.

Gayer, the noted German submarine historian, says that thsee cruises revealed certain defects of design. Chief amongst the modifications advocated were the removal of the telephonic buoy, which, if it floated clear on diving, revealed the position of the submarine ; the provision of alarm gongs to warn all stations below of an imminent emergency dive ; and the enlargement of the bridge (or navigating platform) on the roof of the conning-tower.

In the Heligoland Bight action on August 28 the U-boats took no part ; but, as a result of the British incursion, a halfflotilla was stationed in the Ems.[1] This force was augmented to a full flotilla (of about ten boats) by the addition of the U 27-30 class, as soon as they had completed their trials in the Baltic.

Hersing set out again in September, this time accompanied by U 20 (Droescher). Late at night on the 2nd he crept up the Firth of Forth. He actually penetrated the estuary as far as the Forth Bridge before his presence was detected and the alarm raised. Baffled in his attempt to attack the British warships in the Forth, he ran out of the Firth and made his

---

[1] On the outbreak of war, the German Submarine Force was divided into two flotillas.

way southward. Three days later he made history by sinking the first warship by an automobile torpedo fired from a submarine.

The afternoon of the 5th was stormy. Off St. Abb's Head, Hersing fell in with the leader of the Forth Destroyer Patrol, the scout *Pathfinder*, in company with her flotilla. Although U 21 was plunging wildly, Hersing's luck was in, and the torpedo took the little cruiser under the fore funnel. The fore part of the ship blew up in flames ; as her stern rose out of the water the stricken vessel gave a lurch and within four minutes she had dived to the bottom, bows first, with 259 of her unfortunate crew. So rough were the seas that no glimpse of a torpedo had been seen, and an element of doubt persisted as to the cause of this sudden and overwhelming catastrophe. Brief as was her career, the *Pathfinder* was true to her name ; for even in death she showed the path along which the naval war would progress—that of submarine operations of a virulence deadly to surface vessels, war and mercantile.

Hersing's exploit was the first of those events, in the autumn of 1914, which naturally increased the renown of the German submarine service—a service whose progress had been retarded by the exacting demands of certain naval chiefs, notably Grand-Admiral von Tirpitz, who insisted on 'a serviceable submarine before any submarine at all.' At the same time it very greatly increased the British uneasiness for the safety of the Grand Fleet, lying in its unprotected anchorage in the Orkneys. On this same day, in the hope of finding a safe haven, the Grand Fleet steamed to a new coaling-base in Loch Ewe, on the west coast of Scotland, whilst at Scapa Flow submarine alarms were continual. Although they have been subsequently proved without foundation, these rumours of the presence of an undetected enemy had effects of far-reaching consequence.

The next blow was struck in southern waters and with stunning power. Since the passage of the Expeditionary Force in August, a patrol of old armoured cruisers (the 7th Squadron) had been maintained in the area known as the 'Broad Fourteens,' south of the Dogger Bank, its purpose being to cover the Dover Patrol and to support the Harwich

AN ARM NEW TO NAVAL WARFARE

Force flotillas. This cruiser force, jocularly known as the 'Live Bait Squadron,' only too soon justified its grim nickname. As though even Nature herself conspired with the attacker, the weather on the evening of September 17 necessitated the destroyers seeking shelter in port. It was not until the early hours of September 22 that Commodore Tyrwhitt was able to put to sea from Harwich to provide an anti-submarine screen. During the interval of bad weather these large cruisers had had to maintain their patrol without any destroyer protection. Danger from submarine was thought to be negligible owing to the short steep seas created by the gale; moreover, it was believed that the German U-boats were working farther north, off the Norwegian coast. In accordance with orders, the three cruisers *Aboukir*, *Cressy*, and *Hogue* were steaming in line abreast two miles apart, on a northerly course, at barely ten knots. Dawn on September 22 broke fine and clear; over the shoal waters of Scheveningen a heavy swell was running. At about half-past six, without the slightest warning, a violent explosion shook the *Aboukir*. At once the cruiser listed, and twenty-five minutes later she capsized, leaving most of her crew struggling in the water.

Believing a mine to be the cause of this disaster, the *Hogue* closed in to succour her dying consort. She, in turn, was struck by two torpedoes. Within five minutes her quarterdeck was awash; another five, and she had entirely disappeared. The *Cressy* likewise hove-to to rescue survivors; but she also was hit by two torpedoes, and sank in a quarter of an hour. In the last case the loss of life was particularly heavy, as the *Cressy*'s boats were away, busily engaged in picking up survivors from the other cruisers. Solely through the admirable behaviour of two Dutch steamers and a couple of Lowestoft trawlers (which disregarded the peril of suspected mines), about 837 officers and men were saved. Despite all endeavours at rescue, the tragedy cost this country the lives of 62 officers and 1073 men, many of whom were old reservists and midshipmen.

In this terrible manner was the menace of the submarine driven home. The triple sinking was the work of but one small boat, U 9, commanded by Otto Weddigen. He had during the peace-time exercises signally distinguished himself by the skilful handling of his boat. His career as a warrior was destined to be as dazzling as a meteor's flight—and as brief. From his second-in-command, Lieutenant Johannes Spiess,[1] we know exactly how the attack was carried out. Few such pictures have been given to us of the reverse side of submarine attack as that which he relates so vividly. Sent out on September 20 under sealed orders to molest the transports crossing over to Belgium, Weddigen had considerable trouble with his gyroscopic compass when running down the Dutch coast, and found himself fifty miles off his course. On the evening of the next day, the 21st, he sought refuge for the night on the sea-bed off Scheveningen; but so heavy was the swell that, even when lying in soundings of 16 fathoms (about 100 feet), U 9 was violently bumped on the bottom. Fearing that leaks might be started by the concussions, Weddigen was forced to go up to the surface. Here, above, he found not the rest he sought. Four vessels showing lights bore down on him. Thinking these to be British destroyers, he was compelled to submerge again. There was nothing for it but to run submerged during the dark hours, so throughout the whole course of that autumn night, U 9 prowled to and fro under the waves like a nocturnal marauder of the jungle.

Just before sunrise next morning, U 9 broke surface and began to run the charge into her batteries, now well-nigh exhausted after her restless night. Spiess, conning the submarine, suddenly sighted soaring up above the horizon a tall top-mast of a warship. Then, observing dense clouds of smoke, he had no further doubts. He immediately summoned Weddigen, who gave orders to dive. The approach began. Three 'small four-funnelled' cruisers appeared on the horizon. Spiess went forward to prepare and adjust the spare torpedoes, and on his return to the control-room he was told by Weddigen that the ships were 'Birmingham'-class cruisers. As the unsuspecting vessels came within torpedo range, Weddigen gave orders to go down to fifteen metres immediately after the torpedo had been fired. At 7.20 A.M. the No. 1 bow torpedo

---

[1] *Six Ans de Croisières en Sous-Marins*, Johannes Spiess. (French translation by Lieut. Henry Schricke.)

left its tube. The crew expected something immediate, terrific, and cataclysmic to happen. Nothing happened; Spiess glanced at the depth manometer and clasped his hands around the periscope and waited. Then came to their ears a dull thud, followed by a sonorous noise. Never had they heard the like before—the sound of a torpedo explosion, travelling under water from the recipient target to the attacking submarine. The periscope was raised again. Weddigen, peering into it, saw his first victim in her death-throes. The exultation of U 9's crew was tempered by the fear that leaks might have been sustained from an explosion so near at hand, but a hasty examination proved the hull to be water-tight. Thirty-five minutes later, Weddigen got a double shot into his second target, but he was so close in, that he was forced to go astern on one engine to get clear of the sinking ship. Down again dived U 9. From the chief engineer then came a report that the batteries were almost discharged, and an immediate return to the surface was rapidly becoming inevitable. Nevertheless, Weddigen continued his attack.

In the stern tubes still remained two torpedoes. The last reserve torpedo was reloaded into a bow tube. Taking another sight through the periscope, Weddigen found the third cruiser immobile, presenting a perfect target. Her boats had been lowered and sent away on life-saving work. Weddigen was a chivalrous officer, and his feelings of exultation may well have been tempered with pity for the ship he was to slay. One hour after the first torpedo had sped away he gave orders for both stern tubes to be fired. One torpedo went wide, the other struck its billet. The cruiser seemed undamaged, so the last torpedo was discharged, and the large vessel received her death-blow. A final glimpse through the periscope revealed her heeling over, slightly but irresistibly. From this terrible *noyade* of goodly ships and gallant men U 9 turned away, and at the first possible moment came up to the surface to recharge her batteries. Creeping homewards inshore along the Dutch coast, late in the afternoon they saw on the sea-horizon the Harwich destroyers frantically hunting to and fro, searching and quartering for the slayer of the three big cruisers.

Returning safely to the shelter of the Ems, the U 9's crew received a tremendous ovation. Weddigen had not merely, as he had at first thought, avenged U 15 by sinking three 'Birmingham'-class cruisers : he had sent to the bottom three large armoured cruisers of 12,000 tons each. He had opened a new era in naval warfare ; and, in the immense enthusiasm with which his feat was greeted, demand arose for some enterprise against the Grand Fleet.

Dreadful and shocking as the calamity was, it conveyed salutary lessons. For one thing, a heavy seaway or swell, running over shoal waters, did not prevent a submarine from making her approach undetected, as had been hitherto thought. For another thing, it was now clearly grasped how imprudent was the policy of using old and large cruisers as a patrolling or screening force ; of advancing those cruisers to positions within easy striking range of hostile submarine bases, and of leaving them there unscreened by destroyers. To repeat such dispositions would clearly court another disaster. Indeed, Admiral Mark Kerr has related that he had written a memorandum before the war, advocating withdrawal of all large ships from the North Sea in the event of hostilities, lest a successful attack (such as this) should give impetus to belief in the potency of the submarine arm. By bitter experience did the British learn their lesson, but not until both the French and Italians had likewise suffered heavy loss was the principle accepted of not exposing easy targets to enemy torpedoes.

As a result of this triple sinking, the 7th Cruiser Squadron was abolished ; a mine-field was laid on October 2, about fifty miles north of Ostend, southward of the field laid by the *Königin Luise* in the early days of August. By the end of the year some 2000 British mines had been planted ; but, the type of mine used being defective, British mining work ceased altogether by the following June. The only value these mines possessed lay in their supposed presence, thereby deterring enemy submarines from traversing a suspected area for some time. Excepting such damage as was suffered by our ships, it is questionable whether any injury whatever was wrought by the mines. Indeed, the Germans issued an order, ' British mines do not explode ! ' They asserted that areas declared

AN ARM NEW TO NAVAL WARFARE 11

by the British as mined and dangerous to navigation were sometimes found to contain no mines whatsoever. The outcome in the end was the same. To declare an area dangerous and not to mine it gave the same result as declaring the area dangerous and sowing it with non-effective mines. In either case, whether mines were there or not, no ships would be damaged in that particular locality. Later on, the Germans, thinking we were again bluffing with ' fictitious areas,' went superciliously cruising through areas that *did* contain potent mines—to their own undoing. In the closing stages of the war, mines exacted the highest number of victims amongst the destroyed U-boats. The original failure of British mines had at least this one saving merit—that it lulled the enemy into a contemptuous over-confidence.

Just before the mine-field was laid, a further development of the submarine war occurred. To von Hennig in U 18 belongs the credit of making the first passage through the Dover Straits. Attacking the scout *Attentive* off Dover on September 27, he penetrated the narrows on the 30th, and returned just before the mine-field was laid. In order to ensure that privacy so essential to success in mining operations, it was imperative to postpone the work of laying until nightfall and under destroyer protection. U 18 was possibly the boat which attacked the old British submarine B 3, south of the Goodwins, on October 2. Von Hennig's chief difficulty encountered on this trip was the strong currents; otherwise, he found matters in the Straits to be just the same as in peace-time, with all navigating lights ashore, light-vessels and buoys, working at night as guides to sea-traffic in the defile of the Straits.

Other submarines were operating farther north. On October 1, U 16 (Hansen) started on a record cruise lasting fifteen days. Before this boat returned, Weddigen in U 9 set out again, this time in company with U 17 (Feldkirchner), to attack the Grand Fleet in its anchorage. As it happened, the Canadian Expeditionary Force was even then crossing from Halifax, N.S. Certain dispositions had therefore been made to prevent German ships breaking out into the Atlantic and intercepting the convoy of troopships. Amongst such measures, the 10th Cruiser Squadron (then consisting of the old 'Edgar'-class cruisers) was brought down from its northern blockading line (Iceland-Shetlands) to a position extending eastwards from Aberdeen. On October 15 the two submarines made contact with this cordon. The cruisers were steaming in line abreast, ten miles apart.

Once more U 9 had encountered her enemies at daybreak, and hopes ran high of repeating the triple success of September 22. It was not long, however, before Weddigen and Spiess saw that they had an entirely new situation to deal with. By steaming in set formation, on a steady course and at a uniform speed, the *Aboukir*, *Cressy*, and *Hogue* had made the problems of approach and attack as simple as they could possibly be for the attacking submarine.

But now ? The British had learnt their lesson ! The 'Edgar'-class cruisers kept well apart ; they continually altered course ; they varied their speed, sometimes moving at 7 knots and sometimes spurting up to 14 knots. They were infinitely more difficult targets, since the whole problem of approaching and attacking them changed from minute to minute. Such were the tactics the British had devised, after the triple cruiser disaster, to baffle submarines. And they did so baffle U 9. For hours she dogged the cruisers, trying to work into range and position. In the end, Weddigen and Spiess gave up all hope and went below.

Then the tide of fortune turned in favour of U 9. Word was sent that three cruisers were approaching. Weddigen at once reassumed the command ; every one went to his diving station ; U 9 effaced herself beneath the waves. A glassy calm prevailed, so that the periscope had to be used with great discretion. One brief look revealed that the cruisers were exchanging signals between themselves. A boat was being lowered, probably for the conveyance of orders or a messenger.

Submarine attack is a game of glimpse and guess ; hence it is only natural to find discrepancies between the British and German accounts of this and similar affairs. To a commander less astute, prompt, and resourceful than Weddigen the interweavings of the three cruisers, the continual changes in the situation, would have been almost bewildering. He suddenly found himself in danger of being run down by one of his opponents. (Whether this vessel was the *Hawke* or the *Endymion* is not clear.) He decided to dive under her, and estimated that, when he rose on the farther side of her, he would be in an excellent position for a shot with one of the after tubes. But when he did so rise, it was to find a cruiser ahead instead of astern of him. His reading of events was that, after an ineffectual attempt to ram, one of the cruisers had described a half-circle, and had worked herself round into a position before the bows of the submarine. Here was the opportunity he had striven for, ever since he had first sighted the cruisers at daybreak. He grasped it without an instant's hesitation. A bow tube ejected its torpedo. It was upon the hull of the *Hawke* that the all-shattering explosion impinged. She had hove-to, to take her mails from the *Endymion* ; and for the imprudence the *Hawke* paid with her life. She had received her mails, had got under way, and was moving at 12 to 13 knots, when the explosion came. The old ship took a list at once, heeled over, and sank in eight minutes, taking down with her about 500 of her crew. The other cruisers were out of sight ; but an hour later *Theseus* narrowly avoided a torpedo, fired by U 17. All ships were then ordered to steam north-westwards ; no reply could be got from the *Hawke*, and a search resulted in the discovery of a raft bearing but one officer and a score of men.

Weddigen, after dealing this second blow, carried on to make the first attempt to penetrate Scapa Flow ; off the eastern entrance he attacked a division of destroyers, nearly succeeding in torpedoing the *Alarm*. So preoccupied was he that he suddenly found the *Nymphe* nearly atop of him, and only escaped being rammed by a precipitate dive. The roar of the destroyer's engines and propellers as she raced overhead nearly deafened those inside U 9. When he returned to his base, it was to hear that U 17 had stopped, searched, and scuttled the steamer *Glitra* (866 tons) off Stavanger, on the 20th—an event pregnant with significance, and one to which further reference will be made presently.

In southern waters, U 20 was causing uneasiness. On

October 13 a submarine, sighted off the Isle of Wight by Torpedo Boat No. 116, had to dive hurriedly. Her presence gave rise to great anxiety for the safety of the incoming Canadian convoy. The destination of the troopships was accordingly diverted from Southampton to Plymouth, it being then believed that no submarine would venture so far westward. However, Droescher in U 20 found his return through the Straits too hazardous, and decided to hold on and pass up the western coasts, returning by the north of Scotland. Whether he passed up the Irish Sea or along the western Irish seaboard is not clear. The material point is, his presence was never detected. On the 17th, off the Butt of Lewis, he suddenly came upon four battleships and a destroyer screen; and his astonishment was such that he lost his opportunity of attacking. On the eighteenth day Droescher returned from his great feat of circumnavigating the British Isles.

Off the western Scottish coasts submarine alarms became increasingly frequent, and German submarines now began to pass westward of the Orkneys. The trip of U 20 was kept a close secret by the Germans; but when a submarine was definitely located in Loch Ewe on October 7, there could be no feeling of security for the Grand Fleet. Weddigen, it is true, had failed to penetrate the anchorage at Scapa Flow, more by bad luck than through efficient patrolling work. The decision was made to move the battle-squadrons to Lough Swilly in the north of Ireland, until such time as Scapa Flow could be made secure against the incursion of submarines. That part of the Grand Fleet should have run into the mine-field laid off Lough Swilly by the *Berlin* and so lost one of its most powerful units, the *Audacious*, does not affect the deep significance of this step. It meant that a few submarines had forced the most powerful battle-fleet in history to abandon its base and retreat to a second base, and then to a third, each being progressively more remote from the main theatre of naval hostilities—the North Sea.

The retreat of the Grand Fleet was, in its way, as serious as the German break-through in Flanders during March-April 1918. Gone was the 'containing' position in the Orkneys, and with it the support for the Northern Blockade.

AN ARM NEW TO NAVAL WARFARE

The whole of the East Coast was left perilously exposed to hostile attack : the naval forces in these waters were left unsupported. In a word, the bottom of the whole strategical situation was knocked out for a time by the German U-boats. What tremendous possibilities were opened up by the submarines for combined operations by the German Fleet and Army ! Well was it for us that the Germans failed to seize the enormous opportunity lying within their reach.

Before Droescher returned in U 20, the new boat U 27 (Wegener) started out to relieve him. Hardly had her cruise begun when she encountered the British boat E 3 off Borkum Riff, on the 18th. Wegener says that his torpedo literally blew her in two ; but, fearing lest other submarines should be in the neighbourhood, he could not search for any survivors. He then continued his interrupted trip towards the Dover Straits, followed a few days later by U 19 (Kolbe). This latter boat was to put into Zeebrugge, recently captured by the German troops. Off the Dutch coast, on the night of the 24th, U 19 was run down in pitch darkness by the destroyer *Badger*, and was forced to return in a damaged condition to her base. (Indeed, it may be remarked that this veteran boat survived many perils right through the war, and she sank 36,000 tons of shipping in the Irish Sea in February 1918. At a later stage of hostilities Spiess took over the command : in his book he relates the many and amazing escapes of U 19 in the Baltic, North Sea, Channel, and Atlantic.)

Since U 19 had been placed *hors de combat*, U 24, under Schneider, had to be sent out. Through this substitution Schneider acquired the unenviable distinction of committing the first atrocity of the German submarine warfare. Off Cape Grisnez, on the 26th, he came upon the French steamer *Amiral Ganteaume* (4590 tons),[1] laden with 2500 Belgian refugees, and did not scruple to torpedo her. Although the ship did not sink and was towed into Boulogne, about forty lives were lost in the panic which broke out amongst the terrified countryfolk. Was not the cup of sorrows bitter enough to Belgium without this fresh affliction ? Driven from their homes by the field-grey hordes, these grief-distraught peasants took

[1] Formerly the Allan liner *Hibernian*.

refuge on the sea. Still they found not upon the sea the sanctuary they sought.

A more legitimate success was the sinking of the old cruiser *Hermes* (employed as a seaplane-carrier). Whilst *en route* from Dover to Dunkirk, on October 31, she was struck by two torpedoes from U 27, and her sinking was attended by the loss of twenty-two lives. The presence of Admiral Hood's bombarding squadron off the coast of Flanders was undoubtedly proving a strong magnet to the U-boats; but, beyond adding to the difficulties of the operation, they gained no success against these ships.[1]

The mishap to U 19 merely postponed the arrival of enemy craft at the Flanders ports. On November 9 the first submarine, U 12, entered Zeebrugge; and during the ensuing month she was followed by U 5, 8, 11, and 24. (Zeebrugge at this time was used merely as an advanced post from which the submarines could harass the Channel traffic and enemy warships in southern waters. As a force separate from the High Sea Fleet, the Flanders Flotilla did not come into being until March 29, 1915; up to that date the U-boats merely used the Flemish ports as *points d'appui*.) Two days after U 12 arrived, Forstmann took her down to the Straits and found the old gunboat *Niger* lying totally unprotected at anchor off

[1] The increasing submarine activity is revealed by the number of contacts reported during October :—

October 2. Submarine B 3 attacked in the Dover Straits.
        5-7. U-boat sighted in Dover Straits by destroyers *Mohawk* and *Coquette*; another seen by drifters off Smith's Knoll Spar Buoy; a third in Loch Ewe.
        9. Cruiser *Antrim* attacked by submarine off Skudenaes.
        10. Destroyer *Attack* attacked by submarine off Schouwen Bank.
        11-13. Torpedo Boat No. 116 chased a submarine off Isle of Wight; the monitor *Severn* attacked by submarine in Straits of Dover; and destroyer *Goshawk* attacked off the Dutch coast.
        15. Cruiser *Hawke* sunk by U 9; flotilla-leader *Swift*, rescuing survivors, attacked three times; *Theseus* attacked by U 17 in North Sea.
        16. Destroyer *Alarm* attacked off Orkneys by U 9.
        17. Gunboat *Leda* and leader *Swift* attacked off Scapa Flow.
        21. Destroyer *Lynx* sighted submarine off Cromarty Firth.
        24. Destroyer *Badger* rammed U 19 off Holland; another seen off Lochs Ewe and Shell.
        31. Cruiser *Hermes* sunk in Dover Straits.

AN ARM NEW TO NAVAL WARFARE 17

Deal pier. He promptly sank her. These boats probably effected the reconnaissance preliminary to the battle-cruiser raid on Yarmouth on November 3 ; they formed the screen placed to intercept any pursuit of the retreating German ships.

The scuttling of the steamer *Glitra* on October 20 has been mentioned. The next incident came on November 11, when the Great Eastern packet *Colchester* (1209 tons) was attacked in the North Sea by a submarine, from which she escaped by flight. This was the first attack so frustrated. Twelve days later U 21 appeared off Havre and stopped the steamer *Malachite* (718 tons) ; after allowing the crew sufficient time to abandon ship, Hersing sank her with gunfire. In a similar fashion he treated the *Primo* (1366 tons) on the 26th. In neither case was there any loss of life. Thereafter a lull followed. In December two of these boats—U 5 (Lemmer) and U 11 (Suchodoletz)—vanished ; it is believed they came to grief in the minefield off Zeebrugge.

Besides the craft operating in the southern waters, others were working in the North Sea. During October the withdrawal of the Grand Fleet had resulted in a search made by U 22 for the British battle-squadrons being fruitless ; a second attack was made on November 23, when U 16 and U 18 attempted to penetrate the defences of Scapa Flow. The Grand Fleet was not there ; unknown to the attackers, it was sweeping down towards the Bight, to support the Zeebrugge bombardment by the Dover Patrol. Without any chance of success, von Hennig in U 18 made the attempt. In the early hours of the 23rd he succeeded in getting as far as the boom in the Hoxa entrance, by following in the wake of a steamer. An inspection of the anchorage showed the Grand Fleet was absent, so he altered course to come out. He had not gone far before the armed trawler *Tokio* detected his presence ; soon afterwards he was located by another armed trawler, *Dorothy Grey*, which rammed the intruder. Both periscope and hydroplanes appear to have been damaged, for U 18 dived wildly, hit the bottom, and then broke surface. Rammed again, this time by the destroyer *Garry*, which had joined the hunt, the U 18 once more went down. Yet again she struggled up to the surface ; then, completely

B

disabled, drifted along the Pentland Skerries. Her crew fired star signals, and, as the *Garry* came alongside, U 18 sank off Muckle Skerry. Her crew, realizing escape to be impossible, had scuttled her. All except one were rescued.

Her consort, U 16 (Hansen), also reconnoitred off the southern entrance; but she likewise saw nothing of the Grand Fleet. During the next two days she caused much commotion, claiming to have entered Lerwick (Shetlands), off which port, on the 25th, she was attacked and driven off by the gunboat *Skipjack*. On the same day, also, U 17 put into Norwegian waters in a damaged condition, but she left next day to avoid internment.

After the attempted raid on the Orcadian fleet anchorage, the activity of the U-boats died down. During the Scarborough bombardment on December 16, three submarines were posted off the Humber, following a reconnaissance of the East Coast mine-fields by U 27. Gayer says that the North Sea boats were principally charged with the duty of coastal patrol and defence, it being apprehended that the British would shortly attempt to scuttle block-ships across the mouths of the German rivers. Only once were the submarines called up to search for and attack enemy warships adjacent to Heligoland. On Christmas Day, 1914, an air raid was made on Cuxhaven by British machines flown off aircraft-carriers; on this occasion, U 20, U 22, and U 30 were sent to attack the surface ships. The first-mentioned U-boat fired a torpedo at one of the accompanying light cruisers, but the other two were prevented from attacking by the destroyer screen.

Again, during the battle-cruiser action off the Dogger Bank on January 24, 1915, six U-boats were stationed in the mouth of the Ems and off Heligoland, awaiting orders should they be required to attack pursuing British ships. Quite erroneously, the British squadron of battle-cruisers firmly believed that German submarines were present at the fight. The suspected arrival of U-boats had a most important effect on the chase. It led to the formation of a huge anti-submarine screen around the wounded *Lion* whilst that vessel was under tow back to Rosyth, so that she might be rendered safe against torpedo attack. Against the undamaged British battle-cruisers

AN ARM NEW TO NAVAL WARFARE 19

German submarines would have had a reasonable chance of success, had they been at large. The inactivity of the High Sea Fleet and the paucity of submarines prevented the working out of joint operations between squadrons and submarines at this time. Not until more than a year later were such combined operations seriously undertaken.

The New Year opened with the biggest submarine success yet achieved. It happened that U 24 (Schneider) was cruising in the Western Channel during Christmas week. By a coincidence the 5th Battle Squadron had been withdrawn from the Medway to undergo gunnery practice off Portland. Most unfortunately no destroyer screen was afforded to the battleships, it being presumed that the Western Channel was safe. (It must be recollected that the long cruise of U 20 from the Scillies to the Orkneys was not then known to the Admiralty.) All day long, on December 31, the submarine slunk furtively after the battleships, and the battleships were all unaware of their peril. As night fell they shaped their course for the Isle of Wight, with the intention of resuming practice next day. A strong southerly wind was rising, and the squadron was steaming at low speed in the rough seas. In the early hours of New Year's Day, U 24 struck her blow. The *Formidable* was hit by a torpedo. In compliance with the instructions issued after the triple cruiser sinking in September, the other ships in company were ordered to abstain from closing the doomed battleship. The *Formidable* sank, with the loss of 550 lives.

One result of this tragic event was a plea to the military authorities for the recapture of Zeebrugge and Ostend. In the meantime it was decided to lay drifter nets across the Dover Straits in order to entangle submarines passing through; thereafter, armed yachts or destroyers would come up and despatch the enemy with explosive sweeps. As the depth of these nets was only 60 feet and the diving limit of German submarines at this time was anything up to 164 feet, it was quite possible for the under-water craft to dive below the curtain. Moreover, as the drifters could only be maintained by day, the passing U-boats had merely to await nightfall and then pass the obstacle. Even in the daytime the indicator buoys of the nets were clearly visible to the submarines, and could be given a wide berth. Nets as a submarine antidote were no new idea; they had been tried as far back as 1905. In the Dover Straits the strong tides greatly reduced their value.

Apart from this attempt to hinder the U-boats, the Germans lost two more units from accidental causes. Three boats, U 22, U 31, and U 32, had sailed for the Thames estuary on January 13, but on the ninth day U 32 returned damaged. Hoppe (U 22) came in on January 27, the bearer of a tragic tale. Six days previously, U 22 had encountered a submarine off the Dutch coast; twice he challenged her, but had received no reply. Convinced that she was a British boat, Hoppe had then torpedoed her. One man was picked up from amongst the wreckage—the sole survivor of U 7, commanded by König, Hoppe's best friend. As for the third boat, U 31 (Wachendorff), she never returned; it is surmised that she blew up on a mine off the East Coast. The German version of this mystery is that she foundered during a bad dive, or that defective batteries overcame the crew; further, that six months later she was found by the British, still water-tight, and her crew dead at their stations. It is an interesting tale, but it entirely lacks corroboration. The truth is, the exact circumstances, date, and place of U 31's loss are as much a mystery to-day to the British naval authorities as they are to the German.

Nevertheless, all this pioneer work was to prove invaluable to the enemy, and an experiment far-reaching both in range and consequence was projected. Hersing was selected to extend the zone of the submarine menace into the western waters of England. Leaving Wilhelmshaven on January 21, and passing through the Straits of Dover, he appeared off Walney Island on the 29th and shelled Barrow, causing insignificant damage before he was driven off by the Walney Island batteries. On the next day he sank with bombs the three steamers *Kilcoan* (456 tons), *Linda Blanche* (369 tons), and *Ben Cruachan* (3092 tons), all off the Lancashire coast. Passing south, he was then attacked by the armed yacht *Vanduara* off Fishguard, and eventually returned safely.

AN ARM NEW TO NAVAL WARFARE 21

Little difficulty was experienced by U 21 in passing through the Straits : the nets were located by their buoys and successfully passed ; the mines were avoided by going through at low water when they were near the surface and visible.

Whilst Hersing was out on this cruise, U 19 was working off the Dutch coast ; on the 21st she sank with bombs the steamer *Durward* (1301 tons). In the Channel was Droescher in U 20. He had a different method of sinking : he gave no warning, but fired a torpedo into his unsuspecting victims. By such summary methods he sank, on the 30th, the steamers *Ikaria* (4335 tons), the *Tokomaru* (6084 tons), and the *Oriole* (1489 tons), the last-named with her entire crew, numbering twenty-one souls. Such was the beginning of the long toll of non-combatant life exacted by enemy submarines. From this time until February 1917 (when ' unrestricted ' war, without any pretence at humanity, began), 27 per cent. of the ships destroyed were sunk without any warning. Droescher, as if to emphasize his callous conduct, at dusk on February 1, off Havre, fired a torpedo at, and missed, the large hospital-ship *Asturias* (12,002 tons), although she was brilliantly lighted up and her hull painted the regulation white with green bands punctuated with red crosses.

Beyond the sinking by U 16 of the steamers *Dulwich* (3289 tons) and the *Ville de Lille* (997 tons) off Havre on February 15 (when two lives were lost), no further depredations occurred until the official opening of the 1915 campaign against trade. Up to this point (February 18, 1915) a total of eleven British and one Allied merchantmen had been sunk, and one Allied ship damaged. The Germans had announced that they would attack the numerous troopships leaving British ports ' with every means at their disposal,' but against these ships they did not score a single success.

The first phase had closed. The Germans had found in their hands a weapon wherewith they could strike at their enemy with a freedom denied to their surface ships. These under-water craft had forced the Grand Fleet to retreat from its North Sea anchorage. They had stumbled upon a means of attacking their enemy's trade. Submarines had proved that they possessed far greater powers of endurance than had been credited to them. On the German side, discovery had been made that an intermittent patrol could be maintained in certain areas : on the British side, it had been found feasible, from the very outset of war, to maintain a continuous Diving Patrol in the Bight of Heligoland.

Perhaps unwisely, the Germans experimented with a rather haphazard trade war after the unpremeditated scuttling of the *Glitra*. This initial venture showed the possibility that, at a later stage, a much more serious onslaught might be made on British, Allied, and neutral shipping. Yet it seemed as if little could be done to ward off such a blow, were that blow ever to be delivered. Mine-fields had been laid in the southern North Sea, and a system of drifter nets inaugurated in the Dover Straits. Otherwise, reliance was placed in the chance success of patrols, in the screening of the battle-squadrons, and in advising masters of merchant-ships to use their speed and so escape from their attackers. Eleven British steamers had been sunk, and five others had escaped by flight ; more serious had been the destruction of one battleship, four cruisers, one small cruiser, an aircraft-carrier, an old gunboat, and one submarine. On their side, the Germans had to deplore the disappearance of seven units of their small under-water force. The wastage had not been made good by the completion of three or four new boats. Orders had, however, been placed for twenty large and thirty-three small coastal and mine-laying submarines. In the minds of the German naval leaders there was now no doubt of the intrinsic war-value of the *Unterseeboote*.

CHAPTER II

TRIAL AND ERROR: THE FIRST WAR ON SHIPPING

(FEBRUARY–SEPTEMBER 1915)

I

WHEN did the idea of a war on commerce, waged by submarines, first present itself to the Germans? The answer to this riddle would reveal much that is hidden. The late Sir Julian Corbett emphatically stated [1] that before the war it was recognized that Germany would not scruple to employ submarines in the prosecution of war on and against enemy merchant shipping. Such a procedure would be at variance with German Naval Prize Regulations. Those Regulations, in unison with the international code of maritime law, laid down the following principle: Only in the event of it being found impossible or impracticable to bring a prize into port could the captured vessel be destroyed there and then; such destruction was not to be carried out 'until after all persons on board are placed in safety, with their goods and chattels if possible.'

How were principles so humane as these ever questioned or departed from? To answer the question, a brief outline must be given, showing how the idea of a war by submarines against commerce first arose. But before embarking on such a topic, a preliminary word is necessary as to the development of anti-submarine warfare. Three years after the first British submarines had been ordered, submarines took part in the 1904 manœuvres at Spithead, when both indicator nets and sweeps were improvised as anti-submarine measures. It will be recollected that A 1 was lost during these tests. The disaster led to all research and counter-attacks being given up for the

[1] *Naval Operations*, vol. ii. p. 132.

time. In 1910 a Committee was set up to consider defence against submarines ; and amongst the devices discussed were the smoke-screen, zigzagging, deceptive painting of hulls, mines, hand-grenades, towing-charges, stalking by submarines, and the mounting of guns in submarines.[1] It is to be noted that British opinion was averse to the mounting of guns in submarines ; and there is no case on record of the destruction of a submarine by a gun mounted in another under-water vessel.

All the foregoing methods of attack were considered in relation to *submarine attack on warships*, singly or in squadrons ; and a submarine war on commerce was not discussed. Towards the end of 1913, however, Lord Fisher, assisted by Captain S. S. Hall, prepared a memorandum in which it was prophesied that the Germans would use their submarines for attacking commerce. So utterly repugnant was this novel idea that both the First Lord [2] and the First Sea Lord [3] declared that the paper was 'marred by this suggestion.'

In the British naval manœuvres of 1913, submarines proved astonishingly effective ; whilst the Germans, in the naval manœuvres held during the spring of 1914, also tried a scheme of combined operations by submarines and battle-squadrons. They were so successful that the idea of 'booby-traps' received investigation. Gayer says that it was demonstrated that submarines could carry out operations efficiently with or against surface vessels ; and the results greatly influenced submarine operations during the first stages of the war. The German boats were stationed at Heligoland, to be in proximity to the High Sea Fleet, with which they were to operate ; alternatively, they were to assist in repelling any strong British naval attack on the German North Sea coast, particularly against Borkum and Sylt. Before the war the Germans had an exercise known as 'periscope trawling' ; it was believed to have been a form of explosive sweep towed by destroyers.

Rear-Admiral Spindler emphatically denies that Germany

[1] Brassey's *Naval Annual*, 1919, p. 131.
[2] The Right Hon. Winston S. Churchill, M.P.
[3] Admiral H.S.H. Prince Louis of Battenberg, G.C.B. (later the Marquis of Milford Haven).

THE FIRST WAR ON SHIPPING 25

ever premeditated an attack on commerce by submarines before the war.[1] However, one highly significant and interesting admission has been made. Captain Gayer, discussing the pre-war estimates of the submarine's combatant value, says : ' True, before the outbreak of the war one of the best technical experts in this weapon, Lieutenant-Commander Blum, had calculated the number of submarines necessary to conduct cruiser warfare against England, and had placed this number at 200.' [2] This estimate subsequently proved to be a remarkably accurate one.

The question therefore arises whether Blum prepared his report officially or otherwise. If he did so in response to orders, then Spindler's denial of any premeditated plans remains open to question. However, it must be remembered that so high an authority as the late Admiral Scheer has denied that there was any such preparation, declaring that ' such aggressive ideas were quite foreign to our naval policy.' [3]

Gayer relates that as early as September 1914 an attack on British shipping had been discussed and had been disapproved. The rejection rested, not on the grounds of possible inhumanity, but on the score that the number of submarines at hand was inadequate to conduct such a campaign. The first definite demand for a trade war emanated from the High Sea Fleet during November 1914, after the *Glitra* attack. When Feldkirchner returned to his base in U 17, it was feared that his action would meet with censure ; but, instead of rebuke ensuing, his conduct of the affair was formally approved. The policy of a *guerre de course* by submarines on British shipping began to be openly and actively advocated. 'As England completely disregards International Law, there is

---

[1] ' No preparation had been made in the German Navy for the employment of submarines against enemy commerce prior to the outbreak of the war in 1914. The German naval authorities had developed no plan of operations whereby an enemy, England, could be attacked through her overseas commerce, and thus become possessed of a weapon which would really be effective in operations against the vital nerve of the island empire.' —' The Value of the Submarine in Warfare,' Rear-Admiral Spindler, German Navy, *U.S. Naval Institute Proceedings*, May 1926, p. 837.

[2] *U.S.N.I. Proceedings*, Gayer, April 1926, p. 622.

[3] *High Sea Fleet*, Scheer, p. 224.

not the least reason why we should exercise any restraint in our conduct of the war. . . . We must make use of this weapon, and do so in the way most suitable to its peculiarities. Consequently, a U-boat cannot spare the crews of steamers, but must send them to the bottom with their ships. The shipping world can be warned . . . and all shipping trade with England should cease within a short time.'[1]

The alleged violation of International Law by Britain, here referred to, was the prevention of contraband from reaching Germany, whether carried in neutral or in enemy ships. The German Government was reported (erroneously) to have taken over the control of foodstuffs; consequently, these had been made contraband and had been intercepted, if destined in excessive amounts for Dutch and Danish ports.[2] The allegations made by Germany against Britain were that Britain had added to the list of contraband articles not useful for military purposes, and that she had, for her own benefit, misapplied the doctrine of 'ultimate destination.' Further, the German authorities stated that we had seized German property in neutral vessels, as well as Germans of military age. The enemy also declared that, by proclaiming the North Sea a military area, we had set up a blockade of neutral coasts.

As a consequence of the decision to embark on the trade war, the late Admiral von Tirpitz, the Naval Secretary of State, gave an interview to an American journalist, von Wiegand, hinting that a vigorous campaign against shipping by submarine might be started in the near future. By this *ballon d'essai* an attempt was made to ascertain American opinion on such a form of warfare. At the same time, the ' Wiegand interview ' gave to Germany's adversaries a warning of coming events. Against the policy adumbrated by Tirpitz, as spokesman for the extremists, stood the men of saner views, headed by Bethmann-Hollweg, the Imperial Chancellor. In this way

[1] *High Sea Fleet*, Scheer, p. 222. Extract from Memorandum addressed by the leaders of the Fleet to Admiral von Pohl, Chief of the Naval Staff, in November 1914.

[2] The Declaration of London had never been formally ratified by the British Government, and was therefore non-operative. By conferring immunity from capture on private property at sea, it made successful interception of an enemy's sea-borne supplies illegal, and would therefore have rendered efficient blockade almost impossible.

THE FIRST WAR ON SHIPPING

began that long and bitter quarrel between the naval and military authorities on the one hand, and the diplomatists and economists on the other, each party seeking the support of the Kaiser's personal staff.

To the Chancellor went success on the first round. On December 27 he ruled that, whilst he admitted the legality of the proposed trade war, the time was not ripe for such violent measures. A time more opportune, he said, would come when Germany's position on the Continent had been made absolutely secure ; thereafter, no neutral would dare to pick a quarrel with a State so pre-eminently powerful as the Fatherland. In other words, success in the field must precede ruthless war at sea. Paradoxically, the naval leaders insisted that success on land could be achieved only by ruthless warfare at sea !

An event, however, was about to happen which influenced the controversy profoundly. On January 24, Hipper's raiding battle-cruisers were intercepted off the Dogger Bank and chased homewards by Beatty's battle-cruisers, with the loss to the Germans of the *Blücher*. As a direct outcome of this reverse, Admiral von Ingenohl, the Commander-in-Chief of the High Sea Fleet, was superseded by von Pohl, Chief of the Naval Staff. On February 4 the Kaiser inspected the fleet at Wilhelmshaven, and the commanding officers of the submarines were presented to him. After this ceremony it became known that he was about to sign an order declaring the territorial waters around the British Isles to be a war zone.

On the same day the expected announcement was published, to the following effect :—

' 1. The waters around Great Britain and Ireland, including the whole of the English Channel, are herewith declared to be in the War Zone. From February 18 onward, every merchant-ship met with in this War Zone will be destroyed, nor will it always be possible to obviate the danger with which the crews and passengers are thereby threatened.

' 2. Neutral ships, too, will run a risk in the War Zone, for in view of the misuse of neutral flags ordered by the British Government on January 31, and owing to the hazards of naval warfare, it may not always be possible to prevent the attacks meant for hostile ships from being directed against neutral ships.

'Shipping north of the Shetland Islands, in the eastern part of the North Sea, and on a strip at least 30 nautical miles wide along the Dutch coast, is not threatened with danger.

v. POHL,
Chief of the Naval Staff.'

The misuse of neutral flags, here alleged, alluded to the action taken by the master of the Cunard liner *Lusitania* during the Irish Sea raid in January. Carrying a heavy American passenger list, he had flown the United States colours—a practice perfectly legitimate, and one to which many nations had previously and often resorted in war time.

It is important to realize that there were frequent and sharp divergences of view between the Administrations in London and Washington, and the arguments advanced by the Press of each country did little to help and much to hinder mutual understanding. The first crisis came when a German-American purchased the Hamburg-Amerika liner *Dacia*, loaded her with cotton at Galveston, and despatched her on January 31 for the neutral port of Rotterdam. This deliberate attempt to involve British and American relations was adroitly parried by leaving the seizure to the French. On February 27 the *Dacia* was captured by the French auxiliary cruiser *Europe* off the Scillies.[1]

Imports into the neutral countries adjacent to Germany had risen, even by November 1914, to an unprecedented level. Five times as much copper as in 1913 was passing into these states. Still, food was not actually declared to be contraband until February; such cargoes as were intercepted were diverted into British ports, so that their destination was merely changed. When, on January 25, the German Government definitely announced that it would take over all foodstuffs as from February 1, the issue became plain. In deference to

[1] The Declaration of London proposed exemption from capture of enemy tonnage if it should be re-registered under neutral ownership. Such an innovation had been stoutly withstood by British naval and mercantile opinion, in opposition to political and legal views. Such transfers were not recognized by Britain, France, Germany, and Russia, although both Britain and America conceded their legality if the transfer were a *bona fide* one.

THE FIRST WAR ON SHIPPING 29

American demands, engineered by the influential Southern party, cotton was exempted by the British.

Immediately after the declaration of war on shipping, America made a vigorous protest against the projected infringement of neutral rights; at the same time a Note was sent to Britain concerning the alleged misuse of the United States flag. The British explanation was accepted, and there was at once a noticeable relief in the tension between London and Washington. On the other hand, Count Bernstorff, the German Ambassador at Washington, intimated on February 15 that Germany would abandon the campaign if food for civilians were declared immune from capture. Yet Bismarck himself, thirty years before, had justified the 'hunger blockade' when he declared ' the object for shortening war is justifiable if impartially enforced against all neutral ships.'

The late Admiral von Tirpitz was against the declaration of a war zone around the British Isles. He favoured a much less ambitious plan — the more modest blockade of the Thames only. He was exceedingly annoyed at von Pohl's ' flourish of trumpets.' The Naval Secretary's chagrin was probably aroused by the fact that he had never been consulted over the 'War Zone' declaration. Apart from his long and distinguished service, von Tirpitz was certainly entitled, as Director of Supply and Maintenance, to express an opinion upon so important a change in policy.

To the officers in command of the submarines the following memorandum was issued :—

' The first consideration is the safety of the U-boat. Rising to the surface to examine a ship must be avoided for the boat's safety, because, apart from the danger of a possible surprise attack by enemy ships, there is no guarantee that one is not dealing with an enemy ship even if she bears the distinguishing marks of a neutral. The fact that a steamer flies a neutral flag is no guarantee that it is actually a neutral vessel. Its destruction will therefore be justifiable unless other attendant circumstances indicate its neutrality.'

Scheer suggested that success was denied to the project right away by the hint at consideration being shown towards neutrals, and by the attempt to persuade them to conform to the new conditions as laid down by Germany. A policy so half-hearted held out a promise of future concessions. On February 14 it was declared that ships flying neutral colours, unless definitely identified as being of enemy nationality, would be granted immunity. A last-minute order was issued on the 15th, postponing the outbreak of the campaign until such time as the Kaiser should order its beginning. The order came too late ; U 30 had already left for western waters to initiate the new plan of operations.

Gayer says that, before the blockade was declared, the submarines received guns both for use against shipping in weakly patrolled areas and for the attack of vessels outside effective torpedo range. This additional armament necessitated the stiffening of the submarines' decks and the provision of stowage-space for ammunition. Officers and men received special training for their new work ; they were warned against the possible use of mercantile vessels as decoys for enemy submarines, and were admonished to observe the utmost wariness even when a victim was sinking. They were directed to leave the vicinity of any ship slowly settling down or set on fire, because such a vessel would bring up hostile patrols, surface and under-water, to the spot. It was further pointed out that the longer a submarine remained at work within any confined area, the greater should be the caution observed.

Though the practice of sending a new commanding officer for a training cruise in one of the older boats, handled by an experienced officer, proved very useful, a risk of losing two submarine captains in one hull had to be faced. It was fully realized that new submarines with inexperienced captains were more likely to be lost. Another innovation was the inclusion of a ' war pilot ' in the U-boat's complement ; he was drawn from the merchant service, and could give competent advice concerning the shipping met. Perhaps more than anything else, there was a great dearth of qualified wireless-telegraphy operators.

The trials of new boats and the training of commanding officers and crews took a long time ; and before a U-boat left for her maiden cruise she had to be tested thoroughly and dived, to make certain she left no oil-fuel streaks on the surface.

THE FIRST WAR ON SHIPPING 31

In the later stages of the war, boats were so hastily passed into service that their hulls were sometimes not even water-tight.

With the threat of an onslaught on shipping, particularly on the cross-Channel transports, hasty preparations were made to meet the German menace. The patrol of the Western Channel was reorganized, and during February 4-16, two days before the opening date, a new mine-field, stretching from the north of Dunkirk to Elbow Buoy, near Broadstairs, was laid, to the south-west of the existing field off Ostend. The mines appear to have become non-effective very soon afterwards, either sinking or drifting away. On the 13th, seventeen miles of drifter nets, watched by trawlers and destroyers, were run out in the Straits of Dover, and others were ready for the North and St. George's Channels. Altogether, one thousand miles of wire nets, between six and ten feet in mesh, were ordered. Supported by glass buoys, these nets were towed by the drifters in the hope of catching a submarine and entangling her in the meshes, whereupon the armed patrols would come up and destroy her. In theory the idea was simple; in practice it was most disappointing. The nets carried away or caught in sunken wreckage; the floats of glass or kapok filled or became sodden; the detachable clips to loose the net on a catch being made, gave great trouble. In spite of all these set-backs, the nets were persevered with and certainly resulted in some measure of success. Finally, about fifty fleet colliers and coasters received guns, and all steam-yachts were taken up.

For the first few weeks of the campaign the submarines used the route through the Dover Straits. They would either make the run at night on the surface, or rest on the bottom until the currents changed in their favour, thus assisting passage to the north of Ruytingen Sand. As for the British mines, they were treated with contempt.

On February 18 the U-boats received their orders to sink all hostile ships, but to spare neutrals and hospital-ships (unless the latter were obviously engaged in trooping) and Belgian Relief steamers; moreover, 'if, in spite of the exercise of great care, mistakes should be made, the commanding officers will not be held responsible.'

When the awaited day dawned, twenty U-boats were available, but they were only able to work in three relays. U 30 was already on her station, and U 8 (Stoch) left Heligoland to work in the Channel; U 20 and U 27 did not set out until the 25th. With these four boats the great gamble began. U 30, passing round the north of Scotland, appeared in the Irish Sea and sank the steamers *Cambank* (3112 tons) and *Downshire* (337 tons), the former being torpedoed without warning on the 20th, off Point Lynas, with the loss of four lives. This submarine returned safely, but she had a narrow escape : on the 23rd she fouled the nets of the fishing trawler *Alex Hastie*, about 100 miles east of the Farne Islands, and was erroneously thought to have been capsized and destroyed. U 8's trip also nearly ended in disaster. Passing through the new mine-field on the 20th, she got caught in the nets off the Varne ; these she tore through, and carried on into the Channel, where she sank five steamers off Beachy Head, three lives being lost. She also tried to sink the hospital-ship *St. Andrew* (2528 tons) on the 24th, but the small vessel escaped by flight. Altogether, eleven British ships had been attacked, of which seven were sunk. One vessel, the small collier *Thordis*, during heavy weather on the 28th, rammed a submarine off Beachy Head ; Berlin admitted that she had injured the U-boat ; the latter had, however, safely regained port. In addition, a French vessel was damaged, and the Norwegian tanker *Belridge* (with oil from America for the Dutch Government) was torpedoed without any warning by U 8 off Dover, but was towed into port. This last incident made a great impression at Washington.

These two U-boats (U 8 and U 30) were relieved by U 20 and U 27, the latter pair clearing from the Ems on February 25. Next day, U 27 made a record for a long-distance wireless-telegraphy communication from submarines by conversing with the cruiser *Arkona*, lying in the Ems 140 miles away. During the whole cruise special study was made of the reception and sending of such signals. U 20 passed down the Channel to attack shipping in the Bristol Channel and Irish Sea, whilst the other boat made the north-about run to operate in the area around the Isle of Man. Between them, the brace of

Photo. Abrahams & Sons.

I.   THE LAST MOMENTS OF THE *U. 8*.

A Photograph taken in the Straits of Dover, on March 4, 1915. The Conning Tower of the foundering submarine is seen in the centre of the view; and, towards the right, the crew is lined up on deck, waiting to be rescued by the two approaching boats from the British destroyers *Maori* and *Ghurka*. The *Maori* herself appears in the distance. One of the very few photographs in existence, depicting the actual end of a German Submarine.

THE EXTERMINATION OF *UC. 39*.

The crew are here shewn being taken off, after their boat had been depth-charged and shelled by the destroyer *Thrasher*, off Flamborough Head on February 8, 1917.

THE FIRST WAR ON SHIPPING

raiders sank five or six steamers; amongst their victims was the armed merchant-cruiser *Bayano*, sunk (by U 27 off Wigtownshire on March 11) with heavy loss of life. As a result of the foray, the flotilla-leader *Faulknor* and six destroyers had to be detached by Admiral Jellicoe to augment the Irish Sea patrol, though their services were urgently needed with the Grand Fleet.

There was, however, another side to the picture. U 8 had just left Zeebrugge to renew her depredations. Soon after midday on March 4 she was sighted by the destroyer *Viking*, five miles E.N.E. of the North-East Varne Buoy. About an hour later the drifter *Roburn* noticed an indicator buoy moving fast to the eastward. The sea was calm, with light fog. The destroyer division was hunting close at hand, and, as a periscope was presently seen, the *Viking* fired her explosive sweep over the spot where it had appeared. Beyond another glimpse of the periscope, nothing happened for a further hour. Then the destroyer *Maori* saw the periscope again, this time farther down Channel. Thereupon the *Ghurka* towed her sweep across the track the submarine appeared to be taking; and at 5 P.M. it exploded with dramatic result. The stern of U 8 shot up to the surface almost vertically, and she was greeted with a rapid fire from *Ghurka* and *Maori*. Finding escape impossible, the submarine's crew of four officers and twenty-five men emerged from their sinking craft and surrendered. Ten minutes later, U 8 sank.

Another submarine was found to be foul of nets laid in Start Bay on March 1; and when explosive sweeps were fired over the spot, large quantities of oil came to the surface. It was confidently supposed that the submarine had been destroyed, but she must have been damaged only; she may have been U 29, commanded by Weddigen, late of U 9. This boat appeared off the Scillies on March 12, where she sank four steamers. Another vessel, the *Atalanta* (519 tons), was stopped and set on fire, but was towed in; to her belongs the distinction of being the first armed steamer to escape.

Two other U-boats were working, about this time, in the North Sea. At sunset on March 6 the Aberdeen patrol trawler *Duster* sighted one of them, U 12 (Kratzsch), steering

W.N.W., and gave chase. Not being equipped with wireless, the trawler was unable to pass on the important news until next morning, when she met a steam-yacht. Then began another hunt. On the morning of the 8th the quarry was seen south of Buchan Ness by a trawler; and again at evening, south of Aberdeen. Next morning she was located off Stonehaven, and in the afternoon off Montrose; each time she dived and escaped from her slow and feebly-armed pursuers. U 12 was joined now by her consort. Unsuspicious of their danger, they bore south for the Firth of Forth. Kratzsch did not know that he was running straight into the path of the 4th Flotilla, sent out of Rosyth to assist in the search. Off the Bell Rock he approached the cruiser *Leviathan* in the dusk, but, before he could loose a torpedo, he was driven off by a trawler. To the destroyers it was now apparent that they had overrun the line on their hunt northwards. They were recalled, and on the fourth morning, March 10, U 12 was finally sighted off Fife Ness. At full speed, three destroyers, *Acheron*, *Ariel*, and *Attack*, dashed up on converging courses. The *Attack* opened fire as U 12 dived, and ran over her. A minute or two later, *Ariel* spotted the periscope 200 yards to starboard, and, swinging round, she rammed the submarine amidships just as the latter was breaking surface. Rapid fire was opened on the disabled U 12. Her gun was hit and hurled overboard. Up from the sinking craft tumbled the crew, ten being rescued. One of them, Volckner, the war pilot, afterwards escaped from imprisonment during the following September, seized a small boat, and crossed the North Sea. He was picked up by U 16, outward bound, and so returned to relate the fate of U 12.

Although two more diving boats had been destroyed, more raiders were coming out. In the Channel, U 34, U 35, and U 37 were at work, units of the afterwards famous 'Thirties' class. Off Beachy Head they accounted for four steamers. Yet another boat, U 28, left her base, sending the first prize into Zeebrugge on the 16th. On the 13th, Weddigen in U 29 got as far west as the Fastnet, and then decided to return north-about, hoping to attack the Grand Fleet. The Dreadnought squadrons of that Fleet, engaged in exercises, he did encounter on the 18th, E.S.E. of the Pentland Firth. He fired a bow

THE FIRST WAR ON SHIPPING

shot at the *Neptune* of the 1st Battle Squadron ; it missed its target. Weddigen, it would seem, did not observe the 4th Battle Squadron a little to the northward, making for the Moray Firth ; and before he was aware of his peril, the *Dreadnought* was almost atop of him. Those aboard the battleship had sighted the periscope ahead on the port bow. The *Dreadnought* turned and charged down on her venomous adversary. A brief chase ensued. Turn this way or that, U 29 could neither get under nor get away. As an elephant might tread down the writhing coils of a hooded cobra, so did the immense bulk of the famous battleship crush underfoot her viperine opponent. The bows of the submarine were thrown up, plainly displaying her number ; then the seas covered her riven hull for ever. Such was the end, in ship-to-ship combat, of one of Germany's most chivalrous captains. Brief and brilliant had been his course athwart the dark firmament of war ; flawless was his starry flight, undimmed by any dishonour. His humane conduct had won for him, from his victims off the Scillies, the half-rueful and half-jesting sobriquet of 'polite pirate.'

It is interesting to observe, both here and later, that successful commanders were often appointed to the latest boats. Herein was the latent fallacy that the combination of 'ace' and 'the latest thing' must accomplish wonders. In practice, it often resulted in the undoing of both commander and vessel ; far better would it have been to retain the commanders in the craft in which they had demonstrated their proficiency.[1] Hersing appears to have been the only officer who retained his original command, though there may have been others.

Through the waters traversed by Weddigen in the early stages of his final cruise came Forstner in U 28. There could hardly be types of commander more dissimilar than these two. To Forstner belongs the odium of waging war not only *à l'outrance,* but even to the point of savagery. Off Beachy Head he sank the Dutch steamer *Medea* (1235 tons) by

---

[1] As an instance, Spiess made many successful cruises in U 19. After taking over a larger and later boat, U 52, he met with disaster. Wisely he went back to U 19, scoring further successes with her until she was finally worn out and had to be withdrawn from the fighting line.

bombs. Working west, he destroyed three steamers off the Scillies on March 27, including the Yeoward liner *Aguila* (2114 tons). In this last case he opened fire on the passengers and crew as they were taking to the boats, causing the death of eight. Worse followed on the morrow, when he intercepted the Elder-Dempster liner *Falaba* (4806 tons), outward bound for West Africa with 147 passengers and a crew of 95. She was carrying thirteen tons of ammunition. Even as the passengers and crew were getting out the boats, U 28 shot a torpedo into the stationary liner. Men, women, and children were thrown into the water. Thereupon Forstner and his crew came up on deck and jeered at the agonies of the drowning people. This appalling deed resulted in a death-roll of 104 lives.

The attack upon shipping having so begun, the Admiralty issued instructions to masters that, if a submarine be sighted ahead, the best method to adopt would be to alter course towards the submarine and compel her to submerge; thereafter, escape could be made by steaming away. On March 28, U 33 left Zeebrugge and soon afterwards attacked the G.E.R. packet *Brussels* (1380 tons), off the Maas L.V. Captain Fryatt successfully pursued the advised tactics, and U 33 was forced off her attack. Ten months later came the sequel. The *Brussels* having been captured by torpedo-boats, Captain Fryatt was taken to Bruges and there judicially murdered as a *franc-tireur*.

The U 33 returned to port with further news besides her version of this daring counter-attack; she brought back warning of numerous mines in the approaches to the Straits of Dover. Early in April, U 32 found the nets so dangerous in this locality, that she preferred to return north-about rather than face the Dover defile again. Other boats came back with tales of fearful risks to be confronted. As a consequence of these reports, the larger German submarines were forbidden, for the first time, to attempt the passage of the Straits; and for nearly two years they had to make their way to the western seas round the north of Scotland. This decision was probably strengthened by the mysterious disappearance of U 37 (Wilcke) in the Channel, after leaving Heligoland on

THE FIRST WAR ON SHIPPING

April 20.[1] The lengthened course for the larger boats certainly diminished the sinkings during April. The Eastern Channel was clear. Rear-Admiral Hood, who had been transferred from Dover to Queenstown on account of the apparent failure of his measures to cope with the situation, was fully vindicated, and was appointed to the command of the 3rd Battle Cruiser Squadron.

During March, twenty-seven steamers had been sunk; in April, only eleven British and six neutral vessels were destroyed—mostly by U 24 and U 32. On April 17 the armed steamer *La Rosarina* (8332 tons) had been attacked off the south of Ireland, but she drove off her assailant with her gun. This was the first successful *riposte* made by a defensively armed merchant-ship. Six days previously the transport *Wayfarer* (9599 tons) was damaged in an attack, but was brought into Queenstown. April also produced the first laceration of the North Sea fishing-fleets, several vessels being sunk off the Tyne by U 10. At first sight the raid would appear to be wanton wreaking of havoc for havoc's sake; but from the prizes the enemy secured valuable charts, showing mined areas unsafe for fishing. Later came a time when fishing-craft, above all, were left unmolested—and for a very good reason.

The prohibition of the Dover Straits by the Germans to navigation by their submarines had for us an unfortunate effect, in that it created a false sense of confidence, both in the sufficiency and efficiency of our defensive measures. True it was, that the nets were being continually carried away. Therefore a more enduring obstacle, in the shape of a steel net placed right across the Straits, was proposed. Much material was collected, and then it was diverted to Gallipoli to provide an urgently-needed boom there. In fact, U-boats had experienced little difficulty in passing through, either by night on the surface or by day under the nets. It was only the fear of unknown dangers that prevented the North Sea boats from using the passage.

---

[1] British Records, 1919, show the loss in the North Sea in June. Gayer (vol. ii. p. 20) indicates that the loss took place at an earlier date, and his version has been accepted as probably the more accurate one.

It has been mentioned at an earlier stage that the creation of the Flanders Flotilla, as a separate unit from the High Sea Fleet, dated from March 29, 1915. Two new types of small submarines—the coastal 'UB I'-boats and the mine-laying 'UC I'-boats—had been ordered in October and November 1914; from Kiel, Bremen, and Hamburg they were railed in sections to Antwerp in Flanders and to Pola in the Adriatic. To hasten construction, they were given heavy-oil motors, ready to hand, and originally ordered for small motor-vessels. These UB I- and UC I-boats were of simple design and were extremely feeble. On the surface they were too slow to chase steamers; and when submerged they had neither power nor endurance enough to make headway against strong currents. Their batteries were almost exhausted after an hour's run submerged at 5 knots; and their best performance below water was 50 miles at $2\frac{1}{2}$ knots—of little use against the 8- or 10-knot currents in the Dover Straits. One of their commanders likened his vessel to a 'sewing-machine,' and gives a vivid account of her acrobatic feats when a torpedo was discharged. The wonder is that such 'tin tadpoles' performed what they did.

The earliest unit to be passed into service was UB 10, on March 29, and she was followed by sixteen similar boats. Originally they swam about in the 'Hoofden,' but by July they appeared in the Channel. In August the first of the fifteen UC-boats were at sea. Those detailed for service in Flanders were UB 2, 4, 5, 6, 10, 12,[1] 13, 16, 17, and UC 1, 2, 3, 5, 6, 7, 9, and 11. Their mission was to harass the Channel traffic and the East Coast trade. Later, the improved and larger UB II- and UC II-boats operated as far west as the Bay of Biscay and the western approaches—areas which became Golgothas of the world's shipping. It may be noticed here that not until March 3, 1916, were the first British mines laid off Heligoland by submarine E 24, and she was lost on her next trip. The inferior British mine led to a discontinuance of mining activities during 1915, for German submarines could carry these ineffective engines on their bows, shake them off, or bump against them with impunity. Many German

---

[1] UB 12 was later converted into a mine-layer, carrying eight mines.

THE FIRST WAR ON SHIPPING 39

warships had as a souvenir a British mine mounted on a stand.

In addition to the diminutive submarines referred to above, a number of small torpedo-boats were being assembled at Antwerp, intended for attacking the numerous patrol trawlers and drifters at work in the ' Hoofden.' On May Day came the first burst of activity. Four Yarmouth trawlers had been sent out to hunt a submarine reported near the North Hinder L.V. At the same time, it happened that two of these Flanders torpedo-boats, A 2 and A 6, had been ordered out to see if there were any British destroyers about. Thirty miles to the south-west of the Galloper were two old destroyers, *Brazen* and *Recruit*. Just before noon the *Recruit* was rent in two by a shattering torpedo explosion and sank at once, 26 of her crew being saved. Her assailant was UB 6 (Hacker). A little later another torpedo was fired at one of the armed trawlers engaged in the search. About three hours after, two torpedo-boats were encountered, and the trawler *Columbia* was sunk by torpedo. Thereupon began a general *mêlée* with the small guns. The action was brought to an end by the arrival of four Harwich destroyers. After an hour's chase, the two hostile torpedo-boats were caught and sunk. So the initial enterprise of the newly-established Flanders Flotilla ended ignominiously, after first promising success.

The defences at Dover were still giving a deal of trouble. In the earlier fortnight of April the original Folkestone-Grisnez barrage was completed and run out. Such a herculean task deserved better success. Daily, submarines had carried away the nets without the buoys indicating the damage; a new type of glass buoy gave promise of greater reliability. To supplement this obstruction, a net barrage was also laid off Ostend on April 8; deep mine-fields were also planted off Beachy Head and off Dartmouth, where submarines were wont to lie. As, however, the larger submarines had just been debarred from using the Dover passage, the coincidence of events gave rise to the illusion that the counter-measures were effective.

At the same time the North Channel was taken in hand. Here a modification was adopted, as these straits were both narrower and deeper than the gut separating England from France. Two lines of nets were laid twenty miles apart; between these nets were four or five lines of net drifters, supported by patrols. At each line of nets was a patrol to extend the barrage area. By such means it was hoped to keep a submarine under for a distance of at least thirty miles; at the end of that distance her batteries ought to be almost exhausted by so long a run submerged. The idea was not unlike the famous 1917 Dover barrage, without the mines.

In the St. George's Channel there was a line of some thirty-six drifters; but in the south-west approaches the patrol was subsequently divided into four areas, directed from Falmouth. In these waters an act was now to be perpetrated so defiant of civilized usages that the world stood aghast at the infamy.

On April 30, Schwieger, appointed to the command of U 20, left Borkum Roads to relieve U 24 and U 32 in western waters. A week earlier, notices emanating from the German Embassy in Washington appeared in the American Press, warning intending passengers not to embark in the Cunard liner *Lusitania* (30,396 tons), then about to sail for Liverpool. Nevertheless, the great liner left New York on May 1 (the day following U 20's departure) with over 1200 passengers, of whom 159 were American citizens.

Even before the *Lusitania* had passed Sandy Hook, outward bound, it was apparent that a submarine was coming south, leaving behind her a trail of destruction. On April 28 an Admiralty collier, *Mobile* (1950 tons), was sunk off the Butt of Lewis; on the next day another, the *Cherbury* (3220 tons), succumbed off the coast of Mayo; on the 30th the Russian steamer *Svorono* (3102 tons), and a third collier, *Fulgent* (2008 tons), were put down by U 23 off the south-west of Ireland. Finally, three more vessels were attacked on May 1, off the Scillies, of which one was the American tanker *Gulflight*; this ship did not sink, and was towed in, with her master and two of the crew dead. Clearly, then, the area through which the Cunarder would have to pass was unsafe. Anxiety was in no way allayed when a further steamer was destroyed on May 3, a sailing-ship off the Old Head of Kinsale on the 5th, and the two Harrison liners *Candidate* (5858 tons) and

THE FIRST WAR ON SHIPPING 41

Centurion (5945 tons) on the 6th. The scanty patrols were utterly inadequate in number to deal with the situation, for the appearance of a submarine off the Fastnet on the 4th had caused a further dispersal of strength. All shipping was warned to avoid headlands, and ten trawlers based on Queenstown were spread from Fastnet to the Waterford area.

The morning of May 7 was fine, with fog in patches. As the *Lusitania* entered the danger zone, she passed the Fastnet well to seaward, steaming at about 15 knots. She had reduced her speed of 21 to 18 knots in order to cross the Mersey Bar at dawn when the tide served. On running into a patch of fog, Captain Turner reduced speed further and began to blow his siren. As the weather cleared, speed was increased; and reports were taken in that submarines were off Cape Clear (which he had passed) and off Waterford, which he would pass in the late afternoon. Fine clear weather off the Old Head of Kinsale was found at 2.15 P.M., and nothing was in sight. Then, without the slightest warning, a torpedo was seen racing towards the liner. The missile hit her amidships, exploding with appalling effect; and a second seemed to strike her well aft. The huge ship took a list to starboard, and within twenty minutes had plunged to the bottom, leaving the water black with hundreds of drowning men, women, and children. So sudden was the catastrophe that the rescue vessels, rushing to the scene, could pick up but 800, leaving a death-roll of 1198 as the result of this wanton murder.

Schwieger had arrived off the south-west of Ireland on the morning of May 5, and towards evening had sunk the sailing-vessel already mentioned, following up this attack by destroying the two Harrison liners next day. At about two o'clock on the afternoon of the 7th he sighted ahead what he took to be the masts and funnels of destroyers coming up, but the mass speedily resolved itself into the shape of a large four-funnelled liner with smoke-stacks painted black. By running at high speed he got into position to fire a bow torpedo, which he saw explode just aft of the bridge. He denied that he fired a second torpedo, and suggested that the later explosion was caused by the boilers, or coal, or munitions. Only as the liner heeled over did he recognize the identity of his victim; and, diving to 11 metres, he cleared out of this region and soon afterwards started on his return voyage, arriving at Wilhelmshaven on the 13th.

The *Lusitania* was unarmed, and the 5500 cases of riflecartridge and shrapnel forming part of her cargo were stowed well forward;[1] and the only possible assumption, provided Schwieger's version be correct, is that the second detonation was caused by the explosion of the boilers. Throughout the civilized world went a shudder at the news that a nation should slaughter, in cold blood and with deliberation, a thousand non-combatants. The crime, coming so soon after the *Falaba* outrage, the attack on the *Gulflight* (the first American steamer to be molested by a submarine), and an air attack on the American steamer *Cushing*, evoked a strongly-worded protest from Washington to Berlin, backed by a demand that Germany should cease from sinking passenger ships without adequate warning. For four months did Germany try every expedient to avoid giving way; and, although orders went forth on June 6 to spare large passenger ships, it does not appear that they were seriously observed. Left and right, ships continued to be sunk, as the submarines went about their work. Against the demand of the Imperial Chancellor that the submarine war should be restricted, the naval authorities, supported by the Kaiser, stood firm. Bethmann-Hollweg was told that the campaign must continue, unless he would accept sole responsibility for its cessation. Orders to spare neutral ships were issued. That was the only mollification allowed; all British ships were, without exception, still to be sunk. So petty a concession the Chancellor realized would do little to improve matters; he urged that another *Lusitania* case must on no account occur. At last he won over the Kaiser. Thereafter, and on the whole, the new orders to sink passenger ships without warning were complied with.

II

When the *Lusitania* was sunk, it had been obvious that two or three submarines were cruising in western waters. Hersing

[1] *Naval Operations*, vol. ii. p. 393, footnote 2.

THE FIRST WAR ON SHIPPING 43

in U 21 had left the Ems on April 25, and during the last days of this month was passing south on his historic 4000-mile trip to Cattaro, in the Adriatic. It was in response to Turkey's request for submarine attack upon the naval forces off the Peninsula (and also to begin a war on merchantmen in the Mediterranean) that Hersing had been chosen to make the venture. Avoiding all traffic and eluding the patrols, he made a rendezvous about a week later off Cape Finisterre with the Hamburg-Amerika steamer *Marzala*. Hersing had been promised a supply of food, oil fuel, and lubricating oil from her. Together they went into Rio Corcubion to transfer the supplies. To his dismay, he found the 12 tons of fuel perfectly useless, even after mixing, and he was now confronted with the alternatives of trying to reach his goal or of making his way back. He had started with 56 tons of fuel, and he had but 25 tons left. Moreover, he was not yet half-way to Cattaro. What should he do ? After the most exact calculations, he decided he had a chance, if he could avoid much diving and if the remaining run could be made mostly at low speed on the surface. At dawn on May 6, as he entered the Straits of Gibraltar, he sighted two torpedo-boats; one, Torpedo Boat No. 92, he attacked, and then had to dive. The startling news of his appearance was now out, and he had to exercise greater caution. A steamer was seen, so he dived ; once more he had to efface himself when a French destroyer later came in sight. Nevertheless, he entered the Adriatic base on May 13, with but 1·8 tons of fuel left !

For about ten days after the *Lusitania* attack there was a decided lull in Irish waters. On the 18th the respite was ended by a renewal of sinkings. Three days later such activity had died away, to be again followed by another serious outburst in the Western Channel, when U 34 (Rücker) sank six steamers in three days and attacked others. Her presence caused great anxiety for troopships about to sail from Avonmouth for Gallipoli. Rücker did not confine his attention to large ships ; on June 1 he found a couple of fishing-craft in the St. George's Channel, and one, the *Victoria* (155 tons), unwisely tried to run for it. Rücker thereupon began to pump shell after shell into the helpless little vessel, only desisting when the skipper had been blown to pieces; the mate lay dying with his legs cut clean off; a trimmer had both legs broken, and the engineer and boy were killed.

The fishing-fleets in the North Sea were also suffering, and in May nineteen of their craft were destroyed by submarines. The Dover Straits prohibition had the effect of increasing activity in the North Sea; and, as the U-boats passed westward by the north-about route, the number of attacks and hunts grew accordingly. On May 8 the 3rd Battle Squadron was attacked, about 100 miles E.N.E. of the Firth of Forth, by U 39 (Forstmann, late of U 12), the *Dominion* barely eluding a torpedo fired at her. On May 17 both U 19 and U 25, with a destroyer, took part in the *Hamburg*'s mine-laying trip off the Dogger Bank. The operation was to be supported by the High Sea Fleet, and the submarines were posted as a trap for British ships which might appear. Gayer says that the mine-fields laid by the Germans in 1915 in the North Sea did not prove of much value; their presence was soon revealed by trawlers, and the area was marked down as dangerous. Actually, as the mines sown were not swept up, they constituted an extra peril to the U-boats crossing the North Sea.

On the other hand, the Flanders Flotilla boats were finding the new orders most hampering. The constant flow of neutral shipping in the southern North Sea required visit and search; this could not be carried out within their sphere of operations. However, certain stretches of the Dover-Calais barrage were found through which boats could pass. A fast mine-laying expedition was then made by UC 11 for the deposit of a field close to the South Goodwins L.V. On June 10, Torpedo Boat No. 12 was mined in the Thames estuary; as her consort, No. 10, closed in to take her in tow, the latter also struck a mine. Both boats foundered.[1]

During June, attacks on the North Sea and South Wales fishing-fleets accounted for 58 small craft. Every fishing-vessel was now precious, because hundreds had been previously taken up for patrol and mine-sweeping work. A

---

[1] Official White Paper, 'Navy Losses' (1919), attributed loss to submarine attack. Later information shows loss to have been caused by mines, possibly those laid by UC 11.

THE FIRST WAR ON SHIPPING

determined attempt to combat this danger was therefore made. It was decided to include amongst the fishing-craft a decoy trawler, and the idea was at once crowned with success. On June 5 the decoy trawler *Oceanic II* was attacked by U 14 (Hammerle); other Peterhead trawlers came up and poured a rapid fire into the assailant. Following up this surprise, the *Hawk* rammed U 14 ; the submarine sank. Twenty-seven of the crew were picked up, only Lieutenant Hammerle, who remained behind in his boat, perishing. For a time this area was cleared, but during June 23-24 no fewer than sixteen Orcadian fishing-vessels were destroyed by U 19 and U 25. The latter boat was rammed whilst submerged, and was forced to return home damaged.

The fishing-fleets were, however, to cost Germany another submarine this month. On June 19, as the ships composing the 3rd Cruiser Squadron were sweeping across the North Sea, a line of four submarines was encountered. Attacked as they were, the cruisers parried the thrusts of the enemy. On the next day the *Argyll* narrowly escaped a torpedo from U 40 ; the *Roxburgh* was less fortunate, and suffered damage from another fired by U 38. These two submarines then parted company.

Valentiner in U 38 appeared in the south-west approaches, and sank several ships. He hunted down and destroyed the Leyland liner *Armenian* (8825 tons), whose master was forced to surrender after a chase costing 29 lives. Valentiner (whose name must be marked for future recollection) was relieved by Schwieger in U 20 and Forstmann in U 39. The pair between them sank about twenty Allied and neutral ships, besides attacking a dozen more. Amongst their victims figured the horse-transport *Anglo-Californian* (7333 tons), shelled and chased on July 4. Lieutenant Parslow put up so gallant a defence, albeit at the cost of his life, that he staved off defeat until patrols drove off his assailant. He was posthumously awarded the Victoria Cross in 1919. Schwieger made another 'mistake' on July 9, when he attacked the Cunard liner *Orduna*, asserting that this 15,499-ton ship was 'a small enemy steamer.' To quote the Germans' own proverb : 'The wolf never lacks a pretext against the lamb.'

Soon after Valentiner had parted from U 40 (Fürbringer), the latter boat embroiled herself in an adventure that led to her undoing. She was on her maiden trip, having set off for a cruise on the 18th, and her commander unwisely attacked fishing-craft off Aberdeen. The decoy trawler idea had by this time been further developed. Since May a trawler had been sent to sea with one or even two ' C class ' submarines in tow, inter-connected by telephone with the towing vessel. It was hoped that a German submarine, seeing a tow-line evidently drawing along the nets, would be misled into making an attack on an apparently harmless fishing-vessel. The trawler skipper would thereupon telephone to the submarine in tow the position, course, and procedure of the U-boat. The British submarine could slip the tow and stalk the attacker unseen. On June 8 the trawler *Taranaki* and the submarine C 27, working in such combination, had just failed ; now success was at last to be achieved.

With C 24 in tow, the *Taranaki* sighted U 40 on June 23, some fifty miles south-east of Aberdeen ; according to plan, whilst the trawler engaged the attention of the enemy, C 24 tried to slip her end of the tow. The cable refused to slip, and the trawler was therefore compelled to free her end instead. In spite of 100 fathoms of tow-rope and telephone cable dangling from her bows, C 24 managed to readjust her trim and get into position before the cable became entangled in her propellers. The sight of the trawler's crew abandoning their ship so engrossed the crew of U 40 that they never perceived a periscope near by. A torpedo crashed into the hull of their boat, which promptly blew up ; and only three who were on deck (including Fürbringer) escaped entombment in the shattered U-boat.

On the previous day another German submarine had come to grief. In Borkum Roads, U 30 foundered ; save three men on deck, the entire crew went down, imprisoned in their vessel, to endure a lingering death. There U 30 lay on the bottom for three months. Subsequent to her salvage, she underwent overhaul, but was always described as a ' Jonah.' None the less, she was the sole survivor of her class at the Armistice. In the North Sea, U 25 (Wünsche) was out again after repairs, attacking the cruiser *Hampshire* on July 1, off the Moray Firth, with no success. During July 15-19 a large submarine hunt began off Fair Island; and on the 16th the gunboat *Speedwell* rammed U 41 and damaged her periscope. Another U-boat was reported in the nets off Fair Island; and on the 20th the disguised armed trawlers *Gunner* and *Quickly*, from Granton, had a fight off the Bell Rock with another enemy submarine; they claimed to have sunk her, although no sure proof could be adduced. The action is noteworthy as the first in which depth-charges were reported to have been used.

At this time it was noticed that a U-boat was continuously stationed off the Hebrides to intercept the supply ships for the Grand Fleet; and here, in July, the first Q-boat success was gained. When, in November, the submarines had first appeared in the Channel, a small steamer from St. Malo had been attacked; and the late Admiral Sir Hedworth Meux (the Commander-in-Chief at Portsmouth) had suggested concealing a gun amongst her cargo of vegetables. A decoy ship, the *Victoria*, was fitted out; and she was followed by the Great Eastern Railway packet *Antwerp* (under Lieutenant-Commander Godfrey Herbert, R.N.), normally plying between Harwich and the Hook of Holland. Next, up at Scapa, five old colliers were fitted out; and it was one of these, the *Prince Charles*, which drew first blood. Putting to sea to invite attention from U-boats, the decoy vessel was to lure her attacker within point-blank range, open a sudden fire and overwhelm the enemy. On July 22 the fishing-fleet west of the Orkneys was ravaged by U 36. During this and the next two days the raider accounted for nine fishing-craft and three merchantmen—one French, one Russian, and one Norwegian. She also made a futile attempt against the armed merchant-cruiser *Columbella*. Next she captured the American sailing-vessel *Pass of Balmaha*. Into her prize she put a crew who brought the vessel to a German port. With the *Pass of Balmaha* a British boarding-party was also seized; for, before U 36 fell foul of her, the American ship had been intercepted by the armed merchant-cruiser *Victorian*.[1]

---

[1] Later, this sailing-vessel became the commerce-raider *Seeadler*, whose career ended in the Pacific.

Towards evening on July 24 the *Prince Charles* sighted the U 36 (Graeff), ten miles W.N.W. of North Rona, alongside the Danish steamer *Louise*. Pretending not to see the U-boat, the decoy held on, and observed the submarine leave the Dane to head off herself, the newcomer. At about three miles' range, U 36 opened fire and ordered the disreputable-looking tramp to heave-to. The order was obeyed, and the boats were swung out as though the crew were abandoning ship. The enemy then lay off at 600 yards and continued to pour shell into the steamer. Seeing that the U-boat would not close, the *Prince Charles* (Lieutenant W. P. Mark-Wardlaw, R.N.) decided that the time had come to unmask her guns, run up the ensign, and open fire. The German crew on deck made a frantic rush for the conning-tower; but it was too late. The first shot hit 20 feet abaft the conning-tower; U 36 tried to dive, presenting her other broadside. The *Prince Charles* closed to 300 yards, hitting frequently. The U 36 settled down by the stern; her crew came tumbling up; next the bows rose high in the air, and she slid backwards into the depths. Of her crew of 34, 15 were picked up. Encouraged by this success, the authorities subsequently fitted out many other such decoys.

However, attacks off the Hebrides continued. On the next day the American steamer *Leelanaw* (1924 tons) and the *Grangewood* (3422 tons) were sunk. Their attacker was possibly the new U 68, one of the five boats ordered in Germany by Austria before the war. This U-boat thereafter made her way to the Scillies area, and during the last days of July and the beginning of August she sank several ships, including the three Fleet messengers, *Turquoise, Nugget,* and *Portia,* all *en route* for the Mediterranean. A sister raider, U 66, was also at sea, sinking a Swedish barque on the 19th.

Ere the end of the month arrived, the trawler and submarine combination secured another kill. On July 20 the trawler *Princess Louise* and C 27 were cruising off Fair Island when they fell in with U 23 (Schulthess). Everything went well this time, until C 27 took up her position and fired her torpedo. It went wide, and the U-boat tried to dive; before she could submerge, a second torpedo struck abaft the conning-tower and blew her up. Four officers and six men were

THE FIRST WAR ON SHIPPING 49

captured. Unfortunately, these prisoners were allowed to mingle with certain interned civilians of enemy nationality about to be repatriated, to whom they related their experience. The 'trawler-cum-submarine' trap was thus revealed to the enemy, and for a time that particular lure had to be laid aside. Still, Gayer relates that U 16 narrowly escaped a similar fate from the *Taranaki* and C 24, being hit and sinking to 76 metres before she was got under control. In August the method was revived, consequent on the destruction of large numbers of fishing-craft off Lowestoft and Cromer. It had again to be discontinued after the loss of C 33 and C 29 whilst in company with their consort trawlers. At a yet later date the Queenstown patrols revived the plan, but without obtaining any striking success.

One of the longest duels ever fought between submarine and patrol throughout the war took place towards the end of July. At about 4.15 A.M. on the 27th the trawler *Pearl*, armed with only a 3-pounder gun, was patrolling off Barra Head. The weather was thick, with a freshening south-east wind and a heavy swell, certain indication of a coming gale. U 41 was sighted, steering southward, over 5000 yards distant. The *Pearl* immediately closed in at full speed, and the U-boat altered course to the S.S.W. At 4.25 A.M. the range was down to 500 yards; U 41 was travelling fast and firing across the *Pearl's* bows. An attempt was made by the trawler to ram. At the same time she opened fire; by the fifth and sixth shots, hits were made, and U 41 made a hurried dive. A second attempt to ram was then essayed by the *Pearl*; a short time afterwards, the periscope of the enemy was seen, fired on and shot away at the second round. U 41 then completely submerged; and for an hour both patrol and U-boat kept parallel courses to the south-west, with the *Pearl* on the U 41's starboard bow ready to ram. At the end of that time the German boat turned about to the north-east, and then, half an hour later, changed her course to the north-west. Still the *Pearl* dogged her quarry.

Soon afterwards rain began to fall; despite the impaired visibility, the U 41 was again seen at 9.15 A.M., close to the surface. At 11 A.M. the *Pearl* decided to fire her explosive

D

sweep about 500 yards ahead of the oily wave, but the electric cable got damaged. Towards noon the engineer reported that, in an hour's time, the trawler would have to stop to repair a pump. The hunt was therefore brought to an inconclusive close after an eight hours' chase. The U 41's troubles were not yet at an end; at 9.10 P.M. she was located by the armed yacht *Vanessa* and chased. Next morning other trawlers picked up the scent and continued the harrying for another two hours. Hansen, the commander of U 41, was therefore forced to abandon his cruise and had to return to port, with the conning-tower seriously injured.

In southern waters the Flanders boats were now becoming troublesome. In June, UB 6 (Hacker) made a test run through the Straits to prove that the defences were ineffective. As a consequence, four other UB-boats were sent to attack the Dover-Boulogne line. Owing to fog and bad weather, the two which ran through failed to secure any targets; the third was damaged in a new obstruction between Colbart Sand and Grisnez; the fourth crawled back and was taken in tow (after an absence of eleven days) suffering from machinery breakdown. Steinbrinck reported the Straits to be closely patrolled. The UC mine-layers, on the other hand, were more successful. The appearance of new mine-fields off the East Coast was a puzzling feature in such busy waters, and it was ascribed to neutral fishing-craft. On June 18, fields, laid by UC 1, 2, 3, and 11, were discovered off Harwich and Dover; and on the 30th the old destroyer *Lightning* foundered on one of these mines near the Kentish Knock L.V. Two days later the coaster *Cottingham* (513 tons) accidentally ran down UC 2 (Mey) off Yarmouth; and when this small craft was raised the mystery was revealed. She was found to be fitted with twelve mines, ' wet ' stowage, in six inclined chutes.

The second success against these Flanders boats was again due to the introduction of a decoy, amongst the Lowestoft smacks, at the time when they were suffering severely in August. Four smacks were given a concealed 3-pounder gun ; and by the end of the month three of them (*G. & E., Inverlyon,* and *Pet*) had been in action. On the 15th, *Inverlyon* shelled and sank UB 4 (Karl Gross) off Smith's Knoll Spar Buoy,

Yarmouth. During the bombardment of the Flanders coast by the Dover Patrol, in August and September, the UB-boats were detailed to lie as outposts between the Thornton Ridge and Middelkerke; consequently only the UC mine-layers were available to molest shipping. A further extension of cruising range by these boats was achieved by UC 5. Early on August 20 she left Bruges *via* the Zeebrugge lock, crossed the nets at No. 3 buoy at about 10.20 P.M., and ran through the Straits at full speed on the surface, under cover of the darkness. Off Boulogne she laid twelve mines next morning, and was thus the first submarine mine-layer to penetrate into the Channel. On these mines the steamer *William Dawson* (284 tons) foundered the same day. UC 5 followed up this success by a repetition of her performance on September 7, when she planted six mines before Boulogne and another six in the 'Gate' at Folkestone. Next day the cable-ship *Monarch* (1122 tons) fouled one of these latter and sank, two and a half miles off Folkestone. Off the south-east coast further mines were laid by UC 1, 3, 6, and 7.

With the advent of August the climax of the 1915 campaign was reached. On the 4th and 5th, three submarines sailed to make a big attack in the south-western approaches. On the night of the 13th, U 27 and U 38 made a rendezvous to the north-west of Llandudno, after which U 27 carried on to the south. U 38 hovered about for some days, expecting to pick up three German officers (including von Hennig, taken prisoner when U 18 sank) who had escaped from a prison camp in North Wales. As the third dawn broke and no fugitives were seen on the beach one hundred yards distant, U 38 was forced to abandon the rescue and follow U 27 to the south, eventually returning to Heligoland on the 29th. Unfortunately for themselves, the officers were but five hundred yards away, waiting on another beach, and were hidden from view of U 38 by a projecting rocky headland. They were afterwards recaptured.

Schneider in U 24 appeared off Whitehaven on the 16th, and shelled the benzol and naphtha works there, damaging them so slightly that they were able to resume work in four days. He appears to have had an exciting run south, being three times attacked in the Irish Sea as he tampered with the sea traffic. During the next day two ships went down off Bardsey Island, and five others farther south. By the 19th all three boats—U 24, U 27, and U 38—were at work between Ushant and the St. George's Channel. During the morning four more steamers were sunk. U 24 was shelling the *Dunsley* (4930 tons), fifty miles south of Kinsale, when Schneider noticed a large steamer approaching from the east. She was zigzagging, and Schneider said that he imagined she was trying to ram his boat. He loosed off a torpedo, which took the liner aft. Such havoc did it wreak that his target sank in ten minutes, with forty-four of her passengers and crew. The ship was the White Star liner *Arabic* (15,801 tons), outward bound for America, and no one aboard had seen the slightest sign of the submarine. Schneider appears to have been ignorant of her identity, but by this act he had precipitated another crisis in the diplomatic relations between Germany and the United States.

Two more steamers were destroyed, during the early afternoon, north and westward of the Scilly Isles; and at three o'clock the Leyland liner *Nicosian* (6369 tons), laden with mules, was stopped by U 27 (Wegener) about 100 miles south of Queenstown. Cruising in the neighbourhood was the Q-boat *Baralong* (Lieutenant-Commander Godfrey Herbert, R.N.). Here was her long-awaited opportunity. Almost as her crew sighted the distressed *Nicosian*, calls were received from her that she was being chased; and, a few minutes later, that she had been captured by an enemy submarine. The *Baralong* turned towards the liner, her crew witnessing the scene of destruction with growing anger. The *Nicosian* next reported that she was captured by two submarines; and the decoy further lessened the distance separating her from the U-boats. Not until she was barely two and a half miles off did U 27 appear to notice the stranger's presence, so busy was she shelling the mule-carrier. Trimming down to meet the oncoming vessel, Wegener turned towards her at high speed. The *Baralong* swung to starboard, apparently to pick up the *Nicosian*'s boats; U 27 manned her gun again, and resumed her course to prevent the *Baralong* from reaching the

THE FIRST WAR ON SHIPPING

boats. Whilst the *Nicosian* lay between herself and the submarine, the *Baralong* stopped her engines, struck her neutral colours and ran up her White Ensign. She unmasked her 12-pounder guns and trained them on the spot where U 27 would reappear from behind the *Nicosian*'s bows. Thirty-four rapid rounds at 600 yards, and U 27 disappeared in a boil of water, never again to emerge.

The *Nicosian*'s boats were then called alongside ; it was observed that about a dozen Germans had swum towards their late prize and were clambering up the hanging boat-falls and pilot ladder. Seeing there was nothing to prevent the Germans from scuttling this ship, with her valuable cargo of mules, Lieutenant-Commander Herbert ordered the guns and the marines to open fire. Even so, four Germans got aboard and disappeared below. The commander of the decoy had been informed by the *Nicosian*'s master that arms and ammunition were ready at hand in the chart-house of the abandoned steamer ; the fugitives made no sign of surrender, and were somewhere down below. The *Baralong* went along-side, and the marines were ordered to recover possession of the ship. They were warned against surprise and told to get in the first shot. The Germans were at last discovered in the engine-room, and were all shot at sight by the marines, who believed they had to deal with the assassins of the *Arabic*. The crew of the *Nicosian* then returned to their ship and brought her into Bristol, in spite of the holes made by the submarine's shell-fire.

These are the facts concerning the notorious '*Baralong* incident.' Many were the versions invented or circulated. Berlin was not slow to exploit the affair to its utmost, demanding the arraignment of the *Baralong*'s captain and crew on a charge of murder. The British Government, whilst expressing its willingness to have the whole question of irregularities examined by an impartial tribunal, suggested that three other incidents, which had occurred during the same forty-eight hours, should be investigated at the same time. First, there was the *Arabic* sinking—a large passenger liner sunk without warning ; secondly, a collier, *Ruel*, had been shelled until her crew took to their boats, whereupon the submarine merely transferred her fire from the steamer to the open boats, thereby killing one man and wounding seven others; and lastly, the killing of fifteen of E 13's crew by German destroyers, as this submarine lay stranded on Saltholm Flat, in Danish territorial waters, on her passage into the Baltic. Berlin, quite naturally, declined the British proposal.

The *Baralong* had been taken over for conversion into a Special Service Vessel as far back as March, and her commanding officer was to become one of the Q-boat aces. Her success led to the fitting-out of two more decoys; but even before they were commissioned, yet another U-boat had succumbed to the lure. In October the Q-boat campaign began officially. Considering the skill, the devotion, and the extraordinary amount of care and thought lavished on this service, it is curious that more decisive results were not achieved. Simulating whatever type of ship was being subjected to attack at the time, these decoys embraced sloops, colliers, tramps, coasters, brigs, trawlers, fishing-smacks—in fact, any vessel which presented an objective likely to become attractive to the U-boats. The essence of success lay in a rapid and overwhelming attack at close range; should the submarine be able to dive, great would be the peril of the decoy. An outraged submarine, once again secure in the nether element, would exact a merciless revenge for her deception, forthwith or upon a future meeting. A speedy return to port or a change of disguise at sea gave a slender hope of escaping retribution, for a revealed decoy was a doomed ship.

In Q-boat tactics, therefore, overwhelming attack was essential. Hardly less important was the problem of making an undetected approach. Whether the enemy was to approach the decoy, or the decoy the enemy, entirely depended on the conditions. As the campaign developed in ruthlessness, so did the handling of the decoys become more intricate. It became necessary to suffer torpedoing in order to induce the attacker to become over-confident and expose himself to the return blow. There are cases in which no fewer than three panic parties left the decoy, hoping to inveigle the U-boat to approach the stricken ship and so pass the spot on which the concealed guns could best bear. Yet failure was the only

THE FIRST WAR ON SHIPPING

outcome. Step by step the Q-boats adapted themselves to the submarines' habits, ever changing as the war proceeded. From the five Scapa decoys, the two or three Channel boats, and the half-dozen fishing-craft of 1915, there were at sea by October 1916 some 47 Q-boats; and in 1917—the climax of this service—no fewer than 180 of these vessels roamed the seas offering themselves as prey. Whereas in 1915 there were but eight duels between submarine and decoy, the number next year rose to about two dozen, and in 1917 the total reached 63. Many other U-boats were severely mauled, but only 13 submarines were destroyed by decoy-ships. The capacity of the double-hulled German submarines for surviving the severest punishment was remarkable.

Although U 27 had been destroyed, U 24 and U 38 continued this concerted drive against shipping around the Scillies. During the next four days, August 20-23, they sank ten more ships, bringing the total in this area up to 35 British, 4 neutral, and 2 fishing-vessels. Of this formidable 'bag,' U 38 brought down 22 cargo-steamers and 3 sailing-vessels, together with 5 fishing-craft destroyed on her passage to and from the Scillies. For the greater part, U 38 secured her victims with her gun, only using torpedoes when she wished to complete a rapid sinking and avoid alarming the patrols. Gayer says that Valentiner's success was the greatest ever achieved during the whole of the war around the British Isles. This 'drive' by the diving corsairs died away, and a period of quiescence ensued. It was a startling demonstration of what submarines 'off the leash,' waging unrestricted war, could (and actually would, at a later date) accomplish.

In the North Sea, U 28 and U 25 were at work; but the latter's engines broke down, and she was met to the northward of Horns Reef by a couple of torpedo-boats and towed home. As she was considered to be no longer fit for active service, she joined the Periscope School at Kiel. Another boat, U 22 (Hoppe), was more successful. At the beginning of August she had been sent to attack a British armed merchant-cruiser reported to be permanently stationed to the W.N.W. of Bödo and intercepting German ore-carriers from Narwik. On the 8th she found her quarry—the *India*, a converted

P. & O. liner—and promptly torpedoed her, sending her to the bottom with most of her crew. This was a unique event, for a submarine had been sent out to destroy a definite objective, a hostile vessel, and had successfully accomplished her mission without delay. A contemporary enterprise was the escort given by U 17 to the auxiliary mine-layer *Meteor* on her trip to the Moray Firth, which was mined on the night of the 6th.

About this time Germany lost another submarine. So far, no account has been given of the Baltic Flotilla.[1] When war broke out in August 1914, two boats were detailed for service in this theatre; and in September two others, U 23 and U 25, were withdrawn from the North Sea to join them. Before the long winter months set in, the Baltic submarines gained a notable success: on October 11, U 26 (Count Berckheim) torpedoed and sank the Russian cruiser *Pallada* in the Gulf of Finland, with heavy loss of life. This boat scored another point, on June 4, 1915, when she sank the Russian mine-layer *Yenesei*; but during August or September she set out on a cruise from which she never returned. She is believed to have perished in the Russian mine-barrier off Reval. Across the Gulf of Finland was an immense double line of mine and net barrages through which only one or two U-boats ever penetrated and returned from reconnoitring cruises.[2] The Baltic (Courland) Flotilla reached its greatest strength in the autumn of 1916, when it numbered eleven boats. In December 1917, on the collapse of Russia, all submarines were withdrawn.

The first real increase in its numbers occurred in September 1915, when U 9, U 10, U 17, and UC 4 were added. The transfer resulted from the sinking of U 6 (Lepsius) off Stavanger on September 15. She had been easily sighted and stalked by the British submarine E 16, chiefly through the volumes of dense white smoke given off by the Körting

---

[1] The Baltic (Courland) Flotilla was directly under the control of the C.-in-C. Baltic Forces (Prince Henry of Prussia), and not under the command of the C.-in-C. High Sea Fleet, or Commanding Officer, Submarines.

[2] U 9—Weddigen's famous boat—was a unit of this flotilla, and, under the command of Spiess, was based on Libau. Her duties consisted chiefly in hunting for hostile submarines, in making scouting cruises, and in patrolling off the Gulf of Riga. She was converted into a *surface* mine-layer, and, as such, laid fields in the Finnish Gulf.

heavy-oil motors. Spiess, who took over U 9 from Weddigen, gives a realistic account of those early boats ; he talks of the ' pillar of cloud attending them by day.' To the children of Israel, centuries ago, such a phenomenon was a help—to the U-boat courting invisibility it was a sore handicap. At night the exhaust funnel emitted sparks, and even flames. Little wonder that, as soon as the new Diesel-engined U-boats went into the fighting line, all surviving craft anterior to U 19 were withdrawn from the dangers of the North Sea. To these three Körting-engined boats the small coastal UB 2, UB 5, and UB 20 were added in 1916.

Spiess relates one hazardous experience. He penetrated the Russian mine-fields off Uto, ' the Heligoland of the Finnish Gulf,' late on August 25, and nearly paid with his life for his temerity. Sighting in the twilight, against the rocks, a Russian submarine, with a steam-launch alongside, he decided to attack her. He believed that the officers were about to disembark in the launch, leaving their submarine for the night. He manœuvred to get into position for firing a torpedo. At the next sight through the periscope, he saw, to his horror, the Russian submarine gliding towards U 9, trying to creep up a narrow channel between the reefs. Hurriedly he gave orders to turn about ; U 9 slowly turned, and struck a rock with a dull grinding noise. The Russian sighted them and opened fire at the periscope. On his own initiative the engineer trimmed down U 9 to eight metres and succeeded in getting the boat clear of the reef. Spiess, at the periscope, gave up all hope when he saw a torpedo streaking towards him ; fortunately for him, it missed and sped away. Night had now come on. In pitch darkness, by dead reckoning and great good luck, they groped their way out of that crazy labyrinth of rocks, reefs, and mine-fields. Next day he balanced accounts by sinking a large Russian auxiliary. By April 1916, U 9 was the *doyen* of the boats on active service, and joined the other war-worn craft at the Kiel Periscope School.

To return to western seas, it will be recalled that the sinking of the *Arabic* had again embittered the diplomatic relations between Berlin and Washington. Bearing in mind the fact that the *Lusitania* dispute had not yet been composed, the effect of another outrage acerbated American opinion still further. Tirpitz, the Naval Secretary, and Bachmann, Chief of the Naval Staff, on one side, were brought into acute conflict with Bethmann-Hollweg, the Imperial Chancellor, and von Müller, Chief of the Kaiser's Naval Cabinet, on the other. The latter pair were working for an arbitration settlement of the *Lusitania* case, whereas the two former advocated the continuance of submarine warfare against shipping. On August 26 the Kaiser definitely showed himself to be favourably disposed towards the views of Tirpitz and Bachmann. Two days later the Chancellor sent an unauthorized Note to Washington, promising that ships would not be sunk without previous admonition. To complicate matters further, Bernstorff, the German Ambassador at Washington, stated, without any official sanction, that the submarine commander who had attacked the *Arabic* had exceeded his orders and would be punished.

Bachmann was thereupon retired, and replaced by von Holtzendorff. The differences between the Naval Chiefs and the Supreme Command continued, both Tirpitz and von Pohl, the Commander-in-Chief of the High Sea Fleet, vigorously protesting against the futility of employing submarines in the manner announced by Bethmann-Hollweg. To hedge the boats about with such restrictions, they declared, would be rendering success almost unattainable; and on August 27, orders were issued that no U-boat should leave port until the altercations were settled. Tirpitz suggested the despatch of submarines to the Mediterranean, rather than see them cramped by stipulations and conditions. What if the impediments proposed were accepted? Suppose that shipping be stopped and searched before destruction? Tirpitz asserted that such a procedure would bring about the very state of affairs most desired by the British decoy-ships. Here was a vicious circle indeed—Q-boats had been evolved because merchant-ships were sunk without being stopped and examined by the submarines: now submarines dared not board and search for fear of coming within reach of the mercantile-disguised decoys!

THE FIRST WAR ON SHIPPING 59

On August 30 both Tirpitz and von Pohl protested against a new order that even small passenger-ships must be spared ; and they both asked to be allowed to resign. Their requests were refused. ' We continued the campaign in a form in which it could not live and at the same time could not die,' said Tirpitz. And Bethmann-Hollweg retorted, *à propos* of the unsettled imbroglio with Washington, ' I cannot stay for ever on the top of a volcano.' Eventually a Note was sent to the United States Government expressing regret for the *Arabic* attack, without admitting liability, and offering to submit the case to the Hague Tribunal. Maladroitly an account of the affair was simultaneously sent, asserting that, before the *Arabic* was sunk, orders to spare passenger-ships had been issued. Since this looked like an attempt at justification of the sinking, the flame of public indignation was fanned afresh. Then at length orders were issued, on September 18, for all attacks on commerce to cease around the British coasts as from the 20th. A fortnight later, Schneider's action was formally ' disavowed,' and it was agreed to negotiate an indemnity.

During this political controversy another large passenger-ship, the Allan liner *Hesperian* (10,920 tons), was torpedoed and sunk on September 6 : she was the first armed merchant-ship to succumb to a submarine. Her attacker was no other than Schwieger. Caught 80 miles S.W. by S. from Fastnet on the 4th, the liner was too badly injured to regain port, in spite of great efforts to tow her in. U 20 destroyed two other British steamers and a neutral sailing-vessel during September 4-5, before proceeding southward to interfere with shipping entering La Rochelle. Here Schwieger accounted for four vessels, and then had to make his return. The contention advanced from Berlin that the *Hesperian* struck a mine was so improbable as to verge on the absurd ; submarines had been busy in southern Irish waters, and it was highly unlikely that German boats would be sent to operate at large in an area which they knew (or believed) to be mined.

Other shipping was destroyed during September 4-5, the casualties being caused by U-boats on their passage to the Mediterranean. On August 4, U 34 (Rücker) and U 35

(Kophamel) had both left their home ports; they entered the Mediterranean without incident, and arrived at Cattaro on August 23. U 39 (Forstmann) and U 33 (Gansser) set off for the Adriatic on August 27 and 28 respectively. The latter boat waylaid two British steamers and a neutral sailing-ship, as she was passing through those western waters ravaged by Germany's steel sharks on previous occasions. Off Finisterre the same diving raider added yet another steamer to her toll of destruction and arrived at Cattaro on September 16. These four submarines were later joined by U 38. Under the ablest commanders, they began to garner in shipping in the Mediterranean—the safest, easiest, and most fruitful field for the work, and one wherein they reaped an exceedingly rich harvest.

Another boat of this class, U 41 (Hansen), repaired after her encounter with the *Pearl*, left Wilhelmshaven on September 12 to relieve U 20 in western seas and disturb the incipient calm upon those troubled waters. On the 23rd, Hansen sank the horse-transport *Anglo-Colombian* (4792 tons), the *Chancellor* (4596 tons), and the *Hesione* (3663 tons), one after another, about 80 miles south-west of Fastnet. As Hansen was busily engaged next day in shelling the *Urbino* (6651 tons), 67 miles S.W. by W. from Bishop Rock, he was interrupted by the appearance of another steamer. When the stranger was yet 5 miles distant, U 41 dived. On emerging, the prospective new victim was seen steaming southward. At full speed on the surface, U 41 raced to head off the fugitive, ordering her to stop. Seeing she was flying neutral colours, Hansen (now about $2\frac{1}{2}$ miles distant) signalled her to send over her papers. As the boats were lowered, the stranger unobtrusively edged ever nearer, on a converging course with the submarine. Then, at 700 yards range, Lieutenant-Commander Godfrey Herbert, of the Q-ship *Baralong*, hoisted the White Ensign, unmasked the guns, and opened a rapid and accurate fire. At the second shot, U 41 was hit at the base of the conning-tower; as she tried to dive, shells and bullets rained on her, until, plunging wildly, she slanted down on her death-dive. Only the lieutenant and one man, out of her crew numbering 32, were found alive in the water.

II. THE DEATH THROES OF THE *ANGLIA*.

It was upon a mine, laid by the *UC.5*, that the cross-Channel Hospital Ship *Anglia* struck, on November 17, 1915. Eighty of the wounded and staff on board perished in this disaster. The *Anglia* is seen here near her end. She is heeling over; her bows are submerged, her screws are threshing the surface, and steam is being blown off from the boilers.

THE FIRST WAR ON SHIPPING

With this action the 1915 campaign ended in western waters, if the sporadic raid by U 24 (Schneider) during December is excepted. Made with the obvious intention of detaining in British seas such anti-submarine patrols as might be diverted to the Mediterranean, the foray resulted in one Belgian and three British steamers being destroyed. Among the four vessels deleted was the coaster *Cottingham* (513 tons), which had accidentally sunk UC 2 in July.

So the warfare died down in the west. A portent of future trouble, admitting of no misunderstanding, had been given to the world. With the relaxation came respite for the inadequate and harassed patrols. But if the war against shipping approaching these islands had ceased, the Flanders submarines, now numbering some 17 boats, became ever more active. The small mine-layers, having penetrated the Dover Straits in the late summer, spawned death over the waters outside the south- and east-coast ports. Off Dover they laid 150 mines, off the Nore 180, off Lowestoft 306, and off Grimsby 12—making a total of 648.[1] Altogether, these mines caused the loss of some 94 vessels (of which 32 were British steamships and 24 were of neutral registry), 10 fishing-craft, and 15 mine-sweepers (including the *Duchess of Hamilton, Brighton Queen,* and *Lady Ismay*). Amongst the British casualties was the hospital-ship *Anglia* (1862 tons), carrying cot cases from France; on November 17 she struck one of the mines laid by UC 5, and took down with her about eighty of her staff and wounded soldiers. The two Trinity House vessels *Alert* and *Irene* (543 tons), lent to the Dover Patrol for anchor work in connection with the net and mine barrages, were also numbered with the lost—with most of the crew in the latter ship. Three British destroyers foundered on these mines—the *Maori* sank off Zeebrugge on May 7; the old *Lightning* (as already related) on June 30; and the 30-knotter *Velox* off the Nab L.V. on October 25. The destroyer *Mohawk* was more fortunate, when she hit a mine on June 1, in being towed into port. Mines had also claimed victims in Torpedo Boats Nos. 10 and 12; but the French destroyer *Branlebas,* sunk off Dunkirk on November 9, was torpedoed by UB 17.

[1] *Encyclopædia Britannica* (Capt. A. C. Dewar, R.N.).

Against these sub-surface pests the Allied patrols seemed powerless; and such losses as were suffered by the Flanders Flotilla during this time could not be claimed by the anti-submarine forces. One, UC 8, sent from the Periscope School at Kiel to augment the force at Bruges, stranded off Terschelling on November 6, and, after being refloated, was interned.[1] Another was UC 9 (Schürmann), which blew up on her own mines (probably to the south-east of the Longsands L.V.) during October.

The impunity with which these small boats pursued their tasks caused real exasperation to the patrols. A minor development in political circles brought about a yet greater activity of the Flanders units. On November 5, Washington sent a Note to London protesting against the British blockade, and particularly in regard to the restriction of imports into neutral countries adjacent to Germany. To demonstrate Allied solidarity (as in the *Dacia* case), France requested the temporary use of the armed merchant-cruisers *Digby* and *Oropesa* (which she renamed *Artois* and *Champagne* respectively), since she desired to co-operate in the work of the 10th Cruiser Squadron, blockading the North Sea. Berlin, naturally, construed this U.S. Note as an opportune moment to relax the restrictions imposed on her submarines; and on November 21 the Flanders command received permission to resume attacks on shipping entering ports between Dunkirk and Le Havre. As a result, two small steamers, *Huntly* (1153 tons) and *Belford* (516 tons), were sunk by UB 10 off Boulogne on December 20. If little else was accomplished, the Flanders boats showed British authorities that the Belgian coast mine-field and the Goodwins net barrage were forming no deterrent to their excursions. On the contrary, Gayer says the submarines made the passage on the surface at night, riding over the nets; further, they found the net-supporting buoys and floats, together with lighted and unlighted navigation marks, to be invaluable for taking bearings.

[1] After the British submarine H 6 had been salved from Schiermonnikoog and interned at Nieuwediep, the Netherlands Government suggested taking over both boats. The British and German authorities agreed to the proposal. As M 1, the small German mine-layer became a unit of the Royal Netherlands Navy.

THE FIRST WAR ON SHIPPING 63

With the calling-off of the submarine campaign against shipping in the west, the North Sea Flotilla, numbering ten boats in December, underwent modernization and overhaul. The cruise of U 24 to the west was in the nature of an experimental winter trip, and proved that the season was no obstacle to harassing enemy shipping. Experiments were also made with mines discharged from torpedo-tubes; and early in 1916 the new U 44 did, in fact, successfully lay a field of mines by this method in the Thames estuary. The other North Sea boats were employed in a variety of duties during the winter: thus, between November 16-23, Schwieger in U 20 made a scouting trip preparatory to the laying of a mine-field off Cape Wrath by the raider *Möwe*, on her first ocean-raiding cruise. The raider herself was later escorted across the North Sea by U 68 (Güntzel), on December 27.

Gayer discloses the interesting fact that, at the end of September, only four of the remaining thirteen North Sea boats were available for trade-war in the west without undergoing extensive repairs. It is probable that he refers to U 20, 24, 28, and 32, for Valentiner was preparing to take U 38 on her long voyage to the Adriatic, to join the five already energetically prosecuting the slaughter of ships in the Mediterranean. According to the German official summary, the submarine strength on January 1, 1915, was 26 boats: during the ensuing twelve months 20 units were lost and 62 added, giving a net strength of 68 at the close of the year. These figures deserve further examination, and a more detailed survey should therefore be attempted.

Gayer states that at the end of September 1915, 10 boats were left to the North Sea Flotilla.[1] At the Kiel School were UB 9, UB 11, and UC 8 (he omits any mention of U 1-4, and does not refer to U 25, which had been found unfit for further active service). In the Baltic were U 9, U 10, U 17, and UC 4. In Flanders were eight UB-boats and seven UC-mine-layers.[2] In the Adriatic were five U-boats, two UB-boats, and two UC-boats;[3] at Constantinople were to be found

---

[1] North Sea Flotilla: U 19, 20, 22, 24, 28, 32, 38, 43, 44; UC 10.
[2] Flanders Flotilla: UB 2, 5, 6, 10, 12, 13, 16, 17; UC 1, 3, 5, 6, 7, 9, 11.
[3] Adriatic Flotilla: U 21, 33, 34, 35, 39; UB 1, 15; UC 12, 14.

three UB-boats and two UC-boats.[1] The ex-Austrian boats U 66-70 were on trials, of which U 66 and U 68 appear to have been on active service for several weeks before the close of September 1915.

Of the North Sea boats, U 19 was undergoing a replacement of engines, and U 22 had been giving incessant trouble. U 30, only recently salved, was non-operative. From the Flanders list one boat must be deducted, UC 9; and from those at Constantinople, UC 13. Holland had interned UC 8. The boat to be numbered U 42 was building at Spezia (Italy) in August 1914, but never became a German vessel.[2]

Five German submarines had been lost during 1914, and by the end of 1915 the total had been carried to twenty-four.[3]

Concerning new construction, the last boats of the pre-war programmes, U 43, U 44, and U 45, were delivered by the builders in April 1915. The last of the five repeat vessels (U 46-50), ordered in August 1914, was not delivered until July 1916. As these boats were completed, they were passed into the Ems (3rd) Flotilla. They were under-powered; and, although designed for 15·3 knots, they never could make more than 13·5 knots. The five boats laid down before the war for Austria-Hungary (numbered by Germany as U 66-70) were completed during the summer of 1915. As for the boats intermediately between the two classes just detailed, U 51-56 came into service during the first half of 1916, U 57-62 during the latter half, and U 63-65 in the spring of the same year. From twelve to fifteen months was the building period for these last three boats, due to the appropriation of engines ordered for Russian submarines. In addition, a class of large mine-layers, U 71-80, later known as the 'Children of Sorrow,' was ordered in January 1915, and between October 1915 and June 1916 they began their cheerless careers as belligerents.

As regards the smaller coastal and mine-laying boats, the UB I and UC I types had been completed during the spring and summer months. An enlarged and much-improved

[1] Constantinople Flotilla : UB 7, 8, 14 ; UC 13, 15.
[2] As the Italian *Balilla*, she was torpedoed and sunk by the Austrian Torpedo Boat No. 66, ten miles north of Lissa, on July 14, 1916.
[3] U 5, 6, 7, 8, 11, 12, 13, 14, 15, 18, 23, 26, 27, 29, 31, 36, 37, 40, 41 ; UB 3, 4 ; UC 2, 9, 13. The interned UC 8 is not included in this total.

THE FIRST WAR ON SHIPPING 65

design of coastal boat (UB II type) was ordered in the spring of 1915; they were numbered UB 18-47, and were completed between November and the following August. No boats of the second and improved UC type were available until or after June 1916.

From February 18 until December 1915, in the waters surrounding the British Isles, approximately 166 British merchant-ships and 168 fishing-vessels had been destroyed; the casualties amongst the attacking submarines numbered 16. Mines laid by submarines accounted for about 28 British ships. Far more ominous was the feature manifested in the last quarter—namely, the loss of nearly 50 British steamers in the Mediterranean. High was the mortality to be suffered hereafter by our shipping in this theatre. Nevertheless, Berlin could hardly be satisfied with the results derived from the campaign in the western approaches and in the waters adjacent to the British Isles, for they presented an average of only 20 sinkings per month.

This was, however, but one side of the problem confronting the German authorities. There was every danger of exasperating the United States and other neutrals beyond endurance. The exact limits of their patience were not to be assessed by rule and trammel. Closely interwoven with the hazard of new enemies was the problem of expediency. If it could be established that an unrestricted submarine campaign would win the war for Germany before intervention by the United States could be felt on the battle front, then no niggling over ethics and no scruples of humanity should be allowed to affect the decision. The naval authorities, both at Berlin and Wilhelmshaven, believed decision by the submarine weapon to be possible; the Chancellor held the opposite opinion. So long as this conflict of views existed, then for so long had the decision—for or against unrestricted war on the world's shipping—to be postponed. A year later, Bethmann-Hollweg was beaten, not on the ground of humane conventions, but on the principle of expediency. Which policy would, in the end, best serve Germany—to restrain the U-boats, placate America, and so prolong her neutrality; or to use the submarines without mercy, and so win the war, before America could muster her strength for battle ? Could the Gordian knot of victory be cut quickly enough by the 'sharp sword' of a ruthless onslaught on shipping ? If not, it would be madness to incur the hostility of the most powerful of neutral States. On the issue the Chancellor took his stand—and fell. His fall was as the lightning flash, heralding the coming storm. Then burst the typhoon of terrorism upon the Ocean and the Narrow Seas.

CHAPTER III

THE MEDITERRANEAN : SOWING THE SEED

(1915)

So, in home waters, liner, freighter, and fishing-boat secured a temporary respite from their marauders. But it was now the turn of the Mediterranean, hitherto placid and secure, to be plagued by the new buccaneers. Here, in the great sea-corridor linking the Orient and the Atlantic, were to be found prizes rich and abundant beyond the most roseate dreams of the North Sea corsairs. Thence came the submersible destroyers of sea-borne commerce ; and for many a long day Allied and neutral shipping, plying between the Rock and Suez, was waylaid and murdered. So incessant were the sinkings, they came to be regarded as an ill without cure, and therefore only to be endured. The cruising conditions were ideal for the attackers. Accordingly, the best boats, under the ablest captains, were sent to the Adriatic, from there to prey upon the heavy sea-traffic flowing east or west. Emerging from bases which flanked the shipping routes, the U-boat commanders easily found the track of merchantmen in the high visibility and favourable weather. Inadequate and none too efficient were the counter-measures at first devised by the Allies, as custodians of sea-borne cargoes, against the danger.

It was not her enemy's trade in the Mediterranean which primarily attracted the notice of Germany and induced the naval authorities to send submarines thither. During the spring of 1915, when the naval attack on the Dardanelles was creating alarm in the minds of the Turks, Hersing had been asked if he would attempt to take his boat, U 21, to this land-girt sea and menace the Allied warships lying off the Peninsula. Success attended his venture, yet it was not until the autumn that the first merchant-ship was sunk by submarine in the Mediterranean.

In 1914, when the Triple Alliance dwindled into the Dual Alliance, drastic alterations in the Central Powers' Mediterranean policy became inevitable. The Imperial and Royal Navy of Austria-Hungary was a compact, well-balanced fleet of modest proportions, and included six small submarines belonging to three different types. They could not be regarded as 'Hochseeboote' (ocean-going boats), on account of their limited cruising range, and their activities had, perforce, to be confined to home waters. Five large boats, under construction at Krupps' yard on the outbreak of war, were taken over for the Imperial German Navy.[1] In addition, a small 'demonstration' boat, privately owned by the Whitehead firm at Fiume, was expropriated in August 1914 and commissioned as XII.[2]

With these seven small craft Austria-Hungary was content, until the intrusion of Italy into the war forced her to supplement her resources. The work of the small submarines was confined to the Adriatic, in which Anglo-French forces were constantly patrolling. Not until 1917 were Austro-Hungarian boats employed against commerce; and the conservative policy of the Vienna authorities resulted in friction with the less squeamish Germans. Many and ingenious were the attempts made by Germany to involve her ally in compromising incidents; as, for example, by misuse of the Dual Monarchy's War ensign. It is, however, generally accepted that German submarines were solely responsible for all nefarious deeds committed in the Middle Sea.

[1] They were begun in 1913 for the Austro-Hungarian Navy. When taken over for the Imperial German Navy, they were numbered U 66-70 in the German series.

[2] The Austro-Hungarian submarines were, at first, officially identified by *Roman* numerals only, *without* any prefix of the letter 'U.' At some unknown date during the war the prefix 'U' was adopted, and the style of numeration was also changed from Roman to Arabic characters. Much confusion would, however, be created if the Austrian boats were alluded to as if they were lettered and numbered according to the German method. For example, a reference to U 20 would leave the reader in doubt whether the Austrian U 20 or the German U 20 was being mentioned. Hence, throughout this book the original system of describing the Austro-Hungarian submarines by Roman numerals alone has been adhered to, in order to obviate any misunderstanding.

THE MEDITERRANEAN : SOWING THE SEED 69

The first attack—an entirely legitimate operation of war—came on October 17, 1914, when the French forces were off Cattaro. The cruiser *Waldeck-Rousseau*, assailed by IV, escaped injury. The second presaged the beginning of a new problem for the containing French force, which was in the habit of patrolling waters adjacent to the hostile bases without the least protection against under-water attack. On December 21, XII (Lerch) met the French battleship *Jean Bart* in the Straits of Otranto ; she found the great vessel steaming along at a leisurely speed of 9 knots and entirely unguarded by any screen of destroyers. Fortunate indeed was the French Dreadnought. The torpedo hit her right forward, and such damage as she received was made good by H.M. Dockyard at Malta.

Coincident with the foregoing event, a French submarine, *Curie*, made a gallant but unsuccessful attempt against the Austrian ships in Pola harbour ; she became inextricably entangled in the barrage nets and was forced to rise and surrender. Although scuttled, the *Curie* was raised. She was to a large extent rebuilt by the Austrians. On being commissioned in the following March as the XIV of the Austro-Hungarian Navy, she was a much-improved boat.

A long period of quiescence followed, to be rudely broken by a shattering blow. The lesson of the *Jean Bart* attack had not been taken to heart, and disaster duly ensued. On the night of April 26, 1915, the French armoured cruiser *Leon Gambetta* patrolled the Straits of Otranto at a bare 6·5 knots, and without any destroyer screen. In the later stages of the war such a target was only to be met with in the U-boat commander's dreams. From out of the darkness sped two torpedoes, striking the big cruiser with terrible effect. Plunged into blackness by the wrecking of the dynamos, the crew displayed the greatest coolness. Every officer remained aboard with Admiral Sénès and went down with the ship when she disappeared ten minutes later. Altogether, about 650 souls perished—a heavy price to pay for lessons of experience already learnt by the British in the cruiser catastrophes of the preceding autumn. The attacker was V (von Trapp). As a result of his success, the large French ships watching the Austro-Hungarian Fleet were withdrawn southward, and the blockade was left to destroyers.

About a month after the above disaster, Italy declared for the Allies and relieved the French of the major part of their arduous work, on condition that a British squadron should support the Italian Fleet. Four battleships and four light cruisers had to be withdrawn from the Dardanelles and sent to Taranto. It was one of these reinforcements, the light cruiser *Dublin*, which next fell foul of the submarines. Escorting a convoy along the Montenegrin coast on June 9, off San Giovanni di Medua she was struck by a torpedo from IV (Jüstel), in spite of six screening destroyers. Notwithstanding her injuries, she made her way back to port. The attack was a clear testimony of the increasing skill of the Adriatic submarines.

We have already related how Hersing had left the Ems on April 25 for the Mediterranean, and had made his decision to carry on in spite of the useless fuel taken in from the supply-ship *Marzala* in Rio Corcubion (Spain). From the middle of April rumour ran to the effect that a submarine base was secretly being established by enemy agents at Budrum in the Gulf of Kos. Towards the end of the month, suspicion deepened into certainty that active preparations were being made for the arrival of such a boat. The last vestige of doubt was removed when, at dawn on May 6, Torpedo Boat No. 92 of the Gibraltar Patrol encountered U 21 steering east. The submarine fired a torpedo at her and then dived to avoid being rammed. Next day, Hersing was sighted by a steamer south of Cartagena. These reports caused the greatest anxiety for the safety of the large ships off the Gallipoli Peninsula, and large rewards were offered at this time in neutral ports— particularly Greek—by the Allies for intelligence of U 21. Hersing, however, had not yet entered the eastern basin of the Mediterranean; he had turned northward and made for Cattaro, which haven he reached on May 13. Before he left for the Peninsula, his boat had to go up to Pola for repairs.

When Italy became a belligerent, the Austro-Hungarian naval authorities took immediate steps to increase the small submarine force at their command. Small but useful rein-

THE MEDITERRANEAN : SOWING THE SEED 71

forcements were quickly furnished by the German shipyards. It will be remembered that in October-November 1914, orders for seventeen coastal and fifteen small mine-laying submarines had been placed with Krupps and the Weser Co. by Admiral von Tirpitz. Out of these thirty-two German craft, six coastal boats (UB 1, 3, 7, 8, 14, 15) and four mine-layers (UC 12, 13, 14, 15) were sent in sections to Pola by rail, where they were assembled under German supervision.[1] During 1915, only six new submarines were added to the Austro-Hungarian Navy. One was the captured and reconditioned French *Curie* (renumbered XIV). One or two war cruises seem to have been carried out by UB 1 and UB 15 under German colours, the latter boat achieving several successes ; but in the course of the summer these two German boats were definitely transferred to Austria-Hungary, and became the boats XI and X of her navy. During the autumn, railway trucks brought from Bremen to Pola three more small submarines in sections. They were craft of the German UB I species. The parts were rapidly assembled, and the trio of 'tin tadpoles' went out on active service as the XV, XVI, and XVII.

Before Hersing's arrival at Pola, three of the new small coastal boats had left to attack the Allied naval forces off the Peninsula, carrying with them a cargo of much-needed munitions for the Turks. One, UB 3 (Schmidt), reported herself by wireless some eighty miles from Smyrna, and then completely vanished ;[2] the other two, UB 7 and UB 8, arrived safely at Constantinople, and thereafter were based on the Bulgarian port of Varna, working in the Black Sea against the Russians.

Hersing himself left for the Dardanelles on May 20, passing through the Cerigo Straits and avoiding the mines. Off Dedeagatch he attacked the Russian cruiser *Askold* ; and then, on the 25th, he created consternation by appearing amongst the British ships off Gallipoli. First, but without success, he attacked both the battleships *Swiftsure* and *Vengeance* ; then, encountering the *Triumph* off Gaba Tepe, he had to wait over two hours before he could get in his shot. The torpedo did its

[1] At a later date the German UB 8 became a Bulgarian vessel.
[2] British Records (1919) gave loss off Flanders 24.4.16, which is incorrect.

work; the battleship slowly heeled right over and sank in half an hour, with 75 of her crew. The U 21, rising to observe the result of the hit, was hotly attacked; and Hersing relates that he escaped by making for the stricken battleship, and actually dived under her as she was slowly foundering. Deeming it expedient, he remained submerged for the next twenty-eight hours; then he rose to the surface to recharge his batteries. A cast was made to pick up the *Askold*, but the search was fruitless. As no battleships were to be seen off Gaba Tepe, he made southwards for Cape Helles. Here, early on the morning of May 27, he discovered the *Majestic*. His target had her nets out and was surrounded by patrols and transports; nevertheless, a torpedo sped to its billet through a gap in the encircling shipping, and seven minutes later the gallant old battleship was lying capsized in nine fathoms of water. 'It was a shot the best might envy,' said the late Sir Julian Corbett.[1] Yet Hersing was insatiable, and he cruised around for two days, only to find that the battleships had retired to Mudros. He then put into a coast station on the Turkish coast for a day, returned to the Dardanelles, and, finding no targets, entered the Straits on June 1. At the entrance he got into a terrific whirlpool, had a desperate fight to get free, and on June 5 he arrived at Constantinople with but half a ton of fuel left. Amidst scenes of tremendous enthusiasm, Hersing's great task here ended. He had indeed brought relief and encouragement to the Turks. A paladin encased in steel, he had smitten down, under their very eyes, two of the great sea-dragons which belched death upon the Turkish soldiery. The spectacle of the dying monsters could do naught but dishearten the British troops clinging to the hard-won tip of the Peninsula.

With her mission fulfilled, we leave U 21 and revert to the scene of the Adriatic. The day following the *Dublin* attack, June 10, the newly-completed UB 15 (von Heimburg) made her first trip, and at the same time gained an unexpected success. Off Venice, von Heimburg sighted the Italian submarine *Medusa* on the surface, and promptly sent a torpedo into her. As the torpedo left the bow tube, the German 'sewing-machine' gave a wild leap, her bows tilted up, and the

[1] *Naval Operations*, vol. iii. p. 31.

THE MEDITERRANEAN: SOWING THE SEED

crew had to scramble forward to restore her trim. UB 15 next came to the surface, and there rescued half a dozen Italians.[1]

Another warship destroyed by UB 15 was the Italian armoured cruiser *Amalfi*, a unit embodied in a squadron of cruisers sent up to protect Venice from raids from the sea. On July 7, as she was supporting light forces in the Gulf of Venice, the *Amalfi* was struck by a torpedo and sank with 72 of her crew. Swiftly came the next blow. On July 18 an Italian squadron was shelling the railway at Ragusa, when the *Giuseppe Garibaldi* was hit by a torpedo from IV (Jüstel), and thus another large Allied cruiser was sent to the bottom. Still a further success was scored by the Austrian boats on August 5, when V (Schlosser ?) surprised the Italian submarine *Nereide*, lying hove-to on the surface and unloading stores for the small garrison at Pelagosa, an island temporarily occupied by the Italians on July 11.

Then, at last, Fortune's tide turned from flow to ebb. A French aeroplane claimed to have bombed and damaged XI (von Fernland) on July 1, but the feat still lacks evidential support. Austria's first submarine loss occurred about August 8,[2] when the Whitehead boat XII (Lerch) blew up on the mine-field laid to protect Venice after the *Amalfi* disaster. Five days later the French destroyer *Bisson* bombed and sank III (Strnad) off the Montenegrin coast.[3] After these reverses the activity of the submarines working within the Adriatic dwindled away.

At Constantinople a half-flotilla was formed, consisting of U 21, UB 7 and UB 8, and UC 14 and UC 15. Of these five boats, UB 7 (Werner) worked in the Black Sea, sinking a few ships, notably the British steamer *Patagonia* (6011 tons) off Odessa on September 15. She also attacked the Russian

[1] It is believed that the small Italian Torpedo Boat 5 PN, sunk on June 26, also fell a victim to this submarine.

[2] Date uncertain. Some reports give the 9th and 11th; but the Report, specially prepared by the 'Kriegsarchiv,' Vienna, for this book, gives the 8th as the date of loss.

[3] She is also said to have been rammed by an Italian cruiser (or auxiliary cruiser) on the 11th, and, on the next day (12th), to have been caught on the surface by the *Bisson* and sunk. The 'Kriegsarchiv' Report (Vienna, 1930) gives August 13 as the date of III's loss, and this date has been accepted as being probably the correct one.

battleship *Panteleimon* off Varna on October 27. The UB 8 was ceded to Bulgaria. The UC 15, on her run from the Adriatic, spent an anxious week in the Gulf of Kos repairing defects before she was able to find security up the Straits. Hersing was joined by UB 14 and UC 13 during the summer; and these latter three boats operated both in the Aegean and in the Black Sea.

The first loss to the Constantinople cadre occurred in the closing days of November. Surprised by Russian destroyers with her batteries exhausted, UC 13 (Kirchner) was driven ashore on Kerphen Reef, and then blown up by her crew.[1] The remaining mine-laying submarine, UC 12, carried munitions, money, and German agents to the North African coast to foment insurrection amongst the Senussi against Britain in Egypt, and Italy in Tripolitania and Cyrenaica, although Italy was not yet at war with Germany.

Hersing occasionally visited Beirut and Tripoli during his expeditions to the eastern Mediterranean. He emerged from the Straits on July 4, and sank the empty French transport *Carthage* (5601 tons) off the Peninsula. As he dived to elude the patrols, his boat was nearly wrecked by a mine exploding near by. On August 29 Hersing proceeded on another cruise, and made a second attack on the battleship *Swiftsure* on September 18, again without success. Finding his return barred by mine-fields on the 26th, he made for Pola, where U 21 was laid up for repairs until January 22, 1916. His work, however, was carried on by von Heimburg, now in UB 14. This boat, whilst on passage to Constantinople, succeeded (on August 13) in inflicting the first of the many serious losses suffered by the Allied troopships. Her victim was the *Royal Edward* (11,117 tons), carrying 31 officers and 1335 men from Alexandria to Mudros. The torpedo was fired from 1600 metres, and caught her aft, causing such havoc that she quickly sank with her bows in the air and with a loss of 866 souls. The scene of this attack was close to Budrum,

---

[1] Date variously given as:—
    (*a*) 29.11.15, Michelsen and *Taschenbuch der Kriegsflotten*, 1922.
    (*b*) 24.11.15, Press reports.
    (*c*) —.11.16, Gayer.

THE MEDITERRANEAN : SOWING THE SEED

and there the submarine lurked, waiting for ships to pass. Her patience was rewarded on September 2, when she likewise waylaid the transport *Southland* (11,899 tons) off Strati Island. Forty lives were lost as a result of the torpedo attack; but the ship did not sink, and was brought into Mudros, after the troops had been transhipped to the hospital-ship *Neuralia*.

The sporadic attacks on the Allies' communications next took on a far more serious aspect. On August 4, U 34 (Rücker) and U 35 (Kophamel) had started from home ports on their long voyage to Cattaro, and they were followed on August 27-28 by U 33 (Gansser) and U 39 (Forstmann). The fifth of these famous 'Thirties,' U 38 (Valentiner), joined her sister craft in November. The first two arrived at Cattaro on August 23, and, after necessary repairs, left to attack shipping in the neighbourhood of Crete. They sank five ships, including the French auxiliary cruiser *Indien* on September 8, and the Indian troopship *Ramazan* (3477 tons), which was shelled and sunk on the 19th, with the loss of 305 troops and one of the crew. After this foray, these two boats carried munitions across to the Senussi.

Closely following them came U 33 and U 39. They were sighted off Gibraltar by Torpedo Boat No. 95 of the Gibraltar Patrol, and U 33 was fired upon. Shaking off their pursuers, the newcomers at once began to molest shipping along the Algerian coast, as they passed eastward towards their destination. Organized war on shipping was not opened until the end of September, and the eastern Mediterranean was selected as probably the most fruitful area of operations. Between September 28 and October 11 no fewer than 18 ships were sunk, including the munition-ship *Arabian* (2744 tons) on October 2; many other vessels were also attacked, including the huge White Star liner *Olympic* (46,359 tons) with 5500 troops on board. As all the losses had occurred in a zone under French supervision, a flotilla of French destroyers was detached from the Adriatic. In addition to this augmentation of patrols, the British submarine H 2 was sent to the Aegean to work as a decoy. Certain transports, passing through the dangerous area, were also armed with 12-pounder guns.

For over ten days a lull ensued. During this period a

further burden was added to the Allied naval authorities' task, both by the declaration of war on Bulgaria on October 15, and by the landing of a large Anglo-French force at Salonica. Targets such as the laden troopships and transports offered could scarcely be allowed to escape with impunity. Hither U 35 (Kophamel) was attracted. In the Gulf of Salonica, on the 23rd, she came upon the troopship *Marquette* (7057 tons), with 646 officers, nurses, and men and 541 animals, from Egypt, and he sank her with a torpedo; altogether, 10 nurses, 128 troops, and 29 of the crew were lost. Having delivered this thrust, Kophamel went across to the Gulf of Xeros, where he received orders to put into Budrum to embark a Turkish mission and munitions and take them over to Bardia, on the North African coast. He took on board ten German and Turkish officers, and, with two schooners in tow, left on November 1. Having safely delivered the cargo of munitions and landed the mission three days later, Kophamel next morning (November 5) found the armed boarding-steamer *Tara* entering the port of Sollum on her daily visit to the threatened garrison. He promptly torpedoed the unsuspecting British patrol, and 70 of her crew, who got clear in the boats, were towed by U 35 into Bardia (then in possession of the disaffected Senussi) and were handed over to the Turkish commandant. Kophamel returned to Sollum, where he came upon two Egyptian coastguard gunboats; one, *Abbas*, he sank, and the other, *Abdul Moneim*, he damaged. Later in the day, U 35 appears to have sunk the horse-transport *Moorina* (4944 tons) off Crete. On his return, Kophamel was directed to take charge of the German submarine base at Pola. He handed over U 35 to an officer from Admiral von Pohl's staff—one who was destined to become the 'ace of aces' in the submarine arm, namely, Lothar von Arnauld de la Perière. With the definite establishment of an Adriatic Flotilla, Pola and Fiume became refitting bases for quarterly overhauls; the fortified and land-locked Dalmatian port of Cattaro, with its deep water, admirably met all requirements as a centre of operations.[1]

[1] The Austro-Hungarian submarines were principally based upon Pola and the Gulf of Cattaro, but use was also made of Trieste and Sebenico.

THE MEDITERRANEAN : SOWING THE SEED

During the time U 35 had been so active, U 39 had reappeared off Crete ; after a short spell in those waters she was relieved by U 34. Thereafter, U 33 worked unaided off Malta. In all, during November forty ships were sunk and twelve were attacked but escaped. U 33 claimed to have destroyed fourteen vessels during her cruise (November 15-December 1). Amongst her victims was the *Clan Macleod* (4796 tons). For two hours this steamer by flight eluded capture. When her master surrendered, Gansser opened fire on the crew as they took to the boats, killing twelve and wounding several others. At this early period no escorts could be provided from the Allied naval forces and patrols, and the sole remedy to hand lay in arming the more valuable ships.

The first intimation of U 38's arrival in the Mediterranean was an attack on the troopship *Mercian* (6305 tons) between Gibraltar and Alboran on November 4. The troops were ordered up on deck in expectation of a torpedo striking the crowded liner, but, instead, shells began to fall around and aboard the troopship. A panic ensued. The master himself took the wheel, but the unauthorized lowering of two boats resulted in their capsizing. By zigzagging, the plucky master managed to dodge most of the shells ; but, as his wireless had been shot away, he was unable to call up help. When at length he was relieved at the wheel by a soldier, he got machine-guns going and drove off U 38. His gallant defence had lasted an hour, during which time 23 men had been killed in the troopship and 31 others lost as a result of the boats capsizing.

Continuing his course along the Algerian coast, Valentiner secured further victims, and this officer branded himself by being the first of his kind to commit an act of deliberate savagery in the waters of the Mediterranean ; hence his name appeared on the list of ' war criminals.' On November 7 he had sunk the empty French transport *France IV* (4025 tons) off Sardinia, and then he fell in with the Italian liner *Ancona* (8210 tons). Running up Austrian colours, he opened fire on the passengers and crew as they took to the boats ; and as a result of this wantonly inhuman attack 208 lives were sacrificed. Valentiner later arrived at Cattaro, having sunk

14 ships on his expedition. Six days later another Italian steamer (*Bosnia*, 2561 tons) was sunk, with the loss of 12 lives. Since Berlin had promised Washington that passenger-ships, not committing any hostile act, should be spared, Austria, although innocent, was made to shoulder the blame and so conceal her ally's perfidy.

Another success had lately been gained by the Constantinople boats. Whilst his boat, UB 14, was lying under repair on November 2, von Heimburg was informed that the French submarine *Turquoise* had stranded in the Sea of Marmora and had been captured intact; further, that papers found in her showed that her commander was to make a rendezvous with the British E 20 near Rodosto on November 5. By dint of great exertions, UB 14 was made ready for sea in twenty-four hours; and, instead of the French boat, UB 14 kept the appointment with E 20. Lying on the surface, the British submarine awaited her ally. A torpedo streaked towards her and blew her up; and only nine of her crew could be saved from the sinking craft.

After the first nine days of December a lull set in, to be broken by a serious recurrence of sinkings lasting until January 4. Valentiner in U 38 had left Cattaro on December 9, taking the small UC 12 in tow, the latter being laden with war material for the Senussi. This mission accomplished, he seems to have paid a round of visits, putting into Jaffa, Beirut, and Alexandretta, at which ports he was received with enthusiasm. He then turned his attention to shipping, and from December 27 to January 4 he sank five British and several Allied steamers, with the loss of over 500 lives. Unhampered by any chivalrous or humane feelings, he did not scruple to torpedo without warning the P. & O. liner *Persia* (7974 tons), about 70 miles to the south of Crete, on the 30th; the ship's boilers blew up, and she sank like a stone, with 334 lives. Other ships he destroyed were the *Clan Macfarlane* (4823 tons), with 52 of her crew, on the same day; the *Glengyle* (9395 tons), with 10 of her crew, on January 1; the *Coquet* (4396 tons), with 17 lives, on January 4; the large Japanese liner *Yasaka Maru* (10,932 tons); and the French liner *Ville de la Ciotat* (6390 tons), with 29 lives. On January 2, in the Gulf of Marmarice, he em-

THE MEDITERRANEAN : SOWING THE SEED

barked further war material and a new Turkish mission for transport to Africa. However, the vigilant patrol off the coast of Tripoli prevented him from carrying out the enterprise, and he returned to Cattaro on January 10.

Upon Valentiner's gross violation of the German pledge that passenger-ships should be spared, Washington, very naturally, sent a strongly-worded remonstrance ; but Berlin, with brazen effrontery, denied that any of her commanders were responsible. Austria, however, flatly refused to be made the scapegoat again, as she consistently disapproved of such savage methods. Later, when hospital-ships began to be sunk during the unrestricted war of 1917, German submarines were absolutely forbidden to use Austrian colours.

The German authorities had expected that, by sending submarines to the Mediterranean, all risk of ' incidents ' likely to excite American indignation would be avoided. Any such expectation was extinguished by Valentiner's conduct. As a result of his outrages, German officers in command of submarines were bidden to observe Prize War rules in this theatre, allowing passengers and crew time to disembark before their ship was destroyed. With a few notable exceptions, this procedure was observed until 1917.

So closed the year 1915 in the Mediterranean. During the autumn some 54 British and 38 Allied and neutral ships had been destroyed by half a dozen submarines. Clear warning of coming troubles had been given in no uncertain manner. The problem of trade-defence in the Mediterranean presented especial difficulties ; the Allies did not clarify that problem, but complicated it the more, by dividing up the whole sea into an artificial pattern of ' zones,' fitted together like a mosaic.[1] Bad as such a division of command may have been when viewed from a military standpoint, it was at the time the only possible solution of an intricate political problem. Britain was fighting in alliance with two great Mediterranean

[1] The Italians were responsible for the Adriatic, the western seaboard of Italy, and the waters along the coast of Tripoli ; the French controlled the western Mediterranean, the Tunisian seaboard, the Ionian Sea, and the Syrian coast ; whilst to the British forces were assigned the area east of Gibraltar, the Aegean Sea, and the centre of the Mediterranean as far east as Port Said.

Powers; she had to exercise forbearance and tolerate her Allies' claims to a share in the control of the sea campaign. France and Italy, jointly and vehemently, objected to the idea that they, the two great Latin States of the 'Latin Lake,' should allow their Fleets to be subordinated under any system of unified command wherein Britain would be the paramount and directing power. Through the Mediterranean passed lines of communication vitally essential to all three of the Allies, and each naturally thought its own interests to be every whit as important as those of the other two. Out of this conflict of claims arose the method of localized control. Long did that method, with its inherent defects and difficulties, remain as a weight in the balance against the Allies. So long as the system of fractional commands prevailed, then for so long was one common and coherent system of trade-defence beyond attainment.

Anti-submarine measures were almost non-existent. On the one hand, British opinion leaned towards 'routeing' and patrol; on the other hand, the French favoured a systematic search for bases. The more important transports were armed with guns to repel surface attacks, but nothing feasible could be devised to ensure protection against torpedoes. It was estimated that at least 40 destroyers and 280 trawlers were necessary to patrol the long shipping lanes with any chance of success. Everything was in the submarines' favour. Many were the straits and channels into which the sea-traffic had to converge, and to those focal points the German submarines had only to resort to find the targets that they desired. East to west, and west to east, transports and supply-vessels moved continuously between Gibraltar and Gallipoli, Salonica and Egypt; intercoastal traffic was plentiful; Italy urgently needed the import of vital necessaries. All these factors, combined with weather conditions, made the U-boats' task an easy one. Small wonder, then, that it was the German submarine commanders' ambition to be sent to the Mediterranean. Long and bitter was the struggle to be, before the menace was met, mastered, and fought down.

CHAPTER IV

THE WAR OF LIMITATIONS AND THE RESPITE

(JANUARY–MAY 1916)

IN October 1915, Bulgaria threw in her lot with the Central Powers. To the mind of General Falkenhayn (Chief of the German General Staff), the time was ripe for resuming the submarine campaign around the British Isles. That onslaught had lately been brought to an end through America's remonstrances. Falkenhayn's main contention was that the non-belligerent States would be so impressed by Bulgaria's action, that they would not dare to abandon their neutrality.[1] The next event was the publication of a Note from Washington, on November 5, concerning the Allied policy of blockade, which Germany interpreted as a turn of American opinion in her own favour.[2] A perceptible relaxation in the restrictions governing the submarine war became noticeable. At a conference held in December between the German naval and military leaders the situation was thoroughly discussed; and von Holtzendorff (Chief of the Naval Staff) put forward a proposal for the resumption of the trade-war. Pointing out that British rates of freight had risen tenfold, he said it was estimated that four or five war-stations around the British Isles could now be occupied and maintained by the U-boats, giving a monthly yield of 480,000 tons destroyed. With average Mediterranean sinkings totalling 125,000 tons, and mining operations inflicting a further loss to the Allies of 26,640 tons, it was calculated that enemy shipping could be reduced at the rate of 631,000 tons gross each month. As such loss would be cumulative, he gave it as his opinion, on being pressed by the Imperial Chancellor, that England would be

---

[1] *High Sea Fleet* (Scheer), p. 246.
[2] *U.S.N.I. Proceedings*, April 1926, p. 637.

beaten *within six months* from the initiation of such operations. Tirpitz was all for bold measures. Every loss, so far, had been made good ; the submarine force had been so enlarged that it could now wage a campaign drastic enough to give a decisive turn to the whole conflict on land and sea. But the Chancellor remained unconvinced.

A new Note was addressed to the Allies on January 18 by Washington, wherein the legality of submarine warfare on commerce was admitted, provided that ships were stopped and those aboard were allowed to leave before their vessels were destroyed. It went on to suggest that, by resisting attack, the ships became liable to justifiable destruction. Most important and above everything else was the suggestion that *defensively-armed merchant-ships might be treated as armed merchant cruisers or as auxiliary cruisers*. Now, in October 1915 the Admiralty had issued instructions to masters of armed merchantmen that fire should be opened only if their ships were attacked, and then only by gunners under orders of the master ; that they must not interfere with any other ships ; that correct colours were to be hoisted when fire was opened ; and that fire must not be opened or maintained by a vessel which had stopped, hauled down her flag, or indicated her intention to surrender. Submarines were not to be allowed to close. Lastly, if a ship were sighted in distress with a submarine standing by, fire was not to be opened on the submarine unless the sighting vessel was herself also attacked.

One outcome of mounting defensive armaments in merchant-vessels was that the submarine was forced to abandon the gun and make under-water attack with the torpedo. With the latter and more drastic weapon went the attendant risk that neutral vessels, such as those of America, might be sunk outright.

The impressions to which such a Note would give rise were obvious. Berlin read it as a move designed to weaken the grip of the British blockade. The Chancellor pleaded for a postponement of the unrestricted submarine warfare until April 1 ; but, following the rejection of Germany's peace terms, on February 11, permission was granted to submarine commanders to treat armed merchant-vessels as warships as

THE WAR OF LIMITATIONS AND THE RESPITE 83

from February 29, with the proviso that, before attack, the guns must be distinguished.

Admiral von Pohl, the Commander-in-Chief of the High Sea Fleet, had died on February 5, and had been succeeded by Admiral Scheer. The latter officer had under his immediate command about half of the submarines, and fully realized the futility of these qualified orders. If a U-boat closed, in surface trim, to a range close enough to discover the guns, she would be liable to summary destruction should the ship under examination prove to be a decoy. On the other hand, if the submarine approached submerged, she might be too late to get into position for a torpedo attack. Scheer related [1] that on February 23 the Kaiser fully agreed with him, but held that the time had not yet come to risk the armed intervention of America. The Naval Staff concurred that the military situation was not such as to warrant measures so extreme.

In home waters, therefore, the year 1916 opened quietly. In the North Sea we find the U 70 (Wünsche, late of U 25) convoying the blockade-runner *Marie*, bound for German East Africa ; whilst U 32 was sent on a futile errand to attack the stranded British submarine H 6 off Schiermonnikoog. The adapted mine-layer U 44 made another trip, and laid a field off Blyth and Tees Mouth ; this, incidentally, was the first minefield laid by submarine north of the Humber. Hunted by a couple of torpedo-boats, she claimed to have sunk one of them.[2] U 70 accompanied the raider *Greif* when that disguised corsair made her disastrous run across the North Sea on February 29, to sink and be sunk by the armed merchant-cruiser *Alcantara*.

If the North Sea boats were curbed, the Flanders units continued their mining work without intermission. Many were the losses suffered, and amongst the casualties figured the light cruiser *Arethusa*, whose famous career terminated on February 11. Returning after the German destroyer raid on the mine-sweeping sloops off the Dogger Bank, she struck mines off the North Cutler, stranded, and became a total loss. On February 27 the P. & O. liner *Maloja* (12,431 tons) foundered

[1] *High Sea Fleet* (Scheer), p. 110.
[2] On January 28, Torpedo Boat No. 13 was sunk in collision.

on mines off Dover, with 122 of those on board ; the destroyer *Coquette* and Torpedo Boat No. 11 were similarly lost in the North Sea on March 7 ; and two days later the armed boarding steamer *Fauvette* went down off the East Coast. Many other vessels were also sunk by mines.

With February, deliveries began of the second and enlarged series of ' submarines for coastal waters ' (Unterseeboote für Küstengewasser). Divided into two batches, the component boats were numbered UB 18-29 and UB 30-47, the latter group being slightly longer than the preceding dozen. Steinbrinck was transferred from UB 10 to UB 18. On the night of the 26th he ran through the Straits and sank two French mine-sweepers off Havre, believed to be the *Au Revoir* (1058 tons gross) and *Îles Chanzey*.[1] Two more steamers, *Harmatris* (6387 tons) and the French *Louisiane* (5109 tons), were destroyed off Boulogne and Havre on March 8 and 9 respectively.

During the early weeks of 1916 the German naval authorities were working unceasingly for the resumption of the submarine campaign. On March 4 the Kaiser gave his consent for unrestricted warfare to begin on April 1, whereupon a statement in explanation and condonation of the step was to be put before the U.S. Government. The general situation seemed to be satisfactory : Bulgaria had overrun Serbia ; Austria held Italy ; Turkey kept the Russians at bay at Erzerum ; while in Iraq the British disaster at Kut had relieved the threat to Baghdad ; Egypt was endangered by the Senussi on the one hand and the Turkish Syrian army on the other ; and Ireland was seething with discontent. The Allied blockade had of course to be reckoned with, but its effects were not as yet grave. Blockade was a form of paralysis creeping slowly over the body economic, and it would be many a long day before the German ' will to victory ' was numbed by such a malady.

England could be menaced by a ruthless attack on her sea-

---

[1] According to a 'List of French Navy Losses,' compiled by M. Henri le Masson, and published in *The Navy* (London), Jan. 1930, *Au Revoir* was torpedoed and sunk February 27, 1916. The List makes no allusion to the loss of any second vessel such as *Îles Chanzey*.

THE WAR OF LIMITATIONS AND THE RESPITE 85

borne trade. Neutrals, intimidated and imperilled, would be deterred from bartering with her. The risk of conflict with America could be accepted. Admitted that she would be well able to stand a ten years' war, and that her accession would prove a stimulus to the Allies. But, as the sponsors of unrestricted operations urged, it was the task of the diplomats to stave off America. Should the United States continue to be friendly, concessions could be made, on condition that such pressure would be brought to bear on England as would allow the revival of neutral trade with Germany. American intervention, it was clearly realized, would prolong the war ; but, at the same time, it was considered that the success to be gained would more than counterbalance this danger.[1]

At this stage, on March 6, the Kaiser overruled the decision in favour of unrestricted war in well-defined areas, with exemption allowed to hospital-ships. This fresh vacillation came too late ; orders had gone forth to the submarines and could not be countermanded. Tirpitz, yet again, had not been asked to express his views ; he tendered his resignation.[2]

Already the first mercantile victim of the 1916 campaign had been secured, on March 4, in the steamer *Teutonian* (4824 tons), torpedoed and sunk 36 miles S.W. by W. from Fastnet. On March 16 the large Dutch liner *Tubantia* (13,911 tons), bound for Buenos Ayres and calling at Dover for mail, was torpedoed off the North Hinder L.V., and sank three hours later. It is related that she was carrying German bullion, concealed in cheeses and consigned to German banks abroad ; the German submarine commander being unaware of her freight, by a frolic of fortune destroyed German treasure. A few days later the Dutch steamer *Palembang* (6674 tons) was also sunk.

Far more serious in after results was the attack on the cross-Channel packet *Sussex* (1353 tons) on March 24. She was carrying 380 passengers, including several Americans ; and the torpedo from UB 29 (Pustkuchen) killed 50 of those on board as it exploded against her hull. The ship, however, did not sink and was towed into Boulogne, where fragments of the torpedo were found to be in one of the lifeboats. In the face

---

[1] *High Sea Fleet* (Scheer), p. 240.
[2] He was succeeded by Admiral von Capelle.

of this damning evidence, the excuse first proffered, that a mine had done the work, had to be discarded by the German apologists as untenable. Pustkuchen said that he had mistaken her for a troop transport because of her crowded decks; or, alternatively, for a sloop of the 'Arabis' class. Of the results of this 'incident' more will presently be related.

At the moment when the Kaiser postponed the unrestricted campaign, U-boats had already been sent out to the western seas in pairs. U 22 (Hoppe) and U 32 (Spiegel) were ordered to report on conditions of warfare against armed merchantmen; they returned on March 18, and claimed to have sunk 35,000 tons of shipping. Hoppe's share was four enemy steamers and twelve neutral ships of 20,000 tons; and he had allowed two passenger-ships to pass unmolested. Both boats developed defects and were forced to return.

As a variation from the usual task of commerce destruction, twelve U-boats supported an air raid on Britain on March 5, with only moderate success. On the 25th, U 69 was ordered to attack British forces which had appeared off Sylt as support to the air raid on Tondern airship base. Being unable to come within attacking distance, U 69 attained no result. The U 74 (one of a new class of large mine-layers) laid a field between St. Abb's Head and May Island on March 31, preparatory to projected Fleet operations. These movements had, however, to be abandoned owing to adverse weather. In this field the steamer *Sabbia* (2802 tons) was blown up before the mines were located and swept up.

Discouraging though the results attained by U 22 and U 32 had been, other boats went forth in quest of prey. To U 70 fell a meagre 6200 tons in the Irish Channel; but U 28, attended by better fortune, struck down some 17,700 tons between March 26 and April 1. Operating in the North Channel, U 43 (Jürst) and U 44 (Wagenführ) laid claim to 29,500 tons. On the morning of the 23rd the latter allowed the *Mauretania* to pass unscathed within a hundred metres, although U 44 had all four tubes ready to fire. Amongst the ships destroyed are to be found the *Englishman* (5257 tons), sunk on March 24, 30 miles north-east of Malin Head, with 10 lives; the *Rio Tiete* (7464 tons), four days later, 140 miles west of Ushant ; and the Holt liner *Achilles* (7043 tons), sunk on the 31st, 90 miles W.N.W. of Ushant, with 5 of her crew.

In the south-western approaches, U 68 (Güntzel) appeared. Leaving the Ems on March 16, she fell in with the Q-ship *Farnborough* (Q 5) on the sixth day out. Ever since October this decoy had been cruising in search of U-boats ; the weary months of waiting were now to be rewarded. U 68 fired a shot across the tramp's bows, which had its desired effect of bringing her to. The crew, by all visible evidence, were precipitately abandoning their ship and taking to the boats ; the engineer appeared to be blowing off steam. Güntzel was, however, impatient, and closed in to 800 yards to hasten matters. Suddenly the White Ensign fluttered in the breeze, the screens fell away, and again and again the revealed guns riddled the trapped raider with shell. Where U 68 had gone down, Lieutenant-Commander Gordon Campbell steamed over the spot and dropped depth-charges. The bows of the wounded submarine rose out of the water ; five more rounds were fired into her ; and she vanished for the last time. For this successful fight, Lieutenant-Commander Campbell was promoted to Commander on March 29, and received the D.S.O.

Against shipping the spring campaign continued with varying success. U 66 exterminated 20,000 tons between April 5 and 10 ; U 69 claimed 21,000 tons between April 15 and 20 ; U 19 (R. Weisbach), after her long overhaul and change of engines, destroyed 19,000 tons. Her chief mission at this period was the landing of Sir Roger Casement in Tralee Bay on April 20. She was accompanied part of the way by U 20 (Schwieger), until the latter developed defects and had to return. U 22 (Hoppe) sank 11,000 tons in the Irish Channel, and had a narrow escape from being rammed by a cruiser off Belfast. This boat was notoriously unsafe, and difficult to handle submerged. Her commander had a hair-raising experience when the cruiser loomed out of the mist and compelled an emergency dive. First bows up, and next with stern raised, dropping all the while, U 22 sank to two hundred feet ; water began to seep through the seams ; chlorine gas started to generate ; still, the pressure-hull stood the immense strain. The only course was to blow tanks at high pressure. At first there was little response to the drastic remedy; then the sweep of the pointer-needle around the dial of the manometer began to slow down, crept on a little, and then stopped. The dive at last was checked. U 22 began to rise. Faster and faster she moved upwards; finally, her rate of ascent became so rapid, she went out of control and shot to the surface. Close by lay the cruiser, but never sighted the submarine on its rocket-like projection upwards from the depths. U 22 crept away, with both boat and crew shaken by such submarine acrobatics.

Off Ushant, U 45 obliterated 8000 tons of shipping; then, on April 25, she broadcast the recall to all boats in western waters. This order was taken in by every boat except U 20. All defects and damages in the slayer of the *Lusitania* had been made good, and she had sailed the previous day. Schwieger carried on for the western approaches and sank 23,000 tons, including the *Cymric* (13,370 tons), outward bound for America. This White Star liner he sank on May 8, about 140 miles W.N.W. from Fastnet, with the loss of five lives. She was the thirty-seventh unarmed steamer to be sunk without warning since the *Lusitania* crime. He also set up a long-distance wireless-telegraphy record for submarines of 770 miles, communicating with Germany on his cruise. Amongst the April toll of shipping were included the *Zent* (3890 tons), sunk without warning on the 5th, 28 miles W. by S. ½ S. from Fastnet, with 49 lives; and the *Whitgift* (4397 tons), similarly put down off Ushant on April 20, with 32 souls.

April 1, the date originally fixed for unrestricted warfare, had passed. Washington was threatening to break off diplomatic relations as a consequence of the *Sussex* outrage; and President Wilson told Congress, on April 19, that ' unless the Imperial German Government shall now immediately declare and carry into effect the abandonment of their present method of warfare against passenger and freight-carrying vessels, the Government have no choice but to sever diplomatic relations with the German Government altogether.' To this Berlin replied expressing the regret that ' the sentiments of humanity, which the Government of the United States extends with such fervour to the unhappy victims of the submarine campaign, have not been extended to the millions of women

THE WAR OF LIMITATIONS AND THE RESPITE 89

and children who are being driven to starvation in order that their pangs may force the victorious armies of the Central Empires to dishonourable capitulation. . . . It would be an act which never could be vindicated in the eyes of humanity or of history to allow, after twenty-one months of war, a controversy to assume a development which would seriously menace peace between the German and American peoples.' Therefore the German submarines received the following order: 'In accordance with the general principle of visit, search, and destruction of merchant-vessels recognized by international law, such vessels, both within and without the war zone, shall not be sunk without warning and without saving human lives, unless the ships attempt to escape or offer resistance.' For Pustkuchen, the attacker of the *Sussex*, punishment was promised.

The new orders were promulgated on April 20. Four days later, Scheer sent the recall to all his submarines in western waters; he saw no use in sending out boats to undertake work highly dangerous under ordinary conditions, and rendered doubly hazardous by compliance with the numerous instructions and limitations of their handling. The Kaiser assented to milder courses on the 30th, directing the U-boats to be used for military purposes only. He intimated, however, that whenever the political and military situation allowed, the campaign would be resumed.[1]

In the Flanders Flotilla's area the spring of 1916 was a busy time. In consequence of the attention paid by the submarines to the approaches of Havre, several British drifters were sent to operate off the port in the hope of catching one of the marauders in their nets. On the morning of April 5 a hostile submarine was reported in the roads. Six drifters at once put out, and at 10.15 A.M. the *Pleiades* shot her nets. Just as the *Endurance* followed suit, the enemy was reported foul. The *Comrades* reported feeling a bump and shock beneath, a short while before. Events followed in quick succession. A periscope struck and disabled the rudder of *Endurance*, who played out her nets and let them go, when her skipper judged the U-boat was thoroughly entangled. Encircled by the

[1] *High Sea Fleet* (Scheer), p. 242.

drifters, and attacked by the French torpedo-boat *Trombe* (which dropped three bombs), UB 26 (Smiths) was forced to come to the surface and surrender. This boat had left the Ems on March 19, passing down the Dutch coast about three miles out, and arrived at Zeebrugge on the 21st. She had later left to work in the Channel, crossing the net barrage between the South Goodwins and Outer Ruytingen. UB 26 was easily raised by the French from her shallow resting-place; and, after repairs, the prize was commissioned for further service as the French *Roland Morillot*. For Germany this was a doubly unfortunate stroke of fate : on board were found papers furnishing positive proof that the *Sussex* had fallen victim to a German submarine.

During this same month of April, Fate decreed that a unit of the Flanders Flotilla should be the first to succumb to an innovation in anti-submarine weapons. On the 23rd the small mine-laying UC 3 (Kreysern) got caught in mine-nets off Spar Buoy (Norfolk coast), where she was bombed and blown up by the armed smack *Cheero*. Here, it would seem, is the first recorded instance of a submarine having been located, in war, by hydrophone. Acoustic detection became, later, one of the most successful of all devices employed against under-water craft.

Towards the end of April the first Belgian coast barrage was laid by the Dover Patrol. This sea-zareba was primarily intended to give protection to British war-vessels patrolling about eighteen miles off-shore from the strip of coast held by the enemy. The barrage was not specially designed to impen the U-boats within their bases, nor to prevent those craft from moving up and down the Dover Straits. None the less, this barrier, by reason of its pattern and position, would impede the hostile under-water vessels by hindering free movement. An *enceinte* of mines and nets, completely enclosing the German-Belgian coastal waters, could not be created, because of Dutch neutrality. At the north-eastern extremity of the barrage a considerable gap existed. However, the enemy submarines setting out from the Flanders base for a cruise would have to run north-eastwards, as if making for the German Bight, and cross the mouth of the

THE WAR OF LIMITATIONS AND THE RESPITE 91

Scheldt, before they could reach and round the end of the barrage and start on their south-westerly run, down the Straits. Submarines inward-bound would also have to hold to a north-easterly course for a much longer distance, before they could round the end of the barrage and double back to make their ports.

The whole plan was, of course, to form as complete an off-shore barrage as possible outside Zeebrugge and Ostend, the sea-exits to the inland base at Bruges. On April 24 the work of planting the obstruction began. Starting at 5 A.M., the *Orvieto, Princess Margaret, Paris*, and *Biarritz*, steaming at a speed of 14 knots, laid 1421 mines. At 10.20 A.M., six trawlers, each carrying 24 mines, laid their cargoes in the shallow water at the eastern end.[1] A double line of deep mines, fifteen miles in length, together with over thirteen miles of moored mine-nets and fourteen light-buoys, was laid off Thornton Ridge. During the planting of the deep mines, drifters laid explosive nets to seaward. Farther out still, others laid indicator nets, parallel to the West Hinder Shoal, thirty miles from Ostend, to catch any U-boats returning to their base. Admiral Bacon of the Dover Patrol reported that during the day numerous explosions had occurred; and he believed four or five submarines had been destroyed in the mine-nets. This sanguine estimate was based on good evidence; but, as has since been proved, only two German submarines were snared—one fated to escape and the other to perish. UB 10, fouling the nets, exploded several mines as she endeavoured to free herself; after eight hours' struggling, she got clear and entered her base. UB 13 [2] (Metz) was less fortunate; she fouled the anchor cable of the drifter *Gleaner of the Sea*, stationed with several other drifters off Thornton Ridge. The submarine was next bombed by the *E.E.S.*; and then, to make

---

[1] The line was prolonged during May 1916.

[2] The identity of this loss caused much confusion. British Records (1919) showed: UB 13 lost, March 1916, area and date of loss unknown; UB 3 sunk in North Sea, April 24, 1916. German records give the boat sunk on April 24, 1916, as UB 13. The German version is correct. UB 3 was a Mediterranean boat, and had vanished (on passage to Constantinople) almost a year previously to the incidents related above.

quite sure, explosive sweeps were fired by the destroyer *Afridi*.

The barrage was completed on May 26, and was maintained until October; it was reinforced by mine-fields and mine-nets, and, whenever possible, patrolled. That only an intermittent surveillance could be maintained by surface vessels was a grave but unavoidable defect. Sally-ports were close at hand, from which enemy destroyers might dash out at night, to sink or injure any of the craft posted as sentinels over the nets. All surface patrols had to be withdrawn by dusk, and Schulze relates that at nightfall submarines would tear with grapnels a gap in the nets. Had the type of British mine then in use been more efficient, it is probable that several submarines would have been destroyed immediately after the laying of the barrage. The aircraft and drifter patrol certainly confined the enemy's work of removal to the dark hours, but effected little else. Gayer dates the increasingly effective anti-submarine measures off Flanders from this time. After October the barrage could not be patrolled.[1] There was, moreover, the exit leading into Dutch waters, through which the U-boats passed, by day, unseen and submerged, or, by night, at periscope depth.

Taken as a means whereby a daylight patrol could be established, maintained, and guarded along the Belgian littoral, the barrage scheme was, without doubt, a success. It 'carried war into the enemy's country,' and therefore achieved the purpose for which it was primarily planned. But, regarded in its secondary and subsidiary capacity—that of an obstructive and destructive fence, set up in the face of the hostile submarines—the enterprise fell far short of the mark aimed at. The pity was that the anti-submarine value of the scheme was very much overrated. That mistaken confidence arose from a very natural error, the attribution of an effect to a wrong cause. Immediately after the barrage had been created, submarines became less active. The inference was obvious: it was the new barrage which was

---

[1] In the summer of 1917 it was relaid in preparation for the Great Landing on the Belgian coast—a project never carried out owing to the failure of the armies to capture Passchendaele from the Germans.

THE WAR OF LIMITATIONS AND THE RESPITE 93

hampering the U-boats' operations. But, as it happened, on the same day as the mines were laid, Scheer had ordered the recall of his submarines. Once again, coincidence of change in German submarine policy with the initiation of a new sea-barrier gave the idea that the enemy had received a serious set-back.

Other submarines encountered the perils of this mine barrage. On May 7 more mine-nets were laid; and when, on July 15, these nets were being replaced by the drifters, the eighth net was found to be missing and the mines exploded. During the hauling of nets the body of a German telegraphist rating was brought up; on it was found a pass made out from Bruges and an identity disc marked U 10. Three days later this man's name and twenty-nine others appeared in the German casualty list. The mystery about the whole affair is that, according to German records, U 10 was lost with all hands in the Baltic; but the German authorities do not, by a year, agree amongst themselves as to the date of her loss.[1]

On the day following the barrage-laying (April 25), German battle-cruisers raided Lowestoft. Previous to this sortie, two of the large mine-layers had left to lay fields. U 71's destination was the Moray Firth. Owing, however, to engine trouble and loss of oil fuel, she had to return on the 21st with

[1] Here are the three German versions :—
    (a) *Taschenbuch der Kriegsflotten* (1922) lists U 10 as 'lost in the Baltic (probably by a mine), June 1915.'
    (b) Gayer says U 10 was sent, during May 1916, to a position to the N.W. of Gotska Sands in the Baltic, and never returned.
    (c) Michelsen says U 10 was lost in the Baltic during June 1916, probably by striking a mine.

The *Taschenbuch* places the date of loss about eleven months *before* the Belgian coast barrage was laid: Gayer's explanation fixes it *during* the month the barrage was erected: Michelsen dates the loss to the month *after* the placing of the barrage. British Records, on the strength of the evidence, quoted in the text above, gave U 10 as destroyed during May 1916 by mine, at a position about 25 miles to the N.W. of Zeebrugge. In the autumn of 1915 the earlier U-boats, with Körting heavy-oil motors, were withdrawn from service in the North Sea. U 10 was one of these boats, and (according to Gayer) she was, in Sept. 1915, a unit of the Baltic (Courland) Flotilla. It is extremely dubious if U 10 ever was a unit stationed at Zeebrugge in the spring of 1916. All reliable evidence points to the fact that she was lost in the Baltic, from some unknown cause, during May 1916.

her mission unfulfilled. For similar reasons U 72 did not succeed in mining the Firth of Forth. Other submarines were posted off the Forth; and UB 18 (Steinbrinck) and UB 29 (Pustkuchen, whose punishment for the *Sussex* attack must have been singularly mild) were stationed off Lowestoft. Steinbrinck sighted four British submarines on the surface off Yarmouth, about one mile apart and making 12 knots. He attacked the leading boat. She, having seen his periscope, eluded the torpedo and tried to ram. Steinbrinck dived right under E 22, his assailant, and then rose for another sight. He saw E 22 coming back at full speed, fired both his torpedoes, hitting the British boat with one. As she sank, two of E 22's crew were thrown into the water. Steinbrinck, perfectly aware of the other three submarines' periscopes converging on the spot, kept his stern towards the oncoming enemy craft, picked up the two drowning men, and dived to safety. It was a very gallant deed, and one much admired by his opponents. The other boat, UB 29, torpedoed and damaged the Harwich light cruiser *Penelope.*

Finally, UC 5 (Mohrbutter), after passing through the barrage on the 26th, stranded off Harwich and betrayed her position by sending out wireless calls; she was captured intact by the destroyer *Firedrake* on the next day.

In the North Sea, on May 3 (and during the British attempt to carry out a seaplane raid on the Zeppelin sheds at Tondern), U 24 discovered the Grand Fleet to be at sea, in support of its light forces. She tried to call up by wireless U 51, U 70, and UB 22, patrolling in the vicinity, but without success. She herself could do nothing, for a fire had broken out in the clutch between her Diesel engines and her electric motors.

By this time the spring campaign of 1916 against shipping was virtually at a close. Gayer claims that the U-boats in the western seas had destroyed between 200,000 and 300,000 tons of shipping. He also estimates that the second abandonment of the trade-war conserved, for future Allied use, 1,200,000 tons, in addition to 400,000 tons which the Flanders boats could have destroyed between May and September. Five German submarines had been lost: of these, only one boat, U 68, had succumbed to a snare whilst carrying on the

III. PRIZE OF WAR.

A photograph of *UC. 5* in dry-dock, after her capture on April 27, 1916. So bitter was the campaign that very few submarines fell into enemy hands during the course of hostilities, and those few prizes were only secured as the result of salvage operations.

THE WAR OF LIMITATIONS AND THE RESPITE

drive against the shipping approaches to these islands. This same authority states that the monthly rate of commissioning new boats was never so favourable as between April 1916 and January 1917, averaging ten new craft per month. Twenty-five large and forty-three small boats were in service in March 1916; and of the former, with three exceptions, all were completely fitted out and manned by experienced crews. In addition, fifty-two large and eighty-nine small boats were under construction or about to be delivered.

Gayer remarks that the Allies' anti-submarine measures off the Flanders base showed a notable increase of efficiency, and in particular the air patrol became a never-ending source of worry to the U-boats. On the whole, however, little headway was made in combating the menace of the submarines. True, a respite had been granted to the Allies during the summer, but it also deferred the development of an effective reply. The Allies at that time could not have fully known the reasons underlying the slackening-off of the attack. The wish was father to an erroneous conclusion. It was both convenient and consoling to presume that counter-measures were at last proving effective. For that complacent optimism a bitter price had, a year later, to be paid. For the turning-point in the whole sea war was near at hand. The event was about to occur which led Germany to relegate her battle-squadrons to a secondary position, and to stake her whole future upon the Submarine Arm.

CHAPTER V

THE SUBMARINE AS A MILITARY WEAPON

(MAY–SEPTEMBER 1916)

ALTHOUGH on May 4 the German Government had accepted all the American demands, that submarine warfare henceforth should be conducted along prize war lines, the energetic new Commander-in-Chief of the High Sea Fleet, Admiral Scheer, did not intend to allow his under-water force to rust in idleness. When Schwieger returned from the last cruise of the spring, he was called upon to express his opinion upon the restricted war. In no uncertain terms he declared that 'prize war,' waged according to prize law, gave little promise of decisive results.

An alternative scheme was put forward to allow unrestricted war on warships, transports, and armed merchantmen in the blockaded zone; whilst in other areas the procedure of prize war could be followed. When the American demands were met, a further suggestion was made by the submarine commanders; they proposed to utilize a captured steamer to accommodate the crews of sunken vessels. Commander Bauer [1] (now Commander, Submarine Divisions, and late commanding officer, 1st Flotilla) made a voyage in U 67 to study the conditions himself; and on his return he was more convinced than ever of the danger to which submarines, operating in accordance with prize war, would be exposed.

---

[1] The two submarine flotillas, available for service at the outbreak of war, were later expanded into four flotillas, organized as follows:—

Commanding Officer, Submarines : Commander Bauer.
1st Flotilla, *Brunsbüttelkoog* (commanding officer, Pasquay).

2nd	,,	*Wilhelmshaven*	(	,,	,,	von Rosenberg-Gruszczynski).
3rd	,,	*Emden*	(	,,	,,	Gayer).
4th	,,	*Emden*	(	,,	,,	Prause).

THE SUBMARINE AS A MILITARY WEAPON

Ever since his assumption of the chief command, Scheer had insistently pressed for permission to embark upon offensive operations with the Fleet. After the raid on Lowestoft he decided to plan a bombardment of Sunderland. Such a thrust against the British East Coast, he expected, would draw down a part of the Grand Fleet from its northern bases. Across the tracks of the British battle-squadrons, 'nests' of submarines and mine-fields could be prepared in advance. In mid-May the plans were complete. Submarines were to lie off the British coast so as to gain early intelligence of British forces in movement; and during May 16-17 nine enemy submarines were detected, on departure from their ports, by the Admiralty. Since no attack on shipping ensued, suspicions of some intended new move by the enemy were aroused.

Before this, however, and on the 13th, U 74 (E. Weisbach) left to lay a mine-field south-east of the Bass Rock, off the Firth of Forth. Next, on the 17th, U 43, U 44, and U 52 left their base—the first two to lie off Scapa Flow, and the last to make for the Firth of Forth. On the following day, U 24, U 32, U 63, and U 70 also set out, bound for the Forth. On the 20th, U 47 sailed, to scout off Sunderland and locate mine-fields and channels. Thence she proceeded to lie off Kinnaird Head. On the same day U 75 (Beitzen) put to sea to lay mines off the Orkneys. On the 21st the coastal boats UB 21 and UB 22 sailed for the Humber, UB 27 to lie off May Island, and U 72 to lay mines off May Island on the line Stotfield Head-Kinnaird Head. Lastly, U 46 and U 67 were posted off Terschelling, Commander Prause (of the 4th Flotilla) directing operations from the latter boat. During the next eight days these two last-named units encountered British submarines. In the southern North Sea and off the Thames six boats of the Flanders Flotilla took up positions.[1]

These boats met with varying experiences, and on May 23 U 47 (Metzer) reported the swept channels off Sunderland to

---

[1] *Note.*—Admiralty Narrative (Jutland), page 6 (footnote), gives following disposition on May 30 :—

'Thirteen submarines off British coast—

U 43 } off Scapa.
U 44 }

U 47 off Kinnaird Head.   [*contd. next page* be clear. The weather, however, turned out to be too bad for airship scouting. Aerial reconnaissance was considered essential to the operations in view ; and Scheer waited until the 30th for an improvement. By that date the smaller submarines, holding their stations, were nearing the limit of their endurance. Scheer therefore abandoned the Sunderland scheme and decided to proceed on a cruise northwards instead, his purpose being an attack on Scandinavian traffic with the light craft, supported by the battle-squadrons.

Shortly before noon on May 27 the Peterhead trawler *Searanger* espied a sail and smoke to the northward, moving eastward. Investigation revealed U 74 in this strange guise ; she was greeted with a hot fire from the *Searanger* and two other trawlers, *Oku* and *Rodino*, which had now come up. Mistaking these patrols for harmless fishing-craft engaged in their normal pursuits, U 74 was completely deceived, and paid the penalty for her unwariness. Lowering her sail, she replied with her two guns and concentrated her fire on each of the trawlers in turn. Closing in, the three trawlers poured in an accurate fire, knocking out the submarine's after gun [1] and shooting away the periscope. Hit again and again, U 74 lost

U 24
U 32
U 51
U 63 } off Firth of Forth.
U 66
U 70

U 24 *en route* for Tyne.
UB 21
UB 22 } * off Humber.
U 67 south of Dogger Bank.
UB 27* returned with damage on the 29th.
U 46 returned from Terschelling Light, damaged, on May 30.'

It will be noticed that U 24 occurs *twice* in the list.

To the above list, Scheer (*High Sea Fleet*, p. 139) adds U 22, 53, and 46, but gives no positions. U 64 was in the Ems until after the main action.

Gayer (*U.S.N.I. Proceedings*, April 1926, p. 643) omits U 51 and 66.

* A few of the UB and UC boats were attached to the High Sea Fleet flotillas.

[1] The account here given is based on the version of the fight embodied in Mr. Keble Chatterton's *Auxiliary Patrol*. All German plans, descriptions, and photographs of the submarines comprising the U 71-80 class show these boats to be armed with one Q.F. gun (3·4 inch *or* 4·1 inch) and one small machine-gun, both mounted *abaft* the conning-tower.

THE SUBMARINE AS A MILITARY WEAPON 99

interest in the fight and made some effort to retire under the waves to a place remote from the scene of strife. Such a way of escape was evidently denied to her, for she rose well out of the water, listing heavily to port. Two of the trawlers seized this opportunity to attempt to ram the wounded minelayer, but were frustrated by U 74 making for a fourth trawler, *Kimberley*. Passing within eight feet of this vessel, she received three shots in her hull at point-blank range. Sinking stern first, U 74 disappeared for the last time from human ken, leaving quantities of her life-blood, oil-fuel, on the surface as proof of her demise.

Next day U 72 reported that she had been unable to lay her mines owing to a breakdown of her oil-fuel pump. On the night of May 28-29, U 75 laid her twenty-two mines in groups west of the Orkneys; although considerably hampered by fog in fixing her position, she had laid them in the track used by the Grand Fleet auxiliary vessels, one not usually traversed by the warships. On the same day UB 27 returned and reported that on the 24th she had met four armoured cruisers and destroyers off North Carr Light; moreover, she had penetrated the Forth as far as Inchkeith, being caught three times in the nets and having her port propeller fouled. On the 30th, U 46 (Hillebrand, late of U 16) returned from Terschelling with a damaged periscope, having been attacked by gunfire and by submarine; she also notified numerous mines. Her repairs were at once put in hand.

At 7 A.M. on May 31, U 32 (Spiegel) reported from her position, 155 miles east of the Firth of Forth, two battleships, two cruisers, and destroyers on a south-easterly course.[1] At 9 A.M. a report was received from U 66 (Count Bothmer) of eight battleships, light cruisers, and destroyers in a position 60 miles east of Kinnaird Head on a northerly course; she was prevented by the screen from making an attack.

So much for the lack of success against the Grand Fleet leaving its bases. At ten o'clock on the evening of May 31, as a consequence of the above reports, and upon it becoming known that a fleet action had that day been fought, U 67 and

---

[1] This probably was the submarine which attacked the light cruiser *Galatea*.

all available submarines at the Ems were ordered to leave for the north and report next morning at six o'clock. Because she was resting on the bottom off Terschelling, U 67 did not take in the message. However, a quarter of an hour before midnight U 19 and U 64 left the Ems, followed at 6 A.M. by the repaired U 46. These boats were ordered by Scheer to search for the cruiser *Elbing*, which had actually foundered after collision with the battleship *Posen* during the night. Upon the German directional wireless station reporting a damaged British ship on a course W.S.W. about eight miles west of Horns Reef, U 46, then on a favourable course, was ordered to intercept the injured warship. At half-past twelve the quarry was sighted ahead. It was no other than the *Marlborough*, which had been torpedoed during the fleet action, and after the deployment of the Grand Fleet. She was being escorted by the light cruiser *Fearless* from the scene of the recent battle, and, at 12 knots speed, was making for the Tyne. U 46 got away a torpedo at 3000 yards. The retreating battleship at that moment made a turn of about six points, and those on board the damaged ship saw the torpedo race harmlessly away. Eventually the *Marlborough* entered the Humber on the morning of June 2. Her attacker, instead of dogging the injured battleship and calling up the Flanders boats or U 67, then set a course for the Horns Reef area. The U 67 later received intelligence of the damaged *Marlborough*, but it was so belated that her search was fruitless.

In the hope of intercepting the returning Grand Fleet, U 19, U 22, and U 64 were ordered to make for positions off Peterhead and Scapa Flow, but were forced back by bad weather on June 2. By that time they had got to the westward, and were in the same latitude as the British squadrons. U 46 was ordered to make for Flamborough Head; sighting four small cruisers and ten destroyers, she failed to gain an attacking position. Off Blyth, U 51 (Rumpel) adventured against the damaged *Warspite*, but was driven off by the armed yacht *Mingary*. Scheer claims, however, that both UB 21 (Hashagen) and UB 22 (Putzier) hit a destroyer on June 1.

Finally, on June 5, in heavy weather, the armoured cruiser

THE SUBMARINE AS A MILITARY WEAPON

Hampshire (carrying Field-Marshal Earl Kitchener and his staff), bound for Archangel, struck one of the mines laid by U 75 off Marwick Head and the Brough of Birsay, and sank with all but sixteen of her complement. Of the twenty-two mines sown, fifteen were swept up almost immediately afterwards.

The large, concerted attempt to entrap the Grand Fleet as it steamed out to battle had therefore failed, as also had the disjointed attempts to intercept it on its return to its bases. The inability of the mine-laying submarines to fulfil their missions was due partly to mechanical breakdown, and partly to chance detection by a patrol. More significant was the barren result of the boats posted off the East Coast. They had been ordered to take up stations in the form of an arc ; consequently, as they converged on their focal point their radii of visibility overlapped. No submarines were present at the battle, despite the numerous reports to the contrary. It is doubtful whether they would have achieved any great success. Certainly it would have been extremely perilous for the submarines, and almost impossible to distinguish friend from foe in the wreaths of mist and smoke.

On June 5 we find Scheer urging, not that the Fleet should sally forth again to find another such combat, but that the offensive should be pressed forward by the U-boats. Considering the moral effects of the battle would warrant disdain of neutral protests, he urged the renewal of the war against shipping *à l'outrance*. The Chancellor would no more listen to such proposals then, than on previous occasions. Even attacks on armed merchantmen were prohibited on June 20, and in vain did Scheer press for their resumption. Throughout the summer, therefore, the submarines were forced to remain chafing at the leash. In the expectation that British warships would attack, the seaward terminals of the swept channels, passing through the German mine-fields in the Bight of Heligoland, were patrolled (from July 3 to 13, and July 28 to August 4) by two lines of submarines, distributed on wide arcs. Between these periods, on July 14, U 51 (Rumpel) was torpedoed and sunk in the mouth of the Ems by British submarine H 5, a feat much admired by the Germans for its daring. The Admiralty manifested no immediate approval of the exploit, and, in fact, postponed any recognition for the commanding officer of H 5 for a year. He had left his station without authority and on his own initiative. To carry war into the enemy's camp is one thing, but to absent oneself from an important observation post is another.

Because there was no work for the North Sea submarines, the German Admiralty detached four large boats to the Baltic during the summer. Gayer adds that in the quiescence of this land-locked sea they soon lost the technique of cruiser warfare, and were therefore of little use when that form of fighting was reopened in the North Sea on July 5. The chief victims of this mollified campaign were the North Sea fishing-fleets. Off the East Coast no fewer than thirty-six vessels were so exterminated during this month. The attacks seem to have been made by U 46, 49, 52, and 69 ; and, working in combination, they decoyed the three armed trawlers of the famous Peterhead patrol, *Era*, *Onward*, and *Nellie Nutten*, into a trap and destroyed them. Late in the afternoon of July 11 the *Onward* signalled that a submarine was in sight, 120 miles E.S.E. of Girdle Ness. Both she and *Nellie Nutten* bore down on the U-boat, opening fire but finding themselves absolutely outranged. From the north-east there next appeared a second submarine, and the surprise was completed by the sight of yet a third under-water foe coming out of the south-east. Driven forward between the U-boats and under a long-range cross fire, the three trawlers succumbed to the vastly superior force. The crews of the *Era* and *Onward* were captured, but a Dutch lugger brought into Aberdeen most of *Nellie Nutten's* crew. As a result of this reverse, the East Coast trawlers were supplied with 12-pounder guns in place of the inadequate 3-pounder weapons previously supplied.

On this same day, July 11, a submarine dropped thirty shells into Seaham harbour, but succeeded only in killing one woman. On the previous day the Wilson steamer *Calypso* (2876 tons), which had served earlier in the war as the armed merchant cruiser *Calyx*, fell foul of one of these raiders, and was destroyed with her master and crew of 29. The attacks on the fishing-fleets continued until the 14th, and were re-

THE SUBMARINE AS A MILITARY WEAPON 103

peated during the last days of July. So serious was the view taken of the depredations, that a leader and six destroyers were detached from the 4th Flotilla to patrol the Tyne area. Early in August, twelve destroyers and twenty-four drifters with mine-nets arrived ; and these latter vessels were sent to sea to simulate a fishing-fleet. These measures appear to have discouraged the U-boats from a continuance of their drive against fishing craft, and not until late September did they again put the gleaners of the sea to the sword.

On the other side of the balance was the disappearance of the mine-laying U 77 (E. Günzel) on the 5th.[1] German authorities surmise that she was sunk by a trawler off the East Coast, but no evidence has been adduced by the Admiralty to warrant any such conclusion. One consequence of these attacks on the fishing-fleets was the reintroduction of armed smacks in company with the fishing craft. The combination of a decoy trawler with a submarine in company was resumed, but it met with no success.

A new development now exemplified the increasing power and endurance of under-water craft. On June 23 the mercantile submarine *Deutschland* left Kiel, under the command of Captain König, with a cargo of dyes, mail, and precious stones, bound for America. She arrived at Baltimore on July 9, remained at that port until August 2, and arrived back at Bremen on the 24th with a cargo of zinc, silver, copper, and nickel. A sister boat, *Bremen* (Captain Schwartzkopf), left for Norfolk, Virginia, but she never reached her destination. Speculation still surrounds her fate. A submarine, believed to have been the *Bremen*, was seen 300 miles south of Iceland, holding a course that would bring her to Baltimore. The big armed merchant cruisers of the 10th Cruiser Squadron were spread to intercept the blockade-runner ; and of these, both the *Alsatian* (flagship) and the *Mantua* rammed some heavy, submerged object. The *Deutschland* was unarmed ; and, after inspection, she was recognized as a merchant-vessel by the United States Government. As a reminder that the submarine arm could reach far, the sensational appearance of this novel trader in American

[1] Michelsen gives date as 7th.

waters was effective. Her claim to having set up a record for independent long-distance cruising can be challenged, however. The Canadian-built British submarines of the H class had previously crossed the Atlantic to Gibraltar, in the summer of 1915, unescorted and under their own power, some arriving at British bases, and others joining the Allied naval forces in the Aegean and Adriatic Seas.

Only three British steamers succumbed to submarines in the North Sea during July, whilst mines destroyed five others off the East Anglian coast. In August, again, only three steamers (*Aaro*, 2603 tons; *San Bernardo*, 3803 tons; *Stamfordham*, 921 tons) were torpedoed. A mine accounted for the small steamer *F. Stobart*, off Aldborough Napes Buoy. The North Sea 'Tauchboote' had become strangely quiet, confining their attentions to fishing-vessels. The mining work of the Flanders boats continued unceasingly. Operations by the improved type of UC mine-layer were responsible for the loss of some 70,000 tons of shipping destroyed during the summer of 1916. To one of the early craft—UC 7 (Haag)—fell the unsought distinction of being the first U-boat to perish by depth-charge. Just before midnight on July 6 the motor-boat *Salmon* heard a buzzing sound on her hydrophones. For nearly two hours, at intervals, the noise continued. At last, from the increasing volume of sound, the *Salmon* surmised that the enemy was rapidly approaching. With nice judgment, a depth-charge was dropped overboard at the moment when UC 7 passed beneath. A violent explosion quickly followed. The water was thrown fifty feet high into the air; wreckage of white painted wood, including a grating, bestrewed the surface of the water. There was no doubt that the depth-charge had detonated the mines in UC 7's laying chutes. This incident possesses particular interest, being the first recorded success of the hydrophone and depth-charge combination—a method of counter-attack particularly disliked by the under-water enemy later in the war.

As for the UB boats, they destroyed buoys and navigational aids, which had to be replaced. In the Channel intensive mining warfare was directed against troop traffic. Bartenbach (captain of the Flanders Submarine Flotilla) on August 7 urged the removal of all restrictions upon operations in this area. He cited a test cruise of UB 18 (Steinbrinck), off the Seine, during the first week of August. The boat referred to had made forty-one daylight approaches to determine the character of shipping, either by markings or by the presence of troops on deck. Against these vessels she had been prevented by standing orders from firing a single torpedo. By means of bombs and gunfire she had sunk only seven small steamers and ten sail. In the face of the evidence thus collected, the German Admiralty maintained, none the less, that the situation was not critical enough to warrant a break with Washington ; furthermore, it directed that even transports should be spared.

After the Jutland Battle the Naval Staff again invited Scheer to give his opinion on the conduct of submarine warfare. He replied in no uncertain terms, declaring that, in his view, the submarines should be employed in unrestricted warfare against commerce, or else on purely military operations. At this juncture, June 23, the Chief of the Kaiser's Naval Cabinet, von Müller, tried to play the part of Halifax the 'Trimmer.' Admitting to Scheer that the German Government had been forced 'with rage in our hearts' to make concessions to America, he pointed out that the German submarines could not wholly renounce a limited measure of success such as was obtained by waging a restricted war in the Mediterranean. In his opinion the Commander-in-Chief should endeavour to reconcile the uncompromising attitude of the 'unrestricted war' advocates with the general, political, and military demands. He urged Scheer to try to arrive at some understanding with the Chief of the Naval Staff, von Holtzendorff, lest more U-boats be detached from the North Sea to the Mediterranean. He concluded by expressing his own acceptance of a successful submarine war to the knife.

A week later Scheer received a visit from the Chancellor, who flatly stated that he had no intention of giving his support or assent to the unrestricted campaign, 'which would place the fate of the German Empire in the hands of a U-boat commander.' Holtzendorff, however, had another card to play. He suggested a scheme whereby a submarine could approach her target in a submerged condition to examine the vessel for signs of a gun. If the victim so surveyed proved to be unarmed, the next step was to break surface, secure the papers, and, after the crew had left, sink the prize.

Scheer, however, had other ends in view for the use of his submarines, since he had not abandoned his intention of bombarding Sunderland and entrapping the Grand Fleet. During the night of August 18-19, five boats, U 44, 67, 65, 52, and 53, occupied a line to the north-east of Blyth; and another five, U 63, 49, 45, 66, 64, took up a position off Flamborough Head. Off the Swarte Bank were posted UB 39, 23, 18, and 29; off Terschelling, UB 37, 19, 16, 6, and 12; and off Heligoland, U 48, 69, UB 35, U 55 and 56. Instead of arcs, the submarines formed straight lines this time. In addition, eight Zeppelins acted as fleet scouts over the North Sea. During the evening of the 18th the High Sea Fleet emerged. The Grand Fleet, warned by the Admiralty that at least six enemy submarines had been detected in the North Sea, and that others were probably out, quitted its bases at Scapa Flow, Cromarty, and the Firth of Forth. Early next morning the British submarine E 23 sighted the enemy; by a torpedo she succeeded in crippling the German battleship *Westfalen*, and later reported that hostile forces were out.

Next morning, August 19, at 7 A.M., the light-cruiser screen of the Battle Cruiser Force passed over the Blyth line of submarines. Three torpedoes from U 52 (Hans) hit the *Nottingham* a mortal blow, and the valuable cruiser sank three hours later. Soon after this attack, U 53 (Rose) reported three British battleships and four light cruisers, and thereafter made continuous reports to Scheer. The German Commander-in-Chief, however, was badly misled by the Zeppelin L 13 mistaking the Harwich force for a 'large force of battleships, cruisers, light cruisers, and sixteen destroyers' coming up from the south. When Scheer received this report, he turned to cut them off; thereby he was saved from meeting the Grand Fleet, then but thirty miles distant. In the British squadrons the anxious minutes lengthened to hours; the hopes of a fleet action receded, and disappointment took the place of expectancy. When it was realized that all hope of encountering the High Sea Fleet had vanished, the Grand Fleet turned northwards. At 4.45 p.m. the 3rd Light Cruiser Squadron ran into the Flamborough Head submarine trap, in lat. 54° 27′ N., long. 1° 15′ E. Torpedoes from U 66 (von Bothmer) struck the *Falmouth* at bow and stern, but by the use of depth-charges the screen prevented U 49 (Hartmann) and U 66 from finishing her off. The German boats, after two hours, were forced to abandon their attempts to complete the work. The *Falmouth*, whose engine-rooms were intact, made six knots under her own power; but next day her fate was sealed. In spite of a screen of eight destroyers, U 63 (Otto Schulze) got in two torpedoes, and the luckless cruiser sank eight hours later. Besides these two successes, U 65 claimed she had badly damaged the battle-cruiser *Inflexible* when the Grand Fleet passed through the Blyth line at 8 p.m.

The events of August 18-19 were reviewed by the Naval Staffs and Fleet Commands on both sides of the North Sea. The Germans seem to have been so satisfied with the results obtained that they proposed to carry out again the same general scheme of combined operations by fleet and submarine during the month of October. But when that month arrived, every available submarine was absorbed in the trade war, and the contemplated operations had to be abandoned. On the British side, there was a re-examination of the whole strategical situation in the North Sea, and of our naval policy in relation thereto. Enemy attacks along the English East Coast was one of the subjects then discussed, and with that problem there also went the concomitant question, as to how far it was possible to arrange methods of counteraction, active and passive, against such raids. The difficulty of preventing attacks on the East Coast with the Fleet based at Scapa Flow had, of course, long been recognized; the real deterrent to such attacks lay in the possibility of the High Sea Fleet being brought to action *after the attack*. The problem on the British side was to catch the High Sea Fleet on its return journey, during daylight hours—by no means an easy problem to solve. Interesting as these subjects of national defence are, they lie without the scope of this narrative. One question, and one alone, can be admitted for discussion here : it is the degree to which British naval movements in the North Sea were affected by Scheer's second sortie during 1916.

There could be no doubt whatever that, as anticipated by Sir John Jellicoe, on and before August 19, 1916, the enemy had deliberately set submarine ' barrages ' or ' nests ' with a view to entrapping the Grand Fleet. Moreover, Scheer had, on the whole, succeeded fairly well, both in anticipating British Fleet movements in the south-western part of the North Sea, and in stationing his submarines in that area for the purpose of interception. The problem of divining the possible movements of the British main Fleet was, relatively speaking, a simple one for the German Commander-in-Chief. In the approaches to Sunderland the operational ground for fleets had been cut down to a very restricted area by the large mine-fields laid by the Germans off the Tyne and the Humber and near the Dogger Bank. It was therefore easy to foresee where the British Fleet would go and to station the U-boats accordingly.

In all probability the enemy would again attempt the very same scheme of operations, in which the first part consisted of the deposit of mine-fields and the stationing of submarine-traps. Then, having arranged his sub-surface snares, the enemy would hurry his heavy squadrons across the North Sea for an attack on shipping or patrols along the East Coast ; or for bombardments of seaports and undefended towns ; or even for the landing of troops. If the Grand and Battle Cruiser Fleets were ordered to leave their northern bases, to concentrate and to move southwards against the enemy, under what conditions were they to act ? Was contact with the enemy to be obtained at all costs, regardless of any risks from minefield- and submarine-traps ? Or should the British battle and battle-cruiser squadrons be kept away from those waters wherein the enemy could, with swiftness and all secrecy, forelay his ambushes beneath the surface ? Here was a fundamental point in British naval policy, and in the autumn of 1916 it had to be raised, fully discussed, and settled.

If the more prudent policy was to be followed of avoiding

THE SUBMARINE AS A MILITARY WEAPON 109

endangered waters, then the sea movements of the Grand and Battle Cruiser Fleets would have, perforce, to be confined to the more northern part of the North Sea. But between which points in the North Sea exactly was the dividing line between danger and safety to be drawn—that is, between those waters in which the enemy could prepare traps, anticipatory to his fleet operations, and those in which he had a lesser or no opportunity whatsoever of so preparing his surprises ?

When expressing his views upon the situation, Sir John Jellicoe had therefore to indicate some boundary line across the North Sea, to the southward of which (in his opinion) danger from submarine- and minefield-traps must be expected. The line he marked out was latitude 55° 30′ N. Thus we get the North Sea, as it were, partitioned into two parts, northern and southern. In the northern part, above latitude 55° 30′ N., Sir John Jellicoe felt that he could handle his squadrons with freedom, and with a reasonable degree of safety from pitfalls of the enemy's devising. It was the southern part, lying below lat. 55° 30′ N., which he regarded with distrust, as being likely to contain the sub-surface stratagems concocted by Scheer.

Moreover, Sir John Jellicoe subdivided the southern (and more dangerous) part of the North Sea into halves, eastern and western, along the fourth meridian east of Greenwich. Into the south-eastern part of the North Sea—that is, into the waters lying to the southward of lat. 55° 30′ N. and to the eastward of long. 4° E.—the Commander-in-Chief considered that the Grand Fleet should only go under exceptional circumstances. The reason for his opinion can easily be understood. The area here defined contained the German Bight and the approaches thereto from the westward. It was a region over which the British surface and submarine patrols could not, for one reason and another, keep a close and continuous watch. This, accordingly, was a locality in which the enemy could lay, quickly and privily, submarine- and mine-traps on a large scale.

In the above proposals there was but very slight alteration to the existing understanding, which was that the Fleet should not go to waters south of the Horn Reef (lat. 55° 30′ N.) and east of long. 5° E. unless under exceptional circumstances.

The Commander-in-Chief's view was that, in the western part of the southern North Sea, our patrols could be relied upon to give information as to probable mine-fields, and that the risk of taking the Grand Fleet there could be accepted, *provided that a good opportunity offered of bringing the High Sea Fleet to action in daylight*, but that under such circumstances it was essential that an adequate destroyer screen should be provided for cruisers as well as battleships. The general views of the Commander-in-Chief on this subject were concurred in by the flag officers of the Battle Fleet and Sir David Beatty. Brief and inadequate as this summary may be, it does, in the main, correctly represent the extent to which British naval movements were, after August 19, 1916, influenced by the danger of mine- and submarine-traps.

In August, Schwieger (U 20) left for the Bay of Biscay. He does not appear to have done much damage except to attack the Portuguese gunboat *Ibo* off the Tagus on the 29th, without result. Bartenbach, on September 1, sent UB 18, 23, 29, and 39 to the Western Channel, where, under prize rules, they sank a dozen ships of 70,000 tons. They reported that they were much troubled by 'convoy patrols' and defensively-armed merchantmen. These boats suffered from their low surface speed. Nine knots was the nominal maximum, and the cruising speed only five to six. It was also found necessary to replace the 4-pounder gun, originally mounted, by a 22-pounder piece. In the Pentland Firth, on August 25, the armed boarding-steamer *Duke of Albany* was torpedoed and sunk by UB 27.

September 17 saw U 53 (Rose) westward-bound on a trans-Atlantic trip ; her ostensible mission was to attack British warships, supposed to be lying in wait off Long Island Sound for the mercantile submarine *Bremen*. In reality, her excursion was designed to give America a proof that a combatant submarine could range as far as a mercantile boat like the *Deutschland*—but with a cargo and purpose of a far less pacific nature.[1] Carrying an abnormal quantity of fuel, victuals,

[1] An interesting account of this trip is given in Scheer's *High Sea Fleet*.

THE SUBMARINE AS A MILITARY WEAPON 111

fresh water, etc., for the double voyage, U 53 arrived at Newport on October 7, and immediately left again. Off Nantucket she sank five steamers (three British, one Norwegian, and one Dutch), United States destroyers standing by to rescue the crews. The British naval forces off the New England coast had been informed that President Wilson would take it as an unfriendly act were they to attack the submarine in these waters. Rose was therefore left unmolested, and returned safely to Heligoland on the 28th. The President told Count Bernstorff that such an attack must not be repeated. The appearance of U 53 off America's Atlantic littoral was a shadow cast before and across her threshold : a warning of events to come when she herself was a belligerent. Here was evidence that the zone of danger would progressively expand, and vital focal points for shipping, such as Dakar and Sierra Leone, at some date in the immediate future no longer be safe. Simultaneously, as Rose was recrossing the Atlantic, the *Deutschland* made her second outward trip, appearing at New London on October 31, after a passage of twenty days. She sailed again on November 17 for Bremen, where she arrived on December 10.

Elsewhere, even as far as the Arctic Ocean, the submarines spread their trail of destruction. For two years, from America, England, and elsewhere, an unceasing flow of munition-laden transports had been passing to Archangel, supplying Russia with all those essentials she lacked, and so urgently needed, for the maintenance of her war fronts. Attempts had been made previously to interfere with the traffic. In June 1915, the mine-layer *Meteor* had deposited her field in the entrance to the White Sea ; and during the summer of 1916, submarine mine-layers had laid seventy-two of their ' eggs ' in these northern waters. Of these, thirty were swept up before the ice set in. Towards the end of September, U 43 (Jürst), U 46 (Hillebrand), and U 48 (Buch) were sent to impede the traffic more actively. Though they claimed to have destroyed 50,000 tons of shipping [1] during their operations off the North Cape and along the Murman coast, such an aggregate is an exaggeration. The raid lasted

[1] *U.S.N.I. Proceedings*, April 1926, p. 651 (Gayer).

from October 2 until the 11th ; and the submarines at work sank 6 British ships (totalling 19,229 tons), 1 Russian, and 7 Norwegian vessels. U 46 brought into Wilhelmshaven one valuable prize, freighted with munitions and automobiles. Amongst the British victims were the *Brantingham* (2617 tons), sunk with 24 lives, and the *Astoria* (4262 tons), with 17 of her crew. Other submarines relieved these three raiders. Russian patrols destroyed U 56 (Lorenz) off Lapland on November 2 ; and a second submarine, the mine-laying U 76 (Bender), was damaged by Russian trawlers on January 26, 1917. This latter boat made for Hammerfest (Norway) in a foundering condition ; and, in response to signals of distress, a Norwegian motor-boat went out and rescued all except one of the crew.[1] During the October raid, narrated above, the light cruiser *Fearless* escorted three British submarines to Archangel to counter this fresh extension of the menace. From the 'white man's grave' on the tropical coast of West Africa to the icy desolation of Lapland, and from the shores of New England, past the Pillars of Hercules and the ruins of Troy, even to the farther shore of the Euxine, the steel sharks now ranged. In ocean, sea, and strait, men saw with horror their coming doom in the dorsal fin of the periscope.

[1] Michelsen says, 'Rammed by British steamer and sunk by crew, 27.1.17.'

CHAPTER VI

CRUISER WAR RESUMED

(OCTOBER 1916–FEBRUARY 1917)

ON August 27, Rumania declared war on Austria-Hungary, with the object of establishing 'a Rumanian union on both slopes of the Carpathians.' The German reply to this new accession to the enemy's ranks was quick and decisive. Marshals Hindenburg and Ludendorff were appointed to the supreme command ; and the German populace, believing that the victor of the Mazurian Lakes was a new Bismarck, paired with a new von Moltke, became reassured. At Pless on August 30 a very important conference was held between these military leaders, the chiefs of the Naval Staff and the Marine Office, and the principal Governmental authorities. The inevitable proposal to embark on an unrestricted submarine campaign was brought forward by the Chief of the Naval Staff, Admiral von Holtzendorff. The Foreign Minister, von Jagow, emphasized the danger of arousing the anger of neutrals, and pointed out to his hearers the fundamental difference in German and Allied treatment of neutral trade. Whereas in the former case innocent lives were sacrificed, the Allies' blockade merely diverted the flow of trade from German ports into their own harbours, causing no loss to non-belligerent traders. Helfferich, the Secretary of State, maintained that any statistics forecasting success from unrestricted war were fallacious ; and he plainly declared that the U-boat weapon promised to precipitate a catastrophe. The Chancellor himself expressed doubts concerning the attitude of Denmark and Holland, stating that the entry of Rumania into the conflict prevented the massing of troops to secure the German frontiers.

The proposal was again rejected. None the less, it was

evidently gaining in favour, the Chancellor no longer being the obdurate opponent he once was. The final decision, for or against, was left to the Chief of the General Staff, von Hindenburg. The renewal of unrestricted warfare was therefore postponed until the Rumanian situation cleared up. When the new campaign in the Carpathians had been successfully developed, echelons of defence corps could be assembled near the Dutch and Danish frontiers.

Gayer is emphatic that a great mistake, made at this Pless conference, lay in the failure to sanction any adequate programme, preparatory to the approaching offensive at sea. Only two 800-ton boats (U 115, 116), sixteen of the UB III type (UB 72-87), and nine 'submarine cruisers' (U 142-150) were authorized; and of these, only the UB-boats ever came into service. The same authority says that up to this time no large orders for new submarines had been allocated to the shipyards. Such dilatoriness he attributes to two causes: firstly, to constant changes in the methods of employing submarines; and secondly, to reluctance in embarking on any large-scale building programme before boats of new types had proved their mettle under active-service conditions. Gayer is of the opinion that such indecision as to types and spheres of service should no longer have existed, and that the conference should have approved a large programme. Moreover, the yards which usually built merchant-ships ought to have been turned over to submarine construction earlier than was the case. Spindler, the Director of Submarine Construction at the German Navy Office, encountered much opposition before he could place orders for new boats. Admiral von Capelle, Secretary of State for the Navy, was averse to embarking upon an ambitious programme, considering that a surplus of submarines would be decidedly disadvantageous for the administration and further expansion of the navy as a world-power after the war![1]

Cruiser warfare, in accordance with prize rules, was resumed on October 6. Prior to this, U 57 (von Georg) and U 49 (Hartmann) on their own initiative had left to attack shipping in the North Sea: the former sank a steamer off Flamborough

[1] *U.S.N.I. Proceedings*, April 1926 (Gayer), p. 650.

Head, together with 21 fishing-craft; and the latter sank 3 sail and sent a prize into Emden—a disastrous raid for the Allies, its cost being estimated at £100,000. The new orders brought about an immediate rise in the shipping casualties, and from 131,000 tons the monthly average of sinkings rose to 276,000 tons. The anti-submarine measures were becoming patently inadequate to hold their own against the growing danger; and when the British losses in October were found to have almost doubled the September toll of 84,600 tons, the severity of the menace could not be minimized. Losses were taking place in the Atlantic, in the Arctic, and in the Mediterranean. In the Gulf of Gascony and off Ferrol, U 49 (Hartmann) and U 50 (Berger) destroyed about 40,000 tons of shipping. To accommodate the crews of sunken vessels, a steamer was captured and sent into port when filled with seamen; and this was proof that, under certain conditions, submarine warfare on commerce can be waged humanely.

Mines now began to be found in waters hitherto free. On September 2 the steamer *Kelvinia* (5039 tons) struck one such agent of destruction in the Bristol Channel and sank.[1] Twelve days later the Harrison liner *Counsellor* (4958 tons) foundered on another off Galley Head; and on October 3 a mine-field was laid off the Clyde. The Flanders mine-laying submarines' zone now extended from Flamborough Head as far west as Waterford in the south of Ireland. Off Falmouth, Dartmouth, Portland, and Portsmouth they dumped their deadly freights. These UC boats during 1916 laid 212 mines off Dover, 100 off Dunkirk, 100 off Calais, and 60 off Boulogne. Amongst the losses they caused, mention can only be made here of the steamer *Eretria* (3464 tons), sunk off the Loire on May 13; the Cunard liner *Alaunia* (13,405 tons), two miles south of the Royal Sovereign L.V. on October 19; and the hospital-ship *Galeka*, five miles north-west of Cape La Hague on October 28. Mines had also sunk the destroyer *Lassoo* in the North Sea on August 13, together with five trawlers and about a score of ships, and had damaged the destroyer *Zulu*

---

[1] At the time it was supposed that she fell a victim to torpedo attack, and the incident brought forth a protest from the U.S. Government.

in October. Off Anglesea, on November 4, the steamer *Skerries* (4278 tons) sank ; and two others, *Opal* (599 tons) and *Liverpool* (686 tons), were destroyed in a field laid off the Isle of Man in December. It was therefore evident that the Flanders boats were working farther afield. In fact, the first group of the UC II type (UC 16-33) had come into service during the late summer of 1916.

In western waters during October many large ships perished, notably the Anchor liner *Cabotia* (4309 tons), 120 miles W.N.W. of Tory Island, on the 20th, with her master and 31 of the crew ; the Johnston liner *Rowanmore* (10,320 tons), 128 miles W.N.W. from Fastnet, on the 26th, whose master was captured ; the *Rappahannock* (3871 tons), sent to the bottom 70 miles from the Scilly Isles, with her entire crew of 37, on October 26. The Donaldson liner *Marina* (5204 tons) met her end two days later 30 miles W. of Fastnet, whilst outward bound for America ; and of her crew of 51, 18 were lost, including 6 Americans. On the same day the American steamer *Lanao* (962 tons) was sunk off St. Vincent. On the 23rd the sloop *Genista* sent out a wireless message that she was engaged in a fight with a submarine ; thereafter there was silence : U 59 had won the duel, and another vessel with her entire crew had disappeared. To show the extent of neutral shipping losses, up to October Norway alone had lost 163 steamers (97 sunk without warning, 45 mined, and 21 lost either by mine or torpedo) ; in addition, 58 sail had been destroyed.

So serious was the situation that Admiral Sir John Jellicoe was asked in November to relinquish his command of the Grand Fleet and accept the position of First Sea Lord. Apparently everything had been done that could be done. The Dover Straits defile was an ever-present source of worry, and great were the difficulties there to be surmounted. In the winter of 1914-15, attempts to construct a boom (consisting of huge wooden baulks, each weighing four tons, strung between buoys), extending from Folkestone to Grisnez, had proved a failure. The combination of moored mine-nets and deep mines, as used in the Belgian coast barrage of 1916, served as the pattern for another barrier ranging from the South Goodwin Sands to the Outer Ruytingen,

CRUISER WAR RESUMED

watched by patrols day and night. This obstacle failed to stop the passage of the sub-surface raiders, which would dive below the curtain by day or pass over it by night. The mines dragged at their moorings and fouled the nets, so that by the spring of 1917 the barrage became a menace to the patrols. One submarine only was destroyed, but she was not a victim of any barrier-system, old or new. On August 21, UC 10 (Albrecht) was caught by the British E 54 off the Schouwen L.V., a favourite resting-place for the German boats.[1]

Ineffective as the barrage may have been, as a supposedly impassable obstacle placed athwart the tracks of the submarines, its presence, none the less, irked the enemy. A raid by destroyers, under Commodore Michelsen, therefore took place on the night of October 26, when the destroyer *Flirt* was sunk and the *Nubian* disabled. To the nocturnal foray the British reply was to carry an extension of the nets to the Snou Bank during December.

Barrages were laid not only by the Dover Patrol but by their opponents in Flanders. The UC-boats built up a reef of high-explosives off the Dutch coast from the Maas L.V. to Ymuiden, consisting of 400 mines. Five British destroyers were lost on this obstruction; and the mine-sweepers' task was rendered doubly difficult owing to the liability of a lightning attack from the Flanders torpedo-boats. Off the Forth another barrage was laid to damage the Scandinavian trade; albeit only one steamer succumbed to the 90 mines planted. Off Harwich, 213 of the 265 mines laid were swept up, with the loss of four sweepers and five steamers. Amongst such victims were the sweepers *Ludlow* and *Totnes*, which both struck mines off the Shipwash on December 29. The former vessel sank at anchor, after her stern had been blown off, and was entirely lost; but her sister, brought into Harwich without bows, was repaired, and survived until the Armistice.

Yet another German submarine was expunged, this time no other than the U 20 of infamous memory—the boat

---

[1] British Records (1919) showed the boat sunk on this date, and under the circumstances narrated above, as the UC 7. It has been subsequently ascertained that she was the UC 10.

which, under Schwieger's command, had sunk the *Lusitania*, *Hesperian*, and *Cymric*. She left port on October 13 for the cruise that ended her career. Homeward bound, she picked up a consort off the Norwegian coast, the notoriously unlucky U 30, whose Diesel engines were *en panne*. These boats proceeded in company, and on the next day (November 4) they both went hard aground in a dense fog off Harböere, on the Danish coast. By discharging thirty tons, U 30 managed to refloat two hours later; her companion, however, remained fast. Messages for help were sent out by wireless. In response, a German force, covered by four battleships, the battle-cruiser *Moltke*, and a half-flotilla of destroyers, was sent to rescue the U-boats. The U 20 had to be abandoned. Her bows were blown up, her crew transferred, and the whole squadron started homewards. Suddenly, torpedoes struck both the battleships *Grosser Kürfurst* and *Kronprinz* amidships, inflicting serious damage. The British submarine J 1 had discovered the German force and had evaded the strong screen protecting the more powerful enemy ships. Once again, however, the minute internal subdivision and the efficient precautions for maintaining stability prevented either of the German battleships from sinking, and they regained port. As a consequence, Scheer received a rebuke from the Kaiser for imperilling valuable units of the battle-squadrons. The Commander-in-Chief advanced the plea that the High Sea Fleet must afford every possible support to the active submarines; and from this time forward he put first and foremost the submarine campaign and the destroyer raids on the Dover Straits Patrol.

In western waters the campaign continued, and the Flanders boats began to visit those areas hitherto only frequented by the larger submarines after passing round the north of Scotland. On December 6 the first casualty to these Flanders boats in the south-western approaches occurred, UB 29 (Platsch), the boat which had attacked the *Sussex*, being blown up by explosive sweeps of the destroyer *Ariel*, about twelve miles south-west of Bishop's Rock L.H. Other boats were active, notably U 66. Another, U 57, met the *Deutschland* on her return from American waters and escorted her home. Amongst the vessels destroyed was the *North Wales* (4072 tons), whose wreckage, driven ashore on the Cornish coast, constituted the only evidence of her fate. During the last weeks of 1916, four submarines, believed to be U 32, 52, 64, and 65, were detached to the Mediterranean to augment the Adriatic flotilla.

The Flemish flotilla was now to suffer three further casualties. On November 22, UB 19 (Noodt) left Zeebrugge for the Western Channel, and eight days later fell in with the Q-boat *Penshurst*, twenty-five miles south of Portland Bill. In the fight which ensued the submarine was exterminated. On December 4 the mine-laying UC 19 (Nitzsche) was destroyed with depth-charges by the destroyer *Llewellyn* in the Straits of Dover. Finally, on January 14, 1917, UB 37 (Günther) also fell a victim to the decoy *Penshurst* in the Channel.

Here it is necessary to retrace our steps a little. On September 10, Captain von Bülow was sent by von Holtzendorff to visit Ludendorff at General Headquarters. At the end of the discussion Ludendorff expressed himself in favour of an unrestricted submarine campaign when the military situation cleared. The Chancellor thereupon presented to the Kaiser a memorandum requesting that choice be made between the weapons of diplomacy and the U-boats. At the same time Bernstorff was told to reopen the subject of submarine warfare conduct with President Wilson, with a view to negotiating some arrangement. The instructions came too late, as the President had already determined to postpone any decision until after the Presidential election on November 7. Scheer, on his part, unceasingly urged upon Ludendorff the desirability of inaugurating without further delay a war without restraint, pointing out the peril of half-measures. On November 22 he saw both Hindenburg and Ludendorff, and found both to be in agreement with him. In December the Allies rejected Germany's peace proposals—proposals deliberately framed to be impossible of acceptance, so that Germany could follow the Pilatian precedent of publicly washing her hands and proclaiming her innocence, before she pronounced doom to shipping. On December 22 it was decided to begin the long-delayed warfare ' without limitations ' on mercantile vessels of all nationalities found in the enormously extended war zone. Bethmann-Hollweg, the Chancellor, was beaten at last in his long struggle against the dominant military and naval chiefs.

By ruthless means it was confidently expected to break England's resistance by the autumn of 1917. The German argument ran thus :—England, whose merchant tonnage at this time amounted to 20 million tons gross, was the mainstay of the war-distressed Allies. It was estimated that 3·6 million tons were requisitioned for military purposes ; half a million employed on coast traffic ; about 1 million under repair ; about 2 millions required for the Allied needs,[1] leaving about 8 millions for England's own supplies. The computation of traffic to England during 1916 was put at only $6\frac{3}{4}$ million tons, but to this total was added 3 million tons of neutral shipping and 900,000 tons of ' non-English ' shipping, a total of $10\frac{3}{4}$ million tons. With a bad Argentine harvest and the Canadian wheat-supply ending in February, grain would have to be brought from Australia and India, the longer voyages absorbing $\frac{3}{4}$-million tons. Thus it was expected that, if 600,000 tons a month were destroyed,[2] and about 1,200,000 tons of neutral shipping scared off through terrorism, peace would be obtained in five months. At the end of this period shipping to and from England would have been reduced by 39 per cent., and this loss would be final and beyond replacement. Bread would have to be rationed ; the supply of Danish and Dutch fats would be seriously diminished. Furthermore, the cutting off of the supply of Scandinavian pit-props would mean less coal ; consequently a shortage of munitions would ensue, and this could not be made good from other neutral sources.[3]

[1] The imminent collapse of Russia was not taken into account, for Ludendorff has stated that 'no intelligence came through to us which revealed any striking indications of the disintegration of the Russian Army.'

[2] In April 1917 actually 849,000 tons were destroyed.

[3] As to the origin of 'unrestricted warfare': At the end of 1915 the German Navy Office produced a memorandum advocating an unlimited campaign. To convince the Kaiser, the Imperial Chancellor, and the Foreign Office, statistics were given relating to British food supplies, prices, marine insurance, freights, etc. The memorandum also stated that the condition of the German food supplies warranted the use of extreme measures to

CRUISER WAR RESUMED

War upon sea-borne commerce, under the impediment of accepted prize war rules, yielded a return each month of only 80,000 tons destroyed of the shipping trading with England. 'Restricted' warfare gave results of 350,000 tons. Both systems involved the loss of operating submarines from armed merchantmen. Above all, there was no sign of weakening morale in the resistance of the Allied ranks.

It was emphasized that a declaration of unrestricted warfare coincident with actual commencement would produce a 'holy terror.' As for American intervention, it would result in the seizure of German tonnage lying in the United States ports, but preparations had been made for acts of irreparable *sabotage*, so that such vessels would be useless. Moreover, it was not expected that troops could be brought over from the States in any numbers; and, with England starved out of the war, America must soon give in. Peace, therefore, ought to be secured before the new harvest became available. To this, the only alternative was exhaustion all round.[1]

All the resources of inducement, argument, and even of aggression, were employed to cram the plan through. Not one word of objection or criticism was tolerated. So great a shipping magnate as the late Herr Ballin was not allowed to voice his dissent. The scheme entailed the working of the submarines at the highest pressure, so that the promised results should be attained, month by month. No sooner were the submarines with their tired crews back in port than they were to be turned round and sent to sea again, after scamped overhauls, or no repairs at all. The Germans themselves admit now that the definite promise to achieve a decision in five months' time was a colossal blunder. Thus, a positive promise was made to the German people, and when the people found that pledge was not being fulfilled, and never could be kept,

---

force an early peace. The Chancellor and Foreign Office were averse, mistrusted the figures, and feared an adverse effect on neutrals; whereupon the Navy Office secured the opinions of nine prominent business men, of whom eight predicted success in six months from the date of beginning, and the ninth believed that three months were ample. This referendum doubtless played a considerable part in the decision arrived at in December 1916, as it was regarded as an independent and unbiassed opinion.

[1] *High Sea Fleet* (Scheer), p. 248 *et seq.*

their war-weary hearts were sickened with hope deferred. That the Allies would rise and meet the menace of a merciless, wanton, and wholesale murder of mercantile shipping and crews ; that the Allies would take heroic measures of rationing and ship-replacement ; that the Allies would intensify their war upon the submarines, were all contingencies that entered little or not at all into the German conspectus of future events. Every point in Germany's favour was underscored ; every point against her was minimized, discounted, or scoffed at.

A large-scale building programme was held up by Admiral von Capelle, who was averse to the construction of any boats which could not be completed within a year.[1] In a word, the submarines at hand and in immediate prospect would have to carry out the great ' drive ' against sea-borne commerce. Should any delays arise in the great bid for victory, the gamble was doomed to failure : cohorts of U-boats lying unfinished in the shipyards could not retrieve the situation. It was no use ordering new submarines if their deliveries were to be an affair of the remote future. Put into a nutshell, the whole effort was to be a gigantic ' smash and grab ' raid : the brittle glass of the world's shipping was to be shattered, so that the U-boats could grab the gems of victory and decamp before Policeman America could lay a hand upon them. If the bandits succeeded in getting clear away, and delivered the spoils to their employer, all well and good ! The car they already owned would suffice for all practical purposes. But if they were captured, placing an order for a new car, which could only be delivered months after the raid was over, would be sheer waste of money. Hence von Capelle's reluctance to embark on big programmes based on mass-production methods.

On January 4 there were fresh signs of vacillation ; but on the 9th the Kaiser, against the advice of the Chancellor, gave his assent to the sinking of armed merchantmen without warning as from February 1. The High Sea Fleet received orders to support the U-boats in every possible way.

Before describing the opening of the ruthless campaign, there are a few incidents to be recounted. During January, U 46 (Hillebrand) was active in the Bay of Biscay, and U 55

---

[1] *U.S.N.I. Proceedings,* April 1926 (Gayer), p. 653.

(Werner) and U 85 (Petz) in the western approaches. Two vessels, the Harrison liner *Artist* (3570 tons), torpedoed without warning 58 miles W. by ½ S. from the Smalls on January 27, with her crew of 35, and the fishing-smack *Trevone*, sunk by gunfire 30 miles N.W. from Trevose Head three days later, fell to Werner, a commander whose deeds rival the murderous attacks already related. The liner *Ava* (5076 tons) is believed to have been similarly sunk; but as not a soul of the 92 aboard was ever heard of again, her fate can only be conjectured. The steamer *Lux* (2621 tons) also vanished in the Atlantic with her crew of 29. These tragedies were but a foretaste of the bitter cup to be drunk in the months to come.

From January 29, 1915, until February 1, 1917, there had been sunk 544 British ships, with a loss of 3066 lives : 269 had been torpedoed, of which 148 had been sent to the bottom without any warning. In addition, 129 ships had been attacked but had escaped a summary fate. At this date no fewer than 1337 steamers had been armed. It will be seen, therefore, that during the period here reviewed 27 per cent. of the toll of British shipping destroyed had been sunk without warning.

CHAPTER VII

THE MEDITERRANEAN: REAPING THE WHIRLWIND

(1916)

By the arrival in the Mediterranean, during the autumn of 1915, of the five 'Thirty'-class submarines, under commanders of high proficiency, the Allied naval authorities were brought face to face with a very serious danger. Even before depredations began it had been decided to treat the Straits of Otranto in a fashion similar to the Straits of Dover. Between these two defiles, however, there was a vast difference. Whereas the Dover Straits are shallow, the exit from the Adriatic is anything between three and five hundred fathoms in depth, and it is twice as wide. Against this drawback was the absence of tide in the Otranto channel, a very important factor. With the ideas prevailing at this early period, a surface barrage, at the moment, was the only practical method of denying the enemy submarines an easy passage in or out of the Adriatic. Sixty drifters, therefore, arrived from England in September to form a net barrier across the Straits; and in 1916 the number was increased to one hundred and sixty. The first sixty had hardly arrived before they were called upon to assist in evacuating the remnant of the Serbian army and refugees after the terrible retreat before the hosts of Mackensen. When at length the drifters were released from such unforeseen and extra duties, they shot their line of nets across the Straits from Cape Otranto to Sasseno Island, near Valona. During the winter of 1915 at least two enemy submarines became enmeshed. One of the drifters, *Restore*, was shelled and sunk by U 39 on October 12; and the drifter *Garrigill* had a fight with another submarine on January 20, 1916.

At the beginning of 1916, Hersing in U 21 was cruising in

IV. ARNAULD DE LA PERIÈRE AND OFFICERS OF *U.35*.
The "Ace" (*second from left*) of German Submarine Commanders whose depredations upon shipping amounted to nearly half a million tons sunk.

Syrian waters; UB 7, UB 8, and UB 14 were in the Black Sea; UC 12 was employed in transport work between the Adriatic and North Africa; UC 14 was laying mine-fields in the Adriatic; and UC 15 was in the Black Sea. In this last theatre was also U 33. She appears to have been despatched to Constantinople from the Adriatic early in the spring, since on February 1 she sank the steamer *Belle of France* (3876 tons), with 19 of the crew, in the eastern Mediterranean. Gayer considers that the stationing of this large boat in the Euxine for a whole year was sheer waste. From the German standpoint she could have been far more profitably employed in the Mediterranean, where mercantile targets were plentiful. On Pola were based U 34, 35, 38, and 39 for the war on Allied shipping.

Under her new commander, Lothar von Arnauld de la Perière, U 35 made a raid on the trade routes to the east of Malta. At the same time U 39 was sent to molest the Salonica transports, off which port she torpedoed the large horse-transport *Norseman* (9542 tons) on January 22; the damage inflicted, however, was not fatal, and the vessel was beached. This mission is also criticized by Gayer, who considers that, had U 39 cruised as a freelance, she might have put down between 20,000 and 30,000 tons, working along the regular shipping lanes. Hersing was also cruising in the eastern basin, and on February 8 sighted the old French cruiser *Amiral Charner*. She, like the other antiquated armoured cruisers of the Allied fleets, proved extremely vulnerable to under-water attack, and her end was swift. The sole survivor of her entire crew, numbering 335, was found several days later on a raft, the only narrator of tragic tidings.

Valentiner in U 38 came out again on February 5; towards the end of the month he was relieved by Perière. The latter settled down in earnest to establish that reputation which placed him at the head of the submarine 'aces.' First, on February 25, he sank the French auxiliary cruiser *Provence II* (the 13,753-ton *La Provence*), carrying 1800 troops, of whom 930 were lost. He followed this up on March 1 by accounting for the sloop *Primula* off Port Said. This small ship he found to be the toughest nut he ever cracked; and he related that, although her bows had been blown off, she put her engines full astern and tried to ram U 35 by the highly unorthodox method of butting backwards. She avoided both a second and a third torpedo, and only succumbed at the fourth tube-shot. Many other ships did the gay Lothar sink, mustering in all 22,600 tons. On his next cruise he attacked the large liner *Minneapolis* (13,543 tons), in ballast, damaging her to such an extent that she foundered two days later (March 25). When the Adriatic boats had to withdraw to their bases for overhaul and repair, only 4 British ships were sunk in March and 16 in April.

Besides the current shipping war, mining operations by the two UC-boats also carried on. UC 12 had laid mine-fields on two occasions during the summer months; but now that she was joined by UC 14 (lately returned from Turkish waters), a determined effort was made to interfere with the Serbian evacuation. UC 14 laid a field off Valona on November 26, 1915, causing damage to the Italian auxiliary cruiser *Citta di Messina*. Off Cape Linguetta, on December 4, the Italian transport *Re Umberto*, with troops for Valona, foundered on another mine; 500 troops were, however, rescued by British drifters. Equally unfortunate was the Italian destroyer *Intrepido*, which was destroyed at the same time, but without any loss of life. On January 4, UC 14 laid another field off Cape Linguetta, in which the Italian auxiliary cruiser *Citta di Palermo* (3145 tons) came to grief on the 8th. Two days previously the Italian transport *Brindisi* (863 tons), carrying 425 recruits from America, together with several hundred tons of food for the Serbians, had also struck one of these mines, and sank rapidly, with over 200 of those on board. Mines also brought down another victim in the Italian hospital-ship *Marechiaro* (720 tons) off Cape Laghi on February 21. Two fields were laid off Durazzo by UC 12 on February 15 and 23. A third was planted off Brindisi on March 2; but when her commander, Fröhner, took her out of Cattaro on the 13th to mine the entrance to Taranto, she blew up on her own mines three days later. The shattered hull was quickly salved and repaired, to become the submarine X I of the Royal Italian Navy. This capture by salvage resulted in many mysteries, hitherto a source of bewilderment, being solved. The vessel had been constructed in sections by the Weser Co. of Bremen, and assembled at Pola ; her crew was German, although both Austrian and German colours were carried. Bearing in mind the fact that no state of war yet existed between Rome and Berlin, what reason justified a German submarine in mining the approaches to an Italian port ?

Up to this time Italy had staved off any declaration of war against Germany. Germany, on her side, had not committed any open and avowed act of hostility against Italy. Now, irrefragable proof had been secured — proof that, under cover of her ally's flag, Germany was committing (and had been committing) acts of war against Italy. The formal declaration of war, launched from Rome shortly afterwards (on August 27, 1916), terminated the farcical situation.

Beyond the north-eastern limits of the Aegean, German submarines were busily employed in the Black Sea. The Russian attacks at Erzerum offered scope enough for developing a submarine offensive : such opportunities as presented themselves for inflicting damage on the Russian ships in support of the Grand Duke Nicholas's army could perhaps have been adequately dealt with by craft smaller than U 33 and U 39. The latter boat had joined her sister in May, and remained in the Euxine until August. During the whole of the year the sum-total of their victims numbered but 4 steamers, 4 sailing-vessels, and 2 fishing-craft! Amongst these was the hospital-ship *Portugal* (5358 tons), which Gansser (in U 33) sent to the bottom on March 30, with a loss of 90 lives, including 15 nurses. U 33 was the probable conqueror of the Russian destroyer *Lieutenant Pustchin,* sunk off Varna on March 9. She also sank the steamer *Kiev.* Included amongst her other exploits was the shelling of the Toukhoum lighthouse and of the town of Gradant ; and the same submarine acted in support of the *Breslau* when the latter bombarded Trebizond on April 3. A second Russian hospital-ship, *Vperyed* (859 tons), was sunk on July 9.[1]

At Otranto the drifter nets were proving a futile deterrent ;

[1] British Records (1919) gave date of loss as July 16. Press, *Whitaker's Almanack,* and *Brassey's Naval Annual* (1919) give the above version.

the U-boats could either slip through, on the surface, between the gaps in the nets, or, more rarely, dive below them. In April the top edge of the webbed obstruction was lowered 12 feet farther below its former level underneath the surface ; and at the same time the vertical depth of the reticular panels was increased to 140 feet, thereby making a curtain whose nether edge was 180 feet beneath the surface. Then the first success was achieved. Soon after leaving Cattaro, VI (von Falkenhausen) became entangled on May 13 in the nets. Inasmuch as neither of the watching drifters *Calistoga* and *Dulce Doris* was armed, the *Evening Star II* was called up, and opened an effective fire on the encumbered submarine. Thereupon the German crew scuttled their craft. Incidentally, this was the submarine which had sunk the French destroyer *Renaudin* on March 18 off Durazzo.

In April further mine-fields were laid by UC 14 off Bari and off Corfu ; this submarine had a most fortunate escape, being hit by a torpedo which failed to explode. Upon the Mediterranean scene of maritime operations there appeared the large mine-layers of the U 71-80 class, the craft of a dolorous memory to the combatants of both camps. April 1 was marked by the departure of U 73 from Cuxhaven, bound for the Mediterranean with a cargo of 34 mines. Passing around the north of Scotland, and sinking the sailing-vessel *Inverlyon* (827 tons) off the Fastnet on the 11th, she headed south and appeared off Lisbon on the 17th, there depositing a group of mines, to the subsequent and disastrous detriment of sundry neutral ships. Not until nigh on fifty days had elapsed after the planting of the Tagus field did the cruiser *Hampshire* founder, after striking a submarine-laid mine. In connection with the calamity off the Orcadian coast, Admiral Jellicoe has remarked that, up to the time of the *Hampshire*'s sailing (June 5, 1916), mine-laying by submarine had been confined to waters well south of the Firth of Forth. On the other hand, it is now known from German sources that, on March 31, U 74 laid a ' barrage ' of mines across the southern exit of the Firth of Forth, and in that field the steamer *Sabbia* came to grief on April 20. Had the ' *Sabbia* field,' as well as that deposited off the mouth of the Tagus, been recognized as fields laid by submarines of considerable cruising range, it is possible that the safety of the inshore route to the westward of the Orkneys might have been considered more questionable.

Vigilant patrols and a full moon prevented U 73 from depositing more mines in the vicinity of Gibraltar. After passing the Straits, her commander (Siehs) shaped his course for Malta, in which vicinity he laid his last 22 mines. Part of these he sowed whilst running in surface trim ; being forced under by a destroyer, he submerged and planted his remaining ' pineapples.' Four days later (April 30) he reached Cattaro. Already his deadly cargo had wreaked destruction amongst the Allied warships. Into this field, the day after it had been sown, ran the battleship *Russell* (flagship of Rear-Admiral Sir S. R. Fremantle) and the sloop *Nasturtium*, both ships sinking ; in the former ship the loss of life numbered 126. Next day the armed yacht *Ægusa* also foundered on one of the mines; and even as late as May 4, when the trawler *Crownsin* blew up, this small field continued to claim its victims. Later in the year a second boat, U 72, joined her sister. Despite the fact that another 17 (and smaller) mine-layers arrived and operated in the Mediterranean, only 19 ships were lost by mine from April 1916 until October 1918. In many parts the depth of water was prohibitive to mining, and in shallower areas the danger was lessened by efficient sweeping.

As he was returning from North Africa with a Turkish mission on April 30, Hersing deleted the liner *City of Lucknow* (3677 tons) off Malta, but it was not until May 27 that a serious outbreak of sinkings was reported. During this and the five following days, 10 British steamers were sunk by U 39 off the Algerian coast, and Portoferrajo (Elba) was shelled. Italian shipping in particular suffered heavily, and 30,000 tons were destroyed, the victims being mostly small vessels. Soon afterwards, on June 9, U 35 appeared in the western basin, and during the next three weeks sank 7 British steamers. On June 21 she entered Cartagena with a letter from the Kaiser to Don Alfonso, and left next day to resume her cruise. When she returned on July 4 to her base, she had sunk 40 ships. U 39 then reappeared off the Algerian coast and put down more ships during July 12-25.

Perière's record cruise, during which he claimed to have destroyed no fewer than 54 ships totalling 91,000 tons, lasted from July 26 to August 20. With a 4·1-inch gun mounted and a picked gun-layer from the High Sea Fleet, his usual method was to sink by gunfire, after warning had been given. On this trip he expended 900 rounds of ammunition, as against only four torpedoes, one of which he fired ineffectually at the French cruiser *Waldeck-Rousseau*. His favourite procedure was to open fire at 6000 yards range, closing to 3000 yards, until the ship under attack was abandoned; he then completed the work with a shot at the target's bows and stern. Perière returned to Germany in March 1918 to take command of the submarine U 139; he was then credited with having 'crushed' 500,000 tons of shipping, the equivalent of one-fifth of the total Mediterranean losses in 1916 and 1917. The victims of this redoubtable 'sea-hawk' consisted of 2 war-vessels, 1 auxiliary cruiser, 5 troopships, 125 steamers, and 62 sailing vessels.

Interest now reverts to the Otranto Straits. On June 23 the Austrian XV (Schlosser) had fallen in with the Italian auxiliary cruiser *Citta di Messina* (3495 tons), accompanied by the French destroyer *Fourche*. In spite of the escort, the Italian ship was sunk. The submarine was driven off; yet, a little later, the escorting destroyer was herself torpedoed and went down. The next incident concerned the drifter line. On July 7 a submarine fouled the nets; two days later an Austrian cruiser and torpedo-craft left Cattaro to raid the line of drifters, sinking both the *Astrum Spei* and *Clavis*. Next day a second submarine was reported foul; so, in anticipation of another raid, the drifters were withdrawn southwards to the line Fano Island-Cape Santa Maria di Leuca. This same day (July 10) the Italian destroyer *Impetuoso* was sunk in the lower Adriatic by XVII (Hudecek).

Throughout the year 1916, submarines fouled the nets nine times, and two at least paid the forfeit, the Austrian VI and the German UB 44. This latter was a new boat, being one

V.   A MEETING IN THE MEDITERRANEAN.
A small Submarine of the earliest UB. type alongside *U.35.* The figure on the right, in the uniform of an Officer of the British Army, is Captain Wilson, the King's Messenger, taken prisoner by *U.35.*

FRIEND OR ENEMY?
An approaching aeroplane being anxiously watched by the crews of two German Submarines.

of six put together at Pola in 1916.¹ On July 30 the drifter *Quarry Knowe*, lying to her nets, noticed a submarine foul; she summoned the *Garrigill*, and both drifters clearly observed the nets sinking. A couple of depth-charges were put in, and an explosion followed. Still the dead-weight in the nets continued, and an attempt was made to tow the netted submarine into shoal water. Finally both nets and enmeshed submarine broke away and sank into the depths. So perished Lieutenant Wäger and the crew of UB 44.

Probably in retaliation for this success, three seaplanes attacked the drifter line on August 26, the *Rosies* being bombed and sunk; consequently, anti-aircraft guns were mounted in these little ships. To augment the patrol in its offensive against the under-water foe, a seaplane base was later established. Motor launches were also sent to reinforce the surface patrol. Meanwhile, the submarines passed through the Straits unceasingly. An Italian mine-field was laid off Otranto, and north and south of it patrolled French and Italian ships. Here, in the Gulf of Taranto, the Italian destroyer *Nembo* was torpedoed by XVI (von Zoppa) on October 16; but the explosion of the torpedo detonated the depth-charges in the destroyer's magazine and damaged XVI so much that she sank beside her own victim.² The Italians suffered a heavy blow on the night of December 11, when the battleship *Regina Margherita* hit two mines of a field laid off Valona, and sank with 690 of her officers and crew.

Towards the end of the year there was another burst of activity. During the stormy evening of December 17, XX fouled the nets of the drifter *Fisher Girl*. The help of the *Guerdon* and *D. H. S.* was invoked; depth-charges were scattered around the submarine, and for four hours she lay quiet. Night fell with a gale blowing, and the submarine was reported alongside the *Fisher Girl*. Returning, the *D. H. S.* dropped another depth-charge; oil welled up, calming the

¹ Their numeration was UB 42-47; and of these, UB 43 and 47 were ceded to Austria-Hungary in May 1917, after service under the German flag.

² According to the 'Kriegsarchiv' Report (Vienna, 1930), the submarine XVI was sunk on October 17, 1916, through being rammed by an Italian vessel. This version gives a different date and a different cause of loss to those narrated above.

turbulent sea. When morning broke, an attempt was made to drag the inert mass towards shore, but the wires parted under the strain, and the entangled enemy seemed to drop like a stone to the bottom.[1]

Five days later a cruiser and four destroyers set out to attack the drifters again, but they were chased by a passing French division. It has been assumed that this raid was intended to clear the way for UC 35, which had left Kiel on December 3; after passing through the Dover Straits, she was due to arrive at Cattaro on the 26th. In addition to this boat, six other mine-layers of the UC II type—UC 20, 22, 23, 24, 25, and 34—had already arrived, or were about to join the Adriatic flotilla.

All this time the campaign on commerce proceeded without intermission. The toll taken of shipping mounted steadily. At the end of August, U 38 had replaced U 35 and molested sea-traffic around the Balearics. On August 3 the minesweeper *Clacton* was sunk in the Aegean, and on the 17th the armed yacht *Zaida* was similarly lost in the Gulf of Alexandretta. Perière was at work again during October, and his share of the havoc included the French sloop *Rigel* (destroyed on October 2), and he torpedoed and sank two days later, off Sardinia, the large French auxiliary cruiser *Gallia* (14,966 tons), carrying 2000 French and Serbian troops. He describes this attack as a 'frightful affair.' The *Gallia* was steaming at 18 knots on a zigzag course, and he hit her with his last torpedo at 900 yards range. A wild panic broke and numbers of the troops jumped overboard: 'the sea became a terrible litter of overturned, overcrowded, and swamped lifeboats, and struggling men.' Stern first, the great ship plunged, and over 600 perished.

On the same day the empty troopship *Franconia* (18,150

---

[1] The Austro-Hungarian submarine XX was long supposed to have been destroyed upon the date and under the circumstances narrated above. Actually, she survived this episode in the Otranto Straits, but upon what date she was lost has yet to be proved. The Italians claim that their submarine F 12 sank the Austro-Hungarian XX on July 4, 1918. The 'Kriegsarchiv' Report (alluded to in the preceding footnote) says that XX (under the command of Linienschiffs-Leutnant Ludwig Müller) was torpedoed by an Italian submarine on May 1, 1918.

Photo. Abrahams & Sons.

VI.   THE SINKING OF THE RUSSELL.
This old battleship ran into the minefield laid by U.73 off Malta and sustained fatal injury, on April 27, 1916.

THE MINES' LARGEST VICTIM.
A mine laid by U.73 caused the loss of the huge Hospital Ship *Britannic*, in the Ægean Sea, on November 21, 1916. Completed after the outbreak of war, the 48,000 ton White Star liner was commissioned as a Hospital Ship. The photograph shews the *Britannic* leaving Mudros harbour on the last trip which ended so fatally.

tons) was sent to the bottom off Malta, with 12 of her crew ; on November 6 the P. & O. liner *Arabia* (7933 tons) was torpedoed off Cape Matapan ; on the 14th the French auxiliary cruiser *Burdigala* (better known before the war as *Kaiser Wilhelm*, of 12,009 tons) was sunk, either by mine or torpedo. Mines laid by U 73 in the Zea Channel caused the loss of the huge 48,158-ton White Star liner *Britannic* on the 21st ; she was serving as a hospital-ship, and carried a staff and crew of 1125, but patrolling craft saved all except 21. Two days later, another hospital-ship, the Union-Castle liner *Braemar Castle* (6318 tons), likewise struck a mine, in the Mykoni Channel, but in this case the ship was beached and repaired. On the 29th, mines laid in Suda Bay (Crete) sank the large Atlantic Transport liner *Minnewaska* (14,317 tons) ; and as this bay had often been used by British warships as an anchorage, its pollution by the mine-pest was an unpleasant surprise.

Still more serious was the fact that four more North Sea submarines were being detached to the Mediterranean—U 32, 52, 64, 65. On her long passage to Cattaro, U 52 (Walther Hans) fell in with the old French battleship *Suffren* off Lisbon, on November 25, and found her an easy victim. In urgent need of repair, this gallant old Gallipoli veteran was crawling along at 9 knots for Brest, and absolutely without any escort. Not one of her complement was ever heard of again. On December 4 the defensively-armed liner *Caledonia* (9223 tons) tried to ram her assailant, U 65, before she was sunk off Malta, and grave fears were entertained for the safety of her master, Captain Blaikie, who was captured ; but the hint of reprisals was enough to deter his captors from repeating the Fryatt murder. As for U 65, she was forced to return to Cattaro with serious injuries forward, and was under repair until the following April.

The last month of a disastrous year brought a yet further disquieting development. Although Hans Rose had taken U 53 across the Atlantic and warred on shipping off America's seaboard a few months previously, the raid had not been repeated. That the area of the submarine-infested zone would progressively expand was likely. Over the heads of the Allied Naval Command was therefore suspended a Damoclean sword—the threat that submarines might appear in fresh waters at any moment. Such fears were confirmed when Valentiner in U 38 appeared off Funchal on December 3, torpedoing the French gunboat *Surprise* and the submarine depot- and docking-ship *Kanguru* and the cable-ship *Dacia* (1856 tons) in the Roads. Afterwards he shelled the town for two hours.

December brought no abatement of shipping losses, and U 35 and UC 22 were particularly active. During the last half of 1916 no fewer than 96 British ships of 415,471 tons, 24 French ships of 64,829 tons, and 136 Italian ships of 181,831 tons—a total of 256 vessels of 662,131 tons gross— were destroyed in the Mediterranean. The number of submarines at work was increasing, and in December six large and three smaller boats were known to be out. By January 1917 there were twenty-five based on the Adriatic ports.

Further serious losses had also occurred in December. Those worthy of citation here are the French transport *Magellan* (6207 tons), carrying 1000 troops, sunk off Sicily on the 11th ; the horse-transport *Russian* (8825 tons), sent to the bottom with 28 of her crew on the 14th ; and the steamer *Westminster* (4342 tons), lost on the same day, whose survivors were shelled as they took to the boats. Next, on the 27th, UB 47 (Steinbauer) had found the French battleship *Gaulois* in the Aegean ; he torpedoed her, despite the screen of light cruisers and trawlers. This success he followed up by torpedoing the troopship *Ivernia* (14,278 tons) off Cape Matapan, on New Year's Day ; and owing to the heavy weather 125 lives were lost. He also raided San Pietro (Sardinia).

Closely following upon these disasters came the loss of the battleship *Cornwallis* off Malta, on January 9 ; she was sunk with three torpedoes from one of the newly-arrived boats, U 32 (Hartwig). On January 4 the Russian battleship *Peresviet* (retroceded by Japan to her former foe) was mined and lost off Port Said ; and, finally, the French troopship *Amiral Magon* (5566 tons), carrying 900 troops for Salonica, was torpedoed on the 25th. The vessel sank in ten minutes, and it was only by the strenuous efforts of the French

REAPING THE WHIRLWIND

destroyers *Arc* and *Bombarde* that the loss of life was confined to 93.

If in the Mediterranean the submarines went their way almost unchecked, in the Black Sea there was a different tale to relate. Beginning with the mining of UB 7 (Lütjohann) during September or October, the UB 45 (Palis), lately arrived from the Adriatic, was similarly lost on November 6. Soon afterwards, UB 46 (Bauer) blew up in a mine-field north-west of the Bosporus on December 7.[1] In addition, the small mine-layer UC 15 (Heller), based on Varna, was blown to pieces on her own mines off Sulina during December. Thus within a few weeks the Constantinople half-flotilla had been reduced to two boats.

Hersing left the Mediterranean in February, and his return home in U 21 was marked by an extraordinary incident. Quite unaware that the German Government had granted a 'safe passage' through the danger zone to a convoy of eight Dutch steamers, Hersing sighted a tempting target off Falmouth on February 22. There was, of course, no escort; and one by one he attacked the Dutch ships, sinking six. Only the timely arrival of salvage vessels saved the other two. He returned to port to find that his 'outrage' was the subject of bitter discussion between Holland and Germany. It was an egregious example of the little control Berlin possessed over the forces it had released.

January 1917 marked the end of 'cruiser warfare' in every theatre. Henceforward every ship sighted was to be attacked and sunk, regardless of the plight of those on board. In the months previously reviewed, it had been the ambition of every aspiring submarine commander to be sent to the Mediterranean. There ample targets were to be found, negligible was the danger from the patrols, and any skilful commander hardly needed to fear the passage of the Otranto Straits. Political complications, after the sanguinary despatch of some big liner, scarcely ever arose. Physical geography allowed but small variation in the shipping routes at certain

---

[1] British Records (1919) gave her loss on December 16, 1916, in British mine-field laid outside the Dardanelles after the evacuation. The above is the German version, and is probably correct.

points, and little was the latitude of escape there for the victims. A submarine had only to lie *perdu* and wait for the patrol to pass along the 'beat,' before restarting depredations. The raider could also appear at some distance away, to decoy the patrol from her appointed course, and then get on the line, to harry, sink, and burn. Trawlers were found to be useless for escorting the valuable ships, such as troopships and supply-vessels. Everywhere the cry went up for sloops, destroyers, and depth-charges. It was, however, to be a long day ere the counter-measures, now successful in home waters, could be applied to the harassed Mediterranean.

CHAPTER VIII

THE CRISIS

(February–April 1917)

'Disasters in the sun; and the moist star,
Upon whose influence Neptune's empire stands,
Was sick almost to doomsday with eclipse.'
Hamlet, Act i. Scene i.

On January 31, 1917, the German Note was presented to Washington. Following a preliminary diatribe against the Allies for their rejection of her peace terms—terms deliberately framed to elicit Allied rejection, so that Germany might have an excuse for opening up Unrestricted War—it continued :—

'Every day by which the war is shortened preserves on both sides the lives of thousands of brave fighters, and is a blessing to tortured mankind. The Imperial Government would not be able to answer before its own conscience, before the German people, and before history, if it left any means whatever untried to hasten the end of the war. After the attempt to reach an understanding by negotiation was answered by the enemy with an announcement of an intensified war, the Imperial Government, if it so desires in the high sense to save humanity and not to do wrong against its own countries, must continue the battle forced upon it anew for its existence, with all its weapons. *It must therefore abandon the limitations which it has imposed upon itself in the employment of its fighting weapons.*[1] The Imperial Government hopes that the United States will appreciate the new state of affairs from the high standpoint of impartiality, and will also on their part help to prevent further misery and sacrifice.'

A zone was defined and declared dangerous for all traffic, extending, roughly, from the Dutch coast to Norway, thence to the Faroe Islands and down to Cape Finisterre, the ocean boundary of the prohibited area being about 400 miles

---

[1] The italics are ours.

west of Ireland. The Mediterranean was also included in the proscribed waters, save for a patch south and east of Spain and around the Balearic Islands. A narrow corridor of access to Greece was allowed.[1] Two American steamers would be permitted to ply weekly between New York and Falmouth, provided that they were decorated with large red and white vertical stripes—a tactless condition, seeing that red and white stripes are the American convict marking ! Similarly, a Dutch steamer might ply between Southwold and Flushing daily during the hours of daylight, in like manner bedecked with flags and colours of German choice.

This blend of Pecksniffian sentiments, sublime impudence, hypocrisy, and arrogance was a typical example of German war mentality. Had it not been for the tragedy lurking behind the thinly-veiled threat, the revelation that Germany was troubled in conscience because of her self-imposed limitations might have been greeted with world-wide derision.

If there were any who entertained a lingering hope that there must be some limit to Germany's ruthless campaign, the illusions of those tenacious optimists must have been dispelled by the notification of January 28. In this document Britain was once again accused of employing hospital-ships upon illegal duties. Citation was particularly made of the Gallipoli campaign, during which the British had added to the 59 hospital-ships previously notified another 40 such vessels. Instances were given : for example, there was the allegation that the French *La France* had carried automobiles on her decks ; further, that ships had been used alternately as hospital-ships and transports. As an illustration, the *Copenhagen* was mentioned as having been first used as a transport ; next, as having become a hospital-ship on October 14, 1914 ; thereafter as having reverted to trooping by February 6, 1915 ; and yet again being listed as a hospital-ship on January 1, 1916 ; to be once more deleted from the list on March 4, 1916. Interned German officers in the Isle of Wight declared that cross-Channel hospital-ships went out to France heavily laden, and that high officials made a practice of travelling in these vessels. Moreover, a Dutch subject had

[1] See Chart 1.

THE CRISIS

declared that the German blockade was rendered futile by the British misuse of the Red Cross regulations. Hospital-ships, therefore, would not be tolerated in the area bounded by the lines Flamborough Head-Terschelling and the Land's End-Ushant. On March 29, 1917, Mediterranean hospital-ships were advised by Berlin to touch at Kalamata, in the Peloponnese, and to notify their times of arrival and departure, together with their names, six weeks in advance of such movements. They were then to steam to Gibraltar at a speed that was to be fixed, and an assurance of their *bona fides* was to be given by some neutral official.

To the sworn statements of witnesses, adduced to support the German contentions, the Admiralty immediately and emphatically issued a categorical denial, declaring that their falsity would be proved by a search of any hospital-ship. In November 1915 the *Mauretania* had been inspected at Naples by Danish, Swiss, and United States consuls, who contradicted the allegations. Only in one case was search made by a German submarine, when on February 23, 1917, the *Dunluce Castle* was stopped, and, being found in order, was allowed to proceed on her passage to Gibraltar. But search was now no longer part of German procedure; and after considering the series of deliberate attacks made during the springs of 1917 and 1918, one is inevitably driven to the conclusion that they were the result of carefully-considered orders issued to the submarine commanders, and designed to sap the morale of the masters and men of the merchant service. Had search been made, it would moreover have revealed that the alleged troops carried were khaki-clad R.A.M.C. personnel, and the freight to be medical stores, as sanctioned by the Hague Convention. Germany's excuse for these deliberate murders would then have vanished.

Before the great federated nation of the West the gauntlet was cast down; the challenge was promptly taken up. Three days later, diplomatic relations between the Governments of the United States and Germany were broken off. In a speech to Congress, President Wilson stated :—

'I cannot bring myself to believe that they will destroy American ships and take American lives in wilful prosecution of the ruthless naval programme they have announced. Only overt acts can make me believe this. . . . If American ships and lives should be sacrificed by their naval commanders in heedless contravention of the just and reasonable understanding of international law and of the obvious dictates of humanity, I shall take the liberty of coming again before Congress to ask that authority be given me to use any means that may be necessary for the protection of our seamen and our people in the prosecution of their peaceful, legitimate errands on the high seas. I can do nothing less. I take it for granted that all neutral Governments will take the same course. We are sincere friends of the German people, and earnestly desire to remain at peace with the Government which speaks for them. We do not desire a hostile conflict with the German people until we are obliged to believe them hostile. We seek merely to vindicate our right, justice, and unmolested life. These are the bases of peace, not war. God grant that we may not be challenged to defend them by acts of wilful injustice on the part of the Government of Germany.'

There was to be no chance of misunderstanding Germany's intentions. On January 31 the U 45 held up and demanded oil from the American tanker *Westego*; on the following day the Dutch steamer *Gamma* (2115 tons), from New York to Amsterdam, was attacked without warning and then sunk by bombs and gunfire. On February 3 an American seaman was killed when the boats of the sunken *Eavestone* (1858 tons) were shelled. On the same day Hans Rose in U 53 sank, after warning, the American steamer *Housatonic* (3143 tons). On the 7th the Anchor liner *California* (8669 tons) was sunk without previous admonition, 38 miles W. by S. from the Fastnet, with the loss of 43 lives; the same day brought a similar end to the Johnston liner *Vedamore* (6330 tons), 20 miles west from Fastnet, with 23 of her crew. Yet again, on the 8th, the British India liner *Mantola* (8253 tons) was destroyed, 143 miles W.S.W. from Fastnet, and 7 lives were sacrificed; and four days later the White Star liner *Afric* (11,999 tons) was put down 12 miles S.S.W. from Eddystone, only 5 lives being lost in her case. The 'overt act' was committed on the 25th, when the 18,099-ton Cunard liner *Laconia* was sent to the bottom, 160 miles N.W. by W. from Fastnet, 12 of those aboard perishing.

THE CRISIS

If President Wilson believed that his solemn warning would fall upon heedful ears, such hopes were now at an end. Then came the culminating affront. March 1 brought the revelation of the 'Zimmermann letter.' It was a confidential communication, dated January 19, 1917, from Zimmermann, the German Foreign Secretary, and addressed to the German minister in Mexico. Intercepted in transit and decoded, it was found to contain a proposal that Mexico should be instigated into inviting Japan to join in an attack on the United States, should President Wilson declare war on Germany. American opinion, so curiously passive over the murder of her citizens on the high seas, was thoroughly roused, and a surge of anger swept over the continent. The arming of American merchant-ships was sanctioned on March 4, and next day the President affirmed that America stood on 'armed neutrality.' By the end of February no fewer than 426 neutral vessels had been destroyed since submarines first began to ravage non-combatants' shipping in 1915. War between America and Germany, therefore, could only be a matter of time.

Signs had not been wanting in the fall of 1916 that German submarines were increasing both in range of action and in numbers. Gayer states that, in December, 15 new boats were commissioned. So great an addition was never reached again in any subsequent month, the average monthly rate of commissioning in 1917 being only about 7, and in 1918 about 8. Gayer estimates that between November 1918 and November 1919 the monthly rate of addition would have risen to 25! Michelsen asserts that at the beginning of 1916 there were 41 German submarines in service; on January 10, 1917, the number had risen to 103. As losses during 1916 had amounted to 22, it follows that 84 new boats had been added to the strength during that period. As events proved, October 1917 marked the 'peak' in the strength of German submarine totals, when 140 [1] were available for and on active service, or refitting and repairing; after this month the number dwindled. To this great increase in numbers a corresponding

---

[1] These 140 were 'war-front' boats, and did not include those engaged in training duties.

addition was made to the submarine personnel, who underwent intensive training. Many of the older commanders were appointed to new and larger boats, sometimes to their undoing. For example, R. Weisbach of U 19 was given U 81 ; Bruno Hoppe of U 22 was removed to U 83 ; Schneider of U 24 took over U 87 ; Schwieger of U 20 was appointed to U 88 ; von Spiegel of U 32 went to U 93 ; Wünsche of U 25 was sent to U 97 ; von Georg of U 57 assumed the command of U 101 ; Rücker of U 34 transferred to U 103 ; and so on.

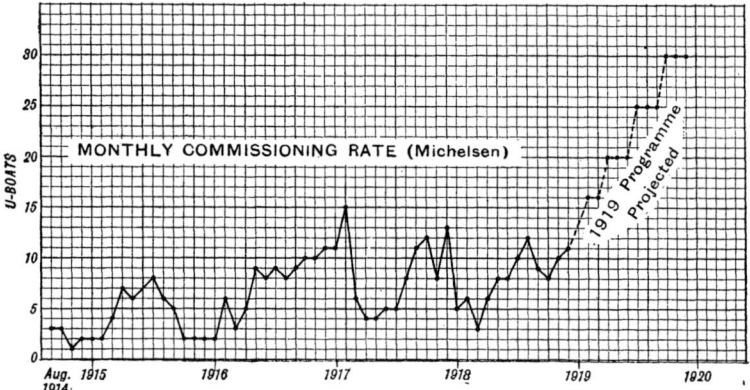

Other commanding officers of the smaller UB- and UC-boats were also posted to boats of later, larger, and improved types.

Although authorities vary considerably in their analyses of the distribution of the submarines on February 1, 1917,[1] we can accept Michelsen as a guide. Taking the ' war front ' boats only, he says there were 49 boats allocated to the North Sea flotillas, 33 in Flanders, 24 in the Adriatic, 3 at Constantinople, and 2 in the Baltic—111 in all. As regards reinforcements from the shipyards, the U 87-92 class were either commissioned or ready for service (the last three boats appear to have been delayed). None of the UB III type was ready until June 1917, when the first boats of the UB 48-71 series appeared. Between November 1916 and June 1917 the second instalment of the UC II-boats (UC 49-79) was ready for service. They were followed by only six more boats of a modified design (UC III) during the following fourteen

[1] Scheer : North Sea 57, Flanders 38, Adriatic 31, Baltic 8.

months. A large type of 'omnibus' submarine, U 117-126, ordered about May 1916, did not come into service until March-November 1918.[1]

Orders were placed in February 1917 for six 810-ton boats (U 158-159, U 160-163), and forty-five 500-ton boats (UB 88-132). Not until June were contracts settled on a much more liberal scale, for nine 850-ton boats (U 164-172), ten 2130-ton cruiser-type boats (U 191-200), thirty-seven 530-ton boats (UB 133-169), and thirty-five mine-layers of 450 tons (UC 84-118). Of these, five of the 850-ton boats and sixteen of the UC series came into commission before the close of hostilities. Another big batch was ordered in December 1917, comprising twelve 850-ton boats (U 201-212), thirty-six UB-boats (UB 170-205), thirty-four UC-boats (UC 119-152), and twenty single-hull craft (UF 1-20). Not one of these boats was finished in time to be of service.[2]

Towards the end of the war, the organization of the submarine force was as follows:—

> (a) Five flotillas, attached to the High Sea Fleet. (The stations and commanding officers of the 1st, 2nd, 3rd, and 4th flotillas have been previously given.[3] The 5th flotilla, stationed at Bremerhaven, was commanded by Jürst.)
> (b) The submarine cruiser flotilla, at Kiel. (This was at first under the orders of the Naval Staff, but was later transferred to the High Sea Fleet.)
> (c) Two flotillas, attached to the Flanders Naval Forces.
> (d) Two flotillas, stationed in the Mediterranean.

Six months had been asked for by the advocates of the ruthless war; by the expiration of that period a decision would be forced. It was estimated that a western station would require five boats—one operating on the station, one coming out on

---

[1] The units of the U 117-126 class were called an 'omnibus' type because in each vessel provision was made for a powerful gun armament, a large torpedo-carrying capacity, and mine-carrying and sowing gear. Thus they were equipped to carry out three methods of attack on shipping.

[2] Michelsen and Gayer do not agree as to the dates on which boats enumerated in this paragraph were ordered.

[3] *Vide* footnote to p. 96.

relief, one returning home, one being opened up for repairs, and the fifth completing overhaul. A week was spent in passage to the south-west of Ireland, and the 800-ton 'medium-size' U-boats had about three weeks' endurance. Of the available strength of 49 North Sea boats, some 23 were at sea during February and 27 in March; and only twice subsequently was this latter total exceeded until October 1918, when every available boat was concentrated in readiness for the final onslaught. In the Mediterranean, rarely was more than a third of the strength at sea. According to established rule, eight stations could be maintained by the North Sea boats; but, when the patrols began to force the U-boats to seek their prey some 200 miles from Fastnet, the effectiveness of their attack was considerably reduced, and in some cases seven boats were required for the maintenance of a single station to provide, by rotation, a single boat in operation. The naval authorities realized that, if the promised success were to be attained in the six months, the employment of the U-boats to their utmost limit must be enforced.

Once again, passage through the Dover Straits for the larger boats was sanctioned. The Flanders boats had found them not impassable; and since 1915 a few experienced commanders of the larger North Sea boats had succeeded in penetrating the Straits. This short cut to the west was therefore ordered; it meant a saving of six out of the twenty-five days usually allotted to North Sea boats, and eight out of the fourteen-day cruise of the Flanders boats. That the submarines were passing through the Dovers Straits became increasingly evident to the British naval authorities. The Senior Naval Officer at Dover was made the subject of a bitter Press attack, although he had done everything possible within his power in the absence of efficient mines. Mines of the Elia type had been laid; they had a large danger zone, and therefore should have been effective as anti-submarine machines; but the firing and mooring gears were faulty. With a fifteen-feet tide, it was difficult to set mines to catch submarines on the surface. Strong currents unduly depressed the mines, and those set to a shallow depth were swung to and fro in a

THE CRISIS

heavy seaway ; the moorings chafed through and parted, and the mines so freed drifted away. Moreover, the mine bodies were porous, and, if not cast adrift, ultimately foundered through seepage. The net-cutters on the submarines' bows and the jumping wires over the hulls cut or threw clear entanglement devices ; mines merely bumped harmlessly against the U-boats, or betrayed their position by floating on the surface ; and there were insufficient patrols to keep the enemy under water. So through this defile poured one long stream of submarines, to spread themselves over the western approaches, where they could extirpate all sea-borne trade as it flowed in from the outer world.

The first of February came, and from the outset the venomous nature of the onslaught allowed of no misconception as to the menace at hand. Thirty-seven had been the average monthly toll of British ships during the last five months of cruiser warfare in all waters, with an additional mean of about 8 from mine injury. Only twice before had 42 British merchant-ships been put down in any one month—in August 1915 and in November 1916. Now, within one short month—February—86 British ships of 256,394 tons gross were sunk by the U-boats, and 12 of 28,413 tons gross were mined, with a loss of 402 lives. In addition, raiders in the outer seas struck down 7 more ships of 28,679 tons.

The returns for March brought no relief ; on the contrary, they exhibited a further upward leap in the losses. The U-boats passed the century mark, destroying 103 ships, totalling 283,647 tons. The number of ships destroyed was almost triple the total for January, and with the rise in vessels deleted the loss of life increased proportionately—630 during March, as compared with 235 in January. Wastage by the mine peril showed but a small advance when compared with February. The March mortality from this danger was 12 ships mined of 26,938 tons, and 51 lives lost. In the outer seas, surface-operating raiders—the *Möwe*, *Wolf*, and *Seeadler*—added their quota, seizing and destroying 9 ships of 41,325 tons, with a sacrifice of 11 lives ; and German destroyers off the East Coast sank 2 further steamers of 1568 tons, 7 lives being lost. The sum-total for all British shipping exterminated during March was 127 vessels of 353,478 tons, and the loss of life one short of 700.

Alarming though these figures were, still worse befell. In April the appalling total of 155 British vessels of 516,394 tons gross succumbed to the diving corsairs, either by torpedo, gunfire, or bomb. Fourteen others of 28,888 tons foundered on mines. The massacre of freighters was accompanied by the loss of 1125 lives at sea. Thus, in the holocaust of April, over half a million tons of British shipping was obliterated. To this work of annihilation must be superadded the ships damaged and temporarily out of employment. Little less were the sufferings of Allied and neutral shipping; and during this dark month no fewer than 336,000 tons was sent to the bottom, whilst another 113,000 tons gross was damaged. Very serious indeed was the decision of Danish, Dutch, Norwegian, and Swedish shipowners to hold up their shipping during the first weeks of the new campaign. Belgian Relief steamers were ruthlessly torpedoed; and when Hersing, returning from the Adriatic in U 21, attacked the eight Dutch steamers (to which a safe-conduct had been guaranteed) off Falmouth on February 22, sinking six of them, the neutrals' alarm was accentuated.

To recapture the tense atmosphere of these weeks at this interval of time is a task almost impossible. Of every 100 steamers that left these shores, 25 never returned; they were sunk outward bound or when returning laden with precious cargoes. Of those steamers which could not yet be armed, three-quarters were destroyed; but three-quarters of the armed steamers escaped destruction. Guns had to be taken from steamers at a port outside the danger zone and remounted on a vessel about to enter the perilous area. American ships began to arm on March 12. Incidentally, the equipping of British merchantmen was one of the great wartime achievements; by the autumn of 1918 not less than 4139 merchant-ships had mounted weapons to thwart their foe.

During the first eighteen days of February, forty fights between submarine and patrol were reported; and in this same period 121 British, 10 Allied, and 50 neutral ships were destroyed or damaged. The U-boats, determined to surpass

VII. THE ORDEAL OF THE NEUTRAL TRADERS.
The pitiable condition of a Danish barque, after being shelled by a German Submarine. Notice the two shell holes in the hull, abaft the stump of the mizzen mast.

all previous performance, were working at their utmost capacity; 23 units of the North Sea flotillas and 9 from the Flanders base were at sea, under tried commanders. As far out as 270 miles W. from Fastnet, shipping was waylaid and wiped out. The patrols hurried to and fro; as soon as they arrived at the scene of a sinking ship, the submarine would have reappeared many miles away, and with little hope of success the hunt began anew. In April, not only did the submarines succeed in destroying the estimated 600,000 tons of shipping, but they actually exceeded this total by 50 per cent. Nearly 900,000 tons gross of merchant-shipping of all nationalities was sent to the bottom during four weeks. Soon there would be nothing left to sink. It was a mathematical certainty that by the end of the year there would be just enough tonnage left to Britain to bring in food; nothing would be left for the transport of troops, nothing for munitions, coal, and other vital necessaries. Collapse faced the Allied leaders.

As previously mentioned, it was in November that Admiral Sir John Jellicoe, Commander-in-Chief of the Grand Fleet, was asked to take up duty as First Sea Lord at Whitehall, expressly to grapple with the ruthless submarine war, then foreseen to be impending and which could not be much longer delayed. With him came Rear-Admiral A. L. Duff, to take charge of a new Anti-Submarine Division, created to control all the patrol and mine-sweeping vessels, as well as aircraft on coastal patrol. Many were the suggestions urged on the Admiralty by naval officers; they ranged from attacks on the German coast and an assault on Zeebrugge, to intensive mining, and protection of commerce.

Under Rear-Admiral Duff the problem was searchingly examined. Amongst the first measures adopted was the forming of 'hunting' patrols, consisting of groups of destroyers and P-boats, based on Portsmouth and Devonport. These new units were formed to obviate the necessity of escorts leaving their mercantile charges to attack a submarine in the vicinity. To the new offensive measures was added organized air-patrol; also, vessels equipped with hydrophones — a device then still in an experimental stage. The mining of the

Bight of Heligoland and the inauguration of a submarine patrol between the Shetlands and the Norwegian coast were also features of the new policy. Wider use of the submarine as a stalker and attacker of submarines was advocated, such as the stationing of a submarine some distance astern of a merchantman, to creep up and destroy the U-boat as the latter preoccupied herself with her selected commercial target.

Amongst the numerous mechanical devices adopted were howitzers to throw a bomb or shell fitted to explode forty or sixty feet below the surface; the introduction of a new projectile for the small 12-pounders; the development of both shore and ship hydrophone-stations; the introduction of the 'Otter' gear for the protection of shipping from mines; the rapid arming of merchantmen; the expansion of the decoy service. A successful method of providing steamers with net-defence was found, and adopted in 1918. These measures were followed by the provision of depth-charge throwers, coastal motor-boats, improved and efficient mines and deep mine-fields in the Bight and at Dover, flares for night work, electrical submarine-detectors, and the dazzle-painting of merchantmen. Convoy was hardly considered, in view of the utter inadequacy of sufficient escorting vessels.

Submarines could not be prevented from emerging from their bases, but attempts to confine them to the North Sea had been made. Such efforts had failed at Dover. In the higher latitudes, organized hunts, intended to keep the quarry submerged until her batteries became exhausted and she was forced to break surface, had likewise little success. A large U-boat could travel, by day, eighty miles submerged at slow speed, and emerge at nightfall. Only a multitude of destroyers and fast patrols could keep her under. Once arrived in western waters, the diving-raiders encountered scanty patrols. Hence it was but necessary to dive as the patrol passed, to resume the work of destruction later or to reappear in another area and so draw the patrols away from the shipping route. Escorts were provided only for important ships; and, even if the attacker were spotted by the escorting destroyer, the chance to the submarine of suffering serious injury from the four depth-

THE CRISIS

charges (then all that could be allowed to each destroyer [1]) was remote. If the patrols became troublesome, the U-boat merely went farther out into the Atlantic to pick up solitary ships. Only from decoys could real danger be apprehended.

No better picture of the difficulties and the baffling nature of the problem can be visualized than a typical hunt in September 1916.[2] On the 3rd, two or three German submarines were located in the western approaches, at times off Ushant, off the Lizard, and even in the Bristol Channel (which was mined). From that day until the 13th, not less than 49 destroyers and 48 torpedo-boats and 468 armed auxiliaries were watching this area, and these two or three enemy submarines were actively hunted by 13 destroyers and 7 Q-boats. In spite of all this fervid activity, the U-boats destroyed more than thirty British and neutral merchant-ships !

Sir Edward Carson, the First Lord, stated, soon after the opening of the new campaign, that forty fights with enemy submarines had taken place during the first eighteen days. One U-boat had been captured ; another had been rammed and sunk ; two had been attacked by patrols and one sunk ; a fifth had been rammed by a destroyer ; a sixth had likewise been rammed ; a seventh had been hit in her conning-tower and was believed destroyed ; an eighth had been bombed ; and a ninth spotted by a seaplane and bombed. Actually, only four enemy under-water pests were exterminated ; but the great difficulty in establishing a loss is illustrated in the case of UC 44. On February 15 she was depth-charged by two destroyers, with the result that her electric-light fittings were smashed. But, by discharging oil and even ejecting chairs from the after torpedo-tube, she deceived her hunters into believing their attack had attained decisive results. Too readily was it assumed that oil, papers, and even fittings rising to the surface were certain evidence that a submarine had received her final quietus.

[1] A great increase in the output of depth-charges was achieved during the latter part of 1917 and during 1918. The accelerated rate of production played a great part in breaking down the German submarine attack on shipping. Some statistics dealing with this point will be found at the end of Appendix I.

[2] The whole operation is described in detail by Sir Henry Newbolt in *Naval Operations*, vol. iv. pp. 333-7.

Immense as the demolition of shipping had been, the cost to the German flotillas was but slight. Four boats only fell victims to patrols or accident. On February 5, UC 39 (Ehrentrant) began to molest the East Coast traffic in the 'war channel,' and during the next three days she sank several vessels. On the 8th, as she was in the act of destroying a ship off Flamborough Head, she was surprised by the destroyer *Thrasher*; too late she dived. A depth-charge explosion inflicted such injury that water poured into the conning-tower and control-room. Inside UC 39, the crew was in a panic. Ehrentrant decided to make his surrender, and the disabled submarine broke surface. Fire was immediately opened on the enemy by the *Thrasher*, killing Ehrentrant as he climbed out of the conning-tower to show his submission. Grasping the perilous situation, the master of the *Hanna Larsen* (1311 tons), a prisoner on board since his vessel had been sunk, climbed up on deck and waved his white handkerchief to the destroyer. The crew, numbering 17, then lined up and were taken off, but UC 39 sank in tow of the *Itchen* before she could be brought in. On the same day UC 46 (Moecke) was rammed and sunk by the destroyer *Liberty* in the Straits of Dover. On the evening of the 23rd, another of these mine-laying craft, UC 32 (Breyer), was hoist with her own petard, being blown up by her own mines off Sunderland as she was fouling the traffic lanes off the port. This boat had narrowly escaped destruction on January 28, whilst attacking fishing-craft in the North Sea; she was surprised by the appearance of an armed trawler, and had to leave a warrant-officer on board one of her intended victims.

Two days later, February 25, UB 30 went aground off Walcheren Island, but was towed into Flushing and interned there. On August 3, however, the Dutch authorities released her.

Three weeks after he had destroyed U 68 (March 23, 1916), Commander Gordon Campbell fell in with another submarine; unfortunately the enemy got away, owing to a premature attack. For many weary months he had ploughed the seas; on February 17, 1917, his patience was rewarded, and in an abrupt manner. Heading straight for the *Farnborough*'s engine-room a torpedo came. To save life, Commander Campbell put the helm over at the last moment and took the hit abaft the engine-room. Water poured into the decoy until two-thirds of the ship was flooded. The ' panic party ' scrambled into the boats and away from the ship, with every sign of agitation and disorder. The still-submerged submarine, at only two hundred yards, watched carefully the sham *sauve qui peut*; closed the boats to scan their occupants, and then came on towards the sinking collier. So close did she pass (at ten to fifteen yards) that Commander Campbell says he could see the whole of her hull under water. When she had gone ahead, she turned to come down the port side. Breaking surface, she made for the boats' crews, over on the port quarter, and the German commander emerged from the conning-tower. At this moment, twenty-five minutes after the torpedo had struck, the White Ensign was broken, screens fell away, and round after round, forty-five in all, was pounded into U 83, at barely a hundred yards range. Hoppe (whom we have previously noticed as in command of U 22) was killed at the first shot; quickly the egg was smashed, and through its shell came scrambling the chicks. Eight of them were seen struggling in the oily water; only an officer and one man could be picked up. The decoy was in a pitiable state. The engineers were waist-deep in water; for half an hour the gun-crews in their tiny gun-houses had lain with their ship sinking beneath them, in momentary expectation that another torpedo would blow them sky-high. Help was called for, and the sloops *Laburnum* and *Buttercup* succeeded in towing the gallant Q-boat into Berehaven, where she was beached. After this event, Commander Gordon Campbell was awarded the Victoria Cross for his extraordinary courage.

Five days later, U 84 (Röhr) had a narrow escape from being sunk by the Q-boat *Penshurst*; and Röhr had to run his boat back to port in surface trim, for so seriously was she damaged that submersion was impossible. Commander Grenfell, of the *Penshurst,* had had another fight only two days earlier; within six weeks he had destroyed two Flanders boats, UB 19 and UB 37. This famous decoy was sunk at length on Christmas Eve 1917, in the St. George's Channel, during her ninth duel.

Many other submarines were damaged in varying degrees during their brushes with the patrols. The defences of the Dover Straits, poor as they were, presented difficulties to the large North Sea boats. The Goodwins-Snou net-barrage, laid in September and extended in December 1916, was proving but a moderate success; between the supporting buoys the net sagged, permitting submarines and even destroyers to pass over it. On February 1, 1917, the UC 17, in attempting the passage, was caught in the nets on the western side, and got clear with forty feet of tangled wire depending from her bows. This encumbrance she got rid of by going ahead and astern. That the nets were at least troublesome was demonstrated on the night of February 25, when German destroyers raided the drifters keeping watch on the nets. The raiders achieved nothing except the killing of a woman and two children, as their shells fell in Margate.

Soon after this raid, the passage of the Straits was forbidden to the North Sea boats for a second time—partly because the weather was now more favourable and permitted the north-about route, and partly because of the numerous patrols. The drifters were not to be left unmolested, and on the night of March 17 two divisions of German destroyers made an attack on the line, simultaneously at each end. During the confused night action the destroyer *Paragon* was sunk by torpedo; the *Llewellyn*, also hit by a torpedo, regained Dover harbour. In addition, the steamer *Greypoint* (894 tons) was sunk in the Downs. The third raid of 1917 ended in disaster for the enemy. When they attempted to repeat the attack, on the night of April 20, two of the raiders, G 42 and G 85, were rammed and sunk by the leaders *Swift* and *Broke*. Thereafter the Dover Patrol was harassed by aircraft only; and it was not until the next year that any further serious effort was made by the enemy to destroy the patrol line.

The U-boats, during the first weeks of the campaign, were sinking ships at the rate of five each day; and they were particularly active in those areas where routes converged. But there were two routes which were hardly molested—the ' French Coal Trade ' and the Scandinavian traffic across the

THE CRISIS

North Sea. The 'French Coal Trade' between South Wales and France began in March 1917; the colliers sailed in batches, under the protection of trawlers, and up to the following August had enjoyed such immunity that only 14 ships out of 8825 sailings were sunk. No doubt the small size of these coal-carrying vessels, taken with their detention in port if a submarine were reported on their proposed route, accounted for part of this freedom from destruction.[1] The protected trade to Scandinavia was screened by destroyers; it had been inaugurated in December 1916, as a result of the big increase in neutrals' losses, and showed, up to August 1917, a mortality of barely 1·2 per cent. Comprising 10,000 sailings, the losses were mainly the result of two raids—one by small German cruisers, and the other by destroyers. In the period subsequent to the second raid, from February to November 1918, there were 4207 ship sailings between Scotland and Scandinavia, of which 18 were lost; this was an equivalent of 0·43 per cent., and most of these vessels were sunk in the great war channel along the East Coast.

With undiminished vigour did the mine-laying boats strew the waters off the headlands and landfalls with their lethal freights; during the year 1917 no fewer than 536 groups of mines were located and 3989 mines were swept up. None the less, the hulls of 170 merchant-ships were fatally riven by the maritime *fougasse*. No longer were the fields confined to the North Sea or the Channel, but even as far as the west coast of Ireland was death spawned upon the seas. Many were the losses caused to tonnage, both of the war and mercantile fleets. In the Channel the French torpedo-boats Nos. 317 and 300 blew up, off Calais on December 29, 1916, and off Le Havre on February 1, 1917, respectively. In the approaches to Lough Swilly and the Clyde 88 mines were laid, and off Belfast 72.

[1] It may be remarked that, until the end of the war, 38,000 vessels carried across to France 30,000,000 tons of coal, with a loss of 0·14 per cent. The Scandinavian Convoy (Old System) and the French Coal Trade can, however, hardly be regarded as representing the convoy in an elementary form. In both cases the routes traversed were short; the passages were made mostly at night, and there was little station-keeping on the part of the merchant-ships themselves. It was more a case of route-protection than the convoy system proper which gave the good results attained by the sailings of the Scandinavian Convoy and the French Coal Trade.

On the bitter winter night of January 23 the armed merchant-cruiser *Laurentic*, bound for New York with 5½ millions of specie, foundered on a mine off Lough Swilly ; sinking in forty minutes, she took down with her very few of the complement, the large death-roll of 349 being due to the severe exposure of the open boats' crews. The large mine-layer U 80 laid about 130 mines during the year off Mull, Stornoway, Coll, Skye, and Harris, of which 76 were located and destroyed. On March 8, Walney Island underwent another bombardment ; next day, mines were discovered in this part of the Irish Sea. Sweepers were put to their work of sterilization, and 48 mines were swept up immediately. In the Irish Sea, mines damaged the large White Star liner *Celtic* (20,904 tons) on February 15 ; happily, this valuable ship was towed safely into Liverpool. Off Harwich during 1917, 680 mines were planted, of which 635 were located and cleared away. The strain on the mine-sweeping flotillas was almost beyond bearing. The 10th Sloop Flotilla was sent from Immingham to Queenstown, both for clearance and for patrol duties : on March 17 and 18 the sloops *Mignonette* and *Alyssum*, sweeping off the west coast of Ireland, blew up, with the loss of 14 lives.

Only off the East Coast, between Cromer and the Humber, was the danger not encountered ; the enemy apparently had no wish to foul waters through which his battleships would have to steam during a coastal raid. When such sorties were relegated to a secondary place in German naval strategy and the efforts of the High Sea Fleet devoted to supporting the U-boats, the East Coast waters, none the less, still remained free from infection. Here was the great British ' war channel '—a long lane, extending right along the south and east coasts of Britain as far north as the Shetlands. Swept daily from end to end, here at least traffic might be assured of a degree of safety impossible in other areas. Even so, the sweepers experienced trouble with a new type of German mine fitted with a delay action, and designed to rise from the bottom after a certain predetermined interval of time. A dangerous area might be swept over and declared free ; next day, mines would be reported again in the very same area. Sweepers would repeat their perilous work of clearance, only to be informed that further mines had cropped up, like noxious weeds, from the sea-bed. Known as 'Monday-Tuesday-Wednesday mines,' these machines further complicated an already difficult problem. Submarines would also follow in the wake of sweepers and foul a stretch of water just worked over; others, again, would torpedo the sweepers. Perilous in the extreme, the duties of these gleaners were unending. Eventually the mine-sweeping force grew to number 726 vessels, consisting of 110 fast mine-sweepers in twenty flotillas, 52 paddle sweepers, 10 'Dance' Class sweepers, and 412 trawlers.[1]

The adoption of the 'Otter' gear appreciably lessened the mine menace. It was a contrivance towed from the bows of a merchant-ship which grappled and cut the mooring cable of the mine, whereupon the mine-body appeared on the surface and might then be sunk as it floated by. For warships the more complicated 'paravane,' in varying forms, was used, as being more suitable for vessels of high speed.

At the end of March, mines were again laid off Liverpool. On March 27 the steamer *Kelvinhead* (3063 tons) foundered on one of them, just off the Mersey Bar. Over a week later the Red Star liner *Lapland* (18,565 tons) struck another in the same locality, but reached Liverpool, on April 8. Next day the American liner *New York* (10,867 tons), carrying as a private passenger Admiral W. S. Sims of the United States Navy, was badly injured by yet another. The sweepers, however, kept the great port clear of mines, and during the year 33 of the 45 laid were destroyed. Other losses included the destroyer *Pheasant*, which blew up on mines laid off the Orkneys on March 1, sinking with all hands; and the torpedo-gunboat *Seagull*, similarly sunk off the west coast of Scotland on April 3.

The enemy paid for this additional attack on the world's shipping, and during 1917 alone 32 mine-laying submarines of the UC types succumbed. Two were destroyed in March —UC 43 (Sebelin) was torpedoed by H.M. submarine G 13 (attached to the Grand Fleet) off Muckle Flugga, on the 10th, as a result of an hour's patient manœuvring. No

---

[1] 'The Mine in the Great War,' *Encyclopœdia Britannica* (Captain A. C. Dewar, R.N.).

survivors were seen in the vast pool of oil. Swiftly change the fortunes of war : elation over this enterprise was followed by lament for a loss. The British boats E 49 and G 13 had been sent to intercept U-boats passing north of the Orkneys, and the former never returned, having struck a mine two days after G 13's exploit. The destroyer *Medea* was believed to have exterminated UC 18 (Kiel) with explosive sweeps off Skinningrove on March 12 ; but later information suggests that the mine-layer succumbed in the Channel, either in the closing days of February or in the early days of March. Another, UC 45, was attacked but not sunk by the decoy schooner *Result*, off the Dogger Bank, on the 15th. Such mine-laying boats, after dumping their cargoes, would pass on to molest shipping before they returned to load up another freight of ' pineapples.'

Besides the above two UC-boats, a large North Sea flotilla submarine was seduced to her doom by another decoy. On March 12 the small steamer *Privet* (Q 19) was cruising off the entrance to the English Channel ; she was sighted and shelled by U 85 (Petz). So destructive was the submarine's fire, that the decoy's steering-gear was disabled and the vessel herself was much shattered. The crew lowered their boats. U 85 closed to obtain from the boats' crew the ship's papers. From the sinking steamer was suddenly poured a deadly stream of lead and steel ; and at the ninth shot U 85 sank with her entire crew. As for the *Privet*, she also foundered off Plymouth Sound, but was raised and, in April, re-hoisted the White Ensign.[1] The moral effect of these decoys ranging at large resulted in great wariness on the part of a submarine approaching any vessel thought to be suspicious. The decoy craft lost heavily ; in 1917, six disguised sloops and eighteen other ' special-service vessels ' were sunk. The Germans knew in 1916 of the existence of such ships,[2] and, adapting the idea, used their own ' trap-ships ' against British submarines.

One other submarine was rendered innocuous during March when, on the 13th, UB 6 (remembered as the first Flanders

---

[1] To this Q-boat belongs the distinction of assisting in the destruction of the last submarine sunk, two days before the Armistice.

[2] For a German description see *Taschenbuch der Kriegsflotten*, 1918, p. 69.

boat to gain a success) stranded off Hellevoetsluis, and was interned by the Dutch authorities.

As has been mentioned above, the shipping losses during March passed the hundred mark. We can do no more than indicate the more prominent casualties, but equally important was the vast number of ships of medium size, carrying cargoes of ever-increasing value, which were exterminated wholesale. On March 1, the R.M.S.P. liner *Drina* (11,483 tons) was sunk without warning, with 15 lives, off Skokholm Island; on the 16th, the *Narragansett* (9196 tons), off the south-west of Ireland, with 46 lives; on the 18th, the Booth liner *Antony* (6446 tons), 19 miles W. by N. from Coninbeg L.V., with 55 lives; the N.Z. Shipping Co. *Rotorua* (11,148 tons), destroyed four days later, 24 miles east from the Start; and the Cunard cargo liner *Thracia* (2891 tons) on the 27th, 12 miles north from Belle Ile, with 36 lives. Worst of all was the sinking of the Union-Castle liner *Alnwick Castle* (5900 tons), which was sent to the bottom without warning, 310 miles W. ½ S. from Bishop Rock, early on the morning of March 19. Passengers and crew, numbering 139, got clear from the sinking ship; but throughout the next few days these boats were tossing about in bitter wintry weather. One boat reached the coast of Spain nine days later with 21 living and 8 dead; another was found with 27 alive; another had 20 living and 5 dead; in the master's boat were 4 dead and the rest too delirious or weak to stir; whilst the fifth and sixth boats were nevermore seen. In all, 40 lives were lost. This month the toll of human life reached 681, of which 630 were due to submarine attack, and 51 to mines.

For the United States the situation had become intolerable. Faced with but one course, President Wilson on April 3 declared before Congress :—

'Civilization itself seems in the balance, but right is more precious than peace, and we shall fight for the thing which we carry nearest to our hearts, for democracy, for the right of those who submit to authority to have a voice in their own government, for the rights and liberties of small nations, for the universal domination of right, for such a concert of free peoples as will bring peace and safety to all nations and make the world itself at last free. To such tasks we dedicate our lives, our fortunes, and everything we have, with the pride of those who know the day has come when America is privileged to spend her blood and might for the principle that gave her birth, happiness and peace. God helping her, she can do no other.'

War was declared on April 5. For nearly three long years the Allies had fought on before America intervened. On both sides the combatants had begun to entertain the belief that American patience was illimitable. Few could appreciate to the full the dependence of the President on the Democratic vote ; the character of the United States political parties ; the problem of a vast population admixed with immigrants of alien birth. Above all, there was the fundamental axiom of the United States' foreign policy to avoid European entanglements and quarrels. Indeed, many on both sides of the Atlantic thought that the President, by tenaciously clinging to the hope that some day he would be called upon to mediate between the warring nations as a peacemaker, was doing naught but prolong the ghastly, gruesome struggle, with its untold agonies of pain and woe. His interventions had encouraged Germany to play fast and loose with her promises. Protest had been made to Berlin, and promises of reform in the anti-shipping war obtained. Protest had been made to Britain, because the blockade measures were unpalatable to the prosperous and politically-powerful Southern States. By these remonstrances the attitude of an impartial neutrality was maintained. But the President, in making complaint against Britain, encouraged Germany to a perfunctory observance of her compacts.

America, on joining the conflict, nominally retained her aloofness from the combinations of European States; she became, not an 'ally,' but merely an 'Associated Power.' Professor M'Laughlin, of Chicago University, who was sent to England by the late President Wilson in 1918 to expound the reasons which induced the United States to lay aside neutrality, summed up the position in a speech at Oxford on May 10. Beginning with the violation of Belgian neutrality and the barbarous treatment meted out to the people of Belgium, he told his audience that, though Americans condemned such practices, they were no inducement to America to take action. When American ships and lives began to be sacrificed by the German U-boats—even after the sinking of the *Lusitania*—the President was content with diplomatic intervention. 'But when it came to this, that all these great world questions were going to be decided and America have no voice—that was more than flesh and blood could stand'— thus spoke his own missionary to the British public. Mr. Spenser Wilkinson stated the position in the words : 'President Wilson entered the war not to defeat Germany, except incidentally, but in order that he himself should dictate the conditions of peace. He brought America into the war, not as an ally, but as an independent belligerent.'[1]

As the precursor of the American naval forces, Admiral W. S. Sims, U.S.N., came to England. Upon the orders of the President, he (and another naval officer) had travelled *incognito* as civilians. On his arrival he was shown at once the actual facts of the situation—facts which could not be made public for fear of dispiriting the nation and encouraging the enemy. The gist of the revelation made by the First Sea Lord (Sir John Jellicoe) to Admiral Sims was this : *The German submarines were winning the war*. The Naval Staff at Berlin had not, after all, been so far out in its calculations. Whereas the U-boats had been pledged to bring about peace by August, it was a mathematical certainty, according to the British Admiralty's estimate, that the war would be lost to the Allies by November, unless some unforeseen check to the enemy should arise. One million tons of the world's shipping lost each month must have such a cumulative effect, that it would be impossible to supply both the armies in the field and the civil populations with the necessaries for continuing their resistance. Neutrals were keeping their shipping in port. Losses were still increasing.

Walter Page, the United States Ambassador in London, declared : 'What we are witnessing is the defeat of Britain.' He was right. Alone and almost unaided, Britain was fighting the insidious menace that was slowly but quite surely undermining the whole Allied resistance.

[1] 'Security,' *Nineteenth Century*, April 1927, pp. 467-8.

160 THE GERMAN SUBMARINE WAR

So Admiral Sims cabled to Washington—again and again—until he drove home to the American politicians and authorities that, unless every available patrolling vessel was sent over, there would be no war in which America could join. It has been estimated that this tardiness in rendering help cost the Allies some 500,000 lives and £3,000,000,000.[1] 'I think that history records few spectacles more heroic than that of the British Navy fighting this hideous and cowardly form of warfare in half a dozen places with pitifully inadequate forces, but with undaunted spirit which remained firm even against the fearful odds. What an opportunity for America!' declared the gallant American admiral.

At last he succeeded in having 6 destroyers sent to Queenstown; they arrived on May 4, and at once undertook a share in the arduous patrol of the western approaches. In this all-important area there were, in February, only 14 destroyers (based on Devonport) and 12 sloops at Queenstown. They were employed without any respite in escorting troopships; and though these patrols were constantly rescuing crews of sunken ships, their very presence served but to point out the shipping tracks to the German sea-guerillas. Cases were reported where, instead of a merchant-vessel being met by a destroyer, a U-boat turned up at the rendezvous after having intercepted radio messages between the incoming ship and her escort. It was estimated that to deal adequately with the menace in this vital area 81 patrols were required.[2] Even with the sloops and destroyers detached from Immingham and the Grand Fleet, they numbered but 40. The submarines, working some two hundred miles out in the Atlantic, would appear in a certain spot to attract the patrols from the closely-watched waters between the coasts of Cornwall and Ireland. By the time the patrols had reached the locality, shipping would be attacked many miles away. So this grim game of blind-man's-buff went on, and the losses rose steadily.

In the month of April the U-boats made their grand onslaught on the world's sea-freightage. Taking British shipping alone, 155 vessels of 516,394 tons were destroyed by

[1] *Battleships in Action*, vol. ii. p. 226 (H. W. Wilson).
[2] *The Crisis of the Naval War* (Jellicoe), p. 111.

submarines, mines accounting for 14 ships of 28,888 tons gross. The death-roll of April reached the terrible total of 1125.

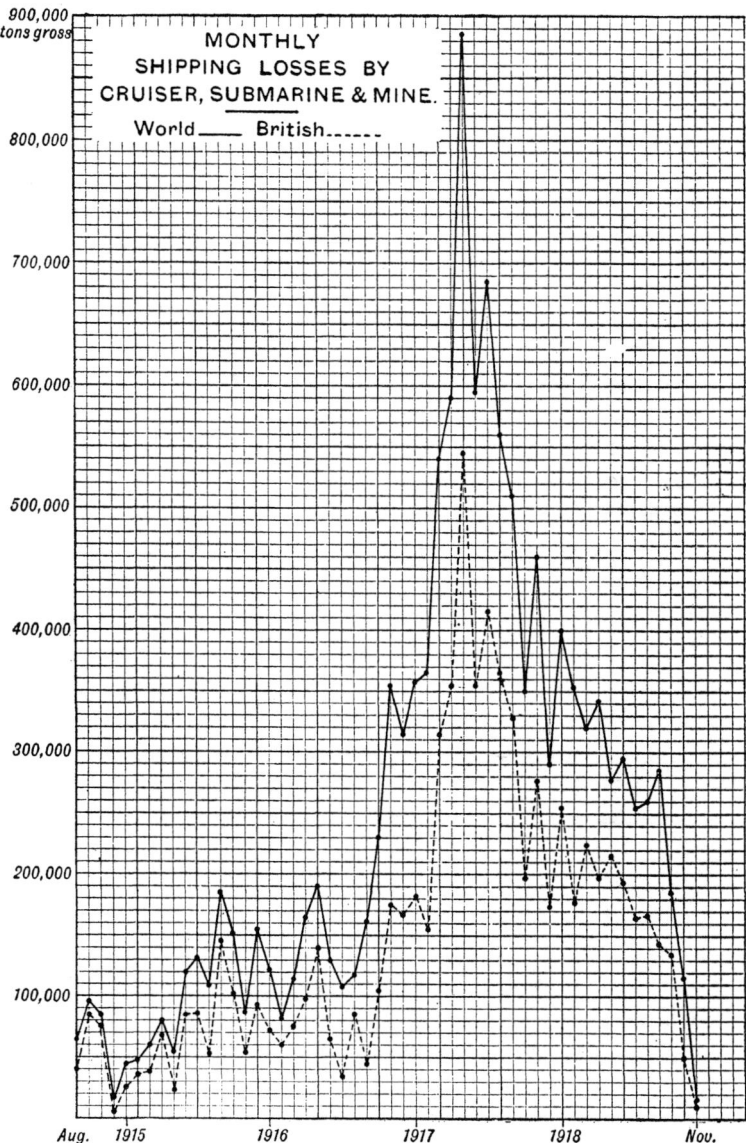

Altogether, not less than 881,000 tons gross of the world's shipping descended into the depths during this single month, one-third of which was lost in the Mediterranean. American shipping was never seriously molested, as the German authorities deemed it inexpedient to embitter this new and powerful enemy. Up to the close of the war, American losses totalled just over half a million tons gross.

Appalling as these figures of British losses were, they presented neither the full sum of devastation nor the extreme gravity of the situation. Besides ships destroyed, there were many damaged and temporarily out of useful employment. In April about 80,000 tons were crippled by torpedo attack, and mines wounded another 47,587 tons. An average of 150 ships repaired each month was maintained for a considerable period. In one particular week there were actually under repair the colossal figure of 2,120,301 tons—more than one-ninth of British mercantile tonnage in 1914. To give a more graphic idea, those two million odd tons represented on an average 600 ships, of 3500 tons each, out of cargo-carrying service.

The replacement of lost ships by new hulls was naturally a problem that rose in urgency progressively with the losses. It seemed to be impossible to protect shipping afloat; so much had been lost that defeat was almost in sight; more and more, new ships were demanded, in the hope that a few might survive the perils of the high seas. In May 1917 Sir Eric Geddes was appointed Shipping Controller of both naval and mercantile tonnage. So far, the claims of the combatant and non-combatant sea-services had been in constant competition; now they were to be dealt with by one authority. In 1915, in the United Kingdom, 688,000 tons of new shipping had been put afloat; in 1916 the figure dropped to 538,000 tons. During the first half of 1917 some 484,000 tons had been built; it was hoped that a million tons would be constructed in the second half; actually the increase proved to be slight, and instead only 620,000 tons were put out from the shipyards. The world's ports were ransacked for tonnage. Decrepit steamers fetched fabulous prices, and even old sailing-vessels, derelict or used as harbour hulks, were reconditioned and sent out to sea again.

Although, with the purchase of other tonnage, new British

THE CRISIS

shipping totalled 1,493,474 tons for the year, the results fell far below the estimated output. In March 1918 Lord Pirrie was appointed Controller-General of Merchant Shipbuilding, and the position improved slightly. In this year, 1,534,110 tons were built, only about half of the hoped-for three millions. In October 1917 Sir Joseph Maclay (who succeeded Sir E. Geddes when the latter was appointed First Lord) warned America that unless she could turn out six million tons of new ships, her military efforts were foredoomed.

When it is considered that in the first half of 1917 over two million tons of British shipping were wiped out, both from hostile action and the ordinary marine risks, and in the latter half another one and three-quarter millions were destroyed, the deficit by tonnage lost, as against tonnage built or acquired, is seen to be two and a quarter millions. Up to the end of 1917, from the outbreak of war, three million tons had been built in the United Kingdom, 780,000 tons of enemy shipping had been captured, but over seven million tons had been destroyed or lost, leaving over three millions as the net wastage of war.

Even this great shipbuilding drive could not master the situation. What was the use of turning out new ships, if they were to be slaughtered as soon as they were completed? Day by day the value of the vessels in service mounted. The ship famine was yet further aggravated by the unavoidable diversions and hold-ups of traffic. No longer did the vessels bound for the East and the Antipodes pass through the Mediterranean; in the Indian trade alone, the loss of time was estimated as an equivalent of forty ships' wastage.

During April, when the climax of this fearful mortality was reached, there were 21 North Sea U-boats out, either returning or setting off or on station; 8 Flanders boats were in the Channel or south Irish waters; and 13 others were ravaging the Mediterranean traffic. It was not by any means the maximum number; yet more submarines appeared at sea in months subsequent to this, but never again did the *noyade* of the sea-traders attain so appalling a total.

One of the worst features of the spring warfare was its

vindictive concentration against hospital-ships, in pursuance of the January warning. So far, mines had been responsible for the accidents to these ships—the *Anglia, Galeka, Britannic,* and *Braemar Castle*—and it is believed that a mine was the cause of the first 1917 casualties. Shortly before midnight on March 1, 1917, the *Glenart Castle* (6807 tons) was off the Owers L.V. when a terrific explosion occurred, plunging the ship into darkness. Fortunately the night was fine, with haze and a smooth sea, enabling the 525 patients, the staff of 68, and crew of 115 to tranship without loss. The vessel herself was brought into Southampton before she foundered.

There was no doubt about the next loss ; Berlin was even anxious to proclaim it as a U-boat success. At midnight on March 20 the *Asturias* (12,002 tons) was attacked for the second time, and was not so fortunate as before. Six days out from Malta, she had landed her wounded at Avonmouth, and was then on her way to Southampton. She was steaming at $14\frac{1}{2}$ knots, fully lighted, and bore all the distinctive markings required by the Hague Convention. The weather was clear, with a choppy sea. Hit aft by the torpedo, she settled down in shallow water off the Start, after all except 41 of the staff and crew had taken to the boats safely. Later she was refloated and brought into Plymouth.

Ten days later, again at midnight, the *Gloucester Castle* (7999 tons) met a similar fate off the Isle of Wight. She was carrying about 400 patients ; and, although the ship was rolling heavily in the rough sea, they were transhipped to the liner *Karnak,* the destroyer *Beagle,* and patrol-boat P 19. Only two of the crew were lost, and one patient died later. This vessel was also towed in and repaired.

It had been assumed that the *Asturias* attack might have been due to a mistake, but the subsequent outrage left no doubt of a deliberate terroristic policy. In consequence, Allied aeroplanes on April 14 bombed the town of Freiburg, in the Black Forest, as a ' measure of reprisal,' causing small damage to the aerodrome but several civilian casualties. The French adopted the plan of carrying German officers on board their hospital-ships, to which the Germans replied by exposing triple the number of French officers in the firing line. Nothing

VIII. THE HOSPITAL SHIP *GLOUCESTER CASTLE* BEACHED.
Torpedoed by a Submarine in the Channel, on March 31, 1917, despite the injury inflicted, the ship was towed into shallow water before she foundered. The photograph shews her with her stern resting on the bottom; later, she was refloated.

THE CRISIS 165

more clearly demonstrated the futility of reprisals and counter-reprisals.

The mining of the *Salta* (7284 tons) on April 10 was most unfortunate. A mine-field had been laid off Le Havre and located during the morning half a mile north of the Whistle Buoy. The hospital-ship was conducted past the field, but, for some unknown reason, the master turned back, and was carried by the heavy seas into the danger area ; the explosion caused such havoc that she sank in five minutes, taking down with her 9 nurses, 42 of the staff, and 79 of the crew. Rescue work by the destroyer *Druid* and the patrol P 26 checked the loss of life greatly ; but an hour later P 26 herself also blew up, with the loss of 16 lives. Mines off Le Havre claimed the destroyer *Derwent* on May 2, when 62 of her complement were missing.

The last attacks on hospital-ships in home waters in 1917 were made on the night of April 17. At about half-past seven in the evening the *Lanfranc* (6287 tons) was 42 miles N. $\frac{1}{2}$ E. from Le Havre, lighted up but escorted by the destroyer *Badger* and P 37. She was carrying 234 British and 167 German wounded, a staff of 52, and a crew of 123. The stricken ship quickly settled down. In spite of the heavy seas running, and the fighting amongst the Germans for a place in the boats (resulting in the capsizing of one), only 4 British and 15 German wounded and 5 of the crew were drowned.

The same evening, about an hour and a half later, the ambulance-transport *Donegal* (1885 tons), escorted by the destroyers *Jackal* and *Liffey*, was struck by a torpedo and the whole of her stern was blown away. Amongst her 639 patients were 33 stretcher cases ; the weather here, 19 miles south from the Dean L.V., was fine and clear, enabling the rescue work to be carried out swiftly. The ship sank within an hour, and the loss of life was confined to 29 wounded and 11 of the crew.

The attacks detailed above proved that, as long as Germany pursued this murderous vendetta against hospital-ships, the brilliant distinguishing lights and marks served only to provide a more distinctive target ; and these symbols of mercy were therefore abandoned. Hospital-ships engaged in cross-

Channel service henceforth ran as ambulance-transports, and so came to share in that extraordinary immunity which, throughout the war, characterized the work of the small troopships. In the case of the ambulance-transport *Donegal*, a gun was carried astern ; she had been chased by a submarine on March 1, before she had received this armament.[1]

These were the last of the 1917 attacks, excepting one in the Mediterranean in May ; and until the early part of 1918 the German submarines stayed their hand. In August 1917 an agreement, whereby eleven Spanish officers were carried aboard the hospital-ships in the Mediterranean, was reached ; the officers were to embark and disembark at Gibraltar. The German Government at the same time affirmed that hospital-ships were free to passage in the Atlantic and North Sea ; but any found in the Channel would be destroyed.

Another feature of the new campaign was the number of attacks on oilers. Sixteen of these valuable vessels were sunk from the end of March to the beginning of September, whilst no fewer than 115 colliers were sent to the bottom in 1917. One consequence of this heavy tanker loss was the reduction of the usual six to eight months' reserve of oil fuel to *eight weeks' supply* ; and it became necessary to provide escorts for these slow and lengthy ships through the danger zone. Steaming of the Grand Fleet had to be restricted, so that on this score, the submarine war on shipping *did* produce a material effect on the purely naval campaign. In this crisis the large liner companies came to the rescue ; and in the

[1] No immunity from legitimate attack at sea was ever claimed for the ambulance-transports. These vessels had therefore the right, in common with all other merchant-ships of the belligerent Powers, to equip themselves with a defensive armament. Ambulance-transports were not allowed to be painted in the colours laid down by the Hague Convention for hospital-ships ; further, they were not allowed to display the illuminated marks or signs at night, indicating the presence of a hospital-ship at sea. Ambulance-transports were, for all practical purposes, military store-ships and carriers, whose liability to attack was admitted. If an ambulance-transport was *legitimately* sunk when carrying wounded, and the wounded suffered injury, the responsibility lay with those who owned, chartered, or controlled the vessel, for using a non-immune mercantile-ship for the conveyance of the wounded. No charge of a contravention of the Hague Convention could, under such circumstances, be made against the enemy.

double bottoms of Cunard liners some 100,000 tons of oil fuel were carried, and in those of the White Star line about 80,000 tons.

Only two submarines were destroyed in April, both mine-laying craft. In this month we find that British submarines based on Scapa Flow, Lough Swilly, Killybegs (in western Ireland), and—in the southern area of the North Sea—the old 'C'-class boats operated against the U-boats. Altogether, 7 hostile submarines were caught by their counterparts on the Allied side in 1917, and 6 in the following year. Value also lay in this antidote by its very threat. The suspected presence of an Allied submarine would cause a German boat to dive hurriedly and decamp to another locality; thus the raider was scared off and suffered impediment in her work. At about half-past three in the morning of April 5, UC 68 (Degetau) was returning to Zeebrugge, when a torpedo shot into her hull and blew her up. The British submarine C 7 had been waiting off the Schouwen gas-buoy, hoping to catch U-boats entering Zeebrugge by this channel, and her expectations were not disappointed. On the 19th, UC 30 (Stenzler) was mined in the North Sea.

In the western seas, however, during April, the U-boats pursued their work of devastation almost unhindered. Between 10 and 15 boats were operating out here, amongst them the veteran U 21, back from the Mediterranean. Daily, 5 British merchant-ships were sent to the bottom; so, in this month alone, the dwindling mercantile marine of the United Kingdom was further reduced by the deletion of 155 hulls. A particularly bad case occurred on the 8th, when Werner of U 55 sank the steamer *Torrington* (5597 tons), 150 miles south-west of the Scillies, with the loss of 34 lives. The master was taken prisoner. On August 31, 1921, he testified at Bow Street police-court that, after the crew had left their ship in two boats, he was ordered on board the submarine, together with his boat's crew. German sailors then entered the boat and rowed across to the sinking steamer. He himself was taken into the U 55; then, to his horror, he found that Werner had ordered his submarine to be submerged with the twenty men still outside on her deck. This submarine commander was one of the most cruel and cowardly of those men who defamed their nation, dishonoured their flag, and disgraced the uniform they wore. As for the other boat's crew, the German sailors certainly boarded her, as the master subsequently saw articles from this boat in their possession. Neither boat nor crew was ever seen again. In precisely the same manner he murdered the crew of the *Toro* (3066 tons) on the 12th, 200 miles W.N.W. from Ushant, after capturing her master.

Werner was but following out the policy later recommended by Count Luxburg, the *chargé d'affaires* at Buenos Ayres, who in May 1917 advised that two small Argentine steamers, *Oran* and *Gauza*, then nearing Bordeaux, should be ' spared if possible, or else sunk without leaving a trace '— (*spurlos versenkt*). Unhappily, many neutral ships were posted as missing during this terrible time, whether due to marine risk, torpedo or mine, will ever remain unknown.

Other notable losses in this memorable month include the Leyland liner *Canadian* (9309 tons) on the 5th, 47 miles N.W. by W. from Fastnet, with her master; the *Powhatan* (6117 tons) on the following day, 25 miles N. by W. from North Rona, with 36 of her crew; the *Vine Branch* (3442 tons), of which no trace was ever found, nor of the 44 comprising her crew; the Elder-Dempster *Aburi* (3730 tons) on the 17th, 125 miles N.W. of Tory Island, with 25 lives; the *Caithness* (3500 tons) on the 19th, 130 miles N.W. by N. from Cape Ortegal, with 47 of her crew; the tanker *San Hilario* (10,157 tons) on the 20th, 270 miles W. by N. from Fastnet, whose master was taken prisoner; the Anchor-Brocklebank *Malakand* (7653 tons) on the same day, 145 miles W. ½ N. from Bishop Rock, with one life lost; the Elder-Dempster *Abosso* (7782 tons) on the 24th, 180 miles W. by N. from Fastnet, with 65 lives; the troopship *Ballarat* (11,120 tons), with Anzacs, on the next day, 24 miles S. by W. from the Wolf Rock, the troops being transhipped without loss; the *Alfalfa* (2993 tons), which disappeared with her entire crew of 24; and the fine P. & O. liner *Medina* (12,350 tons) on the 28th, 3 miles E.N.E. from the Start, with 6 lives. In this month also about 24 British masters were taken prisoner by the U-boats, a practice intended to daunt the spirit of British merchant officers! Amongst the neutral vessels was the American *Aztec* (3727 tons), sunk off Cape Finisterre on the 2nd.

On the other side of the scales there was little to set as counterpoise to the carnage of shipping. There were substantial grounds for hoping that at least one raider had met her doom in western waters, but even this was disproved. On April 13 the new U 93 left Emden on her maiden trip, under Count Spiegel von und zu Peckelsheim, late of U 32. Until the fifth day not a sail or funnel was sighted; but on the 18th Spiegel met the returning U 43 (Jürst), and was advised to steer three hundred miles to the south-west, where plenty of shipping would be found on a new route. Acting on this advice, Spiegel claimed that he sank eleven ships of 27,400 tons, including an American ammunition-carrier, which blew up with every living soul aboard; further, that he took prisoner 5 masters and 12 gunners from the armed merchant-ships. On the morning of the 30th he encountered his *confrère* Hersing in U 21 engaged in sinking a Swedish sailing-vessel; and towards evening he himself came across another sail, a small three-masted schooner, which he brought-to with a warning shell. The crew appeared to have abandoned their ship and had taken to the boats, lying-to on their oars about seventy yards away on the starboard quarter. Whilst Spiegel scrutinized the topsail schooner in every detail, U 93 continued to pump shell after shell into the prize; for forty minutes the little victim endured this hail of death. Unknown to Spiegel, men lay concealed aboard the apparently harmless schooner, waiting to unmask their hidden guns and overwhelm their attacker; they were the crew of the decoy *Prize* (Q 21), under Lieutenant W. E. Sanders, R.N.R. Satisfied that this was no submarine trap, and that the schooner had no submarine in tow, Spiegel closed in to one hundred yards and gave orders to aim for her waterline and sink her. U 93 came up from astern, taking no risks; then she started to pass along on the port side. At that moment Sanders blew his whistle—the sign for the Ensign to be run up and guns to be unmasked. At short range U 93 was speedily disabled. Her conning-tower was wrecked, her forward gun was knocked overboard, and those in the decoy saw a dull glow inside her riddled hull. Four minutes later U 93 disappeared, leaving Spiegel and two seamen in the water, to be captured by the decoy. As for the *Prize*, she was kept afloat by herculean efforts, and made Kinsale two days after. Thence she proceeded across to Milford Haven, narrowly escaping being sunk by U 62. Sanders was awarded the Victoria Cross, but unfortunately his career was only too brief. In June he reported he had met either one or two enemy submarines, which had kept out of range, diving and reappearing. It is believed that the U-boat took a photograph or a sketch of the *Prize* for future recognition. On August 13, when cruising off the Irish coast with a 'D'-class submarine in tow, the decoy fell in with the newly-completed UB 48 (Steinbauer), *en route* for Cattaro, and opened fire at two hundred yards. The U-boat thereupon slid under the surface. The Q-boat's danger became extreme, for, by opening fire, her true nature had been disclosed. During the night the British submarine in company heard a loud explosion; and when she came up to investigate, the gallant Sanders, his ship and her company, had disappeared for ever. Two torpedoes from UB 48 had utterly expunged the three-masted schooner from the face of the waters.

Despite her lurid disappearance at the end of her duel with the *Prize*, U 93 was not sunk. When she was caught by her opponent's broadside, a hit forward stunned the second-in-command, Lieutenant Ziegler. As soon as he recovered, thinking that Spiegel was safely below, he shouted orders to zigzag. U 93, listing heavily to starboard and half-submerged—blind, battered, bleeding—crawled away through a tornado of shell into the merciful obscurity of the dusk. Her conning-tower and the hatch leading to the captain's quarters were wrecked, preventing any hope of escape by diving. Although no damage was reported below, the deck was riddled and the diving- and oil-tanks holed. U 93 was no longer submersible; she had barely enough fuel in her remaining unpierced tanks to bring her into port round the north of Scotland. Incredible though it seemed, Ziegler brought the

IX. THE DESTROYER *TETRARCH* KEEPING WATCH OVER A PATCH OF OIL.

Sometimes, if a German submarine was hotly pressed and heavily attacked by depth-charges, she would " play 'possum " and pretend to be dead. Oil fuel, compressed air, seamen's caps, papers, pieces of wood, etc., were ejected from the submarine, in the hope that her demise would be taken for granted by the hunters above, and the attack would be broken off.

THE CRISIS

wounded boat into List, and from thence was towed to Wilhelmshaven, where the much-lacerated submarine arrived on May 11.

In April another Q-boat was lost. On the 21st, U 62 (Hashagen) had left for the west; and on this—the day on which Spiegel came to grief, April 30—she sank the disguised sloop *Tulip* (Q 12) off the Irish coast, suspicions of true identity having been aroused by a trifling error in the sloop's disguise—the flying of the Red Ensign, an unusual sight in those days. Her commander was taken prisoner. On the previous day another decoy sloop, *Heather* (Q 16), had sighted two boat-crews and a submarine, the latter coming up astern rapidly and opening fire. From the decoy a panic party put off and made towards the U-boat. Just as the submarine moved into a most favourable position, another sloop hove in sight, whereupon the enemy began to submerge. As a final desperate resort, the commander of the *Heather* tried to ram, and dropped overboard depth-charges on the spot where the enemy had disappeared. A torpedo, ineffective in aim, simultaneously streaked from the submarine past the sloop. A couple of further depth-charges ended the duel. Oil and a sheaf of papers came up from the submarine, which might denote a sorely-damaged U-boat or be merely a 'blind.' Certain submarines owed their escape to the release of dummy papers and discharge of oil at moments when they found themselves uncomfortably pressed by the attentions of the enemy above. In this case there were grounds for supposing the U-boat shammed death; for a few days later the *Heather* met a submarine which deliberately shelled her again and again. The panic party put off; the decoy was badly wrecked and her top-bridge hit. Patiently the concealed gunners awaited word to fire. The U-boat ceased to shell the sloop. One of the decoy's crew crawled forward, to find Commander Hallwright dead. The U-boat was diving, and it was too late now to avenge their captain. The *Heather* put back into Queenstown with the body of her gallant commander.

Finally, in the North Sea a U-boat attempted to penetrate Scapa Flow on the night of April 12; but being detected by hydrophones and attacked in Hoxa Sound by motor launches with depth-charges, she failed—as U 18 had failed in November 1914—to enter this inviolate anchorage of the Grand Fleet.

Everywhere the submarines were succeeding in the predicted decimation of England's vital trade; everywhere the defence seemed to make little or no headway against the vindictive and determined onslaught. Upon the graphic chart the line denoting losses had leapt upwards at an appalling slant. Let that gradient be prolonged onwards a few months into the future; it would inevitably intersect the ordinate that meant Starvation !—Defeat !—Surrender ! The crisis of the whole naval war—of her very existence—was upon Great Britain. Her commerce and her merchant navy, built up by the labour of centuries, were both swiftly crumbling, disintegrating before her eyes :

> 'That trade's proud empire hastes to swift decay,
> As ocean sweeps the laboured mole away.'

CHAPTER IX

THE STRUGGLE FOR MASTERY

(May–September 1917)

THE month of May initiated the primal wane of the German drive. After June the curve of shipping casualties caused by the U-boats began to descend steadily. What was the cause of this slow decrease in the rate of destruction ? No single reason can be adduced ; it rather was the collective outcome of many antidotal measures, at last yielding return. When Admiral Jellicoe came to Whitehall in November 1916 to tackle the coming peril, he fully realized that few of the methods he adopted could mature before the following midsummer. No increase of patrol craft could be hoped for until July, and the most that could be done was to use the existing forces to the best possible advantage. Meanwhile, the numerical deficiencies of the patrol craft were daily becoming more evident.

Convoys of merchantmen had already been suggested ; but, owing to the lack of escorting vessels, the idea had not been considered possible or practicable on a large scale. What was required was a number of fast shallow-draught escorts ; everywhere the cry went up for such craft. They were not to be had, or not to be spared. Cruisers and armed merchantcruisers were as open to torpedo attack as their charges ; and owing to the growing famine in shipping, any more merchantships could not be taken over for conversion into combatant vessels. Troop convoys, when passing through the danger zone, had been escorted independently ; and the officers in charge of such groups declared that convoy of ordinary merchant-vessels was not feasible. Determined, however, to leave no avenue unexplored, the Naval Staff conferred with a number of masters in February 1917 on the subject of convoys; and the latter once again expressed their opinion that it would be impossible to keep their ships in station when in company with twelve to twenty other vessels. They believed, however, convoy groups of two, or even three, vessels might be adopted![1] It is but just to state that there were grave and valid objections to the introduction of the convoy method. For one thing, it would entail great delay in the arrival of merchant-ships, inasmuch as the speed of these ships, when assembled in convoys, would perforce have to be that of the slowest unit in company. For another thing, the ports of assembly presented serious difficulties, because the harbours selected for the congregation of shipping into convoys would inevitably become congested. Not until the United States entered the war was the problem solved of finding suitable assembly ports on the farther side of the Atlantic. Finally, should a convoy stumble across a mine-field, the losses that might be sustained by the merchant fleet would be far more severe than those suffered under the method of individual ship-sailings.

Encouraging results had been attained with the French Coal Trade and the Scandinavian Convoy; in March the latter came under the custody of the Grand Fleet destroyers. But (as has been previously remarked) the good results obtained in these two instances were derived more from route-protection than from convoying proper. Convoy in the Atlantic was a very difficult matter. It was estimated that fifty cruisers or armed merchant-ships would be required for homeward traffic alone; an additional twelve would be necessary for outward trade. Only eighteen vessels at that time were available. These large escorts would bring over the convoy to a rendezvous outside the zone of submarine activity, and there hand over the ships to fast shallow-draught escorts. For the latter type of escort it was estimated that eighty-one destroyers or sloops were necessary, with an additional forty-eight trawlers for the slow convoys from Gibraltar. For outward traffic, forty-four additional small escorts were required.

[1] Spiess also says, in his book, that the Germans themselves considered the convoy system to be impracticable with modern steamships.

THE STRUGGLE FOR MASTERY 175

The required escort-ships simply did not exist. An alternative was put forward to convoy a part of the trade and leave the rest entirely undefended, and consequently the crews of these unescorted ships would be lost wholesale. Such an idea could not be entertained, and the augmentation of the existing patrol and escort forces had to be obtained by denuding other spheres of such craft. Although the Harwich force was running the weekly convoy between Holland and the Thames, as well as undertaking its usual arduous duties, certain destroyers were spared from there, and between eight and twelve collected from the Grand Fleet.

The entry of the United States, although it resulted in the addition of six American destroyers to the Queenstown strength on May 4, had a greater effect in releasing from blockade work the majority of the armed merchant-cruisers comprising the famous 10th Cruiser Squadron. Most of the trade entering the neutral countries adjacent to Germany came from the United States; now it was possible to absorb gradually these blockading cruisers into the convoying forces. The dissolution of this squadron began in June. Into the escort service were also pressed old U.S. battleships and cruisers, besides the 2nd Cruiser Squadron of the Grand Fleet, the North American and West Indies Squadron, and battleships from the Mediterranean. To these were further added certain of the faster cargo-steamers, armed with 6-inch guns (but carrying cargo), to serve as convoy cruisers.

Ports of assembly were organized at Gibraltar, Sierra Leone, Dakar, Hampton Roads, New York, Halifax (N.S.), and Sydney (Cape Breton). From these ports in 1917, sailings every eight days were inaugurated, with the exception of Gibraltar and Hampton Roads, from which sailings took place every four days.

The adoption of convoy meant sailing in close formation at night and in fog, without lights and with no certainty of keeping to a constant speed. The fear that convoy might break down under the conditions of modern warfare was soon dissipated, and none can doubt that the system proved the salvation of the Allies. Excepting Gibraltar, the overseas assembly ports for the convoys were remote from the German submarine bases, and so were fairly safe from the raiders. Steamers proceeding singly along the American coast to collect at their assembly ports might be molested, but a sustained attack on those vessels would require large submarines of over 1000 tons in surface displacement. During the earlier half of 1917 Germany possessed no U-boats of such a size. Her boats of 800 to 850 tons could strike out into mid-Atlantic, but, ranging the ocean wastes there, they now had but little hope of picking off solitary victims. The only chance of encountering targets was to lurk about inshore and wait until the convoy approached the coast and its steamers dispersed to their several ports of destination. But operations inshore meant that the U-boats had to work within closely patrolled areas, there to suffer frequent interruptions, attacks, and, very often, final disaster.

That the Scandinavian convoy had already worried the enemy is evident from Spiess, who relates that he had been sent to observe the traffic across the North Sea and study the chances of successful attack on convoys. He reported that the toll of a ship or two, even if exacted from every convoy encountered, would never stop the flow of traffic, and only a raid by surface ships and a wholesale massacre would produce a deterrent effect.[1]

On May 20, 1917, the first convoy reached England from Gibraltar without any loss.[2] It was followed by another, arriving from Hampton Roads, likewise intact. The first assembly numbered 17 ships, and the second 12. By August all homeward-bound ships from Gibraltar, America, and the South Atlantic, with a speed of less than 12 knots, were convoyed ; and, later, fast convoys were sailed. Naturally the U-boats began to devote their attention to the outward-bound ships in preference to the convoyed inward traffic. In spite of elaborate arrangements for escorts to take out a convoy

---

[1] His report bore fruit ; two strong raids, one by light cruisers and the other by destroyers, were afterwards made on the Scandinavian convoy, with very effective results.

[2] A convoy of eleven steamers had left Sierra Leone for the United Kingdom on January 14, 1917, escorted by H.M. armed merchant-cruisers *Almanzora* and *Arlanza*, and had arrived without loss. This convoy had no relation to submarine attack ; it was being escorted home during the *Möwe's* raid.

THE STRUGGLE FOR MASTERY 177

and bring back another inward bound, storms and other causes dislocated or delayed the working system. It was inevitable that the crews of these hard-driven escorting vessels should break down under the additional strain. Nevertheless, by October no fewer than 1502 steamers of 10,656,300 tons d.w. in 99 convoys had been brought into port, with the loss of only 24 vessels ; of these, only 10 had been sunk in convoy. The remainder were lost either after separating or through the disobedience of their masters.

An outstanding feature amongst the results of convoy was that, during the last four months of the year, only 6 ships were sunk farther out to sea than 50 miles, instead of 175 vessels similarly destroyed during the period from April to August. Before the introduction of convoy, ships were being slaughtered at anything up to 300 miles out in the Atlantic. As sinking occurred closer inshore, the loss of life was consequently lessened, and the enemy had to relinquish his practice of taking prisoner the masters of merchant-vessels.

May also brought into practice the 'dazzle' scheme of ship-painting, as perfected by Lieutenant Norman Wilkinson, R.N.V.R. Dazzled models of all types of ships, war and mercantile, were prepared ; then examined at varying angles and under various conditions of light, both by direct vision and periscope. The whole idea was to falsify perspective. It is doubtful whether these dazzle-painted ships caused many submarine commanders at the periscope to mis-estimate the target's course and speed.[1] Other anti-submarine measures included the provision of smoke-boxes to put up a screen between the raider and her victim ; defensive armaments ; the reduction of funnel smoke ; the use of observation kite-balloons with the convoys ; zigzagging courses (which baffled the enemy to a large degree) ; the stationing of trawlers equipped with hydrophones ahead of the convoy ; the inconspicuous rig of the standard cargo-vessels (with short funnel, single light pole mast, and housed derricks and standards) ; and instructional classes for mercantile-marine masters in outwitting the U-boats.

From Spiess we learn of an interesting sidelight on the anti-

[1] *The Merchant Navy*, vol. iii. (Hurd), pp. 212-28.

submarine measures which were being adopted. He relates that the commander of U 49, returning to Emden from a special-duty cruise—observation of the East Coast traffic conditions—reported that he had passed through a new ordeal. He had been attacked by 'marine bombs.' The tidings created a sensation at the Ems base of the U-boats; it was patent that a new peril had to be faced. No longer was the sea a protective cloak; no longer was safety to be found in diving. Spiess himself a short time afterwards experienced his first depth-charge attack, and he did not like it. His boat was plunged into darkness as the lights flickered in and out, and she rocked violently at each concussion. Fortunately for him, the hull stood the strain, and he put as much distance as possible between himself and the convoy he had attacked, and from which he had received so rude a welcome.

This German report of the first depth-charge attack is curious. Ten months earlier—that is, in July 1916—UC 7 had been destroyed by depth-charge; the same month, UB 44 had also been sunk from this cause; in December, UC 19 had been likewise fatally injured. In none of these cases were there any survivors. In one or two other sinkings, depth-charges had been employed to administer the *coup de grâce* to a shelled or rammed submarine. Many other U-boats had actually been attacked by these weapons,[1] but it is clear that the attacked had remained unaware of the new method employed to injure them. U 49 seems to have been the first submarine to bring back definite information of this potent device—an invention used from that time onwards with increasing deadliness. Using this new weapon, war-vessels became a new and formidable force of sea-grenadiers. Immense orders for the supply of depth-charges were placed, but time had to elapse before such contracts could be brought to fruition.

Until the new British mine became available, the vast mining scheme of the Bight of Heligoland could not be undertaken. Three fields were laid in the Bight during January;

---

[1] See action of *Quickly* and *Gunner*, July 1915, p. 47. During December 1916, the Austro-Hungarian XX had been netted and depth-charged by British drifters, but she got back to her base after the ordeal.

they failed to catch a single submarine, and were swept up by the Germans soon after they were laid. Lord Jellicoe has stated that, during experiments, just one-third of British mines exploded against a target submarine ; and that in April 1917 there was a stock of 20,000—of which only 1500 were fit for laying ! In the face of such a crippling handicap, little in the way of decisive success could be expected.

From the earliest days of the war the Germans had established defensive fields off their coast. Outside these were laid the British fields of mines and nets ; but it was not until September 1917 that a reliable type of mine, mooring-gear and sinker, known as Mark H 2, was evolved and became available in quantity.

It will be recalled that in July 1916, U 51 had been destroyed in the estuary of the Ems, far up in the swept channel, by the submarine H 5, whose commanding officer received castigation for infraction of his standing orders in leaving his station, and deferment of his D.S.O. for twelve months. On May 14, 1917, another boat, U 59 (von Firks), was being escorted to the barrage-fields during foggy weather ; failing to pick up the navigational aids to the south-east of Horns Reef, she met with disaster in the German mine-barrier. Salvage craft were rushed to the spot ; but one after another they too blew up, and the work had to be abandoned on the 16th. On the night of May 16-17, U 86 was being taken out to sea when one of her escort, the destroyer S 17 of the Ems outpost flotilla, foundered on a mine. Next day, however, the submarine was got to sea safely. A few days earlier, May 10, the new mine-layer UC 76 (Barten) had been loading up mines at Heligoland, when one of them exploded and detonated the others ; the boat sank at once, with her commander, but was raised later. From extracts which Scheer gives in his diary, a vivid picture is painted of the spring campaign.[1] Daily the mine-laying submarines left for the Bell Rock, the Channel, Irish and Scottish waters, and the Clyde approaches ; and the mortality of these UC-boats grew exceedingly high, no fewer than 52 of the first 79 failing to survive until the close of the war.

[1] *High Sea Fleet* (Scheer), p. 281 *et seq.*

Both from German and Flanders bases the UC-boats worked. On April 30 the UC 26 (von Schmettow) left Ostend to lay mines in the Channel. This boat, which had joined the Flanders flotilla in November 1916, suffered from continuous defects. Just as repairs were completed, a fire broke out in a steamer in the basin at Ostend and further damaged the submarine. At last UC 26 was ready for sea, and duly sailed. Trouble with the motors did not prevent her mining Havre, Ouistreham, and Cherbourg; during such operations she was attacked by aircraft. After this, on May 3, she cruised along the Southampton-Cherbourg-Havre route, hoping to attack shipping. This course proving singularly unprofitable, Schmettow bore up for Zeebrugge on the 8th. He seems to have been an incurable optimist, a trait which cost him dear. As dawn broke on the 9th, UC 26 was discovered by the destroyer *Milne* to the north-west of Calais. Insisting that the patrol had not seen him, Schmettow waited just a little too long before giving the order to dive. The deck was awash as the stem of the *Milne* sheared through the inner pressure-hull. The submarine sank like a stone and crashed heavily on the bottom. Depth-charges dropped by the *Mentor* and *Miranda* sealed her doom; water rushed into the riven UC 26. Two of the crew, who made an air-lock escape to the surface, were the only survivors.[1]

On May 20 another of these mine-layers was destroyed. During 1917 the Flanders boats began to be extremely worried by the vigilant seaplane patrol in the southern North Sea, and six were bombed out of existence during the summer months. The favourite method of attack was to swoop down on the U-boat from out of the sun. Vain was the scan of the heavens by the blinded submarine look-out for the hornet hurtling down from the nave of the solar aureole. Only by rapid diving could a U-boat hope for escape, and even then the water must be deep. The first success was gained on this day (May 20), when UC 36 (Buch) was hit twice by bombs from seaplane 8663, off the West Hinder L.V., the submarine sinking by the stern.

A third of these mine-layers met her end far from her base.

[1] 'Submarine Tragedies,' P. A. Roll (*Revista Marittima*, Rome, Nov. 1925).

Leaving Brunsbüttel on May 25 to lay mines off Valentia Island, on the south-west coast of Ireland, UC 29 (Rosenow) torpedoed and badly damaged a small steamer off the south Irish coast on the morning of June 7. The torpedo wrecked the engines, the stokehold was flooding, and escaping steam added to the perils of the crew, who were seen to be leaving their ship. Rosenow, a very cautious man, waited half-an-hour before he broke surface and, passing the steamer, made for the boat crew, who were starting to pull back to their damaged vessel. Such an impudent action made Rosenow forget his caution, and he opened fire on the boat crew. Still the seamen pulled on, until they lay between the torpedoed steamer and the submarine. For those on board the *Pargust* the awaited moment had come. Commander Gordon Campbell gave the word to fire. Listing badly, UC 29 passed ahead with the crew holding up their hands. Fire was withheld, whereupon UC 29 tried to make off! Again and again was she shelled, until, raked, riddled, and rent, she heeled over on her beam ends and sank, never to reappear. Two Germans were picked up. For his conduct in this, his third successful duel, Commander Campbell was promoted Captain and received a bar to his D.S.O., and Lieutenant Stuart and Seaman Williams received the Victoria Cross by ballot of the crew. As for the shattered *Pargust*, she was taken in tow by the sloop *Crocus*, whilst the sloop *Zinnia* and the American destroyer *Cushing* stood by.

Two other submarines were destroyed in May. On the 1st the large and new U 81 (R. Weisbach) was caught *in flagrante delicto*. She was sinking a steamer, about 150 miles to the south-west of Valentia Island, and was torpedoed and sunk by the British submarine E 54,[1] seven prisoners being taken. On the 17th the decoy schooner *Glen* sank UB 39 (Küstner) in a short duel, about 35 miles south of the Needles, after which action two other submarines appeared and were shelled. This schooner had two further fights in the summer, but on neither occasion did she succeed in sinking her opponent. On the other hand, UC 75 sank the sloop *Lavender* in the Channel on May 5.

The late Admiral Scheer related that U 33, one of the

---

[1] Michelsen says 'by trawler.'

Mediterranean 'Thirties,' was now working from the North Sea bases. Like Hersing's U 21, she had been recalled to join the North Sea flotillas in the great drive. Gansser, her commander, assumed command of the converted mercantile submarine U 156. This boat was a sister of the *Deutschland*; for the whole class of diving blockade-runners had been taken over for the Imperial Navy after the U.S. declaration of war. Ungainly was the build and low the speed of the 'Handels U-boote,' but they possessed the signal merits of high freeboard and great ranging power; and—as war submarines— they had a large torpedo-carrying capacity. Numbered U 151-157, they began to operate in September in the Azores-Canaries area; and the institution of this new war-station cast further burdens on the Allied resources for defence. One boat of the class crossed the Atlantic towards the end of 1917 to cut the trans-oceanic telegraph cables off the American coast.

Contrary to the generally-accepted opinion, the discipline of the German submarine crews was never broken. In May mutiny broke out in the 3rd Squadron of the High Sea Fleet; it was suppressed, but further trouble manifested itself in August aboard other battleships. The perils facing the minesweepers and barrage-breakers were certainly enough to foster unrest amongst the decimated personnel manning such craft. The submarine complements remained steadfast to the last. Cases of insanity, though by no means unknown, were not so prevalent as one might expect. The nervous tension and physical discomforts; the terrible experiences of crews which had escaped death by an hair's-breadth; the ever-increasing losses; the uncertainty as to the fate of those who never returned—all such were factors which might be expected to sap endurance and self-confidence in the bravest. Companionship in danger, active service, adventure—all these things preserved and upheld discipline. No instance has yet come to light of a submarine's crew refusing *en masse* to put to sea, no matter how dangerous an enterprise might be before them. On the other hand, the High Sea Fleet crews, through sheer inactivity, disintegrated into mutiny. The crews of the U-boats were provided with better food, received longer leave, and were allowed other privileges; they were also granted special rewards. The only effect that began to appear was that ratings no longer volunteered for this special branch, and had to be drafted into it, as into the other services. In the later stages of the war, strange cases began to develop, somewhat similar to ' shell-shock ' amongst the soldiers. Men of excellent character, who had cruised for thousands of miles in submarines, and who held highly important control-stations, suddenly collapsed and lost all will-power and sense of responsibility. Others carried out their duties badly, to the grave danger of their boat and shipmates. Spiess recounts that after a bad hydrophone and depth-charge attack the daily practice dives were clumsily carried out, simply because the nerve of the crew had been badly shaken. British submarine crews who had been accidentally attacked by British or United States warships paid full testimony to the unnerving effect of a depth-charge ' pattern.' Of the veterans forming the German submarine personnel in 1914, many perished in 1917 ; others were undergoing training for duty in the new, improved, or larger types of submarine. One noticeable difference was manifested in the crews of the later U-boats : their proficiency deteriorated, as a result of their hasty training and the inclusion of inexperienced hands in the complement. Many of the commanders of 1917-18, by their foolish or imprudent conduct, exhibited their inefficiency. During the last eighteen months of hostilities, submarines, when brought to combat and damaged, surrendered after a feeble resistance.

The month of May, as has been remarked, denoted the first ebb in this tide of destruction. British losses (106 vessels of 320,572 tons torpedoed and 14 others of 28,114 tons mined) showed a reduction of 193,000 tons, and the world total dropped by 284,000 tons. Around the British Isles the same number of boats was operating as in April; in the Mediterranean fewer were cruising. Taking the more notable casualties, we find the Blue Funnel *Troilus* (7625 tons) sunk on May 2, 140 miles W.N.W. from Malin Head ; the Cunard cargo liner *Feltria* (5254 tons) on May 5, 8 miles S.E. from Mine Head, with 45 of her crew ; the Nelson *Highland Corrie* (7583 tons) on the 16th, 4 miles S. from Owers L.V., with 5 lives ; the Federal *Middlesex* (8364 tons) on the same day, 150 miles N.W.

from Tory Island; the Ellerman *City of Corinth* (5870 tons) on the 21st, 12 miles S.W. from the Lizard; the Clan liner *Clan Murray* (4835 tons) sunk on the 29th, 40 miles W. by S. from Fastnet, with 64 souls, whose third officer and probably the third engineer were captured. Altogether, 580 British lives were sacrificed by submarine and mine during this month.

Not only were cargo and passenger-carrying vessels suffering, but the submarines were devoting their attention to the armed merchant cruisers of the 10th Cruiser Squadron, still maintaining the blockade in the high latitudes. Subjected to attack as they traversed the dangerous waters on the way to their bases to coal, four were torpedoed and sunk during 1917; one was torpedoed but regained port; and another survived mine injury. The *Motagua*, which struck a mine on March 16, reached Swarbacks Minn (in the Shetlands). Fortune, however, did not so favour the *Hilary* when on her way to this coaling base on May 25. She had just increased speed to 12½ knots after dropping her paravanes, when a torpedo from U 88 (Schwieger) crashed into her port boiler-room and flooded the furnaces. Another torpedo struck her just under No. 3 boat as it was being lowered, killing four of the crew. An hour later a third torpedo hit her on the starboard side; and the captain, lieutenant-commander, and a steward, who had remained aboard to man a gun, were forced to abandon their ship as she went down quickly.

Insufficient were the destroyers to screen these merchant cruisers on passage to and from their bases. On June 14 the second blow fell. The destroyers *Nessus* and *Noble* had been despatched to meet the *Avenger,* but when they were some thirty miles distant from their charge, early in the morning, the new merchant cruiser was torpedoed in lat. 61° 3′ N., long. 3° 57′ W. She had to be abandoned by the majority of the complement, only the captain and six others remaining on board in the hope of securing a hit on the U-boat should she appear. After an hour and a half, the submarine rose to examine the sinking ship, and then dived and disappeared. Soon afterwards the destroyers arrived, and an hour and a half later the *Noble* sighted a submarine a mile away on the *Avenger*'s port beam. Depth-charges were dropped on the spot, but without result. Shortly after noon the *Avenger* foundered. On June 27, seven of these merchant cruisers were sent to join the ocean convoy forces; for with the inauguration of unrestricted war a great transformation came over the blockade work. No longer was it a question of examining ships trying to run the blockade; Germany was out to sink every ship afloat. The only chance of survival neutral shipping possessed, outside the convoy organization, lay in steaming alone through the danger zone at the highest speed possible. The situation was further simplified when America intervened and examination ports were established outside the danger area. With American control in the western Atlantic, and the Allies' bunkering policy, and agreements with neutral shipping companies, a voyage without the approval of the Allies was rendered most difficult. On December 8, 1917, the 10th Cruiser Squadron ceased to exist, and the last three armed merchant cruisers followed their sisters to the ocean convoy squadron. But before that date they had suffered further loss.

One of the few cases in which a merchant-ship destroyed a submarine occurred on June 20. Early in the morning the Cunard cargo liner *Valeria* (5865 tons), with a cargo from New York, was off the south-west coast of Ireland, when she struck some submerged object. A little later U 99 (Eltester) rose to the surface, bows upward, with one of her periscopes broken. The gunners of the *Valeria* succeeded in depressing their gun so that they were able to hit the disabled submarine at the first shot. The third shot ended the career of U 99, catching her right at the base of the conning-tower.

Important shipping losses during June include the ex-Red Star liner *Southland* (11,899 tons) and the Ellerman *City of Baroda* (5541 tons), both sunk on the 4th to the N.W. of Tory Island, with 10 lives; the *Clan Davidson* (6486 tons) on the 24th, 130 miles S.W. by W. from the Scillies, with 12 lives; the *Don Arturo* (3680 tons), a victim of the *spurlos versenkt* policy in the Atlantic, resulting in the loss of 34 souls; and the empty troopship *Armadale* (6133 tons), sunk 160 miles N.W. from Tory Island, with 27 lives—the first troopship loss in the Atlantic. On the same day, June 27, the Cunard liner

Ultonia (10,402 tons) was sunk 190 miles S.W. from the Fastnet. Submarines were also active in the Bay of Biscay, in which area the French sweeper *Anjou* was mined on the 17th, and the French cruiser *Kléber*, homeward bound from Africa, was likewise lost ten days later.

With the arrival of June the submarines made one great effort to regain the rate of the April sinkings. Compared with 18 North Sea boats at sea in May, there were 27 operating; and it is believed that 12 stations were maintained. Taking into consideration all the various flotillas in the different theatres, never again did so many U-boats scour the seas in search of prey. Sixty-one hostile craft were making an attempt to force the pace before the various anti-submarine measures matured; two-thirds of the allotted six months had passed. The British still showed no signs of weakening. Instead, the counter-attack was becoming more deadly. The convoys were baffling the U-boats.[1]

This month, hydrophone stations were established at Newhaven, Portsmouth, Portland, and Dartmouth,[2] each with a division of motor launches equipped with depth-charges; and in 1918, listening-stations sprang up all around the coast. The introduction of the hydrophone marked the beginning of a new era in anti-submarine warfare. Hitherto, invisibility had cloaked in mystery the movements of the submarine, and had afforded an impenetrable screen to its retreat beneath the waves. As the masked assassin, poignard in hand, lurked behind the arras in mediaeval times, so did the 'gunmen' of the deep conceal their stealthy comings and goings under the league-long rollers of the Atlantic, the sandy shallows of the North Sea, and the turbulent overfalls of the Pentland Firth. The U-boats' campaign was akin to a war-time *Mafia*; like a powerful and virulent secret society, murder and mutilation accompanied by mystery were the marks of its activity.

[1] After the introduction of convoy by the British, the Germans organized a special 'target training convoy' at Kiel, consisting of merchant vessels dazzle-painted on the British system. It used to go out to sea, under escort, to take up the British formations and to zigzag according to British methods. Submarine officers, under training, were taken out to sea to watch the convoy and make practice attacks on it.

[2] So far as can be ascertained, hydrophones first began to be used in the Mediterranean during the autumn of 1917. See p. 255.

THE STRUGGLE FOR MASTERY 187

Here one moment and gone the next; wherever they appeared for one fleeting second, the stain of some vile crime as often as not sullied the purity of the seas. To hunt such malignant phantoms was to the pursuers and agents of justice almost as futile and disheartening a task as the chase of a thousand Vanderdeckens.

At long last the submarine was to be bereft of that secrecy of movement which was her barb in attack and her defence when under assault. Study of submarine sound-waves had proved that, whilst the submarine might deny itself to visual detection, its position might be followed by the auditory sense. And with this advance in methods of retaliation a large measure of the sting was taken from these pestilent sea-scorpions. Compared with the instruments now in use, the Nash Fish, the 'rubber eel,' and the K-tube of 1917-18 seem crude devices, yet they marked a definite step in the elimination of the submarines' power of evanescence and escape.

Most important of all was the moral and psychological effect on the crews. The knowledge that, even as they slunk beneath the waves, they were being followed, followed, followed—twist and turn as they might—by some remorseless pursuer above, that they had lost their hitherto inviolable secrecy of movement, could not but shake their self-control. Much did this invention contribute to breaking the nerve of the men who carried out perilous work in a type of warship hazardous to their lives; who felt every man's hand to be against them; who saw traps and snares all around them; and whose black atrocities often marked the depth of the fear that was in their souls.

To the Lizard Hydrophone Division the first success was accounted, but it was hardly due to the new acoustic apparatus. On June 12 the *Sea King*, one of the group of trawlers, sighted a UC-boat off the Lizard, made straight for her, and forced her to dive. Depth-charges were thereupon dropped on top of her. Nothing could be worse for a mine-laden submarine. Her own engines of destruction detonated; and she blew up. The hydrophones were put over the side; all was as silent as the grave, and the grave it was for the submarine. The reef-strewn sea off England's most southerly point almost ensured fatal injury to a disabled submarine which crashed to so adamantine a bed. The submarine was UC 66, commanded by Pustkuchen (the officer who had made the attack on the *Sussex* when in UB 29), and his destroyer was Commander Godfrey Herbert, R.N. (late of the Q-boat service), in charge of this trawler group.

These hydrophone units worked as far apart as visibility permitted during daylight, and at night they would shut off their engines and drift, listening for the foe, if he were under water, and hoping to catch him on the surface if 'running the charge' into the batteries under cover of darkness. By means of hydrophones, listeners could actually hear a UC-boat laying her mines ; and several groups were thus located.

Not only were these mechanical devices rendering the life of a submarine commander a burden, but the vigilance of the patrols was unceasing. UC 55, in March, laid eighteen mines off the Orkneys, and reported 'the astounding promptness of the counter-measures ; within an hour and a half to two hours after sighting her, twelve destroyers, a submarine chaser, and two sweepers were on the spot.' Again, U 57 reported 'trawlers everywhere, under the coast and thirty miles from it.' Again, UC 77, which left Germany towards the end of May to shell Aberdeen, was frustrated by destroyers, forced to dive and lay her mines off the Forth. These submarines were making strenuous efforts against the trade between England and Holland ; against the traffic entering Lerwick and Kirkwall ; and against all sea-conveyance through the North Channel; and tried to intercept injured vessels making port. Off Harwich alone, five hundred mines were swept up between January and September 1917, at the cost of three trawlers, one paddler, one drifter, but without injury to a single merchant-vessel. Not only were these mines swept up, but other means were taken to interfere with the UC-boats' work ; and UC 77 reported that dummy lighthouses had been erected on the East Anglian coast, to bewilder the mine-layers as they threaded the channels through the banks. The commander of this boat nearly came to grief on the night of June 4-5, when he attacked a patrol, which he mistook for a fishing-trawler ; UC 77 was heavily depth-charged, and her

THE STRUGGLE FOR MASTERY

oil-tanks were burst open, fifteen tons of fuel being lost. She then fouled some nets, but got clear by going ahead and astern. In the St. George's Channel the nets nearly caught UC 65, which had to dive to 197 feet to clear them.

As far back as October 1916, both Norway and Spain had prohibited the use of their waters by belligerent submarines for the purpose of refuelling or replenishing stores and victuals. When the German submarines persistently attacked Spanish fruit-carriers, in direct contravention of guaranteed immunity, the Spanish Government went further. On June 10 the steamer *Loch Lomond* (2619 tons) was attacked by submarine to the west of Gibraltar, escaping destruction by the use of her gun and smoke-boxes, and securing a hit on the enemy. Next day UC 52 was found, with serious engine defects, lying off Cadiz, whither she had been towed by a sister craft and then cast off. At Cadiz she underwent repairs and sailed on the 29th, eluding the British E 38, sent to intercept the German vessel as the latter left to resume her voyage to Cattaro. A decree was then issued by the Spanish that thenceforth any belligerent submarine found in Spanish waters would be interned; and, with one notable exception, this order was afterwards enforced.

About this time UB 36 (Keyserlinck) disappeared in the Channel; and the German War Loss Lists, giving the date as June 24, surmise that she fell a prey to a decoy. Although no such claim was made on the British side, certainly there was a great deal of Q-boat activity during June. It is possible that this U-boat might have been one of the submarines so engaged; she may have crawled away mortally injured from the scene of encounter. First, there was the attack on the decoy *Zylpha* (Q 6), two hundred miles out in the Atlantic, on June 11. The panic party, having abandoned ship, lay on their oars for an hour and a half waiting for the submarine to appear. At last, some distance off, the enemy was seen to break surface and then disappear, paying no heed to the sinking vessel. Helpless, and kept afloat by the ' padding ' of timber, the little decoy lay sorely wounded. When the full bitterness of failure was borne in upon the crew, they called up the United States destroyer *Warrington*, which took off the wounded and stood by the whole day, until shortage of fuel necessitated the destroyer's return to her base. The weather now deteriorated, and those left aboard the *Zylpha* were drenched by the seas sweeping the water-logged vessel. Sail was, however, set, and the Q-boat crept homewards at one and a half knots, in the hope of meeting tugs sent out to her aid. On the 14th she was taken in tow by the sloop *Daffodil*, but just before midnight on the next day the *Zylpha* settled down off the Skelligs.

Another submarine had a fight off the south-west of Ireland, on the 19th, with the disguised collier *Thornhill*. About this time, too, the decoy ketch *Sarah Colebrooke* was damaged in a duel with a U-boat off Beachy Head. On the 20th the sloop *Salvia* (Q 15) was torpedoed by U 62 off the west coast of Ireland ; the explosion detonated her depth-charges, wrecking the engines and destroying the poop. Worst of all, the after gun was hurled overboard. The U 62, with her suspicions thoroughly aroused, pumped shell after shell into the sinking sloop. Five of the crew were killed, and the commander was taken prisoner. On this same day, June 20, in the Bay of Biscay, another Q-boat duel had been enacted, which was resumed at nightfall, between the topsail schooner *Mary B. Mitchell* (Q 9) and a U-boat. On the following day the schooner *Thirza* (Q 30) secured a hit on a disguised submarine during a fight. On the 25th the schooner *Glen* was in action with another submarine off St. Catherine's Point ; and, finally, the barque *Gaelic* (Q 22) encountered yet another U-boat in the Western Channel on the 26th. None of the submarines engaged were claimed to have been sunk ; but the very uncertainty of U-boat warfare leaves ample room for speculation. The simple fact remains that UB 36 'went missing' during June.

July brought a distinct improvement in the total of shipping sunk by torpedo. Compared with the previous month (when 116 British merchantmen of 391,004 tons gross were sunk by torpedo), the number of victims secured by the U-boats fell to 88 ships of 319,931 tons—this was roughly a return to the level of February losses. Mines laid by submarines claimed 9 ships of 30,128 tons—an increase upon the June total ; and in addition, 2 other merchant-vessels foundered on mines laid by ocean raiders. From now onwards the shipping losses became steadily less ; and during the last half of 1917, British shipping was destroyed at the reduced rate of 70 hulls per month. In view of the tonnage famine, it was still a very serious rate of wastage ; by December, about 5,000,000 tons of shipping had been sent to the bottom, and there were fewer ships to destroy. Moreover, in August no fewer than 382 ships of 1,183,000 tons were repaired, out of 708 vessels lying damaged in port. From July onwards the various anti-submarine measures began to exert their full influence on the submarine war ; experienced hands in the U-boat service became fewer and fewer, and the leaven of new and ' raw ' personnel rose in proportion.

The thrust and parry of the warfare continued with unabated fury. In the North Sea, on July 6, the destroyer *Itchen* fell a victim to torpedo attack, but six days later the destroyer *Patriot* sank by depth-charges U 69 (Wilhelms). Then, on the 21st, U 52, returning from a brief spell of service in the Mediterranean, sighted the top of the British submarine C 34's conning-tower off the Shetlands ; she promptly discharged a torpedo at the British boat and blew her up. More serious was the loss to the 10th Cruiser Squadron of the fine vessel *Otway*. This armed merchant cruiser had left Loch Ewe for her patrol during the afternoon of July 22 ; at 10.25 P.M. she was torpedoed in lat. 58° 54′ N., long. 6° 28′ W. Twelve minutes previously a periscope had been seen, but the torpedo could not be avoided, and it hit the *Otway* astern, flooding the engine-room and killing 10 men. Although every effort was made to reach North Rona, the water gained on her crew ; and except for Commodore Colomb, the first lieutenant, and a steward, the ship was abandoned. Soon after midnight the *Otway* sank, and the complement was picked up and taken into Stornoway. After this third loss to the squadron, Admiral Tupper was instructed to take advantage of convoys to pass in his ships ; also to use the destroyer escorts, meeting the incoming convoys, to pass them out. He speedily found there was great delay involved in making for the port of assembly for outward convoys. Further, inward convoys sometimes dispersed soon after leaving Lough Swilly, and the armed merchant cruiser had perforce to proceed alone, as she had previously done. Admiral Tupper suggested that it would be preferable to take the risk of joining the patrol unaccompanied; and on September 21 he was granted permission, with the suggestion that his ships should use the dark hours and moonless nights to cross the danger zone.

In western seas, July was marked by the ghastly tragedy of the steamer *Mariston* (2908 tons), sunk by U 66 on the 15th, 82 miles west from Fastnet. Two explosions quickly destroyed the ship, and 18 of her crew were thrown into the sea. One man alone survived; and he told a terrible tale. One by one, sharks had caught the unfortunate men in the sea, and with piercing shrieks they had been dragged under the water. In all, 29 had perished in this frightful manner; even the submarine commander was so appalled that he dived to escape the sight. Other serious losses include the *Condesa* (8557 tons), sunk on the 7th, 105 miles W. from Bishop Rock; the *Calliope* (2883 tons), lost with all hands (27) in the Atlantic; the *City of Florence* (5399 tons) on the 20th, 188 miles W. $\frac{3}{4}$ N. from Ushant; the tanker *Oakleaf* (8106 tons),[1] sunk on the 25th, 64 miles N.W. $\frac{1}{4}$ N. from the Butt of Lewis; the Federal *Somerset* (8710 tons) on the following day, 230 miles W. by S. $\frac{1}{2}$ S. from Ushant; and the Johnston *Quernmore* (7302 tons), employed as a commissioned escort ship, on the 31st, 160 miles W. by N. $\frac{3}{4}$ N. from Tory Island. The total loss of life for all 88 vessels destroyed by submarine attack during July was 401.

Interest once more centres around the activities of the Flanders flotillas. Now numbering some thirty-eight boats, they were working as far westward as the Bay of Biscay. Severe were their casualties during the next months, and the mortality grew ever higher. On July 24 the small UC 1 (Mildenstein) was spotted off the Thames estuary by five seaplanes. One after the other, in line ahead, they flew over the unhappy craft and dropped their bombs, which 'took effect.' This feat was repeated five days later, when UB 20 (Glimpf) was sighted awash off the North Hinder L.V. by two seaplanes, which bombed her until her sides burst open and she

---

[1] Better known as the Canadian Pacific *Montezuma*, which had been converted into the dummy battleship *Iron Duke* in 1915.

X. SNATCHED FROM THE MAW OF THE SEA.

The R.M.S.P. liner *Demerara*, here exhibited, thrice survived enemy attack during the war. In May, 1915, she was chased by a submarine and escaped; in February, 1916, she found safety by flight from the raider *Möwe*. Lastly, on July 1, 1917, whilst crossing the Bay of Biscay, she was struck by a torpedo from a German submarine. Once again, her luck held; and she remained afloat long enough to be run ashore. She was refloated later, and repaired.

sank with her crew of 24. In connection with this affair, it has been said that Glimpf took his boat to sea, without authority and with a party of military officers and their lady friends on board, to show the landlubbers what a war-time cruise was like. The demonstration seems to have been far more realistic then he ever anticipated! With half of his crew down with influenza, Glimpf was short-handed, and a surprise attack summarily swept him and his boat into oblivion.[1] On the same day, July 29, UB 27 (von Stein) was rammed off Smith's Knoll Spar Buoy by the gunboat *Halcyon*, being finished off with depth-charges. A fourth Flanders boat, UB 23 (Voigt), turned up at Corunna on the 30th, in a dishevelled state. Finding the return to Flanders too hazardous, her commander decided to take refuge in a neutral port and suffer internment.

As the Belgian coast barrage had been successful in allowing the daily patrol to be maintained off the Flemish base, the Admiral at Dover decided to reinstate the coastal net-barrage, which had been allowed to lapse into desuetude during the winter months of 1916-17. It will have been noticed that twice previously the Dover Patrol had been misled into placing too implicit a confidence in barrages. When the wooden boom of 1915 had to be abandoned and be replaced by moored mines, the experience of one or two U-boats, after fouling these entanglements, caused the first ban to be imposed on passage through the Straits. When the Belgian coast barrage was laid in April 1916, by pure coincidence the brief spring campaign was called off. The conclusion was reached by the Admiralty (then unaware of the internal political crisis between the German naval and diplomatic camps) that the counter-measures were eminently satisfactory—the more so, in fact, because of the supposed destruction of five or six U-boats immediately following the laying of the mines and nets. As it was painfully apparent that the Goodwins-Snou nets were failing to debar the use of the Straits to the U-boats, Admiral Bacon believed that the only way of so doing was to lay a mine barrage across the Channel; but no mines were available. He therefore laid a

[1] *Raiders of the Deep* (Lowell Thomas), p. 235.

barrage similar to the coastal mine barrage of 1916. It was designed in preparation for the 'Great Landing' which had so long been planned. Early on the morning of July 25 a minelayer laid 120 deep mines along a line about eighteen miles off the coast, and then the drifters laid fifteen miles of mine-nets in position. On July 27 the line of nets was prolonged still farther. This barrage had to be patrolled day and night. Although it acted as a deterrent, the barrage did not prevent submarines from emerging from their base. Actually, on the very day it was laid, UC 61 (Gerth) left Zeebrugge and passed both this obstruction and the Goodwins-Snou barrier at night, on her way to mine Havre and Boulogne before proceeding farther west. Previously this boat had passed through the Straits five times; on this occasion her luck deserted her, for she stranded in fog off Cape Grisnez. She had to be blown up, and her crew was captured by a patrol of Belgian cavalry next morning. Three days after the coastal barrage was laid, the enemy started to destroy it by tugging gaps in the nets with grapnels; and other damage was done by seaplanes cutting adrift the buoys and wires. Until the new mines became available, there seemed little hope of success in barring the Straits to the U-boats. In February 1917, Admiral Bacon had decided, when it became possible, to lay such a mine-barrage across the Straits.

More fortunate than Gerth of UC 61 was Steinbrinck in UC 65. He passed through the Straits on the 26th, making a record submerged run; and off Beachy Head he sank the old cruiser *Ariadne*, lately converted into a mine-layer for laying out the proposed Northern Barrage between Scotland and Norway.

On July 31, Paul Wagenführ of U 44, a fitting colleague of Werner in U 55, committed an odious outrage on the high seas. After sinking the steamer *Belgian Prince* (4765 tons) towards evening, 175 miles N.W. by W. from Tory Island, he ordered the crew on to the submarine's deck, stripped them of their lifebelts and possessions, and then, with the master as captive below, he gave orders to dive. Thrown into the sea, eight who had managed to conceal their lifebelts lived for a time; and one of them even clambered aboard the still floating steamer. When she was sunk by bombs next morn-

THE STRUGGLE FOR MASTERY

ing he was once more adrift; and altogether, out of the crew of 43, only three survived until the arrival of a destroyer. Due and just retribution for this cruel infamy came swiftly.

In the fascinating book, *Q Ships*, by Mr. Keble Chatterton, there is an account of a duel between a submarine and the decoy *Bracondale*, 125 miles N.W. of Tory Island, on August 5, in which the submarine was hit at 800 yards range. The decoy herself was worsted, and sank, after being thrice torpedoed by her assailant. It is possible that the submarine engaged was U 44, for on August 12 Wagenführ encountered Nemesis off Bergen. Off the Norwegian coast the 3rd Light Cruiser Squadron, with six destroyers acting as a screen, was sweeping northwards. The port wing cruiser *Birkenhead* was guarded by the destroyer *Oracle*. Strong German wireless messages had been intercepted just before dark on the previous evening, indicating the presence of an enemy vessel near by. Next morning, the 12th, the *Oracle*'s officer of the watch espied a trawler's sail on the horizon. Soon afterwards, out of the water on either side of the sail a bow and a stern were seen to emerge. The sail disappeared, and at a distance of between six and seven miles a submarine was revealed. The U-boat dived. Six minutes later, away on the *Oracle*'s port bow, three miles distant, the enemy reappeared, throwing up clouds of spray in her hasty flight. A few seconds later she disappeared. Course was at once altered to cut her off. As though unable to remain submerged, two minutes later the quarry's bows shot up out of the water about half a mile away. At full speed the *Oracle* dashed up to the spot, opening fire on the U-boat's stern, now uplifted. The prow of the destroyer sheered through the submarine at the speed of 27 knots. Struck abaft the conning-tower, terrible injuries were inflicted on the diving-boat. A depth-charge, let go at the exact moment, completed the work of annihilation. As the *Oracle* drifted onwards for some 150 yards, her crew, gazing astern, were rewarded by the sight of the enemy's bows projecting into the air at an angle of 45 degrees, before she plunged to her grave 137 fathoms deep. So perished U 44 and her inhuman commander.[1]

[1] *Submarine and Anti-Submarine* (Sir Henry Newbolt).

Throughout the first six months of this 1917 campaign the mining work of the UC-boats increased twofold. The waters off the south-west of Ireland were an area much frequented by the distributing craft. At the beginning they would lay their whole clutch off headlands and landfalls, and the sweepers would have little difficulty in locating and sweeping up the mines. Then the enemy changed his tactics and began to scatter a few here and there, or would follow in the wake of the sweepers and foul waters as fast as they were cleared. In one month alone the mine-sweepers working from Queenstown swept up 129 mines. But by July the pace started to slacken, and the UC-boats relaxed their intensive efforts perceptibly.

So regular had the mining of certain spots become, that a little ruse is said to have been planned. Fresh fields were discovered in certain areas with such punctuality that the approximate date and place, when and where new mines would appear, could even be forecast with accuracy. Off Waterford, one day, sweepers put out; sundry explosions far out at sea were heard, as if counter-mining were in progress. The sweepers then returned to port. Presumably, submarines off the Irish coast received advice from ashore as to the recent activities of the sweepers. In any case, at 10.30 P.M. on August 4 there was a loud explosion out at sea off Waterford; patrols rushed to the scene, and picked up out of the water the commander of UC 44 (Tebbenjohanns), and a very angry man was he. It appeared that he had already laid eight mines, when his boat blew up on other German mines, laid previously to his arrival. Bitterly did he complain about British carelessness in not clearing the area properly and rendering it safe for *his* operations. The mine-sweepers had actually made a 'dummy counter-mining sweep': they had not cleared away the last-laid patch of German mines, but had left it *in situ*, knowing full well that by a certain date another layer would appear in those very waters to replenish the field. It was a practical joke, admittedly grim, and Tebbenjohanns, perhaps excusably, failed to find any humour in it. Still, his idea that British sweepers toiled unceasingly, to keep British waters safe for German submarines, exhibits an impudence that approaches the sublime.

THE STRUGGLE FOR MASTERY 197

UC 44 was salved, and papers found on board are believed to have furnished conclusive proof that the Dover Straits barrage was presenting little hindrance to passing submarines.

What was probably the epic Q-boat fight of the whole war was fought on August 8.[1] Just before eleven o'clock in the morning, Captain Gordon Campbell, now in the disguised and defensively-armed merchant-steamer *Dunraven*, fell in with Salzwedel, one of the Flanders ' aces,' previously in command of UB 10 and UC 21, and now in UC 71. The decoy was cruising in the Bay of Biscay, in the hope of meeting one of these corsairs. At 5000 yards range UC 71 opened fire, and the *Dunraven*, simulating the procedure of a defensively-armed merchantman, replied with her gun aft. Artfully, Captain Campbell allowed his shells to fall short and ordered speed to be reduced, so that the submarine was induced to close. Dummy wireless messages for help were sent off, and the whole scene of feigned distress was acted perfectly. After forty minutes had elapsed, dense clouds of steam issued from the engine-room (from a specially-devised steam-pipe), but this, unfortunately, obscured the range and return of fire. As the ship was now on fire, the panic party put out, leaving one boat hanging up-ended by the falls. The submarine warily kept astern within an arc upon which the concealed guns could not be brought to bear. The German gunners kept on firing shell after shell into the burning steamer. The decks aft were getting red-hot with the fires raging below ; those who were on board momentarily expected the magazine to go up. None the less, the after-gun crew remained, to keep up the pretence of the defensive gun.

One shell hit the poop and detonated a depth-charge. Thinking that the magazine had exploded, Captain Campbell sent out a genuine call for help ; but this message he quickly negatived when, through the clearing smoke, he saw the poop was still intact. The gun crew stationed there was, however, obviously disabled. Knowing it to be only a question of time before the poop must blow up, Campbell decided to wait for the submarine to pass over to the weather side. Just as UC 71 came under the stern, a terrific explosion shivered the

[1] *My Mystery Ships* (Rear-Admiral Gordon Campbell, V.C., D.S.O., R.N.).

Dunraven. The stern of the ship had blown out, and the after-gun crew was hurled into the air. The UC 71 hastily dived.

The concussion of the explosion caused the fire-gongs to start ringing. At this signal the concealed gun on the boat deck opened fire, the White Ensign was prematurely run up, and the true character of the ship was revealed. Captain Campbell waited for the *coup de grâce* from his opponent, but still refrained from calling up help. During this period of expectancy the wounded were removed below and made as comfortable as possible. After twenty minutes had elapsed, the awaited torpedo was seen coming straight for the ship; ' but,' says Captain Campbell, ' as this was the fifth time we had watched the same thing, it left us rather cold.'

An additional panic party now left the ship, some in the remaining boat and others on a raft. Thirty-four remained on board the shattered vessel. The periscope of UC 71 appeared on the starboard bow, and for an hour the submarine circled round the decoy. Salzwedel eventually came to the surface, hove-to astern of the *Dunraven*, reopened fire, and maintained this shelling for twenty minutes. Then, apparently satisfied with results, he submerged and, with the periscope just showing, cautiously passed close by the decoy. A torpedo, fired by Captain Campbell, barely missed UC 71. The submarine then circled round the *Dunraven*'s bows and passed down the starboard side. The starboard submerged tube was next discharged. The torpedo either hit or just grazed UC 71, but failed to explode. Salzwedel promptly dived deep. Captain Campbell, in expectation of another torpedo attack, arranged for a third panic party, which would leave only one gun crew on board the *Dunraven*. But Salzwedel had had enough of decoys for that day : his torpedoes had all been fired away; he was not risking another attack by gunfire. Accordingly he decamped. Soon afterwards the United States armed yacht *Noma* hove in sight, followed by the destroyers *Attack* and *Christopher*. The wounded were taken off from the sinking Q-ship; the battered *Dunraven* was taken in tow, and an attempt was made to bring her into port. The sea, however, claimed the ship that was unconquered and unconquerable by her enemy. The indomitable *Dunraven* disappeared beneath the waves early next morning, with her colours flying ; and her gallant crew was brought to port. Lieutenant Bonner of the after-gun crew was awarded the Victoria Cross, together with Seaman Pitcher, by ballot of the crew ; and the intrepid leader of this ship's company received yet a second bar to his D.S.O.

Many were the types and variegated were the disguises of the Q-ships, yet one thing they held in common—an unflinching courage in the face of the enemy. Little or great, they fought to the last. Here is another instance of the courage displayed by the crews of 'special service vessels.' Two armed smacks, *Nelson* [1] and *Ethel and Millie*, were attacked by a submarine during the afternoon of August 15, in the North Sea. Aboard the first vessel was Skipper Thomas Crisp, and at the enemy's seventh shot he was hit in the side, the shell passing through the deck and out through the smack's side. Lying terribly wounded, his spirit was still undaunted and his courage undimmed. As the gun-layer went to his aid, his son took the tiller. ' It 's all right, lad. Do your best ! ' he told his son. A little later he ordered a carrier-pigeon to be freed, with the message attached, ' *Nelson* attacked. Skipper killed. Send assistance at once.' Five rounds were now left to the gunner of the little disguised vessel ; with the end near, Skipper Crisp had the confidential books thrown overboard and preparations made for abandoning ship. To his son he cried, ' Tom, I 'm done. Throw me overboard.' But he could not be moved ; and, conscious and dauntless to the last, he went down with his ship. Two days later the survivors were picked up. To Skipper Thomas Crisp was posthumously awarded the Victoria Cross for his devotion and gallantry when so sorely wounded. As for the *Ethel and Millie*, her crew was last seen (by the *Nelson*'s survivors) on the submarine's deck, as that vessel of ill omen disappeared into the darkening east.

Three days later, UB 32 (Ditfurth) was bombed by a seaplane 27 miles N. of Cape Barfleur.[2] Another enemy

[1] Previously known as *G. & E.*, see p. 50.
[2] Michelsen says ' Sept. 1917, English Channel, cause unknown.'

boat was accounted for on the 21st. Like other mine-laying submarines, UC 41 (Foerste) involuntarily immolated herself. She was laying mines off the Tay during the late afternoon, and whilst so occupied was disturbed by the approach of two mine-sweeping trawlers, *Jacinth* and *Thomas Young*. In her haste to efface herself she fouled one of her own mines. The explosion attracted the trawlers to the spot; their sweep fouled a submerged object. Of the enemy's mine-laying activities they had no knowledge, but surmised that the obstruction was a hostile U-boat—a suspicion confirmed by the location of a German mine near by. The *Jacinth* dropped atop of the submarine a couple of depth-charges. Any doubt as to the character of the object beneath the surface was at once dispelled. A series of explosions followed, which could only arise from the detonation of further mines inside the mine-laying craft. A third depth-charge was then dropped; and another trawler, *Chikara*, put over the side four more, causing yet a further explosion of mines on board the doomed UC 41. For two hours the sounds of electric motors running could be heard on the hydrophones; thereafter all was quiet. About a month later, salvage parties brought up from the sunken vessel a 22-pounder gun.

The August shipping losses exhibited little change from the return for the preceding month. The following were noteworthy:—The Elder-Dempster *Karina* (4222 tons), sunk on August 1, 17 miles S.S.W. ½ W. from Hook Point, Waterford, with 11 lives; the Blue Funnel *Laertes* (4541 tons) the same day, 1¼ miles S.S.W. from Prawle Point, with 14 lives; the *Cairnstrath* (2128 tons) on the 4th, 6 miles S.S.W. from Ile du Pilier, with 22 lives; the *Iran* (6250 tons) on the 7th, 200 miles E.S.E. from Santa Anna, Azores; the *War Patrol* (2045 tons) on the 10th, a mile W. from Penmarch, on a mine, with 13 lives; the New Zealand Shipping Co. *Turakina* (9920 tons) on August 13, 120 miles W.S.W. from Bishop Rock, with 2 lives; the Donaldson *Athenia* (8668 tons) on the 16th, 7 miles N. from Instrahull, with 15 lives; the White Star *Delphic* (8273 tons) on the same day, 135 miles S.W. ¾ W. from Bishop Rock, with 5 lives; the *Rosario* (1821 tons) on the 18th, in the Atlantic, with her crew of 20; the *Bulysses*

(6127 tons) on the 20th, 145 miles W.N.W. from the Butt of Lewis; the Cunard cargo steamer *Volodia* (5689 tons) next day, 285 miles W. ¼ S. from Ushant, with 10 lives; the Leyland *Devonian* (10,435 tons) and the Union Steamship Co. of N.Z. *Roscommon* (8238 tons), both sunk on the 21st, 20 miles N.E. from Tory Island; the Lamport & Holt *Verdi* (7120 tons) next day, 115 miles N.W. by N. from Eagle Island, with 6 lives; the *Heatherside* (2767 tons), which went missing with her crew of 27; the Johnston *Sycamore* (6550 tons) on the 25th, 125 miles N.W. from Tory Island, with 11 lives; the British India *Malda* (7895 tons) the same day, 130 miles W. by ½ S. from Bishop Rock, with the heavy toll of 64 lives; the Brocklebank *Assyria* (6370 tons) next day, 34 miles N.W. by N. ½ N. from Tory Island; and the Canadian Pacific *Miniota* (6422 tons) on the 31st, 30 miles S.E. ½ E. from the Start, with 3 lives—this last-named vessel being probably sunk by U 19 (Spiess).

Of the casualties enumerated above, the double sinking of the *Devonian* and the *Roscommon* requires comment, since few other attacks convey a better impression of the conditions under which convoying worked. Early in the morning of the 21st, nineteen steamers left Lough Swilly in single file, proceeding to form six columns—the usual formation for large convoys. They were escorted by two cruisers and six destroyers; and the convoy commodore's ship was the *Devonian*. At 11.30 A.M. the formation was complete. Just before noon, the *Devonian*, at the head of her column, was hit; a second torpedo just missed the Lamport & Holt *Vasari* (10,117 tons), the next astern; but a third torpedo struck the *Roscommon*, second ship of the column to port. The submarine evaded the counter-attack of the destroyers, and the convoy put back. The *Devonian*'s master, Captain Trant, afterwards emphasized the danger of assembling a string of nineteen vessels, twelve miles in length, in unprotected waters; he pointed out that, during the six or seven hours spent in forming the convoy, the submarine had ample time to prepare for attack,[1] which resulted in the loss of two large and valuable merchant-vessels. Hersing, in U 21,

[1] *The Merchant Navy*, vol. iii. (Hurd), p. 270.

relates a similar attack [1] which he made on another convoy during August. Off the south-west of Ireland he met a convoy of fifteen vessels in three parallel lines, escorted by six destroyers on either flank, one eight hundred yards ahead, and another similarly stationed astern. The sea was glassy, with bright sunlight. Taking hurried glances through his periscope, Hersing ran between two of the leading destroyers; took another fleeting glimpse; fired two torpedoes; and then dived to forty metres. After an interval of forty seconds he heard two explosions; thereafter began his ordeal by depth-charge. Every ten seconds came the detonations at ten, twenty-five, and fifty metres' depth. After a terrific concussion from ahead, all electric lights went out. For five hours, all round him the *wasser-bombe* blew up, and destroyers' propellers whirred above him. Profiting by this lurid experience, Hersing made it his practice, later, not to turn away and put as much distance as was possible between his target and himself, but to dive right under the convoy after attacking it.

The loss of the *War Patrol* on the 10th is particularly interesting, since she was the first of the new ' standard cargo-ships ' to be sunk by the enemy. Reference has previously been made to the huge shipbuilding effort in this country to combat the devastating reductions effected by the U-boats. With tonnage at famine prices, old ships long past their prime, old wind-jammers—in fact, almost anything that would float— were being bought and sold at fabulous prices. Not only in this country were thousands of men engaged in turning out new merchant-ships wholesale. In America the gigantic Hog Island shipyard was created; in France, Italy, and Japan existing yards were enlarged; in this country derelict yards revived, new yards were created, standard ship types adopted, and building plans framed on a generous scale. Everywhere went up the cry for ' Tonnage ! Tonnage ! ! Tonnage ! ! ! ! ' Delivery of two to three new ' standard cargo-ships ' on an average per day, built by mass-production methods, was the ideal aimed at. Propaganda, publicity, inter-yard competitions were all used to stimulate output. To build more ships

---

[1] *Raiders of the Deep* (Thomas), p. 217.

THE STRUGGLE FOR MASTERY 203

than the U-boats could sink was the aim. Never was this ideal realised, even though the sinkings fell month by month. The great shipbuilding drive did not fail for lack of originality. Who does not remember the concrete ships, or even the American-built wooden steamers ? Only the 'standard cargo-ships' have endured, and many still form part of the great shipping companies' fleets.

From February 1 to August 31 there had been sunk 736 British vessels ; of these 572 were torpedoed, 505 being sunk without warning—an equivalent of 69 per cent.

For more than six months, merciless warfare had been waged by the submarines. Britain remained unbeaten, and America had been changed from a contemplative neutral into a belligerent hostile to Germany. Such, in the main, was the outcome of the six months' campaign, and in his predictions and warnings Bethmann-Hollweg had shown far more prescience than Holtzendorff, Tirpitz, and Scheer.

CHAPTER X

THE PENUMBRA OF ECLIPSE

(SEPTEMBER–DECEMBER 1917)

IN September, Michelsen, who had succeeded Bauer as Commodore of Submarines, H.S.F., gave orders that the large North Sea boats should once again make the Dover Straits passage. What was the reason for this reversal of policy ? The answer is not far to seek. August 1 had come and had passed, and yet England had not sued for peace. The six months' time-limit for bringing the arch-enemy to his knees had expired. Bitterly have the naval leaders since regretted that this stipulated period, put forward with the greatest secrecy, should ever have come to the public knowledge. Too many had come to know of the undertaking to force a decision before the harvest-reaping. The German nation expected the U-boats would be triumphant by the autumn. They knew the campaign still raged furiously. It was possible for the naval leaders to conceal from public sight the ominous fact that the sinkings achieved in August were but a third of the fearful April total. The question confronting the German naval authorities was simply this : How long could the deception last ? Would it suffice to carry on until such time as the great ' Hindenburg submarine-building programme ' began to mature ? Comfort might be taken in the knowledge that they had very greatly reduced the world's shipping. They knew that Norway, one of the first five merchant-fleet owners in the world, had lost half of her tonnage. They could not but admit, on the other hand, that the introduction of convoy and the Allied counter-offensive against the U-boats were making headway. Heavy toll was being taken of the flotillas. The morale of the crews was beginning to show signs of deterioration —leave was overstayed, and sickness feigned. Faults arising from inexperience had to be overlooked by the officers, and deference had to be shown to old and experienced hands, because such men were getting more scarce every month and their goodwill had to be cultivated. Shorter and shorter became the periods of refit and overhaul. In the autumn,

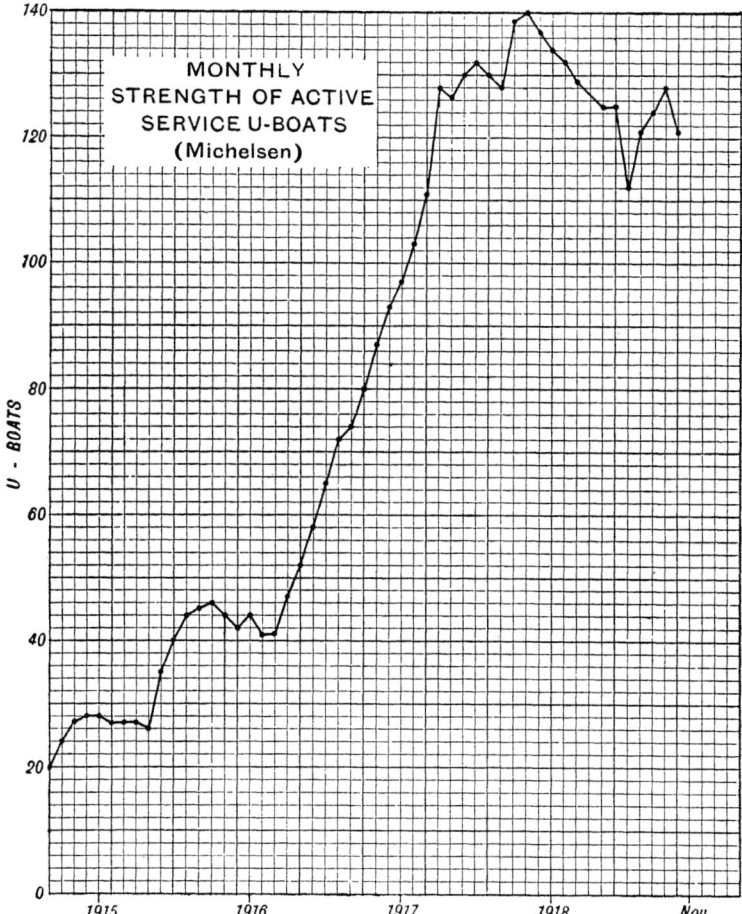

the number of the commissioned submarines, available for service but exclusive of the training boats, mustered a total of 140 boats, a figure never before attained nor afterwards surpassed. With all this array of strength, it was dubious if the great spring drive of February-April could be repeated.

None the less, better results had, at all costs, to be obtained from the forces at command. Less time would have to be wasted by the larger submarines in going out to and returning from the war stations in western waters. Therefore, the bigger boats were ordered by Michelsen to use the shorter but much more dangerous route through the Dover Straits.

In addition to the resumption of the Dover Straits passage by the larger boats, the UC-boats laid mines everywhere—off the north of Ireland, off ports, off landfalls, off headlands, in channels constantly swept; yet so efficient had the British mine-sweeping service become that only eight British merchantmen were lost by mine in September. Hydrophone drifters worked in the Clyde approaches, and also from the Mull of Galloway across to the south of Belfast, to protect the incoming convoys.

As far distant as from the Azores in the south to the White Sea in the north were the submarines operating. Mines had been laid in the Kola Inlet during April by one of the large mine-layers, but it was not until the fall that shipping to and from Archangel began to be molested. Once again, as in 1916, the autumn was marked by submarine activity off the North Cape. On September 2 the munition-laden steamer *Olive Branch* (4649 tons) was attacked in this locality by U 28 (Schmidt), and had to be abandoned. At only 250 yards the submarine opened fire and landed her second shot in the ammunition hold.[1] The steamer blew up, and so violent was the explosion that U 28 was wrecked.[2] The submarine's crew tried to persuade the *Olive Branch*'s people to take them into the heavily-laden boats; but, not unnaturally, their request was refused, and they perished.

Another steamer, *British Transport* (4143 tons), shortly afterwards arrived at Archangel and related that on the night of September 11 she had rammed and sunk U 49 (Hartmann) off the Irish coast. The submarine had fired two torpedoes

---

[1] Mercantile Losses (1919) attributes loss to 'torpedoed without warning.'
[2] Captain R. S. Gwatkin-Williams, R.N., relates, in his book *Under the Black Ensign*, the well-known story that a heavy motor lorry, blown into the air off the deck of the *Olive Branch*, fell upon U 28 and sank her.

at about 9 P.M., but owing to the prompt handling of the merchant-vessel they were avoided. Twenty minutes later, those on board the steamer sighted a luminous patch in the phosphorescent sea on the port bow. Course was altered, and the bows of the merchant-ship sheared through the deck-plating of her attacker, who passed down the side with her bows out of the water. Two shots from the ship's gun settled her fate, and she plunged down into the depths.

Other ships were not so fortunate, but about half of those attacked escaped destruction. In September a marked drop may be observed in the tonnage totalled by the sunken ships. In the preceding month the average size of the victim was about 3500 tons, whereas in this month it dropped to under 2500 tons gross. To large merchant-ships a higher degree of immunity was afforded, since the prophylactic of convoy had been applied to all outgoing as well as incoming traffic. The loss of life was no certain guide; one large ship with a big passenger death-roll would send up the returns and so make it unsafe to draw deductions therefrom regarding the course of the campaign. During the month, the *La Negra* (8312 tons), a Houlder liner carrying a valuable meat cargo, was sunk on the 3rd, 50 miles S.S.W. from the Start, with 4 lives; the Elder-Dempster *Echunga* (6285 tons) on the 5th, 40 miles N. by E. from Ushant, with 9 lives; the Atlantic Transport *Minnehaha* (13,714 tons) on the 7th, 12 miles S.E. from Fastnet, with 43 lives; and the *Boynton* (2578 tons) on the 24th, 5 miles W.N.W. from Cape Cornwall, with 23 lives.

September 1917 is a month particularly important in the chronicles of anti-submarine warfare. It was during this month that the first deliveries of the new type of mine, mooring gear and sinker began to be made. The vast mining scheme in the Bight of Heligoland became possible, and during 1917 not less than 25,150 mines were laid in the 'Wet Triangle,' mostly by the famous 20th Flotilla. This improved pattern, known as Mark H 2, had not been long in use before it changed the contempt of the enemy for British mines into a wholesome fear and respect. Of the 1500 September deliveries, 500 mines were planted in the Bight. In the three following months a total of 10,389 mines was laid both here and at Dover,[1] as the first efficient barrages were gradually built up.

Mention has been made before of the German defensive mine-barriers, and of the mines placed by British layers in January 1917. Outside such previous fields began the new British barriers, spanning the whole Bight from the Danish to the Dutch frontiers. German mine-sweepers, albeit that they suffered heavy casualties, worked feverishly to remove the British fields so as to keep clear three safe and swept channels for the U-boats. In this work they were assisted by Zeppelins, cruising over the waters of the Bight to locate these deadly areas without peril to themselves. One of these routes ran along the Dutch coast past Terschelling, and was considered to be the best ; another extended up to Horns Reef and along the Danish coast ; whilst between the foregoing two lay the third lane. At the exits of these narrow channels British submarines were posted to attack passing U-boats. Inside this arc of British mines was a basin, reaching from the Ems to the north-west of Heligoland. This, in 1917, was kept swept, and through it the submarines were convoyed out to the British mine-barrages. Here they dived, to come up outside and beyond them. As new British fields were sown, so did the arc, enclosing the T.N.T.-tainted waters, grow wider and wider ; longer and longer became the lanes to be cleared by the German mine-sweepers. The casualties to both German sweeping and British laying craft mounted ever higher. The German mine-layers began to distribute mines in areas where it was expected the next British field would be placed ; and they succeeded in so destroying two British layers in the months which followed. As this battle of wits developed, and the German barrage-breakers and sweeping-flotillas were forced to work farther afield, so the more promising did the chances grow of an action between the British and German light forces—that is, between the German ships covering their sweeping craft and the British ships supporting their laying craft. Such actions did actually result.

Here we record the passing of a man who will ever stand out with malignant prominence amongst the corsairs of

[1] *The Crisis of the Naval War* (Jellicoe), p. 92.

1915-18. We refer to Walther Schwieger of *Lusitania* fame, or infamy. The mining of the Bight was in full swing; the British barrier was daily becoming more effective. German submarines were later forced to use Danish or Dutch territorial waters, but the U-boats in the early days of the Bight barrage were reported by British submarines to be diving below the mines and coming up beyond them. Thereupon, nets with mines attached were placed at different depths. On September 7, Schwieger, in command of U 88, left his base in company with another U-boat for a cruise. Passing up the Danish coast, the vessels dived as usual, in order to run under the Horns Reef barrier. Soon after, those on board the other U-boat heard a terrific explosion; so violent was the concussion that it was imagined a mine had been struck. Tanks were blown at once and return made to the surface. When the commanding officer came up and gazed around him, he saw near by a vast ever-widening lagoon of oil-fuel, clotted with wreckage, surrounding the area wherein U 88 had dived. With but a faint hope that U 88 might be only disabled, he remained on the spot awhile, but not a sound broke the silence which once more settled down on those death-strewn waters. Schwieger must have hit a big mine head-on, and possibly detonated his bow torpedoes in one great crash. So perished the man who had struck down the *Lusitania*, the *Hesperian*, and the *Cymric*.[1]

Nor was this the only loss from such a cause. On October 9, complete catastrophe befell U 106 (Hufnagel): by striking these mine-nets as she entered the Bight on her return from a cruise. During the first eleven days of October, two more submarines were caught—U 50 (Berger) and U 66 (Muhle)—as a result of combined operations by destroyers, submarines, and drifters, to the westward of the Dogger Bank. One of these boats is believed to have fouled the mine-nets of the drifter *William Tennant* on the morning of October 2. The hydrophones picked up the sound of a submarine's electric motors; then followed the noise of a heavy explosion in the nets.

---

[1] It should be mentioned that, seven days earlier, British light forces had captured four German mine-sweepers at work in this area.

In the face of the losses just narrated, it might have been expected that the enemy would take energetic measures to remove such impediments to safe navigation. Instead, the North Sea boats were compelled to pass through the Kaiser Wilhelm Canal, Kiel Fjord, the western Baltic, the Belts, and Kattegat to gain the North Sea, thus lengthening their cruises and decreasing their operational time at sea. Scheer is emphatic that only for a few days was this procedure made necessary,[1] but Spiess gives a graphic account of the extra difficulties attending this back-door entrance and exit. He himself narrowly escaped a premature end (in October 1917) by the faulty compensating of tanks when buoyancy was being readjusted between the different salinities of the North Sea and the Baltic. The work was bungled, and the submarine suddenly acquired a heavy negative buoyancy. Down dropped U 52 by the stern like a stone. He had thoughts of teaching his crew a well-needed lesson by letting the boat take the bottom with a crash. Fortunately for himself, he decided otherwise and checked the dive. Had he carried out his original intention, he, his crew, and boat would probably have been blown to pieces by the detonation of the Mark G VII torpedoes, loaded in the after tubes.[2]

The U-cruisers generally worked from Kiel, at first under the direction of the Naval Staff, and later under that of Michelsen, Commodore of the Submarine Flotillas, High Sea Fleet. When it became known that the North Sea boats were emerging from the Belts and Sound, British mine-layers laid a field of 1400 deep mines in the Kattegat. Scheer remarked that, curiously enough, neither British nor German mine-layers were ever caught at such dangerous work. Mines, of course, claimed many of the German sweepers. When it is realized that they had to keep clear lanes through this vast mine area up to a distance of 180 miles northward along the

---

[1] *High Sea Fleet* (Scheer), p. 290.

[2] A few days afterwards, these torpedoes did explode, whilst U 52 was undergoing repairs in one of the basins at the Kiel Dockyard. She foundered at once, but was raised sufficiently by the bows to permit the escape of the survivors. After salvage, she was repaired and re-entered service, but not under the command of Spiess. After this disaster, he went back to his old boat, U 19.

Danish coast, and 140 miles west from the Jade along the Dutch coast, the need for supporting forces is apparent.

That there was such a necessity for prompt assistance by powerful supporting ships was amply proved on November 17, when German sweepers were surprised, under conditions of low visibility, by a strong cruiser force commanded by Admiral Sir R. Phillimore. The British battle-cruisers *Renown* and *Repulse*, and the large cruisers *Courageous* and *Glorious*, with eight light cruisers and several destroyers, swooped down on the German mine-sweepers, capturing the *Kedingen* and driving back the enemy's screening force of light cruisers. The chase was broken off when the battleships *Kaiser* and *Kaiserin* came up to support the four light cruisers and destroyers guarding the German sweepers, and opened an accurate fire on the British ships, mortally wounding the *Calypso*'s captain. When the German force was reinforced by the battle-cruisers *Hindenburg* and *Moltke*, the British squadron fell back upon the Grand Fleet. After this action (in which the British casualties were heavier than those suffered by the force attacked), German supporting battleships occupied an anchorage off the Amrum Bank, at times when sweeping was in progress, to succour the light forces if they were again attacked.

The work of the German barrage-breakers was less enviable. To such *Sperrbrecher* was assigned not only the task of keeping clear the lanes through the fields, but also that of breaking open a path through mined and unswept waters, when ordered to do so, even though such orders virtually meant self-immolation for these naval 'battering-rams.'

From the foregoing it will be seen that everything short of scuttling block-ships in the Bight of Heligoland was attempted to bottle up the U-boats in their North Sea bases.[1] Besides

---

[1] An Inter-Allied Naval Conference was held in London early in September 1917. It was, for the most part, concerned with measures for fighting the enemy's submarine campaign, and its deliberations can be summarized under the following three main headings:—(a) Action against Enemy Bases; (b) Preventive Measures in Areas of Enemy Submarine Operations; and (c) Trade Defence.

(a) *Action against Enemy Bases* (*Blockships and Barrages*).—Sir John Jellicoe brought forward a scheme prepared by the Admiralty which en-the submarines enumerated above as destroyed in September, several others were sunk, the aggregate casualties numbering ten boats. Only once was the monthly total of submarine mortality greater than in this month. On the 10th, UC 42

visaged the scuttling of a considerable number of obsolete warships, as blockships, in the approaches to the German submarine bases in the North Sea. Owing to the dearth of sea freightage, merchant-ships could not be used for such a purpose, and it would therefore be necessary to use old warships. The following table was presented, showing the types and numbers of ships which might be contributed by the Allied and Associated Powers for use as blockships in the German Bight :—

	Britain.	France.	Italy.	Japan.	U.S.A.	Total.
Battleships	18	5	3	2	12 =	40
Cruisers	13	12	3	7	8 =	43

It was not suggested that this scheme should be put into immediate or early execution. The Allied representatives were asked to ascertain if their Governments would be prepared to place the ships at disposal for the purpose indicated. (Offensive operations against enemy bases in the Adriatic were also discussed.)

Other subjects broached were the establishment of a mine- or net-barrage in the Heligoland Bight (or the extension of the existing British mine-fields in that area), and the creation of a mine-barrage completely spanning the North Sea. Sir John Jellicoe pointed out the great difficulties to be overcome, firstly, in devising a pattern of mine suitable for North Sea conditions, and, secondly, in getting that pattern of mine produced in sufficient quantities. To create a complete barrage right across the North Sea from British to Scandinavian waters would require 100,000 mines, and British industry could not supply such a quantity within a reasonable time. (The Anglo-American Northern Barrage, established about a year later, required approximately 70,000 mines.) The Otranto Barrage also came under review, particularly with regard to the provision of adequate destroyer protection for the drifter line.

(b) *Preventive Measures in Areas of Enemy Submarine Operations.*—Sir John Jellicoe called attention to the fact that Allied and neutral shipping had recently been attacked, within the Azores area, by a large German submarine of the ex-mercantile 'Deutschland' type. There was every likelihood that other submarines of the same species would put to sea and operate against shipping in areas outside the existing danger zone. It was therefore necessary to consider what preventive measures should be taken, not only in the Azores but in other remote areas, to guard against large submarines operating at great distances from the German bases. It was decided that certain preventive measures should be taken in the Azores and elsewhere to guard against this danger, particularly to warn shipping, and to prevent the organization of supply services to the submarines. (Operations by hostile submarines in northern Russian waters were also considered.)

(c) *Trade Defence.*—The Conference treated this subject in two divisions : (i) the extension of the existing convoy system in the Atlantic ; and (ii) the

(Müller) blew up on mines off Cork;[1] two days later the British submarine patrol off the north of Ireland secured its first scalp, when D 7 torpedoed U 45 (Sittenfeld) twenty-two minutes after sighting her quarry; and farther in the south, in the St. George's Channel, the disguised patrol-boat PC 61 encountered the mine-layer UC 33 (Arnold) on the 26th, hit her conning-tower with well-directed gunfire, and placed the issue beyond doubt by ramming at a speed of twenty knots. The submarine rolled over under the violent impact. Her mines detonated, and she disappeared in a boil of foam. PC 61 picked up out of this turbulence the commanding officer and a seaman.

UC 72, commanded by Ernst Voigt, a veteran of the Flanders flotilla, was spotted by the seaplane 8695 off the Sunk L.V. on September 22, and was destroyed with one well-aimed bomb. Five days later, UC 21 (Zerboni di Sposetti) came to grief in the North Foreland mine-nets. Yet another

establishment of convoy in the Mediterranean. A report was presented on the existing (and partial) method of convoying in the Atlantic. If the system was to be enlarged so as to protect all shipping in the Atlantic, an additional force, composed of 41 cruisers and 55 destroyers (or sloops)— 96 vessels in all—would have to be found. An examination was made of convoying conditions in the Mediterranean, with a view towards estimating the escort forces required. A system of short-distance routes was mapped out, and for convoys working along these routes it was found that about 290 escort vessels would be required. Actually, a little more than 200 such craft were available at that time. To extend the convoy system in the Atlantic, and to establish it in the Mediterranean, the Allies had therefore to find about 170 to 180 ships for escort duties, ranging from cruisers to trawlers. (They had no ships to spare, and in every area were in want of more. These rough figures give some idea of the difficulties attendant upon the introduction and use of convoys. Convoying, if it is to be done at all, has to be done properly. Assembling merchant-ships in masses, and sending them to sea with inadequate protection, would simply mean presenting the enemy with an opportunity of massacring shipping *en bloc*.) In principle, the Conference was in favour of extending the convoy system. Estimates as to convoying in the Mediterranean were, however, regarded as being merely provisional, inasmuch as an International Commission at Malta was then examining the whole question of trade defence in that sea.

(For details embodied in the above note, use has been made of chapter xxvii. of *With the British Battle Fleet* (Commodore G. von Schoultz, Finnish Navy). Von Schoultz was one of the Russian delegates to the Conference, and gives a full summary of the proceedings.)

[1] The dummy sweep, already described (pp. 196-97) in connection with UC 44, may have referred to this boat.

mine-layer, UC 6 (Reichenbach), was caught on the surface by the seaplane 8676 off the south-west corner of the Thornton Ridge, and was bombed out and blotted out. On the next day, the 29th, far from these perilous waters abounding in mine, air, and patrol dangers, the tenth U-boat was eliminated. As she was patrolling off Lerwick, in the Shetlands, the trawler *Moravia* surprised UC 55 (Lilienstern) laying mines ; the destroyers *Sylvia* and *Tirade* were called up, and sank the marauder by gunfire and depth-charge.

Off the coast of Yorkshire submarines were showing much activity, and it was decided to lay a mine-field six miles east of Whitby. On September 4 a hostile submarine had indulged in a senseless bombardment of Scarborough. The first shells fell amongst mine-sweepers outside the harbour, and the rest were scattered amongst the hotels and shops, killing four people. She was chased off by the mine-sweepers.

All this time the decoys cruised the seas, seeking their prey. In August, Q-boats had eleven actions to their credit ; and in one such combat the *Vala* (Q 7) was sunk between the Fastnet and the Scillies, on the 21st, with all hands. Hitherto decoys had roamed singly ; after the introduction of convoys, solitary ships of low speed were regarded by the enemy with distrust. It now became the practice to include in a convoy a sloop disguised as a merchant-ship. Sometimes these disguised vessels would lag behind to simulate a straggler, ever a tempting target for the U-boat. The convoy sloops gained certain successes during the next months, but suffered heavy loss by reason of their dangerous lot. One such vessel, the *Bergamot*, was sunk in the Atlantic on August 13. Besides losses sustained by patrols in western seas, other warships were sunk in different areas—the new destroyer *Recruit*, mined in the North Sea on August 9 ; the armed boarding-steamer *Dundee*, torpedoed by U 19 in the Channel on September 3, six months after her gallant fight with the raider *Leopard* ; and the destroyer *Contest*, likewise sunk in the Channel on September 18 by a submarine-delivered torpedo.

A mystery of the U-boat war, still awaiting an explanation, dates from September 17. Whilst cruising in the Bay of Biscay, the decoy *Stonecrop* was attacked by gunfire from a submarine which held off at the long range of 10,000 yards. Sending out wireless calls for help, the trap-ship replied to the submarine's fire with her defensive gun, and dropped smoke-boxes. About an hour later the panic party abandoned ship; it included two men in naval uniform to represent the defensive-gun's crew. The submarine's periscope was then seen to be closing in to 400 yards; it passed down the port side of the vessel, under her stern, and then up the starboard side. The U-boat next broke surface 500 yards off on the starboard quarter of the decoy, presenting a full broadside. For three minutes her commander minutely examined the *Stonecrop* through his periscope. Concealed in the decoy, Commander Blackwood waited. As the submarine was about to move towards the boats, the Q-boat dropped her disguise and opened fire with her 4-inch gun and all her howitzers. The fourth shot split open the submarine's conning-tower; the fifth struck the hull just before the mount of the forward gun; the sixth hit just between; and the seventh caught her well aft. The next four shots went home in various parts, tearing up the deck and perforating the hull. After the eleventh hit the enemy disappeared, sinking by the stern. A few seconds later she emerged with a heavy list to starboard, again sinking out of sight. Her crew, seemingly, had made desperate efforts to bring her to the surface, and there seemed little doubt that she was mortally injured. The following day the *Stonecrop* was torpedoed and began to go down slowly. Immediately after the crew had left her—and this time in real earnest—a submarine appeared. For six long days one of the rafts drifted about before it was picked up, by which time 1 officer and 12 men had died of thirst. Their deaths, taken with those of the 3 officers and 28 men who had fallen in action, were indeed lamentable. To tragedy must be added the acerbation of futility, for it has since been proved that no submarine was destroyed. It can only be presumed that the injured U-boat patched up her wounds and broadcast a warning description of the decoy to other U-boats, one of which avenged the attack. For a long time it was believed that the *Stonecrop*'s assailant was Schwieger; but Schwieger was already dead, lying encoffined in U 88 fathoms deep in the mine-strewn North Sea.[1]

Here must be remarked the appearance of the first of the ' UB III ' series of boats, UB 48. This type, a distinct advance on its predecessors, displaced about 510 tons, compared with the 250-ton ' UB II ' boats. They were not far inferior to the 800-ton ' Mittel U-boote ' of the North Sea flotillas. Since the summer of 1916 there had been no deliveries of new UB-boats; now, after an interval of a year, units of the third and enlarged pattern began to appear. The first six boats of consecutive numbering were destined for the Adriatic flotilla. As already related, UB 48 (Steinbauer),[2] on his way to Cattaro, had sunk the Q.-boat *Prize*. The Adriatic haven was reached on September 2. Another, UB 49 (von Mellenthin, late of UB 46), was on her way out. On September 8, such injuries were sustained in a fight with the armed yacht *Narcissus II.*, that the German boat was forced to make for Cadiz, arriving there three days later. She was interned in accordance with the Spanish decree. On the evening of October 6, however, her commander broke his *parole* and took his boat to sea, much to the indignation of the Spanish. The other four units (UB 50-53) of the first six reached the Adriatic without incident, and appear to have been followed soon after by a further half-flotilla, composed of UB 66-71. No new UC-boats were delivered until the summer of 1918.

In the previous autumn U 53 had carried the submarine war across the Atlantic Ocean right to the threshold of American territory. Once again September initiated an expansion in the zone of operations. According to the German apologist Gayer, this month marked the opening of the submarine-cruiser campaign, directly controlled by the German Naval Staff. Actually U 155 (formerly known as the mercantile

---

[1] Prize bounty was awarded in December 1921 to *Stonecrop* for sinking U 88.

[2] Lately in command of UB 47 until that boat, together with UB 43, was ceded to Austria-Hungary. See p. 170.

THE PENUMBRA OF ECLIPSE 217

submarine *Deutschland*) had, under Meusel, made a cruise lasting about 105 days during the summer of 1917. She left Germany about May 24, and returned on September 4. Several interesting features marked this pioneer cruise. It nearly came to an early and disastrous end, for on May 27, near Üdsire Island (off the Norwegian coast), U 155 was stalked and almost sunk by U 19 (Spiess).[1] After passing round the north of Scotland, U 155 went down to the Azores, and shelled San Miguel (Punta Delgada) on the morning of July 4. During her prolonged presence at sea, the big submarine sank 19 merchant-vessels, mostly by scuttling-bombs or gunfire. Ten defenceless neutral ships proved to be easy victims, but of the 19 British and Allied armed merchantmen attacked only 9 could be destroyed. When U 155 got back to Germany she had covered 10,220 miles, of which only 620 had been run submerged. Meusel reported that, during the whole time he had been at sea, only one hostile war-vessel—an armed merchant-cruiser—had been sighted. Good weather prevailed for the greater part of the voyage, and helped materially towards the success of the undertaking. Cruises of equal and even longer duration were afterwards achieved; none the less, the maiden war-cruise of U 155 stands out as one of the longest voyages made by the U-boats.[2] These diving freighters, after their transformation into the war-boats U 151-157, displaced 1870 tons when submerged and 1510 tons in surface trim, and could carry 18 torpedoes. Although clumsy to handle and endowed with bad diving qualities, their endurance was phenomenal; and with their

[1] Spiess explains in his book that British submarines often used to lie in wait near Üdsire, hoping to intercept and sink the U-boats. (U 6 had been caught and sunk by E 16 in this area.) He took U 155 to be a large British boat; he dived and prepared to attack her. But noticing upon the hull of his supposed enemy certain small features peculiar to German submarines, he withheld his attack, rose to the surface, and gave the challenge, which was satisfactorily answered. Spiess was returning from a cruise, and had never been warned, by wireless, of U 155's departure, her appearance, course, etc. The omission (which nearly led to fatal consequences) arose from the divided control of the submarines. U 19 was attached to the High Seas Fleet, whereas U 155 was under the orders of the Naval Staff, Berlin.

[2] 'Submarine Sizes' (Lieutenant-Commander E. W. Burroughs, U.S.N.), *U.S.N.I. Proceedings*, December 1927, p. 1294.

two 5·9-inch and (in some cases) two 3·4-inch guns,[1] they had an awe-inspiring aspect—nothing less than a new type of diving *Möwe*. They pushed the boundary of the U-boat campaign right down to the north-west coast of Africa; so it became necessary to extend the convoy areas to counter this new menace. Still further calls were thus made upon the hard-worked patrol and anti-submarine craft. Grandiloquently dubbed by the Germans 'U-cruisers,' the ex-*Deutschlands* merited no such ornate rating. None the less, these large boats gave the Allies a foretaste of what commerce-raiding might be like were it waged by 'oceanic' submarines of two, three, and four thousand tons displacement. Had the so-called U-cruisers of the 1917 and 1918 programmes ever come to sea in large numbers, the area of depredations might have extended in 1919 to the St. Lawrence, the United States coast, and perhaps even to the Cape, the Caribbean, and the Plate. The cruises of the ex-mercantile craft were apparently intended for training captains and crews in the work projected for the 1919 'U-cruiser' campaign, and as such are worthy of notice.

The two boats, selected to extend the submarine threat into tropical waters, left their bases for cruises of three months' duration. In command of Kophamel, the late commander at Pola, U 151 sailed from Kiel on September 3 for the Azores. During her 12,000-mile trip she destroyed about 30,000 tons of shipping, numbering in all 13 vessels. Amongst her victims was the Italian munition-steamer *Caprera* (5040 tons), whose crew put up a spirited defence with their after gun. Only when a hit by U 151 had started to ignite some ammunition did they hurriedly abandon their ship. Simply on account of the exploding ammunition in the *Caprera*, Kophamel kept clear, and continued a leisurely gunnery practice on the steamer, securing a hit amidships. There was one tremendous explosion; a vast grey billowing cloud darkened the air; and a hail of minute fragments of *débris* descended upon the waters. From the crew, who had left their vessel so precipitately, Kophamel learnt that the *Caprera*, bound from America for Italy, was carrying a

[1] The 3·4-inch guns were not mounted in U 155-7.

thousand tons of dynamite ; and he was devoutly thankful that, when the ship was blown to atoms, he had kept clear of her. In St. Vincent harbour Kophamel sank two Brazilian steamers, and took some copper from a Norwegian ship. At a date during September, U 152 (Meusel) also left for her cruise, which extended to the Portuguese coast, the Azores, and the Canaries. On her return she claimed the destruction of about 40,000 tons. The third cruise was undertaken by U 156 (Gansser) ; her mission included the cutting of the Atlantic cables, five in number, around the Azores. On December 12 she appeared off Funchal, shelled the town, and wrecked the church of Santa Clara, killing or wounding many civilians. Shipping attack in the Azores-Madeira area was another side to the enterprise. The circumstances attendant on the sinking of the sailing-vessel *W. C. M'Kay* with her crew in January are not known ; they were, however, sufficiently revolting to warrant the indictment of Gansser in the British List of War Criminals. Another of his crimes was committed during the destruction of the steamer *Artesia* (2762 tons), sunk by bombs on February 8, 1918, 190 miles E. by N. from Madeira. During the cruise U 156 made nine unsuccessful attacks.

Several events in far different waters are worthy of narration at this point. In the Baltic a half-flotilla of U-boats was still maintained. During the joint naval and military operations against Oesel, in the Gulf of Riga, by the Germans in October, the submarines were detailed to intercept the Russian retreat from the northern part of the Moon Sound. On October 16 the Russian cruiser *Bogatyr* was injured in a torpedo attack by UC 58 ; and on the same day UC 60 sank a transport. One mining-boat, UC 57 (Wissman), disappeared during November, and it was presumed that she blew up on the mines in the Gulf of Finland. After the peace of Brest-Litovsk the Courland half-flotilla was withdrawn. By the end of the year the Baltic U-boats had been transferred to the North Sea flotillas.

In the Arctic, U 46 reappeared after a year's absence, and sank four ships—the *Zillah* (3788 tons) on October 22, the *Ilderton* (3125 tons) and *Obj*, both on the 24th, and the *Baron*

Balfour (3991 tons) on the 28th. Eighteen lives were lost in the first case, one of the *Zillah*'s boats vanishing with its crew. Mines had been laid in the Kola Inlet by a large mine-layer in the previous April, and during the early summer several merchant-vessels had been torpedoed in the high latitudes.

During October the Flanders force was divided into two flotillas. There was no doubt that the Thornton Ridge barrier was hindering free movement, forcing the U-boats to pass eastwards and outside the Schouwen Bank and thence by the West Hinder L.V. To the mines off Zeebrugge, UC 14 (Reserve-officer Feddersen) succumbed on October 3; this boat was one of the craft assembled at Pola in 1915. Since she was incapable of performing the trip from the Adriatic to the North Sea by sea, about January 1917 she was hoisted on a slip, disassembled, and railed from Pola to Bruges for service with the Flanders flotillas. On the 5th, UB 41 (Ploen) was blown up off Scarborough; whether the disaster was due to external contact with a mine or internal explosion has not to this day been determined. Fourteen days later UC 62 [1] (Schmitz) was surprised in the act of sinking a Dutch steamer in the North Sea by the British submarine E 45, and joined her victim on the sea-bottom. Another boat, UC 16 (Reimarus), was sighted off Selsey Bill, on the 23rd, by the destroyer *Melampus* and rammed; explosive paravanes were then fired. Oil welled up, but, as a heavy sea was running at the time, no survivors were seen. It was during bad weather in October that Schneider, the *Arabic*'s assailant, was washed overboard from U 87 and drowned.

Several and prominent were the events marking the month of October. Ships of the 10th Cruiser Squadron (as previously noted) had been ordered, when returning to their base to coal, to join and take cover with the incoming convoys.[2] On October 2 the *Hildebrand*, bound for the Clyde, attached herself to a convoy in charge of the armoured cruiser *Drake*. More unlucky than her sister the *King Alfred* (which on

---

[1] Early records gave UC 79.

[2] On August 21 the *Virginian*, on convoy duty, was torpedoed, but was brought in.

another occasion was beached after she had sustained torpedo injuries), the *Drake* was mortally hit by a torpedo in the North Channel, capsizing later while at anchor in Rathlin Sound. The *Hildebrand* herself escaped attack and reached the Clyde. The incident, however, emphasized the weakness of the arrangement. Further disaster followed on the 9th, when the *Champagne* (ex-*Oropesa*), rejoining her patrol from Liverpool, was torpedoed and sunk in Dundrum Bay. She was hit by two torpedoes at about 6.30 A.M. ; and as the boats pulled away, a third torpedo broke her back. Bad weather resulted in a heavy death-roll of 5 officers and 53 men. Yet a third loss was suffered on the 19th. A convoy of 20 steamers, escorted by the armed merchant cruiser *Orama* and 10 destroyers, was approaching these islands. A hundred miles ahead was the American steamer *J. L. Luckenbach*, sending out S.O.S. calls stating that she was being shelled by a submarine, and that her cotton cargo was alight. Her appeals for help were answered ; she was told that destroyers were coming to her aid, and she was earnestly requested to hold out until their arrival. A running fight ensued between the steamer and U 62 (Hashagen). For over three hours the *J. L. Luckenbach* put up a stout resistance, until at last the United States destroyer *Nicholson* hove in sight. With her second shot she hit the bows of U 62. The submarine dived to escape the rain of depth-charges. Quiet having again descended, Hashagen surfaced ; to his utter amazement he found himself right amongst the convoy. With his last remaining torpedo he struck down the *Orama* and dived. The tip of his periscope had been seen by quick eyes in the American destroyer *Conyngham*, and a depth-charge was put over right above the spot where it had been seen. After the turmoil of the boiling waters had subsided, boards, spars, and other wreckage came up. There seemed little doubt that the hull of U 62 had been riven and had dropped into the depth, freighted with her dead crew. The Admiralty adjudicated the loss of the submarine as a 'probable.' None the less, Hashagen survived and wrought still more damage thereafter. The first casualty amongst the American troopships occurred on the 17th, when the *Antilles* (6878 tons) was sunk ; as she was homeward bound, the loss of life was confined to 70 of the crew.

Other October losses include the Lamport & Holt *Memling* (7307 tons), near Brest on the 3rd ; the Leyland *Memphian* (6305 tons), 7 miles E.N.E. from North Arklow L.V., with 32 lives, and the *Richard de Larrinaga* (5591 tons), 15 miles S.E. $\frac{1}{2}$ S. from Ballycottin Island, by von Georg (probably in U 101), with 35 lives, both on the 8th ; the *Aylevarroo* (908 tons), a victim of *spurlos versenkt*, with her entire crew of 20 ; the P. & O. *Peshawur* (7634 tons) on the 9th, 7 miles S.E. $\frac{1}{2}$ E. from Ballyquintin Point, Co. Down, with 11 lives ; the Leyland *Bostonian* (5736 tons), a commissioned escort ship, on the 10th, 34 miles S. by E. $\frac{1}{2}$ E. from Start, with 4 lives ; the *Hazelwood* (3120 tons) on the 18th, 8 miles S. by E. $\frac{1}{2}$ E. from Anvil Point, with 32 lives ; and the Allan liner *Ionian* (8268 tons) on the 20th, 2 miles W. from St. Govan's Head, with 7 lives. Unfortunately, the loss of life this month from mine and torpedo, in both sunken and damaged ships, totalled 651, a marked increase on the September figure of 408. The number of ships lost was 85, with an addition of 5 fishing-vessels—a slight increase and decrease on the previous month's total of 77 and 7 respectively. The tonnage of the sunken ships was 274,973 tons gross.

It had long been obvious that the mine-nets laid from the Goodwins across to the Outer Ruytingen in September 1916, and extended as far as the Snou in the following December, presented no serious obstacle to the hostile submarines setting out from, or returning to, their Flemish stronghold. From the beginning of 1917 until the end of November no fewer than 253 passages had been made by the U-boats—an average of 23 each month. Between the buoys the nets sagged, enabling both submarines and destroyers to run over this barrier. An attempt to remedy this defect by using more supporting buoys had been made. Nevertheless the mines were a positive danger to the drifters watching the line ; and in the end both mines and nets were taken up. In February 1917, Vice-Admiral Bacon had submitted a scheme for building up a wall of mines, laid at varying depths, from the Varne Shoal to Cape Grisnez ; and, later, he suggested extending the barrage right across to Folkestone. In September he proposed to incorporate in these arrangements a shallow mine-field and four lightships to indicate the barrage to the patrols. When, in November 1917, the new H 2 mark of mine became available in quantity, the first part of the barrage could be undertaken. This section was laid on November 21. Exactly four weeks later the first raider was caught ; and within a few weeks it began to inflict such losses on the passing submarines that in February 1918 the North Sea boats were once again forbidden to attempt the passage. By September 1918 the Straits were effectually sealed, and no more U-boats of any class, large or small, tried to pass. The operations of the Flanders contingent were confined to the North Sea trade alone. Three long years of bitter experience at length brought their reward.[1]

Vice-Admiral Sir Reginald Bacon was averse to the illumination of the Folkestone-Grisnez barrage during the first month after its installation. He did not favour the use of flares (a feature introduced later), on the ground that they would reveal the presence of an obstructive line. He desired the U-boats to hit the mines and be destroyed without an inkling of their fate being given to any other hostile boat in the vicinity. For a similar reason he objected to the massing of patrols above the barrage, pointing out their futility in fog. Moreover, he believed that heavy losses would be inflicted on those craft if hostile torpedo-boats made high-speed raids by night down the Straits. That his opinion was justified is demonstrated by the fact that, after Vice-Admiral Bacon had ceased to be the S.N.O. at Dover, the patrols were massed, and they suffered heavy losses from the very form of enemy attack that he had foreseen. Instead, he advocated a surface mine-field, with gates at Folkestone and Cape Grisnez, illuminated by the lightships ; these and two other

[1] In justice and fairness, Vice-Admiral Sir Reginald Bacon must be awarded all credit and praise for originating the Folkestone-Grisnez barrage and the Zeebrugge-Ostend blockship plans, and for working out all the details connected with those two schemes. Others reaped the harvest which he had sown. He was not allowed the satisfaction of retaining his command at Dover until such time as his plans were put into full execution and without variation from their main lines.

lightships, all having powerful searchlights, and two lights ashore, would, in his opinion, have provided a more efficient illumination than the flares. He decided to keep the patrols to the westward of the lightships, so that they would be able to see the U-boats illuminated by the beams, without they themselves being lit up; further, they would be safe from mine danger.

However, a Barrage Committee, set up by the First Lord (Sir Eric Geddes), made sundry reports and, amongst other things, recommended a reorganization of the patrols. 'The committee ended by reporting that the existing barrage was inefficient (a fact which had become apparent), and made proposals for the establishment of the already approved minefield on the Folkestone-Grisnez line. I do not recollect that any definite new ideas were evolved as the outcome of the labours of this committee.'[1] The Barrage Committee did, however, produce one novelty. It brought into being a pattern of combined maritime martello tower and barrage pillar, in the shape of the so-called 'Southwick monsters' or 'weddingcake ships.' A few of these enormous structures were completed in 1918, but none was ever taken out to sea and sunk into position before the war ended. The Barrage Committee's proposals for re-forming the patrols proved to be of little or no value whatever. Just before the year (1917) closed, both Admiral Sir J. R. Jellicoe and Vice-Admiral Sir R. H. Bacon had been relieved in their positions as First Sea Lord and Admiral at Dover respectively. The first submarine was caught in the new barrage on December 19; the attack on Zeebrugge had been fixed by Vice-Admiral Bacon for February 22; and he wrote that 'there was no time to lose.'

Rear-Admiral Sir Roger Keyes, President of the Operations Committee, succeeded Vice-Admiral Bacon; he introduced a number of innovations. Flares and massed patrols, expedients which, as stated above, Sir Reginald Bacon did not favour, were put into use. The new Senior Naval Officer at Dover also reviewed the plans for the blockship attack on Zeebrugge and Ostend; these plans were left substantially

[1] *The Crisis of the Naval War* (Jellicoe), p. 215.

THE PENUMBRA OF ECLIPSE 225

in the form into which they had been cast by Vice-Admiral Bacon.

During October, Vice-Admiral Bacon had obtained the use of the submarine E 52, his intention being that this British boat should try to catch U-boats passing in and out of Zeebrugge. Previously he had used one or two old C-class submarines, fitted with occulting lights on their conning-towers, so as to simulate the barrage light-buoys by which the U-boats were wont to fix their position as they awaited the tide, to make their run over the nets. These old boats had only bow tubes; and on the one or two occasions, when an enemy had been encountered, they could not bring their bows round quickly enough to attempt a torpedo shot. Success came to E 52 on the night of October 31, as she lay in the area mined in 1914, east of the Goodwins, through which the enemy passed. She suddenly saw the hull of UC 63 (Heydebreck) gliding by, and promptly got a torpedo away. From 'Klaxon' (*The Story of Our Submarines*), it appears that the engineer of the U-boat had just come up to chat with the officer of the watch; the latter thus failed to notice E 52 lying close by, until the moment when the British boat turned to fire. Just one moment's relaxing of vigilance, and out of the void came death for all within the German boat. No further success attended this form of sub-surface attack. UC 63 was returning from a cruise, and had notified her position immediately before she disappeared. The locality of her demise could therefore be easily calculated by the German Naval Command at Bruges, and marked for avoidance as a dangerous area.

Two days after E 52's success, one of the British submarines allocated to the Channel Patrol, C 15, was south of Beachy Head. It was afternoon, and Kapitän-Leutnant Klaus Lafrenz, of UC 65, also homeward bound, sighted the British boat. Being anxious to finish his trip, he took the risk of dodging his opponent's torpedoes. Indeed, just as he was propounding to his second-in-command the doctrine of a quick turn of the helm, he saw the surface air-boil of the expected torpedo. He endeavoured to carry his teaching into effect. The submarine swerved sharply off her course, only

P

to receive, full and square amidships, a hit from a second torpedo. The commanding officer of C 15 had fired a double bow shot, slightly spread, to hit the enemy whichever way he turned. Five survivors were picked up.[1]

The destroyer *Firedrake* scored her second kill by sinking UC 51 (Galster) off Harwich on the 13th ; and four days later two more U-boats ended their careers. One was Steinbrinck's old boat, UB 18, now under Niemeyer ; she ran on to British mines off Start Point. The scene of the other loss was in the western approaches. A division of American destroyers, escorting a convoy of 8 merchant-ships, had just left Queenstown. As the steamers formed into columns, one of the rear destroyers, *Fanning*, spotted the tip of a periscope close to the Dominion liner *Welshman* (5730 tons). It disappeared almost immediately, but not quite quickly enough. The *Fanning* circled round and dropped a depth-charge on the spot where she had seen the periscope ; and the leader of the division, *Nicholson*, put over another ahead of the *Fanning*. As the turmoil subsided, eager eyes scanned the sea for wreckage. Nothing was seen, not even tell-tale oil. Fifteen minutes passed. Then the stern of a U-boat pierced the surface of the water at an angle of thirty degrees, followed by the conning-tower, and finally the whole hull emerged and rode on an even keel. U 58 lay revealed, apparently undamaged. The two destroyers stood by, firing shell at her hull ; and the *Nicholson*, by way of afterthought, dropped another 'ash-can.' This treatment had decisive effect, and out of the conning-tower scrambled Amberger, followed by his crew shouting 'Kamerade !' The destroyers held their fire ; the *Fanning* cautiously approached, whilst the *Nicholson* stood by with guns trained on U 58. Two of the crew were then seen to re-enter the submarine and reappear after a few minutes. U 58 next began to settle ; the crew dived into the water and swam towards the destroyers, which picked them up. Two American seamen jumped into the water to save one German in difficulties ; he died soon afterwards on the deck of the *Fanning*. From the Germans a curious tale was secured. After passing through the Dover Straits on the

[1] *The Story of Our Submarines* ('Klaxon'), pp. 79-83.

XI. AMERICAN WARSHIPS SINK A SUBMARINE.
Although the United States Naval Forces contributed to the destruction of two other U-boats, the only hostile submarine eliminated by U.S. warships unaided was U. 58. On November 17, 1917, the destroyers *Fanning* and *Nicholson* mortally injured U. 58 by gunfire and depth-charge, so that she was compelled to surrender. The German crew is here seen on the after-deck of the sinking U-boat.

French side at 1.52 A.M. on November 14, they had safely arrived in the west. For two days they had waited for this convoy, and were just about to torpedo the *Welshman*, when the periscope revealed the *Fanning* bearing down upon them. The depth-charge which the latter had dropped produced extraordinary effects, wrecking the electric motors and jamming the diving rudders. Unable to navigate, and beyond control, U 58 dropped down to 278 feet, even as her commander was debating whether to perish miserably or to try to blow ballast tanks and come up to surrender. Amberger decided to trust to the mercy of his opponents. The second depth-charge practically wrecked U 58 internally. As this was the only submarine sunk by United States naval forces unaided, the incident claims a fair share of attention. American ships also contributed indirectly to the sinking of three others.

Early on the following morning (November 18), the patrol boat P 57 came upon the mine-laying UC 47 (Wigankow), 24 miles E.S.E. from Flamborough Head. Fifteen seconds after the order to ram had been given, the heavy steel prow of P 57 ripped right through the mine-layer's deck. Her fate was sealed with depth-charges. No survivors were seen in the oil-covered water around. In increasing numbers these submarines were caught as they endeavoured to molest the traffic flowing up and down the great East Coast war channels. Many were attacked, but often escaped from the hornets they had aroused. In this case the wreck was located, and later destroyed.

On November 21, U 48 (Edeling) left Wilhelmshaven for a cruise in the west. By the afternoon of the 23rd, when still sixty miles from Dover, U 48 was spotted by a seaplane and bombed, though not hit. Her commander was seeking a resting-place on the bottom, to await darkness before he started his run through the Straits, near to 2A Buoy (east of the Goodwins). Owing to a strong westerly current and failure of the gyro-compass, U 48 was carried out of her course, and fouled the nets off the North Goodwins. To add to her plight, the nets, entangled in her propellers, made it impossible to use her Diesels, and she was forced to make a surface run on her electric motors. Early next morning, at about 3 A.M., U 48 took the ground on the dreaded Sands.[1] By jettisoning sixty tons of oil-fuel, fresh water, ready-use ammunition, and three torpedoes, U 48 refloated, but could not free herself from the bed she had made. Worse still, the tide was ebbing, and she took the ground once more. Just before dawn she was sighted by the trawler *Meror*, patrolling to the southward; and at the same time two Ramsgate drifters, *Majesty* and *Paramount*, sweeping the war channel, approached from the north-west. Joined by three other drifters (*Present Help*, *Acceptable*, and *Feasible*), the whole pack was after the cornered U-boat in a trice. U 48 was once more afloat and moving south-west. The submarine, it must be noted, was armed with a 4·1-inch gun, a machine-gun, and six torpedo-tubes. The drifters had only 6-pounders, and one had a Maxim in addition, and another had but a 3-pounder. So their intrepid skippers decided to close in as near as they could, and smother the more heavily-armed submarine with concentrated fire if possible. As the fight waxed hot, help arrived from the north in the guise of the old destroyer *Gipsy*, and U 48 was soon reduced to a crippled condition. Edeling, finding his command to be on fire, gave orders to blow up U 48; the crew jumped overboard, and, of the 43, 1 officer and 21 men were picked up out of the water.

The first section of the new mine-barrage between Folkestone and Grisnez was, as previously mentioned, laid on the 21st. The effect of the new obstruction could hardly become apparent until a greater span of the Straits had been sealed; submarines therefore continued to pass up and down. About a week after, in the last days of November, Salzwedel (the officer who had had the thrilling duel with Captain Campbell in the Q-ship *Dunraven*) took his new command, UB 81, through the Straits for the last time. Off the Isle of Wight his boat hit a mine on December 2. With the stern shattered, the submarine's bows emerged, and two men crawled out of the torpedo-tubes; they were picked up by a patrol, which

---

[1] According to Gayer, U 94 also stranded on these banks, but succeeded in getting clear before she had made a bed for herself. U 48 was less fortunate.

rammed the U-boat and sent her to the bottom. With the demise of Salzwedel, the Flanders flotilla lost one of its ablest exponents of the sub-surface warfare. Four days subsequent to this casualty another U-boat came to a singular end. Before the war, it was commonly believed that the risk of collision between under-water craft prohibited their working together. In practice, German submarines had frequently operated in pairs; and the fact that only one serious collision took place showed that the pre-war estimate of risk was too pessimistic. On this day, December 6, U 96 accidentally rammed and sank UC 69 (Thielmann) off Cape Barfleur. Two other losses may be noticed here. The mines off Terschelling accounted for UB 61 (T. Schultz) on November 29; and U 75 (Schmolling) likewise succumbed in the same locality on December 13. The latter, it may be recalled, was the large mine-layer responsible for the laying of the field in which the cruiser *Hampshire* foundered in June 1916.

As for the Q-boats, they kept the seas in all weathers and in all guises. One, the *Begonia* (Q 10), a sloop of mercantile aspect, went to sea in October, and from that time nothing was ever heard of her again. What tragedy is shrouded by this silence will never be known. A second convoy sloop, the *Arbutus*, was torpedoed and sunk in the Bristol Channel on December 16. By the winter of 1917, solitary decoys had passed their zenith, and such successes as were won came only to the convoy decoys; no longer did the German authorities insist on submarine commanders obtaining ships' papers, an insistence that had caused the loss of not a few U-boats with their crews.

There was a general reduction in the November shipping losses, both as regards number, tonnage, and loss of life. Those worthy of notice are: the *Cape Finisterre* (4380 tons) on November 2, 1 mile S.S.E. from the Manacles Buoy, with 35 lives; the Union of New Zealand *Aparima* (5704 tons) on the 19th, 6 miles S.W. ¾ W. from Anvil Point, with 56 lives; the Union-Castle *Aros Castle* (4460 tons) on the 21st, 300 miles W. by S. ¼ S. from Bishop Rock, with 2 lives; the Houlder *La Blanca* (7479 tons), with a valuable cargo of meat, on the

23rd, 10 miles S.S.E. from Berry Head, with 2 lives. In the last-named case the ship had developed engine trouble, necessitating her putting into the nearest port before completing her journey ; and she was sunk after her defects had been remedied. Finally, on November 28, the Elder-Dempster *Apapa* (7832 tons) was sunk by U 96 (Jetz), 3 miles N. by E. of Lynas Point, off the Mersey. This fine ship, a sister of the well-known *Appam*, had left her convoy early in the morning, and at 4 A.M. was struck by a torpedo. She quickly settled on an even keel, and the passengers quietly took to the boats. Before they could be lowered, another torpedo exploded against the liner, causing her to fall over to starboard and crush the unfortunate boats. Sinking stern first, the *Apapa* took down with her 38 passengers and 39 of the crew.

Besides these mercantile casualties, the United States armed yacht *Alcedo* was torpedoed and sunk in the Bay of Biscay on November 15. The American destroyer *Jacob Jones* was also torpedoed on December 6, in the south-western approaches, by U 53 (Rose). It will be recollected that Rose had visited American waters in September 1916, and now he was renewing his acquaintance with his former hosts. Hans Rose sighted the destroyer over 3000 yards distant, and took a flying shot at her ; when he saw her sinking, and her crew in open boats on the wintry waste, he called up Queenstown, gave latitude and longitude of the shipwrecked seamen, and then got away from the area as quickly as possible. Rose, noted as one of the humane submarine-commanders, would on occasion gather together a ship's boats and take them in tow towards land. His work was usually characterized by a sharp, sudden burst of activity, ceasing as unexpectedly as it had begun.

The last month of the terrible year 1917 closed with a few noteworthy events. On October 20, mine-nets had been laid off Flamborough Head to trap U-boats as they approached this headland to fix their position. Already UC 47 had been surprised near the new danger spot, and had paid in full for her temerity. The mine-nets were next to claim as victim the UB 75 (Fr. Walther) on December 10. British mine-fields were laid off many other landfalls where U-boats themselves were prone to lay mines in the early days of mining, and before they themselves desired to use these marks for checking their navigation. The UC-boats were still active, and were confining their work to inshore waters, where shipping hugged the coast to evade the submarines in deeper soundings. Mines were laid far apart instead of in small groups, and fields began to be discovered well out at sea.

The most significant occurrence was the first victim of the new 'deep' barrage. The whole affair was simplicity itself. About midnight on December 19 the UB 56 (H. Valentiner) began her run through the Straits of Dover;[1] exactly at 11.42 P.M. there was a terrific explosion. One German was seen in the water, but he died after he had come to the surface. From now onwards submarines trying to run the gauntlet suffered heavily ; many got through unscathed, and, indeed, 21 passed during the first fortnight. But as the wall of mines was laboriously built up, the greater became the peril to the enemy, until by October 1918 the barrage was complete. The door of the Dover Straits was at last bolted and barred to the modern emulators of 'Blackbeard.'

The December shipping losses showed an increase in number and tonnage : 76 ships of 227,195 tons gross were 'submarined,' and 8 of 23,606 tons mined, with a loss of life totalling 585. The only large vessel sent to the bottom in waters outside the Mediterranean was the Cunard cargo-liner *Vinovia* (7046 tons), sunk on the 19th, 8 miles south of the Wolf Rock, with 9 lives. On the 16th the *Bristol City* (2511 tons) was lost with her entire crew of 30. One submarine was caught red-handed, and paid the penalty. On Christmas Day, Count von Speth-Schülzburg, who had just succeeded the late Rudolf Schneider (so well known in these waters) in the command of U 87, was celebrating the day of peace and goodwill by sinking the Elder-Dempster *Agberi* (4821 tons), 18 miles N.W. of Bardsey Island. As the sloop *Buttercup* circled round the sinking liner, she struck a submerged submarine. Quickly the patrol boat PC 56 dropped a depth-

[1] Michelsen gives all barrage victims as 'in Channel.'

charge and forced U 87 to the surface. She was at once rammed by the patrol boat, and at point-blank range was greeted with a hot fire from the *Buttercup*. No U-boat could stand such drastic treatment, and U 87 broke in two and sank. This success was counterbalanced by a serious mining disaster off the Mersey Bar. On the 28th the pilot vessel *Alfred H. Read* (457 tons) blew up on mines and sank so rapidly that 39 lives were lost, including 16 Liverpool pilots—a very heavy blow to the port.

During the month under review the submarines again turned their attention to the Scandinavian convoys. The raid on October 17 by the cruisers *Bremse* and *Brummer* (resulting in the massacre of 9 Allied and neutral ships, after the loss of the escorting destroyers *Mary Rose* and *Strongbow*) had been followed by a submarine attack on October 24, when one steamer was sunk. Then another raid by surface ships was made, this time with destroyers; and on the night of December 11, 6 British and neutral ships, with the destroyer *Partridge* and the trawlers *Commander Fullerton, Livingstone, Lord Alverstone,* and *Tokio*, were all wiped out. This second German success showed that a larger degree of security must be provided. Methil, in the Firth of Forth, was therefore chosen as the port of departure for the convoys instead of far northern Lerwick. This change incidentally saved the escorts much hardship in facing the stormy weather in the latitudes of the Shetlands. From Methil, the convoys, whilst on passage, were covered by squadrons detached from the Grand Fleet, which made sweeps timed to synchronize with the mercantile sailings. Thereafter, immunity from raids was more or less secured. So did history once again repeat itself, by ships of the line giving direct support and protection to mercantile traffic. On December 8 the armed boarding steamer *Grive* was torpedoed, though it was not until the 24th that she foundered off Lerwick owing to heavy weather. She had only lately returned from Archangel. Another of these boarding steamers, home from the Arctic, the *Stephen Furness*, was torpedoed and sunk in the Irish Sea on the 13th, with heavy loss of life. On the previous day a submarine had attacked the ships in the French Coal Trade.

THE PENUMBRA OF ECLIPSE

A particularly heavy blow was sustained on the 22nd by the Harwich force. These ships were responsible for the Dutch butter convoy and the ' beef-trip.' A mine-field had been located in their track, but for some reason the convoy sailed right into it, resulting in the loss of the new destroyers *Surprise, Tornado*, and *Torrent*. First one destroyer blew up, and the other two shared a similar fate on closing her. Even so, other destroyers came up to the spot and rescued 193 survivors.[1]

In British home waters at the close of the year the Germans were feeling the first effects of the Allied counter-drive against the U-boats. From January 1 to December 31 they had lost 63 submarines, or three times as many as had suffered extinction in 1916. In the autumn of 1917 a large new submarine programme was begun; repair facilities were reorganized on a large scale, and a special ' Submarine Bureau ' was organized under Vice-Admiral Ritter von Mann-Tiechler.[2] Gayer, however, believes that the effort came too late. Had a large programme been ordered immediately after the Pless Conference in September 1916, he thinks sufficient new boats would have been forthcoming to compensate for the heavy losses suffered in the latter part of 1917. Yet, of the boats ordered about September 1916, only one large boat ever went to sea before the end.[3] If the great German shipbuilding resources had been organized in 1916 as they were in the later stages of the war, a plentiful supply of material might possibly have been produced ; but the German military authorities would not release enough skilled artisans from the front to ensure a rapid output of new construction. During the last four months of 1917 an average of 8 submarines was destroyed.

[1] The Germans themselves had sustained a similar disaster in November 1916, when destroyers attempted to raid Libau and six blew up—an event known to the German Navy as ' The Massacre of the Innocents.'

[2] Gayer Lecture (*U.S.N.I. Proceedings*), pp. 655-6, and *High Sea Fleet* (Scheer), p. 328.

[3] U 142, the largest submarine built by the Germans. She had just completed her trials when the war ended, and never saw active service. The Germans do not agree as to whether she was technically ' completed ' or not. Some lists include her amongst ' submarines completed ' by 11th November 1918 ; other lists show her as a submarine completing and unfinished at conclusion of hostilities.

The shipping losses remained fairly constant at about 300,000 tons of British and 100,000 tons of foreign merchant-vessels. New construction was a long way behind the rate of destruction; and of course there was great leeway in unreplaced losses to make up. The November toll (56 British ships of 154,806 tons torpedoed) was below that of any month in the first half of 1918; and of the 892 ships under repair in the shipyards during this month, 542 vessels of 1,509,000 tons were passed out into mercantile service with their injuries made good. But it must be recollected that during 1918 the patrols had to be diverted to some degree from mercantile defence to protection of the American troop-transports. The United States armies were brought over, for the greater part, in British ships, and guarded almost entirely by British escorts and patrols. In home waters, the new year opened with improved and increasingly effective anti-submarine measures coming into fruitful operation; in the Mediterranean, however, the counter-attack still lacked punishing power.

The condition of the world's shipping, after thirty-eight months of hostilities, is shown by the subjoined statistics :—

ADMIRALTY TABLE OF SHIPPING LOSSES, 1914 TO END OF 1917

	British.	Foreign.	World.
Losses	7,079,492	4,478,081	11,557,573
New ships	3,031,555	3,574,720	6,606,275
Enemy ships seized	780,000	1,809,000	2,589,000
	Loss of	Gain of	Loss of
Net result	3,267,937	905,639	2,362,298

By the end of 1917, therefore, the climax of the submarine warfare upon shipping had passed. But the Allies and neutrals, who had to contend with all the anxieties and harassments arising from the contemporary *guerre de course*, could not count on it, as a certainty, that the worst of their troubles were over. February had hitherto been the month chosen by the Germans to cry havoc and hound the U-boats on to the sea-traders, to interdict zones from free navigation, and to declare the conditions under which merchantmen would be attacked. With no little trepidation was the second month of 1918 awaited by those nations which still kept their trading tonnage in active employment. There was a dread that the coming spring would bring another massacre of ships and seafarers, like to the butchery of the past April.

But, by the beginning of 1918, the Great General Staff had secretly recanted its profession of faith in the potency of the U-boats. It is said that, even before the six months' campaign had run its full course, the military chiefs had apostatized from the submarine cult. The Russian collapse had freed entire armies for service on other fighting fronts. Hindenburg and Ludendorff had decided that, if the war was to be won, it was not to be won at sea by the submarines, after all; it was to be won on land, and by means of a new and great offensive on the western front.

CHAPTER XI

THE MEDITERRANEAN HARVEST

(1917)

IN northern waters the climax of the struggle had been passed; the shock of the initial onslaught on the world's shipping had there been met and at fearful cost had been held. Slow, and almost imperceptible at times, was the decline of the enemy's offensive; yet with gathering force were the countermeasures holding and driving back the U-boats' attack. The review of the general situation in the Mediterranean is here resumed at the point at which it was left in January 1917. Far from favourable was the situation. Of the mosaic of Allied zones a description has already been given. The system of control may be summarised as follows: the Commander-in-Chief was the French Admiral Gauchet, flying his flag at Corfu; under him were Rear-Admiral Ballard at Malta, Rear-Admiral Sir C. Thursby in the Aegean watching the Dardanelles, Vice-Admiral Sir Rosslyn Wemyss in Egyptian waters, and Rear-Admiral Heathcoat Grant at Gibraltar. There were in addition French flag-officers in Syria and off Greece, an Allied force was operating in the Straits of Otranto, and in the western basin were French and Italian commands. Each navy was responsible for its own particular zone; with minor events outside its strict limits the force in that zone was not concerned. The results achieved by this partition of the sea and the variegation of commands were unsatisfactory. Napoleon's dictum that ' You cannot wage war in small parcels ' seemed to have been either ignored or entirely flouted.

It is essential that a summary should be presented of the leading characteristics of the Mediterranean situation previous to the opening of unrestricted war in these busy waters. After the Gallipoli evacuation in December 1915, the main

XII.   THE BEGINNING OF A WAR CRUISE.
A 'Medium Size' U-boat (of about 800 tons displacement) leaving the Basin at Heligoland for operations against shipping.

THE LAIR OF THE SEA GUERILLAS.
A Photograph taken at Cattaro, the Adriatic Base of the German Submarines. In the foreground, *U. 35* is seen preparing for one of her devastating cruises. Behind her lies the Austro-Hungarian boat *XXVII*. The two large submarines on the right are probably boats of the German *U. 63-65* class. The Austro-Hungarian cruiser *Sankt Georg* is in the background.

THE MEDITERRANEAN HARVEST 237

task of the naval forces was to guard and keep open the supplies for the Salonica and Egyptian expeditions, totalling some 400,000 men. In December 1915, soon after the violent attacks of the previous month (when 23 British and 18 Allied and neutral ships were sunk), a conference was held at Paris by the Allied naval representatives.[1] Upon essentials the meeting revealed a sharp divergence of views. The French, on the one hand, maintained that hostile submarines were using deserted creeks in the eastern Mediterranean as operational bases, and urged a thorough search by old cruisers of every likely spot. The British, on the other hand, favoured the diversion of shipping to certain routes which would be guarded by every available patrol-vessel. Vice-Admiral Dartige du Fournet (then the French Commander-in-Chief) supported the British view, suggesting that the strength needed for an efficient patrol would be 140 destroyers and 280 trawlers. No such force was available, and other remedies had to be devised. Then were the waters parted and the seas rent into the patchwork of eighteen areas. Slight adjustments followed whereby the French retained their position of supremacy in the Aegean, and the Malta-Egypt troop route was entirely controlled by British ships.

The German submarines of the Adriatic meanwhile had been withdrawn to the bases to undergo refit and repair; their offensive effects accordingly dwindled down to insignificant dimensions. In 1916 the January sinkings totalled 6 ships, those of February 12, and in March only 4 vessels were sunk. Then in April the total rose to 16, and in May the figure had reached 37, the Italian losses being particularly heavy (30,000 tons). With the forces at command, it was only possible to send out solitary naval 'policemen,' to patrol along given 'beats,' so as to save peaceful traders from being bludgeoned to death. Such a system of patrol gave but poor results, either in protecting shipping or in encountering the enemy. The patrols were, more often than not, an assistance to the submarines instead of an annoyance. As before remarked, a U-boat had but to find and watch the patrol to

[1] 'Anti-Submarine Campaign in the Mediterranean, 1916-18' (Capt. C. V. Usborne), R.U.S.I., April 1924.

discover which routes were being used and guarded; she then cruised up and down the lanes so revealed, with the certainty of picking up targets. The approach of any patrol could be easily dodged by a dive. Escorts could only be provided for such shipping as troopships, oilers, meat- and munition-carriers; these important vessels were passed on from zone to zone. Even under these arrangements the system broke down occasionally, with disastrous results. Long were the routes, and traffic at sea would number anything up to 350 ships at a time. To protect their shipping, the Allies could muster (in early 1917) 66 destroyers, 200 trawlers, and 79 sloops, gunboats, and armed boarding-steamers, for escort duty;[1] and many of these were too slow to chase a submarine in surface trim.

The toll of shipping continued to rise. The principal features of the 1916 Mediterranean campaign, and particularly the remarkable cruises of von Arnauld de la Perière in U 35, have been already reviewed. To these historic seas the German naval authorities had sent their submarine 'aces,' because there was less risk of 'regrettable incidents' and diplomatic complications with Washington than in waters where American citizens travelled and got 'submarined.' From the exploits of her Mediterranean submarine commanders Germany learnt that, so long as American lives were not lost, Washington would make no active protest against the sinking of shipping without warning. True, the U-boats only sank without admonition the ships which were armed; this was in compliance with the German intimation that her U-boats would only sink without warning those vessels which attempted to fly or fight. The attacks were most numerous at the western end, in the French zone; and during the last six months of 1916, 96 British ships of 415,471 tons, 24 French ships of 64,829 tons, 136 Italian vessels of 181,831 tons, totalling 256 ships of 662,131 tons gross, were destroyed. The British tonnage loss amounted to 62 per cent. of the whole. On the other hand, the Italians lost about half the total number of ships, a fact accounted for by the large number of

---

[1] It is important to realize that, in order to provide for a continuous patrol at sea, only a part was available whilst the other vessels were under repair or refitting and their crews resting.

THE MEDITERRANEAN HARVEST 239

small vessels sunk. The British ships destroyed were of considerable size.

It may be recalled that in the autumn of 1916 four large submarines [1] had been sent to join the six others (U 21, 33, 34, 35, 38, and 39) which had arrived in the previous spring and autumn; and they were closely followed by U 47 and U 63. Seven mine-laying craft of the improved UC II type also left German ports for the Mediterranean,[2] and during the first six months of 1917 nine other boats went out to these waters.[3] As against this increase in strength, four boats made their return to northern waters.[4] To the large boats, transferred from the North Sea flotillas, were added units of the UB III type, as the latter became available for service in the latter half of 1917.[5] Only three new boats (UB 105, 128, 129) could be sent out during 1918 to compensate for the casualties suffered by and in the Mediterranean flotillas.

In January 1917 thirteen boats still survived. There was the famous U 21, now past her prime but remembered for her pioneer work and exploits off Gallipoli, and about to return to the North Sea. Of the formidable 'Thirties,' U 33, 34, 35, 38, and 39 were still at work. The 'Children of Sorrow,' the slow and clumsy mine-layers of the U 71-80 class, had contributed U 72 and U 73 to the Adriatic flotilla. The coastal UB I design was represented by UB 14; the UB II series by UB 42, 43, and 47. The small mine-layer UC 14 was left as the last specimen of her species.[6] By the beginning of February there were 27 [7] German and 15 Austrian submarines based on Adriatic and Turkish ports.

For the Allies, the Mediterranean position was by January 1917 serious. Within the two last months of 1916 there had been a marked increase in the mercantile sinkings, and the increment no doubt was due to the expansion of the hostile

[1] Believed to be U 32, 52, 64, 65.
[2] UC 20, 22, 23, 24, 25, 34, and 35.
[3] UC 27, 37, 38, 52, 53, 54, 67, 73, and 74.
[4] *High Sea Fleet* (Scheer), p. 260.
[5] UB 48, 49, 50, 51, 52, 53, 66, 67 (?), 68, 69, 70, 71.
[6] Early in 1917, UC 14 was disassembled into sections and sent overland to Flanders. She was mined off Zeebrugge in October 1917.
[7] Includes UC 14.

submarine force. The counter-attack on the U-boats showed little success, past, present, or prospective : in 1915, one boat had been posted as missing, another was sunk in the Black Sea, and 2 Austrian craft in the Adriatic ; in 1916, 4 were destroyed in Turkish waters, 1 German and 1 Austrian craft were caught as they attempted the Otranto Straits, and a German and an Austrian had succumbed off Taranto. Events in the year 1917 justified the gloomy portents of the preceding year ; only two of Germany's under-water pests were exterminated, and an Austrian boat utterly vanished.

Soon after Admiral Ballard came to Malta, in September 1916, he urged the adoption of convoy ; he was informed that the French were responsible for the general policy, and, even if sufficient defensive craft could be collected, this method could not be adopted. The existing system of patrolling routes and providing escort for important vessels seemed to be the utmost that could be then achieved. The weakness of the method of escort from one zone to another was vividly brought home to the authorities by the sinking of the Italian troopship *Minas* (2854 tons), laden with Serbian troops for Salonica. Her Italian escort turned back on reaching the line of demarcation between the Italian and British zones. As Admiral Ballard had not been instructed to send British destroyers to meet the Italian steamer, the troopship went on alone. Off Cape Matapan, on February 15, she was sunk, with the loss of 870 lives. Two days later the French troopship *Athos* (12,644 tons), carrying Senegalese troops and 1000 coolies, also perished. The latter disaster was characterized by the coloured troops' bravery ; after every coolie had been taken off, they lined up in perfect order as the vessel went down. As a result of catastrophes such as these, it was decided that a conference should be convened at Corfu, between the Allied naval authorities, to centralise the escort and patrol organisation. It was held in April, and by then the situation had gone from bad to worse.

Shipping losses in the earlier months of 1917 were on an ascending grade, and the opening of the unrestricted war in all waters brought a still steeper slant in the upward trend. Forty-eight ships of 100,000 tons were sunk in February, and

35 vessels of 54,000 tons in March. Amongst the naval casualties came that of the French mine-laying gunboat *Cassini*, on the night of February 28, in circumstances of especial cruelty. Either the magazine or her mines blew up, killing most of the crew. The survivors clambered aboard a raft ; a voice then hailed them in French out of the darkness, and as they replied they were greeted with machine-gun fire. The biggest individual victim amongst the combatant vessels was the 18,400-ton French battleship *Danton*, sunk off Sardinia. Escorted by the destroyer *Massue* and steering a zigzag course, she was hit at midday on March 19 by two torpedoes from U 64 (Moraht). Attacked by depth-charge, the submarine escaped by a hurried dive, and afterwards extinguished 7 merchant-vessels, including 2 armed British steamers, and 3 Italian sail. She had left Wilhelmshaven for Cattaro on November 26, 1916, and proved herself to be one of the most destructive *loups de mer* in the Mediterranean. As for the *Danton*, she sank in three-quarters of an hour with 806 of her complement, one of the heaviest death-rolls for a single warship in the whole of the naval war. Deplorable also was the accidental sinking of the Italian submarine *Alberto Guglielmotti* on March 10 by the sloop *Cyclamen*. The British patrol discovered the Italian boat off the island of Capraia, and, mistaking her for an enemy, sank her.

Some slight success was gained by the abandonment of the system of fixed routes in favour of the dispersal of shipping over several routes and frequent variation of such steamer tracks. From mid-January to the end of March, British shipping between Egypt and Salonica or Malta enjoyed an encouraging reduction of losses—only 4 ships. Along the Algerian coast, where the route was patrolled by French craft, traffic passed close inshore ; and if a ship were unarmed, she was to sail at night, seeking refuge in some harbour by day. Serious losses were experienced along the Algerian coast towards the end of February ;[1] since armed steamers were as liable to loss at night as their unarmed sisters, the Algerian coast route was given up early in March. Instead, ships

[1] Between February 20 and March 3, seven defensively-armed steamers were torpedoed without warning in broad daylight.

leaving Gibraltar hugged the Spanish coast and thence steered on varying courses. Each ship had its separate track, and these tracks were zigzagged in such a way that, should a U-boat encounter a prize, it would be long before another vessel passed the same spot. These new measures, generally applied to the whole Mediterranean, promised greater security against attacks on the high seas. There were, however, serious impediments, imposed by physical geography, from which there was no escape, namely, that there are only two outlets from the Mediterranean—the Gibraltar Gut to the west, and the Suez Canal to the east. No matter how varied and dispersed the tracks might be, all routes had eventually to converge upon the Canal or the Strait. The enemy was not slow in grasping this fact. Towards the end of March, U 63 appeared on the convergence of tracks off Alexandria and put down 2 armed steamers and an Egyptian sailing-vessel. One of the victims, an Admiralty collier, was escorted by four patrols. In none of these cases was the assailant seen. In this area next appeared U 73, the disseminator of many destructive mines, and laid her steel snares off Alexandria; thence cruising along the North African coast as far as Oran. Four vessels succumbed to the mines. Taken as a whole, however, the Mediterranean was unsuitable for mining operations, excepting only the approaches to certain ports. Little was therefore achieved by the mine-laying boats.[1]

Important shipping losses include the *Clan Farquhar* (5858 tons) on February 26, 80 miles north from Benghazi, with 49 lives; the *Queen Eugenie* (4358 tons) on March 25, 23 miles N.N.E. from Cani Rocks, with 35 lives; and the *Brodness* (5736 tons) on March 31, 5 miles W.N.W. from Port Anzio.

During the month of April the enemy exerted his strength to the full. No fewer than 13 U-boats were out at one time, and 24 separate cruises were detected at another period. They sent to the bottom 51 steamers and 43 sail—a total of 94 vessels of 218,000 tons, representing one-quarter of mercantile loss during April all over the world. Two cruises can

---

[1] The use of small mine-layers as transports to North Africa, from time to time, is a fact attested by Gayer.

XIII. WHAT IS YOUR SHIP? WHERE ARE YOU BOUND?
The crew of a sunken steamer being interrogated from the deck of a German Submarine.

THE ANTI-SHIPPING WAR IN OPERATION.
A photograph, taken in the Mediterranean—during the most intensive phase of the German attack on shipping—shewing a cargo ship being sent to the bottom by U.35, the 'Champion Raider.'

be related in detail, so as to present an epitome of the 1917 conditions and difficulties. As already mentioned, 4 Adriatic boats returned to Germany for repairs, after a spell of duty in the Mediterranean. Hersing had taken U 21 home in February ; Gansser appears to have returned in U 33 early in the summer ; and UC 14 turned up amongst the Flanders flotilla during the autumn. The fourth, U 52 (Hans), before entering the Straits of Gibraltar in November 1916, had been the victor in the encounter with the old French battleship *Suffren*, homeward bound. Now U 52, after her brief stay, was making her return to Germany, and once again left behind her a trail of devastation. After sinking a couple of Italian sail, Hans appeared off Genoa on April 4, torpedoed the Italian liner *Ravenna* (4101 tons) without warning ; sank the American *Missourian* (7924 tons), which surrendered after only one round was fired ; and then, shortly before midnight, found the Ellerman liner *City of Paris* (9239 tons), about 50 miles south of Nice. In the full moonlight Hans had no difficulty in sizing up his target, and promptly torpedoed her. The passengers and crew took to the boats, whereupon U 52 sank the liner with four shots. When the French patrols arrived thirty-six hours later, they found three boats ; in them were 29 dead Lascars. Another drifted ashore with 12 dead, and two other boats were never heard of again. Altogether, 122 perished. On the night of April 13-14, U 52 passed through the Straits of Gibraltar, after claiming 6 more victims ; and outside Lisbon she sank 2 more steamers, bringing her return for this cruise up to 40,964 tons destroyed.

Synchronizing with the above trip by Hans, there was another expedition made by his *confrère* von Arnauld. The latter left Cattaro in U 35, to resume his depredations. His excursion lasted five weeks and cost 65,000 tons of merchant-ships. Making for his favourite hunting-ground, he sank the *Parkgate* (3232 tons) south of Sicily, with the loss of 16 lives, the episode being ' shot ' with a cinematograph camera. The *Maplewood* (3259 tons) on the 7th, south-west of Sardinia, was his next target ; crossing over to the Algerian seaboard, he expected to find the usual stream of prizes, unaware that ships were sailing on dispersed tracks. Disappointed in this move, he steered along the abandoned coastal route westward, eventually passing through the Straits on April 12. At that time, owing to the shortage of guns, ships leaving Gibraltar for Canadian or American ports were ordered to dismount their guns, so that these weapons could be mounted on other vessels about to traverse the dangerous Mediterranean. U 35, therefore, secured an easy victim outside the Straits in the *Patagonier* (3832 tons), sunk on the 14th, 135 miles west from Gibraltar. Von Arnauld had already caught three vessels in the western approaches to the Rock. He proceeded to sink a Greek on the 15th, a Russian and three British on the 17th, the *Sowwell* (3781 tons) on the 19th, 180 miles from Cape Spartel, and the *Lowdale* (2660 tons) and *Nentmoor* (3535 tons) next day. The presence of both U 52 and U 35 in this area caused considerable anxiety, as preparations for the first Gibraltar convoy to the United Kingdom were in hand. Traffic was diverted along the African coast well to the southward. The local patrols were quite unable to cope with the situation, and von Arnauld had little to fear. He repassed the Straits on the 25th after sinking 5 more vessels, having destroyed not less than 17 ships west of Gibraltar. Off Algeria he sank a Greek steamer; and escaping the bombs of a French seaplane, U 35 returned in safety to Cattaro.

Other submarines reaped a rich harvest. April 15 was a particularly disastrous day, for within the space of a few hours three fine ships were sent to the bottom. The British India liner *Mashobra* (8236 tons) was sunk, with 8 lives, 140 miles S.W. from Cape Matapan. Far more serious was the loss of the troopship *Arcadian* (8929 tons), from Salonica to Egypt with 1000 troops; she was torpedoed 26 miles N.E. of Milo, and went down within six minutes, carrying with her 242 troops and 35 of the crew. At the same time, 150 miles E. of Malta, another troopship, the *Cameronia* (10,963 tons), with 2630 troops, from Marseilles to Egypt, and escorted by two destroyers, was also struck by a torpedo and sank with the loss of 129 troops and 11 of the crew. In the case of the *Arcadian*, the loss took place in the French zone, and, three hours after she had sunk, French patrols arrived on the scene.

Both within and without the Mediterranean the small patrol

XIV.   A TROOPSHIP PLUNGING TO THE DEPTHS.

A remarkable photograph shewing the R.M.S.P. liner *Arcadian* in her last agony. On May 15, 1917, three large liners were sent to the bottom in the Mediterranean: in this case, the troopship sank in ten minutes, causing a heavy death-roll of 277. As the foundered ship turned over under water, spars and wreckage shot up to the surface, inflicting fatal injuries to many of those survivors struggling in the water.

THE MEDITERRANEAN HARVEST 245

craft were being overstrained to the point of exhaustion and collapse, both mechanical and human. Though they were worked to the uttermost, they were always too meagre in numbers to give security to the long and multiplied lines of communication. In the Mediterranean a double duty was imposed upon the small craft: they were set the task, not only of guarding the trade routes, but also of defending the Army's lines of supply by sea to the eastern theatres of war. It is little wonder and no discredit to them that, with inadequate strength, so herculean a task proved to be beyond their powers. The military authorities, being in urgent need of reinforcements for the western front, proposed a transfer of troops from Salonica to France. The First Sea Lord also favoured a reduction of the British Expeditionary Force in Macedonia, since such a step would set free patrol forces for employment in other areas and upon other duties. It was, in his opinion, of the utmost importance that there should be a reduction in the lines of communication, and that the import of food supplies should be protected. The support of subsidiary military campaigns in the Near East and Middle East was absorbing far too much of our naval energy and of our minor maritime forces.

On April 27 the Conference began at Corfu on board the French flagship *Provence*. Once again opinions differed: the French favoured the fixture of routes; the British admirals preferred dispersal. The outcome of the discussion was far from satisfactory. Shipping was to hug the coast at night, spending the day in netted harbours of refuge; and when it became necessary to traverse open sea, ships were sent out singly and were to scatter on dispersed routes. Consecutive escort was to be provided for important ships right through all zones, and two other vessels might take advantage of the protection afforded by adding themselves to the escorted ship. More than three vessels in company could not be allowed. Even the use of the very word 'convoy' was anathema and forbidden. Vessels unfit for escort duties were relegated to patrol work.

Very important was the decision to debar passage through the Mediterranean to shipping bound to and from the Far

246 THE GERMAN SUBMARINE WAR

East, and to divert it round the Cape of Good Hope. Troops and material for Egypt and Salonica were to be embarked at Taranto. Another interesting suggestion was put forward by the admiral in command of the British Adriatic Squadron. He stressed the fact that efforts to afford protection by patrol or escort, and to seal the Otranto Straits, were proving of little use; he attributed the failure to the want of small armed vessels. He urged that the 120 drifters at Taranto should be entirely withdrawn and redistributed over the patrol areas. If that measure failed, then they could return to their previous work and be augmented by vessels from the patrol strength, so that the net-barrage should be made fully efficient. The proposal was not entertained. To grasp the significance of his suggestion, the system then in practice at Otranto should be described briefly here. There were 120 drifters, and 30 motor launches supplied with depth-charges and armed with a small gun, the latter quite inadequate for inflicting decisive punishment on a submarine. The drifters maintained a line of nets 44 miles long, from the Italian side to Fano Island. South of the drifters were the motor launches, which remained out at night to force the U-boats to dive into the nets to the north. Northward of the net line was, at times, an Italian force; southward, French vessels from Corfu. No destroyers supported the net-drifters; the Italian ships nominally attached were kept in harbour to await any urgent call from the drifters, but the motor launches watched the nets at the Italian end of the line. Submarines had little difficulty in emerging from the Adriatic. Nine times in 1916 the nets had been fouled: UB 44 and VI had been destroyed, but two Austrian boats, enmeshed and depth-charged on July 8 and 10, had got away. There is no doubt that XX also escaped in December 1916. On April 10, 1917, an entangled submarine had five depth-charges dropped on her, but no wreckage came up. During April the Austrian XXX disappeared; she left Cattaro on March 31, and was never heard of again.[1]

[1] At the time of her loss she was commanded by Linienschiffs-Leutnant Friedrich Fähndrich. These are the only details concerning the end of XXX that can be furnished by the 'Kriegsarchiv,' Vienna. On the Allied side there is not a single item of information to explain this boat's end. Her fate to this day remains a mystery, and it is likely to remain so for ever.

Both the French and the Italian authorities advocated a fixed barrage from Sta. Maria di Leuca to Fano Island, such as had been tried and abandoned in 1915 in the Dover Straits. It was to be constructed of British material and French mines. Later in the year they again pressed forward the scheme known as the 'de Quillac' net. Eventually the idea was absorbed in a later and more comprehensive plan for sealing the Straits. The gravity of the situation may be gauged from Italy's declaration that, unless her demands for shipping were met, she could not maintain the offensive any longer. Judged by after effects, the most important of all the verdicts delivered by the Corfu Conference was, perhaps, the finding that all shipping routes, escorts, and patrols throughout the Mediterranean should be placed under a centralized control.

The recommendations of the Corfu Conference mark an epoch in the Mediterranean. Subsequently, in June, the Allied authorities agreed that the entire anti-submarine campaign and all trade defence should be directed by a British vice-admiral, whose flag should be flown ashore at Malta ; and that the French Commander-in-Chief should be left free to deal with the enemy squadrons in the Adriatic and at Constantinople. The choice of the Admiralty first fell upon Sir Rosslyn Wemyss, but on his return to Whitehall in July he remained there, to serve as Deputy First Sea Lord. On August 6, Vice-Admiral Sir Somerset Gough-Calthorpe was appointed to the new and important post at Malta.

Even whilst the Conference sat, the submarines became more voracious. Six large steamers and eight Italian sail, totalling 27,000 tons, were put down in four days by the eight submarines at work. The victims included the *Pontiac* (3345 tons), the *Karonga* (4665 tons), with 18 lives, and the *Teakwood* (5315 tons). Off Corsica, U 33 was at work ; U 35 was (as before remarked) returning to Cattaro ; and, within sight of Malta, UC 37 sank by gunfire an Italian sailing-vessel.

The waters around Malta were almost unprotected. One drifter (and perhaps a couple of motor launches in fine weather) made up the formidable floating defences of this jewel in the British Crown ! So great was the congestion in the Grand Harbour that merchant-shipping had to be accommodated at moorings in two other open anchorages. Off these two latter refuges the U-boats used to prowl; they could see fleets of fine cargo-vessels riding peacefully to their moorings, but the U-boats never dared to come inshore and raid the anchorages. They saw between themselves and the steamers lines of buoys evidently marking the seaward limits of defensive nets and dangerous mine-fields. Little did the German submarines know that the limit-buoys of the supposed mine-fields were only old, painted oil-drums strung out in a line, and that not a single net or mine actually stood between the freighters and their would-be destroyers! The 'defended anchorages' at Malta were a sheer 'bluff,' but, as such, they were far more successful than the real barrages in Dover and Otranto Straits.[1]

But to revert to UC 37: after laying mines off Cape Rosa, she torpedoed and sank (on April 30) the French troopship *Colbert* (5394 tons), from Marseilles to Salonica, with the loss of 51 lives. On the following day the tanker *British Sun* (5565 tons), with 7000 tons of oil, was torpedoed. She had an escort of 3 armed trawlers, but so unfitted were these little vessels for their duty that the tanker had to reduce speed to $6\frac{1}{2}$ knots, to enable them to keep up with her. The oil was set ablaze, spreading over the water in a sheet of flame, and the valuable ship disappeared in this inferno, a veritable Viking's pyre.

For May, the necrology of shipping exhibited a smaller number of demises. Thirty-eight steamers and 43 sailing-vessels were sunk in place of the 94 put down in April. Amongst them, the most serious casualty was the fine troopship *Transylvania* (14,315 tons), with 3000 troops for Egypt. In February the Japanese Government had offered to send 8 destroyers under a Japanese rear-admiral to co-operate with the British patrols in the Mediterranean. Two of these Japanese destroyers, *Matsu* and *Sakaki*, were escorting the *Transylvania*; and when they were $2\frac{1}{2}$ miles south of Cape Vado, in the Gulf of Genoa, the large liner was twice torpedoed, sinking in less than an hour with 270 of those aboard. The advent of much-needed destroyers from Japan, and the

---

[1] R.U.S.I. (Admiral Ballard), April 1924. The Maltese anchorages here referred to were Marsa Scirco and St. Paul's Bay.

use of similar Hellenic and American craft later on, greatly relieved the strain on the British and French escorts. On June 11 the *Sakaki* was damaged by a torpedo, losing 55 of her crew. A further casualty was suffered on May 29, when the French transport *Yarra* (4163 tons) was sunk and 56 of her passengers were returned as missing.

The first and only torpedoing of a Mediterranean hospital-ship happened in this month of May. At the end of March the German Government had announced that hospital-ships in the Mediterranean, as in the English Channel, would be sunk. These ships, therefore, were kept in harbour until April 15, when they sailed with an escort of two destroyers each. They were still painted white, with the regulation distinctive marks; but they were ordered to zigzag and steam at nights with lights darkened. Towards 7 P.M. on the evening of May 26 the *Dover Castle* and *Karapara* were steaming west, escorted by the destroyers *Cameleon* and *Nemesis*.[1] When the two hospital-ships were 50 miles north of Bona, the *Dover Castle* (8271 tons) was deliberately torpedoed by UC 67 (Neumann). She was on passage from Malta to Gibraltar, with 700 patients and staff and a crew of 141. Six stokers were killed outright, but the wounded were safely transhipped to the *Cameleon*, either direct or from the lowered boats. The *Karapara*, covered by a smoke-screen from the *Nemesis*, made for Bona, and escaped a similar fate. The master and 16 of the crew elected to remain on board the stricken ship, as she did not appear mortally injured; and at 8 P.M. the *Cameleon* left for Bona with 950 souls aboard. Hardly had she departed when a second torpedo hit the *Dover Castle* under the bridge on the starboard side, and within three minutes the ship had plunged into the depths. Those who had remained on board were picked up six hours later. This attack on escorted ships, covered by what was deemed to be adequate protection, was the subject of thorough investigation. The two destroyers had been stationed abaft the beam of their convoy, as it had been found that many escorted ships had been torpedoed from

---

[1] Soon after this attack the British destroyers *Minstrel* and *Nemesis* were 'loaned' to the Japanese, and commissioned as H.I.J.M. ships *Sendan* and *Kanran* respectively.

astern. It was therefore held that if the U-boat were sighted ahead she would be open to rapid counter-attack ; whereas, if the destroyers were stationed ahead and the attack came from astern, the U-boat had disappeared by the time the destroyers had turned in their tracks. In this case, UC 67 was not sighted ; and the new idea of placing the escort abaft the beam of the ships escorted (which meant that the convoy was to some extent exposed as a decoy) was discontinued.

The attack of UC 67 was inexcusable. Three days before, she had sunk the *Elmmoor* (3744 tons), 36 miles E. by S. from Syracuse, and had captured her master. After his release he was able to give full details of the wanton outrage. Neumann sighted the hospital-ships early in the afternoon, and had dogged them for hours. At five o'clock the master of the *Elmmoor* was sent below ; and at that instant he noticed the *Dover Castle* turn to starboard on a 'leg' of her zigzag. Simultaneously Neumann turned to port to intercept her. UC 67 was submerged during the two torpedoings. On June 4, 1921, Neumann stood his trial at Leipzig, but was acquitted on the ground that he was obeying superior orders. He had left Cattaro on May 23, and on the day after his infamous attack he laid a mine-field off Algiers, and is believed to have been the assailant of the *Manchester Trader* (3938 tons). This steamer put up a magnificent defence against the gun-fire directed upon her, the master yawing off his course each time he saw the gun-flash on the submarine. After four and a half hours, the merchant-ship's gun burst ; the submarine closed rapidly, and demanded the surrender of the master. He had changed into dungarees, and in his place the enemy took captive the second mate, afterwards shelling the riven steamer. The arrival of a trawler put the U-boat to flight, but the *Manchester Trader* was beyond help, and sank.

As a result of the *Dover Castle* attack, Berlin promised immunity to Mediterranean hospital-ships if they carried neutral supervisors and proceeded without an escort of armed vessels. In August, negotiations between Madrid and Berlin culminated in the appointment of Spanish supervision officers, who were to be carried as far as Gibraltar. If thence pro-

THE MEDITERRANEAN HARVEST 251

ceeding westward, these ships were to land their wounded at some British port outside the Channel.

During the last part of May a new mine-layer, UC 73, arrived from German waters, after attempting to molest shipping outside the approaches to the Straits of Gibraltar. Another of these boats, UC 52, put into Cadiz on June 11 with damage to her machinery; on the previous day she had been hit during an attack on the armed steamer *Loch Lomond* (2619 tons), but whether her injuries were due to shell-fire or not could not be determined. She was granted an asylum in the Spanish port until she completed repairs. Her commander was informed that he must not attack commerce on his way to Cattaro. On the night of the 29th, UC 52 slipped out during pitch darkness, eluded E 38, 4 torpedo-boats, and 4 motor launches waiting to intercept her, and reached her goal in safety. It was after this visit that Spain declared her intention of interning any submarine taking refuge in her ports.

Von Arnauld spent another fruitful fortnight west of Gibraltar, early in June, sinking 11 ships of about 31,000 tons. Other submarines were also energetically attacking the flow of traffic, and on June 2 the horse-transport *Cameronian* (5861 tons), with mules for Egypt, was caught fifty miles from Alexandria; 52 soldiers and 10 of the crew were lost, the remainder being saved by the escort. On the 19th the French submarine *Ariane* was vanquished in a duel with a U-boat off Cape Bon; and the French auxiliary cruiser *Himalaya* (5620 tons) was sunk by torpedo on the 22nd, off the Algerian seaboard, with 28 of her crew. The Greek destroyer *Doxa*, manned by a French complement, blew up on a mine and sank on the 28th. Mines were found in increasing numbers; and in May and June the approaches to Salonica were fouled by a field laid by UC 23. A second British transport was also torpedoed this month. Four miles S.E. from Skyro, on the morning of June 24, the *Cestrian* (8912 tons), with 800 men and horses from Salonica to Egypt, was torpedoed by UB 42 (Schwartz); and it was solely due to the splendid discipline of the troops that only 3 of the crew were lost. This submarine, working from Constantinople, had torpedoed (but not sunk) the sloop *Veronica*

252 THE GERMAN SUBMARINE WAR

off Alexandria in April. In comparison with the damage they inflicted, these Constantinople boats suffered heavy casualties for the gain of a very few successes.

After June had passed, a welcome reduction became noticeable in the mortality of shipping. At this point a reversion must be made to the situation at the Straits of Otranto. As at Dover, the submarines poured through this defile to reach their happy hunting-grounds. That the drifter-net obstruction, motor launches, and aircraft were annoying the U-boats could not be doubted, but the diving corsairs were usually able to elude the attempts to catch them. They would slip through when bad weather prevented the drifters from maintaining their guard, or else they would dive beneath the nets.

The disappearance of an Austrian boat about this time has been referred to previously. She was numbered XXX, and so high a serial number might be taken as denoting a large expansion of the Austro-Hungarian flotilla. Such was not quite the case, and the actual extent of the increase merits explanation. In July 1916 the destroyer *Impetuoso* had been sunk by a boat numbered XVII. So far as can be traced, there were no boats numbered XVIII and XIX.[1] Four small Whitehead-type boats were built, numbered XX to XXIII; three of these were commissioned during 1916, and the fourth during January 1917. Boats of the German UB II type were very popular with the submarine officers of the Flanders Flotilla, and Austria-Hungary determined to acquire craft of the same pattern. Seven such boats were commissioned between November 1916 and May 1917, bearing the numbers XXVII to XXXII and XL. An eighth boat (XLI) went into

[1] On July 30, 1916, the Italian submarine *Giacinto Pullino* stranded near the Quarnaro, and her wreck fell into Austrian hands. She was reported to have been salved, repaired, and recommissioned for service as the Austro-Hungarian XVIII. The 'Kriegsarchiv' (Vienna) Report, however, contains no reference whatever to the *Giacinto Pullino*, either as the Austrian XVIII or under any other name or number. Probably the Italian boat was so damaged as to be incapable of repair for further war service. About December 1915, Krupps supplied a licence and the necessary plans to Gänz & Co., of the Danubius Yard, Fiume, for the building of two big submarines, which were to have been of the same type as the German U 66-70 class. These two boats were never built; they were, perhaps, to have borne the numbers XVIII and XIX.

service before the end of the war.¹ In August 1917 the two German boats UB 43 and UB 47 (likewise of the UB II type) were definitely transferred to the Austrian flotillas, without change of numbers (XLIII and XLVII). These last-mentioned numbers are, however, not to be regarded as indications that Austria-Hungary, at one time and another, placed forty-three or forty-seven submarines in commission. During the war her boats were never numbered consecutively and in unbroken series, as were the German craft. Frequent and extensive gaps existed in the Austro-Hungarian numeration. Between the numbers I and XLVII, twenty numbers were unassigned. Thus it came about that, although a submarine bearing the number XLVII did put to sea, no more than twenty-seven submarines were ever completed. Of these, six boats existed before the war ; twenty were built or assembled by the shipyards in the Upper Adriatic during the period of hostilities ; and one boat was acquired by capture. Seven units, out of this small force of twenty-seven boats, succumbed during the course of the conflict, and an eighth boat was injured beyond repair. It may be remarked here that Austria-Hungary never had the use of a single big submarine comparable to the German 'Mittel-U' boats of about 800 tons. Her war construction only comprised small coastal craft, which were either of the German UB I and II types, or of the Whitehead pattern.²

The counter-measures in force in the Straits of Otranto were strengthened in May by the establishment of a seaplane base at Taranto, to support the drifters. Before this month the enemy had been irritated into contemplating measures for disrupting the barrier ; and, just as at Dover, a raid by surface ships was planned. Four reconnaissances by Austrian destroyers were made during March and April, and then the

[1] When XLI entered service is uncertain. The *Rivista Marittima* has given her commissioning date as May 1917, but the 'Kriegsarchiv' (Vienna) Report says that XLI was not launched until 1918.
[2] According to Techel, some submarines of the German 'Mittel-U' type (800 to 880 tons) and 'UB III' types (510 to 530 tons) were building for the Austro-Hungarian Navy in 1918, the Diesel engines being supplied by Krupp's. None of these boats was finished when Austria-Hungary ceased to be a belligerent state.

blow fell. A double attack was delivered by surface craft, whilst under-water boats supported the raiders. Three submarines were posted to intercept Anglo-Italian forces. Off Valona, IV (Singule) was stationed; UC 25 was ordered to mine Brindisi; and XXVII (von Fernland *or* Holub) was sent to cruise between Brindisi and Cattaro. The three Austrian fast light cruisers, *Helgoland, Saida,* and *Novara,* were detailed to exterminate the drifters, and two destroyers were sent to attack simultaneously the Italian transports running between Italy and Valona. The latter thrust was delivered early in the morning of May 15, when the Italian destroyer *Borea,* escorting three steamers, was surprised by the enemy ships, disabled at the first round, and left sinking. One of the transports, carrying munitions, blew up.

The main onslaught fell upon the drifter line. The three cruisers, under Captain Horthy, steamed through the line of drifters (being mistaken for British or Italian ships), turned about, and began to destroy piecemeal the small vessels. The Austrians called upon the crews to surrender. Some did so, but others stoutly refused to entertain such an idea. Skipper Watts, of the *Gowan Lea,* heroically charged the Austrians, firing the while with his $2\frac{1}{4}$-inch popgun. Under a withering fire the gallant skipper broke through, and even intended to return to the action, after repairing his puny weapon, disabled by a direct hit. For his action Skipper Watts was awarded the Victoria Cross. Other crews showed the same magnificent courage. Of the 47 drifters, 14 were sunk and 5 damaged, 72 prisoners being taken.

The sound of firing aroused the suspicions of the Sasseno look-outs, and a report was sent to Brindisi, where lay the Anglo-Italian cruisers. An hour and a half elapsed before the first ships could get away, and the chances of intercepting the retreating raiders so began to dwindle. A chase developed, in which the *Dartmouth* received three hits; and the *Bristol* (whose bottom was very foul) was forced to drop behind. At about 10 A.M. reinforcements came out from Cattaro in the form of a large cruiser and five torpedo-boats; the action between the two British cruisers and the three Austrian light cruisers continued ding-dong fashion, now one side scoring a

XV. THE ATTACK ON THE HOSPITAL SHIP *DOVER CASTLE* (1).
This vessel was torpedoed by *UC. 67*, in the Mediterranean, on May 26, 1917. Taken from the Hospital Ship *Karapara* four minutes after the torpedo explosion. the above illustration shews what ineffective cover is afforded if a smoke screen is laid with a following wind. The smoke is lifted from the surface of the sea, and the injured ship is still clearly visible.

XVI. THE ATTACK ON THE HOSPITAL SHIP *DOVER CASTLE* (2).
Taken a few minutes later from a different bearing, this view shews the destroyer to the right steaming into the wind. The smoke screen drops.

XVII.   U.38 AFTER COLLISION.
The track of a steamer with which she had collided is seen across the deck. The distorted periscope, bent rails, overturned gun and the crushed conning-tower are clearly seen.

THE MEDITERRANEAN HARVEST 255

hit, then the other inflicting damage. When the British ships were forced to break off the chase, and whilst the *Dartmouth* was still forty miles from Brindisi, she was torpedoed by UC 25 and seriously damaged. After the crew had been transferred to destroyers, she was towed into port next morning. Finally, the mine-field laid off Brindisi claimed its victim in the French destroyer *Boutefeu*, which had been ordered out to assist the injured *Dartmouth*.

Following on this well-planned raid, the drifter line was again moved farther south and was maintained only by day. The enemy therefore had gained a decided success. As a slight recompense the French submarine *Circé*, watching off Cattaro, discovered UC 24 (Willich) on the 24th, and sank her. On June 3 the Austrian destroyer *Wildfang* succumbed to mine injury off Cattaro.

By June the sinkings in the Mediterranean, though numerically greater than in May, were less than those in April. The tonnage sacrificed had dropped from 218,000 to 133,700. Had the Allied forces in the Mediterranean been well supplied with adequate weapons to fight the submarines, the decrease would have been more marked.[1] Depth-charges were at a premium; only three to six could be allowed to each patrolling ship, and it was not until the end of the year that the 'killer' destroyers were supplied with forty each. The 300-lbs. depth-charge was then a most uneconomical weapon, for the range wherein certain destruction of the U-boat was assured was only 14 feet; up to 28 feet it would disable a submarine; up to 60 feet it would produce a demoralizing effect on the submarine crew.[2] The attacking

---

[1] According to *The Crisis of the Naval War* (Jellicoe), p. 67, an experimental station with a hydrophone training-school was begun at Malta during the autumn of 1917; south of Otranto a hydrophone station was established, and at Gallipoli a hydrophone training-school was instituted before the close of the year. Captain C. V. Usborne, R.N. (in his R.U.S.I. lecture) said that in June 1917 he obtained twelve sets of directional hydrophones and thirty to forty sets of 'plate' or 'shark-fin' hydrophones, for use in the Mediterranean, the latter pattern then being 'the latest thing' in acoustic detection. Various craft were fitted out with these instruments, but the hydrophones were very crude, and the system of submarine-detection by sound-listening could only be carried on very slowly.

[2] *The Crisis of the Naval War* (Jellicoe), p. 61.

vessel had to steam as swiftly as possible to the area in which the submarine had dived, and then ' brown ' that area with a pattern of depth-charges in the hope that one such charge would explode sufficiently near the U-boat to secure a kill. The introduction of mortars for throwing the charges to a distance was a distinct advance in that the attacker had no longer to steam to the point of disappearance and there drop her missiles. Big anti-submarine 11-inch and 7·5-inch howitzers, throwing shell set to explode under water, further enlarged the resources of the counter-offensive, and mercantile vessels so armed could retaliate with effect upon their molesters.

That the anti-submarine craft in the Mediterranean were scantily provided with depth-charges is a matter previously alluded to. Of little avail was it to go a-hunting for U-boats unless weapons were provided for the slaying thereof. Not only were the patrols scant in number, but when they did at last encounter their long-sought diving enemies their powers of attack were feeble and circumscribed. Thanks to the efforts made by the Admiralty and the munition plants, a vastly-increased output of depth-charges was reached towards the end of 1917 and during 1918. With the increment in the supply of anti-submarine weapons there naturally followed a rise in mortality amongst the hostile submarines. Yet again it may be stressed that the expanded output of depth-charges had as much to do with the decline of shipping losses as the introduction of the convoy system itself. Upon this point we have the testimony, at first hand, of the German submarine officers. Time and again they were driven off from their targets, or pinned under water, well-nigh stunned by the crashing salvoes of the new sea-grenades.

Here, as in home waters, the most efficient method of protecting trade was finally adopted. Hitherto it had been a gamble if the patrols would ever blunder across the enemy, with the dice heavily loaded in favour of the submarines. The decisive step was taken on May 22, when the first convoy of four ships with four trawlers left Malta for Alexandria. The policy of individual sailings along patrolled routes had failed, chiefly because the lines to be defended were too long for the

THE MEDITERRANEAN HARVEST 257

patrol forces at command. The policy of arming ships and allowing them to sail alone had also not succeeded. Individual ships, at large upon one route, merely offered the submarine a succession of targets. Further, of the vessels available for patrol, only a percentage could be kept continuously on the work; the balance were steaming to and from their bases, refitting, resting their crews, and refuelling.

Convoys would mass the mercantile vessels into combination for mutual defence. The smaller combatant vessels would no longer be frittered away in patrolling work; they would emerge from port in assembled force, as escorts to the convoys. Then, to get their shipping targets, the U-boat would have to come to the convoys, and with the convoys would be the 'submarine-killers.'[1] If the submarine attacked, she might torpedo one ship or two; but the moment she revealed her presence she would be subjected to a massed attack by her opponents. Against the guns of the escorting warships and the mercantile vessels the submarine would have no chance of success on the surface. She would therefore be forced to employ the short-range torpedo—an uncertain and expensive weapon. The cheapest forms of destruction—gunfire and scuttling by bomb—would be denied the enemy. At one time

[1] Mahan pointed out that, if a hostile force had to be intercepted, it should be met off its port of departure. If that course could not be pursued, then the next best chance of interception lay in meeting the enemy off his most probable point of arrival. It was little use wandering about at large in mid-sea or mid-ocean on the off chance that the enemy might be intercepted there. The Dover and Otranto Straits barrages (and the Heligoland Bight mine-fields) represented attempts to intercept the enemy near his ports of departure—the submarine bases—and such attempts succeeded indifferently well. But the massing of mercantile ships in convoys provided 'the most probable point of enemy arrival'—the one thing that had hitherto been the unknown quantity in anti-submarine operations. Submarines would have to come and attack the convoys, and with the convoys could be sent craft to kill the submarines, provided always that those craft were equipped with sufficient means for slaying the under-water craft. Convoy is therefore justified, in that it deprives the enemy of his power to select his 'point of arrival.' Patrolling the seas with diffused forces had been tried, and, although the method had met with some measure of success, it never could be entirely satisfactory, because contact with a highly-elusive enemy was, more often than not, the outcome of pure chance. Barrage and convoy, respectively covering the enemy's points of departure and probable arrival, became, in the last stages of the war, the main elements of anti-submarine operations, so that Mahan's teaching was, in the final outcome, fully vindicated.

R

the Germans experienced a shortage of torpedoes, and, until production was enlarged, submarines were actually sent out to sea supplied with obsolete, fifteen-year-old bronze torpedoes.

The success of the pioneer convoy service between Malta and Alexandria was striking. From May 22 until July 16 only two ships were lost ! On July 26 a convoy left Gibraltar for the United Kingdom, consisting of 13 vessels, and the only loss was a French ship in collision with an escorting sloop. Convoys between Gibraltar and Italy were equally successful, and 190 ships sailed each month, under the wing of an Italian cruiser and 11 armed merchant-cruisers ; only 1 ship was lost in July—the victim of a night attack. Losses could not be absolutely eliminated. In July, 22 steamers of 85,000 tons were sunk in the Mediterranean. On the 3rd, the British India liner *Mongara* (8205 tons), escorted by an Italian destroyer and trawler, was sunk only a mile and a half from Messina breakwater ; the submarine which torpedoed her also laid mine-fields off Syracuse and Malta, in which the sloops *Aster* and *Azalea* came to grief next day. They were escorting a hospital-ship into Malta ; and although their precious charge escaped, the *Aster* foundered and the *Azalea* suffered much damage. In the sinking of the *Eloby* (6545 tons) on July 19, with troops and munitions, 56 lives were lost as a result of the ship blowing up, 75 miles S.E. by E. from Malta. The P. & O. liner *Mooltan* (9723 tons), escorted by two Japanese destroyers, was sunk on July 26, 53 miles N.N.W. from Cape Serrat, west of Bizerta.

In short, the convoy organization was in full swing for vessels other than those considered entitled to special escort. By the end of August outward sailings from the United Kingdom to Gibraltar were brought under convoy ; and such losses as were suffered occurred only amongst ships sailing independently. In the black month of April 1917 the Mediterranean losses were one-fifth of the total inflicted, amounting to 180,000 tons ; by the autumn the losses in home waters had been reduced by one-half ; and although in the Mediterranean they were also less, they still represented one-third of the tonnage destroyed. By May 1918 the Mediterranean sinkings were half of those achieved by the enemy in all seas, though

THE MEDITERRANEAN HARVEST 259

they again showed an actual reduction. In brief, whilst the losses in home waters had declined from about 700,000 to 160,000 tons a month during the period April 1917-May 1918, ship mortality in the Mediterranean only fell from 294,000 to 128,000 tons a month during the same period. They had come down to roughly one-half, whilst those in home waters had been reduced to nearly one-fifth. Only in August 1918 did an appreciable improvement set in, when the Mediterranean losses were about 49,000 tons, representing one-sixth of the total.[1] This blessed relief was the combined product of increased efficiency in the Otranto barrage and of convoying. To quote Gayer on this point : ' Only in May 1918 were the [submarine] losses serious, when five U-boats were lost. In the early part of 1918 the English took the patrol of the Mediterranean seriously in hand, and took over the patrol of the Otranto Straits from the Italians, thus making it effective for the first time.' [2]

From this anticipation we return to July 1917. In that month the drifter line in the Straits was maintained only when submarines were believed to be passing, and then under warship protection. At night the motor launches, equipped with hydrophones, would lie out in the Straits, listening for passing under-water craft; and this idea spread, until the drifters were also supplied with hydrophones. The patrol was strengthened by the addition of destroyers and submarines, the inception of a complete convoy system for the whole Mediterranean enabling a redistribution of patrol craft to be made.

The autumn of 1917 saw General Allenby's victorious advance in Palestine. A heterogeneous force of warships supported the seaward flank of his army, resting on the Syrian coast. Here was to be found the ancient French battleship *Requin*, the British ' blistered ' cruiser *Grafton*, the small monitors M 15, 29, 31, and 32, the ' China ' gunboats *Aphis* and *Ladybird*, the destroyers *Comet* and *Staunch*, three French

[1] This analysis is to be found in Captain (now Rear-Admiral) C. V. Usborne's lecture, R.U.S.I., April 1924.
[2] *U.S.N.I. Proceedings*, April 1926, p. 630. By making this quotation, the authors do not in the least desire it to be thought that they endorse Captain Gayer's opinion that the barrage was inefficient so long as it remained under Italian control.

destroyers, with attendant trawlers and drifters. The attention of the U-boats was naturally attracted to these ships ; and to guard against such a danger, nets were laid around the bombarding ships. The *Grafton* had already survived torpedo attack, when she had been hit on June 10 and was safely brought into Malta. In spite of the protection afforded, UC 38 (Wendlandt) sank both the *Staunch* and M 15, with 35 of their crews, on November 11. This submarine afterwards returned to Cattaro and set out on another cruise on December 1. In the Ionian Sea, on the 14th, she torpedoed and sank the old French cruiser *Chateaurenault* ; [1] but this time UC 38 reckoned without her host, in the shape of the French destroyers and their depth-charges. The sea around her began to boil in terrible eruptions and burst skywards. With water pouring into her hull, she was forced to seek the surface, only to be met by an implacable gunfire ; a riven wreck, she vanished for ever. In passing, we may notice that the *Comet*, the companion to the *Staunch*, was likewise torpedoed and sunk on August 6, 1918.

Mines were again discovered off Alexandria during August, and off Malta in October. In this latter field the hospital-ship *Goorkha* (6335 tons), bringing 400 wounded from Salonica, was badly damaged on October 17 ; she struck a mine in 70 fathoms of water, about 6 miles from the entrance to the Grand Harbour. Fortunately, her patients were transhipped to the *Braemar Castle*, and the injured ship was brought in. Other contemporary losses include the Italian auxiliary cruiser *Umberto I*. (4720 tons), mined or torpedoed off Gallinara Island, on August 14 ; the French fleet auxiliary *Golo II*. (1380 tons), sunk off Corfu on August 22 ; the *Civilian* (7871 tons) on October 6, 15 miles N. of Alexandria ; the P. & O. liner *Pera* (7635 tons) on October 19, 105 miles E. $\frac{3}{4}$ N. from Marsa Susa ; the *Collegian* (7520 tons) on the next day, 100 miles N.W. by N. from Alexandria ; the P. & O. liner *Namur* (6701 tons) on the 29th, 55 miles E. by S. $\frac{1}{2}$ S. from Gibraltar, all victims to submarine attack.

The introduction of 'through convoy,' from the United Kingdom to Port Said, was begun in October. This step

[1] Reported converted to a mine-layer during 1916.

THE MEDITERRANEAN HARVEST 261

marked the resumption of the Indian and Far Eastern trade through the Mediterranean, which had been diverted round the Cape of Good Hope in 1916. The manifold aspects of convoy arrangements in the Mediterranean are so varied that only a brief summary can be here embodied. The resumed sailings of ships from India, the Far East, and the Antipodes through this sea were equivalent to the setting free of 40 per cent. of ships required to carry essential products from the East. Previously ships had actually taken a month to arrive at Port Said from Malta; such extraordinary delays could now be eliminated by the central control of routes from Malta. The convoys' escorts consisted generally of a couple of trawlers and a sloop or destroyer. Sometimes there were only trawlers; and if a submarine were met with, disaster would befall. As the trawler stopped to rescue the crew of a stricken ship, the submarine would go on and pick off another vessel, and then another. So the convoy, harassed by a sniping torpedo-fire from the submarine, plodded on, whilst the rescue trawler panted after its charge. Had not such events been so tragic, the spectacle would have been ludicrous. Despite incidents of this nature, only 13 vessels in the 'through convoys' were sunk out of 653 ship sailings. In local convoy the results were even more satisfactory, the losses working out at ·32 per cent. of ship sailings. On the other side of the scale, from the beginning of convoy 15 per cent. of the U-boats lost were destroyed whilst attacking the merchant fleets.

The escorts in their arduous work suffered alongside the vessels under their care. The sinking of the sloop *Candytuft* on November 18 was remarkable for the tenacity of her hold on life. She had been repairing damage at Gibraltar, after a fight on the way out from the United Kingdom. She left with her convoy on the 16th, and all went well until the ships were off Cape Sigli. Here a submarine was waiting to attack merchant vessels; she fired her torpedo and hit the sloop. Unfortunately, the torpedo struck below the wardroom during the serving of a meal, killing all but two of her officers. Her stern was blown off, and an attempt was made to beach her; a second torpedo blew her bows away. Almost incredible though it may seem, the midships portion of the ship continued to float, and drifted ashore at Bougie. Nine of her crew were lost. On December 1 the Italian auxiliary cruiser *Citta di Sassari* (2930 tons) was sunk by torpedo off Cape Mele; and the French had to number their patrol, *Paris II.* (551 tons), amongst the fallen. On December 13 she was shelled and sunk by a submarine in the Gulf of Avala, her captain and crew of 16 being captured.

As a mournful close to a most disastrous year came (on December 30) the loss of the troopship *Aragon* (9588 tons). Nearing Alexandria, she was dealt a shattering blow from a torpedo, and rapidly settled down. Trawlers and destroyers at once closed to pick up those who had succeeded in jumping clear. As the destroyer *Attack* was engaged in this work of rescue she was literally blown in two by a mine, and disappeared with 10 of her crew and many of those she had just taken on board. Altogether, 591 soldiers, the master, and 18 of the crew perished. Hardly had the rescue craft finished their search for survivors when, on the next day, the fleet auxiliary *Osmanieh* (4041 tons) also foundered on one of these mines, taking down with her 8 nurses, 166 troops, the master, and 23 of the crew.

XVIII. THE END OF THE *FRANCONIA*.

A Cunard liner, engaged on trooping work, she met her end on October 4, 1916, in the Mediterranean. Only twelve lives were lost, as her troops had been previously disembarked at their destination.

THE TORPEDOING OF A TROOPER.

The havoc created by the torpedo which hit the troopship *Aragon*, off Alexandria, on December 30, 1917, was so extensive that the 9500-ton liner quickly settled. The photograph shews a trawler and ships' boats engaged in rescue work. A destroyer, the *Attack*, also closed, but blew up on a mine. Altogether, the death-roll numbered 610.

CHAPTER XII

THE MEDITERRANEAN FREED

(JANUARY–NOVEMBER 1918)

As time proved, the new year harboured less of disaster ; a gradual improvement began, though in no way comparable to the alleviations enjoyed in northern waters. Gayer recounts that by the beginning of 1918 the situation in the Adriatic, so far as it concerned repair facilities, was 'alarming.' When the German submarines burst into these hitherto secure seas, they found at Cattaro a repair-ship, and at Pola an Austrian dockyard. With such resources the Germans seem to have been content. The inevitable result of so short-sighted a policy soon became manifest. A striking example is revealed by a glance at the situation of the Adriatic boats in January 1918. Not more than 3 new boats arrived from German yards during the year to make good the wastage. Only 5 were waging war on commerce ; the others, numbering 28, were undergoing repair or refit. Scheer related that boats requiring extensive overhaul were forced to return to Germany. It was rather a paradoxical course to make a submarine, in need of thorough repair, undertake a 4000-mile trip, beset by every peril of the enemy's contrivance. The example here cited of the conditions in January is, of course, exceptional ; generally between a third and a quarter of the force was at sea, and in May 1918 the maximum number—16 boats at sea—was reached. Nevertheless, Gayer complains that the repair periods grew longer and longer, until in 1918 orders were placed for docks and shops to be constructed at Pola and Cattaro, and for repair centres at Fiume and Trieste. The remedies came too late to be of benefit ; the Dual Monarchy collapsed before the repair centres were ready. The German boats had to evacuate the Austrian ports just as the Pyovica docks (near Cattaro) were finished. As a result of these delayed schemes, when the end came 10 U-boats had to be abandoned at the Adriatic ports because they were unfit to undertake the long journey to the North Sea.

In June 1917, Kophamel had been succeeded by Pullen as commanding officer of the Mediterranean boats. Under the latter's charge there were now two flotillas. Commander Otto Schultze had the First Flotilla under his orders for a time, until he was relieved by Commander Friedrich Lützow. The Second Flotilla was under Commander Rudolf Ackermann. 'These forces were militarily under the Austrian Naval Command, but in other respects they were controlled by the home (*i.e.* German) authorities.'[1]

When reviewing the last stages of the war in the Mediterranean, interest is focussed round the convoy organization and the sealing of the Otranto Straits. The appointment of Vice-Admiral Sir S. A. Gough-Calthorpe as the British Commander-in-Chief (in August 1917) was the beginning of a centralized and coherent control. Vast and difficult was the problem of frustrating the German attack on the Mediterranean trade. The decision to unify the command was fundamentally sound, for it vested authority over all the Allied anti-submarine forces in one head instead of several. The patchwork quilt of 'zones' was abolished. War was no longer to be waged 'in small parcels.'

The first and most important task was to deny the passage of the Otranto Straits to the U-boats. This defile, 40 miles wide at its narrowest, was, compared with the Dover Straits, tremendously deep; here the bottom was anything between 300 and 500 fathoms, or from 1800 to 3000 feet. Obviously the mining difficulties were greatly increased; and the only favourable feature was the absence of tide and current, which had been found so troublesome at Dover. The system of drifter nets and its indifferent success have been already described. The drifters had actually been withdrawn in the summer of 1917, working only when there seemed a likelihood of trapping passing submarines. The French and Italians had sponsored the ' de Quillac ' net—a fixed net, fitted with mines,

---

[1] *Der U-Bootskrieg*, 1914-18 (Michelsen), p. 49.

THE MEDITERRANEAN FREED

and supported by buoys some distance beneath the surface of the sea. It was begun in October, and on November 10 the first section was laid by the drifters. Suspended 33 feet below the surface, it had a depth of 150 feet. To negotiate the barrage, a submarine would have two courses open to her: either she must take the risk from patrols by passing over the curtain, or else dive below it and risk the danger of great hydrostatic pressure. As the German submarines could withstand the pressure at depths between 180 and 250 feet, there was little to prevent a determined commander from burrowing his way under the nets. Throughout the winter, spring, and following summer this gigantic barrage extended itself across from the eastern end of the deep mine-field off Taranto to Fano Island; and by September 30, 1918, it was reported complete.

Admiral Calthorpe had to decide whether to devote his patrol resources to strong escorts for the convoys, or to reduce the convoy escorting strength and concentrate the mass of his patrols in the Straits. He chose the latter course, and in February 1918, after a conference at Rome, the great scheme was begun. He had the hearty support of the French, but the Italians were not so favourably disposed to this method. Both still regarded the ' de Quillac ' net as the real antidote, and it was incorporated in the general plan.

Admiral Calthorpe's barrage was based on the principle of depth from front to rear, and intensive patrol of a broad band across the Straits, extending far north and south. It was hoped to force submarines to dive soon after leaving Cattaro and remain submerged until they were well clear of the southern approaches to the Straits. There could be no hope for the submarines of 'sleeping on the bottom' whilst the hunt above expended itself in futile search; the water was too deep. The submarines would have to keep on the move continuously. If a submarine stopped her engines, she would either rise to the surface or sink to the bottom, according to her condition of positive or negative buoyancy. German submarines' submerged endurance varied according to type; as a general average, the 800-ton U-boats could travel 100 miles at 3 knots, the improved UB types 70 miles at 3 knots, and the improved UC's 80 miles at 3 knots, provided always that their batteries were fully charged, and that so low a speed was sufficient to give steerage-way. At their lowest speed, therefore, they could remain submerged about 30 hours; at about 4 knots, for 20 hours; at 5 knots, for 12 hours; and at 8 knots, for about 2 hours.

In the lower Adriatic there was a large 'diving area' for the Allied submarines; south of this was the advanced destroyer force; south of this again came the hydrophone trawler line, with three destroyers in support; in the Straits was the fixed-barrage patrol of drifters, with two sloops towing kite-balloons; yet farther south came the area covered by American submarine-chasers; and well to the south of the barrage were kite-balloon sloops, with torpedo-boats and trawlers equipped with 'Fish' hydrophones. When the barrage was completed, it was hoped passing submarines would exhaust their batteries before transit of this extensive area was finished, and so be forced to reveal their presence by coming to the surface. Thereupon the 'killer' destroyers would swoop upon their prey. Finally, to guard against attack by Austrian surface ships, there was at Brindisi a squadron of light cruisers. How far this ambitious scheme succeeded will be shown hereafter.

The year opened quietly, as there were few U-boats operating. On January 20 the armed boarding steamer *Louvain* was sunk in the eastern Mediterranean. Ten days later the Atlantic Transport liner *Minnetonka* (13,528 tons), the last of the four large sisters, fell a victim to U 64 (Moraht), 40 miles E.N.E. of Malta, to which island she was *en route* in ballast. Only 4 of the crew were lost. Moraht claimed to have sunk 5 vessels on this cruise, including a small Italian armed merchant cruiser, probably the *Caprera*, sunk on February 4 off Villa Joiosa. On the next day the *Glenartney* (7263 tons) was sunk 30 miles N.E. from Cape Bon; the *Romford* (3035 tons) was also lost on the 10th, only $2\frac{1}{2}$ miles east of Cape Carthage, 28 of her crew perishing. In March the *Clan Macpherson* (4779 tons), on the 4th, took down with her 18 of the crew when she sank 24 miles north of Cape Serrat; and on the 15th the *Clan Macdougall* (4710 tons) was mortally injured, 60 miles S.E. by E. from Cape Carbonara, sinking with 33

THE MEDITERRANEAN FREED

lives. The Italian mine-layer *Partenope*, on convoy duty, was sunk off Bizerta on the 24th.

Meanwhile, disciplinary conditions in the Adriatic bases were causing serious disquiet to the German authorities. Signs were not wanting that trouble was brewing ; and in the previous October the Austrian Torpedo Boat No. 11 had been taken out from Sebenico by her crew and surrendered to the Italians at Recanati. A serious mutiny broke out in certain of the Austrian warships at Cattaro on February 1 ; and as a result several of the older battleships and cruisers were paid off. The revolt was suppressed, but there could be no doubt that the enforced idleness of the larger warships' crews was sapping morale. About this time, early in 1918, von Arnauld left the Adriatic flotilla to take command of U 139, his departure being a great loss to the Mediterranean force.

Not only had the shipping losses been reduced, but retribution began to be inflicted at last upon the enemy raiders. The past year had been almost barren of success against the U-boats ; now the counter-attack was to be driven home. On January 9 a convoy was passing Bizerta, escorted by the sloop *Cyclamen* ; a submarine being reported close by, she ran out her explosive paravanes, and presently one of them detonated. Out of the violent commotion the bows of UB 69 (Klatt) rose vertically ; then the submarine took her last slant to the bottom, there to stay for ever. Nine days later, January 18, came another convoy 'kill.' Off Cape Bon, the sloop *Campanula*, escorting a convoy of eight steamers, saw the centre ship of the middle column being attacked by submarine. As the sloop came up, two torpedoes were fired ; the *Campanula* then dropped depth-charges over the spot whence they had come, destroying UB 66 (Wernicke). A third success followed on February 21, in the Adriatic. As the transport *Menfi* was on passage between Brindisi and Valona, a torpedo was loosed off at her and missed its billet. The Italian torpedo-boat *Airone* thereupon got to work with depth-charges and explosive sweeps, and promptly sank the attacker, the Austrian XXIII (Korvetten-Kapitan Klemens Ritter von Bézard).[1] As a set-off against this series of exterminations, the

[1] *La Guerre navale dans l'Adriatique* (Thomazi, Paris, 1929).

French submarine *Bernouilli* had a fatal encounter with a hostile submarine in the Adriatic on February 13 ; and on April 17 the Italian submarine H 5 was accidentally torpedoed and sunk by the British H 1. The Italian torpedo-boat *Ardea* claimed to have destroyed the XL (Krsnjavi) by depth-charges on April 26.[1] This, however, cannot be admitted, since XL was interned after the war.

In home waters during the summer of 1917 there had sprung up, around the coasts, listening-stations with hydrophone units in adjacent waters. In the spring of 1918, motor launches equipped with hydrophones were established at Gibraltar, in the Aegean, and in the Otranto Straits. The Gibraltar unit drew first blood. In the early hours of April 21 the ML 413, lying off Almina Point, heard the sound of fast-running engines coming up out of the west. Switching on her lights to avoid a collision, she espied a submarine rapidly moving east. The U-boat altered course sharply, crossed the bows of the motor launch barely ten yards distant, and dived. ML 413 swung round, followed up the wake of the submarine, and put over two depth-charges. After the disturbance had subsided, she listened on her hydrophones. The little vessel heard nothing. As day broke, the sea around was seen to be covered with oil. Upon the greasy lagoon there floated four pieces of woodwork and part of a steel-lined mahogany door, pitted with steel splinters. Thus terminated abruptly and decisively the career of UB 71 (Schapler, late of UC 73).

It has since been ascertained that this submarine was one of three bound for the Adriatic from Germany. On the afternoon of April 24 a convoy of twenty-four vessels from Milford Haven had as usual been met, one day out, by the Gibraltar danger zone escorting-ships. From the masthead of the sloop *Chrysanthemum*, on the flank of the convoy, the look-out sighted the barely submerged form of a submarine, which was promptly attacked. A quick turn of the wheel of fortune very soon dispelled the general satisfaction in the convoy. Shortly before three o'clock on the following morning a torpedo exploded underneath the wardroom of the sloop *Cowslip*, astern of the convoy. Five officers and a steward were killed out-

[1] *La Guerre navale dans l'Adriatique* (Thomazi, Paris, 1929).

right as they lay asleep. The U.S. coastguard cutter *Seneca* quickly appeared on the scene, and rescued 81 survivors. The *Cowslip* disappeared, forty-five minutes after she had been struck, in the waters off Cape Spartel.[1]

May was the open season for the hunters. The enemy seemed to have made special efforts in this month to stem the rising tide of defeat. During the second week not less than 16 boats were operating. Five of these never returned to their base. On the 8th the patrols got a ' double.' Escorted by the destroyer *Basilisk* and the U.S. armed yacht *Lydonia*, a convoy was 80 miles north-east of Algiers when one of the merchantmen, the *Ingleside* (3736 tons), was torpedoed and sunk, with 11 lives. Retaliation quickly followed. Running up the torpedo's track, the *Basilisk* dropped three depth-charges at intervals of a minute. The *Lydonia* followed suit. Patches of brown oil welled to the surface, the only visible evidence that UB 70 (Remy) was lying wrecked on the bottom of the sea. It was not until three months later that the Admiralty was able to verify this loss. The other case involves one of the notorious ' Thirties ' class, and the last of those terrors to come to the Mediterranean. U 32 (Albrecht) was sighted by the sloop *Wallflower*, when the latter vessel was escorting a convoy from Gibraltar to Alexandria. The second unit of the marauding ' Thirties ' was despatched by gunfire.[2]

Eight days later, as the French patrol *Ailly* was escorting two sailing-craft off Sardinia, she fell in with UC 35 (Korsch). Taking the patrol for a merchant vessel, the submarine began to shell her at 6000 yards. The French gunners, however, secured a hit in UC 35's after ballast tank on the port side, starting a leak. Another shell struck the conning-tower, on which stood Korsch and two or three of the crew. Finding escape by diving impossible, the commander gave orders to abandon UC 35. The submarine sank suddenly, and 5 of the crew were picked up. This boat had left Kiel on December 3, 1916, and, passing through the Dover Straits, had arrived at

[1] 'Reminiscences of World War Convoy Work,' *U.S.N.I. Proceedings*, May 1929, p. 388.
[2] Michelsen says ' depth-charge.'

Cattaro on December 26. This was her tenth cruise. She usually worked in the Gulf of Genoa, watching the trade routes, and after mining them would hunt small game.

On the 18th, U 39 (Metzer), remembered as Forstmann's old boat, turned up at Cartagena seriously damaged. She had been towed thither by another submarine, and in accordance with the Spanish decree was interned. Three days previously a submarine had been depth-charged by the U.S. gunboat *Wheeling* and the yachts *Surveyor* and *Venetia*, escorting a Gibraltar-Bizerta convoy. Again, a few days before U 39 appeared at Cartagena, six Allied seaplanes bombed a submarine off the Spanish coast. It is possible that, in either case, the submarine so attacked was U 39.

Gayer says that only in May did the submarine casualties become serious, when five U-boats were lost. The fifth loss was sustained in the Adriatic. At last the Allied submarines, watching outside the Austrian bases, were to receive the reward of their long vigil. They had had 17 fights, but hitherto without success; and they could claim no more than the sinking of two enemy transports off the Dalmatian coast. The fortunate craft was the British submarine H 4; on May 23 she sighted the UB 52 (Launburg) returning from a cruise. Increasing to full speed, H 4 got a couple of torpedoes into the enemy at 250 yards, UB 52 making a sharp and futile turn to avoid them. Of her crew, Launburg and the quartermaster were saved.

Amongst the May torpedo victims were included the Orient liner *Omrah* (8130 tons), sunk on the 12th, 40 miles S.W. $\frac{3}{4}$ S. from Sardinia; and the Union-Castle liner *Leasowe Castle* (9737 tons), on the 26th, 104 miles W. by N. $\frac{1}{2}$ N. from Alexandria. Both formed part of the troop convoy bound from Alexandria to Marseilles. Consisting of 7 large liners, it carried an entire infantry division for the hard-pressed army in Flanders. Many times had the convoy passed backwards and forwards, dogged each time, from the moment the troopships left Alexandria until they landed their precious freight. In spite of the escorting British and Japanese destroyers, the *Omrah* succumbed. As many as three U-boats would attack the convoy simultaneously; and it speaks much for the skill

XIX. A VIKING'S PYRE.

The *UB. 49* standing by the Italian sailing ship *Giovanni Albanesi* (500 tons gross), in the Mediterranean, on May 19, 1918. The Submarines usually destroyed sailing vessels by bombs or gunfire.

THE MEDITERRANEAN FREED 271

displayed by the escort that the threat was so often and so successfully parried. The *Leasowe Castle* was carrying 2900 troops, as well as her crew. An hour and a half after she was struck, she sank. Fortunately, the night was fine and clear, with full moon. Methodically and quietly the work of getting out the boats and filling them proceeded. In three-quarters of an hour 40 boats were in the water. When about 400 troops remained, the ship began to settle quickly. A destroyer came alongside for the men to jump on to her deck. With a loud crash a bulkhead gave way ; the liner suddenly sank by the stern, and the destroyer barely had time to cut herself away from the wreck. Altogether, 92 troops and 9 of the crew lost their lives; the remainder in the boats and on the rafts, guarded by a smoke-screen put around them by two destroyers, were picked up towards noon and brought into port. Another loss was the sinking of the French auxiliary cruiser *Sant' Anna* (9350 tons) on May 10.

The building-up of the Otranto Straits barrage was not likely to proceed without active objection by the Austrians. Indeed, their German allies vehemently urged them to attack and destroy the surface patrol, as they themselves had tried to do at Dover. On the night of April 22, five Austrian destroyers did set out to repeat the raid of the previous spring, but they were driven off by a division of Allied destroyers. On May 14 one of the British destroyers attached to this huge force of 246 vessels, the *Phœnix*, was sunk by torpedo whilst maintaining the patrol in the southern Adriatic. Proof that the new defences were becoming a source of anxiety to the Germans was afforded by the preparations made by the Austrian fleet for an attack in force. With material brought from England, the fixed net was slowly and laboriously extended across these deep waters. More than the net, the submarines found the huge patrolled areas a great handicap when returning from or setting out on a cruise. The Germans therefore succeeded in persuading their reluctant ally to destroy the barrage. As the U-boats due to return from cruises in May failed to arrive, the anxiety deepened. How they had been lost, and at what point of their cruises, could not be ascertained. Admiral Horthy, the leader of the 1917 raid, was therefore despatched to Cattaro, with his four large battleships, to support the projected raid. Leaving Pola in pairs, the battleships set their course along the Dalmatian archipelago. Behind one of the islands, Commander Rizzo, with two small motor boats, was lying in wait. Unobserved in the mists of dawn, on the morning of June 10 he glided through the battleships' destroyer screen and launched his torpedoes at the *Szent Istvan*. The battleship settled down, listed over, capsized, and sank. The preliminary concentration for the raid thus ended in disaster.

Another and a notorious U-boat was fated to perish in an attempt to pick off a unit in a convoy. On June 11, U 64 (Moraht) had left Cattaro on her eighth cruise, passing the Straits at about six in the morning. On the 17th, Moraht found the Marseilles-Malta convoy, passing between Sardinia and Sicily. In the heavy weather the torpedo he fired went under the target, but hit the next astern, *Kandy* (4921 tons). Moraht said afterwards that he imagined he was on the outside of the convoy, until a third steamer loomed up. He dived, but not before his periscope had been seen. The sloop *Lychnis* steamed to the spot and dropped over the side her depth-charges. This drastic treatment disabled the steering gear of U 64, and she thrust her bows out of the water like a great whale coming up to ' blow.' Greeted with shells from *Lychnis* and the trawler *Partridge II.*, Moraht dived to sixty feet, came up, and again broke surface. The sloop was still close by, and Moraht gave the order for an emergency dive. U 64 did not respond, and the bows of *Lychnis* shivered her. Down to the bottom the wounded submarine began to drop stern first. Nothing could be done to check her descent except by blowing her tanks. Reappearing in a circle of ships, she was once again hotly shelled. Although she attempted to return the fire, she was riddled, and sank like a stone. Five survivors, including Moraht, were saved. This commander claimed to have sunk 150,000 tons of shipping. In the same waters where, fifteen months previously, she had conquered the *Danton*, U 64 herself was vanquished.

A further loss occurred on July 9, when the Austrian X (Dürrigl) was completely disabled by mine off Caorle, in the

THE MEDITERRANEAN FREED

upper Adriatic ; and it does not appear that she ever went to sea again.

Now the fixed barrage was to claim its first victim. On August 1, UB 53 (Sprenger) left Pola for an expedition ; two days later, early in the morning, Sprenger dived and travelled under water for 45 miles, hoping to come up hard by Fano Island. At about 5 P.M. he decided to break surface. Instead, he hit the last section of the mine-nets, exploding two mines, and sustaining such damage that water poured in, and the submarine refused to answer her diving controls. At nightfall Sprenger scuttled his crippled craft, the crew swimming to the destroyer *Martin* and the trawler *Whitby Abbey*, by whom they were picked up. On board the trawler the man, listening at the C-tube hydrophone on the forecastle, heard most fearful crashings, which grew louder and louder, and, to his utter amazement, over the gunwale appeared the face of a German seaman. The man had clambered up the C-tube.[1]

At this point the pendulum swings once again : the French submarine *Circé*, remembered as the victorious opponent of UC 24, was found by U 47 off Cape Rodoni on August 20, and blown to pieces by a torpedo. Other important losses to be noticed were the sinking of the French troopship *Djemnah* (3716 tons) on August 2, when 442 lives were lost ; followed by the destruction of the French *Polynesien* (6373 tons) on the 10th, as the result of striking a mine, 19 of the crew being drowned. The *Amiral Charner* (4604 tons) was sunk on September 13, but only 6 lost their lives.[2] Two British armed boarding-steamers, *Snaefell* and *Sarnia*, were also sunk by torpedo attack on June 5 and September 12 respectively, the latter off Alexandria.

The shipping losses during the summer showed a remarkable drop. In May they were still 128,000 tons ; by August they had receded to 49,000 tons. Conspicuous amongst the fallen were the Blue Funnel *Glaucus* (5295 tons), sunk on June 3,

[1] R.U.S.I. (Usborne), April 1924.
[2] She must not be confused with the French cruiser of the same name sunk by U 21 on February 8, 1916. This loss recalled the fate which threatened her sister, one of the first steamers attacked by submarine, the *Amiral Ganteaume*. Both of these vessels were known in this country before the war as the Allan liners *Hibernian* and *Hungarian*.

S

20 miles W. from Cape Granitola (Sicily) ; the *Kosseir* (1855 tons), sunk on July 20, 40 miles N.E. by N. from Alexandria, with 39 of her crew ; the Ellerman *City of Adelaide* (8389 tons), on August 11, 60 miles E.N.E. from Malta, with 4 lives ; the *War Arabis* (5183 tons), on September 9, 88 miles N.E. by E. from Cape Sigli ; the *Wellington* (5600 tons) and *Tasman* (5023 tons), both on September 16, about 200 miles to the N.W. of Cape Villano, with the loss of 9 lives; the *Bylands* (3309 tons), on October 1, in the same vicinity ; and the *Reventazon* (4050 tons), on the 5th, in the Gulf of Salonica, with 15 lives.

Events now followed one another in rapid succession. On September 25 Bulgaria proposed an armistice, and five days later concluded peace. In a futile effort to stop the rot, Germany herself proposed an armistice with the Allied and Associated Powers on October 4, but the terms could not be entertained unless occupied territories were evacuated. With Allied victories in France and Flanders, on the Italian front, in Mesopotamia and Aleppo, the crumbling of the Central Powers went on uninterruptedly. On October 2 an Allied force attacked Durazzo and destroyed the base. During the raid the Austrian destroyers *Dinara* and *Scharfschütze* were sunk, the one by Italian M.A.S. boats, the other by two British destroyers. The Austrian torpedo boat No. 87 was also torpedoed and driven ashore by the small Italian motor boats, and the submarine XXXI (Rigele) was attacked.[1] The only minor success the enemy submarines achieved was when XXVIII (von Trautenegg) blew away with a torpedo the British cruiser *Weymouth*'s rudder.

The end was fast approaching, but the German U-boats remained active down to the last. A convoy was attacked off Malta on October 4 by UB 68 (Dönitz). The submarine was engaged at once by the escort (the sloop *Snapdragon* and the trawler *Cradosin*), and was so damaged by gunfire that she was scuttled by her crew, who were captured. Another U-boat succeeded in twice torpedoing the French battleship *Voltaire*, at ten o'clock on the night of the 18th, in the Cervi Channel off Mudros. The first torpedo blew a hole measuring 16 metres

---

[1] Winterhalder denies Admiral Sims' claim that two submarines were sunk. XXXI was found at Cattaro, after the end of war, and interned there.

THE MEDITERRANEAN FREED

by 4 metres in her side forward, whilst the second exploded before it hit and caused little further injury. The lateral *caisson* protection, 'padded' with empty wine-casks, saved the *Voltaire* from the fate of her sister-ship the *Danton*, and she arrived at Milo safely.

No British shipping was molested in the Mediterranean between October 16 and November 2. In home waters, all German submarines were recalled on October 21. Commander Pullen, at Pola, was left to decide what preparations should be made to evacuate the Mediterranean. The Austrian collapse was imminent. A revolt amongst the Croatian troops broke out at Fiume on October 23; they seized the port, and proclaimed their union with Italy. On the 31st, Hungary proclaimed her independence, and Austria asked for an armistice. Next day the Jugo-Slav flag was hoisted in the Austrian warships; and on the 3rd an armistice with Austria was agreed upon, to come into force at 4 P.M., November 4.[1] Unaware of the imminent cessation of hostilities, two Italian officers succeeded in penetrating Pola harbour and placing a contact-mine against the hull of the battleship *Viribus Unitis*, on the night of November 1-2. The Austrian Dreadnought foundered with heavy loss of life. Meanwhile Turkey had unconditionally surrendered on October 30, the terms of the armistice being signed on board the battleship *Agamemnon*.

Michelsen says that there were 28 German submarines remaining in the Adriatic, but Scheer gave the number as 26. Four boats, still manned at Constantinople (UB 14, UB 42, UC 23, and UC 37), fled to Sevastopol, and were surrendered there on November 26. At Varna the French seized the Bulgarian UB 8. Pullen sent orders to those submarines at sea, on October 28, to return to fill up with fuel and stores, and to make their way back to Kiel. On the 31st they were directed, if this course were not practicable, to put into Spanish ports. Those that could not be made ready for the perilous and long return trip were to be blown up. Accordingly, on the 28th, U 47, U 65, UB 48, UC 25, and UC 53 were destroyed at Pola, and UC 54 at Trieste; on the 30th the

[1] *U.S.N.I. Proceedings*, June 1929. (Letter by Italian Naval Attaché, Washington Embassy.)

large and small mine-layers U 73 and UC 34 were likewise blown up at Pola ; on the 31st the new UB 129 was demolished at Fiume ; and on November 1 the other large mine-layer U 72 was so wrecked at Cattaro. One boat, UC 74, appears to have been at sea ; and she later turned up at Barcelona, and was interned on November 2. The remaining 15[1] left the Adriatic on October 28, to begin the long voyage to the North Sea. With their bases gone, the submarines were homeless. First, Bulgaria had sued for peace ; Turkey had followed suit ; lastly, Austria had fallen. Nowhere was there a resting-place for Germany's under-water raiders; they were fugitives on the face of the deep. That they were loth to leave the scenes of their depredations can be gathered from the final attack on British shipping. Two steamers, the *Surada* (5324 tons) and the *Mercia* (4871 tons), were both sunk without warning off Port Said on November 2 ; and the *War Roach* (5215 tons) was damaged but reached port. The last attack in the Mediterranean was made on the 7th, when the Blue Funnel liner *Sarpedon* (4393 tons) evaded a torpedo fired at her.

As for the 15 refugee U-boats returning home, all of them safely passed through the Straits of Otranto for the last time.[2] As they neared the Straits of Gibraltar, each boat essayed the passage independently. Hartwig, who was in U 63, relates that the Straits were swarming with hunters : destroyers, torpedo-boats, patrols, submarine-chasers, gunboats, seaplanes—all massed in an attempt to prevent the U-boats from passing. Any hopes of running through on the surface were dashed, as the weather was too clear. Groping along, with even periscopes below the surface, he heard the hum of propellers everywhere. Once, when the noise died away, Hartwig rose to fix his position, and found to his dismay that a destroyer was but five hundred yards off. Escaping the stem of his opponent by inches, he hurriedly dived to 30 feet. Fortunately, for him at least, he kept good trim and depth ; both above and below him he heard depth-charges exploding.

[1] U 34, 35, 38, 63 ; UB 49, 50, 51, 105, 128 ; UC 20, 22, 27, 52, 67, and 73.
[2] As the last section of the ' de Quillac ' net was laid on September 30, the whole scheme, so laboriously constructed, seems to have been no obstacle to the U-boats.

Photo. Abrahams & Sons

XX. THE END OF H.M.S. BRITANNIA, OFF CAPE TRAFALGAR.
The largest British warship sunk by a German Submarine. Torpedoed by
UB. 50 on the morning of November 9, 1918, the battleship foundered three
and a half hours after being hit.

THE MEDITERRANEAN FREED

Running between such strata of death, he was compelled to continue well out into the Atlantic before he dared to come up. Eventually he was joined by twelve of his consorts, and together they made their way homewards, passing round the north of Scotland, and put into a Norwegian fjord, where they heard for the first time of the German Revolution.

Of the 15 which had sailed from the Adriatic, 13 reached German ports. As for the other two, U 35 sought refuge in Barcelona and was interned; but U 34 (Klasing) was caught. Just after midnight on November 8-9, the motor launch 155 sighted U 34 off Almina Point, Ceuta, and gave chase. A Very's light fired by ML 373 revealed the quarry diving. At once ML 155 put over a depth-charge. Reinforcements promptly arrived in the form of the Q-ship *Privet*. She sighted the hunted submarine and opened fire, securing a hit on U 34's conning-tower. After firing three 12-pounder shells at the disabled U-boat, she then put in depth-charges; and by half-past twelve the last German submarine to be lost in the war had perished. So phosphorescent was the water that U 34 could be seen, quite distinctly, moving under the water, glowing and outlined by sea-fire. These two raiders, U 34 and U 35, were members of that original band which followed in the track blazed by U 21. Into the Middle Sea they had burst—that ancient avenue of commerce, wherein had plied for centuries the triremes of Rome, the galleys of Venice, the dread Viking keels, and the corsairs of Barbary. So lastly came the Teutonic *Tauchboote* to spread death and desolation wherever they cruised. Many of them were doomed never to see their native ports again.

The U-boats, however, were not to depart without giving a final proof of their virulence. For venom they went not in want, and, striking, they struck down the largest British warship they had yet slain. A few hours after U 34 had been accounted for, UB 50 (Kukat) came upon and sank the battleship *Britannia* off Cape Trafalgar. *Absit omen!* She dealt the 16,350-ton vessel so mortal an injury with two torpedoes, that the battleship sank. Her death-agony of three and a half hours' duration sufficed for most of the crew to be taken off. With this parting blow the

U-boat menace in the Mediterranean came to its appointed end. Five million tons of shipping had been sent to the bottom of this inland sea, for the most part by torpedo. Of all this colossal total, mines destroyed only 19 vessels! The daily sweep of the shipping lanes had saved many a hull. Large areas were also too deep for mining operations such as were accomplished around the British Isles. Long and bloody had been the struggle; at a terrible cost had the Expeditionary Armies in Palestine, Salonica, and Mesopotamia been maintained; and only in the last two or three months had the enemy been prevented from snatching at whatever prize he desired. We are told that Hersing, for instance, would disdain to attack merchant-ships if there were the remotest chance of picking off a warship. To the Mediterranean were sent the tried and experienced commanders; and there they added to their already formidable tally of victims. The Allies handicapped themselves by their parochial system of control, under which the entire Mediterranean Sea was divided into zones, and over these zones their naval forces were separated and scattered.[1] The patrols, themselves sent out to steam along the shipping lanes, by their very movements showed the sea-wolves along which track the mercantile lambs were coming to be slaughtered.[2] Only in the closing stages were sufficient weapons of destruction available. The offensive launched against the depredators came late; the vast Otranto barrage, theoretically almost invincible, could claim but little success. None of the 15 U-boats which fled the Adriatic and poured through the defile was denied its way. The barrage, it is true, had caught one boat; it therefore had the potentiality of catching others. But how often? Was it possible that the wide and deep Otranto Straits would ever have been sealed, as the narrow and shallow Dover Straits were sealed?

[1] See Chart 1. It will be noticed, for example, that a merchant-ship traversing the length of the Mediterranean from west to east would pass from British to French, from French to British, from British to French, and finally into British control. The 'zone' method of trade defence and anti-submarine attack was an outcome of the Paris Naval Conference (December 1915), and it was abolished after the Corfu Conference (April 1917).

[2] R.U.S.I. (April 1924), Usborne.

THE MEDITERRANEAN FREED 279

The U-boats were compelled to issue from three narrow straits to prey upon their enemies' commerce—the Dover Straits, the Otranto Straits, and the Dardanelles. In this narrative little attention has been given to the last exit ; it must not be overlooked that fully 2500 mines were laid across the entrance to the Dardanelles by the end of 1917. At Gibraltar and in two other places mine-fields had also been planned. Only in the case of the Dover Straits were the tremendous efforts rewarded with decisive results. ' If they do these things in a green tree, what shall be done in the dry ? ' If it be so difficult to deter submarines from passage through confined waters, what of the future, if an enemy's submarine bases face and give immediate access to a great ocean ?

On November 1, the Royal and Imperial Navy of Austria-Hungary ceased to exist, inasmuch as all the war-vessels had been surrendered to the Jugo-Slavs. This change of nationality did not, however, save the fleet of the extinct Dual Monarchy. Every combatant vessel in the Adriatic and upon the Danube was taken possession of. A few small patrol-boats were handed back to the new states of Austria and Hungary for police duties on the Danube. Otherwise the entire navy was divided between the Allied nations, great and small. For the submarines there was no escape. At Pola were found I, II, IV, V, XI, XV, XVII, XXI, XXVII, XXVIII, XXXII, and XL ; at Cattaro the remaining boats were located—XXII, XXIX, XXXI, XLI, XLIII, XLVII. Various unfinished craft were found lying in the shipyards.[1] Seven boats had been lost—III, VI, XII, XVI, XX, XXIII,

[1] Thirteen unfinished boats were reported to have been found by the Allied naval authorities after the Armistice, namely :—
    (a) XXIV to XXVI—3 boats completing at Fiume.
    (b) XXXIII to XXXIX—5 boats completing at Pola, 2 boats at Fiume.
    (c) XLIV to XLVI—3 boats lying unfinished at Monfalcone.
But according to a recent and more reliable report (compiled by the ' Kriegsarchiv,' Vienna, during August 1930), the incomplete submarines amounted to no more than eleven, bearing the numbers XLVIII to LI (48 to 51), LIII (53), and CI to CVI (101 to 106). In addition, six other boats, numbered LIV to LIX (54 to 59) had been ordered, but were never actually begun.

In concluding this history of the Austro-Hungarian submarines, the

XXX; and X had been completely disabled. The French took back the *Curie* (renumbered XIV), and the Italians recovered the *Giacinto Pullino*, or whatever remnant there was left of that unfortunate boat.

So closes the record of the German and Austro-Hungarian submarine operations in the Mediterranean. Amongst all the theatres of naval warfare, it was perhaps here that the world received the most appalling demonstration that the new diving corsairs could harry shipping as shipping had never been harried before by pirate, privateer, or frigate. Not for one moment is it intended that these pages should be read as a belittlement of the splendid work done by the patrols. These little ships—often weary ships, manned by weary men—held on grimly to their wearisome task, no matter how insufficient their numbers and weapons might be. 'Naval dust' have they been called; but were they not, after all, that dust in the balance which just turned the scales against the enemy? Many a time did the patrols, in the Middle Sea and around the British Isles, hunt down and kill the U-boats, or help in the extermination of those maleficent agents of a malignant policy. And many a time was a fine merchantman, with a precious cargo, delivered out of the enemy's hands by one of the little vessels.

opportunity may be taken to point out that the following numbers were never borne by any completed craft :—VII (7), VIII (8), IX (9), XIII (13), XVIII (18), XIX (19), XXIV (24), XXV (25), XXVI (26), XXXIII to XXXIX (33 to 39), XLII (42), XLIV (44), XLV (45), and XLVI (46). It is possible that some of these numbers were allotted to submarines which were projected or laid down but never completed. Information regarding the Austro-Hungarian submarines destroyed on the stocks at Monfalcone on the first Italian capture of that port cannot be secured. The twelve submarines found at Pola (whose numbers are indicated in the text above) were taken over by the Italians. The six boats at Cattaro (whose numbers are also given in the text above) were taken charge of by the French and towed away to Bizerta, but XXIX foundered whilst under tow thither. Within twelve months of their deliveries to the Allies, the other seventeen boats were all broken up or scuttled in deep water. The mine-injured X does not seem to have been assigned to any of the Allies. Being unseaworthy and unfit for removal to any French or Italian port, she may have been broken up at (or scuttled outside) whatever Austro-Hungarian port she lay at, under Allied supervision; or the materials in her hull may have been used for the repair of her sister-boats. X may therefore have been partly or wholly broken up by the Austro-Hungarians themselves.

THE MEDITERRANEAN FREED

Above and beyond all, it must be clearly understood that the patrol system, despite all its defects, was the only possible and practical method of trade defence until such time as a sufficient number of fast vessels became available for convoy duty. That the convoy method should have been adopted only in the later stages of the war was in no way whatever due to any blind and dogged conservatism on the part of the naval authorities in clinging obstinately to the patrol method. Those naval authorities had to make the best use possible of the forces at their command. If fast war-vessels were not to be had for the protection of trade, then so long as that deficiency existed the convoy system was impossible, and the protection of trade had to be carried on by the small, slow, and scattered patrols. When combatant vessels of speed were at last at hand for the protection of merchant fleets upon the high seas, then, and only then, could the convoys be organized and put into operation.

CHAPTER XIII

DOWNFALL AND NOT WORLD POWER

(January–November 1918)

AROUND the British Isles the year 1918 opened quietly. Down the Channel still passed the submarines, but from month to month the impediments to their progress became more difficult and dangerous. It could not but be a disquieting thought for any submarine commander to reflect on that, when returning from a cruise, he must pass through waters of great hazard between the Scylla of the mines and the Charybdis of the patrols. The Flanders flotilla was losing one boat each week. It was estimated that the average life of any boat of that flotilla was not more than six trips. Even when they reached their base they were not left at peace. Incessant raids by Allied aircraft, plastering the base at Bruges with bombs, proved a further addition to the strain under which the personnel of these Flanders U-boats lived. Concrete bomb-proof shelters, with roofs six feet thick, were built at Bruges to house the submarines; a few others were constructed at Zeebrugge. Only rarely did the aircraft inflict material damage on the U-boats in their lairs. In the shallow parts of the North Sea, aircraft were dreaded by the under-water craft; there was not water enough to hide in from the penetrating gaze from aloft. Gayer admits that in the spring the British gained the upper hand in the Flanders area, and maintains that it would have been a wiser course to have gradually absorbed the Flanders U-boats and their crews into the North Sea and Mediterranean flotillas. A U-boat setting out on a cruise to the Bay of Biscay was confronted with difficulties formidable even at the beginning of 1918, but which became insurmountable by the late summer. Eighteen miles off the coast lay the Belgian

DOWNFALL AND NOT WORLD POWER

coastal barrage, extending from Dunkirk to the Scheldt, a distance of thirty-five miles. If a long *détour* through Dutch waters was to be avoided, the only course was to try to break out directly through the barrier. The water was too shallow to pass round the ends; neither was there enough depth to dive beneath the nets, festooned with mines and watched by patrols. They could only hope to slip over the coastal barrage by night. This first step negotiated, the U-boat next encountered the Dover nets, from the Goodwins to the Snou Bank. Again the U-boat must only make the attempt to slip over under cover of night, though here the deeper soundings permitted diving below the mined curtain. Now came the critical part of the Dover Straits ordeal. From Folkestone across to Cape Grisnez a great wall of super-sensitive mines was being built up; and over that great sub-surface span of steel and high-explosive, incessant watch was kept by vigilant pickets of patrols. Night was turned into day by giant shore searchlights, whose beams met in mid-Channel, and upon the edges of these hateful shafts of light hovered more patrols. At first, only magnesium flares were supplied to the patrols. Sometimes the flares failed, and the watching and waiting U-boat would seize her opportunity to dash through the dark patch and make a run for it. Indeed, it was her only chance. Beyond this maritime Aceldama, the U-boat might hope to evade the Channel aircraft and submarine patrols. The resting-places, hitherto resorted to by herself and her kindred, had become nests of British mines—deathtraps to be shunned. Any ship, even a decrepit old 'flowerpot' of a brig, might prove to be a dangerous decoy. In the heavens, on the surface, beneath the waves—everywhere was gin and snare, trap and engine of death; patrol and decoy; net and mine. Every wave seemed to pass by, hissing its promise of a certain and horrible end. Out in the ocean the crew could relax their strained nerves. They could snatch at the fleeting present; they could endeavour to forget the ordeal of return, involving probable death almost in sight of their base. Cases of insanity, though they certainly occurred amongst the submarine personnel, were not numerous; but the commanders became prematurely aged. Few of the

Flanders 'aces' survived the war; they could hardly hope to do so, when their less experienced brothers were falling by the dozen. No fewer than 80 Flanders boats were destroyed, with 145 officers and over 1000 men!

The German authorities could roughly ascertain the area of any loss. As to the manner in which a missing U-boat had fallen there existed at least three contingencies. The boat and crew might have perished together; the crew, or part of its complement, might have been saved when their boat was lost; or the U-boat and crew might possibly have been seized. The capture of the crew would become known to the Germans eventually by the exchange of prisoners-of-war lists. Of the manner in which the U-boat had met Nemesis the German authorities could learn but little. On the British side, grim silence, absolute and ominous, reigned. 'Spurlos versenkt' was proving a two-edged sword—merchantman and submarine alike could perish by it.

How wise the British policy of preserving an implacable silence was, Gayer revealed seven years later. 'In consequence of the unexplained loss in January of U 87, 84, 93, and 95 during the passage of the Dover Straits, and reports of additional barriers, Commodore Michelsen thereupon ordered the north-about route to be resumed.'[1] As a matter of fact, none of these boats succumbed in the Straits; all four reached western waters and there met their several and violent ends. Out of the vast void of the Atlantic came no voice, no sign, no trace of their fate.

The manner in which U 87 finished her career has already been described. From her deck Rudolf Schneider of *Arabic* ill-fame had been swept; she became the steel sepulchre of his ill-fated successor. U 93 (Gerlach) was accidentally run down by the steamer *Braeneil* off the Lizard on January 7.[2]

---

[1] *U.S.N.I. Proceedings*, April 1926 (Gayer), p. 655.

[2] British Records (1919) attributed the loss of U 93 to a mine in the Channel on the same date as given above. Later it was ascertained that she was destroyed in the manner here stated. The German *Taschenbuch der Kriegsflotten* (1922) ascribed the loss of U 93 to an encounter with some British decoy-ship in the Channel during 1918. This can be disregarded; it is a typical example of the Germans' uncertainty as to the fate of several of their submarines.

This was Count Spiegel's command, the one in which he had fought the famous decoy *Prize*. He had felt her sinking under his feet, to be left struggling for his life in the water. Ziegler, who brought her home, shattered and leaking, was not on board at the time of her loss, being absent from duty on sick leave. U 95 (Prinz) certainly got into western waters before she mysteriously disappeared. U 84, in command of Röhr, participant in the fierce battle with the decoy *Penshurst* a year earlier, was rammed and sunk by PC 62 in the St. George's Channel on January 26.

The first months of 1918 were marked by a series of outrages on hospital-ships similar to those characterizing the brutal murders of 1917. In August 1917, when Berlin agreed to the appointment of 11 Spanish officers for service in the Mediterranean, the German Government reaffirmed that the Atlantic and the North Sea were free to hospital-ships. Avonmouth was therefore chosen as a suitable port to land wounded and sick from overseas; and into the Bristol Channel throughout the remainder of 1917 poured the large white vessels bearing their living *débris* of the battlefields and trenches. On the night of January 4, one such hospital-ship, the *Rewa* (7308 tons), was steaming up the Bristol Channel at between eight and nine knots, with all the usual distinctive lights brilliantly burning. She was carrying 279 patients, a staff of 79, and a crew of 207, and bound from Malta. The Spanish officer had been landed at Gibraltar, after testifying to the *bona fides* of the ship. At fifteen minutes past eleven the *Rewa* was 19 miles W. ¼ S. from Hartland Point; the night was fine and clear. Out of the darkness raced a torpedo from U 55 (Werner), to explode against the hospital-ship. Four of the crew were killed outright. The *Rewa* at once settled down. The wounded and staff were rapidly transferred to the boats and were picked up by patrols. At two o'clock in the morning the *Rewa* sank. Such an infamy, especially in waters wherein hospital-ships had been guaranteed as safe from attack, prompted Berlin to suggest that the disaster was due to a mine. Mr. A. J. Balfour, Foreign Secretary, pointed out, however, that in the same locality, on this very day, a patrol had been attacked. Two days later the steamers *Spenser* (4186 tons) and *Halber-*

dier (1049 tons) were both torpedoed by submarine in this particular area. No UC-boat would lay mines in waters wherein other German submarines would probably operate. Moreover, a light low down and close to the surface had been seen by those aboard just before the attack. Later, it became known that Werner, a commander already of evil repute and of whom we have not heard the last, had made the wanton and deliberate assault on the helpless wounded.

In January, 57 British merchant-ships were torpedoed and sunk, a decrease of 19 on the previous month. Among those destroyed around the British Isles were the commissioned escort ship *Mechanician* (9044 tons) on the 20th, 8 miles W. from St. Catherine's, with 13 lives ; and the Cunard liner *Andania* (13,405 tons) a week later, 2 miles N.N.E. from Rathlin Island, when 7 lives were lost. Early in 1918, submarines became particularly active off the north of Ireland ; and to protect the approaches to the Clyde, Belfast, and Liverpool, a deep mine-field was laid in the North Channel. The work was carried out by British mine-layers, assisted by the U.S.S. *Baltimore,* a cruiser converted into a layer. The entire field was planned to comprise 10,000 mines ; at the time of the Armistice it was still incomplete, and reliance had to be placed on the hydrophone units and submarine patrols. More than anything else, the suspicion that a hostile submarine lurked on their flanks caused the U-boats great uneasiness. There are cases on record when a U-boat broke surface at the exact moment that a British boat likewise came up. Both hurriedly dived, and the U-boat got away as quickly as possible from that unhealthy spot. Exceedingly hazardous were the conditions under which the Allied submarines worked. They were forbidden to cruise outside a specified patrol square, as destroyers had standing orders to sink at sight any submarine found without that area. British submarine commanders bore witness to the efficiency of the ' hunters ' after they had themselves become, by mischance or misunderstanding, the objectives of assault. Three British and two Italian submarines were sunk accidentally by their own or Allies' patrols. Through the North Channel one continual stream of American troopships passed during 1918, and the enemy submarines made great efforts to intercept and harry them. In the Irish Sea the German commanders complained particularly of the numerous British airships and seaplanes ; they did not fear the bombs dropped around them, but they did dislike having their movements watched and reported.

In addition to the four U-boats whose loss has been narrated, four other boats were destroyed in waters around the British Isles during January. In the Heligoland Bight minefields, one of the coastal boats attached to the North Sea flotillas, UB 22 (Wacker), received her *quietus* on the 19th, to be followed to the bottom next day by three German torpedo-boats. On the 26th, two other submarines came to a sudden end in the Dover area. Whilst patrolling, the destroyer *Leven* sighted a periscope and dropped depth-charges on the spot ; seven of the crew of UB 35 (Stöter) were seen in the water, but only one could be picked up, and he died later. In the other case the drifter *Beryl III.* came upon the large U 109 (Rey), at about eight o'clock in the morning, off Cape Grisnez. She was lying stationary ; fire was opened on her ; she dived, but not before a hit had been registered on her conning-tower. Two hours later a heavy double explosion was heard by the watching vessels around. Along many a coast the legend lives, of provinces submerged and lost, and of church bells ringing under the sea. From England to France, under the waves, now hung Death's great belfry—cast in steel, clappered with doom, ready to knell for the U-boats. In the depths this hideous carillon pealed. The double stroke marked the passing of U 109, one of the best and latest submarines produced by the German shipyards.

Two days after the foregoing two successes—that is, on January 28—the hydrophones of the Granton trawler *W. S. Bailey* detected a submarine off the Firth of Forth, evidently lying in wait for the passing of the Scandinavian convoy. As soon as the enemy's sound was located, depth-charges were put over. Hours passed. No wreckage floated to the surface to denote possible injury. No sound of motors was heard. Then in the moonlight the hull of UB 63 (Gebeschus) emerged ; the periscope was seen to be distorted at an angle of forty-five degrees. Depth-charges were again put in, this time by the trawler *Fort George*, and the wrecked U-boat disappeared for ever.

Sixty-eight British ships of 224,501 tons gross were sunk by the submarines in February, with the loss of 697 lives—the last being attributable to heavy death-rolls in certain cases. On the 4th the Cunard liner *Aurania* (13,936 tons) was sent to the bottom, 15 miles N. $\frac{1}{2}$ W. from Instrahull, with 8 lives; the same day the *Treveal* (4160 tons), sunk off the Skerries, Anglesea, took down 33 of her crew. The next day, February 5, the *Mexico City* (5078 tons) sank 15 miles W. by S. $\frac{1}{2}$ S. from South Stack, Holyhead, with 29 lives. On this day the U-boats secured their first success against the Atlantic troopships. Seven miles north of Rathlin Island the Anchor liner *Tuscania* (14,348 tons), from Halifax to Liverpool with 2000 troops and cargo, was fatally hit by torpedo, sinking two hours later. Partly because boats overturned as they were lowered from the listing liner, and partly as a result of boats making towards land instead of remaining by the ship, the heavy loss of life amounted to 166 soldiers and 44 of the crew. In the sinking of the *Merton Hall* (4327 tons) on the 11th, 30 miles N. by E. from Ushant, 57 lives were sacrificed; and in that of the *Renfrew* (3830 tons) on the 24th, 8 miles S.W. from St. Ann's Head, 40 were drowned. Other ships sank with between 20 and 30 of their crews, but the worst case was the second hospital-ship outrage of 1918. Just before four o'clock on the morning of February 26 the *Glenart Castle* (6824 tons) was torpedoed by UC 56 (Kiesewetter). She was on her way from Newport (Mon.) to embark wounded at Brest, and was carrying a staff of 64 and a crew of 122. Steaming at 10 knots, ablaze with light, she was 10 miles W. of Lundy Island when she was struck on the starboard quarter. The explosion wrecked the dynamo, plunged the ship into darkness, and destroyed the wireless installation. The deck was ripped up and the boats were smashed, leaving insufficient to carry those on board. To make matters worse, a rough sea was running, and the weather was bitterly cold. The Union-Castle liner sank in seven minutes. The survivors called to UC 56 for help in their trouble, but their cries were ignored. In the rough seas the boats were swamped, and, later in the morning, only 30 survivors were found by a French dandy, *Le Faon*, and the American destroyer *Parker*. Altogether, 8 nurses, 7 officers, and 43 ranks of the R.A.M.C., and 95 of the crew died as a result of this deliberate attack. Seven minutes before the torpedo was fired, the submarine had been seen to race ahead to take up a favourable attacking position.

Four German submarines were destroyed in February. On the 4th the UC 50 (Seuffer) was depth-charged off Dungeness by the composite *Zubian*, an event which justified the curious creation of this destroyer.[1] Four nights later, at about 9.30 P.M., UB 38 (Bachmann) was detected by the drifter *Gowan II.* trying to pass through the Straits on the French side. Finding herself revealed in the flares, and to avoid being run down by the drifters, she dived. There followed a triple explosion. Then, to quote Scheer,[2] it was realized that 'the Straits were almost impassable.' Thereafter, only the Flanders boats attempted the passage, but the majority of them gave it up in April. A few of the most intrepid commanders, however, persevered until September.

It was clear that something must be attempted to break down or breach this new and formidable defence. As stone by stone the Wall of Hadrian rose to span England and keep out the barbarian Pict and Scot, so rose, mine by mine, the submarine barrier between the white cliffs of Old Albion and *la doulce France*. Not only in these Straits were the vast walls of mines slowly built up against the U-boats; in the Bight of Heligoland the fields of death grew ever wider. In January a U-boat attempting to leave on a cruise through the Bight exits found a new mine-barrage in her path and was forced to turn back and try the Kattegat route. As a consequence, she arrived off Hartlepool on February 12 with only just enough fuel in hand for immediate return to her base. No longer was the submarine personnel drawn from volunteers; there was a shortage of experienced engineers and petty officers. The submarine commanders had even

---

[1] The *Zubian* was created by joining undamaged after and fore halves of the two injured destroyers *Nubian* and *Zulu*.
[2] *High Sea Fleet* (Scheer), p. 314.

T

to endure the jealousy of their brothers in the High Sea Fleet. It became noticeable that submarines were more willing to surrender now, than present a stubborn defence.

So, on the night of February 14, a flotilla of destroyers under Captain Heinecke set off to destroy the ' flare ' barrier that made night in the Straits like day. Urgent calls from the Flanders corps induced Scheer to detach these fast destroyers from the High Sea Fleet for a determined attack on the patrols. Of the hidden mine-wall below the massed patrols the Germans knew nothing, and the raid was futile. The secret of the deep fields was well kept. In darkness and in mist the German raiders fell upon the barrage force at about midnight ; here they found fifty drifters, half a dozen trawlers, several mine-sweepers, and a destroyer. The patrols were fourteen miles lower down the Straits than they were in the previous raid of October 1916, and they had a much larger destroyer force to protect them ; yet the enemy was able to wipe out 1 trawler and 7 drifters, in addition to damaging other vessels, with a loss on the British side of 22 killed, 54 missing, and 13 wounded. So grievous a blow to the little ships was, as ever, relieved by the heroism displayed by their crews. At once other crews came forward to take the place of their fallen comrades. It was obvious that better protection must be given. Next night the flare barrage was at work and the Straits still remained guarded.

Farther west in the Channel, UB 17 (Branscheid) reached the terminal point of her career when she tried to attack a convoy. The patrols down Channel even bitterly complained that the Dover Patrol would not let submarines through, in the later stages of the war, so rendering their watch inexpressibly monotonous. In this case the destroyer *Onslow*, in charge of the convoy, was off Portland when she sighted a torpedo passing under her keel. It was a simple matter to run up the torpedo's wake and drop depth-charges over the spot from which it had been fired. UB 17 came up, heeled over to port, and sank.

Off the north of Ireland the U-boats continued to ravage shipping. One, U 89 (Bauck), was rammed and sunk with all hands by the armoured cruiser *Roxburgh*, on ocean escort duty, on the night of February 12 ; but other U-boats took her place and secured many large victims. On March 1 an armed merchant cruiser, the large Allan liner *Calgarian*, of 17,515 tons, also on similar duty, fell to the torpedoes of U 19 (Spiess), that relic of Germany's pre-war flotilla. The *Calgarian* was in the North Channel off Rathlin Island when hit by a torpedo at 180 metres range. Spiess, seeing that she still kept afloat, went back to finish his work. Despite a screen of 7 destroyers, 11 trawlers, and 3 sloops, he succeeded in sending in a couple of torpedoes as the *coup de grâce*. The U-boats dealt another heavy blow on the 15th, when the R.M.S.P. *Amazon* (10,037 tons) was sunk 30 miles W. by N. from Malin Head. Towards the end of the month, U 101 (von Georg) was active in the St. George's Channel and U 90 (Jetz) off the Mull of Galloway ; both these commanders were afterwards nominated as war criminals for their attacks. The former sank the *Trinidad* (2592 tons) on March 22, and 39 lives were lost. The loss on the 30th of the small *Lough Fisher* (418 tons), with all hands, twelve miles S.S.E. from Helvick Head, was a second specimen of von Georg's handiwork. One of the larger ships destroyed was the *Etonian* (6515 tons) on the 23rd, thirty-four miles S. by E. ½ E. from the Old Head of Kinsale, after great efforts had been made to tow her in. In the case of the attack on the *Comrie Castle* (5173 tons) in the Channel on the 14th, the U-boat was disguised as a drifter, with a funnel rigged, a sail set aft, and showing a red light. Sounding a blast on her syren, she just cleared the Union-Castle liner and promptly torpedoed her. The liner was beached next morning, in a sinking condition, in St. Helen's Roads.

To despoil and destroy the Atlantic convoys approaching the North Irish coast was a hazard for the U-boats. From Spiess one obtains a glimpse of the perils to be faced by the under-water raiders. On his next cruise in U 19, he unwisely returned to the scene of his last triumph, and barely escaped to return and relate his experiences.[1] Others did not share

---

[1] During the return of U 19 after her narrow escape, there occurred the only proved instance of a U-boat's crew setting foot on British soil. Spiess sent a few members of his crew ashore, on the lonely island of St. Kilda, to shoot some sheep.

his luck. On March 15 the destroyers *Michael* and *Moresby*, patrolling these waters, surprised U 110 (Kroll) just after she had torpedoed a steamer. The destroyers picked up one boat's crew ; then, noticing the surface swirl from a submerged submarine, dropped depth-charges. Forced up to the surface, U 110 was finished off with gunfire, six of the crew being rescued. At the southern end of the Irish Sea the patrols added to their successes when the patrol-boat PC 51 depth-charged to extinction U 61 (Dieckmann) in the St. George's Channel, on the night of the 26th. This case was remarkable in that an original intention to ram had to be given up at the last moment, owing to the helm jamming. PC 51 swung right round, and then headed away from the enemy. Fortunately, the defect was quickly remedied.

To the Dover barrage fell one submarine in March. UB 58 (Löwe) tried to pass through during the early hours of the 10th, found six drifters in her path, and dived to her death. The following day, off the Lincolnshire coast,[1] UB 54 (Hecht) succumbed to depth-charges of the destroyers *Retriever, Sturgeon,* and *Thruster.* The destroyers were just about to form a screen ahead of a light-cruiser squadron engaged on a cruise, when the conning-tower of the U-boat was sighted about a mile distant from the *Sturgeon*'s port bow. The unlucky submarine had appeared right amongst the flotilla. Ahead steamed the *Sturgeon,* to port was revealed the *Retriever* and to starboard the *Thruster.* UB 54 dived at once, and attempted to slip through the rapidly-closing gap between the pursuing *Sturgeon* and the advancing *Retriever.* The *Sturgeon* was too quick for her. Up the U-boat's track ran the keen destroyer and dropped a depth-charge, set at 40 feet, on either side. As the detonations subsided, the bows of UB 54 pierced the surface of the sea at an ominous angle. Once again the insatiable *Sturgeon* turned. UB 54 made a desperate attempt to dive to safety, but even as she was hiding herself beneath the waves the remainder of the *Sturgeon*'s depth-charges followed her down, accompanied by two more from the *Retriever* and another brace from the *Thruster.* Oil and wreckage marked the scene of this spirited attack ; but,

[1] Michelsen says ' Channel.'

as neither survivors were rescued nor bodies seen, the Admiralty report merely listed the U-boat as 'probably sunk.' Seven weeks later, 'subsequent information' dispelled any shred of doubt as to the finality of the attack.[1] Lastly, far away from these inshore waters, UC 48 was so badly damaged in a fight with patrols that she sought refuge at Ferrol on the 24th, and was interned.[2]

On March 10 another hospital-ship was attacked. Ships had been sunk during the day in the Bristol Channel, and towards evening the *Guildford Castle* (8036 tons), from Cape Town to Avonmouth with 438 patients, was nearing the end of her long voyage. At 5.35 P.M. the fourth officer sighted the track of a torpedo about 700 yards distant. The helm was put hard a-starboard, and the liner was struck by some submerged object, shivering and listing four degrees. She recovered, but signals for help were at once sent out. Soundings, however, revealed no injury, and the ship reached port in safety. An examination of the hull showed marks on the length of the ship's port side, where the torpedo had bumped alongside. Further, two or three of the crew had seen a periscope. The ship was, of course, brilliantly lighted up, with the conventional signs of her merciful duties.

In April, 67 British ships of 209,469 tons were sunk by submarines. From this time onward the number and tonnage of destroyed shipping declined, fluctuating slightly but on the whole trending in the downward direction. Michelsen states that 22 North Sea boats were out in April, and this number was increased to 27 in May, when the Germans made their last struggle to win back the ground they had lost. On April 15 the Allan liner *Pomeranian* (4241 tons) sank so rapidly, 9 miles N.W. by W. from Portland Bill, that only one of her crew of 56 survived. He caught hold of the rigging just below the crow's-nest as he came up; the ship was on the bottom, and soon afterwards he was rescued from his precarious perch. On the next day the Canadian Pacific *Lake Michigan* (7640 tons) was sunk 93 miles N.W. from Eagle Island. The

---

[1] *Submarine and Anti-Submarine* (Newbolt), p. 214.

[2] UC 48 was scuttled by her crew on March 14, 1919, before she could be handed over to the Allies.

P.S.N. Co. *Oronsa* (8075 tons) was also sunk, 12 miles W. of Bardsey Island, on the 28th, with 3 of the crew. Two ships were fatally injured by mine; altogether, only 10 British vessels succumbed to mine damage during the whole of 1918!

April 1918 bears an interesting comparison with the same tragic month of the preceding year. In 1918, 67 ships of 209,469 tons were sunk; twelve months before, 155 British vessels of 516,394 tons gross had been destroyed. By September 1918 the losses had been reduced to 48 ships of 136,859 tons. This result was obtained, it should be noted, in spite of the extra duties imposed by the necessity of protecting the American troop-convoys.

The April results of the Dover Barrage numbered two more U-boats. To avoid the vigilance of a drifter division, on the 11th the UB 33 (Gregor) dived to her utter undoing. Weeks later a steel chest, containing confidential code- and signal-books, was recovered from the wreck. The 22nd of the month found UB 55 (Wenninger) running the Straits. A trawler and seven drifters loomed up. UB 55 made a hurried dive; there was an ear-splitting detonation, and the submarine reeled, listed, and dropped to the sea-bed with a crash. Inside UB 55 darkness reigned. Water leaked in through the compartments. She was lying in 100 feet of water, with her intricate internal mechanism smashed. Remorselessly the water seeped in. Efforts were made to open the conning-tower hatch and establish an air-lock as the rising water inside compressed the air. Slowly the hatch opened, and one huge air-bubble surged to the surface. Twenty of the crew escaped from their steel coffin; and at daybreak 3 live Germans were picked up by one drifter, 3 others and a dead man being found by another. During April, UC 79 (Krameyer) vanished. The Germans ascribe her loss to a mine, and her twisted hull probably lies on the wreck-strewn bed of the North Sea, or under the Dover Barrage.

St. George's Day, April 23, will for ever be associated with the immortal fame of the blocking attack. At Zeebrugge the block-ships were sunk in the mouth of the canal; at Ostend the attack failed. The attempt was repeated in May, when the *Vindictive* was put across the canal entrance at Ostend.

DOWNFALL AND NOT WORLD POWER 295

The wrecks of the cruisers prevented large craft, such as destroyers, from emerging into the sea for three weeks, and were a source of danger for two months. Two days after the attack, however, UB 16 worked her way past the Zeebrugge block-ships.[1] At Ostend, when the *Vindictive* was slewed round, the blocking was only partial. By this time the Flanders force had declined from the zenith of its power. It is generally admitted by German authorities that all boats and personnel should have been sent to the Mediterranean or else should have joined the North Sea flotillas in the spring of 1918. From home ports they could still have made descents on the Dutch trade to England or on the Scandinavian traffic. Instead, they remained at the Belgian base until the military collapse forced their withdrawal in October. The Dover barrage was now so far advanced that the old net-barrier was no longer maintained. In August it was laid again, however, but only with mines, extending from the east Goodwins to Gravelines.[2] The coastal barrage off Flanders was allowed to fall into neglect.

After the St. George's Day attack, few of the Flanders boats tried to enter the Channel; their work was curtailed, and, for the smaller boats, their cruising was confined to the North Sea. On what curious labours they spent the summer months is to be detailed at a later point. It may be noted here that the command of the German forces in Flanders—that is, war-vessels, bases, coastal defences, and naval brigades ashore—was vested in Admiral Schröder. In May the naval forces afloat, commanded by Conrad Albrecht, comprised 19 destroyers, 16 'A' torpedo-boats, 7 motor boats, 24 mine-sweeping motor boats, and 4 mine-layers, with two submarine flotillas of 22 UB- and 12 UC-boats. Captain Bartenbach was responsible for the submarine section. The Flanders con-

---

[1] *The British Assault on the German Bases at Zeebrugge and Ostend*, by Captain Karl Schultz, German Navy (retired). Prepared from the documents in the naval archives, *U.S.N.I. Proceedings*, July 1929, p. 582. (NOTE BY AUTHORS.—Schultz says the boat which passed the obstruction was UB 15. This is impossible, inasmuch as UB 15 had been sent to the Adriatic in 1915 and had been handed over to the Austro-Hungarian Navy. The boat in question must have been UB 16.)

[2] *Auxiliary Patrol* (Chatterton), p. 193.

tingent of the U-boat forces claimed to have destroyed altogether 2554 ships of 4,400,000 tons by mine and torpedo—an equivalent of one-third of the shipping sunk. Working from Flamborough Head as far west as the Irish Sea and the distant Bay of Biscay, they lost 80 of their number—an equivalent of nearly one-half the number of U-boats lost at sea when carrying out war-cruises, either through the Allied counter-offensive or from accidental causes.[1]

If the activities of the Flanders boats had been curtailed, the large submarine raiders were now operating far out into the Atlantic, and were carrying out cruises of three months' duration. Kolbe took out one of the converted 'Deutschlands' on December 23, 1917, and did not return until April 19, 1918. His command is said to have been U 152, and during the course of this cruise he went down to the coasts of Portugal and West Africa, and even as far as the Canary Islands. Prolonged as his voyage was, he could not, upon his return, lay claim to more than 30,000 tons of shipping destroyed. On January 14, U 155 set out from Kiel, once more bound for the Azores zone, but this time under Eckelmann's charge. When she came back, on May 4, her commanding officer reported the destruction of 50,000 tons of shipping. Among those vessels deleted was the Italian Fleet collier *Sterope* (9550 tons displacement), from whom she took 45 tons of oil-fuel on April 7. She also looted and sank the Spanish liner *Giralda* (2194 tons), this being the fifty-sixth Spanish ship to be sunk. Another of these converted merchant-submarines, U 157 (under the command of Max Valentiner), intercepted the Spanish liner *Infanta Isabel de Borbon* off Cadiz on March 28. The Italian auxiliary *Prometeo* (4455 tons), sunk by gunfire in the Atlantic on March 18, was probably another victim of these corsairs.

On April 9, U 154 (Gercke) appeared off Monrovia and opened fire on the wireless station; she was busily engaged on this task when the Elder-Dempster liner *Burutu* hove in sight. Gercke appears to have mistaken her for an armed merchant cruiser, since he broke off his bombardment. Next day the *Burutu* was attacked by a large submarine. She

[1] *Marine Rundschau* (Schulze), date not recorded.

evaded the torpedo, and then she was shelled at 3000 yards range by the full broadside of the submarine's four guns.[1] The range opened to between 6000 and 7000 yards ; a chase developed and lasted until dark. Firing her forward gun, the submarine endeavoured to edge the *Burutu* inshore ; but at nightfall Captain Yardley of the *Burutu* eluded his pursuer and made Sierra Leone. The *Burutu* arrived in port listing heavily ; she had been twice hit, and lost 1 killed. U 154 was thereafter joined by U 153 ; and on April 25 they fell in with the Q-boat *Willow Branch* (alias *Bombala*), carrying stores between Gibraltar and Sierra Leone.[2] This ship was nine days out, and was off Cape Blanco, when the two large submarines hove in sight. The brace of U-boats expended thirty rounds before they found the range. For two and a half hours the fight waxed and waned. Finally the *Willow Branch*, a blazing wreck, was abandoned by her crew, numbering 53 ; the third officer was taken prisoner. As for the enemy, his loss was 1 killed and 7 wounded. Terrible were the events that ensued in that tropic clime. After the first day the ship's boats became separated. The master's boat was never seen again. The other drifted about under the blazing sun for eight days, the torments of agonizing thirst torturing the survivors. Some—11 in all—drank sea-water and went mad. On the ninth morning the 14 left made land in the estuary of the Senegal River. Two of the stronger cast about and found a tiny pool of water ; and after drinking a little they tottered back to their comrades, bearing the life-giving fluid. It was too late ; they had died. These two struggled on until next day ; then, found by friendly Arabs, they were taken to a French post.

Retribution did not tarry. On May 11, both of these submarines, U 153 and U 154, were found in the latitude of Cape St. Vincent by E 35, one of the British submarines based on Gibraltar. A thrilling two hours' combat ensued ; finally, U 154 was blown up by a well-directed torpedo from the

---

[1] U 151-154 mounted four guns (two 5·9-inch, two 3·4-inch). No other German submarines, completed and at sea in 1918, mounted so many.

[2] Owing to the shipping shortage, Q-ships were running with genuine cargoes.

British boat. Owing to the presence of U 153, no search could be made for survivors.

Through home waters the American troopships began to pass in ever-increasing numbers, proving a serious strain on the hard-driven patrolling forces. Escorts had to be provided through the danger zone for vessels so precious, even at the cost of relaxing the offensive against the diving marauders. Gayer says there were not enough U-boats wherewith to carry on attack both on trade- and troop-convoys simultaneously; and, since the latter class of vessel could only be attacked by torpedo, it was not interfered with seriously. Trading vessels were the U-boats' selected prey. Scheer points out that concentrations against convoys failed because merchant squadrons were diverted around danger-spots; the U-boats waited in vain for the expected convoys. Nevertheless, attempts *were* made to sink the troopships, and Scheer relates that the ' U-cruisers ' (*sic*) shadowed the convoys, calling up other boats to concentrate for an attack nearer land. He admits, however, that the troop-convoys were too well guarded to make attack easy. The price of such immunity was provided by the simple process of robbing Peter Patrol to protect Paul Troopship. Admiral Sims, U.S.N., testifies that, of the 1,500,000 U.S. troops brought over during the summer of 1918, 1,000,000 were embarked in British bottoms; and this despite the fact that already 6918 ships of 1,694,000 tons had suffered extinction. Of the escorts necessary for the troop movements, 70 per cent. of the vessels were British; of the destroyers, only 14 per cent. were American; and of the auxiliary craft, just 3 per cent. were American. Out of the vast auxiliary patrol force of 3000 vessels, American ships numbered 160.[1] The convoying of the American force involved 393 destroyer- and 51 ocean-escorts. In April there were 150 American ships helping; by July the number had risen to 250. Armed merchant cruisers became troopships, patrols became escorts; and by

[1] The United States ordered 927 anti-submarine craft (279 destroyers, 448 submarine-chasers, 112 Eagle boats, 67 submarines, and 21 sweepers), but the majority of these vessels were not finished in time to take part in war operations.

DOWNFALL AND NOT WORLD POWER 299

June 1,000,000 American troops had been brought over. Fifty-six U.S. troops were lost when the armed merchant cruiser *Moldavia* (9500 tons) was sunk in the Channel on May 23—the only loss the U-boats ever succeeded in inflicting on the American troop convoys. The submarines also caught the westward-bound and empty *President Lincoln* (18,168 tons), sunk by U 90 (Jetz) on May 31, and the *Covington* (ex-Hamburg-Amerika *Cincinnati*, 16,339 tons), put down on the night of July 1 by U 86 (Patzig), with 6 of the crew. Every available ship of any size was pressed into the transport service after March 21, when the great German offensive was launched on the western front and the German troops broke through the Allied lines in France and Flanders.[1] The bulk of the American troops was landed at St. Nazaire ; and from April to October, American troop-convoys reached the Allied ports every four days. The record number carried in one convoy was 31,693. The onrush of German invasion was checked at last.

A significant feature of the 1918 campaign was the complete failure of the UC-boats to cause material injury to British trade. Eight British ships were sunk by mine around the British Isles during the period January 1-November 11. Whereas in 1917 some 32 of these enemy boats had been accounted for, less than a third of this number were sunk by patrols or accident during 1918. In January 1918 there were certainly 37 of the 79 UC-boats left, and they were decidedly busy throughout the summer. What were they doing ?

The task of these mine-layers presents one of the most

[1] After the collapse of Russia, it was hoped that a large number of industrial workers would be released from military service, to assist in the more rapid production of new submarines. The remainder of the troops freed from the eastern front could be used to crush Italy. Such a decisive victory, it was pointed out, would go far to support the submarine campaign in the Mediterranean, where a considerable degree of success had already been obtained with the anti-shipping warfare. The Chief of the Submarine Office energetically advocated these proposals, but other naval and military leaders were at variance regarding their value. Hindenburg and Ludendorff had already decided upon their great offensive upon the western front for the early spring of 1918, and they vetoed all proposals for the diversion of man-power from the eastern front to the shipyards. Later, in 1918, they were not so unwilling to entertain such suggestions. (Gayer, *U.S.N.I. Proceedings*, April 1926, p. 656.)

interesting moves in the closing stages of the naval war. In a great arc about forty-five miles distant from the Bell Rock, off the Firth of Tay, mines began to be discovered; and in an ever-increasing radius more and more were dragged to light. The puzzle as to their position and objective was solved after a time. Quietly and methodically the minesweepers removed the various batches one by one. Unaware of this, the enemy continued to drop whole cargoes outside their previous groups. Throughout the summer, backwards and forwards these UC-boats crossed the North Sea. They loaded up, went out to lay their mines, and went home for more. As fast as they could be freighted and turned round, out they went again. By October the German plan was complete;[1] it was to trap and cripple the Grand Fleet as it emerged from its Scottish bases to join battle when the High Sea Fleet made its final desperate bid for victory. So fondly did the enemy believe in the existence of his great barrage that in November the cruiser *Königsberg* made a wide *détour* to avoid these phantom mines, unaware that long ago they had been swept up by the 60 mine-sweepers based on the Forth and allotted to this dangerous clearance work.[2]

To preserve an outward aspect of normal routine, German mines were still deposited in other places, particularly off Dover and in the path of traffic steaming up the war channel to Methil. On March 27 the old destroyer *Kale* blew up on a mine; and on the following day the armed boarding steamer *Tithonus*, engaged in the Scandinavian traffic con-

[1] The German Minister of Defence has denied, since 1918, that the Bell Rock field had any connection with movements of the High Sea Fleet. The denial is not convincing.

[2] On the morning of November 15, six British light cruisers and ten destroyers left the Forth to meet the *Königsberg*. This German cruiser was bringing over Admiral Meurer to arrange details for the delivery of the High Sea Fleet into British custody. The British naval authorities had, of course, notified a safe route across the North Sea for the German ship. 'The *Königsberg* had been given a course which should bring her to the rendezvous at 2 P.M., but already during the morning the *Cardiff*, the Rear-Admiral's flagship, was in touch with her by wireless, receiving her explanations as to why she had varied the appointed course, and how, in one instance, she had made a *détour* about a German mine-field which our ships had long since swept up.'—*The Triumph of the Royal Navy* (Major Percival Gibbons, R.M.L.I.), p. 4.

voy, was sunk by torpedo. It will be remembered that an abortive raid by the High Sea Fleet on the Scandinavian convoy ended in a fiasco on April 24, 1918. Off Stavanger the battle-cruiser *Moltke* was disabled by machinery trouble, and the whole force returned. Spiess, homeward bound on his last cruise in U 19, sighted the High Sea Fleet off the Norwegian coast, at long range. Not knowing that the German fleet was out, he mistook the German ships for the Grand Fleet. He therefore sent off a wireless message reporting ' large British naval forces ' in a position given off the Norwegian coast. This message was taken in by the High Sea Fleet, which at once went to ' action stations ' to fight a fleet that was no other than its own self !

Although the *Moltke* had been disabled, von Hipper [1] had pushed northward as far as the track taken by the Scandinavian traffic. Fortunately, a convoy was even then entering the Forth and another preparing to sail ; the Germans, therefore, found nothing. As a consequence of this excursion, the convoy track was shifted farther northward. Up the war channel along the East Coast, the traffic flowed ceaselessly ; thence, much of it passed across to Norway, Denmark, and Sweden. Against this trade the submarines gained small success. On May 1 the sweeper *Blackmorevale* was mined, and the convoy sloop *Rhododendron* was sunk by torpedo ; on the other hand, the attraction of this trade for the U-boats had many fatal results.

So far, the drifters in the North Channel had had no luck throughout the long and weary years of watching in bleak and stormy waters. At last they were to contribute their share to the downfall of the enemy. In the late afternoon of April 17 the drifter *Pilot Me*, off Torr Head, spotted a periscope fifty yards distant on the starboard quarter. Zigzagging, the drifter turned towards the spot and heavily depth-charged it. A quarter of an hour later, UB 82 (Becker)

[1] On August 11, 1918, Admiral Scheer relinquished command of the High Sea Fleet to succeed Admiral von Holtzendorff as Chief of the Staff. He handed over his command to Admiral von Hipper. Admiral von Capelle, Secretary of State, was succeeded by Vice-Admiral Ritter von Mann-Tiechler (late of the ' U-boat Office '), and, by this change, it was hoped to further the ambitious submarine construction programme.

broke surface between the *Pilot Me* and another drifter, *Young Fred*. Greeted with fire from other drifters as well, the damaged submarine tried to dive. It was too late ; *Young Fred* dropped another couple of depth-charges over her side. There was a terrific explosion, and wreckage shot up from the shattered submarine. On the last day of the month these drifters scored again. At about dawn on the 30th the drifter *Coreopsis II.* sighted UB 85 (Krech) steering eastwards towards the North Channel. This submarine had left Heligoland on the 16th ; had rounded Scotland, and had been operating in this area for about a week. As she passed ahead of the drifter, she was saluted with three rounds ; the fire did not seem very effective, owing to the swell, and UB 85 carried on, with the drifter in hot chase. All at once, UB 85 fired a Very's light, whilst Krech and his men waved their arms. When the other drifters came up, the crew was taken off, and the submarine sank. To their captors the Germans related that UB 85 had been kept down for two days by patrols. All the torpedoes had missed their targets. To add to their troubles, much chlorine gas had been given off from the batteries, making the crew ill. The conning-tower had been jammed by one of the *Coreopsis'* shells ; and when UB 85 submerged, fifteen tons of water poured in. Her defective batteries were hardly improved thereby. Krech therefore decided to surrender ; and he did not seem unduly distressed about his boat's fate.[1]

Another submarine lost was U 104 (Bernis). She was built to plans which produced one of the most technically successful types of 'Mittel' U-boats ever designed. After she was shelled and sunk by the sloop *Jessamine* off the south of Ireland, on April 25, only 1 of her 40 officers and men aboard could be saved.

With the arrival of May the Germans made their final effort. Twenty-seven North Sea U-boats and 8 Flanders boats were out ; at the same time, 16 other boats were cruising at large in the Mediterranean, and 4 of the largest submarines were working far out in the Atlantic Ocean. Never again did the number of 'war-front' submarines reach so high a total.

[1] *Auxiliary Patrol* (Chatterton), pp. 265-9.

DOWNFALL AND NOT WORLD POWER

In the closing days of the conflict, however, all available boats ready for sea service were assembled in the German North Sea ports for the dramatic *finale*. No fewer than 16 German submarines perished this month, or were rendered innocuous, including 5 in the Mediterranean. By May, only a few submarines got through the *chevaux de frise* of flares and mines at Dover ; and on the 2nd, two more tried the passage and failed. At five minutes past eight in the morning, UB 31 (Braun) dived to elude the drifters *Lord Leitrim, Loyal Friend*, and *Ocean Roamer*, which were being assisted by the airship SSZ 29. UB 31 blew up. Five minutes later, at the eastern side, UC 78 (H. Kukat) was forced to dive by the drifters *Mary, B. T. B.*, and *Our Friend* ; she also hit the mines or was slain by depth-charge. After this double loss the U-boats for a time left the Straits severely alone.

Farther down the Channel, UB 78 (Stosberg) was rammed and sunk by the cross-Channel transport *Queen Alexandra*, just a week later (May 9), and a second success quickly followed. At daybreak on May 12, the White Star liner *Olympic* was coming up the Channel, laden with U.S. troops, and under escort of four American destroyers. On board the huge vessel, the captain and look-outs sighted, simultaneously, one and a half points on the starboard bow, the hull of a submarine breaking surface, about half a mile away. This was U 103, commanded by Claus Rücker. He had already proved his mettle as a raider, by his handling of U 34 in the Mediterranean. Recalled from southern waters, he had been sent out to the west in charge of U 103, his mission being to harry shipping in general, and to pay particular attention to the American troopships. So here he was, presented with a magnificent opportunity and a target of colossal size and value—the biggest trooper against which torpedo could strike. But everything was marred by the incompetence of his crew. He gained his attacking position, only to be informed that the torpedoes in the after tubes were not ready for discharge. There was nothing for it but to try to work into a second position for an attack. Accordingly, Rücker set off on a course parallel to that of the liner, running with the 'asparagus stick '—the Germans' nickname for the periscope of a submarine—just submerged. Again matters seem to have been bungled, for the submarine was allowed to break surface and so betray her presence. A shot from the *Olympic*'s forward gun hurtled over U 103. The submarine went ahead on both engines, as the mammoth altered course and charged down to ram. In the dim light of dawn Rücker saw the immense bulk of the giant ship towering right above him. U 103 made a desperate effort to escape by trying to turn inside the liner's circle. The *Olympic* countered the move by putting her helm hard a-port. At five minutes past three the liner's stem dealt the U-boat a terrific, shattering and swinging knock-out blow. For U 103 it was the end. Those on the liner's bridge heard the paravane chains being torn away; next, they saw the lacerated hull of the defeated submarine standing out of the water, almost on end. The wreck passed astern, and then the liner's after guns opened fire. The White Star leviathan, with a twisted stem, resumed her course for Southampton, and later intercepted a message from the U.S. destroyer *Davis*, to the effect that the latter vessel had picked up seventeen survivors from U 103, ' sunk by gunfire from *Olympic*.' [1] Rücker declared afterwards that the tip of one of the *Olympic*'s propellers had ripped open the hull of his boat. Whether this took place before U 103 was rammed, or afterwards, is not clear. In any case, he declared that he was forced to go to the surface, to save the lives of his men. In the last extremity of distress he had craved mercy and rescue for himself and his crew, and had been granted both. He was the man who, three years before the above event, had massacred the crew of the *Victoria*, simply because that fishing-vessel had dared to offer him her puny resistance ! This same day the submarine D 4, one of the Channel patrol, came upon UB 72 (Träger) off Portland, and slew her with a torpedo, 3 survivors being picked up. Two days before, another British submarine, E 34, had similarly torpedoed

---

[1] Captain Sir Bertram Hayes, K.C.M.G., D.S.O., was in command of the *Olympic* at this time. He gives in his book *Hull Down* (pp. 228-31) a very full account of the ramming of U 103, and it is upon his description that we have drawn for the majority of the facts narrated above.

and sunk the little UB 16 (Lühe) in the swept channel off Harwich.

May was the banner-month of the anti-submarine campaign. In addition to those already mentioned, four other successes were dispersed over an area extending from the Bay of Biscay to the Yorkshire coast. Far behind a convoy from La Pallice steamed a straggler, the steamer *Danae*, shepherded by the United States yacht *Christabel* and seaplanes. Close by, a U-boat was suddenly detected in the calm summer evening sea; she was about to discharge her torpedo, when depth-charges exploded around her. From deep below came up the sound of an ominous roar, followed by surges of black oil and

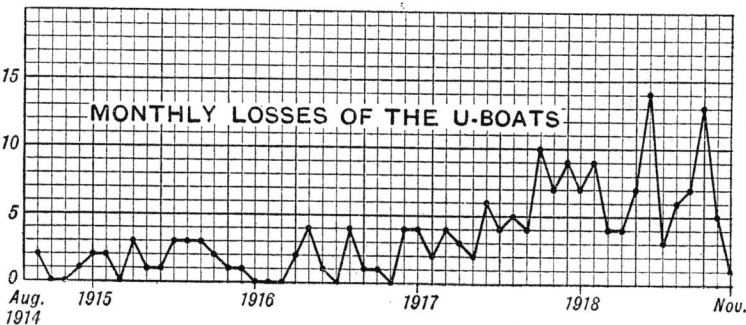

wreckage. A day or so later, on May 24, UC 56 (Kiesewetter) crept into Santander disabled, and was interned. This commander had struck down the hospital-ship *Glenart Castle*, and after the Armistice he was detained in London for examination. As he had a 'safe-conduct' from Spain to Germany, he had ultimately to be released. On the day following the appearance of this corsair, UC 48, lying interned at Ferrol, tried to make her escape but was prevented.

Another success was the sinking of UB 74 (Steindorff) off Portland, on the 26th; she was destroyed by depth-charges from the armed yacht *Lorna*, four of her crew being seen. One who was rescued died three hours later. About this time, also, the new UB 119 (W. Kolbe) went out into the North Sea and disappeared for ever.

As for the remaining loss during the fifth month of 1918, its location was off the East Coast. Here, on May 31, a convoy was attacked off Flamborough Head by UC 75 (Schmitz). The submarine, failing to take proper precautions, was rammed by the twenty-year-old destroyer *Fairy*. Badly damaged, UC 75 lay inert, and the gallant British veteran turned and rammed her adversary again, finally shelling her until she sank, with 26 of her crew. The encounter proved too much for the aged *Fairy*. Her bows were all crumpled in, and she too foundered soon afterwards.

The shipping obituaries in May showed a decrease on the previous month's record : 59 British ships of 188,729 tons were submarined, with the toll of 407 lives, whilst one vessel of 3707 tons was mined. Conspicuous casualties were the Canadian Pacific *Medora* (5135 tons) on the 2nd, 11 miles W.S.W. from the Mull of Galloway ; the New Zealand Shipping Co. *Hurunui* (10,644 tons) on the 18th, 48 miles S. by W. from the Lizard ; the R.M.S.P. *Merionethshire* (4308 tons) and the *Cairnross* (4016 tons), both on the 27th, some 100 miles northward from Flores, in the Azores. On the 30th the Cunard liner *Ausonia* (8153 tons) was sunk by U 62 (Hashagen), 620 miles W. by S. ¾ S. from Fastnet. She had just left her convoy, far out in the Atlantic, when she was struck by a torpedo ; the crew abandoned their sinking ship, which was shelled by U 62. For eight days and nine nights the open boats tossed about in the watery waste before the survivors were found, the death-roll numbering 44. Hashagen says that by this time submarines were forced to find their targets far distant from land, either before the convoy formed or when it dispersed, and he was on his way to the Azores when he chanced upon this lonely vessel.

The German submarines, however, were about to extend their hunting-grounds. The veiled threat behind U 53's visit in 1916 was to be carried into effect, and the submarine war was to be waged along the United States seaboard. The ex-mercantile submarines had proved that extended operations could be carried out ; and their usual hunting-ground was around the Azores and Madeira. Now they were to go farther westward. Altogether, seven cruises were made to American waters during the summer ; four were undertaken by the *Deutschland* (U 151-157) boats, two by the first genuine

XXI. AN OCEAN TRAGEDY.
Six hundred miles out in the Atlantic, the Cunard liner *Ausonia* was torpedoed by *U. 62*, on May 30, 1918. Before the ship's boats were picked up, forty-four of those on board had perished.

DOWNFALL AND NOT WORLD POWER 307

'U-cruisers,' U 139 and U 140, and the seventh by the first of the large mine-layers, U 117. It is possible to trace one or two of these cruises in detail.[1]

The first big raider westward bound, U 151 (von Nostitz und Jänckendorff), sailed on April 14 from Kiel. She had particular orders to avoid shipping until she arrived on the farther side of the Atlantic. In spite of this, she tried to torpedo the steamer *Port Said* on May 2, and was reported by that vessel. Orders were again ignored on May 13, when the *Huntress* (4997 tons) was also attacked, off the Azores. Yet, had the Germans known, they need not have concerned themselves so seriously about concealment of their cruise : Whitehall had already warned Washington to expect a large submarine, such a vessel having left her base on April 19 to begin operations off Delaware Bay about May 20. As a matter of fact, U 151, fitted as a temporary mine-layer, made her landfall on May 21. Within sight of the blazing coastal lights she laid her mines off Cape Henry ; her work was interrupted by a passing armoured cruiser, but was completed as the unsuspecting warship placidly steamed on. U 151 also sighted another armoured cruiser, with a tug towing a target, returning from gunnery practice ; the cruiser was entirely unprotected, not even the most elementary precautions being taken for her security. Off New York, on May 28, U 151 cut two cables—one to Europe and the other to South America. The remainder of her mines she laid in Delaware Bay. On June 3 she picked up a message that a 6000-ton ship had been mined in that field, and that American shipping was disorganised. For the next ten days she preyed on shipping and sank several vessels, including the *Harpathian* (4588 tons) on the 5th, off Cape Henry ; the American steamers *Carolina* (5093 tons) and *Texel* (3210 tons) ; together with other neutral shipping and sailing-vessels. As U 151 retraced her course across the ocean, she came upon the *Dvinsk* (8173 tons) *en route* for Newport News for troops, on June 18. The vessel sank after the crew had taken to their boats, 400 miles N.E. from Bermuda. All that day the boats kept together, but during the night they became separated. For ten days one

[1] *Raiders of the Deep* (Lowell Thomas), p. 285 *et seq.*

of the boats drifted about the stormy Atlantic before she was found ; another was at sea for eight days ; and one, with 22 of the crew, was never seen again. Soon after torpedoing the *Dvinsk*, U 151 saw another large steamer approaching, believed to have been the former *Kronprinz Wilhelm* ; at her another torpedo was fired, and U 151 dived to await the sound of the torpedo exploding. As the allotted interval sped by, a dull thud was heard, then another and another. U 151 was being depth-charged. Down the submarine dived, and nothing could stay her descent. Tested to but fifty metres, she actually touched eighty-three (273 feet). At this depth the tremendous external pressure of the sea prevented the tanks being blown until an immense air-pressure overcame the hydrostatic resistance. After the descent had been checked, U 151 began to rise, slowly at first, but soon she was shooting practically out of control to the surface, where possible enemies might be waiting. The surface of the waters was moved and spewed up Leviathan. With a gasp of relief the commander found nothing to be in sight except the *Dvinsk*'s boats. A few days later the *Mauretania* appeared out of fog, loomed close, and disappeared unscathed. On July 20, U 151 entered Kiel after a cruise of 94 days, in which she had covered 10,915 miles ; her commander claimed to have sunk 23 ships of 61,000 tons, and had laid mines responsible for another 4 vessels.

Admiral Sims, U.S.N., informed Washington on June 29 that another large submarine was then to the west of Ireland and would arrive about July 15. This boat was the first of the 'U-cruisers,' U 140, under Kophamel. She had left on June 22, arrived off the United States coast on July 14, and operated in the western Atlantic until September 1, when she began her return. She claimed to have sunk 30,000 tons of shipping. But before she had set out on her cruise, U 156 (Feldt) had sailed a week previously to lay mines in American waters ; arriving on July 5, she placed her mines and started on her homeward trip on September 1. Until the last leg of the long journey, all went well. Then, on September 25, when 130 miles from Bergen, U 156 hit a mine in the vast Northern Barrage and perished with her crew. On one of her

DOWNFALL AND NOT WORLD POWER 309

mines laid off Fire Island the United States cruiser *San Diego* foundered on July 19.

Early in July the fourth large submarine sailed. She was the new mine-layer U 117 (Droescher, the early commander of U 20), carrying about 34 mines [1] and 24 torpedoes. After disseminating her mines (which caused a loss of 23,000 tons of merchant-shipping), she returned in company with U 140. These last three boats (U 140, U 156, U 117) were active off the American seaboard in an area extending from Cape Hatteras to Newfoundland. Their British victims included the motor vessel *Dornfontein* (766 tons) on August 2, 25 miles W.N.W. from Brier Island, Nova Scotia; the *Luz Blanca* (4868 tons) on the 5th, 35 miles S.W. from the Outer Gas Buoy, Halifax; the *Penistone* (4139 tons) on the 11th, 145 miles S.W. $\frac{1}{2}$ S. from Nantucket Island; the *Mirlo* (6978 tons) on the 16th, half a mile S. by E. from Wimble Shoal Buoy, Cape Hatteras; the Blue Funnel *Diomed* (7523 tons) on the 21st, 195 miles E.S.E. from Nantucket Island; and the small *Erik* (583 tons) on the 25th, 70 miles N.W. by W. from St. Pierre, Newfoundland. As these raiders passed northwards from the southerly waters, they inaugurated a novel method of decimating the fishing-fleet off the Grand Banks. Here, on August 20, they captured the fishing-craft *Triumph*, 60 miles S.W. by S. from Cape Canso, N.S., and converted her into a decoy raider.[2] The extempo-

[1] U 117-126 class: normal mine stowage 34+2 mines in tube elevator, +6 mines loaded into discharge tubes=42. The extra mines, once loaded, could not be got at for adjustment, and the six in discharge tubes were practically 'wet-stowage,' used only on short trips. The number of mines varied according to the amount of stores carried; on a cross-Atlantic trip, the number of mines was cut down to 32-36.—(Lieut.-Comm. W. M. Quigler, U.S.N., in *U.S.N.I. Proceedings*, Aug. 1928.)

[2] It is interesting to notice that on July 4, 1813, during the British blockade of the United States coast, when particular attention was paid to small traders with poultry, sheep, etc., running the blockade, a party of Connecticut fishermen fitted out the smack *Yankee* to capture H.M. sloop-of-war *Eagle*. Concealed in her hold were forty well-armed men; but on deck were three fisherfolk, a goose, a calf, and a sheep. Putting out from New York, the smack was sighted and chased by the *Eagle*. She was stopped; and as the *Eagle* was laid alongside, the forty men rose up, opened fire on the British, drove them below, and carried the sloop into New York. This was a perfect example of decoy work. The decoy idea can, of course, be traced back in history to the wooden horse of Troy. (See *U.S.N.I. Proceedings*, May 1928, p. 440.)

rized corsair then began to prey upon her kind, capturing and sinking by bomb (on the same day) the *Una A. Saunders* and the *Lucille M. Schnare*, and (on the 25th) the *Verna D. Adams*. The fishing-vessels were completely surprised at their toil, never suspecting that one of their number had been transformed into a hostile craft. The submarine also sank another fishing-vessel on the 21st ; and, with the *Triumph*,[1] sank two more on the 25th, *E. B. Walters* and *C. M. Walters*, 35 miles W. by S. from Little Miquelon. Moving thence to St. Pierre, where the *Clayton W. Walters* and the *Marion Adams* were accounted for, on the next day they sank the *Gloaming*, and on the 30th destroyed the *Elsie Porter* and the *Potentate*, 290 miles E. ½ N. from St. John's, Newfoundland.

In August, U 155 (Eckelmann), once the *Deutschland*, paid her return visit to American waters—this time no longer in the guise of a peaceful trader. She arrived on September 7, and retraced her course when the general recall was sounded. Closely following her came U 152 (Franz), which arrived on September 29 and was likewise forced to curtail her cruise. The seventh boat, U 139, under the famous von Arnauld, was recalled before she had passed the Azores. Mines from either U 155 or U 152 appear to have damaged the United States battleship *Minnesota* on September 29, but the injured ship reached port. Altogether, Admiral Sims estimates the damage caused to shipping by these trans-Atlantic raiders as 110,000 tons, mostly comprising small vessels of little value. He relates that no difficulty was found in following their course from the time of their departure until they arrived, owing to the interception of radio messages passing between the German Admiralty and the oceanic destroyers of trade.

After this digression, return must be made to the campaign around the British Isles. By June there was no definite line of demarcation between the zones of the North Sea and Flanders boats. The Bell Rock mine-field was absorbing all the energies of the mine-layers, and the UB-boats had to operate wherever they could. Because of the withdrawal of the patrols to escort the arriving American troop-

---

[1] What subsequently became of the little raider remains to this day a mystery.

XXII. THE LARGEST TYPE OF U-BOAT.
One of the so-called 'Submarine-Cruisers,' probably a unit of the *U. 139-141* class. Each displaced close upon 2,000 tons; was armed with two 5.9-inch guns, and carried 19 torpedoes. Of the only two boats completed in time to undertake a war-cruise, *U. 139* was commanded by von Arnauld de la Perière.

U. 153 : ONE OF THE '*DEUTSCHLAND*' TYPE MERCANTILE SUBMARINES.
These boats, numbering seven, were converted into combatant vessels and appeared in the Atlantic Ocean during the last fifteen months of the war.

DOWNFALL AND NOT WORLD POWER 311

ships, they gained more success than had seemed likely. During this month no enemy submarines were sunk around these islands by patrols ; the two destroyed were claimed by mines—UC 64 (Schwartz) early on the morning of the 20th was forced into the Dover Barrage by a division of 1 trawler and 7 drifters. The pioneer Flanders mine-layer UC 11 (Utke) dissolved herself by contact with mines off Harwich on the 26th.

Important shipping losses, which numbered 49 of 158,660 tons, include the Cunard *Vandalia* (7333 tons) on the 9th, 18 miles W.N.W. from the Smalls ; the *Montebello* (4324 tons) on the 21st, 320 miles W. $\frac{1}{2}$ N. from Ushant, with 41 lives ; the Leyland *Atlantian* (9399 tons) on the 25th, 110 miles N. by W. $\frac{1}{2}$ W. from Eagle Island ; the British India *Orissa* (5358 tons) on the same day, 21 miles S.W. of Skerryvore. In the Bristol Channel the armed merchant cruiser *Patia* was struck down on the 13th, with 16 of her complement ; and the submarine D 6, of the North of Ireland submarine patrol, was torpedoed by an enemy boat and sunk, on the 28th. Overshadowing everything else was the tragic sinking of the hospital-ship *Llandovery Castle* (11,423 tons). It was the culminating outrage on these Red Cross ships, hitherto respected by all belligerent nations, until Germany prostituted her submarines to crime. Returning from Halifax, she carried a staff of 80 R.A.M.C., 14 nurses, and a crew of 164. There were no patients on board, of course. At 9.30 P.M. on the night of June 27, when she was 116 miles west from the Fastnet, she was struck by a torpedo from U 86 (Patzig). Hit in No. 4 hold, the liner quickly filled, and sank ten minutes later. As the boats pulled clear, the sinister hull of the submarine glided up. Patzig ordered the master's boat to come alongside. He questioned Captain Sylvester concerning eight American flight officers who, he alleged, had been aboard ; this allegation was flatly denied, and the master added that he had seven Canadian medical officers with him. Patzig demanded to see one of these ; and Major Lyons was so brutally jostled that he broke a bone in his foot. Still unsatiated with the enormity of his crime, Patzig started to circle his submarine round the ship's boats at high speed, barely missing ramming the master's boat. Those in this boat then heard, a short distance away in the darkness, the submarine open fire on some object. Twelve rounds were fired before U 86 melted into the night. Over a hundred miles from land, the boats were alone—specks in the wilderness of the ocean. The master's boat, 50 miles from the Fastnet, was picked up by the destroyer *Lysander*; in it were 24 survivors. Of the rest, numbering 234, never a trace was found, and there can be little room for doubt that Patzig shelled them.

Warning that such a crime might eventuate had come from Berlin. On April 25 it was declared that papers found on a captured American flying officer proved that American airmen were brought over in Atlantic hospital-ships disguised as members of the American ambulance service. With his lieutenants, Boldt and Dittmar, Patzig was arraigned for trial at Leipzig in 1921; but he did not appear. His subordinate officers each received sentence of four years' imprisonment. Conclusive evidence of his guilt was obtained from the helmsman, who declared that in vain was Patzig begged to spare the hospital-ship. For four hours the U 86 had followed the *Llandovery Castle*, the latter vessel being lighted up and clearly distinguishable for what she was. After the torpedoing, Patzig had sent for his gunner; and these four men, Patzig, Boldt, Dittmar, and the gunner, remained alone on deck as the boats were shelled. The two officers sentenced were allowed to escape shortly after conviction.

Another hospital-ship was sunk this month. On June 5 the Dutch *Koningin Regentes*, carrying repatriated British prisoners-of-war, was torpedoed; but all except 4 were safely transferred to the *Sindoro*.

In the approaches to the North Channel, during July, 7 U-boats concentrated. Several important losses are to be noted. The United States supply-ship *Westover* (5590 tons) was sent to the bottom on the 11th; the sloop *Anchusa*, on the 16th, took down all but 16 of her crew; the well-known Cunarder *Carpathia* (13,603 tons) succumbed on the next day, 170 miles W. by N. from Bishop Rock. The Allan liner

XXIII. THE CONVOY'S GUARD COMES TO GRIEF.
The Commissioned Escort Ship *Mechanician* (formerly a Harrison liner) was twice torpedoed early on the morning of January 20, 1918, off St. Catharines. During an attempt to get her into the Solent, she went ashore on Shingle Sands, near the Needles, at about noon. The guns, mounted fore and aft, can be clearly seen in the photograph.

THE LARGEST VESSEL TO SUCCUMB TO TORPEDO ATTACK BY SUBMARINE.
On July 19, 1918, the 32,000-ton liner *Justicia* was subjected to one of the most determined and prolonged attacks made by the U-boats, sinking with six torpedo wounds, twenty hours after the first had struck her.

DOWNFALL AND NOT WORLD POWER 313

Mongolian (4892 tons) met her end on the 21st, 5 miles S.E. from Filey Brig, with 36 lives. The *Barunga* (7484 tons), carrying invalided Anzacs home, was caught on the 15th, 150 miles W. by S. from the Bishop Rock, but fortunately no lives were lost when she sank. Off the south of Ireland the armed merchant-cruiser *Marmora* was likewise sunk, on the 23rd.

The most remarkable case concerned the sinking of the huge new White Star liner *Justicia* (32,234 tons), the U-boats' second largest victim. In 1914 this ship was building for the Holland-Amerika line as the *Statendam*. She had been completed and taken over by the White Star line, proving herself a very valuable addition to the fleet of troopships. She had just left Belfast for America, escorted by twelve patrols ; and when 20 miles W. by N. from Skerryvore she was hit by a torpedo from UB 64 (von Schrader). It was about four o'clock on the afternoon of the 19th. At once the escort put over thirty-five depth-charges. Two hours later a couple of torpedoes came from the submarine ; a success that was greeted by the distribution of twenty-three ' ash-cans.' Listing heavily, the wounded giant was taken in tow. Two and a half -hours elapsed, and UB 64 shot her fourth torpedo. Once again the sea was plastered, this time with eleven more depth-charges. The submarine, now leaking badly, exuded oil; whilst the liner still fought for life. Until noon next day, when she was 20 miles W. by N. ¾ N. from Skerryvore, the big White Star liner lived ; but a torpedo from U 54 (von Ruckteschell) proved too much for her endurance, and she sank at midday on July 20. Both submarines got away, in spite of the enormous number of depth-charges expended. It was during the hunt by the destroyers *Marne, Milbrook*, and *Pigeon* for the attackers that contact was made with UB 124 (Wutsdorff), and the interloper they sank with depth-charges ; by this time forty patrol craft had been collected. Survivors from UB 124 declared that serious leaks had been caused by the fearful concussions, and in an endeavour to escape they had dived right under the sinking liner.

On the same day, July 19, UB 110 (Fürbringer), in attacking a convoy off Roker, was rammed by the destroyer *Garry* and finally sunk by ML 263 with depth-charges. When this submarine was raised by the Admiralty salvage section, her log proved to be of great interest. Even before she had arrived at her Flanders base she had been attacked by two seaplanes. Leaving Zeebrugge on the 5th, she had experienced daily attacks by depth-charge from the 7th until the 18th, on which latter day twenty-six explosions were counted by those on board. This *rafale* of 'ash-cans' was the reward for the torpedoing of an oil-tanker. In the fatal attack on the convoy, the charges damaged her diving-rudders, preventing her from getting down before the crash with the destroyer. In the same neighbourhood, off Whitby, UB 107 (Prittwitz und Gaffron) was depth-charged out of existence by the armed yacht *Vanessa* and three trawlers, on the 27th. During this month, UB 108 (W. Amberger) disappeared in the Channel; the cause of her loss remains unexplained to this hour.

Two other boats made their exit during July. UC 77 (Ries) essayed a performance now beyond attainment even by submarines under the command of experienced officers. Ries was a novice, and neglected to take the most elementary precautions. As he tried to run the Dover Straits on the evening of the 10th, he left behind him a surface trail of air-bubbles and oil from a leak. Two trawlers, sighting this glaring evidence of a U-boat's presence, promptly abolished UC 77 with depth-charges. On the same day a curious incident occurred off Cape Clear. The American submarine L 2, one of seven working from Berehaven, encountered UB 65 (Schelle); but before L 2 could loose off her torpedoes, 'something distressing happened to UB 65' (to quote Admiral Sims). There was a terrific explosion. What had happened? Two theories have been advanced: some believe that two German submarines were present, and UB 65 had been accidentally torpedoed by her consort; others hold that UB 65 passed so close to L 2, that the magnetic pistol in the nose of one of the German torpedoes functioned prematurely, whilst still in the tube. Still another theory, and one more fantastic, was that UB 65 did fire a torpedo, but it took an erratic course, circled, and crashed into the boat from which it had sprung forth.[1]

[1] Michelsen gives the cause as 'disguised steamer' (*i.e.* sunk by a decoy).

DOWNFALL AND NOT WORLD POWER 315

July produced the lowest toll of ships sunk since unrestricted war was launched in February 1917 ; and this despite the fact that 22 of the North Sea and 8 of the Flanders boats were out. In the North Sea a vast barricade of mines was slowly being built up by American and British mine-layers. Stretching from the Orkneys right across to the Norwegian coast, this barrage was intended to deny the U-boats an entry into the Atlantic. It was a colossal task, and there were many who pinned their faith on the mine-fields nearer the German Bight. The first mines were laid on March 3 ; they were of the antennæ type. So unsatisfactory were they, that after 43 per cent. of these had been laid they had to be swept up. On these mines the sloop *Gaillardia* was lost on March 28. With deliveries of the new pattern of mine, the work began again, and on June 8 the Northern Barrage took its place in the great offensive against the U-boats. On the day the work began, two enemy submarines were damaged by the mines ; returning home, they brought the tidings of yet further obstacles to be faced. By November, 70,117[1] mines had been planted, mostly by American ships. It must be remarked that, after Norway prohibited under-water craft from using her territorial waters in October 1916, the U-boats had paid scant heed to such behests. In August 1918 many coastal lights were extinguished by the Norwegians ; and finally, in October, a mine-field was laid co-extensive with the eastern end of this 240-mile Anglo-American barrage. ' Even when near completion, the barrage was not so effective as many had hoped for, in spite of the great expenditure of labour and material. The number of submarines accounted for was known to be disappointing,' writes Lord Jellicoe.[2]

In other areas the mining warfare continued. The enterprising and audacious 20th Mine Laying Flotilla lost the destroyers *Ariel* and *Vehement* on August 2, when both were blown up in the Bight, with a loss of 97 lives. A new field, in which it is believed that the German torpedo-boats S 63, S 66,

[1] The laying of the Northern Barrage began on June 8, 1918. By October 26 the U.S. layers had planted 56,571 mines : by October 11 the British layers had deposited 13,546 mines. The U.S. mines were very hastily manufactured, and many detonated prematurely after being laid.

[2] *The Crisis of the Naval War* (Jellicoe), p. 95.

S 138, and A 79 came to grief, was laid on the 11th by motor boats. The Harwich force sustained another loss on the 15th, when the leader *Scott* and the destroyer *Ulleswater* both fell as victims to torpedo attack by submarines.

In August the Germans ran a leader-cable along the Thornton Ridge to guide their submarines; albeit, the utility of the Flanders base was fast declining. The East Coast traffic still attracted the smaller craft; and when UB 30 (Stier) attacked a convoy off the Tyne on the 13th, she paid the penalty. Rammed by the trawler *John Gillman*, she was then treated to a dose of depth-charges; two hours later she was compelled to come up, seriously injured, only to be shelled and again depth-charged. Divers afterwards located the wreck. Again, on the 28th, UC 70 (Dobberstein) was spotted by a seaplane off Whitby; the destroyer *Ouse* was called up, and she, with the invaluable depth-charge, dismissed UC 70 from the ranks of the combatants.

One of the last Q-boat fights of the war was staged in the western Channel on July 30. The disguised small coasting-steamer *Stockforce* (732 tons) was cruising at sea; at this belated stage of hostilities there was little expectation left that the U-boats could be inveigled into making surface attacks. Suddenly the decoy was dealt a shattering blow by a torpedo. Not the slightest warning had been given, and the small vessel lay completely disabled. Upon the departure of the panic party, the submarine appeared and began to shell the wrecked *Stockforce*. The U-boat closed in to 300 yards, and the order to fire was given by Lieutenant H. Auten, R.N.R. The conning-tower of U 98 was blown off, her deck was ripped open, and with twenty distinct hits registered on her hull she sank by the stern. The decoy herself sank off Bolt Head; U 98, severe as her laceration had been, survived to make a home port safely. Yet another instance was given of the German double-hulled diving-boats' capacity for enduring heavy punishment inflicted at almost point-blank range.

In August, 41 British ships of 145,721 tons were sunk by submarines. The average size of those lost was now little over 3000 tons, although several larger merchant-vessels were still struck down. On the 3rd, the ambulance transport *Warilda* (7713 tons), from Havre to Southampton, escorted by the patrol-boats P 39 and P 45, was torpedoed at about half-past one in the morning. She was carrying 614 wounded and sick, 70 R.A.M.C. staff, and a crew of 117. Hit between the engine-room and No. 4 hold, the explosion not only killed the engineers and staff below, but also resulted in the loss of 101 patients lying in an improvised ward in this hold. The ship sank by the stern, touched the bottom, and fell over. Altogether, 113 patients, 1 nurse, 2 of the staff, and 7 of the crew perished. Probably the same submarine sank the *Clan Macnab* (4675 tons) next day, 14 miles N.N.W. from Pendeen L.H., with a death-roll of 22 lives. Other important casualties were the Nelson *Highland Harris* (6032 tons) on the 6th, 82 miles N. $\frac{3}{4}$ W. from Eagle Island, with a loss of 24 lives ; the *Clan Macvey* (5815 tons) on the 8th, half a mile S.E. from Anvil Point, with 7 lives ; the Ellerman *City of Brisbane* (7094 tons), one and a half miles S.S.W. from Newhaven, on the 13th ; the Cunard cargo-liner *Flavia* (9291 tons) on the 24th, 30 miles N.W. by N. from Tory Island ; and the Canadian Pacific *Milwaukee* (7323 tons) on the 31st, 260 miles S.W. from Fastnet, the second torpedo almost cutting this ship in two.

For the submarines, two courses only were now open—to prowl for their prizes far out in the ocean, or to slink along inshore. To the west of Brest, 400 miles out into the Atlantic, the old French cruiser *Dupetit-Thouars* steamed along to pick up a convoy and shepherd it into port. The sun on August 7 descended into the placid sea, all aflame towards the western horizon. The tranquillity of the great ocean was rudely dispelled by man's brutal work of destruction. The old cruiser reeled under two square hits from torpedoes fired by U 62 (Hashagen) ; the stricken warship took a heavy list and sank in twenty minutes. Her captain forbade all ships near by to close, lest they should share a similar fate. Nine days later the French steamer *Lyndiane* (1564 tons) met a summary end off the north coast of Spain ; and in this case the utmost barbarity was shown by the submarine. The ship's boat, the whaler, and even a raft were all rammed by the U-boat, evidently commanded by a staunch adherent of the *spurlos versenkt* policy. Towards the close of the war the U-boat commanders, on the whole, showed more humanity in their work. It is only just to record that there were cases of the submarines giving assistance to the boats' crews of their prizes by the provision of medical aid and physical comforts.

On August 8 the Torbay hydrophone unit (consisting of the old destroyer *Opossum* and 7 ML's) located a submarine 4 miles south by west of Berry Head; and so thoroughly did they lard the area with depth-charges, that the UC 49 (Kükenthal) then and there passed out of existence. The wreck was found later.[1] The new mines continued to demonstrate their powers of prompt detonation and destruction. The small UB 12 (Schoeller)—now converted into a layer, capable of carrying 8 mines—came to an abrupt end off Heligoland during August. On the 14th, UB 57 (Losz) hit the coastal barrier off Zeebrugge. This officer, known to his brethren as 'the blithesome spirit of Flanders,' contemned all obstacles placed in his path. 'Go through the barriers on the surface,' he advised, adding the boast : 'The patrols are blind. I go through under their noses.'[2] True it is that UB 109 (Ramien) passed through the Dover Straits during July, *en route* to the Azores. Unfortunately for herself, a month elapsed before she essayed her return, and during that period the defences had been further strengthened. On the 29th of August, homeward bound, she blew up off Folkestone. The last submarine to perish in the Dover Barrage was UB 103 (Hundius); on September 16 she was driven into the mines by the airship SSZ 1 and some drifters, and was shattered by bombs. UB 103 was one of two boats that made the final attempt to run the gauntlet.

This was the second instance of successful combination between airship and surface patrol. The first example had been that of UB 31 in May. Increasing efficiency in the combined hunts by seaplane and patrol was one more nail in the U-boat's coffin. All round the coast of the British Isles there had sprung up aerodromes, airship bases, and seaplane stations

---

[1] Michelsen says ' probably lost in the Hoofden ' : this can be ignored.
[2] *Raiders of the Deep* (Lowell Thomas).

for anti-submarine work. There were nearly a hundred small airships in service, comprising the various S.S. (Submarine Scouting) types;[1] in addition, there were the Coastal Patrol (C.P.), C. Star, and North Sea (N.S.) types. The last were designed for scouting work with the Grand Fleet; each had two Rolls-Royce engines or two 240-h.p. F.I.A.T. engines. Non-rigid airships (or 'Blimps') carried out patrols, or escorted convoys in and out. Upon dispersal of convoys, the small airships were delegated to accompany the more important steamers carrying valuable cargoes. To these aerial scouts, hovering like hawks over their prey, much could be seen that was hidden from the vision of surface ships. Little to the liking of the enemy was this aerial surveillance. When the *Ouse* exterminated UC 70, her partner in the sky dropped Very's lights along the track of the submarine. In this way the position and course of the quarry were indicated to the surface slayer. The kite-balloons, towed by the convoy sloops or trawlers, must not be overlooked in this very brief outline of the aerial offensive against the U-boats.

The month of September showed, on the one hand, an increase in the number of British ships destroyed, but, on the other, a decline in the amount of tonnage lost. Unhappily, the loss of life was rendered heavy by one tragic case. The figures were 48 ships of 136,859 tons, with 521 lives. On the 1st, both the Atlantic Transport *Mesaba* (6833 tons) and the Ellerman *City of Glasgow* (6545 tons) were sunk, 21 miles E. ¼ N. from the Tuskar, with 32 lives; and two days later another ship, *Highcliffe* (3238 tons), was sunk in the same area. On the 9th, the Canadian Pacific *Missanabie* (12,469 tons) was mortally hit, 52 miles S. by E. ½ E. from Daunt's Rock; and as the liner fell over, a funnel crashed on to the boats and killed 45 people. The outstanding

---

[1] S.S. classes of airship :—
  S.S. type : one 75-h.p. Renault engine or one 75-h.p. Rolls-Royce engine.
  S.S.P. type ⎫ one 100-h.p. Green or one 110-h.p. Berliet or one 75-h.p.
  S.S.Z. type ⎭   Rolls-Royce engine.
  S.S.E. type (experimental) : two 75-h.p. Rolls-Royce engines.
  S.S.T. type : twin engines, two 75-h.p. Rolls-Royce or two 110-h.p. Berliet.

loss was the sinking of the *Galway Castle* (7988 tons) by U 82 (Adam), on the 12th. Torpedoed 160 miles S.W. ½ S. from Fastnet in a rough sea, many of the boats were swamped, and altogether the death-roll was 143.

Heavy losses of life occurred in the following cases : the *Ruysdael* (3478 tons), sunk on the 7th, 228 miles W. ¾ S. from Ushant, with 12 souls ; the *Buffalo* (286 tons) on the 13th, off Corsewall Point, with 10 lives ; the *Gibel-Haman* (647 tons) on the 14th, off Abbotsbury (Dorset), with 21 of the crew ; the *Kendal Castle* (3885 tons) next day, 4 miles S.E. from Berry Head, when 18 were lost ; the *Acadian* (2305 tons) on the 16th, 11 miles S.W. by W. from Trevose Head, with 25 lives. A similar number of casualties resulted from the sinking of the *Lavernock* (2406 tons) next day, 5 miles N.W. from Trevose Head. In the same vicinity, on the succeeding day, the *John o' Scott* (1235 tons) was sent to the bottom with 18 of her crew. On the 19th the Harrison liner *Barrister* (4952 tons) was mortally injured by torpedo 9 miles W. ½ N. from Chicken Head, taking down with her 30 of the crew. Two days later the *Polesley* (4221 tons) was likewise attacked and sunk 1 mile N. from Pendeen Lighthouse, 43 souls perishing. It is probable that the last 9 of these victims, all sunk within nine days off the south-western extremity of the United Kingdom, were struck down by one submarine, with a resultant toll of 202 lives.

Hans Rose, in U 53, was nearly finished off by American destroyers on September 2. His meeting-place with two other U-boats had been deduced from intercepted wireless communications, and he barely escaped the trap set for him. The bill of U-boat mortality for September relates mostly to the Northern Barrage. The German authorities still persist in denying that more than two boats succumbed in these mines ; but it is certain that U 92 (Ehrlich) was blown up in the barrier on September 9 ; and ten days later UB 104 (Bieber) shared a similar fate. UB 127 (Scheffler) also appears to have left her bones under the barrage.[1] All these casualties

---

[1] When Group 9 of mines at the western end of the Northern Barrage was being cleared away by U.S. mine-sweepers after the war, the sweeping-wire of the U.S.S. *Heron* and *Sanderling* fouled the wreck of a German sub-

DOWNFALL AND NOT WORLD POWER 321

occurred at its western end. Off Bergen took place (as previously recorded) the fatal termination of U 156's Atlantic cruise. Right in the centre of the barrage, U 102 blew up in September; she was commanded by Beitzen, who had laid the mines that destroyed the *Hampshire*. So, by poetic justice, did he himself fall a victim to that same murderous mechanism. Just south of the western limit, near the Orkneys, UB 83 (Buntebardt) was suppressed for good by depth-charge from the destroyer *Ophelia*, on the 10th;[1] UB 113 (Pilzecker) disappeared in the Channel this month, but there is no certain evidence as to her exact mode of death. Lastly, off the Northumbrian coast on the 29th the great British airship R 29 was patrolling; spotting a patch of oil on the face of the waters, she drew the attention of the destroyers *Ouse* and *Star* and six trawlers to this promising clue. No time was lost in despatching UB 115 (Thomsen) with depth-charges.

If the submarines had scourged the seas with whips, they themselves were now being flagellated with scorpions. As proof that the counter-measures were at last harrying the enemy at every turn, we have the late Admiral Scheer's testimony:[2] 'The gradual decline in the monthly sinkings by the U-boats filled one with anxiety. Many a U-boat with a splendid and experienced crew did not return.' Again: 'The results of the last months had shown that the successes of individual boats had steadily decreased. This reduction in successes was due mainly to the stronger and more perfect measures of defence taken by the enemy, and also to the loss of some of the older and more experienced commanders. Taking into consideration the then rate of U-boat construction, we had to expect, in spite of the steady increase in the

marine, and parted. 'From the records at the Admiralty, the wreck was presumed to be the UB 127': 'The Removal of the North Sea Mine-Barrier,' by Lieut.-Commander Noel Davis, U.S.N. (*National Geographic Magazine*, Washington, February 1920, p. 119).

[1] It is said that a German submarine heard the sound of mines exploding prematurely in the Northern Barrage, and, believing herself to be under a heavy depth-charge attack, came to the surface. She was at once pounced upon by British destroyers and sunk. UB 83 may have been the victim of such a mistake.

[2] *High Sea Fleet* (Scheer), pp. 328 and 334.

x

number of U-boats, that the figures of the monthly sinkings, which had already diminished to 500,000 [1] tons, would be still further reduced. Judging from the reports as to mercantile shipbuilding, it was to be feared that within a short time the newly-constructed tonnage would be greater than the amount sunk. The success of the campaign would be greatly diminished. It was therefore absolutely necessary for us to develop our only means of an offensive with all the strength at Germany's disposal, so as to attain our goal—a tolerable peace.'

The last month of the submarine horror was marked by several tragedies in western waters. On October 1 the Canadian Pacific *Montfort* (6578 tons) went to the bottom with 5 of her crew, 170 miles W. by S. ¾ S. from Bishop Rock ; and the loss of the tanker *Arca* (4839 tons) next day, 40 miles N.W. by W. from Tory Island, was attended by the sacrifice of 52 lives. Even worse was the work of a submarine in the Irish Sea. During a violent storm on October 4, the Japanese liner *Hirano Maru* (7936 tons) was struck by a torpedo, and rapidly sank ; the rescue work of the United States destroyer *Sterett* was impeded by the U-boat, and the death-roll, including many children, numbered 292. Six days later, in heavy weather, the Irish mail-boat *Leinster* (2646 tons) was just leaving Kingstown for Holyhead with 720 souls on board. Hit by two torpedoes, there could be no hope for the shattered packet; her engine-room was blown out, and she sank in thirteen minutes, 7 miles E.S.E. from Kish L.V. The old destroyers *Lively* and *Mallard* performed splendid rescue work ; but the wild wintry seas claimed 176 men, women, and children. Commenting on this catastrophe, Mr. Arthur Balfour said : ' I ask whether those who had made mankind pale with horror over the early barbarities and brutal excesses in Belgium showed the least sign, after four years of war, that they had in any material respect improved their disposition. Brutes they were when they began the war, and, as far as I can judge, brutes they remain at the present moment. I speak, perhaps, with a warmth of indignation unbefitting a Foreign Secretary ; but, with the news of this outrage in the

[1] Actually the August world losses were down to 283,800 tons.

Irish Channel, I confess I find it difficult to measure my epithets; for, if I rightly understand the story, this Irish packet-boat, crammed as it always is with men, women, and children, in broad daylight, was deliberately torpedoed by a German submarine. It was carrying no military stores, it was serving no military purpose. It was pure barbarism—it was pure frightfulness—deliberately carried out. I cannot measure the wicked folly of the proceedings of which they have been guilty. Let us not forget that this is only one, and not the most destructive, most cowardly, or most brutal thing which at this moment, when they are seeking peace, they are perpetrating upon helpless civilians or still more helpless prisoners-of-war.'

The First Lord (Sir Eric Geddes) on October 25 made the following significant remarks: 'The German submarine menace was decreasing up to last May, when it became necessary to divert our hunting flotillas from chasing to escorting. Owing to this sacrifice of offensive, the submarines have been gaining upon us . . . and we may be in the position of having a very formidable campaign to face.' Again: 'A great renewed effort is impending . . . and the menace is to-day greater than it ever was.' Gayer corroborates these warnings when he relates that thirty new submarines were delivered from the builders in September. The Marine Office had at last wrung from the military authorities several thousand shipyard hands for work on the 'Hindenburg submarine-building programme,' and it was hoped that, during the months ahead, many belated boats would be delivered. When, a few weeks later, the submarines were surrendered, about a hundred new hulls were found, either afloat and completing or in the final stages of construction.[1] Trained personnel was lacking; the Allied counter-offensive was steadily expanding and improving. It was not doubted that a grim final struggle was looming ahead in the spring of 1919.

The end, however, was drawing very near. The Dover Straits were sealed, the Flanders U-boats could hope for no

---

[1] Another 125 boats (or thereabout) had been laid down, but were still unlaunched.

more than six voyages on an average before being destroyed; the Otranto Straits were closing; the Northern Barrage was becoming troublesome; and the combination of convoy, airship, and seaplane patrol, hydrophone listening-stations and units, taken with the peril of mine and depth-charge, had robbed the under-water raider of a great measure of its sting. On October 1 the Marine Corps was ordered to evacuate the Flanders base. Twenty-four torpedo-boats and 20 submarines made their return to German ports; but UB 10, UB 40, UB 59, and UC 4, together with 8 torpedo-boats, were blown up during October 1-2. On the 17th, Ostend was evacuated, Zeebrugge and Bruges on the 19th, and the Flanders coast was clear on the 20th.

Prince Max of Baden, the new Imperial Chancellor, had appealed for an armistice on October 5. He was informed that all Allied territory must be evacuated first; and on the 14th, as the Allied troops poured through the German defences on the western front, President Wilson enjoined that all inhuman acts must cease forthwith. (It was apparently the news of the *Leinster* sinking that called forth this stern remonstrance.) The Kaiser, by a previous arrangement, went from Potsdam to Berlin to urge upon the Chancellor the continuation of the campaign at sea. With Prince Max he found Count Lerchenfeld (the Bavarian envoy); both statesmen desired to arrest the submarine campaign, so that a favourable atmosphere might be prepared for their armistice proposals. In vain the Kaiser tried to persuade them that the campaign must proceed; that the terms of the Wilson Note were humiliating; and that Germany must not part with her means of waging war effectively against the Allies. By so doing she would sacrifice a most valuable bargaining asset; it was the Imperial view that a suspension of submarine warfare should be balanced by liberal concessions to Germany. Prince Max and Lerchenfeld were adamant; the latter even dared to draw attention to the fact that the Wilson Note contained no demand for abdication. Such a demand might come later; and if it did come, it might have to be accepted unconditionally. Prince Max appeared to be of the same mind as the Bavarian envoy on the point. From

DOWNFALL AND NOT WORLD POWER 325

this moment all sympathy between the Kaiser and his Chancellor ceased, and the beaten monarch retired to Spa.

Orders, therefore, went out to all submarines, on October 21, that attacks on passenger-ships must cease forthwith. On this day the last merchant-vessel torpedoed in British waters was destroyed—the *St. Barchan* (362 tons), sunk without warning 4 miles from St. John's Point, Co. Down, with 8 of her crew. On the following day the packets *Duke of Cumberland* (2056 tons) and *Duke of Connaught* (1564 tons) were both attacked in the Irish Channel; in the former case the torpedo was avoided, and the latter escaped by flight. The last naval loss around the British Isles, attributed to hostile submarines, was that of the mine-sweeper *Ascot*, believed torpedoed off Farne Island on November 10, 1918.

The submarines had, as recorded, been recalled on the Trafalgar Anniversary of 1918. Upon return they were concentrated in the North Sea, to participate in the projected final sortie by the High Sea Fleet. All through the summer the Germans had worked at their plans. Daily, almost hourly, grew the expectancy in the British ships of the first German move. When the submarines abandoned the outer seas, every available British trawler and drifter was sent up to the Firth of Forth for emergency sweeping duties. So secure seemed the western area that outward-bound ships were permitted to sail from Liverpool, independently and unescorted, on the 26th. But the 'last sortie' never came.

There yet remained one submarine far out in the western ocean. Von Arnauld de la Perière had taken over the U-cruiser U 139 (ex *Korvetten-Kapitan Schwieger*)[1] in the spring of 1918, and had sailed for American waters in September. These large U-cruisers (U 139-141), according to Gayer, were hampered in their work by leaks in their pressure hulls, and

---

[1] It was at one time intended that the new 'U-cruisers' should be named after famous and deceased officers of the submarine branch, such as Weddigen, Schwieger, etc. This intention was abandoned, and the boats were numerated in accordance with the established system. The big submarines were, however, often referred to as the 'Helder-boote' or the 'hero-boats,' although the original proposal for naming them after 'the submarine heroes' was never put into effect.

they suffered from poor stability and diving powers. Von Arnauld, on October 1, encountered a convoy of 10 large ships off Cape Finisterre. Escorted by two armed merchant cruisers, one stationed ahead and the other astern, together with patrols flanking the columns, the convoy was zigzagging. His torpedo fired at a freighter missed its billet. The convoy passed over the U 139. As the sound of the ships receded, U 139 thrust her hull out of the sea, opened fire with her guns, and received a hot reply. Hastily diving to avoid these attentions, U 139 experienced her baptism of depth-charges. A little later, von Arnauld decided to renew the fray. Chasing the convoy, he secured a hit on one steamer. Again he was forced to dive by one of the escorts. Several hours later, U 139 tried to finish off the vessel already damaged, but was compelled to seek the sub-surface once more, and von Arnauld then secured a torpedo-hit on the injured ship. Hardly had the sound of the explosion died away when there came a shattering crash overhead. Within the submarine the lights went out; water percolated through the hull; U 139 listed over. Down, down she went, sinking like a stone in soundings 3000 feet deep; the conning-tower hatch had jammed. Von Arnauld believes that he had inadvertently passed right under the sinking steamer and was pinned beneath the vast bulk plunging to the depths. By exerting air-pressure on all tanks, U 139 was freed from her incubus, only to shoot to the surface and be greeted with depth-charges. With three periscopes snapped off, she was forced to grope her way along blindly, just beneath the surface, to escape from the hornet's nest she had raised. On receiving the recall, von Arnauld brought his boat back to Kiel on the 14th, to find that the Revolution had broken out.[1]

As the submarines had deserted the shipping lanes, to take part in North Sea fleet operations, opportunity for attacking the U-boats became greatly less; such losses as occurred were all to be found east of the British Isles. First, UB 90 (Meyer) was torpedoed and sunk in the Skagerrak, on the 16th, by the British submarine L 12; likewise did the large mine-layer

[1] *Raiders of the Deep* (Lowell Thomas).

DOWNFALL AND NOT WORLD POWER

U 78 (Bolbrecht) succumb to the attentions of G 2 on the 28th, in waters west of the Jutland Battle area. The Northern Barrage exacted its final victim in UB 123 (Kamm), blown up off the Orkneys on the 19th.

The manner in which the last submarine of the North Sea flotilla met its end was far more heroic than the fate of her many consorts previously deceased. UB 116 (Emsmann) set off with a volunteer crew of officers, bent on a gallant attempt to penetrate into Scapa Flow and there sink the British flagship. The forlorn venture was sadly misdirected, since the Grand Fleet was at that time in the Firth of Forth. On October 28 the submarine was located on the screen connected with electrical detectors of the outer Hoxa defences. When she was well over the field of controlled mines, the circuit was closed. This, incidentally, was the only time, during the whole war, that a submarine was destroyed from a shore control-station.

The final episode completed the cycle. As the German submarines began their operations in 1914, so did they end them in 1918, by an attempt to find the Grand Fleet in its war anchorage. In the last resort they sought an honourable objective, as they did at the outset ; but, between beginning and end, how far did they travel in ways of dishonour and what infamies did they achieve !

The German battleships were ordered out on the last desperate enterprise on October 28, but the crews refused to go out to what they believed would be certain death. Spiess, who had been appointed to the command of U 135 (but had not yet undertaken any war cruise in her), dramatically reveals the disintegration of the High Sea Fleet.[1] Suddenly summoned by Michelsen (Commodore of Submarines), Spiess was informed that the crews of the battleships *Ostfriesland* [2] and *Thüringen*, lying in the Schillig Roads, had mutinied. He was ordered to take U 135 out to the scene, and thereafter act upon orders from the Fleet Command. What lay behind these orders could easily be guessed at : the big submarine was to attack and sink the two rebel battleships if called

---

[1] *Six Ans de Croisières en Sous-Marins* (Spiess).
[2] In some accounts of the mutiny, this ship is referred to as the *Helgoland*.

upon. With an eye to future contingencies, Spiess considered it advisable to ask for written orders. He therefore went on board the hulk-flagship *Kaiser Wilhelm II.*, and made a request to Admiral von Trotha. The Chief of Staff did not find it expedient to commit any orders to writing. The written word endureth! Anything in black-and-white might be highly inconvenient and compromising—if the mutineers won!

From von Trotha, Spiess went to von Hipper, but even from the Commander-in-Chief himself he could obtain no clear instructions or orders. Von Hipper merely made a few vague remarks, and with a formal bow indicated that the interview was at an end. Spiess therefore returned to U 135, to announce his amazing news and orders to the officers. He informed them that they must exact implicit obedience from their men, even if it should be at the point of the revolver.

U 135 convoyed out to the Schillig Roads two small steamers, laden with armed boarding-parties. The *Thüringen* was the first rebel vessel to be tackled. Soldiers under the command of Lieutenant Grimm, of the Naval Staff, drove the mutineers forward and confined them below hatches. Five minutes were allowed for a surrender. On the expiration of the fifth minute, all other ships, whose crews had taken no part in the revolt, were ordered to move out of range. U 135 was cleared for action, and stood off to gain her attacking position. A torpedo-boat dashed up, flying a signal intimating that she was about to open fire with shell upon the recalcitrant seamen. The execution of the signal was delayed. The mutineers of the *Thüringen* shortly afterwards surrendered.

The other renegade ship, the *Ostfriesland*, suddenly and menacingly trained her whole broadside battery on the U 135, at 500 yards range. It was the last effort at resistance. Grimm and his soldiers boarded the battleship and regained control. The insubordinate seamen were bundled into the boarding-steamers, and taken ashore under armed guard. Thus the mutiny of October 31 collapsed.

The end, though deferred, was still nigh at hand. Admiral Kraft took his battle-squadron to Kiel; the insurrection broke out afresh and with increased violence. The smouldering discontent blazed up into a conflagration which consumed not only the High Sea Fleet but the German monarchy. Commodore Michelsen hoisted his broad pennant in U 135 and left for Heligoland, there to collect a force still loyal to the old *régime*, comprising about 50 submarines, torpedo-craft, and patrols. Forced by the disaffected garrison to seek a safer anchorage, he made for Lister Deep, off the Schleswig coast, only to find that part of the German Empire rent by civil war. On board the cruiser *Graudenz* a General Council of officers was held. For hour after hour one expedient after another was discussed and rejected. Wilhelmshaven, Cuxhaven, and Kiel—the three chief naval ports—were in the hands of the revolutionaries. Heligoland, Borkum, and Sylt were no longer safe. Michelsen's ships were bereft of any secure refuge. In the end, after hours of debate, the bitter, humiliating and inevitable course had to be accepted—to take the ships back to port and surrender them to the ' Soldiers' Councils.'[1]

Michelsen, with his broad pennant in the *Graudenz*, steamed down the line and for the last time took the salute from the submarines of the Imperial Navy.

On November 5 the Allies announced that they were ready to discuss terms of peace, and at eleven o'clock on November 11 hostilities ceased on all fronts.

---

[1] It was feared that the revolutionaries would carry out reprisals against Spiess and his crew for the part they had played in quelling the mutiny of October 31. Spiess was given leave to take shelter in some neutral port, and he decided to make for Memel, in the Baltic. Soon after leaving Lister Deep, he took in a wireless message raising the alarm that British warships had appeared to the north-west of Borkum. This warning was followed by the orders: ' British destroyers have broken through into the Bight. First Submarine Flotilla cover the Elbe, Second cover Heligoland, Third the Jade, and Fourth Emden.' Spiess hurried back in U 135 to take up the station assigned to his flotilla, but it all proved to be a false alarm. He was ordered to put into Wilhelmshaven, and there he turned over U 135 to the battleship-hulk *Braunschweig*, parent vessel of the 3rd Submarine Flotilla.

CHAPTER XIV

SURRENDER

THE U-boat weapon had broken in the hand of Germany ; it had brought ruin and disaster instead of swift and decisive victory. It had made America enter the raging conflict on the side of Germany's enemies, whereas, by adroit handling, Berlin had at certain periods a chance of winning the great Republic of the West to her side. By her manifestation of folly, her improvidence, her disregard of consequences almost inevitable, she had ensured her own defeat. The U-boat was the weapon which indirectly caused her own doom. It ranged the whole of the civilized world against her ; the victory promised to the German nation by its agency had not been gained. Hope deferred broke down the civil morale of the Central Powers. Upon a fertile ground of disillusionment and war-weariness the communistic theorists sowed their unwholesome seed. From the mutiny of the High Sea Fleet on October 28, the weeds of rebellion spread until they choked the good wheat of the German nation and strangled the lilies of the monarchies of Prussia, Bavaria, and Saxony.

For the submarines, the end, utter and ignominious, had come. The *élite* of the High Sea Fleet was to be handed over to the Allies for internment, until such decisions were arrived at as would decide its fate. Not so for the under-water raiders. For them it was *Væ victis* ! Surrender, absolute and final, was implacably demanded. Why did the Germans never scuttle the U-boats in their own ports, as they later scuttled the High Sea Fleet in Scapa Flow ? The answer to that question is : Immediately after the Armistice, plans for scuttling all the submarines were being discussed, when the stunning warning was flashed across the North Sea that if every submarine was not handed over, the Allies would

XXIV. THE IMMOLATION OF THE FLANDERS U-BOATS.
One of the raiders from Flanders, believed to be UB. 59, blown up by the Germans when they evacuated the Belgian coast.

SURRENDER.
The papers of a German officer are being examined, on board a surrendered submarine at Harwich, November, 1918.

SURRENDER 331

permanently occupy Heligoland. That was the final and crushing blow.

The naval conditions of the Armistice of November 11 included the following :—

' To surrender at the ports specified by the Allies and the United States all submarines at present in existence (including all submarine-cruisers and mine-layers), with armament and equipment complete. Those that cannot put to sea shall be deprived of armament and equipment, and shall remain under the supervision of the Allies and the United States. Submarines ready to put to sea shall be prepared to leave German ports immediately on receipt of wireless orders to sail to the port of surrender, the remainder to follow as soon as possible. The conditions of this Article shall be completed within fourteen days of the signing of the Armistice.'

Harwich was chosen as the port of surrender. As the mists of dawn dispersed on the morning of November 20, the long, low-lying, sinister forms of 20 German submarines were seen being shepherded into captivity by the Harwich ships. Twenty miles from port, British crews boarded the U-boats and took them over from the Germans ; and, as they passed the gates, the White Ensign was hoisted above the German flag. This humiliating scene was repeated next day. Another 20 boats were sent over ; but only 19 arrived, as the twentieth boat, U 97, foundered on the voyage across. They were navigated by crews paid for each trip ; and German commanding officers took no part in the ignominy of surrender. On the 22nd, a further 20 were handed over to the Harwich force ; three days later, a larger batch of 28 crossed the North Sea ; and on the 27th, when 27 were delivered by the German crews, the total number of boats surrendered had reached 114. Eight arrived on December 1 ; thereafter, further groups were yielded up as soon as the boats could be made fit for the passage, or be rendered seaworthy if still unfinished. During February 1919, 6 additional boats—UB 89, UC 40, UC 71, UC 91, U 16, and the famous U 21—foundered on their way to Harwich. Eight old boats—U 1,[1] U 2,[1] U 4, U 17,

[1] It is not certain if these were broken up during the war, for the sake of the materials they contained, or if they were destroyed after the Armistice.

UB 2, UB 5, UB 9, and UB 11—were broken up in Germany, being unfit to make the last sea-trip.

In neutral ports lay 9 U-boats. On November 11 the large converted merchantman U 157 took refuge at Trondhjem, and two days later the large mine-layer U 124 put into Karlskrona. U 35 and UC 74 had sought safety at Barcelona. Six U-boats had been interned during hostilities : UC 8 and UB 6 in Dutch ports, and U 39, UB 23, UC 48, and UC 56 in Spanish ports. These internees were all handed over to the Allies, with two exceptions—UC 8 had been acquired by Holland, and the crew of UC 48 scuttled their boat at Ferrol on March 14, 1919, before Spain could deliver her to the Allies. The total number of submarines surrendered was 176, including the 4 at Sevastopol ;[1] they were allocated as follows—Britain 105, France 46, Italy 10, Japan 7, United States 6, Belgium 2.[2] Of these, France retained 10 for incorporation in her fleet by special permission. Japan temporarily kept her 7 for experimental and research work, and rendered them incapable of military service by July 1, 1921. Engines, armament, and equipment of German submarines were not allowed to be built into hulls of new submarines or other war-vessels, without special agreement.

On the conclusion of hostilities there were 158 German submarines in the various enemy ports (including the 8 old boats broken up in Germany after the war), 5 were lying interned in neutral ports, 3 had fled to ports of the non-belligerents during the final *débâcle* of November.[3] These 166 boats were ready for surrender. To this number were added 18 others rendered seaworthy for delivery, and these make up the 184 demanded by the Allies.[4] From such total there must be deducted the 7 boats that foundered *en route* to Harwich and 1 scuttled.[5]

[1] UB 14, UB 42 ; UC 23, UC 37.

[2] Re-assigned to Belgium after delivery to Great Britain.

[3] U 124 is not included in this figure, as her whereabouts on November 11 is not known. She is included amongst those lying in German ports.

[4] The famous U 9 was not demanded for surrender, but was brought over by the German seamen to obtain passage-money. She had been converted into a surface-operating mine-layer, and, apparently, had long ceased to be a submarine at all.

[5] UB 8, seized at Varna by the French, is not here included.

SURRENDER 333

The total war losses were 178; if the 14 scuttled at Adriatic and Flanders bases be added, the total is raised to 192. The death-roll amounted to 515 officers and 4849 warrant officers and men.[1]

The submarines sank 11,153,000 tons of shipping. Of this colossal total, Britain's loss was 2099 ships of 6,635,059 tons gross, with 12,723 civilian lives, and 578 fishing-craft of 57,583 tons (with 98 fisherfolk), sunk by submarine; and 259 British merchant-ships of 673,417 tons, with 1493 lives, sunk by mine (not all laid by submarines), and 63 fishing-vessels of 8545 tons with 332 lives, mined. Submarines damaged 1727 British ships of 7,335,827 tons, resulting in a loss of another 512 lives; and mines injured 84 ships of 432,446 tons, with 64 lives lost. When to these huge totals are added vessels sunk and molested by cruisers, ocean

[1] Extracted from German Naval Staff Report, 1922. The totals for officers were made up as follows:—

	Active List.	Reserve.	Total.
Non-specialist branches	296	72	368
Engineer officers	130	14	144
Surgeons	2	..	2
Torpedo branch	1	..	1

The following classification of losses by ranks accounts for only 511 officers:—

	Active List.	Reserve.
Commanders	2	..
Lieutenant-commanders	73	..
Lieutenants	160	12
Sub-lieutenants	61	60
Lieutenant-commanders (E)	29	1
Lieutenants (E)	42	12
Probationary lieutenants (E)	19	1
Probationary sub-lieutenants (E)	39	..

Admiral Spindler (to whom allusion has previously been made) gives the following estimate: 'In Germany, the total personnel required for the manning, overhaul, repair, and replacement-building of the submarines and at the dockyards amounted to 113,000. . . . In the German submarines at the front there were, according to the most careful estimates, about 13,000 men in all. Of these, 5087 were killed.'—('The Value of the Submarine in Naval Warfare,' *U.S.N.I. Proceedings*, May 1926, pp. 841-2.)

Of the junior officers of the German Navy killed during the war, about one-half of the lieutenant-commanders, and about one-third of the lieutenants and sub-lieutenants, lost their lives in the submarine warfare. For this reason the naval war was often referred to in Germany as 'the war of the lieutenants.'

raiders, and aircraft, as well as the ever-present toll of marine risk (and many large ships were lost through collision and stranding during the war), the British total is increased to about 9,055,000 tons gross.[1] The French lost 238 ships of 696,845 tons by enemy action, the Italians lost 238 ships of 769,450 tons, the United States (who did not employ her shipping to any extent in the danger zone) 80 ships of 341,512 tons, and the Japanese 29 vessels of 120,176 tons. Second only to Britain came a neutral, Norway; her losses were assessed at 1,172,000 tons. Greece lost 415,000 tons, Sweden 264,000 tons, Denmark 245,000 tons, Spain 238,000 tons, Holland 229,000 tons, Belgium 105,000 tons, and Brazil 31,000 tons.

Merchant Fleet losses :— [2]

	Tons gross.
Argentina	4,275
Belgium	85,758
Brazil	25,464
Denmark	243,707
France	899,358
Great Britain	7,759,090
Greece	345,516
Holland	211,969
Italy	872,341
Japan	120,176
Norway	1,180,316
Portugal	94,946
Russia	183,083
Spain	168,391
Sweden	201,276
United States of America	397,059
Other countries	12,177
	12,804,902

[1] Of the British total of 2099 ships sunk, 243 mercantile-vessels, chartered or controlled by the Admiralty, are duplicated in the official return, 'Navy Losses.'

[2] *The Italian Navy in the World War, 1915-1918.* Issued by the Chief of the Staff of the Royal Italian Navy (Historical Section), Rome (1927).

British naval losses by submarine were :—

Battleships	5	Mine-carriers	*2
Cruisers	5	Mine-sweeper	1
Light cruisers	3	Fleet messengers	*6
Torpedo gunboat	1	Commissioned escorts	*3
Monitor	1	Miscellaneous	*2
Sloops	11	Colliers	*193
Flotilla leader	1	Oilers	*35
Destroyers	7	Special Service Ships	
Submarines	4	(Q-boats)	22
Aircraft-carrier	1	Tug	1
Mine-layer	1	Yachts	2
Armed merchant cruisers	11	Admiralty trawlers	3
Armed boarding-steamers	9	Hired trawlers	14
Naval hospital-ship	*1	Drifters	3
Frozen meat carrier	*1		
			349

* These ships are also included in the lists and totals of the official return, 'Merchant Shipping (Losses).'

Mines laid by submarines were responsible for sinking—

Battleship	1	Destroyers	9
Cruiser	1	Torpedo-boats	2
Light cruiser	1	Submarine	1
Torpedo gunboat	1	Patrol-boat	1
Sloops	4	Armed boarding-steamer	1

Of the 225 auxiliary vessels which succumbed to mine injury, the majority probably fell victim to submarine-laid mines.

The enemy laid about 11,000 mines in 1360 groups around the British Isles. Of all the mines laid by German vessels, only two groups were undetected after the Armistice—namely, one laid by the raider *Wolf* in the Indian Ocean, and the other in the Arctic. The great work of mine-clearance began in 1919, and continued until October, when 11,487 fixed and 12,386 drifting mines had been swept up or destroyed, dating these figures from that far-distant month of August 1914.

Barrages, fields laid by the enemy in the early days, and dangerous areas had all to be scoured clean. British and German sweepers had to free the North Sea danger-areas; and a British sweeping-flotilla based on Scheveningen was occupied for months in clearing the Dutch waters. Ten years after the end of hostilities it was stated that 49 British ships had foundered on mines since the Armistice; the clearance work inevitably entailed further losses to the hard-worked mine-sweeping force.

The war-weary nations scarcely paid heed to the naval losses sustained from these grim reminders of terrible years passed through. The armed yacht *Goissa* was the first victim, foundering on a mine during the clearance of the Dardanelles on November 15; the trawler *Glenboyne* was thus lost off the north of Ireland on January 4, 1919; the drifter *John Robert*, on passage from Messina to Alexandretta, is believed to have been similarly lost on February 1; the sweeper *Erin's Isle* was lost off the Nore on the 7th; the sweeper *Cupar* in the North Sea on May 5; the sweepers *Kinross* and *Duchess of Richmond* in the Aegean on June 16 and 26 respectively; and the sweeper *Princess Mary II.*, also in the Aegean, was beached before she settled down, on August 2. In the White Sea, mines claimed the sweepers *Sword Dance* and *Fandango* on June 24 and July 2; and in the Baltic Sea the light cruiser *Cassandra* was fatally injured by mine on December 5, 1918, the sloops *Gentian* and *Myrtle* on July 16, 1919, and the destroyer *Verulam* on September 4. This was the price exacted after the war, both from mine-clearance and accidental contact with the deadly machines.

During the first three months of unrestricted warfare, an average of 130·1 ships per month of all nations was destroyed in home waters, and 33·3 in the Mediterranean. In the last three months of the campaign the figures had been decreased to 38 and 11 respectively—a reduction of 71 per cent. and 67 per cent. respectively. The intensity of the war in the later stages is illustrated by the fact that from May 1 to November 2, 1918, there were sunk 252 British ships; and of these, 228 were torpedoed without warning. Ninety thousand ships of 97,000,000 tons were convoyed by British escorts, and only 436

SURRENDER

ships were lost under naval charge : this was an equivalent of 0·5 per cent.

*   *   *   *   *

So did the seamen of the war and merchant navies and of the fishing-fleets meet and master the greatest peril that ever menaced the integrity of the Commonwealth of the British Nations.

> ' So shall Thy people, with joyful devotion,
>   Praise Thy Name, delivered from perils abhorred ;
> Singing in chorus, from Ocean to Ocean,
>   Peace unto the Nations, and Peace in the Lord.'
>
>   (The Old Russian National Anthem,
>   ' God the All-Terrible.')

APPENDIX I

The Triumph of Convoy

A.—SHIPS IN ORGANISED ATLANTIC CONVOYS
July 26, 1917, to October 5, 1918 *

Direction.	No. Convoyed.	Casualties.	Per cent. Loss.	Gross Tonnage. Convoyed.	Lost.	Per cent Loss.
Homeward	8194	74	0·9	43,196,740	364,842	0·84
Outward	6774	44	0·65	33,860,491	289,446	0·85
	14,968	118	0·79	77,057,231	654,288	0·85

* Not inclusive of convoys on passage on October 5, 1918.

B.—WORLD'S DAILY AVERAGE LOSS OF SHIPS

Quarter of Year.		No. of Ships.	Tons Gross.
1917	1st	7·6	16,350
	2nd	10·43	23,550
	3rd	6·22	15,270
	4th	5·04	12,500
1918	1st	4·5	10,740
	2nd	3·37	8,600
	3rd	2·91	7,813

62 per cent. United States troops were carried in British ships.
Argentine wheat convoy: 307 ships of 1,466,000 tons gross;
1 ship lost.

C.—CONVOYS up to OCTOBER 26, 1918 (cessation of submarine warfare)

Convoy Route.	No. of Convoys.	No. of Ships in Convoy.	Losses.	Per cent.
ATLANTIC:				
North Atlantic .	306	5,416	40	0·74
Gibraltar .	133	1,979	30	1·5
West African ports .	105	944	6	0·64
Rio de Janeiro .	22	307	1	0·32
	566	8,646	77	0·89

APPENDIX I

Convoy Route.	No. of Convoys.	No. of Ships in Convoy.	Losses.	Per cent.
OUTWARD:				
Various sailings from British ports.	508	7,110	45	0·63
OTHER CONVOYS:				
Scandinavian (old system).		6,475	75	1·15
,, (new system)		3,923	16	0·41
French coal-trade		37,221	53	0·14
Local Mediterranean.		10,275	127	1·24
East Coast (N. of Humber)		12,122	40	0·51
		85,772	433	0·52
Total (Outward and other Convoys)		77,126	356	
Add for Atlantic Convoys as above		8,646	77	
Grand Total		85,772	433	

THE OUTPUT OF DEPTH-CHARGES

Amongst the counter-measures adopted to meet the German 1917-18 attack on shipping, the output of depth-charges played a part almost as important as that of the convoy system. It is perhaps not too much to say that convoy and depth-charge, taken together, were the two measures primarily responsible for the collapse of the German onslaught on shipping.

In July 1917 the weekly output of depth-charges was only 140. After Admiral Sir John Jellicoe took up duty at the Admiralty in November 1916 as First Sea Lord, every means possible was adopted to increase the rate of production. By the end of 1917 the weekly output had risen to 800, and was still mounting rapidly. During 1917 between 100 and 300 depth-charges were used per month; but during the last six months of hostilities *two thousand* depth-charges per month (on an average) were being expended in attacks upon the German submarines.

APPENDIX II

A SHORT HISTORY OF GERMAN SUBMARINE DESIGN, 1904-1914 [1]

To the late Marshal Foch is attributed the saying : 'The next war will begin where the last one ended.' In a certain sense, every new war is a continuation of its predecessor. Hence, it is in the Russo-Japanese War of 1904-5 that we find the germ of the German submarines—that service which was destined to play so large a part in the conflict of 1914-18.

Under the old hierarchy of sea power, as we knew it up to 1918, Germany was the last great naval Power to adopt the submarine. She did, in fact, only order her first boat about ten years before the outbreak of the World War. Her dilatoriness in accepting the new arm of sea warfare was, in a large measure, due to the stubborn opposition of the late Admiral von Tirpitz—the very man who, from 1915 to 1917, urged the waging of submarine warfare à l'outrance.

Speaking in the Reichstag in 1901, von Tirpitz said that Germany, thanks to the configuration of her coasts and the geographical situation of her ports, had no need whatever of submarines, which he considered to be purely defensive weapons.[2] And again, in another speech, von Tirpitz declared : 'We have no money to waste on experimental vessels. We must leave such luxuries to wealthier States like France and England.'[3]

In the *Memoirs* he wrote and published after the end of the Great War, von Tirpitz has dealt with his responsibility for the belated introduction of submarines into the German Navy.[4] It was his settled policy never to adopt any new weapon until its military usefulness had been clearly demonstrated, albeit that this rule of conduct laid him open to the gibes of disappointed inventors and impatient patriots. He therefore refused to throw away good

---
[1] The technical facts embodied in this historical summary are for the most part taken from Dr. H. Techel's *Der Bau von Unterseebooten auf der Germaniawerft* (Berlin, 1923).

[2] *Sous-Marins, Torpilles et Mines*, MM. Laubeuf and Stroh (Paris, 1923), p. 75.

[3] *Engineer* (London), April 13, 1923.   [4] *Memoirs*, vol. i. p. 138.

APPENDIX II 341

money on the building of submarines, when the only submarines that could be built would have been feeble little things, just capable of creeping up and down the coast. Such craft would have been of no use to Germany. As soon as sea-going boats were produced, he was the first to encourage their building on a large scale. In spite of financial restrictions, he went as far as the limits of technical production would then allow.

D'EQUEVILLEY AND KRUPPS

Early in 1902 an engineer named d'Equevilley approached Fried. Krupp of Essen and proposed that the great German firm should avail itself of his experimental work and research upon the construction of submarines. Where d'Equevilley conducted his experiments, and where he gained his practical knowledge, has never been explained. He has been described as having been both a French and a Spanish engineer. Suffice it to say that such submarines as were built to d'Equevilley's plans bore a most remarkable resemblance, in hull-form and construction, to the 'submersibles' designed by the French naval architect, M. Maxime Laubeuf, for the French Navy between 1897 and 1902.

Krupps had about that time (1902) bought the Germania Yard at Gaarden, near Kiel. D'Equevilley's proposals with regard to submarine construction were therefore referred to the technical staff at Kiel for consideration and report. The verdict given was favourable.

THE 'FOREL'

In February 1902 the Germania Yard began to work out plans for a small experimental submarine.[1] This boat was built at the firm's own expense and upon its own initiative and responsibility. At that time the German Navy Office refused to apportion any money for the building of under-water craft. The idea was that Krupps should gain some practical knowledge, at first hand, of submarine construction, and possess the means of carrying out research work upon problems of sub-surface navigation. With the experience so acquired, a step forward could be taken towards the building of bigger boats. The experimental boat was laid down during July 1902, and was built with great secrecy, although there was nothing very original in her design. From the technical point of view, Krupps' 1902 boat represented little or no advance

[1] It may be mentioned here that no reliable proof can be found to support statements made in naval annuals, twenty-five years ago, to the effect that, about 1890-99, submarines of the Nordenfelt type were built at Kiel for the German Navy.

upon the *Gymnote*, built to the designs of the French engineer Gustave Zédé in 1886. Judging by the plans, d'Equevilley had nothing to do with the experimental boat. This primitive vessel displaced 15½ tons in surface trim; her only means of propulsion was by electric batteries and a motor, and she had a very feeble radius of action—4½ miles at 3½ knots when carrying both her outboard torpedo-discharges.

First trials were run in June 1903; a month later, a submerged run was made, and a target moored three miles from the submarine's point of departure was successfully attacked. She also made a demonstration run before H.M. the German Emperor, and on September 23, 1903, Prince Henry of Prussia made a brief cruise in her. She also appears to have been demonstrated before the German naval authorities. In every respect she is alleged to have been a success, save in one point: she never made her designed speeds.

Russia, at the outbreak of her disastrous war with Japan, became a liberal (and none too discriminating) patron of experimental submarines. The Krupp experimental boat was acquired by Russia and became the *Forel* (=*Trout*) of the Imperial Navy; she carried out diving and surface-running trials near Petersburg (Leningrad) in June and August 1904. In a complete state she was loaded on a double-bogie railway-truck for overland transport to Vladivostock. Whether she ever arrived there, and whether she ever attempted to take part in the Russo-Japanese War, or not, are matters which are still numbered among the petty conundrums of naval history. Her end, like the fate of many of the early Russian submarines, is obscure. The *Forel* was reported to be still in existence in 1911; but she does not appear among the submarines listed in a 1914 (pre-war) edition of a Russian Naval Annual.

The 'Karp' Class

It was early in 1904 that the Russo-Japanese War broke out, and in June of the same year Russia ordered from Krupps three submarines, known later as the *Karp* class (*Karp, Karas, Kambala*). These three boats were destined to have a marked influence on the development of the German submarine service.

Before the little experimental boat (*Forel*) had been finished, Krupps were at work upon the plans for a larger 'autonomous' submarine. The *Forel* had this grave defect: before making each run, she had to have her batteries recharged with current, generated outside her own hull; as, for example, at a shore electric-

APPENDIX II

power station. In the improved design, Krupps intended to use a combination of internal-combustion engines, dynamos, and electric motors, as is now the standard practice for the propulsion of submarines.[1] Upon one point the Germans had made up their minds : it was that the stowage and use of petrol, within and by a submarine, was dangerous—so dangerous as to verge on the suicidal. In such a conclusion they were right. There had been frequent explosions and fires—sometimes attended with fatal results—within the hulls of the petrol-propelled submarines used by foreign navies. The Germans therefore decided that, if any volatile fuel was to be carried for use in an internal-combustion engine, that fuel must not be stowed within the working-compartments, but outside of them. In 1904, d'Equevilley patented his design for a double-hull submarine, with fuel stowage located without the pressure-hull. Benzine or petrol the Germans would only tolerate for the starting-up of engines. Once started up and warmed, the internal-combustion engines were to run on petroleum, paraffin, or some other 'heavy' oil. So much, in fact, had been decided upon when the Russians placed their order for the three *Karp* boats in June 1904.

The next problem was to get engines built that would burn a 'safety fuel.' The firm of Körting Brothers had constructed small heavy-oil engines for the propulsion of automobiles, lorries, launches, etc., but they had built no engine bigger than 8 h.p. Krupps approached Körtings, and the latter firm agreed to try to produce the heavy-oil engines for the new Russian submarines. The first attempt was an experimental engine, consisting of only one cylinder. This engine gave indifferent results under test; it exhibited signs of rapid wear, and the fuel consumption was excessive. However, it solved certain technical problems; and, profiting by the experience so gained, Körtings next produced engines of vastly improved performance and power.

For the three Russian submarines, six sets of 200-B.H.P. Körting heavy-oil motors were ordered—two sets to each boat. The *Karp*-class boats each displaced 207 tons (in surface trim), and, with heavy-oil motors totalling 400 B.H.P., could make 10·8 knots.

---

[1] The American Alstitt is said to have been the first to propose this combination of machinery for the propulsion of submarines. Little is heard of Alstitt ; some reference books on the history of submarine navigation simply do not allude to him at all. He was the man who indicated the successful solution of the propulsion problem, after ' bottled steam,' ' chemical boilers,' compressed air, electricity, treadmills, handmills, clockwork, and other fantastic ideas had all been tried and found hopelessly inefficient.

The engines were efficient in the development of power, but were still deficient from the view-point of durability. For one thing, the uncooled pistons cracked through overheating; therefore, after a given length of service the engines had to be opened up and new pistons fitted. The contact-breakers of the electric ignition wore away so quickly, that each boat had to carry a complete spare set. A tall and heavy exhaust-funnel had to be erected before the engines could be started up and the boat run in surface trim : the same funnel had to be lowered and stowed away before the boat could submerge—a procedure which added considerably to the time required for preparations before the boat could submerge. Fuel consumption was very heavy, and such quantities of heavy oil were burnt in the cylinders, that vast volumes of billowing white smoke belched out of the exhaust funnel, making the submarines conspicuously visible at long range. At night the funnel would emit showers of sparks, and even flames. Although Körtings' type of heavy-oil engine was subsequently much improved, these handicaps against inconspicuous cruising on the surface were never overcome. With Körting-engined submarines, tactics had to conform to the limitations imposed by the machinery. If the submarine was running on the surface, and a vessel, presumed to be hostile, was sighted at long range, the submarine closed down her heavy-oil motors, lowered her funnel, and made the first part of her 'approach' on the surface, running on her electric motors ; then she dived, to make the second part of her 'approach' and the attack. This course made considerable inroads into the current available for submerged running, the actual attack, and subsequent retreat.

The First Four Experimental Boats

The *Karp*-class boats passed through their trials, and made the run to the Russian port of Libau under their own power. They represent the real beginning of German submarine design, for the first submarine built for the German Navy, U 1, was merely an improved and slightly enlarged version of the *Karp*-class design. In these three Russian boats is seen the genesis of the German submarine—the combination of the d'Equevilley double-hull with the Körting heavy-oil engine. Both in the design of the earliest under-water boats, and in the training of their personnel, the German policy, through and through, was one of 'safety first.'

The Berlin Navy Office had therefore little to do with the initiation of submarine construction in Germany. It was Russia

APPENDIX II

who bought the *Forel*, and so defrayed Krupps' expenditure on first experiments; and again, it was thanks to a Russian order that the first three U-boats of typical German design were built and tried out.

'For experiments connected with submarines, with a view to building at least one boat of this type: 1,500,000 marks [£73,421]': so ran the first money vote in the German Navy estimates, 1905-6. Despite statements made elsewhere to the contrary, the first German submarine (U 1) was not launched until April 16, 1906, and she was completed on December 14 of the same year.[1] She displaced 237 metric tons and measured $138\frac{3}{4}$ feet in length (over all), with a beam (maximum) of $12\frac{1}{4}$ feet, and a draught just over 10 feet; this pioneer boasted a single torpedo-tube in her bows. Three 17·7 inch (45 cm.) torpedoes were carried.

In brief, up to 1904, von Tirpitz was adamant in his opposition to the building of small and unreliable submarines of an experimental nature. The naval authorities inspected the *Forel*, but would have nothing to do with her. If the German Navy was to have submarines, those submarines must have a real, practical value. When Krupps demonstrated with the *Karp* class for Russia that a submarine type of real fighting worth had been produced, then, and only then, did the Germans order a boat of similar pattern for their own fleet.

U 1, however, proved but an indifferent success: 'The U 1, commanded by Lieutenant Bartenbach,[2] has undergone trials in the North Sea (July 1908) with a complement of 19 men. Her small displacement renders this boat unfitted for operations at any distance from the coast, as observations taken showed that her employment in the high seas is attended with danger.'[3]

U 2 was built by the Imperial Dockyard at Danzig. It is believed she was begun in March 1906; she was launched during June 1908 in an advanced state, and was completed on July 18 of the last-mentioned year. She was also an experimental boat, her design being based on that of U 1, with modifications devised by the Navy Office. Larger and more powerfully armed and engined than U 1, she was little more successful than her predecessor.

---

[1] When U 1 was laid down is uncertain: possibly it was on the date commonly reported to be that of her launch—August 30, 1905. Another version is that she was ordered on December 3, 1904, and laid down in February 1905.

[2] From 1914 to 1918, Captain (S), Flanders Naval Forces.

[3] She had a cruising range of 1000 miles on the surface, but this was a nominal computation.

The German policy of caution is exemplified by the fact that, in 1908, France possessed 60 submarines, Britain had about 68 under-water vessels, and the United States about a dozen. The majority of these boats were small and feeble craft, fit only for coastal defence. Many, also, were elementary experimental vessels, and were almost worthless for combatant duties.

U 3 and U 4 (also built at Danzig Dockyard in 1907-9) were even larger than the two preceding boats. On January 17, 1911, occurred Germany's sole peace-time disaster with submarines. U 3 foundered in Kiel Harbour; it was presumed that her water-ballast tanks had accidentally flooded. Divers placed a chain sling around the sunken hull, and a small floating crane at hand succeeded in bringing her bows to the surface. Nearly all of the crew were extricated through a torpedo-tube. Three officers, including the commander, however, elected to remain on board during the rest of the salvage operations by the submarine-salvage vessel *Vulkan*, which had been sent for. It is believed that the floating crane then let go her sling to enable the *Vulkan* to pass her hawsers. Unfortunately, during the lifting operations a ventilator appears to have given way. In poured the sea, drowning like rats in a trap the three officers inside.[1]

The above four boats, U 1, 2, 3, and 4, did not take part in any active military operations during the war, so far as can be ascertained.

The 'Desiderata' Boats

About the end of 1907 the Navy Office formulated the following points as essential military qualities to be embodied in any future submarines :—

(a) Speeds : 15 knots on surface, $10\frac{1}{2}$ knots submerged.
(b) Endurance : 2000 miles at high speed on the surface.
(c) Complement : 20 officers and men, for whom an air supply of 72 hours' duration was to be provided.
(d) Torpedo-tubes : 4 (2 bow, 2 stern). 6 torpedoes.

There were also to be improvements in screws and the accumulator batteries.

Here follow fourteen boats, viz.: U 5-8 class, U 9-12 class, U 13-15 class, U 16 (special boat), U 17-18 class, which were ordered between May 1908 and May 1910. They represent the efforts made by the Germans to produce submarines that would fulfil the *desiderata* tabulated above. Hence we refer to all these craft generically as the 'Desiderata' boats.

[1] *Navy League Annual*, 1911-12, p. 76.

APPENDIX II 347

The four essential qualities just enumerated could not be incorporated in a boat of much less than 500 tons surface displacement. To make the required surface speed of 15 knots, each 500-ton boat would have to be fitted with motors totalling 1000 to 1200 B.H.P. But the Körting heavy-oil motor could not be successfully built in units developing more than (about) 300 to 350 B.H.P.

The Germans therefore took the peculiar step of placing *four* sets of heavy-oil engines in each submarine's hull, the four engines being placed in pairs, tandem-wise, on each shaft. Other navies have tried the same system of four-engine grouping on two shafts, and have found the results to be very unsatisfactory. The earlier 'Desiderata' boats certainly could not make the 15 knots stipulated, or anything like it. About $13\frac{1}{2}$ knots was the average result attained on trials for the U 5-8 class. The U 9-12 class reached about $14\frac{1}{2}$ knots on trials. During the World War, U 9 could not overhaul a British trawler that was doing 12 knots.

Körting engines of 'mixed' powers were even linked together in one hull. For example, in a boat of the U 9-12 class the forward pair of engines were each 300-B.H.P. (8-cylinder) units; the after pair were each 225-B.H.P. (6-cylinder) units. The aggregate power for all four engines was 1050 B.H.P.

The U 13-15 class managed to get $14\frac{3}{4}$ knots on the surface during trials, but only the last three boats (U 16 and U 17-18) ever attained the 15 knots specified in the 1906 'Desiderata' design.

THE FIRST DIESEL-ENGINED BOATS

Bigger submarines were required, demanding more powerful engines for their propulsion. But the Körting heavy-oil motor seemed to have reached the absolute limit of development. The 'four-engine drive' system, used in the 'Desiderata' boats, had proved none too reliable or satisfactory. It represented the best that could be done with that particular type of engine. The path to further progress would have been barred had not the Germans, by patience and foresight, provided means for surmounting the technical obstacles now confronting them.

The advantages of the Diesel engine had from the first been patent; the introduction of this type of engine was, however, retarded by the very severe restrictions imposed by the Navy Office on over-all dimensions and weight. The first Diesel engine designed for the propulsion of submarines was built at Krupps' Germania Yard in 1906-7—that is, contemporaneously with the first German submarine, U 1. Investigation had to be carried out into the weights and performances of the four-cycle and two-cycle types of Diesel engine. Krupps, therefore, also built an experimental two-cycle engine for comparative tests.

About two years were occupied in trials and research. By November 1908 the Navy Office was so satisfied with the progress made, that it ordered an 850-B.H.P. two-cycle Diesel engine from Krupps. The famous M.A.N. Co. was also working along lines parallel to Krupps upon the problem of building reliable high-power Diesel engines for submarine propulsion.

The satisfactory performance, during severe and prolonged tests, of the Krupp 850-B.H.P. two-cycle engine (and also of a four-cycle engine of similar power, produced by the M.A.N. Co.) solved the problem of how to build bigger internal-combustion engines than Körtings could produce. So the way was opened to the building of still bigger submarines of 650 to 800 tons surface displacement.

On account of difficulties with the drawings, preparations of castings, patterns, metallurgical research, etc., the Krupp 850-B.H.P. engine was not ready for tests until May 1911. It demonstrated its reliability to the entire satisfaction of the naval authorities. Seven duplicate engines were ordered, and these, with the original experimental motor, made up eight sets. These eight Krupp Diesel engines were used to engine the four submarines of the U 23-26 class.

The first Diesel-engined submarine built by Krupps was not, however, built to German order. She was the Italian *Atropo* (built 1910-12), engined with two small Krupp Diesels, each of 350 B.H.P. There is also some reason for supposing that U 3, whilst under refit after her salvage, was fitted with small Diesels. Both U 3 and U 4 appear to have been extensively overhauled and modernized during the two or three years prior to the war.

The first Diesel-engined submarines for the German Navy were the four boats of the U 19-22 class. Each of these had two sets of 850-B.H.P. Diesels of the M.A.N. type. The first boat, U 19, was not completed until July 1913. The first of the Krupp Diesel-engined boats, U 23, is understood to have been completed about September 1913. Hence it was only about a year before the outbreak of war that Germany received her first real ocean-going boats of the Diesel-engined 'Mittel-U' species. As was inevitable with a new type of propulsion, prolonged trials had to be run, modifications made, and experiments carried out.

Gayer says that Germany had only eighteen serviceable submarines in July 1914, as U 23 and U 25 were still running their

APPENDIX II 349

trials and did not yet possess any real fighting value. Michelsen, on the other hand, gives the strength as twenty boats; and it seems certain that U 24 and U 26 were then in service. Techel, another German authority, says that U 26 was also running trials. There was another class in process of delivery, of which the component units, U 27-30, were commissioned during October 1914. The 'Thirty' class of ten boats, U 31-41 (afterwards to become so notorious) was delivered during the autumn, and began to appear at sea early in 1915. The U 42, building at Spezia (Italy), was acquired by the Italians and became the *Balilla*, under which name she was torpedoed and sunk by the Austrian torpedo-boat No. 66 on July 14, 1916. The next class was numbered U 43-50, of which U 43-45 were ordered in July 1913 and the remainder immediately following the outbreak of war. Admiral von Capelle, giving evidence before the Reichstag ' War Failures Committee,' stated that forty-five boats were ordered before the war; and the German Fleet Law, 1912, contemplated the construction of seventy-two submarines, at the rate of six per annum, by the year 1920.

The German submarines, early in 1914, were divided into two flotillas; and the hulk *Acheron* was the headquarters of the Periscope School at Kiel, corresponding roughly to the British *Dolphin* establishment. Attached as tenders were various torpedo-boats, which would accompany the submarines to sea.

Admiral Jellicoe has testified in his books that little was known of the details of the German submarines, particularly as regards their endurance and power, which were greatly underestimated. He says that, excepting only U 1-4, they were comparable with the nine British E-class boats. In the middle and later stages of the war the Admiralty went to the other extreme and overestimated the size of the earlier German craft. As a matter of fact, the U 5-16 ('Desiderata') boats were only about 500 tons (surface) displacement as against the 652 tons (surface) displacement of the earlier British E-boats; and only U 19-22 and U 23-26 were equal in size to contemporaneous British craft. In speed, excepting U 5-8 and U 9-12, the German boats were as good as the British boats; in armament they were almost as good; but in endurance the British E-boats were much inferior. The German boats were horribly cramped, crowded, and complicated internally. The double-hull design of the German submarine allowed a 500-ton boat living and working spaces only equal to those for a 300-ton single-hull craft; yet these German *Unterseeboote* carried a crew as numerous as the larger British E class, as they required so many hands to control all their complicated gear.

Before the war it had been considered something of a feat for a submarine to remain at sea, off the coast, for five to seven days. The first war-cruise of the U-boats, including the fifth German submarine built for the Imperial German Navy, lasted six days, and extended right across the North Sea as far as the eastern Scottish coast. The feature of the first year of war was the unsuspected sea-keeping endurance displayed by submarines generally.

Conclusion

German submarine development may therefore be treated as consisting of three phases of design : (a) the Russian *Karp* class and the four primitive experimental boats U 1-4 ; (b) the ' Desiderata ' boats with Körting four-engine drive ; and (c) the first Diesel-engined boats, the pioneers of the real ' overseas striking force.'

It is sometimes conjectured : ' What would have happened had Germany possessed one hundred submarines at the beginning of the Great War ? ' To this it may be replied that, if Germany *had* possessed one hundred submarines in 1914, the majority of these boats would have been either crudities like the U 1-4, or unreliable craft such as were the ' Desiderata ' boats. Vessels such as these would have been utterly unfit to face the Atlantic.[1] Only by the end of 1911 did Germany know she had at last produced powerful and reliable Diesel engines wherewith to propel big ocean-going submarines. She had confined the building of submarines to two shipyards—the Imperial Dockyard at Danzig and Krupps' Germania Yard at Kiel. The output of Diesel engines had likewise been restricted to two centres—Krupps and the M.A.N. Co. Hence her sources of production were very limited. With all her powers of organization, Germany could hardly have built a hundred big Diesel-engined boats between 1912 and 1914, much less train personnel to man these hundred boats when ready.

The training of personnel for the submarine service is entirely another matter. Suffice it to say, that it was marked by caution verging almost upon timidity. The way in which Germany used her submarines in the very earliest stages of the war showed that she had little or no idea as to the immense power of the weapon lying in her hands.

[1] In October 1914, Weddigen tried to drive U 9—one of the 500-ton ' Desiderata ' boats—to the westward of the Orkneys. Faced with the Atlantic, U 9 pitched and rolled so excessively, that the attempt had to be given up. (Spiess, *Six Ans de Croisières en Sous-Marins*.)

APPENDIX III

Note

(a) The various German authorities (Michelsen, Schürer, Techel, Schwarthe, Weyer, etc.) do not agree as to whether certain submarines were 'building' or 'completed' at the end of the war. Hence, totals for submarines built and completing, given by these authorities, vary.

(b) Further, there is no accepted definition of a 'war loss.' Certain German lists only regard as 'war losses' those boats which were lost at sea on war cruises. Other lists include the boats blown up by the Germans at Flemish and Adriatic bases; also, boats interned, ceded to Austria-Hungary, etc. Because of the uncertainty as to (a) number of submarines actually completed, and (b) nature and total number of 'war losses,' the net strength of the German submarine force, November 1918, is also a variable quantity.

(c) The surface displacements of German submarines also vary somewhat, between list and list. Statistics for total tonnage-output, prepared from displacement figures given by one German authority, will therefore vary if compared with a list compiled from another German authority.

A

THE GERMAN SUBMARINE STRENGTH

ADMIRAL VON CAPELLE, giving evidence before the Reichstag 'War Failures' Committee, 1919, stated that the number of German submarines built, building, and projected up to November 1918 was 810. The series composing this total were 276 U-boats, 1 UA-boat, 249 UB-boats, 192 UC-boats, and 92 UF-boats. (Michelsen makes the total 811 by adding a U-cruiser, K 44, of which no details are known.)

The 810 submarines are accounted for as follows :—

	U.	UA.	UB.	UC.	UF.	Total.
Lost in the war	62	..	64	52	..	178
Surrendered	69	1	64	42	..	176
Scuttled	4	..	5	5	..	14
Ceded	..	..	5	..	..	5
Lost *en route* to surrender	3	..	1	3	..	7
Interned and *not* surrendered	..	..	..	2*	..	2
Broken up in Germany	4	..	4	..	..	8
BUILT	142	1	143	104	..	390†
BUILDING AND PROJECTED	59	..	59	48	41	207
PROJECTED	74	..	47	40	51	212
	275‡	1	249	192	92	809‡

* UC 8 acquired by Holland : UC 48 scuttled at Ferrol.
† Includes three U-, seven UB-, and nine UC-boats completed for surrender after 11.11.18.
‡ Excluding U 42 (which was never a German warship).

Losses according to Types

	U.	UB.	UC.	Total.
1914	5	..	..	5
1915	14	2	3	19
1916	7	8	7	22
1917	19	12	32	63
1918	17	42	10	69
	62	64	52	178

B

GERMAN SUBMARINE TYPES (MICHELSEN)

Peace
- 16 heavy-oil engine boats . . (U 3-18.)
- 26 Diesel boats . . . (U 19-41, 43-45.)
- 1 Fiat boat . . . . (U 42.)

War
- 1 acquired Norwegian boat . (UA.)
- 131 medium-size boats . (U 46-65, 81-116, 158-172, 201-212, 229-276.)
- 5 Austrian boats taken over . (U 66-70.)
- 10 large mine-layers . . (U 71-80.)
- 10 improved large mine-layers . (U 117-126.)
- 28 improved medium-size boats . (U 127-138, 213-228.)*
- 3 cruisers . . . . (U 139-141.)
- 37 improved cruisers . . (U 142-150, 173-200.)
- 7 ex-mercantile cruisers . . (U 151-157.)
- 1 UD-cruiser . . . (K 44.) †
- 17 UB I-boats . . . . (UB 1-17.)
- 30 UB II-boats . . . (UB 18-47.)
- 202 UB III-boats . . . (UB 48-249.)
- 15 UC I-boats . . . . (UC 1-15.)
- 64 UC II-boats . . . (UC 16-79.)
- 113 UC III-boats . . . (UC 80-192.)
- 92 UF single-hulled boats . . (UF 1-92.)

811 submarines.‡

* These boats appear to have been rated at one time as 'cruisers.' Gayer refers to them as the 'fast 1200-ton type.' Michelsen's description of them, as the 'improved medium-size' type, is the one now generally accepted.

† Nothing is known about this boat. Michelsen gives the bare mention of her, in his Table of Peace and War Construction, as set out above. Neither he nor any other German authority gives any technical details of K 44. It may be explained here that UA was an ex-Norwegian boat; the UB designs were for coastal and small ocean-going boats; the UC designs were for small mine-laying boats; the UD design was probably for an experimental cruiser-type boat provisionally numbered K 44. The UE design was for the improved large mine-layers of the U 117-126 class. The UF design was for a new type of single-hulled boat.

‡ This is Michelsen's total, but actually he only includes 809 boats in his Table. The remaining two boats are probably the old U 1 and U 2, which he has omitted to include, both under the category of 'heavy-oil engine boats' and in the total.

C

MONTHLY RATE OF COMMISSIONING (MICHELSEN)

	1914.	1915.	1916.	1917.	1918.	1919 (projected).
Jan.	..	2	3	6	3	20
Feb.	..	4	5	4	6	20
Mar.	..	7	9	4	8	20
Apr.	..	6	8	5	8	25
May	..	8	9	5	10	25
June	..	6	8	8	12	25
July	..	5	9	11	9	30
Aug.	3	2	10	12	8	30
Sept.	3	2	10	8	10	30
Oct.	1	2	11	13	11	..
Nov.	2	2	11	5	(16)	..
Dec.	2	6	15	6	(16)	..
	11	52	108	87	85	Total=343

N.B.—Compare with Official German Summary (Appendix G).

D

DISTRIBUTION OF GERMAN SUBMARINES (MICHELSEN).

10th of a Month	Total				Baltic				Constantinople				Adriatic				Flanders				North Sea				U-Cruisers			
	Total	At Works	In Dock	At Sea	Total	At Works	In Dock	At Sea	Total	At Works	In Dock	At Sea	Total	At Works	In Dock	At Sea	Total	At Works	In Dock	At Sea	Total	At Works	In Dock	At Sea	Total	At Works	In Dock	At Sea
1914																												
Aug.	20	4	16	—	2	—	2	—	—	—	—	—	—	—	—	—	—	—	—	—	18	4	14	—	—	—	—	—
Sept.	24	2	20	2	2	—	2	—	—	—	—	—	—	—	—	—	—	—	—	—	21	2	18	2	—	—	—	—
Oct.	27	5	14	8	6	—	3	3	—	—	—	—	—	—	—	—	—	—	—	—	21	5	11	5	—	—	—	—
Nov.	28	10	15	3	7	1	6	1	—	—	—	—	—	—	—	—	—	—	—	—	21	9	9	3	—	—	—	—
Dec.	28	9	15	4	7	2	4	1	—	—	—	—	—	—	—	—	—	—	—	—	21	7	11	3	—	—	—	—
1915																												
Jan.	27	11	12	4	7	6	—	1	—	—	—	—	—	—	—	—	—	—	—	—	20	5	12	3	—	—	—	—
Feb.	27	11	15	1	6	4	1	1	—	—	—	—	—	—	—	—	—	—	—	—	21	7	14	—	—	—	—	—
Mar.	27	15	6	6	5	3	2	—	—	—	—	—	—	—	—	—	—	—	—	—	22	12	4	6	—	—	—	—
Apr.	26	15	5	6	3	2	1	—	—	—	—	—	—	—	—	—	—	—	—	—	23	13	4	6	—	—	—	—
May	35	19	8	8	3	1	1	1	3*	—	3	—	—	—	—	—	—	—	—	—	25	11	7	7	—	—	—	—
June	40	15	15	10	2	1	—	1	4*	—	4	—	—	—	—	—	7	—	4	2	24	14	8	4	—	—	—	—
July	44	12	22	10	3	—	1	2	4*	—	4	—	—	—	—	—	10	1	5	4	20	12	4	4	—	—	—	—
Aug.	45	9	23	13	6	1	5	—	12*	—	2	5	—	—	—	—	13	—	7	3	15	8	7	5	—	—	—	—
Sept.	46	14	18	14	4	1	1	2	12*	5	3	2	—	—	—	—	15	—	10	5	11	8	2	1	—	—	—	—
Oct.	44	18	19	7	5	3	1	1	—	7	—	—	13*	5	5	3	16	1	13	2	9	3	5	1	—	—	—	—
Nov.	42	11	22	9	7	2	2	3	—	—	—	—	8	3	1	4	13	1	0	2	10	3	6	—	—	—	—	—
Dec.	44	12	24	8	7	1	6	—	5	2	3	—	—	—	—	—	14	2	8	4	10	4	6	—	—	—	—	—

* Mediterranean War Forces.

APPENDIX III

	1916	1917	1918
Jan.	41 14 23 4 4 — 3 — 4 1 3 — 8 5 — 3 14 — 13 — 11 7 4 — — — —	103 51 32 20 8 — — 1 3 — 2 — 25 20 — 5 22 1 18 3 45 21 12 12 — — — —	132 70 29 33 — — — — 4 2 1 — 33 28 — 5 30 4 19 7 59 35 8 16 6 1 — 4
Feb.	41 20 11 10 3 2 1 1 4 1 — 2 8 6 — 2 17 — 8 — 12 10 2 — — — — —	111 42 31 38 2 2 — — 3 1 — 1 24 17 1 5 33 2 22 5 49 20 6 23 — — — —	129 50 29 50 — — — 1 4 4 — 1 33 18 1 14 30 4 19 7 55 22 8 25 7 2 — 4
Mar.	47 16 20 11 4 2 2 2 4 — 3 — 8 5 1 3 17 1 12 — 14 8 3 3 — — — —	128 49 43 36 2 1 3 1 3 — 3 — 26 17 — 6 38 2 33 6 59 28 — 27 — — — —	127 72 18 37 — — — — 3 2 — — 33 24 1 9 29 4 17 6 55 42 — 13 7 1 — 6
Apr.	52 9 23 20 7 1 4 2 4 — 3 1 9 2 1 2 16 — 10 — 17 17 5 3 — — — —	127 45 40 42 3 1 3 1 3 — — 1 25 11 — 13 35 3 22 6 61 30 4 21 1 — — —	125 63 17 44 — — — — 3 3 — — 34 24 — 9 26 4 16 — 55 33 4 22 8 4 — 5
May	58 26 25 15 8 2 2 3 3 — — — 12 8 — 3 15 2 12 — 24 19 4 6 — — — —	130 63 28 61 8 1 2 4 3 1 — 1 26 12 1 5 33 2 16 1 58 40 — 18 1 — — 1	125 53 15 55 — — — — 3 — — — 34 18 — 6 25 2 14 — 55 28 1 27 9 5 — 4
June	65 32 18 28 9 3 5 2 3 1 — 1 13 9 — 3 16 1 9 1 27 19 5 7 — — — —	132 47 24 61 5 1 2 3 3 — — 1 27 19 1 8 37 7 19 1 60 28 5 27 2 1 — 1	112 61 17 36 — — — — 3 — 3 — 28 19 — 9 23 3 9 1 49 34 — 15 9 3 2 1
July	72 23 21 21 10 4 6 — 5 2 2 — 28 20 2 9 35 2 22 3 31 17 2 5 — — — —	130 60 28 42 5 — 2 — 3 — — — 29 20 — 9 35 4 19 1 57 30 5 20 4 1 — 1	121 59 17 45 — — — — 3 — 3 — 30 18 — 11 24 3 17 4 58 33 — 22 12 4 — 5
Aug.	74 23 27 17 10 3 3 4 3 2 3 2 27 19 1 6 35 2 22 — 37 17 — 3 — — — —	128 53 30 45 5 — 2 — 4 — 3 — 29 19 — 9 37 — 20 7 61 27 2 29 4 1 2 1	121 69 10 45 — — — 1 2 — 3 1 29 18 — 11 22 5 7 — 58 39 1 19 11 4 — 5
Sept.	80 26 36 29 10 3 2 — 5 4 2 3 32 18 — 9 37 — 17 2 38 23 2 8 — — — —	139 39 27 55 6 — 4 1 4 4 — — 29 20 1 7 35 1 20 5 55 24 2 31 2 — — 1	124 80 10 43 — — — 1 3 — 2 1 30 23 — 7 22 5 3 7 67 45 — 22 11 7 — 7
Nov.	87 39 25 17 10 5 5 2 4 1 — 1 14 7 1 6 20 — 16 — 38 23 2 9 — — — —	137 81 26 30 6 4 1 — 4 — — — 32 24 1 13 35 1 27 7 61 43 4 10 4 1 — —	
Dec.	93 29 29 29 10 7 — 5 2 3 — 5 17 10 2 7 24 2 16 3 38 23 6 14 — — — —		
Oct.	97 43 20 24 10 10 7 1 2 7 3 1 18 9 2 7 25 1 10 13 42 24 4 — — — — —	134 57 17 60 1 — 1 1 4 4 1 1 34 21 1 12 34 5 12 17 56 26 3 27 5 1 — 3	121 67 — 54 — — — — 3 — 1 2 28 18 — 10 13 5 — 8 67 37 — 30 10 6 — 4

356 THE GERMAN SUBMARINE WAR

E
DETAILS OF THE GERM.

U-boat.	Date of Order.	Date of Completion. (Month and Year.)	Displacement (tons).		Torpedo and Mine Equipment.			
			Surface.	Submerged.	Torpedoes.		Mines.	
					Above Water.	Below Water.	Number. Cm.	Laying Gears.
					Tubes.	*Tubes.*		
3-4	8.07	5-7.09	420	510	—	2B, 2S	6:45	—
5-12	4.08	7.10-8.11	500	620	—	2B, 2S	6:45	—
13-16	8.09	12.11-4.12	540	635	—	2B, 2S	6:45	—
17-18	5.10	11.12	560	690	—	2B, 2S	6:45	—
19-22	11.10	7.13-11.13	650	840	—	2B, 2S	9:50	—
23-26	3.11	9.13-5.14	670	860	—	2B, 2S	9:50	—
27-30	2.12	5.14-8.14	680	870	—	2B, 2S	10:50	—
31-41	6.12	9.14-2.15	680	870	—	2B, 2S	6:50	—
42	?	Not delivered	690	—	—	—	—	—
43-50	7.13-8.14	4.15-7.16	720	940	—	4B, 2S	6:50	—
51-56	8.14	2.16-6.16	720	902	—	2B, 2S	8:50	—
57-62	10.14	7.16-12.16	780	950	—	2B, 2S	7:50	—
63-65	3.15	3.16-5.16	810	930	—	2B, 2S	8:50	—
66-70	?	7.15-9.15	810	930	—	4B, 1S	12:45	—
71-80	1.15	10.15-6.16	750	830	1B, 1S	—	4:50	2S
81-86	6.15	8.16-12.16	810	950	—	2B, 2S	10:50	—
87-92	6.15	2.17-10.17	760	1000	—	4B, 2S	12:50	—
93-98	9.15	2.17-5.17	850	1000	—	4B, 2S	16:50	—
99-104	9.15	3.17-8.17	750	950	—	2B, 2S	12:50	—
105-114	5.16	7.17-6.18	800	1000	—	4B, 2S	16:50	—
115-116	9.16	Unfinished	880	1230	—	4B, 2S	13:50	—
117-121	5.16	3.18-8.18	1160	1510	—	4B	24:50	2S ⎫
122-126	5.16	5.18-10.18	1160	1470	—	4B	12-22:50	2S ⎭
127-130	5.16	Unfinished	1220	1650	—	4B	14:50	—
131-134	5.16	Unfinished	1160	1530	—	4B	14:50	—
135-138	5.16	6.18-8.18	1180	1530	—	4B	14:50	—
139-141	8.16	3.18-6.18	1930	2480	—	4B	19:50	—
142-150	11.16	Unfinished	2160	2770	—	4B	19:50	—
151-157	2.17	5.17-2.18	1510	1870	—	2B	18:50	—
158-159	2.17	Unfinished	810	1030	—	4B, 2S	14:50	—
160-172	2.17	5 boats by 5.18-10.18	820	1000	—	4B, 2S	14:50	—
173-200	6.17-12.17	⎫ Never came into service ⎭	2130	2780	—	4B, 2S	19:50	—
201-212	12.17		820	1000	—	4B, 2S	16:50	—
213-228	5.18-6.18		1380	1880	2*	4B, 2S	18:50	—
229-276	6.18		900	1210	—	4B, 2S	12-13:50	—

* Training bar discharge (*Schwenkbar*).   B—Bow tube.   S—Stern tu[be]

APPENDIX III

BMARINES (MICHELSEN)

	Endurance				Speed		Diving Period in secs.	Engines		Crew	
	Surface		Submerged		Surface, Knots.	Submerged, Knots.		Surface (H.P.)	Submerged (Electric)	Officers	Men
	Miles.	At Knots.	Miles.	At Knots.							
	3,000	9	55	4·5	11·5	9·5	60	2×200	2×505	3	19
	3,400	8·6	80	5	14·2	8·1	65	4×225	2×580	4	24
	1,920	14·8	90	5	15	10·7	40	2×350	2×550	4	24
or	1,210	13·5	75	5	15	9·5	70	2×250 4×350	2×550	4	24
	5,200	8	80	5	15·5	9·6	75	2×850	2×550	4	35
	5,020	8	85	5	16·8	10·3	84	2×900	2×550	4	35
	5,520	8	85	5	16·7	9·9	45	2×1000	2×550	4	35
	4,440	8	80	5	16·5	9·5	50	2×925	2×550	4	35
	1,500	18	24	8	18	10	30	2×1250			
	4,840	8	51	5	15·2	9·3	?	2×1000	2×550	4	35
·8	5,260	8	55	5	17	9·2	?	2×1100	2×550	4	35
·8	5,800	8	50	5	16·5	8·5	?	2×1100	2×550	4	35
	6,620	8	60	5	16·6	9·1	?	2×1100	2×550	4	35
	3,980	8	115	5	16	10·6	?	2×1150	2×630	4	35
	4,610	7	83	4	10·6	8	40	2×450	2×450	4	35
·8	7,630	8	56	5	16·8	9·1	?	2×1200	2×550	4	35
	7,660	8	56	5	15·6	8·6	45	2×1200	2×550	4	35
·8	3,800	8	50	5	16·8	8·6	45	2×1200	2×550	4	35
·8	4,080	8	45	5	16·5	8·2	45	2×1200	2×550	4	35
·8	3,900	8	50	5	16·4	8·5	45	2×1200	2×550	4	35
	5,860	8	35	4·5	16	8·5	30	2×1200	2×550	4	35
	6,080	8	60	4·5	14·7	7·1	30	2×1200	2×600	4	36
	5,520	8	60	4·5	14·7	7·1	30	2×1200	2×600	4	36
	2,780	8	50	4·5	18	8·5	30	2×1700	2×890	4	42
	2,780	8	50	4·5	18	8·5	30	2×1700	2×890 2 300KW*	4	42
	2,780	8	50	4·5	18	8·5	30	2×1700	2×890	4	42
	4,000	8	53	4·5	17·7	8·1	30	2×1750	1 300KW*	6	56
or	5,400	6	70	4·5	17·5	8·6	30	2×3000	2×1300 1 300KW*	1† 6	20 56
or	13,130	5·5	65	3	12·4	5·3	?	2×400	2×400	6 1†	50 19
	4,950	8	55	5	16	9	35	2×1200	2×550	4	35
	2,900	8	62	4·5	16·2	8·2	45	2×1200	2×550	4	35
	5,300	6	70	4·5	17·5	8·5	30	2×3000	2×1300 1 300KW*	6 1†	56 20
	2,900	8	60	4·5	16	9	30	2×1200	2×550	4	35
	?	?	90	4·5	18	9·5	30	2×1750	2×890 2 300KW*	4	42
	5,860	8	60	4·5	16·2	8·5	30	2×1450	2×550	4	35

* For recharging.   † Prize crew.

DETAILS OF THE GERM.

U-Boat.	Date of Order. (Month and Year.)	Date of Completion.	Displacement (tons).		Torpedo and Mine Equipment.			
			Surface.	Submerged.	Torpedoes.			Min(
					Above Water.	Below Water.	Number. Cm.	Minelaying Chutes.
UA	?	8.14	270	340	—	2B, 1S	5:45	–
UB 1-17	11.14	1.15-5.15	127	142	—	2B	2:45	–
UB 12	11.14	3.15	147	161	—	—	—	4
UB 18-47	4.15-7.15	11.15-8.16	260	290	—	2B	4:50	–
UB 48-71	5.16	6.17-11.17	510	650	—	4B, 1S	10:50	–
UB 72-87	9.16	9.17-12.17	520	650	—	4B, 1S	10:50	–
UB 88-132	2.17	12.17-7.18	510	640	—	4B, 1S	10:50	–
UB 133-141	6.17	Never came into service	530	660	—	4B, 1S	10:50	–
UB 142-169	6.17		530	660	—	4B, 2S	10:50	–
UB 170-205	12.17		540	670	—	4B, 2S	10:50	–
UB 206-249	6.18		550	670	—	4B, 2S	10:50	–
UC 1-15	11.14	4.15-7.15	168	183	—	—	—	6
UC 16-33	8.15	6.16-9.16	410	490	2B	1S	7:50	6
UC 34-48	11.15	9.16-11.16	420	500	2B	1S	7:50	6
UC 49-79	1.16	11.16-6.17	420	500	2B	1S	7:50	6
UC 80-118	6.17	7.18-10.18 (six boats)	480	560	2B	1S	7:50	6
UC 119-192	12.17	Never finished	510	580	2B	1S	7:50	5
UF 1-92	12.17-7.18		360	380		4S 1S*	7:50	–

B = Bow tube.   S = Stern tube.

* In the German text this is annotated as '*Abgangsrohr*,' which literally means going tube.' The purpose of this tube is unknown. It may possibly have pr ome means of escape for the crew. It may also have been a tube adaptal lternative use, either for the firing of torpedoes or for the sowing of mines.

APPENDIX III

JBMARINES (MICHELSEN)

	Endurance.				Speed.		Diving Period in secs.	Engines.		Crew.	
	Surface.		Submerged.		Surface, Knots.	Submerged, Knots.		Surface (H.P.).	Submerged (Electric).	Officers.	Crew.
s.	Miles.	At Knots.	Miles.	At Knots.							
	950	9·7	76	3·3	14·2	7·3	67	2 × 450	2 × 190	3	1
G.	1650	5	45	4	6·7	6	22	1 × 60	1 × 120	1	1
G.	1650	5	45	4	6·7	6	22	1 × 60	1 × 120	1	1
r	5700	6	45	4	9·2	5·8	32	2 × 140	2 × 140	2	2
or 5	4200	6	55	4	13·4	7·8	30	2 × 550	2 × 380	3	3
or 5	4000	6	50	4	13·4	7·7	30	2 × 550	2 × 380	3	3
or 5	3500	6	50	4	13·5	7·5	30	2 × 550	2 × 380	3	3
5	4240	6	50	4	12·5	7·5	30	2 × 550	2 × 380	3	3
5	3400	6	50	4	12·5	7·5	30	2 × 530	2 × 380	3	3
5	3700	6	50	4	12·5	7·5	30	2 × 530	2 × 380	3	3
5	3400	6	50	4	12·5	7·5	30	2 × 530	2 × 380	3	3
G.	850	5	50	4	8·4	5·5	23	1 × 90	1 × 175	1	1
	6910	7	55	4	11·5	6·9	40	2 × 250	2 × 230	3	2
	7100	7	55	4	11·7	6·9	40	2 × 250	2 × 230	3	2
	8000	7	59	4	12	7·2	33	2 × 300	2 × 310	3	2
5	8200	7	40	4·5	11·5	6·6	15	2 × 300	2 × 310	3	2
5	8200	7	40	4·5	11·5	6·6	30	2 × 400	2 × 310	3	2
	3500 (ca.)	—	64	4	11	7	15	2 × 300	2 × 300	2	2

F

SUBMARINE PROGRAMMES

	No. of Boats.
(a) Ordered before the war by Admiral von Tirpitz	45
(b) Ordered during Aug. 1914-Feb. 1916 by von Tirpitz	186
(c) Ordered during Feb. 1916-Dec. 1916 by von Capelle	86
(d) Ordered during 1917 by von Capelle	273
(e) Ordered during Jan. 1918-Sept. 1918 by von Capelle	220
	810

(a) Körting heavy-oil motors	U 1-18	
Diesel engines	U 19-45	
whose sizes increased from below 400 tons (surface) to 720 tons.		
		45
(b) Aug. 1914. Repeat order for five 720-ton boats	U 46-50	
Aug.-Oct. 1914. Repeat order for six 720-ton boats	U 51-56	
Oct. 1914 Six 780-ton boats	U 57-62	
Acquired boats—five 810-ton Austrian craft	U 66-70	
Acquired boat—one 270-ton Norwegian craft	UA	
Nov. 1914 Seventeen 127-ton coastal boats	UB 1-17 *	
Nov. 1914. Fifteen 168-ton mine-layers	UC 1-15	
Jan. 1915. Ten large mine-layers	U 71-80	
Mar. 1915. Three 810-ton boats	U 63-65 †	
Apr.-July 1915. Thirty improved coastal boats	UB 18-47	
June 1915. Twelve 760/810-ton boats	U 81-92	
Aug. 1915. Twelve 750/850-ton boats	U 93-104	
Aug. 1915. Eighteen improved small mine-layers (410 tons)	UC 16-33	
Nov. 1915. Fifteen additional improved small mine-layers (420 tons)	UC 34-48	
Jan. 1916. Thirty-one additional improved small mine-layers (420 tons)	UC 49-79	
		186
(c) May 1916. Twenty-two large boats, viz.—		
(i) ten 800-ton boats, and	U 105-114	
(ii) twelve improved medium-size 1200-ton boats	U 127-138	
	Carry forward,	22

* Schürer says fifteen of these boats were ordered in October 1914, and the other two in November 1914.

† Gayer gives U 63-65 among the boats ordered during August and September 1914.

APPENDIX III

			No. of Boats.
	Brought forward,		22
May 1916.	Ten large 1160-ton mine-layers	U 117-126	
May 1916.	Twenty-four improved coastal boats	UB 48-71	=37
Aug. 1916.	Three 1930-ton cruisers .	U 139-141	
Sept. 1916.	PLESS programme :—		
	Two 880-ton boats	U 115-116	
Sept. 1916.	Sixteen improved coastal boats	UB 72-87	
Nov. 1916.	Nine cruisers, 2160-ton boats	U 142-150 =	27
			86
(d) Feb. 1917.	Six 800-ton boats .	U 158-163	
Feb. 1917.	Forty-five 400-ton improved coastal boats .	UB 88-132	
Feb. 1917.	The intervention of America caused the acquisition of the *Deutschland* commercial boats, and three more ordered * .	U 151-157	
June 1917.	Nine 800-ton boats	U 164-172	
June 1917.	Ten 2000-ton cruisers .	U 173-182	
June 1917.	Thirty-seven improved coastal boats .	UB 133-169	
June 1917.	Thirty-nine improved mine-layers	UC 80-118	
June-Dec. 1917.	Eighteen 1200-ton cruisers	U 183-200	
Dec. 1917.	Twelve 820-ton improved medium-size boats .	U 201-212	
Dec. 1917.	Thirty-six 540-ton coastal boats	UB 170-205	
Dec. 1917.	Thirty-four 510-ton mine-layers	UC 119-152	
Dec. 1917.	Twenty 360-ton single-hull boats	UF 1-20	
			273
(e) May-June 1918.	Sixteen 1380-ton improved medium-size boats .	U 213-228	
June 1918.	Forty-eight 900-ton boats .	U 229-276	
June 1918.	Forty-four improved coastal boats .	UB 206-249	
1918.	Forty 510-ton mine-layers .	UC 153-192	
Jan.-July 1918.	Seventy-two 360-ton single-hull boats .	UF 21-92	
			220
	Total .	. .	810

Remarks :

May 1916 programme—U 127-134, 137, 138 were never completed.

* *High Sea Fleet* (Scheer), p. 335.

May 1916 programme—U 121 finished after Armistice.
Sept. 1916   do.   —U 115-116 never completed.
Nov. 1916   do.   —U 142-150 never completed. U 142 had just run trials, but was broken up in Germany.
Feb. 1917   do.   —U 158-159 never completed.
June 1917   do.   —U 165, 168-172 never completed, but U 166-167 were finished after the Armistice.
June 1917 programme—UB 133, 136, 144, 145, 150, 154, 155 were completed after the Armistice; remainder never completed.
—UC 106-114 completed for surrender; UC 115-118 never completed.

Later programmes—None completed.

The boats ordered in Feb. 1917 (begun in the summer and completed in summer 1918) were surrendered, as also were the ex-mercantile boats.

Of the boats ordered in June 1917 (begun in summer), a few were completed in Nov. 1918, and surrendered 80 per cent. complete.

The boats ordered in Dec. 1917 and in 1918 were never completed.

To show how the programmes became in arrears, the UC 80-89 should have been finished before 1918, but were completed after the Armistice.

It is interesting to observe that Lord Jellicoe (*The Crisis of the Naval War*, page 48) compares the building times of British and German yards. The Germans took longer to build heavy ships, but German destroyers were built in little over 12 months, compared with 24 months in British yards. British submarines were completed in two years normally; and, although during 1916 and 1917 this time was reduced to a little over 18 months, it is certain that the original UB- and UC-boats were turned out within 5 months, and the improved classes in about 10 months. The 'Medium-size' or 'Mittel' U-boats took about 18 months to build. U-cruisers ordered during 1916 were still unfinished 24 months later (Nov. 1918).

Conclusions

1. Arrears began to develop towards the autumn of 1916.
2. These arrears appear due to the diversion of dockyard and shipyard labour and materials from submarine construction to the repairing of the High Sea Fleet after the Jutland battle. So much is admitted by Scheer.
3. These arrears were further accentuated by the Pless decision to build U-cruisers, which (as it later proved) took far more time to complete than the 'Mittel' U-boats, and were twice as intricate to build.
4. Consequently, the 1917 anti-shipping war was affected.
5. These arrears were never overtaken. They became worse

APPENDIX III

towards the end of the War, when over 200 boats (part of the Dec. 1917 and 1918 programmes) had not even been laid down.

6. The calling-in of the smaller Stinnes yards for the building of the UF class is evidence of the congestion at the larger building-yards.
7. The expected increase of the 1919 output, which Gayer emphasized, is questionable. By the end of 1919 (according to Scheer) it was hoped to turn out 30 boats monthly.*
8. About Aug.-Sept. 1918, the German Admiralty's demand for the release of workmen from the Army to speed up the work in the shipyards and to increase the production of submarines was met. This would no doubt have resulted in an intensified effort to sharpen the submarine campaign. The loss of valuable submarine *personnel* was, however, a serious factor. The veteran crews of the older U-boats had to be broken up so that the complements of the new submarines might at least contain a few ratings with first-hand experience of cruising under war conditions.

G
AN OFFICIAL GERMAN SUMMARY (1920) OF SUBMARINE TOTALS

No. of S/m.	In service on.	Built.	Lost.	Gain/ Loss.	In service on	No. of S/m.
28	4.8.14	+ 3	−5	−2	31.12.14	26
26	1.1.15	+62	−20	+42	31.12.15	68
68	1.1.16	+95	−25	+70	31.12.16	138
138	1.1.17	+103	−72	+31	31.12.17	169
169	1.1.18	+81	−81	±0	11.11.18	169
		+344	−203	+141		

Note.—December losses were probably not known until January.

   344 built : This figure agrees with Schwarthe, *Die Technik im Weltkrieg*, but Schürer gives 345 by counting U 121 as completed, which boat was, however, only finished after the Armistice.
   203 lost : 178 War loss ; 14 scuttled ; 6 interned ; 4 ceded to Austria ; 1 ceded to Bulgaria.

   * Michelsen (p. 132) says that by October 1918 the rate of delivery was 13 boats per month (*cf.* Appendix C), but it was hoped that the output would thereafter be accelerated thus :—By April 1919, 22 boats per month ; by August, 33 ; by December, 37 boats per month. For the first few months of 1920, deliveries were to be at the rate of 33 boats per month.

FINAL SUMMARY

A. BY CONSTRUCTION (Pre-War and War Building Programmes)

- 28 boats built before War (14,625 tons displacement).
- 344 boats built during War (including U 42, building at Spezia, 198,330 tons displacement).
- 226 boats building Nov. 1918.
- 212 boats projected.

810

B. BY DESTRUCTION (Losses, Cessions, Surrenders, Demolitions, and Building Programmes not carried out in full)

- 178 lost in War.
- 14 scuttled.
- 5 ceded to Austria and Bulgaria.
- 1 internee purchased by Holland.
- 1 internee scuttled before surrender.
- 7 foundered *en route* to surrender.
- 176 surrendered to Allies (including 18 finished for delivery).
- 8 old craft broken up in Germany.
- 208 incomplete boats broken up on stocks or dismantled.
- 212 projected.

810

H

GERMAN SUBMARINE CONSTRUCTION, ETC.

TOTAL TONNAGE OUTPUT OF GERMAN SUBMARINES

(By calendar years. From Schwarthe's *Die Technik im Weltkrieg*)

COMPLETED

	Number of Boats.	Tonnage.
August 1914	28	15,204
Aug.-Dec. 31, 1914	3	1,618
1915	62	26,418
1916	95	47,390
1917	103	65,528
Jan.-Nov. 1918	81	52,888
Total	372	209,046

Total construction during war period, Aug. 1914-Nov. 1918, was 344 boats, totalling 193,842 tons.

APPENDIX III

Completion of Boats by 'War Years'

ACTUAL OUTPUT

From 1st Aug. 1914 to 1st Aug. 1915	19 boats, totalling 16,075 tons.
From 1st Aug. 1915 to 1st Aug. 1916	65 ,, ,, 32,959 ,,
From 1st Aug. 1916 to 1st Aug. 1917	101 ,, ,, 56,453 ,,
From 1st Aug. 1917 to 1st Aug. 1918	99 ,, ,, 68,671 ,,

ESTIMATED OUTPUT

From 1st Aug. 1918 to 1st Aug. 1919	167 boats totalling 121,061 tons.

Output of German Shipbuilding Yards

(Arranged in descending order. From *The Engineer*, April 21, 1922. By November 11, 1918)

Firm.	Boats built.	Boats building.	Total.
Vulkan, Hamburg	89	37	126
Krupp-Germania, Kiel	79	28	107
Blohm & Voss, Hamburg	67	39	106
A. G. Weser, Bremen	74	27	101
Imperial Dockyard, Danzig	32	32	64
Bremer-Vulkan, Vegesack	4	20	24
Smaller yards	..	41	41
Totals	345	224	569

Note.—Out of the 28 submarines completed before outbreak of war, 10 were built by Krupps and 18 by the Imperial Dockyard, Danzig. If these boats be included—

(a) Krupps built 89 boats and had 28 building : total—117.
(b) Imperial Dockyard, Danzig, built 50 boats and had 32 building : total—82.
(c) Total for boats built becomes 373.
(d) Total for boats built+building becomes 597.

I (a)

MONTHLY ANALYSIS OF LOSSES

Month.	1914.	1915.	1916.	1917.	1918.	Total.	Average.
Jan.	..	2	..	2	9	13	3·25
Feb.	..	..	..	4	4	8	2
Mar.	..	3	2	3	4	12	3
Apr.	..	1	4	2	7	14	3·5
May	..	1	2	6	14	23	5·75
June	..	2	..	4	3	9	2·25
July	..	3	4	5	6	18	4·5
Aug.	2	3	1	4	7	17	3·4
Sept.	..	2	1	10	9	22	4·4
Oct.	..	1	..	7	5	13	2·6
Nov.	1	1	4	9	1	16	3·2
Dec.	2	..	4	7	..	13	3·25
Total	5	19	22	63	69	178	3·42
Monthly average	1	1·59	1·83	5·17	6·4	3·42	

Maximum months : May 1918, September 1917.
Heaviest losses : May, September.
Lightest losses : February, June, October.
22 months were above the average of 3·42.

The above analysis is based on the German Naval Staff Report, 1922, but has been corrected to embody information subsequently received.

I (b)

LOSSES RECOUPED BY SALVAGE

In 1919, Captain Persius, an outspoken critic of his country's conduct of the naval war, declared that, in the later stages of hostilities, the training of new *personnel* for service in submarines was so hastily and inefficiently carried out that several boats foundered with their entire crews. He cited the accidental losses of UB 79, 84, 106, and of a UC-boat whose number he did not record. It is also said that UB 114 was lost whilst she was running her trials. The four UB-boats here enumerated were all surrendered after the war, so if they were accidentally lost they must have been salved. Other accident losses alluded to are : U 30 (p. 46), UC 76 (p. 179), U 52 (p. 210, footnote 2) : these three boats were also recovered by salvage.

APPENDIX III

(1) Area

Area	North Sea.	Channel.	Dover Area.	S.W. Waters.	East Coast.	Scottish Waters.	North of Ireland.	Atlantic.	Flanders Area.	Bight.	Norwegian Waters.	Danish Waters.	Mediterranean.	Black Sea.	Adriatic Sea.	Baltic Sea.	Arctic Ocean.	Total.
1914	—	—	—	—	—	2	—	—	2	1	—	—	—	—	—	—	—	5
1915	1	1	1	2	4	6	—	—	—	1	1	—	1	1	—	1	—	19
1916	1	2	1	2	3	1	—	—	2	1	—	1	—	4	2	1	1	22
1917	5	12	8	9	11	2	1	2	5	—	1	2	1	—	1	1	2	63
1918	7	9	13	6	9	3	5	1	2	1	—	2	9	—	2	—	—	69
	14	24	23	19	27	14	6	3	11	4	2	5	11	5	5	3	3	178

NOTE.—It is only possible to hazard a guess as to the totals, for the destruction of a submarine sometimes involved the simultaneous use of several methods. Many boats were sunk by gunfire after being forced to the surface by depth-charges.

(2) Cause

CAUSE OF DESTRUCTION.	Mine.	Depth-charge.	Submarine (Torpedo).	Gunfire.	Ramming.	Decoys.	Aircraft.	Mine-nets, Nets, etc.	H.E. Sweeps.	Accident.	Captured.	Wrecked.	Unknown.	Total.
1914	3	—	—	—	2	—	—	—	—	—	—	—	—	5
1915	3	—	3	2	4	3	—	—	1	1	—	—	2	19
1916	6	2	2	3	—	2	—	2	2	—	1	1	1	22
1917	14	12	8	5	3	5	6	3	1	2	—	—	4	63
1918	18	24	6	6	5	2	—	1	1	1	—	—	5	69
	44	38	19	16	14	12	6	6	5	4	1	1	12	178

Alternative analyses can show :—

21 by decoy means (Q. boats 11, decoy P boats 3, disguised fishing-vessels 3, Q convoy-sloops 2, submarine with trawler 2).
17 in submarine duels.
9 by aircraft (bombed 6, airship with patrols 2, seaplane with patrol 1).
65 by patrols (rammed 6, gunfire 11, depth-charge 28, explosive sweeps 4, nets and d.c. 6, rammed and d.c. 2, rammed and

K

(a) Lost in War: 178			(b) Surrendered: 176		
Serial Numbers:—			Serial Numbers:—		
U-	UB-	UC-	U-	UB-	UC-
5	3	1	3	6†	17
6	4	2	9	14	20
7	7	3	19	21	22
8	12	5	22	23†	23
10	13	6	24	24	27
11	16	7	25	25	28
12	17	9	30	28	31
13	18	10	33	34	37
14	19	11	35	42	45
15	20	12	38	49	52
18	22	13	39†	50	56†
20	26	14	43	51	58
23	27	15	46	60	59
26	29	16	52	62	60
27	30	18	53	64	67
28	31	19	54	67	73
29	32	21	55	73	74
31	33	24	57	76	76
32	35	26	60	77	90
34	36	29	62	79	92
36	37	30	63	80	93
37	38	32	67	84	94
40	39	33	70	86	95
41	41	35	71	87	96
44	44	36	79	88	97
45	45	38	80	91	98
48	46	39	82	92	99
49	52	41	86	93	100
50	53	42	90	94	101
51	54	43	91	95	102
56	55	44	94	96	103
58	56	46	96	97	104
59	57	47	98	98	105
61	58	49	100	99	106*
64	61	50	101	100	107*
66	63	51	105	101	108*
68	65	55	107	102	109*
69	66	57	108	105	110*
74	68	61	111	106	111*
(Continued on left side of next page.)			(Continued on right side of next page.)		

* Completed after Armistice for surrender.   † Interned.

APPENDIX III

Lost in War (contd.) Serial Numbers:—			Surrendered (contd.) Serial Numbers:—		
U-	UB-	UC-	U-	UB-	UC-
75	69	62	112	111	112*
76	70	63	113	112	113*
77	71	64	114	114	114*
78	72	65	117	117	..
81	74	66	118	118	..
83	75	68	119	120	..
84	78	69	120	121	..
85	81	70	121*	122	..
87	82	72	122	125	..
88	83	75	123	126	..
89	85	77	124	128	..
92	90	78	125	130	..
93	103	79	126	131	..
95	104	..	135	132	..
99	107	..	136	133*	..
102	108	..	139	136*	..
103	109	..	140	142	..
104	110	..	141	143	..
106	113	..	151	144*	..
109	115	..	152	145*	..
110	116	..	153	148	..
154	119	..	155	149	..
156	123	..	157	150*	..
..	124	..	160	154*	..
..	127	..	161	155*	..
			162	..	..
			163	..	..
			164	..	..
			166*	..	..
			167*	..	..
			UA		

SCUTTLED : 14

U-	UB-	UC-
47	10	4
65	40	25
72	48	34
73	59	53
..	129	54

FOUNDERED EN ROUTE TO SURRENDER : 7
U 16, 21, 97
UB 89
UC 40, 71, 91

INTERNEES, NOT SURRENDERED : 2
UC 8, 48.

CEDED CRAFT : 5
UB 1, 15, 43, 47—to Austria.
UB 8—to Bulgaria.

BROKEN UP IN GERMANY : 8
U 1, 2, 4, 17
UB 2, 5, 9, 11

* Completed after Armistice for surrender.

L

GERMAN SUBMARINE LOSSES : 178
(Chronologically arranged.)

1914.		CAUSE.	LOCALITY.
August 9	.	U 15 (K/L R. Pohle).* Rammed by *Birmingham*.	Off Fair Island.
,, 12	.	U 13 (K/L Graf A. von Schweinitz).* Mined.	Off Heligoland.
November 23		U 18 (K/L von Hennig).† Rammed by trawler.	Off Scapa Flow.
December	.	U 5 (K/L J. Lemmer).* Mined.	Off Zeebrugge.
,,	.	U 11 (K/L F. von Suchodoletz).* Mined.	Off Zeebrugge.
1915.			
January	.	U 31 (O/L Wachendorff).* Mined ?	Off East Coast.
,, 21		U 7 (K/L G. König).† Torpedoed by U 22.	North Sea.
March 4	.	U 8 (K/L A. Stoch).† Explosive sweeps.	Dover Straits.
,, 10	.	U 12 (K/L Kratzsch).* Rammed by *Ariel*.	Off Fife Ness.
,, 18		U 29 (K/L O. Weddigen).* Rammed by *Dreadnought*.	Off Pentland Firth
April	.	U 37 (K/L E. Wilcke).* Missing ?	Channel.
May	.	UB 3 (O/L S. Schmidt).* Missing ?	Aegean Sea.
June 5	.	U 14 (O/L M. Hammerle).* Rammed by trawler.	Off Peterhead.
,, 23	.	U 40 (K/L G. Fürbringer).† Torpedoed by C 24.	Off Aberdeen.
July 2	.	UC 2 (O/L K. Mey).* Run down by s.s. *Cottingham*.	Off Yarmouth.
,, 20	.	U 23 (O/L H. Schulthess).† Torpedoed by C 27.	Off Fair Island.
,, 24	.	U 36 (K/L E. Gräff).† Gunfire of Q-boat *Prince Charles*.	Off Hebrides.
August 15	.	UB 4 (O/L C. Gross).* Gunfire of trawler.	Off Yarmouth.
,, 19	.	U 27 (K/L B. Wegener).* Gunfire of Q.-boat *Baralong*.	Off Scillies.
Aug./Sept.	.	U 26 (K/L von Berckheim).* Mined ?	Baltic.

NOTE.—K/K denotes Korvetten-Kapitän.
K/L denotes Kapitän-Leutnant.
O/L denotes Ober-Leutnant zur See.
* denotes killed or died after capture.
† denotes captured.

APPENDIX III

1915.		CAUSE.	LOCALITY.
Sept. 15	.	U 6 (K/L R. Lepsius).* Torpedoed by E 16.	Off Stavanger.
,, 24	.	U 41 (K/L K. Hansen).* Gunfire of Q-boat *Baralong*.	Off Scillies.
October	.	UC 9 (O/L P. Schürmann).* Blown up by own mines ?	E. of Longsands L.V.
November 6		UC 8 stranded. (Acquired by Holland.)	Off Terschelling.
,, 29		UC 13 (O/L Kirchner). Stranded and destroyed by Russian t.b.d.	In Black Sea.
1916.			
March 16	.	UC 12 (O/L E. Fröhner).* Blown up by own mines.	Off Taranto.
,, 22	.	U 68 (K/L L. Güntzel).* Gunfire of Q-boat *Farnborough*.	S.W. of Ireland.
April 5	.	UB 26 (O/L W. Smiths).† Netted by Allied patrols.	Off Havre.
,, 23	.	UC 3 (O/L G. Kreysern).* Mine-nets of smack *Cheero*.	Off Norfolk.
,, 24	.	UB 13 (O/L A. Metz).* Bombed by drifter.	Off Walcheren.
,, 27	.	UC 5 (O/L Mohrbutter).† Stranded and captured.	Off Harwich.
May 27	.	U 74 (K/L E. Weisbach).* Gunfire of trawler.	Off Aberdeen.
June	.	U 10 (K/L F. Stuhr).* Mined ?	Baltic.
July 5	.	U 77 (K/L E. Günzel).* Missing ?	North Sea.
,, 6	.	UC 7 (O/L G. Haag).* Depth-charge of motor-boat *Salmon*.	Off Lowestoft.
,, 14	.	U 51 (K/L W. Rumpel).* Torpedoed by H 5.	Estuary of Ems.
,, 30	.	UB 44 (O/L F. Wäger).* Netted and depth-charged.	Otranto Straits.
August 21	.	UC 10 (O/L W. Albrecht).* Torpedoed by E 54.	Off Schouwen Bank.
Sept./Oct.	.	UB 7 (O/L H. Lütjohann).* Mined .	Black Sea.
November 2		U 56 (K/L H. Lorenz).* Gunfire of Russian patrols.	Off Lapland.
,, 4		U 20 (K/L W. Schwieger). Stranded.	Off Jutland.
,, 6		UB 45 (K/L K. Palis).* Mined .	Black Sea.
,, 30		UB 19 (O/L E. Noodt).† Gunfire of Q-boat *Penshurst*.	Channel.
Nov./Dec.	.	UC 15 (O/L B. Heller).* Mined .	Off Sulina.
December 4		UC 19 (O/L A. Nitzsche).* Depth-charge of *Llewellyn*.	Dover Straits
,, 6		UB 29 (O/L E. Platsch).* Explosive sweeps of *Ariel*.	S. of Ireland.
,, 7		UB 46 (K/L C. Bauer).* Mined .	Bosphorus.
1917.			
January 14		UB 37 (O/L P. Günther).* Gunfire of Q-boat *Penshurst*.	Channel.
,, 26		U 76 (K/L W. Bender). Gunfire of Russian trawlers.	Arctic Sea.

THE GERMAN SUBMARINE WAR

1917.		CAUSE.	LOCALITY.
February	8	UC 39 (O/L O. Ehrentraut).* Gunfire of *Thrasher*.	Off Flamboro' Hd.
,,	8	UC 46 (O/L F. Moecke).* Rammed by *Liberty*.	Dover Straits.
,,	17	U 83 (K/L B. Hoppe).* Gunfire of Q-boat *Farnborough*.	S.W. of Ireland.
,,	23	UC 32 (O/L H. Breyer).† Blown up by own mines.	Off Sunderland.
Feb./Mar.		UC 18 (O/L W. Kiel).* Missing?	Channel.
March 10	.	UC 43 (K/L E. Sebelin).* Torpedoed by G 13.	Off Muckle Flugga.
,, 12	.	U 85 (K/L W. Petz).* Gunfire of Q-boat *Privet*.	Western Channel.
,, 13	.	UB 6. Stranded and interned.	Hellevoetsluis.
April 5	.	UC 68 (O/L H. Degetau).* Torpedoed by C 7.	Schouwen Bank.
,, 19	.	UC 30 (O/L H. Stenzler)*. Mined.	North Sea.
May 1	.	U 81 (K/L R. Weisbach).† Torpedoed by E 54.	Off Valentia Island.
,, 9	.	UC 26 (O/L Graf von Schmettow).* Rammed and d.c. by destroyers.	Thames Estuary.
,, 14	.	U 59 (K/L von Firks).* Mined.	Horns Reef.
,, 17	.	UB 39 (O/L H. Küstner).* Gunfire of Q-boat *Glen*.	Off Isle of Wight.
,, 20	.	UC 36 (K/L G. Buch).* Bombed by seaplane 8663.	Off W. Hinder L.V.
,, 24	.	UC 24 (K/L K. Willich).* Torpedoed by French s/m *Circe*.	Off Cattaro.
June 7	.	UC 29 (K/L E. Rosenow).* Gunfire of Q-boat *Pargust*.	South of Ireland.
,, 12	.	UC 66 (O/L S. Pustkuchen).* Depth-charge of trawlers.	Off Lizard.
,, 20	.	U 99 (K/L M. Eltester).* Gunfire of s.s. *Valeria*.	Atlantic.
,, 24	.	UB 36 (O/L von Keyserlinck).* Missing?	Channel.
July 12	.	U 69 (K/L E. Wilhelms).* Probably depth-charge by *Patriot*.	In North Sea.
,, 24	.	UC 1 (O/L Mildenstein).* Bombed by seaplanes.	Near Sunk L.V.
,, 26	.	UC 61 (K/L G. Gerth).† Stranded and blown up.	Cape Grisnez.
,, 29	.	UB 20 (O/L H. Glimpf).* Bombed by seaplanes.	Off Flanders.
,, 29	.	UB 27 (O/L von Stein).* Rammed and d.c. by *Halcyon*.	Off Harwich.
,, 30	.	UB 23. Damaged and interned.	Corunna.
August 4	.	UC 44 (K/L Tebbenjohanns).† Blown up by own mines.	Off Waterford.
,, 12	.	U 44 (K/L P. Wagenführ).* Rammed by *Oracle*.	South of Bergen.
,, 18	.	UB 32 (O/L B. von Ditfurth).* Bombed by seaplane.	Off Cape Barfleur.

APPENDIX III

1917.		CAUSE.	LOCALITY.
August 21	.	UC 41 (O/L H. Foerste).* Depth-charged by trawlers.	Firth of Tay.
Sept. 2	.	U 28 (K/L G. Schmidt).* Lost in sinking munition-ship.	White Sea.
,, 7	.	U 88 (K/L W. Schwieger).* Mined.	Off Denmark.
,, 10	.	UC 42 (O/L H. Müller).* Blown up by own mines.	Off Cork.
,, 11	.	U 49 (K/L R. Hartmann).* Gunfire of s.s. *British Transport*.	Atlantic.
,, 12	.	U 45 (K/L R. Sittenfeld).* Torpedoed by D 7.	North of Ireland.
,, 22	.	UC 72 (O/L E. Voigt).* Bombed by seaplanes.	Near Sunk L.V.
,, 26	.	UC 33 (O/L A. Arnold).† Gunfire and rammed by PC 61.	Off Waterford.
,, 27	.	UC 21 (O/L von Zerboni di Sposetti).* Mine-nets.	North Foreland.
,, 28	.	UC 6 (O/L G. Reichenbach).* Bombed by seaplane.	Near Sunk L.V.
,, 29	.	UC 55 (O/L Ruhle von Lilienstern).* Gunfire and d.c. of destroyers.	Off Lerwick.
,, October 1/11	.	U 50 (K/L G. Berger).* U 66 (K/L G. Muhle).* } Mined in combined operations by t.b.d., s/m, net drifters.	Near Dogger Bank.
,, 3		UC 14 (O/L der Res. Feddersen).* Mined.	Off Zeebrugge.
,, 5	.	UB 41 (O/L M. Ploen).* Explosion.	Off Scarborough.
,, 9	.	U 106 (K/L H. Hufnagel) * Mined.	Entrance to Heligoland Bight.
,, 19	.	UC 62 (O/L M. Schmitz).* Torpedoed by E 45.	East of Lowestoft.
,, 23	.	UC 16 (O/L G. Reimarus).* Explosive sweeps of *Melampus*.	Channel.
November 1		UC 63 (O/L von Heydebreck).* Torpedoed by E 52.	Dover Straits.
,, 3		UC 65 (K/L K. Lafrenz).† Torpedoed by C 15.	Channel.
,, 13		UC 51 (O/L H. Galster).* Sunk (?) by *Firedrake*.	Off Lowestoft.
, 17		UB 18 (O/L G. Niemeyer).* Mined.	Start Point.
,, 17		U 58 (K/L G. Amberger).† Depth-charge by U.S. destroyers.	Queenstown.
, 18		UC 47 (O/L Wigankow).* Rammed and d.c. by P 57.	Off Flamboro' Head.
,, 19/22		UC 57 (K/L F. Wissman).* Missing?	Baltic.
,, 24		U 48 (K/L C. Edeling).* Stranded and shelled.	Goodwin Sands.
,, 29		UB 61 (O/L T. Schultz).* Mined.	Off Terschelling.
December 2		UB 81 (O/L Salzwedel).* Mined.	Off Isle of Wight.
,, 6		UC 69 (O/L H. Thielmann). Accidentally rammed by U 96.	Cape Barfleur.

1917.		CAUSE.	LOCALITY.
December	10	UB 75 (O/L F. Walther).* Mine-nets	Off Flamboro' Head.
,,	13	U 75 (K/L Schmolling). Mine-nets	Off Terschelling.
,,	14	UC 38 (O/L H. Wendlandt).† Depth-charge of French t.b.d.	Ionian Sea.
,,	19	UB 56 (O/L H. Valentiner).* Mined.	Dover Barrage.
,,	25	U 87 (K/L von Speth-Schülzburg).* Rammed and d.c. by *Buttercup* and PC 56.	Off Bardsey Island.
1918.			
January	7	U 93 (K/L H. Gerlach).* Sunk by s.s. *Braeneil*.	Off Lizard.
,,	9	UB 69 (O/L A. Klatt).* Explosive sweeps of *Cyclamen*.	Cape Bon (Med.).
,,	18	UB 66 (K/L F. Wernicke).* Depth-charge of *Campanula*.	Cape Bon (Med.).
,,	19	UB 22 (O/L K. Wacker).* Mined	Heligoland Bight.
,,	26	U 84 (K/L W. Röhr).* Rammed by PC 62.	St. George's Channel.
,,	26	U 109 (K/L O. Rey).* Gunfire of drifter.	Dover Straits.
,,	26	UB 35 (O/L K. Stöter).* Depth-charge of *Leven*.	Dover Straits.
,,	28	UB 63 (O/L R. Gebeschus).* Depth-charge of trawlers.	Firth of Forth.
,,		U 95 (K/L A. Prinz).* Missing ?	Western waters.
February	4	UC 50 (K/L R. Seuffer).* Depth-charge of *Zubian*.	Channel.
,,	8	UB 38 (O/L G. Bachmann).* Mined.	Dover Barrage.
,,	12	U 89 (K/L W. Bauck).* Rammed by *Roxburgh*.	North of Ireland.
,,	25	UB 17 (O/L A. Branscheid).* Depth-charge of *Onslow*.	Channel.
March	10	UB 58 (O/L W. Löwe).* Mined	Dover Barrage.
,,	11	UB 54 (O/L E. Hecht).* Depth-charged by destroyers.	Off Lincolnshire.
,,	15	U 110 (K/K K. Kroll).* Depth-charged by destroyers.	North of Ireland.
,,	24	UC 48. Damaged and interned	Corunna.
,,	26	U 61 (K/L V. Dieckmann).* Depth-charged by PC 51.	St. George's Channel.
April	11	UB 33 (O/L F. Gregor).* Mined	Dover Barrage.
,,	17	UB 82 (K/L W. Becker).* Gunfire and d.c. of drifters.	North of Ireland.
,,	21	UB 71 (K/L K. Schapler).* Depth-charge of ML 413.	Str. of Gibraltar.
,,	22	UB 55 (O/L Wenninger).† Mined	Dover Barrage.
,,		UC 79 (O/L A. Krameyer).* Mined.	Dover Barrage.
,,	25	U 104 (K/L K. Bernis).* Gunfire of *Jessamine*.	South of Ireland.
,,	30	UB 85 (K/L Krech).† Gunfire of drifter.	North Channel.
May	2	UB 31 (O/L der Res. W. Braun).* Depth-charge of drifters.	Dover Straits.

APPENDIX III 375

1918.		CAUSE.	LOCALITY.
May 2	.	UC 78 (K/L H. Kukat).* Depth-charge of drifters.	Dover Straits.
,, 8	.	UB 70 (K/L J. Remy).* Depth-charge of convoy escort.	Mediterranean.
,, 8	.	U 32 (K/L K. Albrecht).* Gunfire of *Wallflower*.	Mediterranean.
,, 9	.	UB 78 (O/L A. Stossberg).* Rammed by s.s. *Queen Alexandra*.	Channel.
,, 10	.	UB 16 (O/L von der Lühe).† Torpedoed by E 34.	Off Essex.
,, 11	.	U 154 (K/K H. Gercke).* Torpedoed by E 35.	Off C. St. Vincent.
,, 12	.	UB 72 (O/L F. Träger).* Torpedoed by D 4.	Channel.
,, 12	.	U 103 (K/L C. Rücker).† Rammed by s.s. *Olympic*.	Channel.
,, 16	.	UC 35 (O/L H. P. Korsch).* Gunfire of French patrol *Ailly*.	Sardinia.
,, 18	.	U 39. Damaged by seaplanes and interned.	Cartagena.
,, 23	.	UB 52 (O/L Launburg).† Torpedoed by H 4.	Otranto Straits.
,, 24	.	UC 56 (K/L der Res. Kiesewetter). Damaged and interned.	Santander.
,, 26	.	UB 74 (O/L E. Steindorff).* Depth-charge of yacht *Lorna*.	Portland.
,, 31	.	UC 75 (O/L W. Schmitz).† Rammed and gunfire of *Fairy*.	Off Yorkshire.
,,	.	UB 119 (O/L W. Kolbe).* Missing ?	North Sea.
June 17	.	U 64 (K/L R. Moraht).† Gunfire of convoy escort.	Mediterranean.
,, 20	.	UC 64 (O/L F. Schwartz).* Mined .	Dover Barrage.
,, 26	.	UC 11 (O/L K. Utke).† Mined .	East of Harwich.
July 10	.	UC 77 (O/L J. Ries).* Depth-charge of trawlers.	Dover Straits.
,, 10	.	UB 65 (K/L M. Schelle).* Blown up in fight with L 2.	Off Cape Clear.
,, 19	.	UB 124 (O/L Wutsdorff).† Depth-charge of destroyers.	North Channel.
,, 19	.	UB 110 (K/L W. Fürbringer).† Depth-charge of t.b.d. and ML.	Off Durham Coast.
,, 27	.	UB 107 (K/L von Prittwitz und Gaffron).* Depth-charge of trawlers.	Off Scarborough.
,,	.	UB 108 (K/L W. Amberger).* Missing?	Channel.
August 3	.	UB 53 (K/L Sprenger).† Mine-nets .	Otranto Straits.
,, 8	.	UC 49 (O/L H. Kükenthal).* Depth-charge of t.b.d. and ML's.	Off Torbay.
,, 13	.	UB 30 (O/L R. Stier).* Rammed and depth-charge of trawler.	Off Whitby.
,, 14	.	UB 57 (O/L J. Losz).* Mined .	Off Zeebrugge.
,, 28	.	UC 70 (O/L K. Dobberstein).* Depth-charge of *Ouse*, with seaplane.	Off Whitby.
,,	.	UB 12 (O/L E. Schoeller).* Mined .	Off Heligoland.

1918.		CAUSE.	LOCALITY.
August 29	.	UB 109 (K/L Ramien).† Mined	Dover Barrage.
Sept. 9	.	U 92 (K/L G. Ehrlich).* Mined	Northern Barrage.
,, 10	.	UB 83 (O/L H. Buntebardt).* Depth-charge of *Ophelia*.	Pentland Skerries.
,, 16	.	UB 103 (K/L P. Hundius).* Depth-charge of drifters.	Dover Straits.
,, 19	.	UB 104 (O/L T. Bieber).* Mined	Northern Barrage.
,, 25	.	U 156 (K/L R. Feldt).* Mined	Northern Barrage.
,,	.	U 102 (K/L K. Beitzen).* Mined	Northern Barrage.
,,	.	UB 127 (O/L W. Scheffler).* Mined	Northern Barrage.
,, 29	.	UB 115 (O/L R. Thomsen).* Depth-charge of t.b.d. and trawlers.	Off N.E. coast.
Sept./Oct.	.	UB 113 (O/L U. Pilzeder).* Missing ?	Channel.
October 4	.	UB 68 (O/L Dönitz).† Scuttled after gunfire of convoy escort.	Malta.
,, 16	.	UB 90 (O/L G. von Mayer).* Torpedoed by L 12.	In Skagerrak.
,, 19	.	UB 123 (O/L R. Kamm).* Mined	Northern Barrage.
,, 28	.	U 78 (O/L J. Bolbrecht).* Torpedoed by G 2.	Off Horns Reef.
,, 28	.	UB 116 (O/L H. J. Emsmann).* Mined	Off Scapa Flow.
November 9		U 34 (K/L J. Klasing).* Gunfire and depth-charge of Q-boat *Privet* and ML's.	Off Gibraltar.

SCUTTLED CRAFT : 14

Oct.	1, 1918	UB 10	Blown up on evacuation of Flanders.			Bruges.
,,	2, ,,	UB 40	,,	,,	,,	,,
,,	,, ,,	UB 59	,,	,,	,,	,,
,,	,, ,,	UC 4	,,	,,	,,	,,
,,	28, ,,	U 47	Blown up on evacuation of Adriatic.			Pola.
,,	,, ,,	U 65	,,	,,	,,	,,
,,	,, ,,	UB 48	,,	,,	,,	,,
,,	,, ,,	UC 25	,,	,,	,,	,,
,,	,, ,,	UC 53	,,	,,	,,	,,
,,	,, ,,	UC 54	,,	,,	,,	Trieste.
,,	30, ,,	U 73	,,	,,	,,	Pola.
,,	,, ,,	UC 34	,,	,,	,,	,,
,,	31, ,,	UB 129	,,	,,	,,	Fiume.
Nov.	1, ,,	U 72	,,	,,	,,	Cattaro.

INTERNED CRAFT : 6. (Included in War Loss List, but not included in total losses.)

Nov.	6, 1915	UC 8	Holland	.	Acquired and became M 1.
Mar.	13, 1917	UB 6	,,	.	Surrendered to Allies, 25.2.19.
July	30, ,,	UB 23	Ferrol	.	Surrendered to Allies, 1919.
Mar.	24, 1918	UC 48	,,	.	Scuttled prior to delivery to Allies, 14.3.19.
May	18, ,,	U 39	Cartagena		Surrendered to Allies, 17.5.19.
,,	24, ,,	UC 56	Santander		Surrendered to Allies, 1919.

APPENDIX III

REFUGEE CRAFT IN NOVEMBER 1918 : 8

Nov. -, 1918, U 35 arrived at Barcelona. ⎫ Mediterranean fugitives.
,, 2, ,, UC 74 arrived at Barcelona. ⎭
,, 11, ,, U 157 arrived at Trondjhem. ⎫ Took refuge during Revolution.
,, 13, ,, U 124 arrived at Karlskrona. ⎭
,, 26, ,, UB 14, UB 42, UC 23, UC 37.   Surrendered at Sevastopol.

Of the above interned and refugee boats, all except UC 8 and UC 48 were surrendered.

POST-ARMISTICE LOSSES : 7

Nov. 21, 1918 U 97 foundered *en route* to surrender, in North Sea.
Feb. 10, 1919 UC 91   ,,   ,,   ,,   ,,
,,   20 ,,   UC 71   ,,   ,,   ,,   off Heligoland.
,,   21 ,,   UC 40   ,,   ,,   ,,   ?
,,   22 ,,   U 16   ,,   ,,   ,,   in River Elbe.
,,   22 ,,   U 21   ,,   ,,   ,,   in North Sea.
,,   ,,   UB 89   ,,   ,,   ,,   ?

SURRENDERED, NOVEMBER 1918–MAY 1919 : 176. (Those in heavy figures retained.)

Partition of boats :—

France (46) : U 25, 38, 39, 57, 71, **79, 105, 108**, 113, 118, **119**, 121, 136, **139**, 151, 157, 160, **162, 166**. UA. UB 6, 14, 23, 24, 73, 84, **94, 99**, 114, 121, 126, 130, 142, 154, **155**. UC 22, **23**, 27, 28, 56, 58, 74, 100, 103, 104, 107.
Italy (10) : U 54, 114, 120, 163. UB 80, 95, 102. UC 93, 94, 98.
Japan (7) : U **46, 55, 125**. UB **125, 143**. UC **90, 99** (temporarily retained).
U.S.A. (6) : U 111, 117, 140. UB 88, 148. UC 97.
Belgium (2) : U 91, 112.*
Britain (105) : U 3, 9, 19, 22, 24, 30, 33, 35, 43, 52, 53, 60, 62, 63, 67, 70, 80, 82, 86, 90, 94, 96, 98, 100, 101, 107, 122, 123, 124, 126, 135, 141, 152, 153, 155, 161, 164, 167. UB 21, 25, 28, 34, 42, 49, 50, 51, 60, 62, 64, 67, 76, 77, 79, 86, 87, 91, 92, 93, 96, 97, 98, 100, 101, 105, 106, 111, 112, 117, 118, 120, 122, 128, 131, 132, 133, 136, 144, 145, 149, 150. UC 17, 20, 31, 37, 45, 52, 59, 60, 67, 73, 76, 92, 95, 96, 101, 102, 105, 106, 108, 109, 110, 111, 112, 113, 114.

All the above were broken up or used as targets, except as above stated.

* Re-assigned to Belgium after surrender to Britain.

M

A LIST OF GERMAN SUBMARINE 'ACES' (MICHELSEN)

(N.S. = North Sea.)

	Cruises.	Tonnage Sunk.
K/L Lothar von Arnauld de la Perière (U 35, U 139)	10 (Med.)	400,000
,, Walther Forstmann (U 12, U 39)	16 (N.S., Med.)	380,000
,, Max Valentiner (U 38, U 157)	17 (N.S., Med.)	300,000
,, Hans Rose (U 53)	12 (N.S.)	210,000
,, Otto Steinbrinck (UB 10, UB 18, UB 57, UC 65)	24 (Flanders)	210,000
,, Kophamel (U 35, U 151, U 140)	10 (N.S., Med.)	190,000
,, Walther Schwieger (U 20, U 88)	12 (North Sea)	190,000
,, Hans von Mellenthin (UB 43, UB 49)	11 (Med.)	170,000
,, Rücker (U 34, U 103)	14 (N.S., Med.)	170,000
,, Wünsche (U 25, U 70, U 97)	12 (North Sea)	160,000
O/L Salzwedel (UB 10, UB 81, UC 21, UC 71)	12 (Flanders)	150,000
,, Steinbauer (UB 47, UB 48)	10 (Med.)	140,000
K/L Gansser (U 33, U 156)	8 (N.S., Med.)	140,000
,, Robert Moraht (U 64)	9 (N.S., Med.)	130,000
,, Wilhelm Werner (U 55)	10 (North Sea)	130,000
,, Leo Hillebrand (U 16, U 46)	12 (North Sea)	130,000
,, Otto Schultze (U 63)	6 (North Sea)	130,000
,, Rudolf Schneider (U 24, U 87)	10 (North Sea)	130,000
,, Ernst Hashagen (UB 21, U 62)	8 (North Sea)	130,000
,, Hartwig (U 32, U 63)	10 (Med.)	130,000

Under 100,000 tons :—

O/L Marschall (UC 74, UB 105)	Mediterranean.
K/L Ritter von Georg (U 57, U 101)	North Sea.
,, Jetz (U 79, U 96, U 90)	North Sea.
,, Raimund Weisbach (U 19, U 81)	North Sea.
,, Wassner (UB 38, U 59, U 117, UC 69)	North Sea.
,, Gerhard Berger (U 50)	North Sea.
,, Alfred von Glasenapp	North Sea.
,, Dieckmann (U 61)	North Sea.
,, Wilhelms (U 69)	North Sea.
O/L Howaldt	Flanders.
K/L Ramien (UB 109)	Flanders.
,, Siess (U 73)	Mediterranean.
,, Hersing (U 21)	Mediterranean.
,, Karl Schuster	?
,, Jürst (U 43)	North Sea.
O/L Viebeg	Flanders.
K/L Johannes Klasing (U 34)	Mediterranean.
O/L Losz (UB 57)	Flanders.
K/L Adam (U 52)	**North Sea.**

APPENDIX III 379

O/L Bieber (UB 104) . . . . North Sea.
K/L Richard Hartmann (U 49) . . . . . North Sea.
„ Ernst Krafft . . . .
O/L Pustkuchen (UB 29, UC 66) . . . . . Flanders.
„ Karl Neumann (UC 67) . . . . . . Mediterranean.
„ Hans Valentiner (UB 56) . . . . . Flanders.

NOTE.—The totals of tonnage sunk are from German estimates, and must be regarded with reserve.

The following Commanders were listed as war criminals by Great Britain :—

K/L Kiesewetter (UC 56) for sinking the hospital-ship *Glenart Castle*, 26.2.18.
K/L Patzig (U 86) for sinking the hospital-ship *Llandovery Castle*, 27.5.18.
K/L Max Valentiner (U 38) for sinking without warning the *Glenby*, 17.8.15 ; and the *Persia*, 30.12.15.
K/L Werner (U 55) for sinking without warning the *Clearfield*, Oct. 1916 ; the *Artist*, 27.1.17 ; the *Trevone*, 31.1.17 ; the *Torrington*, 8.4.17 ; and the hospital-ships *Rewa*, 4.1.18, and the *Guildford Castle*, 10.3.18.
K/L Jetz (U 96, U 90) for sinking without warning the *Apapa*, 28.11.17 ; the *Destro*, 25.3.18 ; the *Inkosi*, 28.3.18.
K/L Adam (U 82) for sinking the *Galway Castle*, 12.9.18.
K/L Aust for sinking the *Golden Hope*, 9.6.17.
K/L Bothmer (U 66) for sinking the *Mariston*, 15.7.17.
K/L Droescher (U 20) for sinking the *Ikaria* and *Tokomaru*, 30.1.15.
K/L Gansser (U 33, U 156) for sinking the *Clan Macleod*, 1.12.15 ; the *Belle of France*, 1.2.16 ; the *W. C. M'Kay*, ?.1.18 ; the *Artesia*, 8.2.18.
K/L Georg (U 57, U 101) for sinking the *Refugio*, 12.5.17 ; the *Arlington Court*, 14.5.17 (attacked); the *Jersey City*, 24.5.17 ; the *Teal*, 1.6.17 ; the *Richard de Larrinaga*, 8.10.17 ; the *Glenford*, 20.3.18 ; the *Trinidad*, 22.3.18 ; the *John G. Walter*, 24.3.18 ; the *Lough Fisher*, 30.3.18.
K/L Glasenapp for sinking the *Haileybury*, 22.2.18 ; the *Birchleaf*, 23.2.18 ; the *Landonia*, 21.4.18 ; the *Baron Herries*, 22.4.18 ; the *Ethel*, 26.4.18.
K/L Nostitz und Jaenkendorf (U 151) for sinking the *Dvinsk*, 18.6.18.
K/L Kolbe (U 152) for sinking the *Clan Murray*, 29.5.17 ; the *Fernley*, 30.5.17 (attacked) ; the *Ellaston*, 16.3.18 ; the *Elsie Birdett*, ?.4.18.
O/L Neumann (UC 67) for sinking the hospital-ship *Dover Castle*, 26.5.17.
K/L Rücker (U 103) for sinking the *Victoria*, ?.?.17.
K/L von Schrader (UB 64) for sinking the *Dartmoor*, 27.5.17.
K/L Wassner (UB 38 or UC 69) for sinking the *Addah*, 15.6.17.

Italy placed the name of Arnauld de la Perière on the list for sinking the Italian ships *Siena*, *Dores*, and *Lilla*.
Neumann was tried at Leipzig on June 4, 1921, and acquitted on the ground that he obeyed superior orders.
Patzig escaped to Danzig prior to his trial in July 1921. Lieutenants Boldt and Dittmar each received four years' imprisonment.

N

(The following analyses are extracted from Michelsen.)

THE SHIPPING LOSSES CAUSED BY GERMAN WARSHIPS

I. WHITE PAPER LIST

Period by Campaigns.	Number of Ships over 100 British Reg. Tonnage.	Gross Tonnage.
Aug. 1914–Sept. 30, 1915	431	791,705
Oct. 1, 1915–Apr. 30, 1916	359	898,794
June 1, 1916–Jan. 31, 1917	1152	2,099,523
Feb. 1, 1917–Dec. 31, 1917	2566	5,753,751
Jan. 1, 1918–Nov. 2, 1918	1046	2,648,223
	5554	12,191,996

Notice large total sunk in period prior to Unrestricted Campaign.

II. LLOYD'S REGISTER OF SHIPPING

Year.	Number of Ships over 100 British Reg. Tonnage.	Gross Tonnage.
1914	162	372,277
1915	726	1,438,173
1916	1187	2,328,688
1917	2734	6,350,362
1918	1052	2,744,172
	5861	13,233,672

NOTE.—The excess of 307 ships of 1,041,676 tons (gross) in this estimate is due to the inclusion of shipping sunk by the ocean raiders, aircraft, destroyers, and more particularly the mercantile tonnage commissioned by the naval authorities as auxiliary cruisers, etc. Notice large 1916 total.

III. AN ESTIMATE (MINIMUM) OF U-BOAT SINKINGS

	Number of Ships.	Tons Capacity.
North Sea	2364	5,154,605
Flanders	1590	2,054,249
Mediterranean	1409	3,286,462
Baltic	19	11,626
?	326	511,923
	6520*	12,243,090*

* Totals here shown are incorrect. They should read 5708 ships of 11,018,865 tons capacity.

APPENDIX III

AN ESTIMATED ANALYSIS OF NATIONALITY TONNAGE SUNK BY TORPEDO AND MINE

	U.K.	U.S.A.	Denmark.	Holland.	France.	Italy.	Japan.	Norway.	Russia.	Spain.	Sweden.	Europe.	S. America.	Others.
1914	3	(No	min	es	were	laid	by	sub	mari	ne	in 19	14.)		
1915	417	5	16	12	37	14	3	65	23	2	28	55	1	1
1916	467	5	52	26	119	142	5	192	25	20	52	41	1	1
1917	1227	70	113	53	235	178	16	413	61	26	56	133	14	3
1918	560	49	31	12	85	66	4	95	18	28	29	59	3	1
	2744	129	212	93	476	400	27	765	137	76	165	288	19	6

The above figures are not accurate, because mines were laid during 1915-1917 by the *Meteor*, *Möwe*, *Wolf*, on the high seas. This analysis is made by the authors.

O

SHIPPING LOSSES CAUSED BY CRUISERS, SUBMARINES, AND MINES (FAYLE)

1914.	British.	World.	1916.	British.	World.
Aug.	40,200	62,700	Jan.	62,200	81,200
Sept.	88,200	98,300	Feb.	75,800	117,500
Oct.	77,800	87,900	Mar.	99,000	167,000
Nov.	8,800	19,400	Apr.	141,100	191,600
Dec.	26,000	44,100	May	64,500	129,100
1915.			June	36,900	108,800
Jan.	32,000	47,900	July	82,400	118,200
Feb.	36,300	59,900	Aug.	43,300	162,700
Mar.	71,400	80,700	Sept.	104,500	230,400
Apr.	22,400	55,700	Oct.	176,200	353,600
May	84,300	120,000	Nov.	168,800	311,500
June	83,100	131,400	Dec.	182,200	355,100
July	52,800	109,600	1917.		
Aug.	148,400	185,800	Jan.	153,600	368,500
Sept.	101,600	151,800	Feb.	313,400	540,000
Oct.	54,100	88,500	Mar.	353,400	593,800
Nov.	94,400	153,000	Apr.	545,200	881,000
Dec.	74,400	123,100	May	352,200	596,600

SHIPPING LOSSES CAUSED BY CRUISERS, SUBMARINES, AND MINES (FAYLE)—*(continued)*

1917.	British.	World.
June	417,800	687,500
July	364,800	557,900
Aug.	329,800	511,700
Sept.	196,200	351,700
Oct.	276,100	458,500
Nov.	173,500	289,200
Dec.	253,000	399,100
1918.		
Jan.	179,900	356,600
Feb.	226,800	318,900
Mar.	199,400	342,500
Apr.	215,500	278,700
May	192,400	295,500
June	162,900	255,500
July	165,400	260,900
Aug.	145,700	283,800
Sept.	136,800	187,800
Oct.	59,200	118,500
Nov.	10,100	17,600

Total of British Shipping Sunk.

By submarine	6,692,000 tons
By mine	682,000 tons
By cruisers, etc.	448,000 tons
By aircraft	7,900 tons
	7,829,900 tons

Damaged by submarines	7,335,800 tons
Damaged by mine	432,400 tons
Damaged by aircraft	89,200 tons
Damaged by cruisers, etc.	150,500 tons
	7,807,900
Interned in hostile ports	184,000 tons

World Losses (registered tonnage).

United Kingdom	9,055,000 tons
Norway	1,172,000 ,,
Italy	862,000 ,,
France	807,000 ,,
United States	531,000 ,,
Greece	415,000 ,,
Japan	270,000 ,,
Sweden	264,000 ,,
Denmark	245,000 ,,
Spain	238,000 ,,
Holland	229,000 ,,
Belgium	105,000 ,,
Brazil	31,000 ,,

APPENDIX IV

P

SUBMARINES OF THE LATE AUSTRO-HUNGARIAN NAVY

I. Technical Details

(a) The following List is based upon a Report, specially prepared for this book, by the ' Kriegsarchiv ' (Official War Records Office of Vienna, dated the 14th August 1930, and entitled ' Daten über Unterseeboote der ehem. k. und k. Kriegsmarine.'

(b) Double numbers are given below for each boat. The Roman numerals were used up to (and after) the outbreak of war, but were not used for the later boats. This system of identification has, however, been used throughout this book, for the purpose of distinguishing the Austro-Hungarian submarines from the German. In the latter stages of the war, all Austro-Hungarian submarines were identified by the German method, i.e. by the letter ' U ' followed by Arabic numerals. Numeration by this method is also shown below.

(c) The ' Kriegsarchiv ' information regarding the launching dates and dimensions of the boats built before the outbreak of war is open to question.

(d) Under ' Size ' and ' Machinery,' where two groups of figures occur divided by a stroke, the first set of figures relate to conditions when in surface-running trim ; the second group to conditions when submerged. Tons (displacement and fuel) are in *metric* tons.

(e) The ' Comments ' are remarks, appended by the Authors, amplifying or correcting statements in the ' Kriegsarchiv ' Report. The ' Commissioning Dates ' have been extracted from a Report furnished by courtesy of the Directorate of the *Rivista Marittima*, Rome.

Number.	Where built.	Year of launch.
I (U 1)	Pola Dockyard	1911
II (U 2)		1910

SIZE :—230/270 tons. Dimensions : 27·9 × 3·63 × 3·03 metres (about 97' 6" × 11' 9" × 10' 3").

MACHINERY :—Two sets of Diesels (320 B.H.P. each) ; two electric motors (100 H.P. each). Speeds 11/7·5 knots. Radius of action 1200/35 miles. Fuel 10·8 tons.

ARMAMENT :—Three 17·7" (45 cm.) torpedo tubes (2 bow, 1 stern). Three torpedoes carried (five could be carried, if need arose).

(COMMENTS :—Authorised 1906. Built to plans by the Lake Torpedo Boat Co., Bridgeport, U.S.A. These boats reported to have been re-engined about 1912, but the 'Diesels' referred to above are questionable; heavy-oil engines are more likely. Complement 14.)

Number.	Where built.	Date of launch.
III (U 3) **IV (U 4)**	Krupps' Germania Yard, Kiel	1909

SIZE :—240/300 tons. Dimensions : $27 \cdot 9 \times 3 \cdot 75 \times 3 \cdot 03$ metres (about 97' 5" × 12' 3" × 10' 0").

MACHINERY :—Two sets, Körting heavy-oil engines (300 B.H.P. each); two electric motors (170 H.P. each). Speeds 12/8·75 knots. Radius of action 1200/45·5 miles. Fuel 25·24 tons.

ARMAMENT :—Two bow 17·7" (45 cm.) torpedo tubes. Three torpedoes carried.

(COMMENTS :—Authorised 1906 and ordered Oct. 1907. Were improvements on Krupps' design for U 1 of the German Navy. Complement 17. **U 3** a war loss.)

Number.	Where built.	Date of launch.
V (U 5) **VI (U 6)**	Whitehead & Co., Fiume	1910

SIZE :—235/273 tons. Dimensions $27 \cdot 9 \times 3 \cdot 15 \times 3 \cdot 03$ metres (about 97' 6" × 10' 6" × 10' 0").

MACHINERY :—Two sets, petrol engines (250 B.H.P. each); two electric motors (115 H.P. each). Speeds 10·75/8·5 knots. Radius of action 800/48 miles. Fuel 13 tons.

ARMAMENT :—One 1-pdr. (37 mm.) Q.F. gun (not mounted in **VI/U 6**) and two bow 17·7" (45 cm.) torpedo tubes. Four torpedoes carried.

(COMMENTS :—Authorised 1906 and built by Whitehead's under licence from the Electric Boat Co., U.S.A. Complement 14. **VI/U 6** a war loss. For another boat, **XII/U 12**, listed by the 'Kriegsarchiv' with the above two, see below.

Five submarines were authorised 1911-12, and ordered, as **VII-XI**, from Krupps' Germania Yard, Kiel. After the outbreak of war they were taken over for the German Navy and became the German U 66-70.

A boat of about 700/1070 tons was authorised in 1912, to be numbered **XII,** but was never laid down.

Number.	Where built.	Date of launch.
XII (U 12)	Whitehead & Co., Fiume	1910

All details for Size, Machinery, and Armament as **V (U 5)** and **VI (U 6)** above, but this boat had two sets of petrol engines (300 B.H.P. each). Also one 1-pdr. Q.F. gun as in **V/U 5.**

(COMMENTS :—The history of this boat is rather obscure, but is

APPENDIX IV

believed to have been as follows. She was ordered and built as **VII**, being of the same size and armament as **V** and **VI** above, but was to have been propelled, above and below water, by electric motors. **VII**, however, did not come up to expectation on trials, and was not accepted for the Navy. She became the private property of the Whitehead Co., and was used as an experimental and demonstration boat by that firm. Either before or after the outset of the war she was rebuilt with petrol motors for surface-running. She was requisitioned for the Navy on the outbreak of hostilities; was allotted the number **XII**, and became a war loss during 1915.)

Number.	Where built.	Date of launch.
X (U 10) : XI (U 11) : **XV (U 15) : XVI (U 16) :** **XVII (U 17).**	Weser Co., Bremen	1915

SIZE :—127/141 tons. Dimensions $27 \cdot 9 \times 3 \cdot 15 \times 3 \cdot 03$ metres (about 97' 6" × 10' 6" × 10' 0").

MACHINERY :—One heavy-oil engine (60 B.H.P.); one electric motor (120 H.P.). Speeds 6·6/5 knots. Radius of action 1400/65 miles. Fuel 3·2 tons.

ARMAMENT :—1-8 mm. M.G. and two bow 17·7" (45 cm.) torpedo tubes. Two torpedoes carried.

(COMMENTS :—Boats of the German 'UB I' type. Two of these —probably **XI** and **X**—were the German UB 1 and UB 15, ceded by Germany to Austria-Hungary. UB 1 was built by Krupps' Germania Yard; the other four by Weser Co. Each boat was sent overland in three sections, on railway trucks. The boats were despatched from the German shipyards during 1915 as follows : **X,** June ; **XI,** May ; **XV** and **XVI,** Sept. ; **XVII,** Oct. Assembled at Pola Dockyard and launched, ready for sea, fourteen days after arrival. Complement 14. **XVI** was a war loss.)

XIV (U 14) . . Captured ex-French submarine *Curie*.

SIZE :—407/554 tons. Dimensions $52 \cdot 15 \times 5 \cdot 42 \times 3 \cdot 2$ metres (about 171' 1" × 17' 9" × 10' 6").

MACHINERY :—Two sets, Diesels (430 B.H.P. each); two electric motors (330 H.P. each). Speeds 12·2/8·2 knots. Radius of action 1200/115 miles. Fuel 38 tons.

ARMAMENT :—One small Q.F. gun (calibre not stated); one bow 17·7" (45 cm.) torpedo tube; and six external discharge gears. Eight torpedoes carried.

(COMMENTS :— Launched at Toulon Dockyard, July 1912, and completed 1913. Attempted to penetrate Pola Harbour, Dec. 1914, but was completely netted and had to surrender. Recommissioned March 1915 as the Austro-Hungarian **XIV**. Recovered by the French on the cessation of hostilities.)

Number.	Where built.	Date of launch.
U 20 (XX) : U 22 (XXII)	Pola Dockyard	1916
U 21 (XXI) : U 23 (XXIII)	'Ubag'	

SIZE :—173/210 tons. Dimensions 38·76 × 3·64 × 3·61 metres (about 127' 2" × 11' 11" × 11' 10").

MACHINERY :—One Diesel (450 B.H.P.) ; one electric motor (160 H.P.). Speeds 12/8 knots. Radius of action 1700/71 miles. Fuel 10 tons.

ARMAMENT :—One 8 mm. M.G. ; two 17·7" (45 cm.) bow torpedo tubes. Four torpedoes carried.

(COMMENTS :—Whitehead-type boats. The reference to 'Ubag' is obscure. It can only be suggested that this word embodies the initial letters of some firm's title, e.g. ' U-Boots Aktien Gesellschaft ' (The Submarine Building Co.). If any such firm existed, the centre of its submarine-building activities is unknown to us. The 'Diesel' referred to above was more probably a heavy-oil engine. Commissioning dates : **U 20/XX** and **U 21/XXI**, Aug. 1916 ; **U 23/XXIII**, Oct. 1916 ; **U 22/XXII**, Jan. 1917. **U 20** and **U 22** lost during the war.

Number.	Where built.	Date of launch.
U 27 (XXVII) : U 28 (XXVIII)	Cantiere Navale	
U 40 (XL)		1916
U 29 (XXIX) : U 30 (XXX) :	Gänz & Co., Danubius	
U 31 (XXXI) : U 32 (XXXII)	Yard, Fiume.	

SIZE :—268/306 tons. Dimensions 36·125 × 4·37 × 3·665 m. (about 118' 6" × 14' 3" × 11' 11½").

MACHINERY :—Two Diesels (150 B.H.P. each); two electric motors (140 H.P. each). Speeds 9/5 knots. Radius of action 6600/130 miles. Fuel 20 tons.

ARMAMENT :—One 4-pdr. (5-cm.) Q.F. gun ; one 8-mm. M.G. ; two bow torpedo tubes (size not stated). Four torpedoes carried.

(COMMENTS :—Boats of the German ' UB II ' type. The ' Cantiere Navale ' referred to above was probably the Cantiere Navale Triestino, at Monfalcone, near Fiume. Gänz & Co. built their boats under licence from (and with the help of) Krupps' Germania Yard, Kiel. The ' Diesel engines ' mentioned above are doubtful ; all the German boats of this type had heavy-oil engines. These boats were probably armed with German 50-cm. (19·7") tubes and torpedoes. Commissioning dates : **U 27 /XVII**, Nov. 1916 ; **U 28/ XXVIII**, —— 1916 ; **U 29/XXIX**, Nov. 1916 ; **U 30/XXX**, Jan. 1917 ; **U 31/XXXI**, March 1917 ; **U 32/XXXII**, April 1917 ; **U 40/ XL**, May 1917. Complement 23. **U 30** lost during the war.)

Number.	Where built.	Date of launch.
U 41 (XLI)	Cantiere Navale	1918

SIZE :—Displacements and dimensions as **U 27-32** and **U 40** above.

APPENDIX IV

MACHINERY :—Two heavy-oil engines (150 B.H.P. each); two electric motors (60 H.P. each). Speeds 9·35/5·1 knots. Radius of action 8000/127 miles. Fuel 30·5 tons.
ARMAMENT :—Not reported.
(COMMENTS :—Apparently a modification of the German ' UB II ' type. May have been armed as **U 27-32** and **U 40** above, or may have been a small mine-laying boat (on the lines of the adapted German UB 12) carrying about eight mines. Commissioning date reported as May 1917, but this is unlikely if the 1918 launching date given above is correct.)

Number.	Where built.	
U 43 (XLIII) **U 47 (XLVII)**	Weser Co., Bremen	(Purchased from Germany, 1917.)

SIZE :—272/306 tons. Dimensions 36·9 × 4·37 × 3·665 metres (about 121' 0" × 14' 3" × 11' 11½").
MACHINERY :—Two heavy-oil engines (150 B.H.P. each); two electric motors (140 H.P. each). Speeds 9/5·1 knots. Radius of action 6600/130 miles. Fuel 27 tons.
ARMAMENT :—Not reported.
(COMMENTS :—German UB II-type boats. These two originally belonged to the German group UB 42-47, which was sent overland in sections, assembled and launched at Pola Dockyard. The German UB 43 and UB 47 were transferred to the Austro-Hungarian Navy about Aug. 1917, whereupon the letter ' B ' was dropped from their numbers. The armament was probably the same as that in the other German boats of this type, *viz.* one 3·4" (8·8 cm.) gun, one M.G., two bow 19·7" (50 cm.) torpedo tubes. Four torpedoes carried. Complement 23.)

Numbers.	Condition (1st Oct. 1918).
U 48 (XLVIII) : U 49 (XLIX) : U 50 (L) : **U 51 (LI) : U 53 (LIII).** **U 101 (CI) : U 102 (CII) : U 103 (CIII) :** **U 104 (CIV) : U 105 (CV) : U 106 (CVI)**	Building on cessation of hostilities. No details given.
U 54 (LIV) : U 55 (LV) : U 56 (LVI) : **U 57 (LVII) : U 58 (LVIII) : U 59 (LIX).**	Ordered but never begun. No details given.

(COMMENTS :—From Dr. Techel's *Der Bau von den Unterseebooten auf der Germaniawerft*, it appears that—

(a) some of the above boats (at least two) were to have been of the German ' Mittel-U ' type (about 800 to 850 tons surface displacement); and
(b) other boats (at least two) were to have been of the German ' UB III ' type (about 510 to 530 tons surface displacement).

For these boats, licences, plans, technical advice, etc., were supplied by Krupps to Gänz & Co., Danubius Yard, near Fiume.

The Diesel engines were to have been built, partly by Krupps and partly at the Budapest works of the Gänz Co.)

II. Summary of Austro-Hungarian Submarine Totals

No. of submarines.	In service on	Built or added.	Lost.	Gain or Loss.	In service on	No. of Submarines.
6	4.8.14	+1	±0	+1	31.12.14	7
7	1.1.15	+6	−2	+4	31.12.15	11
11	1.1.16	+4	−2	+2	31.12.16	13
13	1.1.17	+7	−1	+6	31.12.17	19
19	1.1.18	+1	−2	−1	1.10.18	18

III. Losses (7)

1915.   CAUSE.   LOCALITY.

Aug. 8 — **XII** (E. Lerch). Mined. — Gulf of Venice.

" 13 — **III** (K. Strnad). Bombed by French destroyer *Bisson*. — Off Montenegro.

1916.

May 13 — **VI** (von Falkenhausen). Netted and shelled by drifters. — Str. of Otranto.

Oct. 17 — **XVI** (von Zoppa). Depth-charged by Italian destroyer *Nembo*. — Gulf of Taranto.

1917.

April — **XXX** (F. Fähndrich). Missing. — Adriatic or Mediterranean.

1918.

Feb. 21 — **XXIII** (von Bézard). Depth-charged by Italian torpedo-boat *Airone*. — Adriatic.

May 1 — **XX** (L. Müller). Torpedoed by Italian submarine. — Adriatic (?).

IV.

Cause of Loss:

   Nets and gunfire 1
   Depth-charge 2
   Torpedoed by enemy submarine . . 1
   Mined 1*
   Bombed 1
   Missing 1

    * Also **X** permanently disabled by mine, July 9, 1918.

Interned and Disposed of (1919):
   At Pola : **I, II, XI, XV, XVII, XXVII, XXXII.**
   At Venice : **V, XXI, XXVIII, XL.**
   At Fiume : **IV.**

The above twelve submarines were assigned to Italy.

APPENDIX IV

At Cattaro : **XXII, XXIX, XXXI, XLI, XLIII, XLVII**.

The above six submarines were taken over by the French and towed from Cattaro to Bizerta, but **XXIX** foundered whilst under tow.

The five boats which arrived at Bizerta, and the twelve boats taken over by Italy, were all broken up or scuttled in deep water, within twelve months from the dates of their deliveries to French and Italian custody.

CEDED BY GERMANY :

UB 1 ⎫
UB 15 ⎭ probably became **X** and **XI**.
UB 43   ,,   ,,   **XLIII**.
UB 47   ,,   ,,   **XLVII**.

V.

The following is a list of commanding officers * of Austro-Hungarian submarines, with the dates of service in some cases :—

I 1915-16, L/L Franz Nejebsy ; 1917, L/L Eugen Hornyak.
II 1915, L/L Karl Edl. v. Unczowski ; 1916-17, L/L Otto Kasseroller ; 1918, L/L Ivan Ulmansky v. Vracsevgaj.
III 1915, L/L Karl Strnad.
IV 1915, L/L Herman Jüstel; 1916-17, L/L Rudolf Singule ; 1918, L/L Zdenko Knötgen.
V 1915-16, L/L Friedrich Schlosser ; 1918, L/L Alfons Graf Montecuccoli.
VI 1915, L/L Nikolaus Halavanja ; 1916, L/L Hugo von Falkenhausen.
X 1915, L/L Leo Prasil ; 1916, L/L Hermann Rigele ; 1917, L/L Robert Dürrigl.
XI 1915, L/L Robert Teufl v. Fernland ; 1916, L/L Johann Krsnjavi ; 1917, L/L Vladimir Pfeifer ; 1918, L/L Alois Sernetz.
XII 1915, L/L Egon Lerch.
XIV 1915-17, L/L Georg Ritter von Trapp ; 1918, L/L Hugo Pistel.
XV L/L Friedrich Schlosser ; Fried. Fähndrich ; Ludwig Müller ; Andreas Korparic.
XVI L/L Eugen Hornyak ; Orest Ritter von Zoppa.
XVII L/L Zdenko Hudecek ; Hermann Rigele ; Vladimir Pfeifer.
XX 1916, L/L Klemens Ritter von Bézard ; Franz Rzemenovsky von Trautenegg.
XXI L/L Josef Holub ; Hugo Freiherr von Seyffertitz Robert Dürrigl.

* L/L denotes Linienschiffs-Leutnant.

XXII	L/L Josef Holub ; Friedrich Sterz.
XXIII	L/L Klemens Ritter von Bézard.
XXVII	L/L Robert Teufl v. Fernland ; Josef Holub.
XXVIII	L/L Zdenko Hudecek ; Franz Rzemenovsky von Trautenegg.
XXIX	L/L Leo Prasil.
XXX	L/L Friedrich Fähndrich.
XXXI	L/L Franz Nejebsy ; Hermann Rigele.
XXXII	L/L Gaston Vio ; Otto Kasseroller.
XL	L/L Johann Krsnjavi.
XLI	L/L Edgar Wolf.
XLIII	L/L Friedrich Schlosser ; Eugen Hornyak.
XLVII	L/L Otto Molitor ; Hugo Freiherr von Seyffertitz.

Q

TURKEY

(a) The French submarine *Turquoise* was disabled by gunfire of Turkish vessels in the Sea of Marmora on October 31, 1915. She was either driven ashore or sunk in shallow water. She was salved on November 3, docked at Pera, and renamed *Mustedji Ombaschi* by the Turks. She was restored to France in December 1918.

(b) There is a doubtful report that during the war an effort was made to modernise and recondition two antiquated Turkish submarines of the Nordenfelt type (built 1885) so that they might be made capable of war service.

R

FINAL SUMMARY—ENEMY SUBMARINES (ALL NATIONALITIES)

Total boats put into service (German, Austro-Hungarian, Bulgarian and Turkish)	419
Total boats lost on war cruises (ditto)	186
Total residue surviving at end of the war (ditto)	233
Surrendered to or recovered by the Allies	196

INDEX

ABBREVIATIONS

A.B.S. = Armed boarding steamer.
A.M.C. = Armed merchant cruiser.
A/S. = Anti-submarine.
B.C. = Battle cruiser.
B.S. = Battleship.
C.S. = Cruiser Squadron.
D.A.M.S. = Defensively armed merchant ship.
Dftr. = Drifter.

G.B. = Gunboat.
H.S. = Hospital ship.
H.S.F. = High Sea Fleet.
L.C. = Light cruiser.
M/L. = Minelayer.
M/S. = Minesweeper.
N.A.W.I. = N. America & W. Indies.
S/M. = Submarine.
S.S. = Steamship.

T.B. = Torpedo-boat.
T.B.D. = Torpedo-boat destroyer.
T.G.B. = Torpedo gunboat.
Trlr. = Trawler.
A.-H. = Austro-Hungarian.
Brit. = British.
Fr. = French.
Ger. = German.
It. = Italian.
Rus. = Russian.

	PAGE
Aaro (Brit. S.S.) sk.,	104
Abbas (Egypt. coastguard vessel) sk.,	76
Abdul Moneim (Egypt. coastguard vessel) attkd.,	76
Abosso (Brit. S.S.) sk.,	168
Aboukir (Brit. cruiser) sk. by U 9,	7-9, 12
Aburi (Brit. S.S.) sk.,	168
Acadian (Brit. S.S.) sk.,	320
Acceptable (Brit. dftr.),	228
Acheron (Brit. T.B.D.),	34
Achilles (Brit. S.S.) sk.,	87
Action, North Sea (Nov. 17, 1917),	211
Admiralty (Anti-S/M.Division): situation reviewed and measures adopted,	147
instructions to mercantile masters,	36
Adriatic, Brit. Squadron sent to, composition of,	70
Ægusa (Brit. armed yacht) sk.,	129
Afric (Brit. S.S.) sk.,	140
Afridi (Brit. T.B.D.),	92
Agamemnon (Brit. B.S.),Turkish armistice signed on board,	275
Agberi (Brit. S.S.) sk.,	231
Aguila (Brit. S.S.) sk.,	36
Ailly (Fr. patrol vessel),	269
Airone (It. T.B.D.),	267
Airships, Naval:	
British—	
R 29,	321
SSZ 1,	318
SSZ 29,	303
types of,	318-19, 319 n.
as escorts, scouts,	319

	PAGE
Airships, Naval (*contd.*):	
German—	
L 13,	106
act as fleet scouts,	106
used as mine-searchers,	208
Ajax (Brit. B.S.),	2
Alarm (Brit. T.B.D.) attkd. by U 9,	13, 16 n.
Alaunia (Brit. S.S.) sk.,	115
Albatross (Ger. M/L.),	5
Albrecht, Conrad, Cmre. G.N., in command of Flanders forces: ships under command of,	295
Alcantara (Brit. A.M.C.) sk.,	83
Alcedo (U.S. armed yacht) sk.,	230
Alert (Trinity House vessel lent to Dover Patrol) sk.,	61
Alex Hastie (Brit. fishing-vessel),	32
Alfalfa (Brit. S.S.) sk.,	168
Alfonso XIII. (King of Spain),	129
Alfred H. Read (Brit. pilot vessel) sk.,	232
Allenby, General,	259
Alnwick Castle (Brit. S.S.) sk.,	157
Alsatian (Brit. A.M.C., Flag. 10th C.S.),	103
Alyssum (Brit. sloop) sk.,	154
Amalfi (It. cruiser) sk.,	73
Amazon (Brit. S.S.) sk.,	291
Ambulance transports,	165, 166, 166 n., 316, 317
America, United States of:	
divergence of view with Brit. Govt.,	28
capture of S.S. *Dacia*,	28
protests against S/M. war on shipping,	29, 42

391

392 THE GERMAN SUBMARINE WAR

America, United States of (*contd.*):
  protests against use of U.S.
    colours, ... 29
  attack on S.S. *Belridge*, . 32
  tension over sinking of
    Arabic, ... 57-8
  protests against Brit. blockade, 62
  protests against shipping war
    in Mediterranean, . . 79
  Note on Allied blockade
    policy, ... 81
  Note on legality of S/M. anti-
    shipping war, . . . 82
  threatens diplomatic rupture
    with Germany, . . . 88
  protests against sinking of
    S.S. *Kelvinia*, . . 115 n.
  German conditions for steam-
    ship service to Europe, . 138
  rupture of diplomatic rela-
    tions with Germany, Feb.
    1917, ... 139
  policy of non-intervention—
    'Associated Power,' . 158
    independent belligerent, . 159
  cost of dilatoriness to Allies,
    estimate, ... 160
  warned of raid by large sub-
    marines, 1918, . . . 307
Amiral Charner (Fr. cruiser)
  sk., . . . 125, 273 n.
Amiral Charner (Fr. S.S.) sk.,
              273, 273 n.
Amiral Ganteaume (Fr. S.S.)
  sk., ... 15, 273n.
Amiral Magon (Fr. troopship)
  sk., ... 134-5
Ancona (It. S.S.) sk., . . 77
Andania (Brit. S.S.) sk., . 286
Anglia (Brit. H.S.) sk., . 61, 164
Anglo-Californian (Brit. horse-
  transport), ... 45
Anglo-Columbian (Brit. horse-
  transport), ... 60
Anjou (Fr. M/S.) sk., . . 186
Antilles (U.S. troopship), . 221-2
Anti-submarine measures :
  early stages of war, . . 22
  Admiralty instructions to
    mercantile masters, . 36
  weapons :
    mines, ... 11
    first British trials (1904), 23
    committee set up (1910), 24
    'periscope trawling,' . 24
    minefields (deep), . . 39
    depth charges first used, . 47
  (*See also* Defensive arma-
    ments ; Depth charges ;

Anti-submarine measures (*contd.*) :
  Depth-charge mortars ;
  Hydrophones.)
Antony (Brit. S.S.) sk., . . 157
Antrim (Brit. cruiser) attkd., . 16 n.
Antwerp (Brit. decoy, Lt.-Com.
  G. Herbert), . . . 47
Apapa (Brit. S.S.) sk., . . 230
Aparima (Brit. S.S.) sk., . 229
Aphis (Brit. ' China ' G.B.), . 259
Appam (Brit. S.S.), . . . 230
Arabia (Brit. S.S.) sk., . . 133
Arabian (Brit. munition carrier)
  sk., ... 75
Arabic (Brit. S.S.) sk.,
  52, 53, 57, 58, 59, 220, 284
Aragon (Brit. troopship) sk., . 262
Arbutus (Brit. convoy sloop) sk., 229
Arc (Fr. T.B.D.), . . . 135
Arca (Brit. S.S.) sk., . . 322
Arcadian (Brit. troopship) sk., 244
Ardea (It. T.B.), . . . 268
Arethusa (Brit. L.C.) sk., . 83
Argyll (Brit. cruiser) attkd. by
  U 40, ... 45
Ariadne (Brit. M/L., ex-cruiser)
  sk. by UC 65, . . . 194
Ariel (Brit. T.B.D.), . . 34
  sinks UB 29, ... 118
  adapted for mine-laying, sk. 315
Arkona (Ger. L.C. and S/M.
  parent vessel, Emden), . 32
Armadale (Brit. troopship) sk., 185
Armed boarding steamers
  (A.B.S.), (Brit.).
  (See *Dundee, Duke of Albany,*
    Fauvette, Grive, Louvain,
    Sarnia, Snaefell, Stephen
    Furness, Tara, Tithonus.)
Armed merchant cruisers
  (A.M.C.), (Brit.)—
  additional not available, . 173
  used as troopships for U.S.
    Exped. Force, . . . 298
  (See also *Alcantara, Alsa-*
    tian, Artois (ex *Digby*),
    Avenger, Bayano, Calyx,
    Champagne (ex *Oropesa*),
    Columbella, Hilary, Hilde-
    brand, India, Laurentic,
    Mantua, Marmora, Mol-
    davia, Motagua, Orama,
    Otway, Patia, Victorian,
    and 'Cruiser Squadron,
    10th.')
Armed yachts (Brit.).
  (See *Ægusa, Goissa, Lorna,*
    Mingary, Narcissus II.,
    Vanduara, Vanessa, Zaida.)

INDEX

Armed yachts (U.S.).
(See *Alcedo, Christabel, Lydonia, Noma, Surveyor, Venetia*.)
Armenian (Brit. S.S.) sk., . 45
Armistice:
  Bulgaria, . . . 274, 276
  German proposals for (Oct. 1918), refused, . . 274
  asked for by Austria; agreed upon; date of commencement, ... 275, 276
  Turkey, ... 275, 276
  German proposal and Allied conditions (Oct. 1918), . 324
  of Nov. 11, 1918, . . . 329
  relative to German S/M., . 331
Aros Castle (Brit. S.S.) sk., . 229
Artesia (Brit. S.S.) sk., . . 219
Artist (Brit. S.S.) sk., . . 123
Artois (Brit. A.M.C.) lent to France, ... 62
Askold (Russ. cruiser) attkd., 71
Assyria (Brit. S.S.) sk., . . 201
Aster (Brit. sloop) sk., . . 258
Astoria (Brit. S.S.) sk., . . 112
Astrum Spei (Brit. dftr.) sk., . 130
Asturias (Brit. H.S.) attkd. (i), 21
  attkd. (ii), ... 164
Atalanta (Brit. S.S.) attkd., . 33
Athenia (Brit. S.S.) sk., . . 200
Athos (Fr. troopship) sk., . 240
Atlantian (Brit. S.S.) sk., . 311
Attack (Brit. T.B.D.) attkd., 16 n., 34, 198; sk., 262
Attentive (Brit. L.C.) attkd. by U 18, ... 11
Audacious (Brit. B.S.), loss of, 14
Aurania (Brit. S.S.) sk., . . 288
Au Revoir (Fr. M/S.) sk., . 84
Ausonia (Brit. S.S.) sk., . . 306
Auten, H., Lieut. R.N.R., . 316
Ava (Brit. S.S.), loss of, . . 123
Avenger (Brit. A.M.C.) sk., 184-5
Aylevarroo (Brit. S.S.) sk., . 222
Azalea (Brit. sloop), . . 258
Azores:
  Canaries zone, U 151-157 begin to operate in, . . 182
  raid by 'cruiser-submarines' and preventive measures, 211-13 n.
  raids (1917) by U 151, 152, 155, 156, . 211-13 n., 216-19
  raids (1918) by U 152, 155, . 296
Aztec (U.S. S.S.) sk., . . 169

Bachmann, Adm. G.N. (Chief of Naval Staff), . . 58

Bacon, Sir Reginald (Brit. Adm., S.N.O. Dover), 91, 144, 193
  revives Belgian coast barrage, ... 193
  proposes mine barrage Grisnez-Varne Shoal, . . 222
  to be extended to Folkestone, ... 223
  adds lightships, . . . 223
  barrage begun, . . . 223
  credit for barrage and blockships plans, . . 223 n.
  barrage and drifter line, 223-4
  relinquishes command at Dover, ... 224
  uses S/M. against U-boats, . 225
  belief and decision regarding cross-Channel mine-barrage, ... 194
Badger (Brit. T.B.D.) rams U 19, . . . 15, 16 n., 165
Balfour, the Rt. Hon. A. J., P.C., M.P. (Secy. Foreign Affairs), . . . 285-6
  quoted, ... 322-3
Ballarat (Brit. troopship) sk., 168
Ballard, G. A. (Rear-Adm. R.N.), ... 236
  urges adoption of convoy in Mediterranean, 1916, . 240
  quoted, ... 248
Ballin, the late Herr, . . 121
Baltimore (U.S. M/L. ex cruiser), ... 286
Baralong (Brit. decoy) (Lt.-Com. G. Herbert, R.N.), 52-3, 54, 60
Baron Balfour (Brit. S.S.) sk., 219-20
Barrage, Committee's Report, 224
  wooden boom, Folkestone-Grisnez, 1914-15, . . 116
  Nets—
    North Channel (1915), . 40
    Dover (1915), . . . 39
    St. George's Channel (1915), 40
  Dover Straits, enemy S/M. find way through, 44, 197
  Nets and mines:
    Belgian coast (first)—
      described, . . . 90-2
      laid, ... 91
      extended, . . 91 n., 93
      Ger. S/M. damaged, . 92
      value overrated, . . 92-3
      (second) . . . 92 n.
      decided to reinstate, . 193
      laid, ... 194
      U-boats passed through, 194

Barrage (contd.):
  Nets and mines (contd.)—
    Belgian coast (second) (contd.)—
      damaged by enemy, . 194
      abandoned, . . . 295
    S. Goodwins - Outer Ruy-
      tingen, . . 90, 116-17
      moderate success, . . 152
      not effective, . . . 193-4
      number of 1917 pas-
        sages, ... 222
      no longer maintained, . 295
    Folkestone-Grisnez, 1917—
      first plans for, . . . 222-3
      begun, . . . 223, 228
      first S/M. sk., . 223-4, 231
      Sir Reginald Bacon's auth-
        orship, . . . 223 n.
      his views on illumination
        and drifter line, . 223-4
      modifications by Sir R.
        Keyes, ... 224
      early defects with flares, . 283
      U 109 sk. in, . . . 287
      UB 38 sk. in, . . . 289
      regarded as 'almost im-
        passable,' . . . 289
      raid on drifters, etc.. by
        German T.B.D., . . 290
      secret of deep fields kept, 290
      UB 58 sk. in, . . . 292
      UB 33 sk. in, . . . 294
      UB 55 sk. in, . . . 294
      UB 31 sk. in, . . . 303
      UC 78 sk. in ?, . . . 303
      UC 64 sk. in, . . . 311
      UB 103 sk. in, . . . 318
      UB 109 sk. in, . . . 318
    Northern—
      proposed, ... 194
      begun and swept up, re-
        laid and completed, . 315
      number of mines, totals
        laid by Brit. and U.S.
        vessels, ... 315 n.
      defective mines, . . 321 n.
      U 156, U 192, UB 104,
        UB 127, U 102, and
        UB 83 sk. in, . . 320-1
    Gulf of Finland (mine and net), 56
    Heligoland Bight and across
      North Sea, estimated re-
      quirement, . . 211-13 n.
  Barrage-breakers (German),
    182, 208, 211
  Indicator nets, Folkestone-
    Grisnez (1915), . . . 39
    off Ostend, ... 39
    Goodwins, ... 62

Barrage (contd.):
  Otranto Straits (net) (Cape
    Otranto - Sasseno Is.,
    1915) established, . . 124
  easily passed by S/M., . 127-8
  deepened, ... 128
  S/M. foul in, raided by
    Austrian warships, line
    moved south to Fano Is.-
    Sta. Maria di Leuca, . 130
  raided by Austrian sea-
    planes, ... 131
  motor launches and sea-
    plane base in support, . 131
  S/M. pass through, . . 131
  attempted Austrian raid
    defeated, . . . 132
  better destroyer support
    for, ... 211-13 n.
  proposal to send drifters
    to patrol work or bring
    patrols to barrage, . 246
  system in use in 1917
    described, . . . 246
  'de Quillac' net proposed
    and adopted, . . 247
  enemy S/M. continue to
    pass, ... 252
  seaplane base added, . 253
  raided, ... 254-5
  drifters again moved south, 255
  system in July 1917, ex-
    tended use of hydro-
    phones : redistribution
    of forces on establish-
    ment of complete Medi-
    terranean convoy system, 259
  compared with Dover: net
    barrages and drifters, . 264
  'de Quillac' net begun and
    completed : form of, 264-5
  Adm. Calthorpe's barrage
    system described, . . 365-6
  attempt by Austrian
    T.B.D. to raid, defeated, 271
  concentration of Austrian
    B.S. begun for attack
    on, ... 271-2
  operations abandoned, . 271-2
  safely passed by 15 fugi-
    tive German S/M., . 276
  Otranto and Dover : re-
    lative success of, . . 278-9
Submarine (German)—
  round Heligoland, . . 1
  posted to trap Brit. ships,
    May 1915, . . . 44
  found by 3rd C.S., June
    1915, ... 45

INDEX

Barrage (contd.) :
  Submarine (German) (contd.)—
    for Sunderland bombardment, ... 97
    in Heligoland Bight (July-Aug. 1916), . . . 101
    for Sunderland plan (Aug. 1916), ... 106
    German success of (Aug. 1916), ... 108
Barrister (Brit. S.S.) sk., . 320
Barrow-in-Furness shelled by U 21, ... 20
Bartenbach, Capt. (S.) G.N., Flanders Flot., 104, 110, 295
Barunga (Brit. S.S.) sk., . . 313
Basilisk (Brit. T.B.D.), . . 269
Battle squadrons (Brit.) : 3rd attkd. by U 39, . . . 44
  5th, ... 19
Bauer, Capt. G.N., . . 96, 204
Bayano (Brit. A.M.C.) sk. by U 27, ... 33
Beagle (Brit. T.B.D.), . . 164
Beatty, Sir David (Adm., S.N.O., B.C.F.), . . . 110
Begonia (Q 10) (Brit. sloop), loss of, ... 229
Belford (Brit. S.S.) sk., . . 62
Belgian Prince (Brit. S.S.) sk., 194
Belgian relief steamers torpedoed, ... 146
Belle of France (Brit. S.S.) sk., ... 125
Belridge (Brit. S.S.) attkd., . 32
Ben Cruachan (Brit. S.S.) sk., 20
Bergamot (Brit. convoy sloop) sk., ... 214
Berlin (Ger. aux. M/L.), . . 14
Bernstorff, Count (Ger. Ambass. to U.S.A.) :
  proposed exemption of foodstuffs, ... 29
  58, 111, 119.
Beryl III. (Brit. dftr.), . . 287
Bethmann-Hollweg, Herr von, Ger. Chancellor, opposes S/M. warfare on shipping 26-7
  requests restriction of S/M. war, ... 42
  58, 81, 82.
  opposes unrestricted warfare, ... 65-6
  persists in opposing unrestricted warfare, . . 101
  refuses assent to unrestricted warfare, ... 105
  opposition to unrestricted warfare weakens, . 113-14

Bethmann-Hollweg, Herr von (contd.) :
  memorandum to Kaiser, . 119
  defeated on issue of 'unrestricted warfare,' . . 120
  scepticism of estimates, 120-1 n.
  advice ignored by Kaiser, . 122
  opinions on 'unrestricted warfare' vindicated, . 203
Biarritz (Brit. M/L.), . . 91
Birmingham (Brit. L.C.) sinks U 15, ... 3
  'class' cruisers, . . . 8, 10
Birkenhead (Brit. L.C.), . . 195
Bismarck, the late Prince von, views on blockade, . . 29
Bisson (Fr. T.B.D.) sinks III, 73, 73 n.
Blackmorevale (Brit. M/S.) sk., 301
Blackwood, M. B. R., Cmr. R.N., D.S.O., . . . 215
Blaikie, Capt. (master of S.S. *Caledonia*), fears for safety of, ... 133
Blockade :
  British and German compared, ... 113
  simplified by U.S. declaration of war and unrestricted S/M. campaign, agreements with neutrals, bunkering, . . . 185
Blockships :
  German fear of British use of, 18
  proposals to scuttle, in Heligoland Bight, . 211-13 n.
  Zeebrugge and Ostend attacks ; Sir R. Bacon's authorship of, . 223 n.
  date fixed by him, . . 224
  modifications made by Sir R. Keyes, ... 224
  attacks on Zeebrugge and Ostend ; ports not sealed, 294-5
Blum, Lt.-Cmr. G.N., . . 25
Bogatyr (Russ. cruiser) attkd., 219
Boldt, Lt. G.N. (U 86), . . 312
Bombala, alias *Willow Branch* : see S/M. decoy vessel.
Bombarde (Fr. T.B.D.), . . 135
Bombardments by S/M.
  (*See* Barrow-in-Furness, Funchal, Gradant, Monrovia, W/T. Station, Portoferrajo, San Miguel, San Pietro, Scarborough, Seaham, Toukhoum L.H., Trebizond, Walney Is., Whitehaven.)

396 THE GERMAN SUBMARINE WAR

Bonner, Charles G. (Lt. R.N.R.), awarded V.C., . . . 199
Borea (It. T.B.D.) sk., . . 254
Bosnia (It. S.S.) sk., . . 78
Bostonian (Brit. comm. escort ship) sk., ... 222
Boutefeu (Fr. T.B.D.) sk., . 255
Boynton (Brit. S.S.) sk., . . 207
Bracondale (Brit. decoy) sk., . 195
Braemar Castle (Brit. H.S.), 133, 164, 260
Braeneil (Brit. S.S), . . . 284
Branlebas (Fr. T.B.D.) sk. by UB 17, ... 61
Brantingham (Brit. S.S.) sk., . 112
Braunschweig (Ger. B.S., parent vessel 3rd S/M. Flot.), 329 n.
Brazen (Brit. T.B.D.), . . 39
Bremen (see Submarines, German, mercantile).
Bremse (Ger. cruiser M/L.), . 232
Breslau (Ger. L.C.) shells Trebizond, . . . 127
Brighton Queen (Brit. M/S.) sk., 61
Brindisi (It. transport) sk., . 126
Bristol (Brit. L.C.), . . . 254
Bristol City (Brit. S.S.) sk., . 231
Britannia (Brit. B.S.) sk. by UB 50, ... 277
Britannic (Brit. H.S.) sk., 133, 164
British Sun (Brit. S.S.) sk., . 248
British Transport (Brit. S.S.) sinks U 49, . . 206-7
' Broad Fourteens,' . . . 6
Brodness (Brit. S.S.) sk., . 242
Broke (Brit. Flot. leader), . 152
Brummer (Ger. cruiser M/L.), 232
Brussels (Brit. S.S.) forces U 33 under (Mar. 1915); capt. (June 1916), . . . 36
B. T. B. (Brit. dftr.), . . 303
Budrum, . . . 70, 74-5, 76
Buffalo (Brit. S.S.) sk., . . 320
Bülow, von (Capt. G.N.), . 119
Bulysses (Brit. S.S.) sk., . 200-1
Burdigala (Fr. aux. cruiser) sk., 133
Burutu (Brit. S.S.), . . . 296
attkd., ... 297
Buttercup (Brit. sloop), 151, 231-2
Bylands (Brit. S.S.) sk., . . 274

Cabotia (Brit. S.S.) sk., . . 116
Cairnross (Brit. S.S.) sk., . 306
Cairnstrath (Brit. S.S.) sk., . 200
Caithness (Brit. S.S.) sk., . 168
Caledonia (Brit. S.S., D.A.M.S.) sk., ... 133
Calgarian (Brit. A.M.C.) sk. by U 19, ... 291

California (Brit. S.S.) sk., . 140
Calistoga (Brit. dftr.), . . 128
Calliope (Brit. S.S.) sk., . . 192
Calypso (Brit. L.C.), . . 211
Calypso (Brit. S.S., ex A.M.C. Calyx) sk., ... 102
Calyx. See Calypso.
Cambank (Brit. S.S.) sk., . 32
Cameleon (Brit. T.B.D.), . 249
Cameronia (Brit. troopship) sk., 244
Cameronian (Brit. horse-transport) sk., ... 251
Campanula (Brit. sloop), . 267
Campbell, Gordon (Lt.-Cmr. R.N.), awarded D.S.O., . 87
Cmr., awarded V.C., . 150-1
promoted Capt., awarded bar to D.S.O., ... 181
awarded 2nd bar to D.S.O., 197-9
Capt. R.N., V.C., D.S.O., . 228
Canadian (Brit. S.S.) sk., . 168
Candidate (Brit. S.S.) sk., . 40
Candytuft (Brit. convoy sloop) sk., 261-2
Cape Finisterre (Brit. S.S.) sk., 229
Capelle, von (Adm. G.N.), . 85 n.
Secy. for Navy, . . . 114
holds up S/M. building plan, 122
succeeded by Adm. R. von Mann-Tiechler, . . 301 n.
Caprera (It. munition-carrier) sk., 218-19
Caprera (It. aux. cruiser) sk., 266
Cardiff (Brit. L.C.), . . 300 n.
Carolina (U.S. S.S.) sk., . . 307
Carpathia (Brit. S.S.) sk., . 312
Carson, Sir Edward, M.P. (1st Lord), statement on actions with enemy S/M., Feb. 1-18, 1917, . . . 149
Cartagena visited by U 35, . 129
Carthage (Fr. transport) sk., . 74
Casement, Sir Roger, . . 87
Cassandra (Brit. L.C.) sk. after War, ... 336
Cassini (Fr. M/L. G.B.), . . 241
Celtic (Brit. S.S.), . . . 154
Centurion (Brit. S.S.) sk., . 41
Cestrian (Brit. transport) sk., . 251
Champagne (ex Oropesa, Brit. A.M.C.) :
lent to France, . . . 62
sk., ... 221
Chancellor (Brit. S.S.) sk., . 60
Chancellor (Brit. S.S.) sk., . 115
Channel, North, . . . 39
Chateaurenault (Fr. cruiser M/L.) sk. by UC 38, 260, 260 n.

INDEX

	PAGE
Chatterton, E. Keble,	195
Cheero (Brit. armed smack),	90
Cherbury (Brit. Admy. collier) sk.,	40
Chikara (Brit. trlr.),	200
'Children of Sorrow,' the (*see* Ger. S/M., U 71-80 class),	239
Christabel (U.S. armed yacht),	305
Christopher (Br. T.B.D.),	198
Chrysanthemum (Brit. convoy sloop),	268
Citta di Messina (It. aux. cruiser),	126
sk.,	130
Citta di Palermo (It. aux. cruiser) sk.,	126
Citta di Sassari (It. aux. cruiser) sk.,	262
City of Adelaide (Brit. S.S.) sk.,	274
City of Baroda (Brit. S.S.) sk.,	185
City of Brisbane (Brit. S.S.), sk.,	317
City of Corinth (Brit. S.S.) sk.,	184
City of Florence (Brit. S.S.) sk.,	192
City of Glasgow (Brit. S.S.) sk.,	319
City of Lucknow (Brit. S.S.) sk.,	129
City of Paris (Brit. S.S.) sk.,	243
Civilian (Brit. S.S.) sk.,	260
Clacton (Brit. M/S.) sk.,	132
Clan Davidson (Brit. S.S.) sk.,	185
Clan Farquhar (Brit. S.S.) sk.,	242
Clan MacDougall (Brit. S.S.) sk.,	266-7
Clan MacFarlane (Brit. S.S.) sk.,	78
Clan MacLeod (Brit. S.S.) sk.,	77
Clan MacNab (Brit. S.S.) sk.,	317
Clan MacPherson (Brit. S.S.) sk.,	266
Clan Macvey (Brit. S.S.), sk.,	317
Clan Murray (Brit. S.S.) sk.,	184
Clavis (Brit. dftr.) sk.,	130
Clayton W. Walters (Brit. fishing vessel) sk.,	310
C. M. Walters (Brit. fishing vessel) sk.,	310
Coastal motor boats (C.M.B.),	148
Colbert (Fr. troopship) sk.,	248
Colchester (G.E. Rly. Co. S.S.) attkd.,	17
Collegian (Brit. S.S.) sk.,	260
Colliers, Admiralty (or Fleet), arming of,	31
(See *Cherbury, Fulgent, Mobile.*)	
Colliers lost in 1917,	166
Colomb, P. H. (Comre. R.N.),	191
Columbella (Brit. A.M.C.) attkd. by U 36,	47
Columbia (Brit. trlr.) sk.,	39

	PAGE
Combined operations :	
S/M. and airships, German, (May 1916) Fleet and S/M.	86
plans for Sunderland bombardment,	97
stations of S/M.,	97
abandoned,	98
failure of,	101
(Aug. 1916) stations of S/M.,	106
projected Sunderland bombardment, operations by S/M.,	106-7
projected operations for Oct. 1916 abandoned,	107
British precautions against,	107-9
naval and military, S/M. participate in Riga attack,	219
British war-vessels support advance in Palestine : losses sustained,	259
Comet (Brit. T.B.D.),	259
sk.,	260
Commander Fullerton (Brit. trlr.) sk.,	232
Commerce, German S/M. war on :	
first ideas of, British premonitions,	23
Fisher Memorandum,	24
Spindler's denial,	24-5, 25 n.
Blum's estimate,	25
discussed and demanded by flag officers, High Sea Fleet,	25-6
(from sinking of S.S. *Glitra*, Oct. 20, 1914, to sinking of S.S. *Dulwich*, Feb. 15, 1915),	13, 17, 20, 21, 22, 25
N. & W. European waters, etc.	
(from Feb. 15, 1915, sinking of S.S. *Cambank*, to Dec. 25, 1915, sinking of S.S. *El Zorro*) :	
'Wiegand interview,'	26
instructions to C.O. of S/M.,	29
immunity of neutral ships,	30
U 30 begins campaign,	30, 32
preparations in S/M. for trade war,	30
orders to attack ships,	31
shipping attacked,	32-7, 40-5, 47, 48, 51-2, 57-8
orders to spare large passenger-carrying vessels and neutrals,	42
political disputes arise ; sailing of S/M. suspended,	58

Commerce, German S/M. war on:
  N. & W. European waters, etc.
        (contd.).
    new orders for conduct of
      trade war, ... 59
    orders issued suspending
      trade war around British
      Isles, ... 59
    shipping sunk, . . 59-60
    short raid by U 24, . . 61
    attacks renewed in Channel, 62
    statistics of losses, . . 65

  Mediterranean and Black Sea.
    war on shipping begun, 75, 77-8
    U.S. protests against, . . 79
    prize war rules to be ob-
      served, ... 79
    British shipping losses, Mar.-
      Apr. 1916, ... 126
    shipping attacked in Black
      Sea, 1916, ... 127
    German S/M. carry on
      'cruiser war,' . . . 238

  N. & W. European waters.
        Atlantic
    (from sinking of S.S. Teuton-
      ian, Mar. 4, 1916, to sink-
      ing of S.S. Dundee, Jan.
      31, 1917):
    orders issued for recom-
      mencement of anti-ship-
      ping war without re-
      strictions, ... 84
    shipping attacked, . . 85-8
    recall of all S/M. at sea, . 88
    compliance with Interna-
      tional Law ordered, . . 89
    Scheer recalls S/M. attached
      to H.S.F. from trade war,
                              89, 93
    suggestions for modified
      forms of war on com-
      merce, ... 96
    D.A.M.S. not to be attacked, 101
    'cruiser war' resumed, . 102
    restrictions upheld and
      enemy transports not to
      be attacked, . . . 105
    resumption of 'cruiser war,'
                              110, 114
    raid by U 53 off U.S. coast, 111
    shipping attacked in north-
      ern Russian waters, 111-12
    monthly averages of ship-
      ping sunk under 'prize
      war' and 'restricted war'
      systems, ... 121

Commerce, German S/M. war on:
  N. & W. European waters.
        Atlantic (contd.).
    shipping sunk down to Jan.
      1917, ... 123
  'Unrestricted campaign':
    Kaiser and Naval Staff
      defer commencement, . 83
    Kaiser gives orders to
      begin, ... 84
    Kaiser postpones, . 85, 86
    proposed at Pless Confer-
      ence, Aug. 1916, and
      deferred, . . . 113-14
    Scheer urges adoption, . 119
    decision to begin, . 119, 120
    estimates of British and
      neutral shipping in ser-
      vice, and forecast of
      losses, ... 120
    Navy Office Memorandum
      and business men's re-
      ferendum, . 120, 120 n.
    to commence simultane-
      ously with declaration, 120
    criticism not tolerated, . 121
    orders issued for sinking
      of D.A.M.S., . . 122
    German Note presented at
      Washington, Jan. 31,
      1917, announces adop-
      tion of campaign and
      immediate commence-
      ment, ... 137
    attack on shipping begins, 140
    from sinking of S.S. Eave-
      stone, Feb. 1, 1917, to
      sinking of S.S. Sarpedon
      on Nov. 7, 1918: see
      Shipping losses, stat-
      istics of; 'Six months
      plan.'
    orders for suspension of
      all attacks on shipping
      issued Oct. 1918, . . 325
  Glitra episode, . . . 13
  Commissioned escort ships
    (Brit.). (See Bostonian,
    Mechanician, Quernmore.)
  Comrades (Brit. dftr.), . . 89
  Comrie Castle (Brit. S.S.) attkd., 291
  Condesa (Brit. S.S.) sk., . . 192
  Conferences:
    Inter-Allied Naval—
      at Paris (Dec. 1915), . 237
      at Corfu (April 1917), de-
        cision to hold, . . 240
      recommendations of: dis-
        persed routes, consecu-

INDEX 399

Conferences: Inter-Allied Naval (*contd.*)—
  tive escort, centralised control, diversion of trade around Cape of Good Hope adopted, at London (Sept. 1917), 211 n.-213 n.   245-7
  German—
    (Dec. 1915), . . . 81
    at Pless (Aug. 1916), 113, 233
    criticised by Gayer, . 114
Contest (Brit. T.B.D.) sk., . 214
'Continuous voyage,' doctrine of, ... 26
Contraband:
  foodstuffs declared, by Brit. Govt., ... 26-8
  neutral trade with Germany, 28
Contraband trade, British measures against, . . 26
  cotton exempt, . . . 29
Convoys:
  system not considered, as escorts not available, . 148
  suggested: escort required for cruisers and A.M.C. not suitable, . . 172-3
  Naval Staff confers with mercantile masters (2/17), and opinion against: objections to use of, . . 173-4
  Atlantic, estimate of cruisers and A.M.C., inward and outward: actual number available: method of working, ... 174
  partial system rejected, . 175
  weekly Holland-Thames 'beef trip,' . . 175, 233
  sailing intervals of (4-8 days), ... 175
  ports of assembly for, . . 175
  remoteness from enemy S/M. bases, ... 175-6
  dangers of and fears of breakdown, . . . 175
  'convoy cruisers,' . . 175
  German 'target training,' . 186 n.
  first inward arrives, . . 176
  form of inward by Aug. 1917, 176
  fast, organised, . . . 176
  occasional failure of system, 176-7
  statistics of, by Oct. 1917:
    number of ships, total tonnage, losses, . . 177
  distance off-shore ships sunk at, April-Aug. and Sept.-Dec. 1917, . . . 177

Convoys (*contd.*):
  distance off-shore sinkings lessened by, . . . 177
  capture of mercantile officers prevented by, . . . 177
  A.M.C. recommended to join, ... 191-2
  outward- and inward-bound vessels, ... 207
  danger attendant on delay in assuming formation (sinking of *Devonian* and *Roscommon*), ... 201
  attacks on, described by Hersing, . . . 201-2
  additional ocean escort for complete organisation of Atlantic, and escorts for Mediterranean, . 211-13 n.
  disguised sloops included with, as decoys, . . 214
  want of fast escorts prevents earlier adoption, . . 281
  Scheer's excuse for S/M. lack of success against, . . 298
  L. v. Arn. de la Perière, experiences in an attack on, 326
  number and total tonnage of ships escorted: percentage of losses, . . . 336-7
  suspension of, for outward-bound ships (Oct. 1918), . 325
  the Triumph of. *See* Appendix I. pp. 338-9.
  German S/M. sunk in attacking.
    (*See* U 32, U 58, U 64, UB 17, UB 30, UB 66, UB 68, UB 69, UB 70, UB 110, UC 75.)
  first Gibraltar-U.K., . . 176
  anxieties for safety of, . 244
  first outward sailing, . 258
  Scandinavian (old system), 152, 153, 153 n.
  under Grand Fleet destroyers, . . . 174
  watched and reported on by Spiess; surface ships attack advised and adopted, . 176, 176 n.
  attack by German cruisers and destroyers, port of departure changed, sailings covered by Grand Fleet, ... 232
  attempt by H.S.F. to attack — convoy route altered, ... 301

THE GERMAN SUBMARINE WAR

Convoys (contd.):
  Mediterranean—
    adoption urged (1916), . 240
    escorted groups allowed,
      convoy forbidden, . . 245
    adopted (1917) first Malta-
      Alexandria, . . . 256
      advantages of system, 257
    success of Gib.-Alexandria,
      Gib.-Italy routes, and
      large escorts for, . . 258
    'Through' (U.K. - Port
      Said) begun, . 260-1
    saving of tonnage upon
      resumption of routes to
      India and Far East, etc., 261
    escorts for, . . 261
    unsuitability of trawlers,. 261
    local, losses in, . . . 261
Conyngham (U.S. T.B.D.), . 221
Copenhagen (Brit. H.S. and
  transport), . . . 138
Coquet (Brit. S.S.) sk., . . 78
Coquette (Brit. T.B.D.), 16 n., lost 84
Corbett, the late Sir Julian, . 23
Corcubion, Rio, . . . 43, 70
Coreopsis II. (Brit. dftr.), . 302
Cornwallis (Brit. B.S.) sk. by
  U 32, ... 134
Cottingham (Brit. S.S.) sinks
  UC 2, ... 50
  sk., ... 61
Courageous (Brit. cruiser), . 211
Covington (U.S. troop-carrier)
  sk., ... 299
Cowslip (Brit. sloop) sk., 268-9
Cradosin (Brit. trlr.), . . 274
Cressy (Brit. cruiser) sk. by U 9,
                   7-9, 12
Crisp, T., skipper R.N.R.,
  awarded V.C. posthum-
  ously, ... 199
Crocus (Brit. sloop), . . 181
Crownsin (Brit. Adm. trlr) sk., 129
Cruiser Squadrons:
  2nd and N.A.W.I., . . 175
  3rd attkd., ... 45
  7th (covering Dover Patrol
    and Harwich Force), . 6, 10
  10th, . . . 12, 62, 191
    spread to intercept Bremen, 103
    release of majority of
      A.M.C. from blockade, 175
    attkd. by S/M., . . . 184
    insufficient destroyer
      screen, ... 184
    ships of, sent to ocean
      escort duty, . . . 185
    disbanded, . . . 185

Cruiser Squadrons (contd.):
  10th (contd.)—
    ships of, join convoys—
      method unsuitable, . 191-2
    ordered to take cover with
      convoys, . . 220-1
    1st Light, ... 3
    3rd Light, . . . 107, 195
Cupar (Brit. M/S.) sk. after War, 336
Cushing (U.S. T.B.D.), . . 181
Cushing (U.S. S.S.) attkd. by
  aircraft, ... 42
Cuxhaven, British air raid on, 18
Cyclamen (Brit. sloop), . 241, 267
Cymric (Brit. S.S.) sk., 88, 118, 209
Cyrenaica, ... 74

Dacia (Ger. S.S.), capture of, . 28
Dacia (Brit. cable-ship) sk., . 134
Daffodil (Brit. sloop), . . 190
Danae (Brit. S.S.), . . . 305
Danger zone :
  expansion of, . . 111, 112, 133-4
  declared by Germany, Jan.
    28, 1917, ... 137-8
  distance off-shore shipping
    sunk out in Atlantic, . 147
  convoys diminish off-shore
    losses, ... 177
  unconvoyed neutrals cross at
    high speed, . . . 185
  enlarged by operations of
    German 'cruiser-submar-
    ines,' 216-19
Danton (Fr. B.S.) sk. by U 64,
             241, 272, 275
Dardanelles : Gallipoli materials
  for A/S. boom, . . . 37
Dartmouth (Brit. L.C.), . 254, 255
Davis (U.S. T.B.D.), . . 304
Dazzle painting, . . . 148
  method of preparation, pur-
  •pose of, success doubtful,
               117, 177
Decoy vessels, with S/M. in
  company :
  German warning against, . 30
  method, ... 46, 48
  first vessels used, . . . 47
  Taranaki and C 24, . . 49
  system revealed, discontinued 49
  revived, discontinued, again
    revived, ... 49
  additional vessels taken up, 54
  campaign opens, tactics of, 55
  number of fights and S/M.
    sunk by, ... 55
  reintroduced 1916, . . 103
  drifters simulate fishing fleet, 103

INDEX

Decoy vessels (contd.):
armed smacks with fishing
fleet, ... 103
moral effect of, . . 156
losses of (1917), . . . 156
German knowledge of, and
use of, . . 156, 156 n.
S/M. disguised as buoys, . 225
uses of, by end of 1917, . 229
example of use in War of
1812, ... 309 n.
Q ships or special service
vessels, Brit.
(See *Antwerp, Baralong,
Bracondale, Dunraven,
Ethel and Millie, Farnborough* (Q 5), *Gaelic* (Q 22),
Glen, Gunner (Q 31), *Mary
B. Mitchell* (Q 9), *Nelson,
Oceanic II., Pargust, Penshurst* (Q 7), *Privet* (Q 19),
Prize (Q 21), *Quickly, Result, Prince Charles, Sarah
Colebrooke, Stockforce,
Stonecrop, Thirza* (Q 30),
Thornhill, Vala (Q 8), *Willow Branch, Zylpha* (Q 6),
Also sloops *Begonia* (Q 10),
Heather (Q 16), *Salvia*
(Q 15), *Tulip* (Q 12); convoy sloops *Anchusa, Arbutus, Bergamot, Candytuft,
Cowslip, Rhododendron.*)
P boats, PC craft.
(operating with S/M.) *Princess
Louise, Prize, Taranaki.*
Defensive armaments:
for transports in Mediterranean, . . . 75, 77, 80
D.A.M.S., number armed by
Feb. 1917, ... 123
sanctioned for U.S. vessels, 141
D.A.M.S., percentage of
escapes, ... 146
D.A.M.S., total ships armed
(autumn 1918), . . 146
transferred from ship to ship,
146, 244
first mounted in U.S. ships, 146
accelerated, ... 148
177.
losses in Mediterranean, Feb.-
Mar. 1917, . . . 241 n.
Delphic (Brit. S.S.) sk., . . 200
Depth-charges:
first S/M. sunk by, . 104, 117
use (in sinking UC 19), . 119
(in sinking XX), . . 131
(in sinking UB 41), . . 131

Depth-charges (contd.):
mortars, ... 148
small allowance, . . 148-9
increased output of 1917-18,
149 n.
large orders for, . . . 178
first German knowledge of
(May 1917), . . . 178
used against German S/M.
(July-Dec. 1916), . . 178
used against enemy S/M.—
47, 104, 119, 131, 149, 150, 171,
172, 178, 180, 182, 183, 188, 191,
193, 195, 200, 202, 214, 221,
226-7, 231-2, 241, 246, 260, 267,
268, 269, 270, 272, 276-7, 287,
289, 290, 292, 301-2, 303, 305,
308, 313-14, 316, 318, 321, 326.
British S/M. attacked with, 183
demoralising effects of attack by, ... 183
attack described by Hersing, 202
Mediterranean inadequate
supply (1917), . . 255-6
destructive power of 300-lb.
pattern, ... 255
method of use, . . . 256
mortars for throwing, . . 256
increased supply of, and decline in shipping losses, . 256
disliked by enemy S/M., . 256
production of, and number
used (*see* Appendix I., p. 339).
with hydrophone, . 183, 287
'De Quillac' net begun and
completed, design of,
264-5, 276 n.
(*See* Barrages, Otranto
Straits.)
Derwent (Brit. T.B.D.) sk., . 165
Destroyer screen:
absence in loss of 'Three
Cressies', ... 7
absence in loss of *Formidable*, 19
beats off S/M. attack, . 18
U.S. arrival at Queenstown,
160, 175
Japanese arrival in Mediterranean 248
Greek and U.S. in Mediterranean 249
British loaned to Japanese, 249 n.
Detectors, S/M., electrical, . 148
(*Also see* Hydrophone.)
Deutschland. (*See* Submarines,
German, Mercantile.)
Devonian (Brit. S.S.) sk., . 201
D.H.S. (Brit. dftr.), . . . 131
Digby. (See *Artois.*)

2 C

402 THE GERMAN SUBMARINE WAR

Dinara (A.-H. T.B.D.) sk., . 274
Diomed (Brit. S.S.) sk., . . 309
Dittmar, Lt. G.N. (U 84), . 312
Djemnah (Fr. troopship) sk., . 273
Dogger Bank, action of Jan. 24, 1915, ... 18
Dominion (Brit. B.S.), . . 44
Don Arturis (Brit. S.S.) sk., . 185
Donegal (Brit. Amb. Transport) sk., . . 165, 166, 166 n.
Dornfontein (Brit. M.V.) sk., . 309
Dorothy Grey (Brit. trlr.), . . 17
Dover Castle (Brit. H.S.) sk., 249-50
  evidence of master of S.S. Elmmoor, ... 250
Dover Patrol, ... 6
  bombards Zeebrugge, . . 17
Dover Straits :
  first passed by U 18, . . 11
  drifter nets in, . . 19, 20
  A/S. nets laid, defects of, S/M. pass, ... 31
  U 32, U 33 find dangerous, . 36
  first prohibition to larger German S/M., . . . 36
  enemy S/M. find way through nets, ... 44
  Flanders S/M. ordered to go through, ... 50
  Flanders S/M. find no difficulty, ... 62
  failure of A/S. measures, . 116
  German destroyer raid, Oct. 1916, ... 117
  passage by larger S/M. ordered, 1917, . . . 144
  time saved by passage, . 144
  passage again forbidden to North Sea boats, . . 152
  raids by German destroyers, 152
  difficult for North Sea boats, 152
  over-confidence in 1915-16 barrages, ... 193
  North Sea S/M. ordered to use again (Sept. 1917), and surmises on origin of the order, ... 204-6
  passage again forbidden to North Sea boats (1918), impassable for all S/M., . 223, 284, 289
  destroyer raid, . . . 290
Downshire (Brit. S.S.) sk., . 32
Doxa (Gr. T.B.D., Fr.-manned) sk., ... 251
Drake (Brit. cruiser) sk., . 220-1
Dreadnought (Brit. B.S.), . 3
  sinks U 9, ... 35
Drina (Brit. S.S.) sk., . . 157

Druid (Brit. T.B.D.), . . 165
Dublin (Brit. L.C.) attkd., . 70
Duchess of Hamilton (Brit. M/S.) sk., ... 61
Duchess of Richmond (Brit. M/S.) sk. after War, . . 336
Duff, Rear Adm. A. L. (Director, Anti-Submarine Division, Admiralty), . . 147
Duke of Albany (Brit. A.B.S.) sk., ... 110
Duke of Connaught (Brit. S.S.) attkd., ... 325
Duke of Cumberland (Brit. S.S.) attkd., ... 325
Dulcie Doris (Brit. dftr.), . . 128
Dulwich (Brit. S.S.), sk., . 21
Dummy lighthouses, . . 188
Dundee (Brit. A.B.S.) sk., by U 19, ... 214
Dunluce Castle (Brit. H.S.) inspected by German S/M., 139
Dunraven (Brit. decoy), fight with UC 71, . . 197-9, 228
Dunsley (Brit. S.S.) sk., . . 52
Dupetit Thouars (Fr. cruiser) sk. by U 62, . . . 317
Durazzo, Allied attack upon, 274
Durward (Brit. S.S.) sk., . 21
Duster (Brit. trlr.), . . . 33
Dvinsk (Brit. S.S.) sk., . 307, 308

Eavestone (Brit. S.S.) sk., . 140
E. B. Walters (Brit. freight-vessel) sk., ... 310
Echunga (Brit. S.S.), sk., . 207
' Edgar '-class cruisers, . . 12
E.E.S. (Brit. dftr.), . . . 91
Elbing (Ger. L.C.) sk., . . 100
Elmmoor (Brit. S.S.) sk., . 250
  master's evidence on sinking of Dover Castle, . . 250
Eloby (Brit. transport) sk., . 258
Elsie Porter (Brit. freight-vessel) sk., ... 310
Ems River, ... 5, 18
Endurance (Brit. dftr.), . . 89
Endymion (Brit. cruiser), . 13
Englishman (Brit. S.S.) sk., . 86
Era (Brit. trlr.) sk., . . . 102
Eretria (Brit. S.S.) sk., . . 115
Erik (Brit. S.S.) sk., . . 309
Erin's Isle (Brit. M/S.) sk. after War, ... 336
Escorts 147
  unsuitability of trlrs., . . 136
  for important ships and troopships, . . 148, 173
  fast vessels essential, . . 281

INDEX 403

Escorts (contd.):
- in-shore, breakdown in working system, . . 176-7
- estimate of numbers for working Atlantic in and out convoys, . . . 174-5
- ocean : battleships, cruisers, A.M.C. used, . . . 174
- for U.S. troopships, collected at cost of trade defence, . 298
- proportions British and U.S. furnished for protection of cross-Atlantic troop-carriers 298
- number of ocean and destroyer escorts for U.S. troopships, . . . 298
- estimate for Mediterranean and Atlantic convoys (complete), . . 211-13 n.
- Mediterranean (1915-16), only for important ships, . 238
- interzone method, its defects, 240
- consecutive, adopted for Mediterranean, unsuitable vessels for patrols, escorted groups allowed, . 245
- for Mediterranean convoys, trlrs. unsuitable, . . 261

Ethel and Millie (Brit. decoy) sk., ... 199
Etonian (Brit. S.S.) sk., . . 291
Europe (Fr. aux. cruiser), . 28
Evening Star II. (Brit. dftr.), 128
Expeditionary forces :
- B.E.F. crosses to France, . 4
- Canadian E.F., . . 11, 14
- Salonica E.F., reduction recommended, . . 237, 245
- American E.F., U.S. transport of, . . 286-7, 298-9
- U-boats insufficient to molest, 298
- number of U.S. troops carried by Brit. ships, . . 298
- maximum number of troops in one convoy, . . . 299

Explosive sweeps, . . . 118

Fair Island, Ger. S/M. off, Aug. 1914, ... 2
Fairy (Brit. T.B.D.) founders after sinking UC 75, . . 306
Falaba (Brit. S.S.) sk., . 36, 42
Falkenhayn, General (Ger.), . 81
Falmouth, ... 40
Falmouth (Brit. L.C.) sk., . 107
Fandango (Brit. M/S.) sk. after War, ... 336
Fanning (U.S. T.B.D.), . 226-7

Farnborough (Q 5) (Brit. decoy)
- sinks U 68, ... 87
- sinks U 83, ... 150-1
Faulknor (Brit. Flot. leader), . 33
Fauvette (Brit. A.B.S.) sk., . 84
Fearless (Brit. L.C.), . 100, 112
Feasible (Brit. dftr.), . . 228
Feltria (Brit. S.S.) sk., . . 183
Firedrake (Brit. T.B.D.) captures UC 5, . . . 94
sinks UC 51, ... 226
First war cruise by Ger. S/M., 2
- contact Ger. S/M. with Brit. warships, ... 2
- torpedo attack, U 15 v. *Monarch*, . . . 2, 3, 4
- counter attack against S/M., 3
- S/M. sunk by mine, U 13 ? . 3
- S/M. sunk during War (Ger. U 15 by *Birmingham*), 3, 4
- warship sunk by S/M. (*Pathfinder* by U 21), . . 6
- Ger. S/M. to pass the Dover Straits (U 18), . . . 11
- steamer sunk by S/M. (S.S. *Glitra*), ... 13
- circumnavigation of British Isles by S/M. (U 20), . 14
- S/M. sunk by S/M. (E 3 by U 27), ... 15
- merchant-vessel torpedoed by S/M. (*Amiral Ganteaume* by U 24), . . 15
- Ger. S/M. at Zeebrugge (U 12), ... 16
- S/M. attack on merchant-vessel frustrated by flight (S.S. *Colchester*). . . 17
- ships torpedoed without warning (*Ikaria, Tokomaru, Oriole*). . . . 21
- ships torpedoed without warning and lost with all hands (*Oriole*), . . . 21
- H.S. attacked (*Asturias*), . 21
- D.A.M.S. escapes (S.S. *Atalanta*), ... 33
- D.A.M.S. to drive off S/M. by gunfire (*La Rosarina*), . 37
- Brit. mines off Heligoland, . 38
- U.S. merchant-vessel attkd. by S/M. (*Gulflight*), . 40, 42
- minefield laid by Ger. S/M. (UC 11), ... 44
- use of depth-charge, . . 47
- D.A.M.S. sunk (*Hesperian*), 59
Fisher, Lord, Adm. of the Fleet, ... 24
Fisher Girl (Brit. dftr.), . . 131

THE GERMAN SUBMARINE WAR

Fishing craft (Brit.) attkd., 37, 43-4, 44, 45, 46, 47, 49, 50
   statistics of losses, . . 65
   off East Coast (July 1916), 102
   destroyers sent to protect, . 103
   renewal of S/M. attacks (Sept. 1916), . . . 103
   by U 57, . . . 114-15
   by UC 32, ... 150
Flags, German use of Austrian, 68, 127
   forbidden, ... 79
Flanders: German Naval Forces (May 1918), commands and composition of, 295
Flares, ... 148
Flavia (Brit. S.S.) sk., . . 317
Fleet, Austro-Hungarian:
   mutinies at Cattaro (Feb. 1918), ... 267
   final collapse of, . . . 275
   vessels hoist Jugo-Slav flag, 275
   final disposal of, . . . 279
Fleet, Battle Cruiser (Brit.), danger from S/M. and minefield traps, . . 108-9
Fleet, Grand:
   fears for security of, at Scapa Flow, ... 4, 6
   coaling base at Loch Ewe, . 6
   proposals for German S/M. attack on, . . . 10, 11
   German S/M. leave to attack, 10, 11
   fears for security of Loch Ewe, ... 14
   at Lough Swilly, . . . 14
   loss of strategical position in Orkneys, . . . 14-15
   absent during S/M. attack, in support of Dover Patrol, 17
   97, 99, 101.
   bases (Scapa Flow, Cromarty, Firth of Forth), . . 106
   bases, leaves for action (Aug. 1916), . . . 106
   turns northwards, . . 107
   defects of Scapa Flow, . 107
   danger from S/M. and minefield traps, ... 108-9
   steaming endangered owing to fuel shortage, . . 166
   destroyers detached for patrol and escort duties, . 175
   German mining offensive against, 1918 . . . 300
   first and final attempts by German S/M. to enter anchorage 327
Fleet, High Sea, . . . 19, 44
   (*See also* Adms. von Ingenohl, von Pohl, Scheer, von Hipper.)
   difficulty of bringing to action, ... 107
   operations against English East Coast (Sunderland plan), ... 106-8
   support for S/M. and destroyer raids, . . 118, 122
   S/M. flotillas attached to (1918), ... 143
   mutiny in May (3rd Squadron) and Aug. 1917, . . 182
   plan for operns. by autumn 1918, ... 300
   sortie (April 1918), . . 301
   final sortie preparations, recall of S/M., . . . 325
   mutiny of Oct. 31, 1918, suppressed, . . . 327-8
   further mutiny breaks out and revolution begun, . 328-9
   internment of, . . . 330
Fleet messengers (Brit.). (See *Nugget, Osmanieh, Portia, Turquoise*.)
Flirt (Brit. T.B.D.) sk., . . 117
Flotillas:
   Destroyer (Brit.), 20th M/L. 207, 315
   Destroyer (Brit.), hunts for and sinks U 8, . . . 34
   Flanders (Ger.) established, 38
Formidable (Brit. B.S.) sk. by U 24, ... 19
Fort George (Brit. trlr.), . . 288
Forth, Firth of, entered by U 21, ... 5
Fourche (Fr. T.B.D.) sk., . 130
Fournet, Dartige du (Adm. Fr. Navy), C.-in-C. Mediterranean. 237
France IV. (Fr. transport) sk., 77
Franconia (Brit. troopship) sk., 132-3
Freiburg bombed as reprisal for attacks on hospital ships, ... 164
'French Coal Trade,' 152, 153, 153 n., 174, 232
Fryatt, Capt. (S.S. *Brussels*), judicial murder of, . . 36
F. Stobart (Brit. S.S.) sk., . 104
Fulgent (Brit. S.S. and Adm. Collier) sk., . . . 40
Funchal shelled by U 38, . 134
   shelled by U 156, . . . 219

INDEX

G. 42 (Ger. T.B.D.) sk., . . 152
G. 83 (Ger. T.B.D.) sk., . . 152
G. & E. (Brit. disguised trlr.),
                 50, 199 n.
  (See also *Nelson*.)
Gaelic (Brit. decoy, Q 22), . 190
Gaillardia (Brit. convoy sloop)
  sk., ... 315
Galatea (Brit. L.C.) attkd., . 99 n.
Galeka (Brit. H.S.) sk., . 115, 164
Gallia (Fr. aux. cruiser and
  troop-carrier) sk., . . 132
Galway Castle (Brit. S.S.) sk., . 320
Gamma (Dutch S.S.) sk., . 140
Garrigill (Brit. dftr.), . 124, 131
Garry (Brit. T.B.D.), 17, 18, 313
Gauchet (Adm. Fr. N., C.-in-C.
  Mediterranean), . . . 236
Gaulois (Fr. B.S.) sk., . . 134
Gauza (Arg. S.S.), . . . 168
Gayer (Capt. A., G.N.) quoted,
  5, 18, 24, 25, 30, 44, 49, 55, 62, 63,
  92, 93 n., 94-5, 102, 111 n., 114,
  125, 141, 216, 228 n., 233, 233 n.,
  242 n., 259, 259 n., 263, 270,
  282, 284, 298, 299 n., 323, 325.
  Cmr. G.N. and Cmr. 3rd S/M.
  Flot.), ... 96 n.
  on defects of construction
    programme, . . . 114
  criticises operations by U 33
    and U 39, ... 125
Geddes, Sir E., Shipping Con-
  troller, ... 162
  First Lord, . . 163, 224, 323
  predicts intensified struggle, 323
General Council of Officers
  (Ger.) on board *Graudenz*
  in Lister Deep, . . . 329
Genista (Brit. sloop) sk., . . 116
Gentian (Brit. sloop) sk. after
  War, ... 336
Ghurka (Brit. T.B.D.), . . 33
Gibel-Haman (Brit. S.S.) sk., . 320
Gibraltar, Straits of, concentra-
  tion of patrols on evacua-
  tion of Ger. S/M. in Medi-
  terranean, ... 276
Gipsy (Brit. T.B.D.), . . 228
Giralda (Sp. S.S.) sk., . . 296
Giuseppe Garibaldi (It. cruiser)
  sk., ... 73
Glaucus (Brit. S.S.) sk., . . 273
Gleaner of the Sea (Brit. dftr.), 91
Glen (Brit. decoy) sinks UB 39, 181
  other fights, ... 190
Glenart Castle (Brit. H.S.)
  sk., ... 288-9, 305
Glenartney (Brit. S.S.) sk., . 266

Glenboyne (Brit. trlr.) sk. after
  War, ... 336
Glengyle (Brit. S.S.) sk., . . 78
Glitra (Brit. S.S.) sk., . 13, 25
Gloaming (Brit. fishing-vessel)
  sk., ... 310
Glorious (Brit. cruiser), . . 211
Gloucester Castle (Brit. H.S.), . 164
Goissa (Brit. yacht) sk. after
  War, ... 336
Golo II. (Fr. Fleet aux.) sk., . 260
Goorkha (Brit. H.S.), . . 260
Goshawk (Brit. T.B.D.), . . 16 n.
Gough-Calthorpe, the Hon.
  Sir S. (Vice-Adm.):
  became S.N.O. of Malta
    Conference, . . . 247
  assumes command in Medi-
    terranean, ... 264
  decisions as to Otranto
    Barrage, ... 265
Government (Brit.):
  blockade policy, . . . 28
  U.S. note on use of U.S.
    colours, ... 29
  proposes arbitration on *Bara-*
    long, Ruel, Arabic, E 13
    incidents, ... 53
Government (Ger.):
  Lusitania, sinking of, . . 42
  Baralong incident, . . 52
  Note to U.S. regarding
    Arabic sinking, . . . 59
  opinion on U.S. Note to Brit.
    Govt., ... 62
  reply to U.S. on *Sussex* affair,
                             88-9
  Note to U.S., Jan. 31, 1917,
    on ' unrestricted war,' . 137
Gowan II. (Brit. dftr.), . . 289
Gowan Lea (Brit. dftr.), . . 254
Gradant (Black Sea town)
  shelled by S/M., . . 127
Grafton (Brit. ' blister ' cruiser), 259
  attkd., ... 260
Grangewood (Brit. S.S.) sk., . 48
Grant, Heathcoat S. (Rear-
  Adm. R.N.), . . . 236
Graudenz (Ger. L.C.), . . 329
' Great Landing,' the, 92 n., 194
Greif (Ger. raider) sk., . . 83
Greypoint (Brit. S.S.) sk., . 152
Grimm (Lt. G.N. Staff, H.S.F.), 328
Grive (Brit. A.B.S.) sk., . . 232
Grosser Kürfurst (Ger. B.S.)
  attkd., ... 118
Guerdon (Brit. dftr.), . . 131
Guildford Castle (Brit. H.S.)
  attkd., ... 293

Gulflight (U.S. S.S.) attkd., 40, 42
Gunner (Brit. disguised trlr.), 47, 178 n.
Gwatkin-Williams, R. S. (Capt. R.N.) quoted, . . . 206 n.

Halberdier (Brit. S.S.) sk., . 286
Halcyon (Brit. T.G.B.) sinks UB 27, ... 193
Hall, S. S., Capt. R.N., . . 24
Hallwright, W. W., Cmr. R.N., 171
Hamburg (Ger. L.C.), . . 44
Hampshire (Brit. cruiser) attkd. by U.25, ... 46-7
sk., . . 100-1, 128-9, 229, 321
'Handels U-Boote,' . . . 182
Hanna Larsen (Brit. S.S.), master of, ... 150
Harmatris (Brit. S.S.) sk., . 84
Harpathian (Brit. S.S.) sk., . 307
Harwich Force, . . 7, 106
destroyers detached from, . 175
convoying and losses from mines, ... 233
Hawk (Brit. trlr.), . . . 45
Hawke (Brit. cruiser) sk. by U 9 . . . . 13, 16 n.
Hayes, Sir Bertram, Capt. (S.S. *Olympic*), quoted, 303-4, 304 n.
Hazelwood (Brit. S.S.) sk., . 222
Heather (Q 16) (Brit. sloop), . 171
Heatherside (Brit. S.S.) sk., . 201
Heinecke, Capt. G.N., . . 290
Helfferich, Herr (Ger. Sec. of State), ... 113
Helgoland (Ger. B.S.), . 327 n.
Helgoland (A.-H. L.C.), . . 254
Heligoland, Bight of, action Aug. 1914, . . . 5
Heligoland, S/M. stationed round, ... 1, 18
Allied threat to occupy, 330-1
Herbert, Godfrey (Cmr. R.N., D.S.O.), . 47, 52-3, 60, 188
Hermes (Brit. seaplane-carrier, ex-cruiser) sk. by U 27, 16, 16 n.
Hersing (U 21), Ger. S/M. officer 20
Hesione (Brit. S.S.) sk., . . 60
Hesperian (Brit. S.S.) sk., 59, 118, 209
Highcliffe (Brit. S.S.) sk., . 319
Highland Corrie (Brit. S.S.) sk., 183
Highland Harris (Brit. S.S.) sk., 317
Hilary (Brit. A.M.C.) sk. by U 88, ... 184
Hildebrand (Brit. A.M.C.), . 220
Himalaya (Fr. aux. cruiser) sk., 251

Hindenburg, Ger. Field-Marshal, . . 113-14, 119, 299 n.
Hindenburg (Ger. B.C.), . . 211
Hipper, Adm. von, C.-in-C. H.S.F., . 301, 301 n., 328
Hirano Maru (Jap. S.S.) sk., . 322
Hogue(Brit. cruiser) sk. byU9, 7-9, 12
Holtzendorff, Adm. G.N. :
Ch. of Naval Staff, . . 58
proposes resumption of trade war, ... 81, 105
at Pless, ... 113
sends Capt. v. Bülow to G.H.Q., ... 119
203.
succeeded by Scheer, . 301 n.
Hood, Rear-Adm. the Hon. H. L. A., . . . 16, 37
'Hoofden,' the, definition of, 4, 38, 39, 310 n.
Horns Reef, German S/M. stationed off, Aug. 1914, . 2
Horthy, Capt. A.-H. Navy, 254, 271-2
Hospital ships :
German attacks upon, 1917 and 1918, . 139, 164-6, 285-6
renewed German allegations of British misuse : *Copenhagen* cited, . 138-9, 312
German conditions for use of, . . . 139, 166, 285
allegations denied by Admiralty (inspection of *Mauretania* and *Dunluce Castle* cited), . . . 139
cross-Channel service, . . 165-6
Spanish control officers for Mediterranean arranged, 166, 250-1, 285
(See also Brit. H.S. : *Anglia, Asturias, Braemar Castle, Britannic, Copenhagen, Dover Castle, Dunluce Castle, Galeka, Glenart Castle, Gloucester Castle, Guildford Castle, Goorkha, Karapara, Lanfranc, Llandovery Castle, Mauretania, Neuralia, Rewa, St. Andrew, Salta.*
Dutch : *Koningin Regentes.*
French : *La France.*
Italian : *Marechiaro.*
Russian : See *Portugal, Vperyed.*)
(*Also* Ambulance Transports.)

INDEX 407

Housatonic (U.S. S.S.) sk., . 140
Howitzers, A/S., . . 148, 256
Huntly (Brit. S.S.) sk., . . 62
Huntress (Brit. S.S.) attkd., . 307
Hurunui (Brit. S.S.) sk., . . 306
Hydrophones :
  first use of, . . . 90, 186 n.
  first use with depth-charge, . 104
  shore stations and ships, . 148
  trlrs. ahead of convoys with, 177
  Lizard Division, . . . 187
  stations established with
    M/L. attached, . . . 186
  types and moral effect of, . 187
  used in attack—
    against UC 66, . . 187-8
    against UC 41, . . . 200
    against U 50, . . . 209
    against UB 63, . . . 287
  units, methods of working, . 188
  laying of mines detected by, 188
  drifters with, and bases, . 206
  expl. and instructional shore
    station, Malta; instruc-
    tional station at Gallipoli
    (S. Italy); shore station
    S. of Otranto, 1917, 255 n.
  'plate' and 'shark fin'
    pattern for S/M. craft in
    Mediterranean, 1917, 255 n.
  extended use in Otranto
    Straits, ... 259
  'fish' type, ... 266
  shore stations, home waters, 268
  M/L. fitted with (Mediter-
    ranean), ... 268
  'C' tube used by German
    seaman, ... 273
  units in North Channel, . 286
  Torbay unit, ... 318

Ibo (Port. G.B.) attkd., . . 110
Ikaria (Brit. S.S.) sk., . . 21
Ilderton (Brit. S.S.) sk., . . 219
Îles Chanzey (Fr. M/S.) sk., . 84
Impetuoso (It. T.B.D.) sk., 130, 252
India (Brit. A.M.C.) sk. by U 27, 55
Indien (Fr. aux. cruiser) sk., . 75
Infanta Isabel de Borbon (Sp.
  S.S.), ... 296
Inflexible (Brit. B.C.), . . 107
Ingenohl, Adm. von (C.-in-C.
  H.S.F.), succeeded by
  Rear-Adm. von Pohl, . 27
Ingleside (Brit. S.S.) sk., . . 269
Intrepido (It. T.B.D.) sk., . 126
Inverlyon (Brit. decoy), . . 50
Inverlyon (Brit. sailing vessel)
  sk., ... 128

Ionian (Brit. S.S.) sk., . . 222
Iran (Brit. S.S.) sk., . . 200
Irene (Trinity House vessel
  lent to Dover Patrol) sk., 61
Iron Duke (Brit. B.S., flagship
  of C.-in-C. Grand Fleet), . 3
Itchen (Brit. T.B.D.), . . 150
  sk., ... 191
Ivernia (Brit. troopship), . 134

Jacinth (Brit. trlr.), . . . 200
Jackal (Brit. T.B.D.), . . 165
Jacob Jones (U.S. T.B.D.) sk., 230
Jagow, Herr von (Ger. Foreign
  Minister), ... 113
Jean Bart (Fr. B.S.) attkd., . 69
Jellicoe, Adm. Sir John, C.-in-C.
  Grand Fleet :
  detaches leader and de-
    stroyers, ... 33
  anticipates S/M. and mine-
    field traps, ... 108
  indicates 'danger line' of
    North Sea, . . . 109
  views on possibilities of fleet
    action in southern parts of
    North Sea, . . . 109-10
  First Sea Lord, Nov. 1916, . 116
  quoted on S/M.-laid mine-
    fields up to June 1916, . 128
  asked to deal with imminent
    S/M. warfare, . . . 147
  explains gravity of situation
    to Adm. Sims, U.S.N., . 159
  quoted, . 160, 179, 207-8, 224,
    255 n., 315
  recognises delay in maturing
    of A/S. measures, . . 173
  at Inter-Allied Naval Con-
    ference (Sept. 1917), 211-13 n.
  ceases to be First Sea Lord
    and Chief of Naval Staff, 224
  recommends reduction of
    Salonica force, . . . 245
Jessamine (Brit. sloop) sinks
  U 104, ... 302
J. L. Luckenbach (U.S. S.S.), . 221
John Gillman (Brit. trlr.), . 316
John o' Scott (Brit. S.S.) sk., . 320
John Roberts (Brit. dftr.) sk.
  after War, ... 336
Justicia (ex *Statendam*) (Brit.
  troopship) sk., . . . 313
Jutland Battle, German S/M.
  dispositions before, dur-
    ing, and after, . . 98-101

Kaiser (Ger. B.S.), . . . 211
Kaiserin (Ger. B.S.), . . 211

	PAGE
Kaiser Wilhelm II. (Ger. B.S., Hulk-Flagship H.S.F.),	328
Kale (Brit. T.B.D.), sk.,	300
Kandy (Brit. S.S.),	272
Kanguru (Fr. S/M. depot and docking ship) sk.,	134
Kanran (T.B.D. lent to Japan). (See *Nemesis.*)	
Karapara (Brit. H.S.),	249
Karina (Br. S.S.) sk.,	200
Karnak (Brit. S.S.),	164
Karonga (Brit. S.S.) sk.,	247
Kedingen (Ger. M/S.) capt.,	211
Kelvinhead (Brit. S.S.) sk.,	155
Kelvinia (Brit. S.S.) sk.,	115
Kerr, Adm. Mark E. F., R.N.	10
Keyes, Sir Roger (Vice-Adm.), Pres. Operns. Committee, becomes S.N.O. Dover; modifies barrage and blockship plans,	224-5
Kiev (Russ. S.S.) sk.,	127
Kilcoan (Brit. S.S.) sk.,	20
' Killer ' boats (destroyers),	255, 257, 266
Kimberley (Brit. trlr.),	99
King Alfred (Brit. cruiser) attkd.,	220-1
Kinross (Brit. M/S.) sk. after War,	336
Kitchener, Field-Marshal Earl,	101
Kite balloons:	
sloops with,	266
observation with convoy,	177
Kléber (Fr. cruiser) sk.,	186
Königsberg (Ger. L.C.), 300,	300 n.
Königin Luise (Ger. M/L.),	10
Koningin Regentes (Dutch H.S. repatriating Brit. prisoners of war) sk.,	312
Kosseir (Brit. S.S.) sk.,	274
Kraft, Adm. G.N.,	328
Kronprinz (Ger. B.S.) attkd.,	118
Kronprinz Wilhelm. (See *Von Steuben.*)	
Krupps,	71
La Blanca (Brit. S.S.) sk.,	229
Laburnum (Brit. sloop),	151
Ladybird (Brit. ' China ' G.B.),	259
Lady Ismay (Brit. M/S.),	61
Laertes (Brit. S.S.) sk.,	200
La France (Fr. H.S.),	138
Lake Michigan (Brit. S.S.) sk.,	293
Lanao (U.S. S.S.) sk.,	116
La Negra (Brit. S.S.) sk.,	207
Lanfranc (Brit. H.S.) sk.,	165
Lapland (Brit. S.S.),	155
La Provence. (See *Provence II.*)	
La Rosarina (Brit. S.S.) attkd.,	37

	PAGE
Lassoo (Brit. T.B.D.) sk.,	115
Laurentic (Brit. A.M.C.) sk.,	154
Lavender (Brit. sloop) sk. by UC 75,	181
Lavernock (Brit. S.S.) sk.,	320
Law, International, German allegation of Brit. violation,	26
Leader-cable,	316
Leasowe Castle (Brit. troopship) sk.,	270-1
Leda (Brit. G.B.) attkd.	16 n.
Leelanaw (U.S. S.S.) sk.,	48
Le Faon (Fr. fishing-vessel),	289
Leinster (Brit. S.S.) sk.,	322
Leon Gambetta (Fr. cruiser) sk.,	69
Leopard (Ger. raider),	214
Lerchenfeld, Count (Bavarian envoy),	324
Leven (Brit. T.B.D.) sinks UB 35,	287
Leviathan (Brit. cruiser),	34
Liberty (Brit. T.B.D.) sinks UC 46,	150
Lieutenant Pustchin (Russ. T.B.D.) sk.,	127
Liffey (Brit. T.B.D.),	165
Lightning (Brit. T.B.D.) sk.,	50, 61
Linda Blanche (Brit. S.S.) sk.,	20
Lion (Brit. B.C.), Dogger Bank,	18
' Live Bait Squadron,'	7
Lively (Brit. T.B.D.),	322
Liverpool (Brit. S.S.) sk.,	116
Livingstone (Brit. trlr.) sk.,	232
Llandovery Castle (Brit. H.S.) sk.,	311-12
Llewellyn (Brit. T.B.D.) sinks UC 19,	119
damaged,	152
Loch Ewe,	6, 14
Loch Lomond (Brit. S.S.) attkd.,	189, 251
London, Declaration of,	26 n., 28 n.
Lord Alverstone (Brit. trlr.) sk.,	232
Lord Leitrim (Brit. dftr.),	303
Lorna (Brit. yacht),	305
Lough Fisher (Brit. S.S.) sk.,	291
Lough Swilly,	14
Louise (Dan. S.S.),	48
Louisiane (Fr. S.S.) sk.,	84
Louvain (Brit. A.B.S.) sk.,	266
Lowdale (Brit. S.S.) sk.,	244
Lowestoft, bombardment of,	93
Loyal Friend (Brit. dftr.),	303
Lucille M. Schnare (Brit. fishing-vessel), sk.	310
Ludendorff, German General,	113, 119, 235, 299 n.
in favour of unrestricted warfare,	119

INDEX 409

	PAGE
Ludlow (Brit. paddle M/S.) sk.,	117
Lusitania (Brit. S.S.), use of U.S. colours by,	28
sk., . . 40-2, 58, 118,	209
Lux (Brit. S.S.), loss of, .	123
Luxburg, Count (Ger. chargé d'affaires, Buenos Ayres),	168
Luz Blanca (Brit. S.S.) sk., .	309
Lychnis (Brit. convoy sloop), .	272
Lydonia (U.S. yacht), .	269
Lyndiane (Fr. S.S.) sk., .	317
Lynx (Brit. T.B.D.) sk., .	16 n.
Lysander (Brit. T.B.D.), .	312
M 15 (Brit. monitor), .	259
sk. by UC 38, .	260
M 29 (Brit. monitor), .	259
M 31 (Brit. monitor), .	259
M 32 (Brit. monitor), .	259
Maclay, Sir Joseph (Shipping Controller), .	163
Magellan (Fr. transport) sk., .	134
Mahan, the late Adm. A. T. (U.S.N.), views on interception of enemy forces compared with war experiences, .	257 n.
Majesty (Brit. dftr.), .	228
Malachite (Brit. S.S.) sk., .	17
Malakand (Brit. S.S.) sk., .	168
Malda (Brit. S.S.) sk., .	201
Mallard (Brit. T.B.D.), .	322
Maloja (Brit. S.S.) sk., .	83-4
'Malta Commission,' 211-13 n.	
Malta : dummy barrages,	248
Manchester Trader (Brit. S.S.) sk., .	250
Mann-Tiechler, Ritter v. (Adm. G.N.), Chief of new 'Submarine Bureau,' 233, 299 n.	
Secy. of State for Navy,	301 n.
Manœuvres, naval, (1913) Brit., (1914) German,	24
Mantola (Brit. S.S.) sk., .	140
Mantua (Brit. A.M.C.), .	103
Maori (Brit. T.B.D.), .	33
sk., .	61
Maplewood (Brit. S.S.) sk., .	243
Marechiaro (It. H.S.) sk., .	126
Margate shelled by German destroyers, .	152
Marie (Ger. S.S.) runs blockade, .	83
Marina (Brit. S.S.) sk., .	116
Marion Adams (Brit. fishing-vessel) sk. .	310
Mariston (Brit. S.S.) sk., .	192
Mark-Wardlaw, W. P., Lt.R.N.,	48
Marlborough (Brit. B.S.) attkd.,	100

	PAGE
Marmora (Brit. A.M.C.) sk., .	313
Marne (Brit. T.B.D.), .	313
Marquette (Brit. troopship) sk.,	76
Martin (Brit. T.B.D.), .	273
Mary (Brit. dftr.), .	303
Mary B. Mitchell (Q 9) (Brit. decoy), .	190
Mary Rose (Brit. T.B.D.) sk., .	232
Marzala (Ger. S.S.), . 43, 70	
'Massacre of the Innocents,' 233 n.	
Mashobra (Brit. S.S.) sk., .	244
Massue (Fr. T.B.D.), .	241
Matsu (Jap. T.B.D.), .	248
Mauretania (Brit. S.S.), . 86, 308	
(H.S.) inspected by neutral consuls, .	139
M'Laughlin, Prof. (Chicago Univ.), .	158-9
Mechanician (Brit. commissioned escort ship) sk., .	286
Medea (Brit. T.B.D.), .	156
Medea (Dutch S.S.) sk., .	35
Medina (Brit. S.S.) sk., .	168
Mediterranean :	
suitable conditions for cruiser warfare, . 67, 80, 135-6, 238	
unsuitable for mine-laying, 129, 242, 278	
Division and Allied naval commands, . 236, 278	
dispersed shipping routes, 241-2	
Algerian coast route given up	241
convergence of shipping routes, .	242
Medora (Brit. S.S.) sk., .	306
Melampus (Brit. T.B.D.) sinks UC 16, .	220
Memling (Brit. S.S.) sk., .	222
Memphian (Brit. S.S.) sk., .	222
Menfi (It. transport), .	267
Mentor (Brit. T.B.D.), .	180
Mercantile shipping :	
replacement tonnage, concrete ships, Allied building efforts, .	202-3
1914-17, British and foreign (Admy. Table), .	234
repair of : number and tonnage—	
Aug. 1917 .	191
Nov. 1917, .	234
seizure of enemy, 1914-17 (Admy. Table), .	234
sabotage of enemy ships lying in neutral ports, .	121
defensive armaments, Admy. instructions to masters of,	82
instructional courses for officers of, .	177

410 THE GERMAN SUBMARINE WAR

Mercantile shipping (*contd.*):
  capture of masters of, April
    1917, ... 168-9
  abandoned by German
    S/M., ... 177
Merchant Navy (Brit.):
  1917, total, ... 162-3
  1914-17, built, captured, lost,
    deficit, ... 163
Mercia (Brit. S.S.) sk., . . 276
Mercian (Brit. troopship) attkd. 77
Merionethshire (Brit. S.S.) sk., 306
Meror (Brit. trlr.), . . . 228
Merton Hall (Brit. S.S.) sk., . 288
Mesaba (Brit. S.S.) sk., . . 319
Meteor (Ger. aux. M/L.), 56, 111
Meurer, Adm. G.N., 300 n.
Meux, the late Adm. Sir Hed-
  worth, ... 47
Mexico City (Brit. S.S.) sk., . 288
Michael (Brit. T.B.D.), . . 292
Michelsen, Andreas, Adm. G.N.:
  quoted, . 93 n., 117, 141, 142,
    264 n., 275, 293
  orders large S/M. to pass
    Dover Straits, . . . 204
  forbids large S/M. to pass
    Dover Straits, . . . 284
  during mutiny, . . . 327-39
Middlesex (Brit. S.S.) sk., 183-4
Mignonette (Brit. sloop) sk., . 154
Milbrook (Brit. T.B.D.), . . 313
Milne (Brit. T.B.D.), . . 180
Milwaukee (Brit. S.S.) sk., . 317
Minas (It. troopship) sk., . 240
Minefields:
  off Humber (Ger.), 1914, . 5
  laid by *Königin Luise* (Ger.), 10
  off Ostend (Brit.), 10, 11, 31, 62
  off Tory Is., laid by *Berlin*
    (Ger.), ... 14
  off Zeebrugge, . . . 17
  Dunkirk - Broadstairs, Feb.
    1915, ... 31
  Britain, deep, off Beachy
    Head and Dartmouth, . 39
  German, North Sea, . . 44
  British, Bight, laid by E 24, 38
  German, laid by *Hamburg*, . 44
  Gayer's opinion of, . . 44
  German—
    off E. Coast, Harwich and
      Dover, ... 50
    off Boulogne, Folkestone,
      S.E. Coast, . . . 51
    laid by surface vessels
      (U 9), Finnish Gulf, . 56 n.
    laid by surface vessels
      (*Meteor*), Moray Firth, . 56

Minefields—German (*contd.*):
  laid by surface vessels
    (*Möwe*), Cape Wrath, . 63
  laid by surface vessels
    (*Meteor*), White Sea
    (1915), ... 111
  off Dover, Nore, Lowe-
    stoft, Grimsby. . . 61
  Thames Estuary by U 44, 63
  Tees Mouth by U 44, . 83
  W. of Orkneys by U 75, 99, 101
  Tyne, Humber, Dogger
    Bank, approaches to
    Sunderland, . . . 108
  White Sea by S/M. (1916), 111
  laid in new areas, . . 115-16
  statistics and localities
    (1916), ... 115
  Mass L.V.-Ymuiden, . 117
    loss of British T.B.D., . 117
  off Forth against Scandi-
    navian convoy, . . 117
  off Harwich, . . . 117
  off Forth (*Sabbia* field) by
    U 74, . . . 86, 128
  off Valona by UC 14, . 126
  Adriatic by UC 12, . . 126
  off Durazzo by UC 12, . 126
  off Brindisi by UC 12, . 126
  off Cape Linguetta by UC 14, 126
  off Bari and Corfu, . . 128
  off Lisbon by U 73, . 128-9
  off Malta by U 73, . . 129
  Italian—
    off Otranto (surface ships), 131
  German—
    in Zea Channel by U 73, 133
    in Mykoni Channel, . . 133
    in Suda Bay, . . . 133
  British—
    laid outside Dardanelles
      by surface ships, . 135 n.
    Heligoland Bight A/S. bar-
      rage adopted, . 147-8
    Heligoland Bight and
      Dover (deep) adopted, . 148
  German—
    off Sunderland by UC 32, 150
    number laid, swept up,
      casualties, areas of
      (1917), ... 153
    in Western Isles by U 80, 154
    off Barrow-in-Furness, . 154
    off Harwich and in Irish
      Sea, ... 154
    immunity of E. Coast, . 154
    tactics of German S/M.
      M/L., ... 154
    off Liverpool, . . . 155

INDEX

Minefields—German (contd.):
  off Orkneys, . . 155, 188
  off Forth, ... 188
  off Harwich, 1917, . . 188
  Bell Rock, Clyde, Channel, 179
  Havre, Ouistreham, Cherbourg by UC 26, . . 180
  defensive in Heligoland Bight, ... 179
  British—
    failure of, in Heligoland Bight (Jan. 1917), . . 178-9
  German—
    M/S. and naval losses in Bight, ... 179
    redoubled mining activity (Feb. 1917) in S.W. Irish waters, punctuality of laying, ... 196
    intensive campaign and little result, . . . 206
  British—
    number of mines laid in Heligoland Bight and Dover, 1917, . . . 207-8
    Heligoland Bight, German-swept channels through, 208
    Heligoland Bight, German S/M. dive under, . . 208
    Heligoland Bight, mines and nets added, . . 209
    Kattegat, ... 210
    Heligoland Bight, temporarily impassable, . . 210
    off Whitby, . . . 214
  German—
    in Kola Inlet (Apr. 1917), losses from, . . . 220
  British—
    laid off landfalls to catch S/M., ... 230-1
  German—
    pattern and positions of (end of 1917), . . 231
    laid off Alexandria by U 73, ... 242
    laid off Alexandria and Malta (Oct. 1917), . 260
    laid off Cape Rosa by UC 37, ... 248
    laid off Salonica by UC 23, 251
    laid off Brindisi by UC 25, 254, 255
    laid off Syracuse and Malta (1917), . . 258
  British—
    laid off Dardanelles and Gibraltar, . . 135, 279
    laid in Heligoland Bight,

Minefields—British (contd.):
  sk. UB 22 and three T.B.D., ... 287
  laid in North Channel (deep), incomplete Nov. 1918, ... 286
  laid in Heligoland Bight extended, force S/M. to use Kattegat exit, . 289
  German—
    laid off Cape Henry and in Delaware Bay by U 151, 307
    laid off U.S. coast by U 156, 308
    laid off U.S. coast by U 117, 309
    laid off U.S. coast by U 152 or 155, ... 310
    laid off Bell Rock, purpose of, swept up by British as laid, . . 300
    Number of M/S. working, 310, 325
  British—
    Scapa Flow defences (1918) sk. UB 116, . . . 327
  German—
    Arctic fields, . . 220, 335
    laid by surface ships in Indian Ocean by *Wolf*, 335
    groups and number of mines laid, 1914-18, . 335
    clearance, post-war Aug. 1914-Nov. 1918, number of mines swept up, . 335
    losses from mines, 1918-1919, ... 336
Minefields. *See also* Barrages.
Mine nets:
  off North Foreland, sk. UC 21, 213
  laid off Flamborough Head, 230
  Otranto Straits barrage, disable UB 53, . . . 273
Mines, British:
  defects of,
    10, 11, 31, 38, 39, 92, 144-5, 179
  first laid off Heligoland, . 38
  Elia pattern (Brit.), . . 144
  action of currents, . . 144
  improved pattern, . . 148
  useless stock of, . . . 179
  delivery of Mark H 2, 179, 207-8, 223
  number planted in Bight, 207-8
  defects of (Northern Barrage), 315, 315 n.
  laid off Start Point sk. UB 18, ... 226
  laid off Is. of W. sk. UB 81, 228
  laid off Terschelling sk. UB 61 and U 75, . . 229

412   THE GERMAN SUBMARINE WAR

Mines, German :
  average British ships sunk by, 145
  last 5 months' ' cruiser war,' 145
  number laid off Harwich, Jan.-Sept. 1917, . . 188
  ' Monday-Tuesday-Wednesday ' type of, . . . 154-5
Minesweepers, British :
  sk., ... 61
  paddle-wheel, . . . 155
  ' Dance ' class, . . . 155
  force and strength of, types, 155
  off Liverpool, . . . 155
  10th Sloop Flot. sent to Queenstown, . . 154, 196
  of War Channel, . . . 154
  loss off Harwich, 1917 (number of types), . . . 188
  efficiency of, ... 206
  number in Firth of Forth, 1918, ... 300
  (See also *Blackmorevale, Brighton Queen, Clacton, Cupar, Duchess of Hamilton, Duchess of Richmond, Erin's Isle, Fandango, Kinross, Lady Ismay, Ludlow, Princess Mary II., Sword Dance, Totnes.*)
Minesweepers (German) :
  extension of swept channels through British fields in Bight, . . 208, 210-11
  sweepers capt. by British, 209 n., 211
  losses, . . . 210-11, 211
  battleships in support of, . 211
Mingary (Brit. yacht), . . 100
Miniota (Brit. S.S.) sk., . . 201
Minneapolis (Brit. S.S.) sk., . 126
Minnehaha (Brit. S.S.) sk., . 207
Minnesota (U.S. B.S.), . . 310
Minnetonka (Brit. S.S.) sk., . 266
Minnewaska (Brit. S.S.) sk., . 133
Minstrel (Brit. T.B.D.), . . 249
Miranda (Brit. T.B.D.), . . 180
Mirlo (Brit. S.S.) sk., . . 309
Missanabie (Brit. S.S.) sk., . 319
Missourian (U.S. S.S.) sk., . 243
Mobile (Brit. S.S. and Admy. collier) sk., ... 40
Mohawk (Brit. T.B.D.), . . 16 n.
  mine injury, ... 61
Moldavia (Brit. A.M.C. carrying U.S. troops) sk., . 299
Moltke (Ger. B.C.), 118, 211, 301
Monarch (Brit. B.S.) attkd. by U 15, . . . 2, 3, 4
Monarch (cable-ship) sk., . 51

Mongara (Brit. S.S.) sk., . 258
Mongolian (Brit. S.S.) sk., 312-13
Monrovia, W/T. station shelled by U 154, ... 296
Montebello (Brit. S.S.) sk., . 311
Montfort (Brit. S.S.) sk., . . 322
Mooltan (Brit. S.S.) sk., . . 258
Moorina (Brit. transport) sk., 76
Moravia (Brit. trlr.), . . 214
Moresby (Brit. T.B.D.), . . 292
Motagua (Brit. A.M.C.), . . 184
Motor launches (M.L.) (Brit.) :
  No. 155, ... 277
  No. 263, ... 314
  No. 373, ... 277
  No. 413, ... 268
  sent to Otranto Straits, . 131
  used as M/S., . . 315-16
Möwe (Ger. raider and aux. M/L.), ... 63, 145
Müller, von, Adm. G.N., . . 58
  opinion on conduct of War, . 105
Myrtle (Brit. sloop) sk. after War, ... 336

Namur (Brit. S.S.) sk., . . 260
Narcissus II. (Brit. yacht), . 216
Narragansett (Brit. S.S.) sk., . 157
Nasturtium (Brit. sloop) sk., . 129
Naval administration (Ger.), ' Submarine Bureau,' . 233
Naval losses (Brit.) tabulated (combatant and commissioned vessels, aux. patrol and Fleet aux.), by S/M. and mine, ... 335
Naval policy (Brit.) reviewed after Aug. 18-19, 1916, . 107-9
Nellie Nutten (Brit. trlr.) sk., . 102
Nelson (Brit. decoy), sk. . . 199
Nembo (It. T.B.D.) sk., . . 131
Nemesis (Brit. T.B.D.), 249, 249 n.
Nentmoor (Brit. S.S.) sk., . 244
Neptune (Brit. B.S.), . . 35
Nessus (Brit. T.B.D.), . . 184
Netherlands :
  anger with Germany over U 21's attack on eight ships, ... 135, 146
  German conditions for steamer service to England, ... 137
Nets :
  A/S. defence for merchant vessels, ... 148
  drifter :
    decided to lay across Dover Straits, . 19, 31, 37
    defects of, . . . 19-20, 39

INDEX

Nets (*contd.*):
  indicator, first tried (1904), 23
  laid in North Channel, . 31
  laid in St. George's Channel, 31, 189
  laid in Start Bay, . . 33
  materials for Dover Straits sent to Gallipoli, . . 37
  UC 65 escapes from nets in St. George's Channel, . 189
Neuralia (Brit. H.S.), . . 75
Neutrals:
  increase of trade with Germany, ... 28
  immunity from attack, . 30
  decision to lay up shipping, 146
New York (U.S. S.S.), . . 155
Nicholas, Grand Duke, . . 127
Nicholson (U.S. T.B.D.), . 221, 226
Nicosian (Brit. S.S.) attkd., . 52-3
Niger (Brit. T.G.B.) sk. by U 12, ... 16, 17
Noble (Brit. T.B.D.), . . 184
Noma (U.S. yacht), . . . 198
Norseman (Brit. S.S., horse-transport) attkd., . . 125
'North-about route,' 14, 36, 37, 152
  U 32 returns by, . . . 36
  effect of, on shipping losses, 37
North Channel, . . . 31
Northern Russian waters, 206, 211-13 n., 219
North Wales (Brit. S.S.) sk., . 119
Norway:
  loss of tonnage, . . . 204
  forbids use of territorial waters to S/M., . . 189
Nottingham (Brit. L.C.) sk., . 106
Novara (A.-H. L.C.), . . 254
Nubian (Brit. T.B.D.) attkd., 117
Nugget (Brit. Fleet messenger) sk., ... 48
Nymphe (Brit. T.B.D.) attacks U 9, ... 13

Oakleaf (Brit. S.S.) sk., . . 192
Oceanic II. (Brit. decoy) attkd., 45
Ocean Roamer (Brit. dftr.), . 303
Oilers (oil-tankers), losses, Mar.-Sept. 1917, . . . 166
Oil fuel, shortage of (1917); reserves reduced; Grand Fleet steaming reduced; carried in liners' double bottoms, . . . 166-7
Oku (Brit. trlr.), . . . 98
Olive Branch (Brit. S.S.) sk., 206, 206 n.
Olympic (Brit. troop-carrier) attkd., ... 75
  sinks U 103, ... 303-4
Omrah (Brit. troopship) sk., . 270
Onslow (Brit. T.B.D.) sinks UB 17, ... 290
Onward (Brit. trlr.) sk., . . 102
Opal (Brit. S.S.) sk., . . 116
Operations, combined, 15, 19, 24
Ophelia (Brit. T.B.D.), 321, 321 n.
Opossum (Brit. T.B.D.), . . 318
Oracle (Brit. T.B.D.), . . 195
Orama (Brit. A.M.C.) sk., . 221
Oran (Arg. S.S.), . . . 168
Orduna (Brit. S.S.) attkd., . 45
Oriole (Brit. S.S.) sk., . . 21
Orion (Brit. B.S.), . . . 2
Orissa (Brit. S.S.) sk., . . 311
Orkneys, ... 14
Oronsa (Brit. S.S.) sk., . 293-4
Oropesa. (See *Champagne*.)
Orvieto (Brit. M/L.), . . 91
Osmanieh (Brit. Fleet messenger) sk., . . . 262
Ostend, proposals for recapture of, ... 19
Ostfriesland (Ger. B.S.), mutiny on board, ... 327-8
Otranto, Straits of:
  compared with Dover, . . 124
  net drifters sent to, . . 124
  action of May 15, 1917, 254-5
'Otter' gear, . . . 148, 155
Otway (Brit. A.M.C.) sk., . 191
Our Friend (Brit. dftr.), . . 303
Ouse (Brit. T.B.D.), . 316, 319, 321

Page, Walter (U.S. ambassador, London) quoted, . . 159
Palembang (Dutch S.S.) sk., . 85
Pallada (Russ. cruiser) sk. by U 26, ... 56
Panteleimon (Russ. B.S.) attkd., 74
Paragon (Brit. T.B.D.) sk., . 152
Paramount (Brit. dftr.), . . 228
Paravanes, ... 155
Pargust (Brit. decoy) sinks UC 29, ... 181
Paris (Brit. M/L.), . . . 91
Paris II. (Fr. patrol vessel) sk., 262
Parker (U.S. T.B.D.), . . 289
Parkgate (Brit. S.S.) sk., . . 243
Parslow, F., Lieut. R.N.R., V.C., ... 45
Partenope (It. M/L., convoy escort) sk., ... 267
Partridge (Brit. T.B.D.) sk., . 232
Partridge II. (Brit. trlr.), . 272

Pass of Balmaha (U.S. sailing
    vessel) captured, . 47, 47 n.
Patagonia (Brit. S.S.) sk., . 73
Patagonier (Brit. S.S.) sk., . 244
Patia (Brit. A.M.C.) sk., . . 311
Patriot (Brit. T.B.D.), sinks
    U 69 191
Patrol boats (Brit.) (for PC boats
    see Decoy Vessels) :
  P 19, ... 164
  P 26, ... 165
  P 37, ... 165
  P 39, ... 317
  P 45, ... 317
  PC 51, sinks U 61, . . 292
  PC 56, sinks U 87, . 231-2
  P 57, sinks UC 47, . . 227
  PC 61, sinks UC 33, . . 213
  PC 62 sinks U 84, . . 285
Patrols (Brit.) :
  East Coast, ... 5
  Forth, ... 6
  Channel organised, . . 31
  Irish Sea, ... 33
  S.W. approaches, . . 40, 160
  inadequacy of, 41, 61, 62, 244-5
  estimate for Mediterranean, 80, 237
  show shipping tracks to S/M.,
        136, 160, 237-8
  fights with S/M., Feb. 1-18,
    1917, ... 146
  air, adopted,
    147, 180, 192, 213, 214, 287
  'hunting,' formation and
    adoption of, . . . 147
  activity of little use, . . 147
  by British S/M. Shetlands-
    Norway adopted, . . 148
  inadequate to keep S/M. sub-
    merged, ... 148-9
  avoided by enemy S/M., . 148-9
  typical and ineffective hunt,
    Sept. 1916, . . . 149
  fights with S/M., . . . 152
  estimate of force required for
    S.W. approaches, . . 160
  no increase until July 1918,
    numerical deficiency, 173, 256-7
  in-shore danger to enemy
    S/M. from, ... 176
  seaplane, worry Flanders
    S/M., method of attack,
    first success, . . . 180
  vigilance and ubiquity re-
    ported by German S/M., 188
  seaplane :
    destroys UC 1, UB 20, 192-3
    destroys UC 72, . . 213
    destroys UC 6, . . . 214

Patrols (Brit.) (*contd.*) :
  diverted from trade defence
    to cover U.S. troopships,
        234, 311
  Mediterranean, Paris Confer-
    ence, estimate of number
    required, number of vessels
    available, ... 237-8
  proposal to allot Otranto
    dftrs., or concentrate on
    Straits, ... 246
  inadequate number of, and
    insufficiently armed, . 256-7
  excellent work of, . . 280
  only possible system of trade
    protection until convoy
    could be carried out, . 281
  North Channel S/M. patrol, 286
  airships and seaplanes in
    Irish Sea, ... 287
Patrols (U.S.) :
  total force and number of
    vessels therein, . 298, 298 n.
  used as escorts for troopships, 298
Patrols (Russ.) :
  sk. U 56, ... 112
  trlrs. attack U 76, . . 112
Peace proposals :
  by Germany (Dec. 1916) re-
    jected by Allies, . . 119
  by Germany (1917) rejected
    by Allies, ... 137
Pearl (Brit. trlr.), . . 49-50
Pelagosa Island, . . . 73
Pelikan (Ger. M/L.), . . 5
Penelope (Brit. L.C.) attkd., . 94
Penistone (Brit. S.S.) sk., . 309
Penshurst (Q. 7) (Brit. decoy) :
  sinks UB 19 and UB 37, . 119
  fight with U 84, later sk., 151, 285
Pera (Brit. S.S.) sk., . . 260
Peresviet (Russ. B.S.) (ex Jap.
  Sagami) sk., . . . 134
Perière, Lothar v. Arn. de la
  (U 35), . . . 76, 132
Persia (Brit. S.S.) sk., . . 78
Peshawur (Brit. S.S.) sk., . 222
Pet (Brit. decoy), . . . 50
Pheasant (Brit. T.B.D.) sk., . 155
Phillimore, Sir Rich. (Adm.
  R.N.), ... 211
Phoenix (Brit. T.B.D.) sk,, . 271
Pigeon (Brit. T.B.D.), . . 313
Pilot Me (Brit. dftr.), . . 301-2
Pirrie, Lord (Controller-General
  of Merchant Shipbuilding), 163
Pitcher, E. (seaman R.N.),
  awarded V.C., . . . 199
Pleiades (Brit. dftr.), . . 89

INDEX 415

Pohl, von (Adm. G.N.), Chief of Staff:
  declares war zones, . 27-8
  becomes C.-in-C. H.S.F., 27, 58, 59, 83
Polesley (Brit. S.S.) sk., . . 320
Polynesien (Fr. S.S.) sk., . 273
Pomeranian (Brit. S.S.) sk., . 293
Pontiac (Brit. S.S.) sk., . . 247
Portia (Brit. Fleet messenger) sk., 48
Portoferrajo (Elba) shelled by S/M., ... 129
Port Said (Brit. S.S.) attkd., . 307
Portugal (Russ. H.S.) sk., . 127
Posen (Ger. B.S.), . . . 100
Potentate (Brit. fishing vessel) sk., ... 310
Powhatan (Brit. S.S.) sk., . 168
Present Help (Brit. dftr.), . 228
President Lincoln (U.S. troop-carrier) sk., ... 299
Primo (Brit. S.S.) sk., . . 17
Primula (Brit. sloop) sk., . 125
Prince Charles (Brit. decoy) sks.
  U 36, ... 47-8
Prince Max of Baden (Imperial Chancellor), . . . 324-5
Princess Louise (Brit. decoy) and C 27 sink U 23, . 48
Princess Margaret (Brit. M/L.), 91
Princess Mary II. (Brit. M/S.) sk. after War, . . . 336
Prisoners of war, attempt to rescue by S/M., . . 51
Privet (Q 19) (Brit. decoy) :
  sinks U 85, . . 156, 156 n.
  sinks U 34, ... 277
Prize (Q 21) (Brit. decoy) :
  fight with U 93, . . 169-70
  sk. by UB 48, . 170, 216, 285
'Prize war,' regulations of, . 23
Prometeo (It. Fleet aux.) sk., . 296
Provence (Fr. B.S.), . . . 245
Provence II. (Fr. aux. cruiser) sk., ... 125
Pullen, Cmr. :
  Capt. (S.) Adriatic S/M. Force, . . . 264, 275
  orders for evacuation of Mediterranean by German S/M., ... 275

Quarry Knowe (Brit. dftr), . 131
Queen Alexandra (Brit. transport), ... 303
Queen Eugenie (Brit. S.S.) sk., 242
Quernmore (Brit. S.S.) sk., . 192
Quickly (Brit. decoy), . 47, 178 n.

Raids by German destroyers, 117, 152
Ramazan (Brit. troopship), . 75
Rappahannock (Brit. S.S.) sk., 116
Ravenna (It. S.S.) sk., . . 243
'Receiving ships,' used by German S/M., ... 115
Recruit (old) (Brit. T.B.D.) sk., 39
Recruit (new) (Brit. T.B.D.) sk., 214
Regina Margherita (It. B.S.) sk., 131
Renaudin (Fr. T.B.D.) sk., . 128
Renfrew (Brit. S.S.) sk., . . 288
Renown (Brit. B.C.), . . 211
Reprisals, . . . 133, 164-5
Repulse (Brit. B.C.), . . 211
Requin (Fr. B.S.), . . . 259
Restore (Brit. dftr.) sk., . . 124
Result (Brit. decoy), . . 156
Retriever (Brit. T.B.D.), . . 292
Re Umberto (It. transport) sk., 126
Reventazon (Brit. S.S.) sk., . 274
Rewa (Brit. H.S.) sk., . . 285
Rhododendron (Brit. convoy sloop) sk., ... 301
Richard da Larrinaga (Brit. S.S.), ... 222
Rigel (Fr. sloop) sk., . . 132
Rio Tiete (Brit. S.S.) sk.,. . 86-7
Rizzo (Cmr. It. Navy) sinks *Svent Istvan*, . . . 272
Roburn (Brit. dftr.), . . 33
Rodino (Brit. trlr.), . . . 98
Romford (Brit. S.S.) sk., . . 266
Rosario (Brit. S.S.) sk., . . 200
Roscommon (Brit. S.S.) sk., . 201
Rosies (Brit. dftr.) sk., . . 131
Rotorua (Brit. S.S.) sk., . . 157
Rowanmore (Brit. S.S.) sk., . 116
Roxburgh (Brit. cruiser) :
  attkd. by U 39, . . . 45
  sinks U 89, ... 290
Royal Edward (Brit. troop-carrier) sk., ... 74
Ruel (Brit. S.S.) sk., . . 53
Russell (Brit. B.S.) sk., . . 129
Russia, collapse of :
  not foreseen by Germany, 120 n.
  proposals to accelerate S/M.
  building after, . . 299 n.
Russian (Brit. horse-transport) sk., ... 134
Ruysdael (Brit. S.S.), . . 320

S 17 (Ger. T.B.D.) sk., . . 179
S 63 (Ger. T.B.D.) sk., . . 315
S 66 (Ger. T.B.D.) sk., . . 315
S 138 (Ger. T.B.D.) sk., . . 316
Sabbia (Brit. S.S.) sk., . 86, 128
Saida (A.-H. L.C.), . . . 254

416 THE GERMAN SUBMARINE WAR

St. Andrew (Brit. H.S.) attkd.
  by U 8, ... 32
St. Barchan (Brit. S.S.) sk., last
  vessel torpedoed in British
  home waters, . . . 325
St. George's Channel, . . 31
St. Kilda, German landing on, 291
Sakaki (Jap. T.B.D.), . 248, 249
Salonica, Exped. Force landed at, 76
Salmon (Brit. motor-boat), . 104
Salta (Brit. H.S.) sk., . . 165
Salvia (Q 15) (Brit. sloop) sk.
  by U 62, ... 190
San Bernardo (Brit. S.S.) sk., 104
Sanders, W. E., Lieut. R.N.R., 169
  awarded V.C., . . . 170
San Diego (U.S. cruiser) sk., . 309
San Hilario (Brit. S.S.) sk., . 168
San Miguel shelled by U 155, . 217
San Pietro raided by UB 47, . 134
Sant' Anna (Fr. aux. cruiser)
  sk., ... 271
Sarah Colebrooke (Brit. decoy), 190
Sarnia (Brit. A.B.S.) sk., . 273
Sarpedon (Brit. S.S.) attkd.,
  last S/M. attk. in Medi-
  terranean, 1918, . . 276
Scapa Flow :
  German S/M. attempts to
    enter, 13, 14, 17, 18, 171-2, 327
  fears for security of, . . 4, 6
Scarborough :
  bombardment of, . . . 18
  shelled by S/M., . . . 214
Scharfschüze (A.-H. T.B.D.) sk., 274
Scheer, Rr.-Adm. G.N. :
  denies premeditation of S/M.
    war on shipping, . . 25
  protests against lenience to
    neutral shipping, . . 29
  opinion on ' war of limita-
    tions,'. 83
Scheer, C.-in-C. H.S.F. :
  recalls S/M., ... 89, 96
  abandons Sunderland plan,
    May 1916 ; orders search
    for Elbing ; claims S/M.
    success, ... 97-8
  advocates S/M. offensive
    against shipping, . . 101
  protests against limitation
    war, ... 96, 101
  opinion on conduct of S/M.
    war, ... 105
  revives Sunderland plan, . 106
  operations, Aug. 18, 1916, 106-7
  success of S/M. dispositions, 108
  reproof and rejoinder to
    Kaiser, ... 118

Scheer, C.-in-C. H.S.F. (contd.) :
  interview with Hindenburg, 119
  quoted, . 121, 179, 181-2, 203,
    210, 239, 263, 275, 289, 298,
    321-2.
  detaches destroyers for raid
    on Dover Straits, . . 290
  becomes Chief of Naval Staff,
    301 n.
Scheveningen, ... 7, 8
Schoultz, Cmre. G. von (Fin.
  Navy), quoted, . . 211-13 n.
Schröder, Adm. G.N., C.-in-C.
  German Naval Forces,
  Flanders, ... 295
Schultz, Karl (Capt. G.N.),
  quoted, ... 295 n.
Schulze, E. E. (Capt. G.N.),
  quoted, . . . 92, 296 n.
Scott (Brit. Flot. leader) sk., . 316
Seagull (Brit. T.G.B.) sk., . 155
Seaham shelled by S/M., . 102
Sea King (Brit. trlr., Lizard
  H.D.), ... 187
Searanger (Brit. trlr.), . . 98
Seeadler (Ger. raider) . 47 n., 145
Sendan (Brit. T.B.D. lent to
  Japan). See Minstrel.
Seneca (U.S. patrol vessel, ex
  coastguard cutter), . . 269
Sénès, Adm. French Navy, . 69
Senussi, the, . . . 74, 76, 78
Serbian army, evacuation of, 124
Severn (Brit. monitor) attkd., 16 n.
' Sewing-machines,' . . 38, 72
Shipbuilding (mercantile) sta-
  tistics :
  (Brit.) 1915, 1916, 1917, 1st
    half, 2nd half estimated
    and actual, . . . 162
  1918, tonnage built, . . 163
  1914-1917, built in U.K., . 163
  replacement of lost tonnage, 162
  warning to America, . . 163
  (Brit.) 1917, inadequate to
    cover losses, . . . 163
Shipping losses, statistics of :
  by S/M.-laid mines, 1915, . 61
  Mediterranean, . . . 65
  Oct. 1914-Feb. 1915, . 21, 22
  Feb. 1915-Dec. 1915, . . 65

1915

March, April, . . . 37
Autumn (Mediterranean), . 79
Dec. : German estimate of
  future shipping destruction, ... 81

INDEX 417

Shipping losses, statistics of (*contd.*):

1916

Gayer's estimate of results, rise in monthly average of losses on resumption of 'cruiser warfare,' . . 115
Norwegian losses up to Oct. 116
'cruiser war': British shipping lost (all areas) during last five months of, . . 145

1917

monthly rate of losses under 'unrestricted war,' as predicted by Germany, . 120

1915-17

from Jan. 29, 1915-Feb. 1, 1917: British ships torpedoed without warning, 21, 123

1916

(Medn.) Apl. 1916-Oct. 1918: ships sunk by mines, . 129
(Medn.) Italian losses, May 1916 129
(Medn.) British, French, and Italian losses, latter half of 1916, ... 134

1915-17

1915-Feb. 1917: number of neutral ships sunk, . . 141

1917

Feb.: comparison with losses, Aug. 1915 and Nov. 1916, . . . 145
Feb.: number of British ships, total tonnage, lives by S/M., mines, and ocean raiders, ... 145
Mar.: number of ships, total tonnage and lives, by S/M., mines, destroyer raids, and ocean raiders, . . 145-6
April: number of British ships, total tonnage, and lives, by S/M. and mines; British Allied and neutral losses; percentages of escapes, ... 146-7
Feb. 1-18 : British, Allied, and neutral ships sunk or damaged 146
daily average sinkings during first weeks of 'unrestricted warfare,' . . 152

Shipping losses, statistics of (*contd.*):

1917 (*contd.*)

Mar. 1917-Aug. 1918 : sailings and losses of 'French coal trade,' . . 153, 153 n.
Dec. 1916-Aug. 1917, and Feb.-Nov. 1918 : sailings and losses of Scandinavian convoy . . 153, 153 n.
Mar. : loss of life, . . 157
Apr. : British shipping damaged, ... 162
(1917) : British shipping repaired and under repair, . 162
Jan.-June and July-Dec. : British shipping lost by enemy action and marine risks (totals), . . . 163
colliers and oil-tankers sk., . 166
Apr. : average daily British loss, ... 167
May : number of British ships ; British total tonnage and world total tonnage, by S/M. and mine, . 183
May : lives lost in British ships sk., ... 184
June : number of British ships and total tonnage torpedoed by S/M., . . 190
July : number of British ships and total tonnage sk. by S/M. and mine, . . 190
latter half of : average monthly rate of British loss per month, . . . 191
Aug. 1914-Dec. 1917 : total loss (British), . . . 191
Aug. : number and total tonnage repaired of ships lying damaged in British ports, ... 191
July : loss of life in British ships, ... 192
Feb. 1-Aug. 31: total British ships sk., torpedoed without warning, . . . 203
Sept. : British ships mined, 206
average size of sunken ships compared ; Aug., Sept. : proportion of escapes to attacks, ... 207
Sept. and Oct. : number of British vessels, total tonnage and lives lost, . . 222
Nov.: number of British ships and total tonnage sk., 234
Nov.: number and total

2 D

Shipping losses, statistics of (*contd.*):
  1917 (*contd.*)
    tonnage of British ships repaired, ... 234
  Dec.: number of British ships, total tonnage and lives lost (S/M. and mine), 231
  1914-17
    Admiralty Table: British, foreign, world tonnage (losses, new ships, etc.), . 234
  1915-16
    (Medn.) Nov. 1915-May 1916: number of ships (British, allied, and neutral) sk., . 237
  1916
    (Medn.) July-Dec.: number and tonnage of British and allied ships sk., . 238-9
  1917
    (Medn.) Feb.-Mar.: number of ships and total tonnage sk., ... 240-1
    (Medn.) Apr.: number of ships and total tonnage sk., ... 242, 258
    (Medn.) losses during Corfu Conference, . . . 247
    (Medn.) May: number of ships sk., ... 248
    (Medn.) June: tonnage lost, 255
    (Medn.) July: number and tonnage of S.S. lost, . . 258
    reductions of losses in home waters, Atlantic, etc., compared with Medn., . 258-9
  1917-18
    (Medn.) ' through ' convoys, ships sk. out of sailings; ' local ' convoys, percentage of loss, . . . 261
  1918
    (Medn.) May and Aug.: tonnage sk., ... 273
  1915-18
    (Medn.) total shipping destroyed in, ... 278
  1918
    Jan.: number of British ships sk., ... 286
    Feb.: number and total tonnage of British ships sk. by S/M., ... 288

Shipping losses, statistics of (*contd.*):
  1918 (*contd.*)
    Apr.: number and total tonnage British ships sk. (compared with Apr. 1917), 293-4
    Jan. 1-Nov. 11: number of British ships sk. by mines around British Isles, . 299
    May: number of British ships, total tonnage and lives lost, by S/M. and mine, ... 306
    June: number of British ships and total tonnage lost, ... 311
    Aug.: number of British ships and total tonnage destroyed by S/M., . . 316
    Sept.: number of British ships, total tonnage, and lives lost, ... 319
  1914-18
    British merchant-vessels and fishing-craft sk. or damaged by S/M. (number of ships, tonnage, loss of life), 333
    allied and neutral losses, 333-4
  1917-18
    comparison between first three and last three months of ' unrestricted campaign,' 336-7
    Also see Appendix I. (The Triumph of Convoy) and Appendix III. (N and O).
Sims, W. S. (Adm. U.S.N.):
  arrives at Liverpool, . . 155
  interview with Sir John Jellicoe, ... 159
  represents gravity of position to U.S. Govt., . . . 160
  quoted, ... 160, 298
  warns U.S. Govt. of coming raids by large enemy S/M., 307-8
  estimates damage caused by S/M. off U.S. coast, . . 310
  enemy easily tracked, . . 310
  314.
Sindoro (Dutch H.S.), . . 312
Six months plan:
  estimate first mentioned, 81-82
  (*Also see* Commerce, German S/M. war on; ' Unrestricted campaign,' 1917-18.)

INDEX

Six months plan (contd.):
  forecasts of five months, three months, and six months, . . . 120-1 n.
  recognised as mistake, . 121
  boats required for 'war stations,' 143-4
  April 1917 : estimate exceeded, ... 147
  probable success of, foreseen, 147, 159, 172
  progress to June 1917, . 186
  expiration of period, . . 203
  promised results not attained, 204, 235
  Scheer's admission of breakdown, ... 321-2
Skerries (Brit. S.S.) sk., . . 116
Skipjack (Brit. T.G.B.) attacks U 16, ... 18
'Smoke boxes,'. . . . 177
Smoke, reduction of, from ships' funnels, ... 177
Snaefell (Brit. A.B.S.) sk., . 273
Snapdragon (Brit. sloop), . 274
Somerset (Brit. S.S.) sk., . . 192
Southland (Brit. transport) attkd., ... 75
  (Brit. S.S.) sk., . . . 185
'Southwick monsters,' . . 224
Sowwell (Brit. S.S.) sk., . . 244
Spain :
  Govt. of, forbids territorial waters to S/M., . . 189
  internment decree, . 189, 251
  interns UB 49, . . . 216
'Special service vessels.' See Decoy vessels, S/M.
Speedwell (Brit. T.G.B.) rams U 41, ... 47
Spenser (Brit. S.S.) sk., . . 285-6
'Sperrbrecher.' See Barragebreakers.
Spindler, Adm. G.N., quoted, 24, 25, 25 n., 114, 333 n.
'Spurlos versenkt' (sk. without trace), origin of term, 168
Stamfordham (Brit. S.S.) sk., . 104
Standard cargo-ships, . 177, 202-3
Star (Brit. T.B.D.), . . . 321
Statendam. See Justicia.
Staunch (Brit. T.B.D.) sk. by UC 38, ... 259-60
Stephen Furness (Brit. A.B.S.) sk., ... 232
Sterope (It. Fleet collier) sk., . 296
Sterrett (U.S. T.B.D.), . . 322
Stockforce (Brit. decoy) fights U 98, ... 316

Stonecrop (Brit. decoy) sk., . 215
Strongbow (Brit. T.B.D.) sk., . 232
Stuart, Ronald N. (Lieut. R.N.R.), D.S.O., awarded V.C., ... 181
Sturgeon (Brit. T.B.D.), . . 292
Submarines :
  British—
  A 1, loss of (1904), . . 23
  B 3 attkd. by U 18, . 11, 16 n.
  'C'-class operate against U-boats, . . . 167
  C 7 sinks UC 68, . . 167
  C 15 sinks UC 65, . . 225-6
  C 24, with Taranaki, attks. U 16 49
  C 24, with Taranaki, sinks U 40, ... 46
  C 27, with Taranaki, attks. S/M., ... 46
  C 27, with Princess Louise, sinks U 23, . . . 48
  C 29, loss of, . . . 49
  C 33, loss of, . . . 49
  C 34, sk. by U 52, . . 191
  D 4 sinks UB 72, . . 304
  D 6 sk., ... 311
  D 7, sinks U 45, . . 213
  E 3 sk. by U 27, . . 15
  E 13, loss of, . . . 54
  E 16 sinks U 16 56, 217 n.
  E 20 sk. by UB 14, . . 78
  E 22 sk. by UB 18, . . 94
  E 23 attacks Westfalen, . 106
  E 24 (M/L.), loss of, . 38
  E 34 sinks UB 16, . 304-5
  E 35 sinks U 154, . . 297
  E 38, ... 189, 251
  E 45 sinks UC 62, . . 220
  E 49 sk., ... 156
  E 52 sinks UC 63, . . 225
  E 54 sinks UC 10, . . 117
  sinks U 81, . . . 181
  G 2 sinks U 78, . . 326-7
  G 13 sinks UC 43, . 155-6
  'H'-class, cross Atlantic, 104
  H 1, ... 268
  H 2 as decoy, . . . 75
  H 4 sinks UB 52, . . 270
  H 5 sinks U 51, . 101, 179
  H 6 interned and transferred to Royal Netherlands Navy, . . 62 n., 83
  J 1, ... 118
  L 12 sinks UB 90, . . 326
  bases for A/S. patrols (1917), ... 167
  watch at terminals of Bight swept channels, . 208

420 THE GERMAN SUBMARINE WAR

Submarines:
French—
- Ariane sk., . . . 251
- Bernouilli sk., . . . 268
- Circé sinks U C24, . . 255
  - sk. by U 47, . . . 273
- Curie, captured, 69, 71, 280
- Roland Morillot, ex UB 26, 90
- Turquoise, captured, 78, 390

Italian—
- Alberto Guglielmotti sk., . 241
- Atropo (see Appendix II.), 348
- Balilla (ex U 42,) loss of, . 64 n.
- F 12, ... 132 n.
- Giacinto Pullino destroyed, 252, 280
- H 5 sk. accidentally by H 1, ... 268
- Medusa sk. by UB 15, . 72
- Nereide sk. by V, . . 73
- X I, ex German UC 12, . 126-7

Russian—
- Forel (see Appendix II.), 341-2
- Karp, Karas, Kambala (see Appendix II.), . . 342-4

Turkish—
- Mustedji Ombaschi, ex French Turquoise, . 390
- Nordenfelt ' boats (old), attempt to recondition, 390
- see Appendix IV. (Q), . 390

U.S.—
- L 2 (AL 2), . . . 314
- Enemy (all nationalities: summary of, see Appendix IV. (R), ... 390

Austro-Hungarian—
- I/U 1, ... 279
- II/U 2, ... 279
- III/U 3 (Strnad) sk., 73, 73 n., 279
- IV/U 4 attacks Waldeck-Rousseau, . . . 69
  - attacks Dublin, . . 70
- IV/U 4 (Jüstel) sinks Garibaldi, ... 73
- IV/U 4 (Singule), . 254, 279
- V/U 5 (v. Trapp) sinks L. Gambetta, . . . 69
- V/U 5 (Schlosser ?) sinks Nereide, . . 73, 279
- VI/U 6 (v. Falkenhausen) sk., . 128, 130, 246, 279
- X/U 10 (Dürrigl), ex German S/M., . . . 71
  - disabled by mine, 272-3, 280
- XI/U 11 (v. Fernland), ex German S/M., 71, 73, 279

Submarines, Austro-Hungarian (contd.):
- XII/U 12 (Lerch), . . 68
  - attacks Jean Bart, . 69
  - sk., ... 73, 73 n.
- XIV/U 14, ex French Curie, 69, 71, 279, 280
- XV/U 15 (Schlosser), 71, 130
- XVI/U 16 (v. Zoppa), . 71
  - sk., . . 131, 131 n., 279
- XVII/U 17 (Hudecek), 71, 130, 252, 279
- XVIII, XIX, non-existence of, . 252, 252 n.
- XX/U 20 netted, . . 131
- XX/U 20 (Müller) sk., . 132 n., 178 n., 246, 279
- XXI/U 21, ... 279
- XXII/U22, . . . 279
- XXIII/U 23 (v. Bézard) sk., . . . 267, 279
- XXVII/U 27 (v. Fernland or Holub), . . 254, 279
- XXVIII/U 28 (v. Trautenegg), . . . 274, 279
- XXIX/U 29, founders, 279, 279-80 n.
- XXX/U 30 (Fähndrich), loss of, 246, 246 n., 252
- XXXI/U 31 (Rigele), 274, 274 n., 279
- XXXII/U 32, . . . 279
- XL/U 40 (Krsnjavi), 268, 279
- XLI/U 41, ... 279
- XLIII/U 43, ex German UB 43, . . . 279
- XLVII/U 47, ex German UB 47, . . . 279

Austro-Hungarian commanding officers:
- Bézard, K. Ritter v. (XXIII/U 23), . . 267
- Dürrigl (X/U 10), . . 272
- Fähndrich, Fr. (XXX/U 30), . 246 n.
- Falkenhausen, v. (VI/U 6), 128
- Fernland, v. (XI/U 11), . 73
  - (XXVII/U 27), . . 254
- Holub (XXVII/U 27), . 254
- Hudecek (XVII/U 17), . 130
- Jüstel (IV/U 4), . 70, 73
- Krsnjavi (XL/U 40), . 268
- Lerch (XII/U 12), . 69, 73
- Müller, L. (XX/U 20), 132 n.
- Rigele (XXXI/U 31), . 274
- Schlosser (V/U 5 ?), . 73, 130
- Strnad (III/U 3), . . 73
- Singule (IV/U 4), . . 254
- Trapp, v. (V/U 5), . . 69

INDEX 421

Submarines, Austro-Hungarian commanding officers (*contd.*):
Trautenegg, v. (XXVIII/U 28), . . 274
Zoppa, v. (XVI/U 16), . 131
Austro-Hungarian S/M. : .
  taken over by Germany, . 64, 68
  strength, 1914, . . 68, 253
  numeration of, . 68 n., 253
  operations by, . . . 68
  bases, ... 76 n.
  losses, 1915-17, . . . 240
  strength, 1917, . . . 239
  construction of, and prize additions, 253, 279-280 n.
  strength on conclusion of War ; boats at Cattaro and Pola ; losses, 253, 279
  boats unfinished ; missing numbers ; division of S/M. between France and Italy, 279 n.-280 n.
  classes of : XX-XXIII (U 20-23) ; XXVII-XXXII, XL, XLI, (U 27-32, 40, 41) ; XLIII-XLVII (U 43, U 47), ex German UB 43, UB 47, 252, 253 n.
  ceded craft, received from German Navy (*see* Appendix IV., P), . 389
  commanding officers of (*see* Appendix IV., P), 389-90
  internment of and disposal of, between France and Italy (*see* Appendix IV., P), . . 388-9
  losses and causes of loss analysed (*see* Appendix IV., P), . . 388
  chronological list (*see* Appendix IV., P), . . 388
  strength, summary of, by calendar years, War period 1914-18 (*see* Appendix IV., P), . 388
  technical details of (*see* Appendix IV., P), 383-8

German U-boats :
1 broken up, . 331, 331 n.
2 broken up, . 331, 331 n.
4 broken up, . 331, 331 n.
5, first War cruise, . . 2
  at Zeebrugge, . . 16
  (Lemmer) loss of, . 17, 64 n.
6 (Lepsius) sk. by E. 16, 56-7, 64 n., 217n.

Submarines, German U-boats (*contd.*)
7 (König), first War cruise, 2
  loss of, . . . 20, 64 n.
8 (Stoch), first War cruise, 2
  at Zeebrugge, . . 16
  fouls nets, sinks shipping, attacks *St. Andrew*, ... 32-3
  sk., ... 33, 64 n.
9 (Weddigen), first War cruise, . . . 2
  engine defects, and returns, . . . 2
  sinks *Aboukir*, *Cressy*, *Hogue*, . . 7, 8, 9, 10
  sinks *Hawke*, . . 11, 12, 13
9 (Spiess), based on Libau, converted to M/L., 56, 56 n., 57
  Courland Flot., . 63, 332 n.
10 (Stuhr), Baltic, . 56, 63
  loss of, . . . 93, 93 n.
11 (v. Suchodoletz), at Zeebrugge, . . . 16
  loss of, . . . 17, 64 n.
12 (Kratzsch), at Zeebrugge, 16
  sinks *Niger*, . . 16, 17
  loss of, . . 33, 34, 64 n.
13 (v. Schweinitz), first War cruise, and sk., 2, 3, 64 n.
14 (Hammerle), first War cruise, . . . 2
  sk., . . . 45, 64 n.
15 (Pohle), first War cruise, 2
  sk. by *Birmingham*, 3, 64 n.
16 (Hansen), first War cruise, 2
  record cruise (15 days), 11
  attempt to enter Scapa Flow, . . . 17, 18
  attkd. off Lerwick by *Skipjack*, . . . 18
  attacks shipping, . . 21
  picks up escaped 'war pilot' in the North Sea, ... 34
  nearly sunk by decoy, . 49
  founders on passage to Harwich to surrender, 331
17 (Feldkirchner), firstWar cruise, . . . 2
  attacks *Theseus*, sinks *Glitra*, . . 11, 13, 25
  damaged, enters Norwegian waters, . . 18
  to Baltic, . . 56, 63
  convoys *Meteor*, . . 56
  broken up, . . . 331

THE GERMAN SUBMARINE WAR

Submarines, German U-boats (contd.)
18 (v. Hennig), first War
    cruise, . . . 2
    first run through Dover
      Straits, . . . 11
    attacks *Attentive* and
      B 3, ... 11
    sk. in attempt to enter
      Scapa Flow,
        17-18, 64 n., 172
19, first War cruise, . . 4, 5
    attkd. by *Badger*,
        15, 16, 16 n.
    attacks shipping, . . 21
    (Spiess), worn out, . 35 n.
    North Sea,
      44, 45, 57, 63 n., 64
    (R. Weisbach), . 87, 100
    (Spiess), ... 201
    sinks *Dundee*, . . 214
    nearly sinks U 155,
        217, 217 n.
    sinks *Calgarian*,
      291, 291 n., 301
20 (Droescher), first War
    cruise, . . . 5
    in Southern waters, . 13
    returns north about, . 14
    cruise kept secret, 14, 15, 19
    Cuxhaven air raid, sent
      out to attack British
      ships, . . . 18
    sinks shipping, . 21, 32
20 (Schwieger) sinks *Lusitania*, . . 40-2, 45, 58
    sinks *Hesperian*, . 59, 60
    scouting trip, 63, 63 n., 87
    sinks *Cymric*, . . 88
    off Tagus, . . . 110
    loss of, . . . 117-18
21 (Hersing), first War
    cruise, . . . 4, 5
    sinks *Pathfinder*, . . 6
    attacks shipping, attkd.
      by *Vanduara*, . . 20
    sinks shipping off Havre, 21
    proceeds to Cattaro,
      42-3, 63 n., 67, 70
    sinks *Triumph* and *Majestic* off Gallipoli, 71-2
    at Constantinople, 72, 73
    in Aegean, at Pola, 74, 124-5
    sinks *Amiral Charner*, 125, 273
    sinks *City of Lucknow*, . 129
    leaves for Germany,
      attacks Dutch shipping off Falmouth, . 135,
      146; also 167, 169, 182,
      201-2, 239, 243, 277.

Submarines, German U-boats (contd.)
21 founders on passage to
    Harwich to surrender, 331
22 (Hoppe), first War cruise, 4
    scouts off Humber, . 5
    searches for Grand Fleet, 17
    Cuxhaven raid, sent to
      attack British ships, . 18
    sinks U 7, . . . 20
    sinks *India*, . 55-6, 63 n.,
      64, 86, 87-8, 97-8 n., 100.
23 (Schulthess), . . 40
    sk., ... 48-9
    in Baltic, . . . 56
    loss of, ... 64 n.
24 (Schneider), first War
    cruise, . . . 4
    attacks *Amiral Ganteaume*, . . . 15
    at Zeebrugge, . . 16
    sinks *Formidable*, . . 19
    shipping war, . 37, 40
    shells Whitehaven, . 51
    attacks shipping, . . 52
    sinks *Arabic*, . . 52, 55
    short raid, . . . 61
    test winter cruise, 1915, 61, 63
      also 63 n., 95, 97-8 n.
25 (Wünsche), . . . 44
    damaged, . . . 45
    attacks *Hampshire*, . 46-7
    towed home, and joins
      Periscope School, Kiel, 55
    Baltic, . . . 56, 63
26 (Fr. Berckheim) sinks
    Pallade, *Yenesei*, loss
    of, ... 56, 64 n.
27 (Wegener), sinks E 3, . 15
    sinks *Hermes*, . . 16
    examines East Coast
      minefields, . . 18, 32
    sinks *Bayano*, . . 33
    off Llandudno, . . 51
    sk. by *Baralong*,
      52-3, 55, 64 n.
28 (Forstner), sends prize
    into Zeebrugge, . 34
    sinks *Aguila* and *Falaba*
    (crime cases), . 35, 36:
      55, 63, 63 n., 86
28 (Schmidt), sk., . . . 206
29 (Weddigen), probably
    netted in Start Bay,
    attacks shipping near
      Scillies, . . . 33
    reaches Fastnet, attacks
      Grand Fleet, sk. by
      Dreadnought, 34-5, 64 n.

INDEX 423

Submarines, German U-boats (*contd.*)
30 (——), Cuxhaven air raid, sent to attack British warships, . 18
begins war on shipping, Feb. 1915, . . 30, 32
sinks *Cambank, Downshire,* 32
fouls nets, . . . 32
sk., and salved, 46, 64, 118
31 (Wachendorff), loss of, 20, 64 n.
32, returns damaged, . 20
finds Dover Straits dangerous, returns north about, . . 36
shipping war, 37, 40, 63, 63 n., 83
32 (Spiegel), 86, 97, 97-8 n., 99, 99 n.
(Hartwig), for Mediterranean, . 119, 133
sinks *Cornwallis* . 134. 239 n.
32 (Albrecht) sk., . . 269
33, forced under by S.S. *Brussels,* reported off Dover Straits, . . 36
33 (Gansser), leaves for Mediterranean, 60, 63 n., 75
sinks *Clan MacLeod,* . 77
in Black Sea, Gayer's comments on, . . 125
sinks *Portugal,* . . 127
recalled from Mediterranean, 181-2, 239, 243, 247
34 (Rücker) in Channel, 34, 43
leaves for Mediterranean, 59-60, 63 n., 75, 125, 239, 303
leaves Adriatic, . . 276 n.
sk. in Straits of Gibraltar (last Ger. S/M. destroyed), . . . 277
35 (Kophamel), in Channel, 34
leaves for Mediterranean, 59-60, 63 n., 75
sinks *Marquette, Tara, Abbas,* . . . 76
35 (Perière, L. v. A. de la), 76, 77, 125
sinks *Provence II, Primula,* 125
sinks 22,600 tons, . 126
at Cartagena, . . 129
results of raid, . . 130
record raid, 91,000 tons 130
methods used, total ships sk. by, 1915-18, 130

Submarines, German U-boats (*contd.*)
35 sinks *Rigel, Gallia,* . 132
also 134, 238, 239
5 weeks' cruise, 65,000 tons sk., operations to W. of Gibraltar, 243-4, 247, 276 n.
interned at Barcelona, 277, 332
36 (Graeff), sk., 47-48, 64 n.
37 (Wilcke), in Channel, . 34
loss of, . 36, 37, 37 n., 64 n.
38 (Valentiner), attacks *Roxburgh,* . . . 45
off Llandudno, . 51, 52
maximum destruction of shipping round British Isles, . . 55
leaves for Mediterranean, 60, 63, 63 n., 75
attacks *Mercian,* . . 77
sinks *France IV, Ancona,* 77
sinks *Persia,* . . . 78-9
also 125, 132
shells Funchal, . . 134
also 239, 276 n., 277
39 (Forstmann), attacks 3rd B.S., . . 44, 45
leaves for Mediterranean, 60, 63 n., 75, 77
sinks *Restore,* . 124, 125
in Black Sea, . . . 127
also 129, 130, 239
39 (Metzer), interned, 270, 332
40 (Fürbringer), attacks *Argyll,* . . . 45
sk., ... 46, 64 n.
41 (Hansen), rammed by *Speedwell,* . . 47
fight with *Pearl,* . . 49-50
sk. by *Baralong,* . 60, 64 n.
42. See *Balilla.*
43 (Jürst), North Sea, 63 n., 64, 86, 97, 97-8 n., 111, 169
44 (Wagenführ), . 63 n., 64
adapted for M/L., 63, 83
allows *Mauretania* to escape, . . . 86
also 97, 97-8 n., 106
sinks *Belgian Prince,* . 194
sk., ... 195
45 (Sittenfeldt), 64, 88, 106
demands oil from U.S. vessel, . . . 140
sk., ... 213
46 (Hillebrand), 97, 97-8 n., 99, 100
attacks *Marlborough,* . 100
also 102, 111, 112, 122, 219

424 THE GERMAN SUBMARINE WAR

Submarines, German U-boats (*contd.*)
47 (Metzer), 97, 97-8 n., 239
  sinks *Circé*, . . . 273
  blown up, . . . 275
48 (Buch), . . . 106, 111
48 (Edeling), destroyed,
    227-8, 228 n.
49 (Hartmann),
  102, 106, 107, 114, 115
  brings first report of
  depth-charge attack, 178
  sk. by *British Transport*, 206-7
50 (Berger), . . . 115
  sk., ... 209
51 (Rumpel), . 94, 97-8 n.
  sk., ... 101-2, 179
52 (Hans), . . . 97, 102
  sinks *Nottingham*, . 106
  for Mediterranean, . . 119
  sinks *Suffren*, . . 133
  returns from Mediterranean, sinks C 34,
    191, 243, 244
52 (Spiess), . . . 35 n.
  escape of, . . . 210
  founders and is salved,
    210 n., 239 n.
53 (Rose), . . 97-8 n., 106
  crosses Atlantic, . 110, 111
  sinks shipping off U.S.
  coast and returns,
    111, 133, 216, 306
  sinks *Housatonic*, . . 140
  sinks *Jacob Jones*, . 230
  escapes trap, . . . 320
54 (v. Ruckteschell), . 313
55 (Werner), . 106, 122-3
  sinks *Torrington, Rewa,*
  and attacks *Guildford
  Castle* (criminal cases),
    167-8, 194 ; 285 ; 293
56 (Lorenz), . . . 106
  sk., ... 112
57 (v. Georg), . 114-15, 188
58 (Amberger), sk., . . 226-7
59 (v. Firks), sinks *Genista*, 116
  sk., ... 179
61 (Dieckmann), sk., . 292
62 (Hashagen), . . . 170
  sinks *Tulip* (Q 12), . 171
  sinks *Salvia* (Q 15), . 190
  sinks *Orama*, . . . 221
  sinks *Ausonia*, . . 306
  sinks *Dupetit Thouars*, 317
63 (Otto Schulze),
    97, 97-8 n., 106
  sinks *Falmouth*, . . 107
63 (Hartwig),
    230, 242, 276-7, 276 n.

Submarines, German U-boats (*contd.*)
64 (Moraht), 97-8 n., 100, 106
  for Mediterranean,
    119, 133, 239 n.
  sinks *Danton*, . . 241
  sinks *Minnetonka*, . 266
  sk., ... 272
65 (——), . . . 106, 107
  for Mediterranean,
    119, 133, 239 n.
  blown up, . . . 275
66 (v. Bothmer),
  48, 87, 97-8 n., 99, 106, 107
  attacks *Falmouth*, . 107
66 (Muhle) sk., . . . 209
67 (——), . 96, 97, 97-8 n., 99,
    100, 106
68 (Güntzel), . . . 48
  escorts *Möwe*, . . 63
  sk., . . . 87, 94-5, 150
69 (Wilhelms), 86, 87, 102, 106
  sk. by *Patriot*, . . 191
70 (Wünsche), escorts S.S.
  Marie and *Greif*, 83, 86,
    94, 97, 97-8 n.
71 (——), ... 93-4
72 (——), . . . 94, 97, 99
  Mediterranean, . 129, 239
  blown up, . . . 276
73 (Siehs), proceeds to
  Mediterranean,
    128-9, 133, 239, 242
  blown up, . . . 276
74 (E. Weisbach), . 86, 97
  sk., ... 98-9
75 (Beitzen), leaves to
  mine Orkneys, . . 97
  lays mines, . . . 99
  Hampshire sk., . . 101
75 (Schmolling), sk., . 229
76 (Bender), sk., . . 112
77 (E. Günzel), loss of, . 103
78 (Bolbrecht), sk., . . 326-7
80 (——), ... 154
81 (R. Weisbach), sk. by
  E 54, ... 181
82 (Adam), ... 320
83 (Hoppe), sk. by *Farnborough*, . . . 150-1
84 (Röhr), damaged by
  Penshurst, . . . 151
  sk., ... 284, 285
85 (Petz), ... 123
  sk., by *Privet*, . . 156
86 (Patzig), . . 179, 299
  sinks *Llandovery Castle*
  (criminal case), . 311-12
87 (v. Speth-Schülzburg) 220
  sk., . . . 231-2, 284

INDEX 425

Submarines, German U-boats *(contd.)*
  88 (Schwieger), sinks *Hilary*, 184
    sk., . . . 209, 216, 216 n.
  89 (Bauck) sk. by *Roxburgh*, ... 290
  90 (Jetz), . . . 291, 299
  92 (Ehrlich) sk., . . 320
  93 (Spiegel von und zu Peckelsheim), attack on shipping, fight with *Prize*, . . . 169-70
  returns badly damaged, 170-1
  93 (Gerlach) sk., 284-5, 284 n.
  94 (———), . . . 228 n.
  95 (Prinz), loss of, . 284, 285
  96 (Jetz) sinks UC 69, 229, 230
  97 (———), founders on passage to Harwich to surrender, . . . 331
  98 (———), fight with *Stockforce*, ... 316
  99 (Eltester) sk. by S.S. *Valeria*, . . . 185
  101 (v. Georg), . . . 222
  sinks *Trinidad* and *Lough Fisher*, . . 291
  102 (Beitzen) sk., . . 321
  103 (Rücker) sk. by *Olympic*, . 303-4, 304 n.
  104 (Bernis) sk., . . 302
  106 (Hufnagel) sk., . . 209
  109 (Rey) sk., . . . 287
  110 (Kröll) sk., . . . 292
  115 (———), . . . 114
  116 (———), . . . 114
  117 (Droescher), 307, 309, 309 n.
  124 (———) arrives at Karlskrona (Nov. 13, 1918), . . 332, 332 n.
  135 (Spiess), . 327-8, 329 n.
  139 (L. v. A. de la Perière), 130, 267, 307, 310, 325-6
  140 (Kophamel), cross-Atlantic raid, . 308-9
  142 (———), . . . 233 n.
  151 (Kophamel), makes 12,000 miles voyage, 218-19
  151 (Nostitz u. Jänckendorff crosses Atlantic, cuts cables, mines U.S. coast, sinks shipping, ... 307-8
  152 (Meusel), . . . 219
  152 (Kolbe), . . . 296
  152 (Franz), . . . 310
  153 (———), action with *Willow Branch*, . 297-8

Submarines, German U-boats *(contd.)*
  154 (Gercke) shells Monrovia W/T. station, action with *Willow Branch*, sk. by E 35, 296-8
  155 (Meusel), ex-mercantile *Deutschland*, makes cruise of 105 days : operations in Azores area, . . . 216-17
  155 (Eckelmann), . 296, 310
  156 (Gansser), . . 182, 219
  156 (Feldt) lays mines off U.S. coast ; sk. in Northern barrage, 308-9, 321
  157 (Valentiner), . . 296
  arrives at Trondhjem (Nov. 11, 1918), . 332
UB-boats (German)—
  1 (———), Adriatic Flot., . 63 n.
  becomes A.-H. S/M., . 71
  (*Also see* A.-H. Navy XI/U 11.)
  2 (———), Baltic Flot., . 57
  Flanders Flot., . 38, 63 n.
  broken up, . . . 332
  3 (Schmidt), Adriatic Flot., sk., 64 n., 71, 71 n., 91 n.
  4 (Karl Gross), Flanders Flot., ... 38
  sk., ... 50, 64 n.
  5 (———), Baltic Flot., . 57
  Flanders Flot., . 38, 63 n.
  broken up, . . . 332
  6 (Hacker), Flanders Flot., 38
  sinks *Brazen*, . . 39
  test run through Dover Straits, . 50, 63 n., 106
  interned by Dutch, 156-7, 332
  7 (Lütjohanns), Adriatic Flot. and Constantinople, . 64 n., 71, 73, 125
  sk., ... 135
  8 (———), Constantinople Flot., . . . 64 n., 71
  becomes Bulgarian, 71, 73, 74, 125
  seized by French, 275, 332 n.
  9 (———), Kiel Periscope School, ... 63
  broken up, . . . 332
  10 (Salzwedel), Flanders Flot., 38, 62, 63 n., 91, 197
  blown up, . . . 324
  11 (———), Kiel Periscope School, ... 63
  broken up, . . . 332
  12 (———), Flanders Flot., 38, 38 n., 63 n., 106

426 THE GERMAN SUBMARINE WAR

Submarines,German UB-boats *(cont.)*
12 (Schoeller), sk., . . 318
13 (Metz), Flanders Flot.,
                   38, 63 n.
  sk., . . . 91-2, 91 n.
14 (v. Heimburg), Adriatic
  Flot. and Constantinople Flot.,
            64 n., 71, 74, 75
  sinks E 20, . . . 78
  125, 239.
  surrender of, . . 332 n.
15 (v. Heimburg), Adriatic
  Flot., ... 63 n.
  sinks *Medusa*, . . 72
  sinks *Amalfi*, . . 73
  becomes A.-H. S/M., . 71
  (*Also see* A.-H. Navy, X/U 10.)
16 (——), Flanders Flot.,
             38, 63 n., 106
  passes Zeebrugge blockships, . . 295, 295 n.
16 (Lühe) sk., . . . 304-5
17 (——), Flanders Flot., 38
  sinks *Branlebas*, 61, 63 n.
17 (Branscheid) sk., . . 290
18 (Steinbrinck), Flanders
  Flot., ... 94
  test cruise, . . 105, 110
18 (Niemeyer) sk., . . 226
19 (Noodt), Flanders Flot., 106
  sk., ... 119
20, Baltic Flot., . . 57
20 (Glimpf), Flanders Flot.,
  sk., ... 192-3
21 (Hashagen), North Sea
  Flot., . 97, 97-8 n., 100
22 (Putzier), North Sea
  Flot., . 94, 97, 97-8 n., 100
22 (Wacker) sk., . . 287
23 (Voigt), Flanders Flot., 110
  interned at Corunna, 193, 332
26 (Smiths), Flanders Flot.,
  sk., ... 89-90
  (*Also see Roland Morillot*.)
27 (——), . . 97, 97-8 n., 99
  sinks *Duke of Albany*, . 110
27 (v. Stein) sk. by *Halcyon*, ... 193
29 (Pustküchen), Flanders
  Flot., attacks *Sussex*,
                  85, 188
  attacks *Penelope*, . . 94
  test cruise, . . . 110
29 (Platsch) sk., . . 118, 188
30 (——) interned and released by Dutch, 1917, 150
30 (Stier) sk., . . . 316
31 (Braun) sk., . . 303, 318

Submarines,German UB-boats *(cont.)*
32 (Ditfurth) sk., 199, 199 n.
33 (Gregor) sk., . . . 294
35 (Stöter), . . . 106
  sk. by *Leven*, . . 287
36 (Keyserlinck), loss of, 189
  surmises as to cause of,
                   189-90
37 (Günther) sk., . . 119
38 (Bachmann) sk., . . 289
39 (Küstner), . . 106, 110
  sk. by *Glen*, . . . 181
40 (——) blown up, . 324
41 (Ploen) sk., . . . 220
42 (Schwartz), Constantinople Flot., 239, 251
  surrender of, . 275, 332 n.
43 (——) ceded to Austria,
      131 n., 216 n., 239, 253
44 (Wäger), Adriatic Flot.,
  sk., . 130-1, 178, 246
45 (Palis), Constantinople
  Flot., sk., . . . 135
46 (Bauer), Constantinople
  Flot., sk., . 135, 135 n.
47 (Steinhauer), Adriatic
  Flot., sinks *Gaulois*, . 134
  ceded to Austria,
      131 n., 216 n., 239, 253
48 (Steinhauer) sinks *Prize*, 170
  Adriatic Flot., 216, 239 n.
  blown up, . . . 275
49 (v. Mellenthin) interned
  at and escapes from
  Cadiz, 216, 239 n., 276 n.
50 (Kukat), 216, 239 n., 276 n.
  sinks *Britannia*, . . 277
51 (——), . 216, 239 n., 276 n.
52 (Launburg), . . . 216
  sk., ... 270
53 (Sprenger), . 216, 239 n.
  sk., ... 273
54 (Hecht) sk., . . . 292-3
55 (Wenninger) sk., . . 294
56 (H. Valentiner) sk., . 231
57 (Losz) sk., . . . 318
58 (Löwe) sk., . . . 292
59 (——), blown up, . . 324
61 (T. Schultz) sk., . . 229
63 (Gebeschus) sk., . 287-8
64 (v. Schrader), . . 313
65 (Schelle) sk., 314, 314 n.
66 (Wernicke), . 216, 239 n.
  sk., ... 267
67 (——) (?), . 216, 239 n.
68 (Dönitz), . . 216, 239 n.
  sk., ... 274
69 (Klatt), . . 216, 239 n.
  sk., ... 267

INDEX

Submarines, German UB-boats (*cont.*)
70 (Remy), . 216, 239 n.
  sk., ... 269
71 (Schapler), . 216, 239 n.
  sk., ... 268
72 (Träger) sk., . . . 304
74 (Steindorff) sk., . . 305
75 (Fr. Walther) sk., . 230
78 (Stosberg) sk., . . 303
81 (Salzwedel) sk., . 228-9
82 (Becker) sk., . 301-2
83 (Buntebardt) sk., . . 321
85 (Krech) sk., . . . 302
89 (———) founders on passage to Harwich for surrender, . . . 331
90 (Meyer) sk., . . . 326
103 (Hundius) sk., . . 318
104 (Bieber) sk., . . 320
105 (———), . 239, 276 n.
107 (Prittwitz und Gaffron) sk., . . . 314
108 (W. Amberger), loss of, 314
109 (Ramien) sk., . . 318
110 (Fürbringer), sk., 313-14
113 (Pilzecker), loss of, . 321
115 (Thomsen) sk., . . 321
116 (Emsmann) sk., . 327
119 (W. Kolbe), loss of, . 305
124 (Wutsdorff) sk., . . 313
127 (Scheffler), sk., 320, 320 n.
128 (———), . . 239, 276 n.
129 (———), ... 239
  blown up, . . . 276

UC-boats (German)—
1 (Mildenstein), Flanders Flot., 38, 50, 51, 63 n.
  sk., ... 192
2 (Mey), Flanders Flot., 38
  loss of, . . 50, 61, 64 n.
3 (Kreysern), Flanders Flot., 38, 50, 51, 63 n.
  sk., ... 90
4, Baltic (———), . 56, 63
  Flanders Flot., blown up, ... 324
5 (Mohrbutter), Flanders Flot., ... 38
  first to penetrate Dover Straits and lay mines in Channel, . 51, 63 n.
  captured, . . . 94
6 (Reichenbach), Flanders Flot., . . 38, 51, 63 n.
  sk., ... 214
7 (Haag), Flanders Flot., 38, 51, 63 n.
  sk., . . 104, 117 n., 178

Submarines, German UC-boats (*cont.*)
8 (———), Kiel Periscope School; interned and transferred to Holland, . 62, 62 n., 63, 332
9 (Schurmann), Flanders Flot., ... 38
  sk., . . 62, 63 n., 64, 64 n.
10 (Albrecht), North Sea, 63 n.
  sk., . . . 117, 117 n.
11 (Utke), Flanders Flot., 38, 44, 50, 63 n.
  sk., ... 311
12 (Fröhner), Adriatic Flot., 63 n., 71, 74, 78
  munition-carrier, . . 125
  sk., ... 126
  (*See also* X 1 (It.).)
13 (Kirchner), Adriatic Flot. and Constantinople Flot., sk., 64, 64 n., 71, 74, 74 n.
14 (Feddersen), Adriatic Flot., . . 63 n., 71
  Constantinople Flot., . 73
  Adriatic, 125, 126, 239 n.
  Flanders Flot., sk., 220, 243
15 (Heller), Adriatic Flot. and Constantinople Flot., 64 n., 71, 73, 74, 125
  sk., ... 135
16 (Reimarus), Flanders Flot., sk., . . . 220
17 (———) caught in nets, and escapes, . . 152
18 (Kiel) sk. or lost, . 156
19 (Nitzsche) sk., . 119, 178
20 (———), Adriatic Flot., 132, 239 n., 276 n.
21 (Salzwedel), Flanders Flot., ... 197
21 (Zerboni d. Sposetti), sk., ... 213
22 (———), Adriatic Flot., 132, 134, 239 n., 276 n.
23 (———), Adriatic Flot., 132, 239 n., 251
  surrender of, . 275, 332 n.
24 (Willich), Adriatic Flot., 132, 239 n.
  sk. by *Circé*, . . 255, 273
25 (———), Adriatic Flot., 132, 239 n., 254
  attacks *Dartmouth*, . 255
  blown up, . . . 275
26 (v. Schmettow), Flanders Flot., sk., . . 180
27 (———), Adriatic Flot., 239 n., 276 n.

428 THE GERMAN SUBMARINE WAR

Submarines, German UC-boats (*cont.*)
  29 (Rosenow), North Sea
    Flot., sk. by *Pargust*, 180-1
  30 (Stenzler) sk., . . . 167
  32 (Breyer) escapes Jan.
    1917, sk. Feb. 1917,   150
  33 (Arnold) sk. by PC 61, 213
  34 (———), Adriatic Flot.,
             132, 239 n.
    blown up, . . . 276
  35 (Korsch), Adriatic Flot.,
    joins, . . 132, 239 n.
    sk., ... 269-70
  36 (Buch), sk., . . . 180
  37 (———), Adriatic Flot.,
          239 n., 247, 248
    surrender of, at Sevastopol, . . 275, 332
  38 (Wendlandt), Adriatic
    Flot., . . . 239 n.
    sinks *Staunch* and M 15,
      Chateaurenault; sk., 260
  39 (Ehrentrant), North
    Sea Flot., sk., . . 150
  40 (———) founders on passage to Harwich for
    surrender, . . . 331
  41 (Foerste) sk., . . 200
  42 (Müller) sk., 212-13, 213 n.
  43 (Sebelin) sk. by G 13, 155-6
  44 (Tebbenjohanns) feigns
    death and escapes, . 149
    sk., . . . 196, 213 n.
    salvage and capture of
    papers, . . . 197
  45 (———) attkd. by *Result*, 156
  46 (Moecke) sk., . . 150
  47 (Wigankow) sk., . 227, 230
  48 (———) interned at Ferrol, ... 293
    scuttled (1919), 293 n., 332
    attempts to break out of
      internment, . . 305
    interned, . . . 332
  49 (Kükenthal) sk., . . 318
  50 (Seuffer) sk., . . 289
  51 (Galster) sk., . . 226
  52 (———) puts into Cadiz
    damaged, and leaves,
               189, 251
    Adriatic Flot., 239 n., 276 n.
  53 (———), Adriatic Flot., 239 n.
    blown up, . . . 275
  54 (———), Adriatic Flot., 239 n.
    blown up, . . . 275
  55 (Lilienstern), . . 188
    sk., ... 214
  56 (Kiesewetter) sinks
    Glenart Castle, . . 288

Submarines, German UC-boats (*cont.*)
  56 interned at Santander,
              305, 332
  57 (Wissman), Baltic Flot.,
    loss of, . . . 219
  58 (———), Baltic Flot., . 219
  60 (———), Baltic Flot., . 219
  61 (Gerth) stranded and
    destroyed, . . . 194
  62 (Schmitz) sk. by E 45, 220
  63 (Heydebreck) sk. by
    E 52, ... 225
  64 (Schwartz) sk., . . 311
  65 (Steinbrinck), Flanders
    Flot., ... 189
    sinks *Ariadne*, . . 194
  65 (Lafrenz) sk. by C 15,
              225-6
  66 (Pustkuchen), Flanders
    Flot., sk., . . 187-8
  67 (Neumann), Adriatic
    Flot., . . 239 n., 276 n.
    sinks *Dover Castle*, 249-50
  68 (Degetau), Flanders
    Flot., sk. by C 7, . . 167
  69 (Thielmann) sk. by
    U 96, ... 229
  70 (Dobberstein) sk., 316, 319
  71 (Salzwedel), fight with
    Dunraven, . . . 197-8
    founders on passage to
    surrender at Harwich, 331
  72 (Voigt) sk., . . . 213
  73 (———), Adriatic Flot.,
        239 n., 251, 276 n.
  74 (———), Adriatic Flot.,
            239 n., 276
    interned at Barcelona, 332
  75 (Schmitz) sinks *Lavender*, ... 181
    sk., ... 306
  76 (Barten) blows up at
    Heligoland, . . 179
  77 (Ries), . . . 188-9
    sk., ... 314
  78 (H. Kukat) sk., . . 303
  79 (Krameyer), . . 220 n.
    loss of, ... 294
  91 founders on passage to
    surrender at Harwich, 331
  commanding officers (German)—
    Ackermann, Rudolf, Cmr.
    2nd S/M. Flot. (Adriatic),
                264
    Adam (U 82), . . . 320
    Albrecht, K. (U 32), . 269
    Albrecht, W. (UC 10), . 117
    Amberger, G. (U 58), 226-7
    Amberger, W. (UB 108), . 314

INDEX

Submarines, German (*contd.*):
commanding officers (*contd.*)—

	PAGE
Arnauld, von. *See* Perière.	
Arnold (UC 33),	213
Bachmann (UB 38),	289
Barten (UC 76),	179
Bauck (U 89),	290
Bauer (UB 46),	135
Becker (UB 82),	301
Beitzen (U 75),	97
(U 102),	321
Bender (U 76),	112
Berckheim (U 26),	56
Berger (U 50),	115, 209
Bernis (U 104),	302
Bieber (UB 104),	320
Bolbrecht (U 78),	327
Bothmer, Count (U 66),	99, 107
Branscheid (UB 17),	290
Braun (UB 31),	303
Breyer (UC 32),	150
Buch (U 48),	111
(UC 36),	180
Buntebardt (UB 83),	321
Degetau (UC 68),	167
Dieckmann (U 61),	292
Ditfurth (UB 32),	199
Dobberstein (UC 70),	316
Dönitz (UB 68),	274
Droescher (U 20), 5, 14, 15, 20, 21	
(U 117),	309
Eckelmann (U 155),	296, 310
Edeling (U 48),	227-8
Ehrentrant (UC 39),	150
Ehrlich (U 92),	320
Eltester (U 99),	185
Emsmann (UB 116),	327
Feddersen (UC 14),	220
Feldkirchner (U 17),	11, 25
Feldt (U 156),	308
Firks, v. (U 59),	179
Foerste (UC 41),	200
Forstmann (U 12),	16
(U 39),	44, 45, 60, 75
Forstner (U 28),	35
Franz (U 152),	310
Fröhner (UC 12),	126
Fürbringer, G. (U 40),	45-6
Fürbringer, W. (UB 110),	313
Galster (UC 51),	226
Gansser (U 33), 60, 75, 77, 127, 243	
(U 156),	182, 219
Gebeschus (UB 63),	287
Georg, v. (U57),	114
(U101),	142, 222, 291
Gercke (U 154),	296
Gerlach (U 93),	284

Submarines, German (*contd.*):
commanding officers (*contd.*)—

	PAGE
Gerth (UC 61),	194
Glimpf (UB 20),	192-3
Graeff (U 36),	48
Gregor (UB 33),	294
Gross (UB 4),	50
Günther (UB 37),	119
Güntzel, L. (U 68),	63, 87
Günzel, E. (U 77),	103
Haag (UC 7),	104
Hacker (UB 6),	39, 50
Hammerle (U 14),	45
Hans, W. (U 52),	106, 133, 243
Hansen (U 16),	11
(U 41),	50, 60
Hartmann (U 49), 107, 114, 115, 206	
Hartwig (U 32),	134
(U 63),	276-7
Hashagen (UB 21),	100
(U 62),	171, 221, 306, 317
Hecht (UB 54),	292
Heimburg, v. (UB 15),	72
(UB 14),	74, 75, 78
Heller (UC 15),	135
Hennig, v. (U 18),	11, 17-18
attempt to escape,	51
Hersing (U 21), 4, 5, 17, 35, 42-3, 67, 70, 71, 72, 74, 124, 125, 129, 135, 146, 169, 182, 201-2, 243, 278	
Heydebreck (UC 63),	225
Hillebrand (U 46),	99, 111, 122
Hoppe (U 22),	5, 20, 55, 86, 87-8
(U 83),	142, 151
Hufnagel (U 106),	209
Hundius (UB 103),	318
Jetz (U 96),	230
(U 90),	291, 299
Jürst (U 43),	86, 111, 169
(C.O. 5th Flot.),	143
Keyserlinck (UB 36),	189
Kiel (UC 18),	156
Kiesewetter (UC 56),	288, 305
Kirchner (UC 13),	74
Klasing (U 34),	277
Klatt (UB 69),	267
Kolbe (U 19),	15
(U 152),	296
Kolbe, W. (UB 119),	305
König (U 7),	20
König, Capt. (master of merc. S/M. *Deutschland*),	103
Kophamel (U 35),	59-60, 75, 76
(C.O. Adriatic Flotillas),	264
(U 151),	218-19
(U 140),	308

430 THE GERMAN SUBMARINE WAR

Submarines, German (contd.):
commanding officers (contd.)—

Korsch (UC 35), . .	269
Krameyer (UC 79), . .	294
Kratzsch (U 12), .	33, 34
Krech (UB 85), . .	302
Kreysern (UC 3), . .	90
Kroll (U 110), . . .	292
Kukat, H. (UC 78), . .	303
Kukat (UB 50), . .	277
Kükenthal (UC 49), . .	318
Küstner (UB 39), . .	181
Lafrenz (UC 65),. .	225-6
Launburg (UB 52), . .	270
Lemmer (U 5), . . .	17
Lorenz (U 56), . . .	112
Losz (UB 57), . . .	318
Löwe (UB 58), . . .	292
Lühe (UB 16), . . .	305
Lütjohann (UB 7), . .	135
Lützow, Fr. (Cmr. G.N.), 1st S/M. Flot., Adriatic, ...	264
Mellenthin, v. (UB 46, UB 49), . . .	216
Metz (UB 13), . . .	91
Metzer (U 47), . .	97
(U 39), ...	270
Meusel (U 155), . .	217
(U 152), ...	219
Mey (UC 2), . . .	50
Meyer (UB 90), . .	326
Mildenstein (UC 1), . .	192
Moecke (UC 46), . .	150
Mohrbutter (UC 5), . .	94
Moraht (U 64), 241, 266,	272
Muhle (U 66), . . .	209
Müller (UC 42), .	212-13
Neumann (UC 67), .	249-50
trial at Leipzig, . .	250
Niemeyer (UB 18), . .	226
Nitzsche (UC 19), . .	119
Noodt (UB 19), . .	119
Nostitz v. und Jänckendorff (U 151), . .	307
Palis (UB 45), . . .	135
Patzig (U 86), . 299, 311-12	
Perière, Lothar v. Arnauld de la (U 35), . 125, 126, 130, 238, 243, 251 (U 139), . . 267, 325-6	
Petz (U 85), . . 123, 156	
Pilzecker (UB 113), . .	321
Platsch (UB 29), . .	118
Ploen (UB 41), . . .	220
Pohle (U 15), . . .	2, 3
Prause (Cmr. G.N.), C.O. 4th S/M. Flot., . .	96
Prinz (U 95), . . .	285

Submarines, German (contd.):
commanding officers (contd.)—

Prittwitz u. Gaffron (UB 107), ...	314
Pullen (Capt. G.N.), Adriatic Flotillas, . .	264
Pustkuchen (UB 29), 85, 86, 89, 94	
(UC 66), ...	188
Putzier (UB 22), . .	100
Ramien (UB 109), . .	318
Reichenbach (UC 6), .	214
Reimarus (UC 16), . .	220
Remy (UB 70), . . .	269
Rey (U 109), . . .	287
Ries (UC 77), . . .	314
Röhr (U 84), . . 151,	285
Rose (U 53), 106, 110-11, 140, 230, 320	
Rosenow (UC 29), . .	181
Rücker (U 34), 43, 59, 60, 75 (U 103), . . 142, 303-4	
Ruckteschell, v. (U 54), .	313
Rumpel (U 51), . 100,	101
Salzwedel (UB 10, UC 21, UC 71), . . .	197
(UB 81), . . 228-9	
Schapler (UC 73, UB 71),	268
Scheffler (UB 127), . .	320
Schelle (UB 65), . .	314
Schmettow, v. (UC 26), .	180
Schmidt, G. (U 28), . .	206
Schmidt, S. (UB 3), . .	71
Schmitz, M. (UC 62), .	220
Schmitz, W. (UC 75), .	306
Schmolling (U 75), . .	229
Schneider (U 24), 15, 19, 51-2, 59, 61 (U 87), . 142, 220, 231, 284	
Schoeller (UB 12), . .	318
Schrader, v. (UB 64), .	313
Schulthess (U 23), . .	48
Schultz, T. (UB 61), . .	229
Schulze (U 63), . . .	107
(Cmr. G.N.) 1st S/M. Flot., Adriatic . .	264
Schürmann (U 25), . .	62
Schwartz, F. (UC 64), .	311
Schwartz (UB 42), . .	251
Schwartzkopf, Capt. (master of merc. S/M. Bremen), . . .	103
Schweinitz, v. (U 13), .	3
Schwieger (U 20), 40-2, 45, 59, 63, 87, 88, 96, 110, 118	
(U 88), . . 142, 184, 209, 216, 216 n., 325 n.	
Sebelin (UC 43), . .	155

INDEX

Submarines, German (contd.):
commanding officers (contd.)—
Seuffer (UC 50), . . 289
Siehs (U 73), . . . 129
Sittenfeld (U 45), . . 213
Smiths (UB 26), . . 90
Speth - Schülzburg, v.
(U 87), . . . 231
Spiegel von u. zu Peckels-
heim (U 32), . 86, 99
(U 93), . 142, 169-70, 285
Spiess (in U 9), quoted, 8, 8 n.,
9, 12, 13, 15, 57
(U 19, U 52, U 19),
35 n., 174 n., 183, 201,
217, 291, 291 n., 301
(in U 19), quoted, . 217
(U 135), . . 327-8, 329 n.
Sposetti, Zerboni di (UC
21), ... 213
Sprenger (UB 53), . . 273
Stein, v. (UB 27), . . 193
Steinbauer (UB 47), 134, 216 n.
(UB 48), . . 170, 216
Steinbrinck (UB 10), . 50
(UB 18), . 84, 94, 105
(UC 61), ... 194
Steindorff (UB 74), . . 305
Stenzler (UC 30), . . 167
Stier (UB 30), . . . 316
Stoch (U 8), . . 32, 33
Stosberg (UB 78), . . 303
Stöter (UB 35), . . 287
Suchodoletz (U 11), . . 17
Tebbenjohanns (UC 44), . 196
Thielmann (UC 69), . . 229
Thomsen (UB 115), . . 321
Träger (UB 72), . . 304
Utke (UC 11), . . . 311
Valentiner, H. (UB 56), . 231
Valentiner, M. (U 38),
45, 63, 75, 77, 78, 125, 134
(U 157), ... 296
Voigt, E. (UC 72), . . 213
Voigt (UB 23), . . . 193
Wachendorff (U 31), . 20
Wacker (UB 22), . . 287
Wagenführ (U 44), . 86, 194-5
Wäger (UB 44), . . 131
Walther (UB 75), . . 230
Weddigen (U 9),
7, 8, 9, 10, 11, 12,
13, 14, 57, 325 n.
(U 29), . . . 33, 34-5
Wegener (U 27), . 15, 52-3
Weisbach, E. (U 74), 97, 98, 99
Weisbach, R. (U 19), . 87
(U 81), . . . 142, 181
Wendlandt (UC 38), . . 260

Submarines, German (contd.):
commanding officers (contd.)—
Wenninger (UB 55), . 294
Werner (UB 7), . . 73
Werner, W. (U 55),
122-3, 167-8, 194, 286
Wernicke (UB 66), . . 267
Wigankow (UC 47), . . 227
Wilcke (U 37), . 36-7, 37 n.
Wilhelms (U 69), . . 191
Willich (UC 24), . . 255
Wissman (UC 57), . . 219
Wünsche (U 25), . . 46
(U 70), ... 83
(U 97), ... 142
Wutsdorff, (UB 124), . 313
Ziegler (Lieut. in U 93),
170-1, 285
barrages, . . . 17, 18
bases—
Adriatic, ... 76
1st-4th Flotillas, . . 96 n.
classes of—
U 1-4, ... 63
U 27-30, ... 5
'Thirties' (U 31-41),
34, 75, 126, 269
U 43-50, defects of U 46-50, 64
U 51-56, ... 64
U 57-62, ... 64
U 63-64, ... 64
U 66-70 (ex A.-H. VII-
XI), . . . 64, 68 n.
U 71-80 (mine-layers), 64, 128
U 87-92, ... 142
U 117-126 (mine-carrying
capacity of), . . 309 n.
U 139-141, 'Helder boote'
(Hero class), . 325, 325 n.
U 158, 159, 160-172, 191-
200, 200-212, . . 143
U 151-157 (merc. S/M.
taken over), 182, 217, 297 n.
UB 1-17, ... 38
UB 18-47, ... 65
UB 48-71, ... 142
UB 88-132,. . . . 143
UB 133-169, 170-205, . 142
UC 1-15, ... 38
UC 16-48, ... 65
UC 49-79, . . : . 142
UC 84-118, 119-152, . 142
UF 1-20, ... 142
commissioning, monthly rate
of (see Appendix III., C), 353
construction programmes for—
orders placed, . . . 22
ordered, Feb., June, Dec.
1917, ... 142

432 THE GERMAN SUBMARINE WAR

Submarines, German (*contd.*):
construction programmes for
(*contd.*)—
progress to Feb. 1, 1917, 142-3
'Hindenburg' programme,
204, 323
large S/M. begun, criticised
by Gayer, . . . 233
labour shortage, proposals
to remedy, not approved
by German Gen. Staff, 299 n.
boats commissioned Sept.
1918 : labour for yards;
boats unfinished at end
of War, . . 323, 323 n.
programmes for construction of (*see* Appendix
III., F), ... 360-3
official summary showing
progressive rise and
strength by calendar
years (War period) (*see*
Appendix III., G), . 363
final summary, 'By construction' and 'Destruction' (*see* Appendix
III., G),. . . . 364
tonnage output by calendar
and War years, and shipbuilding yards (*see* Appendix III., H), . 364-5
counter-attack by British
S/M. disliked by Germans ; its perils and
experiences of accidental
depth - charge attack ;
losses suffered from own
or Allied patrols, . . 286
design—
improvement after first
War cruise, . . . 5
defects of Körting engines, 56-7
design and construction,
1904-5 (*see* Appendix II.),
340-350
'desiderata' boats (*see*
Appendix II.), . 346-7
Diesel-engined boats, first
(*see* Appendix II.), 347-50
details (technical) of. *See*
Appendix III., E (1)
and E (2).
distribution of (*see* Appendix III., D, . 354-5, 356-9
diving limit (1918), . . 265
submerged endurances, 265-6
escort vessels, . . . 1, 2
escorts of merchant-vessels,
proposed as, . . . 148

Submarines, German (*contd.*):
flotillas—
Pasquay (Cmr. G.N., C.O.
1st S/M. Flot.), . . 96 n.
Prause (4th Flot.), . 96 n.
Rosenberg-Gruszczynski,
von (Cmr. G.N., C.O.
2nd S/M. Flot.), . 96 n.
1st, 2nd, 3rd, 4th, 96 n., 329
towards end of War, . 143
5th S/M. Flot, . . . 143
Adriatic (Mediterranean,
boats on passage to), 59, 60,
63, 63 n., 119, 129, 239
established, . . . 76
boats at sea, Dec. 1916, 134
strength, Jan. 1917, . 134
losses, 1915-17, . . 240
withdrawals, 239, 239 n., 243
want of repair facilities ;
under repair, Jan.
1918 ; order to enlarge repair facilities
too late, . . . 263
destroyed on evacuation
of, . . . 264, 275-6
C.O. and Flotillas, administration of, . 264
Michelsen's and Scheer's
estimates of strength
on collapse of A.-H., 275
evacuation of, . . 276-7
loss of U 34, . . . 277
Baltic—
1914-16 losses; strength
of ; inaction during
winter ; abolition of,
56-7, 219
(Courland), . . . 93 n.
boats sent from North
Sea, ... 102
Constantinople—
strength, Sept. 1915,
63-4, 64 n.
formation of, losses of,
73, 74, 135, 252
strength on surrender of
Turkey, flight and
surrender of, . 275, 332
Ems : 3rd Flot., . . 5, 64
Flanders—
established, . . . 16
early type of UB and
UC boats, . . 38, 44
increase in strength and
activity, . . . 61
Sept. 1915, . . 63 n.
activities in 1916,
89, 90, 104-5

INDEX 433

Submarines, German (contd.):
flotillas (contd.)—
  Flanders—
    extended area for mine-
      layers, . . . 115
    appear in Western ap-
      proaches, . . . 118
    losses, . . . 118-19
    strength in July 1917,
      and area of operations, 192
    divided, ... 220
    forced to work in North
      Sea only, . . . 223
    heavy losses and short
      lives of S/M., . . 282
    concrete shelters for, . 282
    Gayer's opinion on aboli-
      tion of, . . . 282
    dangers encountered by, 282
    losses of (S/M. officers
      and men), 1915-18, . 284
    decline of value during
      1918 ; delay of aboli-
      tion, ... 295
    total of shipping claimed
      to have been sunk by, 296
    evacuation of bases ;
      S/M. blown up, . 324
  Kiel : Periscope School—
    U 25, ... 55
    U 9, ... 57
    UC 8, ... 62
  North Sea—
    small number available,
      Sept. 1915, . 63, 63 n.
  interned boats (Nov. 1918), 332
losses and strength—
  1914, . . . 22, 64
  1914-15, ... 64
  1915-16, ... 63
  1915, ... 65
  1916, ... 94-5
  1916-17, ... 141
  1917, 1918, . . . 167
  value of threat by S/M.
    against, . . . 167
  1917, average of last
    four months, . . 233
  percentage sustained in
    attacking convoys, . 261
  German uncertainty as
    to causes of, . . 284
  total losses, . . . 333
  causes, analysis of (see
    Appendix III., J (2)), . 367
  chronology, analysis of
    (see Appendix III., L), 370-7
  localities, analysis of (see
    Appendix III., J (1)), . 367

Submarines, German (contd.):
losses and strength (contd.)—
  monthly, analysis of (see
    Appendix III., I (a)), . 366
  recouped by salvage (see
    Appendix III., I (b)), . 366
  serial letters (see Appendix
    III., A), ... 351
  serial numbers (see Ap-
    pendix III., K), . 368-9
  broken up in Germany—
    (see Appendix III., A), 351
    (see Appendix III., K), 369
  ceded craft—
    (see Appendix III., A), 351
    (see Appendix III., K), 369
  foundered on passage for
    surrender—
    serial letters (see Ap-
      pendix III., A), . 351
    serial numbers (see Ap-
      pendix III., K), . 369
    chronological list (see
      Appendix III., L), . 377
  interned craft—
    chronological list (see
      Appendix III., L), . 376
    not surrendered (see Ap-
      pendix III., A), . 351
  scuttled craft—
    chronological list (see
      Appendix III., L), . 376
    serial letters (see Ap-
      pendix III., A), . 351
    serial numbers (see Ap-
      pendix III., K), . 369
  surrendered craft—
    serial letters (see Ap-
      pendix III., A), . 351
    serial numbers (see Ap-
      pendix III., K (a)), 368-9
    distribution of, between
      Allied and associated
      Powers (see Appendix
      III., L), . . . 377
personnel—
  training of (pre-War), . 1
  discipline unbroken, . 182
  dangers and rewards of, . 182
  volunteers for crews, . 183
  insanity and nerve cases
    amongst, . . . 182-3
  deterioration in efficiency
    and fighting spirit, 183, 204-5
  decline in morale, . 204-5
  no volunteers, shortage of
    experienced officers,
    animosity of H.S.F.
    officers, . . . 289-90

2 E

Submarines, German (contd.):
  personnel (contd.)—
    casualties, officers and
      men, . . 333, 333 n.
    ' aces ' (see Appendix III.,
      M), ... 378-9
    C.O.'s—
      1st-4th Flotillas, . . 96 n.
      appointed to new craft, 142
      (See also Aces and
        War Criminals List,
        Appendix III., M), 378-9
    War Criminals List, Appendix III., M, . . 379
  preparation of, for war on
    shipping, . . . 30
  radius of action—
    underestimated by British, ... 4
    size of, for trans-Atlantic
      raid, . . . 175-6
    recalled to bases (Oct. 1918), 275
  repairs, facilities improved,
      233, 263
  submarines sunk by S/M.—
    German by British. (See
      U 6, U 45, U 51, U 78,
      U 81, U 154, UB 16,
      UB 52, UB 72, UB 90,
      UC 10, UC 43, UC 62,
      UC 63, UC 65, UC 68.)
    British by German. (See
      C 34, D 6, E 3, E 20,
      E 22.)
    French by German. (See
      Circé.)
    Italian by A.-H. (See
      Medusa, Nereide.)
    A.-H. by Ital. (See XX.)
  surrender of—
    plans for scuttling frustrated, . . . 330-31
    conditions for armistice, . 331
    delivery at Harwich, . 331
    total number of, . . 332
    boats at Sevastopol, . 332 n.
    allocation of, . 332, 332 n.
    prohibition regarding reuse of, ... 332
  types—
    designs for UA, UB, UC,
      UD (?), UE, UF, UK,
      medium size (see Appendix III., B), . 352 n.
    UB I. (UB 1-17) ordered,
      sent to Antwerp and
        Pola, . . . 51, 64
      defects of, . . . 38
      for A.-H. navy, . 71, 239

Submarines, German (contd.):
  types (contd.)—
    UB II. (UB 18-71), 38, 64-5, 84
      defects of, . 110, 131 n.
      popularity with Flanders
        Flot., boats for A.-H.
        Navy, . 239, 252-3
      design used by A.-H. Navy, 253
    UB III. (UB 72-87), . 114, 142
      compared with UB II.
      boats, sent to Mediterranean, . . 216, 239
      building for A.-H. Navy,
          253, 279 n.
    UC I. (UC 1-15) ordered,
      sent to Antwerp and
        Pola, defects of, 38, 64
      losses, ... 179
    UC II. (UC 16-79), 38, 65, 116
      sent to Adriatic, . 132, 142
      losses, . . . 179, 239
    UC III., ... 142-3
    UC boats, losses of, 1917,
          155, 216
    cruisers—
      S/M. (U 142-50), . . 114
      base and commands, . 210
    mercantile—
      Deutschland (Capt. König):
        first voyage, . 103-4
        second voyage, . 110-11,
              118-19
        (See U 155 for further
          history.)
      Bremen (Capt. Schwartzkopf), loss of, . 103, 110
    mine-layers. (See U 9, U
      44, U 71-80, U 117-
      126, UB 12.)
    U 9 (non-submersible), 56 n.
    Flanders Flot., mines
      planted, . . . 61
    attack commerce, . . 156
    losses, 1917 and 1918;
      number of UC-boats,
        Jan. 1918; activities,
        1918, . . . 299-300
    munition-carriers, as,
      71, 74, 76, 78, 79, 125, 242 n.
    ' omnibus ' (U 117-126),
          143, 143 n.
    with Körting engines, . 93 n.
    (Michelsen's analysis) Appendix III., B, . . 352
    maximum and average,
      prediction of, 1918-19;
      rate of commissioning, 141
    ' War front ' boats—
      total, 1917 and 1918, . 141

INDEX 435

Submarines, German (*contd.*):
  types (*contd.*)—
    'War front' boats—
      maximum number attained, . . . 141
      distribution of Feb. 1, 1917, ... 142
      Mediterranean average at sea, . . . 144
      Flanders and North Sea, at sea, Feb. Apr. 1917, 144
        Feb. 1918, . . 147
        Apr. 1917, . . 163
      in Western waters, Apr. 1917, ... 167
      in Western waters and Mediterranean, May 1917, ... 183
      maximum number of North Sea boats at sea, 186
      total of commissioned boats, autumn 1917, 205
      Mediterranean, Apr. 1917, ... 242
      Mediterranean, Jan. 1918, ... 263
      maximum number at sea, . . . 263, 269
      North Sea boats operating, 1918, . . . 293
      total boats at sea, May 1918, ... 302
      North Sea and Flanders boats at sea, July 1918, ... 315
      Aug. 1914-Nov. 1918 (*see* Appendix III., D), 354-5
  W/T.—
    shortage of operators, . 30
    record transmission, 32, 88
Submarine-chasers (SC boats), U.S., ... 266
Suffren (Fr. B.S.) sk. by U 52, 133, 243
Sunderland :
  bombardment of, proposed, . 97
  S/M. stationed for, . . 106
Surada (Brit. S.S.) sk., . . 276
Surprise (Brit. T.B.D.) sk., . 233
Surprise (Fr. G.B.) sk., . . 134
Surveyor (U.S. yacht), . . 270
Sussex (Brit. S.S.) attkd., 85, 88, 89, 90, 94, 118, 188
Svorono (Russ. S.S.) sk., . . 40
Swift (Brit. Flot. leader) attkd., 16 n. in action, ... 152
Swiftsure (Brit. B.S.) attkd., 71, 74
Sword Dance (Brit. M/S.) sk. after War, ... 336

Sycamore (Brit. S.S.) sk., . 201
Sylvia (Brit. T.B.D.), . . 214
Szent Istvan (A.-H. B.S.) sk. by It. C.M.B., . . . 272

Tara (Brit. A.B.S.) sk. by U 35, 76
Taranaki (Brit. decoy), in company of C 24, sinks U 40, 46
Taschenbuch der Kriegsflotten (quoted), ... 93 n.
Tasman (Brit. S.S.) sk., . . 274
Teakwood (Brit. S.S.) sk., . 247
Techel, Dr. (Ger. naval architect), quoted, . . 253 n.
Teutonian (Brit. S.S.) sk., . 85
Texel (U.S. S.S.) sk., . . 307
Theseus (Brit. cruiser) attkd. by U 17, . . . 13, 16 n.
Thirza (Q 30) (Brit. decoy), . 190
Thomas Young (Brit. trlr.), . 200
Thordis (Brit. S.S.) rams S/M., 32
Thornhill (Brit. decoy), . . 190
Thracia (Brit. S.S.) sk., . . 157
Thrasher (Brit. T.B.D.) sinks UC 39, ... 150
'Three cruisers':
  loss of, ... 6-10
  lessons of, . . 10, 12, 19
  (Also see *Aboukir, Cressy, Hogue*.)
Thruster (Brit. T.B.D.), . . 292
Thüringen (Ger. B.S.), mutiny on board, ... 327-8
Thursby, Sir Cecil (Rr.-Adm. R.N.), ... 236
Tirade (Brit. T.B.D.), . . 214
Tirpitz, Grand Adm. von :
  demands of, before building of first S/M., . . . 6
  ('Wiegand' interview), . 26
  opposes 'war zone,' . . 29
  suggests despatch of S/M. to the Mediterranean, . . 58
  tenders resignation, . . 59 71.
  resigns, ... 85
  advocates 'six months plan,' 82 203.
Tithonus (Brit. A.B.S.) sk., . 300
Tokio (Brit. trlr.), . . . 17
  sk., ... 232
Tokomaru (Brit. S.S.) sk., . 21
Tondern (Ger. airship base), 86, 94
Tonnage famine, . 162, 163, 202
Tornado (Brit. T.B.D.) sk., . 233
Toro (Brit. S.S.) sk., . . 168
Torpedo-boats :
  British—
    No. 10 sk., . 44, 44 n., 61
    No. 11 sk., . . . 84

436 THE GERMAN SUBMARINE WAR

Torpedo-boats (*contd.*):
British (*contd.*)—
No. 12 sk., . 44, 44 n., 61
No. 92, . . . 43, 70
No. 95, ... 75
No. 116, . . 14, 16 n.
French—
No. 300 sk., . . . 153
No. 317 sk., . . . 153
Italian—
5 PN, loss of, . . . 73 n.
Austro-Hungarian—
No. 11 deserts, . . . 267
No. 87 disabled, . . 274
German, small ' A ' types—
A 2 sk., ... 39
A 6 sk., ... 39
A 76 sk., ... 316
Torpedoes (German) :
Mark G VII, . . 210, 210 n.
shortage of, ... 257-8
Torrent (Brit. T.B.D.) sk., . 233
Torrington (Brit. S.S.) sk., . 167
master gives evidence, . . 167
Totnes (Brit. paddle M/S.), . 117
Toukhoum lighthouse shelled
by S/M., ... 127
Trade, Mediterranean, diversion
around Cape of Good
Hope, ... 163
re-started, . . . 260-1
' Trafalgar Day ' (Oct. 21,
1918), recall of Ger. S/M.
from commerce war, . 325
Transports :
ambulance : see *Donegal,
Warilda.*
(Brit.): see *Copenhagen, Cestrian, Queen Alexandra,
Southland, Wayfarer.*
(Brit.) (horse) : see *Anglo-Californian, Cameronian,
Moorina, Norseman, Russian.*
(Brit.) (munition-carrier) :
see *Arabian.*
(Fr.) : see *Carthage, France
IV., Magellan, Yarra.*
Transylvania (Brit. troopship)
sk., ... 248
Trant, Capt., master of S.S.
Devonian, ... 201
Trebizond, shelled by *Breslau,* 127
Treveal (Brit. S.S.) sk., . . 288
Trevone (Brit. fishing-vessel) sk., 123
Trinidad (Brit. S.S.) sk., . 291
Tripolitania, ... 74
Triumph (Brit. B.S.) sk. by
U 21, ... 71-2

Triumph (Brit. fishing-vessel)
captured by German S/M.
and converted into aux.
raider, . . . 309-10, 310 n.
Troilus (Brit. S.S.) sk., . . 183
Trombe (Fr. T.B.), . . . 90
Troopships :
Germans announce intention
to attack, ... 21
(Brit.) : see *Aragon, Arcadian, Armadale, Ballarat,
Franconia, Ivernia, Justicia, Leasowe Castle, Marquette, Mercian, Moldavia*
(A.M.C.), *Olympic, Omrah,
Ramazan, Royal Edward,
Transylvania, Tuscania.*
(Fr.) : see *Athos, Amiral
Magon, Burdigala, Colbert,
Djemmah.*
(It.) : see *Minas.*
(U.S.) : see *Antilles, Covington, President Lincoln, Von
Steuben.*
Trotha, von (Adm. G.N.), . 328
Tubantia (Dutch S.S.) sk., . 85
Tulip (Q 12) (Brit. sloop) sk.
by U 62, ... 171
Tupper, Sir Reginald G. (Vice-
Adm. R.N.), . . . 191-2
Turakina (Brit. S.S.) sk., . . 200
Turner, Capt. (master of *Lusitania*), ... 41
Turquoise (Brit. Fleet messenger) sk., ... 48
Tuscania (Brit. troopship) sk., 288
Tyrwhitt, Sir R. Y., Cmre. (T.)
R.N., ... 7

Üdsire Island, ... 217
Ulleswater (Brit. T.B.D.) sk., . 316
Ultonia (Brit. S.S.) sk., . . 185-6
Umberto I. (It. aux. cruiser) sk., 260
Una A. Saunders (Brit. fishing-
vessel) sk., ... 310
Urbino (Brit. S.S.) sk., . . 60
Uto Island (Baltic), . . . 57

Vala (Q 8) (Brit. decoy) sk., . 214
Valeria (Brit. S.S.) sinks U 99, 185
Vandalia (Brit. S.S.) sk., . . 311
Vanduara (Brit. yacht) attacks
U 21, ... 20
Vanessa (Brit. yacht), . 50, 314
Varna, German S/M. base, . 71
Vedamore (Brit. S.S.) sk., . 140
Vehement (Brit. M/L. T.B.D.)
sk., ... 315
Velox (Brit. T.B.D.) sk., . . 61

INDEX

437

Venetia (Brit. yacht), . . 270
Vengeance (Brit. B.S.) attkd., 71
Verdi (Brit. S.S.) sk., . . 201
Verna D. Adams (Brit. fishing-
 vessel) sk., . . . 310
Veronica (Brit. sloop) attkd., 251-2
Verulam (Brit. T.B.D.) sk.
 after War, ... 336
Victoria (Brit. fishing-vessel)
 sk. by U 34, . . . 43-4, 304
Victoria (Brit. decoy), . . 47
Victorian (Brit. A.M.C.), . . 47
Viking (Brit. T.B.D.), . . 33
Ville de la Ciotat (Fr. S.S.) sk., 78
Ville de Lille (Fr. S.S.) sk., . 21
Vindictive (Brit. L.C. used as
 blockship), . . . 295
Vine Branch (Brit. S.S.) sk., . 168
Vinovia (Brit. S.S.) sk., . . 231
Viribus Unitis (Austrian B.S.)
 sk., ... 275
Volckner, 'war pilot' (U 8),
 escape of, ... 34
Volodia (Brit. S.S.) sk., . . 201
Voltaire (Fr. B.S.) attkd., . 274-5
Von Steuben (U.S. troopship,
 ex Ger. *Kronprinz Wil-
 helm*), ... 308
Vperyed (Russ. H.S.) sk., . 127

Waldeck-Rousseau (Fr. B.S.)
 attkd., . . . 69, 130
Wallflower (Brit. sloop), . . 269
Walney Island :
 batteries drive off U 21, . 20
 shelled by S/M., . . . 154
War Arabis (Brit. S.S.) sk., . 274
'War channel,' E. Coast, 154, 301
War, declarations of :
 Britain against Germany, . 2
 Italy against Austria-Hun-
 gary, ... 68, 70
 Britain against Bulgaria, 76, 81
 Rumania against Austria-
 Hungary, ... 113
 Italy against Germany, . 127
 imminent between U.S.A.
 and Germany, . . . 141
 U.S.A. against Germany, . 158
Warilda (Brit. ambulance
 transport) sk., . . 316-17
War Patrol (Brit. S.S.) sk., 200, 202
'War pilot,' . . . 30, 34
War Roach (Brit. S.S.) attkd., 276
Warrington (U.S. T.B.D.), 189-90
Warspite (Brit. B.S.) attkd., . 100
'War zones,' German declara-
 tion of, ... 27-8
Watts, skipper, awarded V.C., 254

Wayfarer (Brit. transport)
 attkd., ... 37
W. C. *M'Kay* (Brit. sailing-
 vessel) sk., ... 219
'Wedding-cake ships,' . . 224
Wellington (Brit. S.S.) sk., . 274
Welshman (Brit. S.S.), . 226, 227
Wemyss, Sir R. (Vice-Adm.
 R.N.), ... 236
 chosen as Senior Naval
 Officer of Malta Commis-
 sion ; becomes Deputy
 First Sea Lord, . . 247
Weser Co., Bremen, . . 71
Westego (U.S. S.S.), . . . 140
Westfalen (Ger. B.S.) attkd., . 106
Westminster (Brit. S.S.) sk., . 134
Westover (U.S. supply ship) sk., 312
Weymouth (Brit. L.C.) attkd., 274
Wheeling (U.S. G.B.), . . 270
Whitby Abbey (Brit. trlr.), . 273
Whitehaven shelled by U 24, . 51
Whitgift (Brit. S.S.) sk., . . 88
Wildfang (A.-H. T.B.D.) sk., . 255
Wilkinson, Norman, Lieut.
 R.N.V.R., ... 177
Wilkinson, Spencer, quoted, . 159
William II. :
 Emperor of Germany,
 27, 42, 58, 83, 84, 89
 reproves Scheer, . . 118, 119
 assents to sinking of armed
 merchant - vessels, Jan.
 1917, . . . 120 n., 122
 Potsdam interview, urges
 continuance of S/M. war-
 fare ; abdicates, . 324-5
William Dawson (Brit. S.S.) sk., 51
William Tennant (Brit. dftr.), 209
Williams, Wm. (seaman
 R.N.R., D.S.M.), awarded
 V.C., ... 181
Willow Branch (alias *Bombala*)
 (Brit. decoy) sk., . . 297
Wilson, Woodrow :
 President U.S.A.,
 88, 111, 119, 324
 views on U 53's raid, . . 111
 speech to Congress quoted, 139-40
 'armed neutrality of U.S.', 141
 message to Congress, Apr. 3,
 1917, quoted, . . . 157-8
 maintenance of U.S. neu-
 trality, 1914-17, . . 158
 plans to participate in peace
 negotiations, . . . 158-9
Wireless telegraphy by S/M.,
 U 20's record, . . . 88
Wolf (Ger. raider), . . 145, 335

W. S. Bailey (Brit. hydrophone
    trlr.), ... 287
Yardley, Capt., master of S.S.
    Burutu, ... 297
Yarmouth (E. Coast), raid on, 17
Yarra (Fr. transport) sk., . 249
Yasaka Maru (Jap. S.S.) sk., 78
Yenesei (Russ. M/L.) sk. by
    U 26, ... 56
Young Fred (Brit. dftr.), . 302

Zaida (Brit. yacht) sk., . . 132
Zeebrugge, ... 15
    as advanced base for S/M., . 16
    proposals for recapture of, . 19

Zent (Brit. S.S.) sk., . . 88
Zeppelins. (*See* Airships, naval.)
' Zigzagging,' 177
Zillah (Brit. S.S.) sk., . 219, 220
' Zimmermann letter,' . . 141
Zinnia (Brit. sloop), . . 181
Zones :
    partition of Mediterranean
      into, ... 79-80
    amended partition, . . 236-7
    abolished in favour of unified
      commands, . . . 247
Zubian (Brit. T.B.D.), 289, 289 n.
Zulu (Brit. T.B.D.), . . 115-16
Zylpha (Q 6) (Brit. decoy) sk.,
    189-90